GU

WHO'S WHO
IN SOCCER

*Completely Revised
and Updated*

JACK ROLLIN

GUINNESS BOOKS ////

Editor: Beatrice Frei
Design: David Roberts

Published in Great Britain by Guinness Superlatives Ltd,
33 London Road, Enfield, Middlesex

Typeset in 7/8pt Times
Printed and bound in Great Britain by
Redwood Burn Limited, Trowbridge, Wiltshire.

British Library Cataloguing in Publication Data
Rollin, Jack
Guinness who's who in soccer.
1. Soccer—Great Britain—Biography
I. Title
796.334′092′2   GV942.7.A1

ISBN 0–85112–464–X

Cover illustrations, left to right: Norman Whiteside (Manchester
United), Glenn Hoddle (Spurs), Neville Southall (Everton) and
Willie Miller (Aberdeen).
Photos supplied by Bob Thomas and Sporting Pictures

THE AUTHOR

Jack Rollin was born in London in 1932 and educated at King's, Harrow. There he played soccer, while later at Westcliff-on-Sea High School it was rugby. Within ten days of joining the Royal Air Force he was playing in a Welsh Cup tie for RAF Bridgnorth and in the services he learned shorthand and typing, resuming his career in journalism and covering the 1954 World Cup in Switzerland in a freelance capacity.

In 1958 an ankle injury ended his own career during which, at the age of 14, he had been offered a trial with the United States club Chicago Maroons. He wisely declined a one-off re-appearance in 1971 against the European Cup finalists Panathinaikos of Greece.

For ten years Jack Rollin was Editor of the weekly magazine *Soccer Star* and its companion monthly *World Soccer* before becoming a freelance again in 1970. Since then he has researched football for BBC Television, acted as an assistant to commentators on 'Match of the Day', spoken on radio and appeared on television programmes. He has contributed to *Radio Times* and in 1975 he won the Designers and Art Directors Association Silver Award for *Radio Times World Cup Special* for the most outstanding specialist feature of the year.

In 1972 he became one of the compilers of the *Rothmans Football Yearbook* and later became its Editor. He has provided advice on the football section of the *Guinness Book of Records* and he reports football regularly for the *Sunday Telegraph*.

Jack Rollin contributed to three part-works: *The Game* (8 vols. 1970); *Books of Football* (6 vols. 1972) and *Football Handbook* (1979–80). His articles have appeared in programmes for matches at Wembley Stadium since 1963. He has produced handbooks which include *World Soccer Digest* 1961, 1962 and 1963 and *World Cup Digest* 1966.

In 1978 he carried out the international research for the BBC Television series 'The Game of the Century' and produced the first edition of *The Guinness Book of Soccer Facts and Feats*.

Other books he has written: *England's World Cup Triumph* (1966), *A Source Book of Football* (1971), *The History of Aldershot Football Club* (1975), *World Cup Guide* (1982), *Who's Who in Soccer* (1984), *Soccer at War 1939–45* (1985) and *Soccer: The Records* (1985). In 1974 he contributed the South American section for John Moynihan's *Football Fever*.

The author is married to June and has a daughter Glenda.

FOREWORD

I am delighted to welcome the second edition of the *Guinness Who's Who in Soccer* by Jack Rollin. It is certainly on a par with all the quality reference books in the Guinness library and will prove an invaluable help to all administrators, managers, soccer writers and supporters of football throughout the United Kingdom.

It is a difficult task to keep abreast of the changing face of personnel at clubs and Jack Rollin is to be congratulated on achieving this task successfully. There are precise details of every professional player in England, Wales and Scotland which can be found by quick and easy alphabetical reference. The inclusion in the second edition of the Scottish league players provides all the information necessary for a football fact-finder.

The book will occupy a prominent place on my desk and I do not hesitate to recommend it.

Gordon Taylor

Gordon Taylor,
Secretary, The Professional Footballers' Association

INTRODUCTION

This book features the statistical League careers of all players who made Canon League appearances during the 1985–86 season as well as those in the Scottish Premier Division. It also includes others who were contracted professionally with Football League clubs at the start of the 1985–86 season and who remained there during the season and others recently in Italy and Spain.

Players on non-contract forms have been designated as amateur for reasons of non-professional uniformity as this was the status accepted before amateurism was abolished 12 years ago. Club names in italics indicate temporary transfers where they have not become permanent moves in the same season.

The Editor would like to thank Alan Elliott for providing details of Scottish League players and also acknowledge the co-operation and assistance of the Football League in the compilation of this book and in particular League Secretary Graham Kelly, Mike Foster, Sheila Murphy and Debbie Singleton. Thanks also to Christine Phillips.

Bibliography: *Rothmans Football Yearbook*
              Sunday Telegraph Canon Football Year Book

Also published by Guinness Books:
Soccer Facts and Feats, 5th Edition
Soccer: The Records
Guinness Book of Records

Season	Club	League Appearances/Goals		Season	Club	League Appearances/Goals	

ABBOTT, Greg

Born Coventry 14.12.63.   Ht 5 9   Wt 10 7
Midfield. From Apprentice.

1981–82	Coventry C	—	—
1982–83	Bradford C	11	—
1983–84		35	3
1984–85		42	6
1985–86		39	10

ABEL, Graham

Born Runcorn 17.9.60.
Defender. From Northwich V and Runcorn

| 1985–86 | Chester | 23 | 2 |

ABERCROMBY, William

Born Glasgow 14.9.58   Ht 5 9   Wt 10 5
Midfield. From St Mirren B.C.

1975–76	St Mirren	—	—
1976–77		3	—
1977–78		30	3
1978–79		31	2
1979–80		15	—
1980–81		29	1
1981–82		30	—
1982–83		25	1
1983–84		34	4
1984–85		31	2
1985–86		23	2

ABLETT, Gary

Born Liverpool 19.11.65.   Ht 6 1¼   Wt 10 11
Midfield. From Apprentice.

1983–84	Liverpool	—	—
1984–85		—	—
1984–85	*Derby Co*	6	—
1985–86	Liverpool	—	—

ACHAMPONG, Kenny

Born London 26.6.66.   Ht 5 9½   Wt 10 10
Forward. From Apprentice

| 1984–85 | Fulham | 10 | 3 |
| 1985–86 | | 35 | 3 |

ADAMS, Mick

Born Sheffield 8.11.61.   Ht 5 8   Wt 11 6
Forward. From Apprentice. England Youth.

1979–80	Gillingham	4	—
1980–81		13	—
1981–82		31	2
1982–83		44	3
1983–84	Coventry C	17	1
1984–85		31	3
1985–86		31	3

ADAMS, Neil

Born Stoke 23.11.65.   Ht 5 8   Wt 10 1
Forward. From Local.

| 1985–86 | Stoke C | 32 | 4 |

ADAMS, Tony

Born London 10.10.66.   Ht 6 1   Wt 12 1
Defender. From Apprentice. England
Youth, Under-21.

1983–84	Arsenal	3	—
1984–85		16	—
1985–86		10	—

ADCOCK, Tony

Born Bethnal Green 27.2.63.   Ht 5 10
Wt 10 8
Midfield. From Apprentice.

1980–81	Colchester U	1	—
1981–82		40	5
1982–83		30	17
1983–84		43	26
1984–85		28	24
1985–86		33	15

ADKINS, Nigel

Born Birkenhead 11.3.65.   Ht 6 0   Wt 12 7
Goalkeeper. From Apprentice. England
Schools.

Season	Club	League Appearances/Goals		Season	Club	League Appearances/Goals	
1982–83	Tranmere R	10	—	1975–76		35	2
1983–84		4	—	1976–77		17	2
1984–85		38	—	1977–78		35	4
1985–86		34	—	1978–79	Birmingham C	31	2
				1979–80		37	6
				1980–81		40	8

AGBOOLA, Reuben

Born London 30.5.62.   Ht 5 9½   Wt 11 0
Defender. From Apprentice.

Season	Club	League Appearances/Goals	
1979–80	Southampton	—	—
1980–81		6	—
1981–82		5	—
1982–83		37	—
1983–84		33	—
1984–85		9	—
1984–85	Sunderland	8	—
1985–86		12	—

1981–82	Everton	17	2
1982–83		11	1
1982–83	*Barnsley*	2	—

From Eastern

1984–85	Wolverhampton W	42	5
1985–86		16	—
1985–86	Blackburn R	5	2

AIREY, Carl

Born Wakefield 6.2.65.   Ht 6 0   Wt 12 5
Forward. From Apprentice.

1982–83	Barnsley	11	2
1983–84		27	3
1983–84	*Bradford C*	5	—
1984–85	Darlington	41	16
1985–86		34	12

AGNEW, Paul

Born Lisburn 15.8.65.   Ht 5 9½   Wt 10 4
Defender. From Cliftonville. Northern
Ireland Youth.

1983–84	Grimsby T	1	—
1984–85		12	—
1985–86		16	—

AITKEN, Roy

Born Irvine 24.11.58.   Ht 6 0   Wt 13 0
Midfield. From Celtic B.C. Scotland Schools,
Under-21, 20 full caps.

1975–76	Celtic	12	—
1976–77		33	5
1977–78		33	2
1978–79		36	5
1979–80		35	3
1980–81		33	4
1981–82		33	3
1982–83		33	6
1983–84		31	5
1984–85		33	3
1985–86		36	—

AGNEW, Steve

Born Shipley 9.11.65.   Ht 5 9   Wt 10 6
Forward. From Apprentice.

1983–84	Barnsley	1	—
1984–85		10	1
1985–86		2	—

AINSCOW, Alan

Born Bolton 15.7.53.   Ht 5 8   Wt 11 5
Forward. From Apprentice. England Youth.

1971–72	Blackpool	18	3
1972–73		37	10
1973–74		19	3
1974–75		31	4

AIZLEWOOD, Mark

Born Newport 1.10.59.   Ht 6 0   Wt 12 8
Defender. From Apprentice. Wales
Under-21, 3 full caps.

Season	Club	League Appearances/Goals		Season	Club	League Appearances/Goals	
1975–76	Newport Co	6	—	1983–84		28	20
1976–77		5	—	1983–84	Oxford U	8	4
1977–78		27	1	1984–85		42	30
1977–78	Luton T	—	—	1985–86		39	23
1978–79		39	—				
1979–80		10	—				
1980–81		23	—				
1981–82		26	3				
1982–83		—	—				
1982–83	Charlton Ath	22	1				
1983–84		31	1				
1984–85		38	3				
1985–86		35	3				

ALEXANDER, Rowan

Born Ayr 28.1.61. Ht 5 9 Wt 11 0
Forward.

1978–79	Queen of the South	2	—
1979–80		37	21
1980–81		36	14
1981–82		23	11
1982–83		38	22
1983–84	St. Mirren	16	3
1984–85		1	—
1984–85	Brentford	19	2
1985–86		28	4

ALBISTON, Arthur

Born Edinburgh 14.7.57. Ht 5 8 Wt 10 13
Defender. From Apprentice. Scotland
Schoolboy, Under-21, 13 full caps.

1974–75	Manchester U	2	—
1975–76		3	—
1976–77		17	—
1977–78		28	—
1978–79		33	—
1979–80		25	—
1980–81		42	1
1981–82		42	1
1982–83		38	1
1983–84		40	2
1984–85		39	—
1985–86		37	1

ALLARDYCE, Sam

Born Dudley 19.10.54. Ht 6 1½ Wt 14 0
Defender. From Apprentice.

1971–72	Bolton W	—	—
1972–73		—	—
1973–74		7	—
1974–75		18	3
1975–76		40	5
1976–77		41	6
1977–78		41	4
1978–79		20	1
1979–80		17	2
1980–81	Sunderland	25	2
1981–82		—	—
1981–82	Millwall	36	1
1982–83		27	1
1983–84	Coventry C	28	1
1984–85	Huddersfield T	37	—
1985–86	Bolton W	14	—

ALDRED, Graeme

Born Ferryhill 11.9.66. Ht 5 10 Wt 11 0
Forward. From Newcastle U.

1984–85	Darlington	28	1
1985–86		16	—

ALDRIDGE, John

Born Liverpool 18.9.58. Ht 5 11 Wt 11 6
Forward. From South Liverpool. Eire 2 caps

1978–79	Newport Co	—	—
1979–80		38	14
1980–81		27	7
1981–82		36	11
1982–83		41	17

ALLATT, Vernon

Born Hednesford 28.5.59. Ht 5 11 Wt 12 7
Forward. From Hednesford T.

1979–80	Walsall	—	—
1979–80	Halifax T	16	—

All appearances include those as substitute

Season	Club	League Appearances/Goals

Season	Club	League Appearances/Goals
1980–81	....	30	3
1981–82	....	24	4
1982–83	....	28	7
1982–83	Bolton W	—	—
1983–84	Rochdale	40	8
1984–85	Crewe Alex	30	7
1985–86	....	9	1
1985–86	Preston NE	19	3

ALLEN, Clive

Born London 20.5.61.   Ht 5 10   Wt 12 3
Forward. From Apprentice. England
Schoolboy, Youth, Under-21, 3 full caps.

1978–79	QPR...........................	10	4
1979–80	....	39	28
1980–81	Arsenal	—	—
1980–81	Crystal Palace	25	9
1981–82	QPR.............................	37	13
1982–83	....	25	13
1983–84	....	25	14
1984–85	Tottenham H	13	7
1985–86	....	19	9

ALLEN, Greg

Born London 18.10.67.   Ht 5 9   Wt 11 10
Midfield. From Apprentice.

1985–86	Arsenal	—	—

ALLEN, Kenny

Born Thornaby 12.1.52.   Ht 6 4   Wt 13 8
Goalkeeper. From Bath C.

1978–79	Bournemouth	46	—
1979–80	....	34	—
1980–81	....	44	—
1981–82	....	10	—
1982–83	....	18	—
1983–84	Bury	—	—
1983–84	Peterborough U.............	—	—
1983–84	Torquay U	11	—
1984–85	....	43	—
1985–86	....	4	—
1985–86	Swindon T...................	40	—

ALLEN, Malcolm

Born Dioniolen 21.3.67.   Ht 5 8½ Wt 10 6
Forward. From Apprentice. Wales 3 full caps.

1984–85	Watford	—	—
1985–86	....	13	2

ALLEN, Martin

Born Reading 14.8.65   Ht 5 10   Wt 11 0
Midfield. From school. England Youth.

1983–84	QPR.............................	—	—
1984–85	....	5	—
1985–86	....	31	3

ALLEN, Paul

Born Aveley 28.8.62.   Ht 5 7   Wt 10 10
Midfield. From Apprentice. England Youth,
Under-21.

1979–80	West Ham U	31	2
1980–81	....	3	1
1981–82	....	28	—
1982–83	....	33	—
1983–84	....	19	—
1984–85	....	38	3
1985–86	Tottenham H	33	1

ALLEN, Paul

Born Leeds 30.7.67.   Ht 5 11¾   Wt 11 3
Goalkeeper. From Local.

1983–84	Bradford C..................	—	—
1984–85	Doncaster R	1	—
1985–86	....	3	—
1985–86	Scunthorpe U	—	—

ALLINSON, Ian

Born Hitchin 1.10.57.   Ht 5 10   Wt 11 0
Forward. From Apprentice.

1974–75	Colchester U	1	—
1975–76	....	5	—
1976–77	....	39	7
1977–78	....	45	6
1978–79	....	46	5
1979–80	....	38	2
1980–81	....	46	6

Season	Club	League Appearances/Goals		Season	Club	League Appearances/Goals	
1981–82	....	42	21				
1982–83	....	46	22				
1983–84	Arsenal	9	—				
1984–85	....	27	10				
1985–86	....	33	6				

ALLON, Joe

Born Gateshead 12.11.66. Ht 5 11 Wt 11 2
Forward. From YTS. England Youth.

1984–85	Newcastle U	1	—
1985–86	....	3	1

ANDERSON, Colin

Born Newcastle 26.4.62. Ht 5 9 Wt 10 7
Forward. From Apprentice.

1979–80	Burnley	—	—
1980–81	....	2	—
1981–82	....	4	—
1982–83	Torquay U	42	5
1983–84	....	39	4
1984–85	....	28	2
1984–85	*QPR*............................	—	—
1984–85	WBA	—	—
1985–86	....	11	—

ANDERSON, Darren

Born Merton 6.9.66. Ht 6 1 Wt 13 5
Defender. From QPR Schoolboy and
Coventry C Apprentice. England Youth.

1983–84	Charlton Ath	1	—
1984–85	....	9	1
1985–86	....	—	—
1985–86	*Crewe Alex*..................	5	—

ANDERSON, Dougie

Born Hong Kong 29.8.63. Ht 6 0 Wt 10 5
Forward. From Port Glasgow.

1980–81	Oldham Ath	—	—
1981–82	....	2	—
1982–83	....	5	—
1983–84	....	2	—
1984–85	Tranmere R.................	45	2
1985–86	....	46	11

ANDERSON, John

Born Dublin 7.11.59. Ht 5 11 Wt 11 8
Defender. From Apprentice. Eire Under-21.
7 full caps.

1977–78	WBA..........................	—	—
1978–79	....	—	—
1979–80	Preston	5	—
1980–81	....	8	—
1981–82	....	38	—
1982–83	Newcastle U	33	1
1983–84	....	41	1
1984–85	....	35	1
1985–86	....	38	3

ANDERSON, Viv

Born Nottingham 29.8.56. Ht 6 0 Wt 11 1
Defender. From Apprentice. England
Under-21 'B', 21 full caps, Football League.

1974–75	Nottingham F	16	—
1975–76	....	21	—
1976–77	....	38	1
1977–78	....	37	3
1978–79	....	40	1
1979–80	....	41	3
1980–81	....	31	—
1981–82	....	39	—
1982–83	....	25	1
1983–84	....	40	6
1984–85	Arsenal	41	3
1985–86	....	39	2

ANDREWS, Gary

Born Nottingham 12.5.68. Ht 5 11
Wt 11 13½
Defender. From Apprentice.

1985–86	Nottingham F	—	—

ANDREWS, Ian

Born Nottingham 1.12.64. Ht 6 1½ Wt 12 6
Goalkeeper. From Apprentice. England
Youth.

Season	Club	League Appearances/Goals		Season	Club	League Appearances/Goals	

1982–83	Leicester C	—	—
1983–84		2	—
1983–84	*Swindon T*	1	—
1984–85	Leicester C	31	—
1985–86		39	—

ANDREWS, Keri

Born Swansea 28.4.68.
Forward. From Apprentice. Wales Youth.

| 1984–85 | Swansea C | 1 | — |
| 1985–86 | | 1 | — |

ANGELL, Darren

Born Newbury 19.1.67.   Ht 6 2   Wt 11 4
Defender. From Reading amateur.

| 1985–86 | Portsmouth | — | — |

ANGUS, Ian

Born Glasgow 19.11.61.   Ht 5 10   Wt 10 3
Midfield. From Eastercraigs.

1979–80	Aberdeen	—	—
1980–81		19	1
1981–82		1	1
1982–83		5	3
1983–84		12	
1984–85		28	2
1985–86		17	2

ARCHDEACON, Owen

Born Greenock 4.3.66.   Ht 5 9   Wt 10 8
Forward. From Gourock United. Scotland Youth.

1982–83	Celtic	—	—
1983–84		1	—
1984–85		3	1
1985–86		23	3

ARCHIBALD, Steve

Born Glasgow 27.9.56.   Ht 5 10   Wt 11 2
Forward. From Fernhill Ath. Scotland
Under-21, 26 full caps.

1974–75	Clyde	4	—
1975–76		16	2
1976–77		31	3
1977–78		14	2
1977–78	Aberdeen	10	4
1978–79		32	13
1979–80		34	12
1980–81	Tottenham H	41	20
1981–82		27	6
1982–83		31	11
1983–84		32	21
1984–85	Barcelona	32	15
1985–86		13	4

ARDILES, Ossie

Born Cordoba, Argentina 3.8.52.   Ht 5 6
Wt 9 10
Midfield. From Huracan. Argentina 42 full
caps.

1978–79	Tottenham H	38	3
1979–80		40	3
1980–81		36	5
1981–82		26	2
1982–83	Paris St. Germain	14	1
1982–83	Tottenham H	2	—
1983–84		9	—
1984–85		11	2
1985–86		23	1

ARMES, Chris

Born Norwich 30.6.67.
Midfield. From Apprentice.

| 1984–85 | Norwich C | — | — |
| 1985–86 | | — | — |

Season	Club	League Appearances/Goals

ARMSTRONG, David

Born Durham 26.12.54. Ht 5 8 Wt 11 5
Midfield. From Apprentice. England Under-23, 'B', 3 full caps.

Season	Club	League Appearances/Goals	
1971–72	Middlesbrough	6	—
1972–73		20	1
1973–74		42	5
1974–75		42	5
1975–76		42	6
1976–77		42	8
1977–78		42	6
1978–79		42	11
1979–80		42	11
1980–81		39	6
1981–82	Southampton	41	15
1982–83		41	8
1983–84		42	15
1984–85		35	10
1985–86		41	10

ARMSTRONG, Gary

Born London 2.1.58. Ht 5 8 Wt 10 7
Defender. Local.

Season	Club	League Appearances/Goals	
1975–76	Gillingham	1	—
1976–77		30	—
1977–78		28	1
1978–79		26	1
1979–80		1	—
1979–80	Wimbledon	5	—
1980–81		35	—
1981–82		31	—
From Finland			
1983–84	Gillingham	8	—
1984–85	Crewe Alex	31	—
1985–86		—	—

ARMSTRONG, Gerry

Born Belfast 23.5.54. Ht 5 11 Wt 13 2
Forward. From Bangor. Northern Ireland 62
full caps.

Season	Club	League Appearances/Goals	
1975–76	Tottenham H	—	—
1976–77		21	3

Season	Club	League Appearances/Goals	
1977–78		19	2
1978–79		10	1
1979–80		30	4
1980–81		4	—
1980–81	Watford	24	3
1981–82		33	7
1982–83		19	2
From Mallorca			
1985–86	WBA	8	—
1985–86	Chesterfield	12	1

ARMSTRONG, Gordon

Born Newcastle 15.7.67. Ht 6 0 Wt 11 2
Forward. From Apprentice.

Season	Club	League Appearances/Goals	
1984–85	Sunderland	4	—
1985–86		14	2

ARMSTRONG, Kenny

Born Bridgnorth 31.1.59. Ht 6 2 Wt 13 7.
Defender. From Beith Jun.

Season	Club	League Appearances/Goals	
1977–78	Kilmarnock	—	—
1978–79		4	—
1979–80		3	—
1980–81		22	1
1981–82		39	2
1982–83		19	—
1983–84	Southampton	26	—
1983–84	*Notts Co*	10	—
1984–85	Birmingham C	36	—
1985–86		22	1
1985–86	Walsall	—	—

ARNOLD, Jim

Born Stafford 6.8.50. Ht 6 1 Wt 11 6
Goalkeeper. From Stafford Rangers.

Season	Club	League Appearances/Goals	
1979–80	Blackburn R	38	—
1980–81		20	—
1981–82	Everton	16	—
1982–83		25	—
1982–83	*Preston NE*	6	—
1983–84	Everton	7	—
1984–85		—	—
1985–86	Port Vale	41	—

Season	Club	League Appearances/Goals		Season	Club	League Appearances/Goals	

ARNOTT, Kevin

Born Bensham 28.9.58. Ht 5 10 Wt 11 12
Midfield. From Apprentice.

Season	Club	App	Goals
1976–77	Sunderland	20	3
1977–78		21	3
1978–79		15	—
1979–80		37	8
1980–81		34	2
1981–82		6	—
1981–82	*Blackburn R*	17	2
1982–83	Sheffield U	7	1
1982–83	*Blackburn R*	12	1
1982–83	*Rotherham U*	9	2
1983–84	Sheffield U	46	6
1984–85		27	3
1985–86		18	1

ASH, Mark

Born Sheffield 22.1.68.   Ht 5 9½ Wt 11 4
Defender. From Apprentice.

Season	Club	App	Goals
1985–86	Rotherham U	—	—

ASHCROFT, Billy

Born Liverpool 1.10.52.   Ht 6 1   Wt 14 4
Defender. From Juniors.

Season	Club	App	Goals
1970–71	Wrexham	19	8
1971–72		29	5
1972–73		35	14
1973–74		28	6
1974–75		23	4
1975–76		42	14
1976–77		40	20
1977–78		3	1
1977–78	Middlesbrough	36	6
1978–79		37	6
1979–80		35	3
1980–81		30	2
1981–82		21	4
From Twente			
1985–86	Tranmere R	23	2

ASHURST, Jack

Born Coatbridge 12.10.54.   Ht 6 0   Wt 12 2
Defender. From Apprentice.

Season	Club	App	Goals
1971–72	Sunderland	—	—
1972–73		11	—
1973–74		19	1
1974–75		6	—
1975–76		21	—
1976–77		31	—
1977–78		38	2
1978–79		11	1
1979–80		3	—
1979–80	Blackpool	25	—
1980–81		28	3
1981–82	Carlisle U	46	1
1982–83		30	—
1983–84		41	1
1984–85		42	—
1985–86		35	—

ASHWORTH, Neil

Born Southend 16.1.68.   Ht 5 11
Forward. From YTS.

Season	Club	App	Goals
1984–85	Rochdale	1	—
1985–86		—	—

ASKEW, Billy

Born Lumley 2.10.59.   Ht 5 5   Wt 10 0
Midfield. From Apprentice.

Season	Club	App	Goals
1977–78	Middlesbrough	—	—
1978–79		—	—
1979–80		1	—
1980–81		5	—
1981–82		6	—
1981–82	*Blackburn R*	—	—
1982–83	Hull C	36	6
1983–84		33	1
1984–85		46	6
1985–86		33	2

Season	Club	League Appearances/Goals		Season	Club	League Appearances/Goals

ASPIN, Neil

Born Gateshead 12.4.65.   Ht 6 1   Wt 12 3
Defender. From Apprentice.

1981–82	Leeds U	1	—
1982–83		15	—
1983–84		21	1
1984–85		32	1
1985–86		38	2

ASPINALL, Warren

Born Wigan 13.9.67.   Ht 5 8   Wt 10 6
Midfield. From Apprentice. England Youth.

1984–85	Wigan Ath	10	1
1985–86		—	—
1985–86	Everton	1	—
1985–86	*Wigan Ath*	41	21

ASTBURY, Mike

Born Leeds 22.1.64.   Ht 5 11   Wt 13 0
Goalkeeper. From Apprentice.

1980–81	York C	1	—
1981–82		15	—
1982–83		4	—
1983–84		5	—
1984–85		7	—
1985–86		16	—
1985–86	*Peterborough U*	4	—
1985–86	Darlington	14	—

ATKINS, Bob

Born Leicester 16.10.62.   Ht 6 0½   Wt 12 1½
Defender. Local.

1982–83	Sheffield U	8	—
1983–84		16	3
1984–85		16	—
1984–85	Preston NE	13	—
1985–86		34	2

ATKINS, Ian

Born Birmingham 16.1.57.   Ht 6 0
Wt 11 13
Midfield. From Apprentice.

1974–75	Shrewsbury T	—	—
1975–76		32	4
1976–77		43	7
1977–78		41	10
1978–79		44	11
1979–80		39	3
1980–81		39	6
1981–82		40	17
1982–83	Sunderland	37	4
1983–84		40	2
1984–85		—	—
1984–85	Everton	6	1
1985–86		1	—
1985–86	Ipswich T	21	2

ATKINSON, Dalian

Born Shrewsbury 21.3.68.   Ht 5 11   Wt 11 1
Forward.

| 1985–86 | Ipswich T | 1 | — |

ATKINSON, Paul

Born Chester-le-Street 19.1.66.   Ht 5 9¼
Wt 10 2
Midfield. From Apprentice. England Youth.

1983–84	Sunderland	8	1
1984–85		9	1
1985–86		13	—

ATKINSON, Paul

Born Otley 14.8.61.   Ht 5 10   Wt 11 5
Forward. From Apprentice.

1979–80	Oldham Ath	38	6
1980–81		30	2
1981–82		33	—
1982–83		42	3
1983–84	Watford	11	—
1984–85		—	—
1985–86	Oldham Ath	26	1

Season	Club	League Appearances/Goals

AULD, Stuart

Born Glasgow 22.2.58. Ht 5 11 Wt 12 7
Defender. From Pollok.

1985–86	Clydebank	27	1

AYLOTT, Trevor

Born London 26.11.57. Ht 6 1½ Wt 14 0
Forward. From Apprentice.

1976–77	Chelsea	—	—
1976–77	*QPR*	—	—
1977–78	Chelsea	11	2
1978–79		15	—
1979–80		3	—
1979–80	Barnsley	18	4
1980–81		37	11
1981–82		41	11
1982–83	Millwall	32	5
1982–83	Luton T	12	2
1983–84		20	8
1984–85	Crystal Palace	35	8
1985–86		18	4
1985–86	*Barnsley*	9	—

AYRE, Bill

Born Crookhill 7.5.52. Ht 5 10 Wt 11 4
Defender. From Scarborough.

1977–78	Hartlepool U	46	12
1978–79		42	5
1979–80		43	9
1980–81		10	1
1980–81	Halifax T	19	1
1981–82		44	4
1982–83	Mansfield T	42	3
1983–84		25	4
1984–85	Halifax T	22	2
1985–86		10	—

BADOCK, Steve

Born Kensington 10.9.58. Ht 6 0 Wt 12 0
Forward. From Portway Bristol.

1985–86	Bristol R	17	3

BAILEY, Gary

Born Ipswich 9.8.58. Ht 6 1½ Wt 13 2
Goalkeeper. From Witts Univ., S. Africa.
England Under–21, 'B', 2 full caps.

1977–78	Manchester U	—	—
1978–79		28	—
1979–80		42	—
1980–81		40	—
1981–82		39	—
1982–83		37	—
1983–84		40	—
1984–85		38	—
1985–86		25	—

BAILEY, John

Born Liverpool 1.4.57. Ht 5 8 Wt 11 3
Defender. From Apprentice.

1975–76	Blackburn R.	6	—
1976–77		34	—
1977–78		41	1
1978–79		39	—
1979–80	Everton	42	2
1980–81		31	—
1981–82		12	—
1982–83		37	1
1983–84		33	—
1984–85		15	—
1985–86		1	—
1985–86	Newcastle U	28	—

BAILEY, Neil

Born Wigan 26.9.58. Ht 5 6 Wt 11 4
Midfield. From Apprentice.

1976–77	Burnley	—	—
1977–78		—	—
1978–79	Newport Co	21	1

Season	Club	League Appearances/Goals
1979–80	....	29 1
1980–81	....	21 1
1981–82	....	18 —
1982–83	....	40 4
1983–84	....	5 —
1983–84	Wigan Ath	23 1
1984–85	....	12 —
1985–86	....	6 1

BAILIE, Colin

Born Belfast 31.3.64.   Ht 5 11   Wt 10 11
Defender. From Apprentice.

Season	Club	League Appearances/Goals
1981–82	Swindon T...........	1 —
1982–83	....	26 1
1983–84	....	38 3
1984–85	....	42 —
1985–86	Reading	26 —

BAIN, Alan

Born Glasgow 5.6.62.   Ht 5 9   Wt 10 8
Forward. From Campsie Black Watch.

Season	Club	League Appearances/Goals
1984–85	Clydebank	21 4
1985–86	....	12 1

BAINES, Steve

Born Newark 23.6.54.   Ht 6 0   Wt 12 12
Defender. From Apprentice.

Season	Club	League Appearances/Goals
1972–73	Nottingham F	2 —
1973–74	....	— —
1974–75	....	— —
1975–76	Huddersfield T	41 1
1976–77	....	44 5
1977–78	....	29 4
1977–78	Bradford C	11 1
1978–79	....	43 10
1979–80	....	45 6
1980–81	Walsall	38 4
1981–82	....	10 1
1981–82	Bury	7 —
1982–83	Scunthorpe U	38 1
1983–84	Chesterfield........	45 2
1984–85	....	46 3
1985–86	....	38 3

BAIRD, Ian

Born Rotherham 1.4.64.   Ht 6 0   Wt 12 10
Forward. From Apprentice.
England Schools.

Season	Club	League Appearances/Goals
1981–82	Southampton	— —
1982–83	....	11 2
1983–84	....	6 1
1983–84	Cardiff C	12 6
1984–85	Southampton	5 2
1984–85	Newcastle U	5 1
1984–85	Leeds U..............	10 6
1985–86	....	35 12

BAKER, Clive

Born N. Walsham 14.3.59.   Ht 5 9   Wt 11 0
Goalkeeper. From Amateur.

Season	Club	League Appearances/Goals
1977–78	Norwich C............	2 —
1978–79	....	2 —
1979–80	....	— —
1980–81	....	10 —
1981–82	....	— —
1982–83	....	— —
1983–84	....	— —
1984–85	Barnsley	37 —
1985–86	....	42 —

BAKER, David

Born Newcastle 5.1.63.   Ht 6 1   Wt 12 10
Defender. From Bishop Auckland.

Season	Club	League Appearances/Goals
1984–85	Southampton	— —
1985–86	Carlisle U	35 2

BAKER, Graham

Born Southampton 3.12.58.   Ht 5 9
Wt 10 8
Midfield. From Apprentice. England
Under-21.

Season	Club	League Appearances/Goals
1977–78	Southampton	3 1
1978–79	....	22 5
1979–80	....	23 4

Season	Club	League Appearances/Goals		Season	Club	League Appearances/Goals	
1980–81	....	39	8				
1981–82	....	26	4				
1982–83	Manchester C	27	4				
1983–84	....	36	8				
1984–85	....	29	4				
1985–86	....	10	—				

BAKER, Steve

Born Southampton 16.6.62   Ht 5 5   Wt 10 2
Defender. From Apprentice.

Season	Club	League Appearances/Goals	
1979–80	Southampton...............	—	—
1980–81	....	1	—
1981–82	....	5	—
1982–83	....	7	—
1983–84	....	8	—
1983–84	*Burnley*	10	—
1984–85	Southampton...............	9	—
1985–86	....	13	—

BAKER, Terry

Born Rochford 3.11.65.   Ht 5 11   Wt 12 4½
Defender. From Apprentice.

Season	Club	League Appearances/Goals	
1983–84	West Ham U................	—	—
From Billericay T.			
1985–86	Colchester U	21	2

BAKHOLT, Kurt

Born Odense 12.8.63.
Midfield. From Vejle. Denmark Under-21.

Season	Club	League Appearances/Goals	
1985–86	*Aston Villa*	—	—
1985–86	QPR..........................	1	—

BALL, Kevin

Born Hastings 12.11.64.   Ht 5 9   Wt 11 6
Defender. From Apprentice.

Season	Club	League Appearances/Goals	
1983–84	Portsmouth	1	—
1984–85	....	—	—
1985–86	....	9	—

BAMBER, Dave

Born St. Helens 1.2.59.   Ht 6 3   Wt 13 10
Forward. From Manchester Univ.

Season	Club	League Appearances/Goals	
1979–80	Blackpool	7	1
1980–81	....	15	3
1981–82	....	38	15
1982–83	....	26	10
1983–84	Coventry C.................	19	3
1983–84	Walsall......................	10	3
1984–85	....	10	4
1984–85	Portsmouth	4	1
1985–86	....	—	—
1985–86	Swindon T..................	23	9

BANKS, Chris

Born Stone 12.11.65.   Ht 5 8   Wt 10 8
Defender. Local.

Season	Club	League Appearances/Goals	
1982–83	Port Vale	—	—
1983–84	....	—	—
1984–85	....	7	—
1985–86	....	19	1

BANKS, Ian

Born Mexborough 9.1.61.   Ht 5 9   Wt 11 13
Midfield. From Apprentice.

Season	Club	League Appearances/Goals	
1978–79	Barnsley.....................	2	—
1979–80	....	38	3
1980–81	....	45	14
1981–82	....	42	15
1982–83	....	37	5
1983–84	Leicester C..................	26	3
1984–85	....	33	9
1985–86	....	31	2

BANNISTER, Gary

Born Warrington 22.7.60.   Ht 5 8½   Wt 11 3
Forward. From Apprentice.
England Under-21.

Season	Club	League Appearances/Goals	
1978–79	Coventry C..................	4	1
1979–80	....	7	—
1980–81	....	11	2

Season	Club	League Appearances/Goals		Season	Club	League Appearances/Goals	
1981–82	Sheffield W	42	21	1979–80	West Ham U	4	—
1982–83		39	20	1980–81		—	—
1983–84		37	14	1981–82		1	—
1984–85	QPR	42	17	1982–83	Aldershot	45	24
1985–86		36	16	1983–84		46	19
				1984–85		15	4
				1984–85	York C	30	12
				1985–86		35	10

BANNON, Eamonn

Born Edinburgh 18.4.58.   Ht 5 9   Wt 11 11
Midfield. From Links B.C.
Scotland Schools, Under-21, 9 full caps.

BAPTIE, Crawford

Born Glasgow 24.2.59.   Ht 6 1   Wt 11 7
Midfield. From Baillieston Juniors.

Season	Club	League Appearances/Goals	
1976–77	Hearts	13	1
1977–78		39	12
1978–79		19	5
1978–79	Chelsea	19	1
1979–80		6	—
1979–80	Dundee U	24	4
1980–81		34	8
1981–82		36	12
1982–83		32	10
1983–84		33	7
1984–85		35	10
1985–86		31	11

Season	Club	League Appearances/Goals	
1984–85	Falkirk	26	4
1985–86		19	2
1985–86	Motherwell	16	3

BARBER, Fred

Born Ferryhill 26.8.63.   Ht 5 11   Wt 11 7
Goalkeeper. From Apprentice.

Season	Club	League Appearances/Goals	
1981–82	Darlington	—	—
1982–83		12	—
1983–84		46	—
1984–85		45	—
1985–86		32	—
1985–86	Everton	—	—

BANNON, Paul

Born Dublin 15.11.56.   Ht 6 2   Wt 12 9
Forward. From Bridgend T.

Season	Club	League Appearances/Goals	
1978–79	Carlisle U	2	—
1979–80		44	19
1980–81		30	5
1981–82		25	9
1982–83		34	11
1983–84		4	1
1983–84	*Darlington*	2	—
1983–84	Bristol R	11	3
1984–85		18	5
1984–85	*Cardiff C*	4	—
1984–85	*Plymouth Arg*	2	—
To NAC Breda			

BARBER, Philip

Born Tring 10.6.65.   Ht 5 11   Wt 12 6
Forward. From Aylesbury.

Season	Club	League Appearances/Goals	
1983–84	Crystal Palace	9	2
1984–85		23	4
1985–86		39	9

BARDSLEY, David

Born Manchester 11.9.64.   Ht 5 9   Wt 10 10
Defender. From Apprentice. England Youth

Season	Club	League Appearances/Goals	
1981–82	Blackpool	1	—
1982–83		28	—
1983–84		16	—
1983–84	Watford	25	—
1984–85		17	—
1985–86		13	2

BANTON, Dale

Born Kensington 15.5.61.   Ht 5 10
Wt 10 10
Midfield. From Apprentice

Season	Club	League Appearances/Goals		Season	Club	League Appearances/Goals	

BARHAM, Mark

Born Folkestone 12.7.62. Ht 5 7 Wt 11 0
Midfield. From Apprentice. England Youth,
2 full caps.

Season	Club	App	Goals
1979–80	Norwich C	4	—
1980–81		35	1
1981–82		27	4
1982–83		38	4
1983–84		11	2
1984–85		14	1
1985–86		35	10

BARKER, Simon

Born Farnworth 4.11.64. Ht 5 9 Wt 10 11
Midfield. From Apprentice. England Under-
21.

Season	Club	App	Goals
1982–83	Blackburn R	—	—
1983–84		28	3
1984–85		38	2
1985–86		41	10

BARLOW, Andy

Born Oldham 24.11.65. Ht 5 9 Wt 11 1
Defender.

Season	Club	App	Goals
1984–85	Oldham Ath	33	—
1985–86		26	—

BARNARD, Leigh

Born Worsley 29.10.58. Ht 5 8 Wt 11 7
Midfield. From Apprentice.

Season	Club	App	Goals
1977–78	Portsmouth	11	—
1978–79		28	7
1979–80		5	—
1980–81		18	1
1981–82		17	—
1981–82	*Peterborough U*	4	—
1982–83	Swindon T	46	4
1983–84		36	7
1984–85		32	2
1984–85	*Exeter C*	6	2
1985–86	Swindon T	38	3

BARNES, Bobby

Born Kingston 17.12.62. Ht 5 7 Wt 10 5
Forward. From Apprentice.

Season	Club	App	Goals
1980–81	West Ham	6	1
1981–82		3	—
1982–83		—	—
1983–84		13	2
1984–85		20	2
1985–86		1	—
1985–86	*Scunthorpe U*	6	—
1985–86	Aldershot	14	8

BARNES, David

Born London 16.11.61. Ht 5 10 Wt 11 1
Defender. From Apprentice.
England Youth.

Season	Club	App	Goals
1979–80	Coventry C	3	—
1980–81		—	—
1981–82		6	—
1981–82	Ipswich T	—	—
1982–83		6	—
1983–84		11	—
1984–85		—	—
1984–85	Wolves	23	1
1985–86		38	1

BARNES, John

Born Jamaica 7.11.63. Ht 5 11 Wt 12 0
Forward. From Sudbury Court.
England Under-21, 27 full caps.

Season	Club	App	Goals
1981–82	Watford	36	13
1982–83		42	10
1983–84		39	11
1984–85		40	12
1985–86		39	9

BARNES, Mike

Born Reading 17.9.63. Ht 6 4 Wt 13 4
Defender. From Apprentice.

Season	Club	App	Goals
1980–81	Reading	1	—
1981–82		6	—
1982–83		21	2
1983–84		6	—
1984–85	Northampton T	19	1
1985–86		—	—

Season	Club	League Appearances/Goals	Season	Club	League Appearances/Goals

BARNES, Paul

Born Leicester 16.11.67.   Ht 5 10½   Wt 10 2
Forward. From Apprentice.

1985–86	Notts Co	14	4

BARNES, Peter

Born Manchester 10.6.57.   Ht 5 10   Wt 11 0
Forward. From Apprentice. England Youth,
Under-21 'B', 22 full caps, Football League.

1974–75	Manchester C	3	1
1975–76	....	28	3
1976–77	....	21	2
1977–78	....	34	8
1978–79	....	29	1
1979–80	WBA	38	15
1980–81	....	39	8
1981–82	Leeds U	30	1
From Real Betis			
1983–84	Leeds U	27	4
1984–85	....	—	—
1984–85	*Manchester U*	—	—
1984–85	Coventry C	18	2
1985–86	Manchester U	13	2

BARNETT, Gary

Born Stratford 11.3.63.   Ht 5 5   Wt 9 4
Midfield. From Apprentice.

1980–81	Coventry C	—	—
1981–82	....	—	—
1982–83	Oxford U	22	2
1982–83	*Wimbledon*	5	1
1983–84	Oxford U	19	7
1984–85	....	2	—
1984–85	*Fulham*	2	1
1985–86	Oxford U	2	—
1985–86	Fulham	36	6

BARNSLEY, Andy

Born Sheffield 9.6.62.   Ht 6 0   Wt 11 11
Defender. From Denaby U.

1984–85	Rotherham U	—	—
1985–86	....	28	—

BARRATT, Tony

Born Salford 18.10.65.   Ht 5 8   Wt 10 2
Defender. From Billingham T.

1985–86	Grimsby T	22	—

BARRETT, Earl

Born Rochdale 28.4.67.
Defender. From Apprentice.

1984–85	Manchester C	—	—
1985–86	....	1	—
1985–86	*Chester C*	12	—

BARRETT, Scott

Born Derby 2.4.63.   Ht 6 0   Wt 12 11
Goalkeeper. From Ilkeston T.

1984–85	Wolverhampton W	4	—
1985–86	....	21	—

BARRON, Paul

Born London 16.9.53.   Ht 6 2   Wt 13 5
Goalkeeper. From Slough T.

1976–77	Plymouth Arg	3	—
1977–78	....	41	—
1978–79	Arsenal	3	—
1979–80	....	5	—
1980–81	Crystal Palace	33	—
1981–82	....	40	—
1982–83	....	17	—
1982–83	WBA	20	—
1983–84	....	42	—
1984–85	....	1	—
1984–85	*Stoke C*	1	—
1984–85	QPR	—	—
1985–86	....	31	—

BARROW, Graham

Born Chorley 13.6.54.   Ht 6 2   Wt 13 7
Midfield. From Altrincham.

Season	Club	League Appearances/Goals		Season	Club	League Appearances/Goals

Season	Club	Appearances	Goals
1981–82	Wigan Ath	41	12
1982–83		28	3
1983–84		42	5
1984–85		38	9
1985–86		30	7

BARTRAM, Vince

Born Birmingham 7.8.68.   Ht 6 2   Wt 13 4
Goalkeeper. From Local.

Season	Club	Appearances	Goals
1985–86	Wolverhampton W	—	—

BATCH, Nigel

Born Huddersfield 9.11.57.   Ht 5 10
Wt 12 7
Goalkeeper. From Derby Co. Apprentice.

Season	Club	Appearances	Goals
1976–77	Grimsby T	8	—
1977–78		10	—
1978–79		46	—
1979–80		46	—
1980–81		42	—
1981–82		42	—
1982–83		38	—
1983–84		42	—
1984–85		23	—
1985–86		30	—

BATER, Phil

Born Cardiff 26.10.55.   Ht 5 10½   Wt 12 12.
Defender. From Apprentice. Wales
Under-21.

Season	Club	Appearances	Goals
1973–74	Bristol R	—	—
1974–75		30	—
1975–76		17	—
1976–77		30	1
1977–78		41	—
1978–79		36	—
1979–80		34	1
1980–81		24	—
1981–82		—	—
1981–82	Wrexham	36	1
1982–83		37	—
1983–84		—	—
1983–84	Bristol R	32	1
1984–85		39	—
1985–86		27	—

BATES, Chic

Born West Bromwich 28.11.49.   Ht 6 1
Wt 11 6
Forward. From Stourbridge.

Season	Club	Appearances	Goals
1974–75	Shrewsbury T	46	17
1975–76		43	7
1976–77		45	13
1977–78		26	8
1977–78	Swindon T	14	1
1978–79		42	14
1979–80		7	—
1979–80	Bristol R	11	2
1980–81		18	2
1980–81	Shrewsbury T	15	2
1981–82		40	4
1982–83		38	9
1983–84		16	3
1984–85		20	1
1985–86		5	—

BATTY, Lawrence

Born London 15.2.64.
Goalkeeper.

Season	Club	Appearances	Goals
1984–85	Fulham	—	—
1985–86		2	—

BATTY, Paul

Born Edington 9.1.64.   Ht 5 7   Wt 10 7
Midfield. From Apprentice.

Season	Club	Appearances	Goals
1981–82	Swindon T	—	—
1982–83		39	1
1983–84		41	4
1984–85		28	2
1985–86	Chesterfield	26	—

BEACOCK, Garry

Born Scunthorpe 22.1.60   Ht 5 10   Wt 11 10
Midfield. From Local.

All appearances include those as substitute

Season	Club	League Appearances/Goals
1980–81	Grimsby T	2 —
1981–82		13 —
1982–83		1 —
1983–84	Hereford U	14 3
1984–85		— —
1985–86		13 1

BEAGRIE, Peter

Born Middlesbrough 28.11.65.   Ht 5 8¼
Wt 9 9¾
Defender. From Local.

1983–84	Middlesbrough	— —
1984–85		7 1
1985–86		26 1

BEARDSLEY, Peter

Born Newcastle 18.1.61.   Ht 5 8   Wt 11 4
Forward. From Wallsend B.C. England 5 full
caps

1979–80	Carlisle U	37 8
1980–81		43 10
1981–82		22 4
From Vancouver Whitecaps		
1982–83	Manchester U	— —
From Vancouver Whitecaps		
1983–84	Newcastle U	35 20
1984–85		38 17
1985–86		42 19

BEASANT, Dave

Born Willesden 20.3.59.   Ht 6 4   Wt 13 0
Goalkeeper. From Edgware T.

1979–80	Wimbledon	2 —
1980–81		34 —
1981–82		46 —
1982–83		46 —
1983–84		46 —
1984–85		42 —
1985–86		42 —

BEASLEY, Andy

Born Sedgley 5.2.64.   Ht 6 2   Wt 12 2
Goalkeeper. From Apprentice.

1981–82	Luton T	— —
1982–83		— —
1983–84		— —
1983–84	*Mansfield T*	— —
1983–84	*Gillingham*	— —
1984–85	Mansfield T	3 —
1985–86		— —

BEATTIE, Andy

Born Liverpool. 9.2.64.   Ht 6 2   Wt 11 10
Defender. From Apprentice.

1981–82	Cambridge U	— —
1982–83		— —
1983–84		21 —
1984–85		18 —
1985–86		23 —

BEATTIE, Stuart

Born Stevenston 10.7.67.   Ht 6 2   Wt 11 10
Defender. From Ardeer Recreation B.C.

1985–86	Rangers	5 —

BEAUMONT, David

Born Edinburgh 10.12.63.   Ht 5 10   Wt 11 5
Defender. 'S' Form. Scotland Youth, Under-
21.

1980–81	Dundee U	— —
1981–82		— —
1982–83		— —
1983–84		2 —
1984–85		18 1
1985–86		13 —

BEAUMONT, Nigel

Born Pontefract 11.2.67.   Ht 6 1   Wt 12 7
Defender.

1984–85	Bradford C	— —
1985–86		2 —

17

Season	Club	League Appearances/Goals	Season	Club	League Appearances/Goals

BEAVON, Stuart

Born Wolverhampton 30.11.58.   Ht 5 6½
Wt 10 4
Midfield. From Apprentice.

1976–77	Tottenham H	— —
1977–78		— —
1978–79		1 —
1979–80		3 —
1979–80	*Notts Co*	6 —
1980–81	Reading	37 6
1981–82		40 5
1982–83		46 4
1983–84		36 7
1984–85		46 2
1985–86		44 3

BECK, John

Born Edmonton 25.5.54.   Ht 5 10½   Wt 11 9
Midfield. From Apprentice.

1972–73	QPR	1 —
1973–74		5 —
1974–75		29 1
1975–76		5 —
1976–77	Coventry C	40 3
1977–78		23 2
1978–79		6 1
1978–79	Fulham	32 2
1979–80		40 2
1980–81		37 8
1981–82		5 1
1982–83		— —
1982–83	*Bournemouth*	4 1
1982–83	Bournemouth	11 3
1983–84		45 3
1984–85		36 1
1985–86		41 5

BECKFORD, Darren

Born Manchester 12.5.67.   Ht 6 1   Wt 11 1
Forward. From Apprentice.

1984–85	Manchester C	4 —
1985–86		3 —
1985–86	*Bury*	12 5

BEEBY, Shane

Born Leeds 27.2.67.
Midfield. From Apprentice.

1984–85	Bradford C	— —
1985–86		— —

BEEDIE, Stuart

Born Aberdeen 16.8.60.   Ht 5 10   Wt 11 0
Midfield. From Sunnybank.

1978–79	Montrose	10 —
1979–80		34 4
1980–81		36 9
1981–82	St Johnstone	26 5
1982–83		34 2
1983–84		34 2
1984–85	Dundee U	26 3
1985–86		18 3

BEESLEY, Paul

Born Wigan 21.7.65.
Defender. From Local.

1984–85	Wigan Ath	2 —
1985–86		17 —

BEESTON, Carl

Born Stoke 30.6.67.   Ht 5 9   Wt 10 3
Midfield. From Apprentice.

1984–85	Stoke C	1 —
1985–86		5 —

BEGGS, Billy

Born Ballymena 27.8.67.
Forward. From Apprentice.

1985–86	QPR	— —

Season	Club	League Appearances/Goals		Season	Club	League Appearances/Goals	

BEGLIN, Jim

Born Waterford 29.7.63.   Ht 5 11   Wt 11 0
Defender. From Shamrock R. Eire 12 full
caps.

Season	Club	App	Goals
1982–83	Liverpool	—	—
1983–84		—	—
1984–85		10	1
1985–86		34	1

BELFORD, Dale

Born Burton 11.7.67.
Goalkeeper. From Apprentice.

Season	Club	App	Goals
1985–86	Aston Villa	—	—

BELL, Derek

Born Wyberton 30.11.56.   Ht 5 9   Wt 10 9
Forward. From Apprentice.

Season	Club	App	Goals
1975–76	Halifax T	31	7
1975–76	*Sheffield W*	5	1
1976–77	Halifax T	26	2
1977–78		44	9
1978–79		11	3
1978–79	Barnsley	32	18
1979–80		14	2
1979–80	Lincoln C	25	5
1980–81		9	—
1981–82		14	5
1982–83		35	23
1983–84	Chesterfield	17	3
1983–84	Scunthorpe U	19	5
1984–85		3	2
1985–86		—	—

BELL, Doug

Born Paisley 5.9.59.   Ht 5 11   Wt 12 1
Midfield. From Cumbernauld.
Scotland Under-21.

Season	Club	App	Goals
1977–78	St Mirren	2	1
1978–79		—	—
1979–80	Aberdeen	9	—
1980–81		17	1
1981–82		13	1
1982–83		23	1
1983–84		24	3
1984–85		22	—
1985–86	Rangers	23	—

BELL, Graham

Born Middleton 30.3.55.   Ht 5 9   Wt 10 6
Midfield. From Chadderton F.C. England
Youth.

Season	Club	App	Goals
1973–74	Oldham	—	—
1974–75		35	—
1975–76		40	3
1976–77		36	4
1977–78		36	—
1978–79		23	2
1978–79	Preston NE	10	1
1979–80		36	2
1980–81		35	1
1981–82		22	1
1981–82	*Huddersfield T*	2	—
1982–83	Preston NE	40	4
1983–84	Carlisle U	14	—
1983–84	Bolton W	20	1
1984–85		36	—
1985–86		36	2

BELLAMY, Gary

Born Worksop 4.7.62.   Ht 6 2   Wt 11 5
Defender. From Apprentice.

Season	Club	App	Goals
1980–81	Chesterfield	3	—
1981–82		25	—
1982–83		42	—
1983–84		38	1
1984–85		22	2
1985–86		12	2

Season	Club	League Appearances/Goals		Season	Club	League Appearances/Goals	

BENJAMIN, Ian

Born Nottingham 11.12.61.   Ht 5 11
Wt 12 0
Midfield. From Apprentice. England Youth.

Season	Club	Apps	Goals
1978–79	Sheffield U	2	2
1979–80		3	1
1979–80	WBA	—	—
1980–81		2	—
1981–82	Notts Co	—	—
1982–83	Peterborough U	46	6
1983–84		34	8
1984–85	Northampton T	44	18
1985–86		46	22

BENJAMIN, Tristan

Born St. Kitts 1.4.57.   Ht 6 0   Wt 11 1
Defender. From Apprentice.

Season	Club	Apps	Goals
1974–75	Notts Co	2	—
1975–76		5	2
1976–77		7	—
1977–78		16	—
1978–79		27	—
1979–80		34	2
1980–81		42	—
1981–82		41	—
1982–83		34	—
1983–84		15	—
1984–85		21	—
1985–86		43	—

BENNETT, Dave

Born Manchester 11.7.59.   Ht 6 0   Wt 11 2
Forward. From Amateur.

Season	Club	Apps	Goals
1978–79	Manchester C	1	—
1979–80		25	2
1980–81		26	7
1981–82		—	—
1981–82	Cardiff C	36	6
1982–83		41	12
1983–84	Coventry C	34	6

Season	Club	Apps	Goals
1984–85		34	2
1985–86		38	6

BENNETT, Gary

Born Manchester 4.12.61. Ht 6 1   Wt 11 11½
Defender. From Amateur.

Season	Club	Apps	Goals
1979–80	Manchester C	—	—
1980–81		—	—
1981–82	Cardiff C	19	1
1982–83		36	8
1983–84		32	2
1984–85	Sunderland	37	3
1985–86		28	3

BENNETT, Gary

Born Liverpool 20.9.63.
Midfield. Local.

Season	Club	Apps	Goals
1984–85	Wigan Ath	20	3
1985–86	Chester C	43	13

BENNETT, Martyn

Born Birmingham 4.8.61.   Ht 6 0   Wt 12 12
Defender. From Apprentice. England
Schoolboy.

Season	Club	Apps	Goals
1978–79	WBA	1	—
1979–80		4	—
1980–81		16	1
1981–82		23	2
1982–83		23	1
1983–84		29	—
1984–85		39	—
1985–86		25	2

BENNETT, Mike

Born Bolton 24.12.62.   Ht. 5 7   Wt 10 6
Defender. From Apprentice.
England Youth.

Season	Club	League Appearances/Goals		Season	Club	League Appearances/Goals	
1979–80	Bolton W	8	—				
1980–81		6	1				
1981–82		35	—				
1982–83		16	—				
1983–84	Wolverhampton W	6	—				
1983–84	Cambridge U	11	—				
1984–85		34	—				
1985–86		31	—				

BENSTEAD, Graham

Born Aldersot 20.8.63.   Ht 6 1   Wt 12 11
Goalkeeper. From Apprentice. England
Youth.

Season	Club	League Appearances/Goals	
1981–82	QPR	—	—
1982–83		—	—
1983–84		—	—
1984–85		—	—
1984–85	*Norwich C*	1	—
1985–86	Norwich C	—	—

BERESFORD, John

Born Sheffield 4.9.66.   Ht 5 5   Wt 10 4
Midfield. From Apprentice.
England Schools, Youth.

Season	Club	League Appearances/Goals	
1983–84	Manchester C	—	—
1984–85		—	—
1985–86		—	—

BERRY, George

Born West Germany 19.11.57.   Ht 6 0
Wt 13 4
Defender. From Apprentice. Wales 5 full caps.

Season	Club	League Appearances/Goals	
1975–76	Wolverhampton W	—	—
1976–77		1	—
1977–78		7	—
1978–79		30	3
1979–80		41	—
1980–81		25	1
1981–82		20	—
1982–83	Stoke C	31	5
1983–84		8	—
1984–85		32	1
1984–85	*Doncaster R*	1	—
1985–86	Stoke C	41	3

BERRY, Les

Born Plumstead 4.5.56.   Ht 6 2   Wt 11 13
Defender. From Apprentice.

Season	Club	League Appearances/Goals	
1973–74	Charlton Ath	—	—
1974–75		—	—
1975–76		15	1
1976–77		39	2
1977–78		41	2
1978–79		38	1
1979–80		42	2
1980–81		44	2
1981–82		25	—
1982–83		39	1
1983–84		42	—
1984–85		26	—
1985–86		7	—

BERRY, Neil

Born Edinburgh 6.4.63.   Ht 6 0   Wt 12 0
Defender.   From   Apprentice.   Scotland
Youth.

Season	Club	League Appearances/Goals	
1980–81	Bolton W	—	—
1981–82		3	—
1982–83		9	—
1983–84		14	—
1984–85		6	—
1984–85	Hearts	3	—
1985–86		32	2

BERRY, Steve

Born Gosport 4.4.63.   Ht 5 7   Wt 11 6
Midfield. From Apprentice.

Season	Club	League Appearances/Goals	
1980–81	Portsmouth	—	—
1981–82		27	2
1982–83		1	—
1983–84		—	—
1983–84	*Aldershot*	7	—
1984–85	Sunderland	34	2
1985–86		1	—
1985–86	Newport Co	26	3

Season	Club	League Appearances/Goals		Season	Club	League Appearances/Goals	

BERTSCHIN, Keith

Born Enfield 25.8.56. Ht 6 1 Wt 11 8
Forward. From Barnet. England Youth, Under-21.

Season	Club	App	Goals
1973–74	Ipswich T	—	—
1974–75		—	—
1975–76		3	2
1976–77		29	6
1977–78	Birmingham C	42	11
1978–79		9	2
1979–80		37	12
1980–81		30	4
1981–82	Norwich C	36	12
1982–83		40	8
1983–84		33	7
1984–85		5	2
1984–85	Stoke C	25	2
1985–86		42	19

BESTE, Robin

Born Bermondsey 16.3.66. Ht 5 10 Wt 11 0
Forward. From Apprentice.

Season	Club	App	Goals
1984–85	Chelsea	—	—
1985–86		—	—

BETT, Jim

Born Hamilton 25.11.59. Ht 5 11 Wt 12 3
Midfield. From school. Scotland Schools, Under-21, 16 full caps.

Season	Club	App	Goals
1976–77	Airdrieonians	1	—
1977–78		7	—
From Iceland and Lokeren			
1980–81	Rangers	34	4
1981–82		35	11
1982–83		35	6
From Lokeren			
1985–86	Aberdeen	24	3

BIGGINS, Steve

Born Walsall 20.6.54. Ht 6 0 Wt 11 12
Forward. From Hednesford T.

Season	Club	App	Goals
1977–78	Shrewsbury T	9	7
1978–79		45	9
1979–80		37	13
1980–81		33	9
1981–82		22	3
1982–83	Oxford U	10	1
1983–84		42	19
1984–85		7	2
1984–85	Derby C	10	1
1984–85	*Wolves*	4	—
1985–86	Derby Co	—	—
1985–86	*Port Vale*	4	—

BIGGINS, Wayne

Born Sheffield 20.11.61. Ht 5 11 Wt 11 0
Forward. From Apprentice.

Season	Club	App	Goals
1979–80	Lincoln C	—	—
1980–81		8	1
From Matlock Town and King's Lynn			
1983–84	Burnley	20	8
1984–85		46	18
1985–86		12	3
1985–86	Norwich C	28	7

BILEY, Alan

Born Leighton Buzzard 26.2.57. Ht 5 8
Wt 11 11
Forward. From Luton T. Apprentice.

Season	Club	App	Goals
1975–76	Cambridge U	12	3
1976–77		46	19
1977–78		44	21
1978–79		41	19
1979–80		22	12
1979–80	Derby C	18	9
1980–81		29	10
1981–82	Everton	19	3
1981–82	*Stoke C*	8	1
1982–83	Portsmouth	46	23
1983–84		37	16
1984–85		22	12
1984–85	Brighton & HA	13	4
1985–86		22	4

Season	Club	League Appearances/Goals		Season	Club	League Appearances/Goals

BILLINGE, Peter

Born Liverpool 24.10.64.
Defender. From South Liverpool.

1985–86	Everton	1	—

BIRCH, Alan

Born West Bromwich 12.8.56. Ht 5 6
Wt 10 5
Forward. From Apprentice.

1972–73	Walsall	8	—
1973–74		14	1
1974–75		24	2
1975–76		24	1
1976–77		25	6
1977–78		31	4
1978–79		45	9
1979–80	Chesterfield	45	13
1980–81		45	22
1981–82	Wolves	15	—
1981–82	Barnsley	17	5
1982–83		27	5
1983–84	Chesterfield	32	5
1983–84	Rotherham U	14	10
1984–85		42	6
1985–86		45	12

BIRCH, Paul

Born West Bromwich 20.11.62   Ht 5 6
Wt 10 4
Midfield. From Apprentice.

1980–81	Aston Villa	—	—
1981–82		—	—
1982–83		—	—
1983–84		22	2
1984–85		25	3
1985–86		27	2

BIRTLES, Garry

Born Nottingham 27.7.56.   Ht 6 0   Wt 12 0
Forward. From Long Eaton U.
England Under-21, 'B', 3 full caps.

1976–77	Nottingham F	1	—
1977–78		—	—
1978–79		35	14
1979–80		42	12
1980–81		9	6
1980–81	Manchester U	25	—
1981–82		33	11
1982–83		—	—
1982–83	Nottingham F	25	7
1983–84		34	15
1984–85		13	2
1985–86		25	—

BISHOP, Ian

Born Liverpool 29.5.65.   Ht 5 9½   Wt 10 6
Midfield. From Apprentice.

1983–84	Everton	1	—
1983–84	*Crewe Alex*	4	—
1984–85	Everton	—	—
1984–85	Carlisle U	30	2
1985–86		36	6

BLACK, Eric

Born Bellshill 1.10.63.   Ht 5 8   Wt 10 4
Forward. Unattached. Scotland Schools,
Youth, Under-21.

1981–82	Aberdeen	13	3
1982–83		31	12
1983–84		18	6
1984–85		27	17
1985–86		26	8

BLACK, Kenny

Born Stenhousemuir 29.11.63.   Ht 5 8
Wt 10 11
Defender. From Linlithgow Rose. Scotland
Schools, Youth.

1980–81	Rangers	—	—
1981–82		8	—
1982–83		14	1
1983–84	Motherwell	17	—
1984–85	Hearts	32	7
1985–86		29	2

Season	Club	League Appearances/Goals	Season	Club	League Appearances/Goals

BLACK, Russell

Born Dumfries 29.7.60.   Ht 5 9½   Wt 11 6
Forward. From Gretna Green.

Season	Club	Apps	Goals
1984–85	Sheffield U	12	—
1985–86		2	—
1985–86	*Dundee*	1	1

BLACKBURN, Eddie

Born Houghton Le Spring 18.4.57.   Ht 5 9
Wt 10 5
Goalkeeper. From Apprentice.

Season	Club	Apps	Goals
1974–75	Hull C	2	—
1975–76		—	—
1976–77		—	—
1977–78		19	—
1978–79		18	—
1979–80		29	—
1979–80	York C	—	—
1980–81		45	—
1981–82		31	—
1982–83		—	—
1982–83	Hartlepool U	20	—
1983–84		41	—
1984–85		9	—
1985–86		46	—

BLACKMORE, Clayton

Born Neath 23.9.64   Ht 5 8   Wt 11 3
Midfield. From Apprentice.
Wales Youth, Under-21, 6 full caps.

Season	Club	Apps	Goals
1982–83	Manchester U	—	—
1983–84		1	—
1984–85		1	—
1985–86		12	3

BLADES, Paul

Born Peterborough 5.1.65.   Ht 6 0
Wt 10 12
Defender. From Apprentice. England Youth.

Season	Club	Apps	Goals
1982–83	Derby Co	6	—
1983–84		4	—
1984–85		22	—
1985–86		30	—

BLAIR, Andy

Born Bedworth 18.12.59.   Ht 5 8   Wt 10 4
Midfield. From Apprentice.
Scotland Under-21.

Season	Club	Apps	Goals
1977–78	Coventry C	—	—
1978–79		26	1
1979–80		32	1
1980–81		35	4
1981–82	Aston Villa	18	—
1982–83		7	—
1983–84		9	—
1983–84	*Wolverhampton W*	10	—
1984–85	Sheffield W	41	3
1985–86		17	—
1985–86	Aston Villa	12	—

BLAIR, Raymond

Born Falkirk 12.11.58.   Ht 5 9   Wt 11 4
Forward. From Dunipace.

Season	Club	Apps	Goals
1976–77	Dumbarton	13	—
1977–78		19	2
1978–79		26	9
1979–80		33	8
1980–81		29	8
1981–82		39	9
1982–83		29	10
1982–83	St Johnstone	10	1
1983–84		36	4
1984–85		6	—
1984–85	Motherwell	31	6
1985–86		20	2

BLAKE, Mark

Born Portsmouth 19.12.67.
Defender. From Apprentice. England Youth.

Season	Club	Apps	Goals
1985–86	Southampton	1	—

BLAKE, Noel

Born Jamaica 12.1.62.   Ht 6 0   Wt 13 5
Defender. From Walsall Amateur and
Sutton Coldfield T.

All appearances include those as substitute

Season	Club	League Appearances/Goals		Season	Club	League Appearances/Goals	
1979–80	Aston Villa	3	—	1980–81		42	11
1980–81		—	—	1981–82		40	19
1981–82		1	—	1982–83		41	27
1981–82	*Shrewsbury T*	6	—	1983–84	AC Milan	30	5
1982–83	Aston Villa	—	—	1984–85	Watford	41	21
1982–83	Birmingham C	37	3	1985–86		23	7
1983–84		39	2				
1984–85	Portsmouth	42	3				
1985–86		42	4				

BLANKLEY, Barry

Born Aldershot, 27.10.64. Ht 5 8½ Wt 10 5
Defender. From Apprentice.

1982–83	Southampton	—	—
1983–84		—	—
1984–85		—	—
1984–85	Aldershot	28	—
1985–86		38	—

BLEASE, Rory

Born Bebbington 16.8.60.
Midfield. From Caernarvon.

1984–85	Chester C	4	—
1985–86		—	—

BLISSETT, Gary

Born Manchester 29.6.64. Ht 5 11 Wt 10 4
Forward. From Manchester C., Manchester
U. amateur, and Altrincham.

1983–84	Crewe Alex	22	3
1984–85		29	9
1985–86		38	11

BLISSETT, Luther

Born W. Indies 1.2.58. Ht 5 11 Wt 12 0
Forward. From Juniors. England Under-21,
14 full caps.

1975–76	Watford	3	1
1976–77		4	—
1977–78		33	6
1978–79		41	21
1979–80		42	10

BLOOMER, Bob

Born Sheffield 21.6.66.
Midfield.

1985–86	Chesterfield	6	—

BLOTT, John

Born Middlesbrough 26.2.65. Ht 5 11
Wt 12 2
Goalkeeper. Local.

1982–83	Manchester C	—	—
1983–84		—	—
1984–85	Carlisle U	2	—
1985–86	Scunthorpe U	—	—

BODLEY, Mike

Born Hayes 14.9.67. Ht 5 11 Wt 12 0
Defender. From Apprentice.

1985–86	Chelsea	—	—

BOGIE, Ian

Born Newcastle 6.12.67.
Midfield. From Apprentice. England
Schools.

1985–86	Newcastle U	—	—

BOLDER, Bob

Born Dover 2.10.58. Ht 6 1 Wt 14 8
Goalkeeper. From Dover.

1976–77	Sheffield W	—	—
1977–78		23	—
1978–79		19	—
1979–80		31	—
1980–81		39	—
1981–82		42	—
1982–83		42	—

Season	Club	League Appearances/Goals		Season	Club	League Appearances/Goals	
1983–84	Liverpool	—	—	1982–83		40	3
1984–85		—	—	1983–84		34	4
1985–86		—	—	1984–85		3	1
1985–86	Sunderland	22	—	1984–85	Southampton	33	1
1985–86	Luton T	—	—	1985–86		34	1

BOLTON, Joe

Born Birtley 2.2.55. Ht 5 11½ Wt 12 11
Defender. From Apprentice.

Season	Club	App	Goals
1971–72	Sunderland	4	—
1972–73		12	1
1973–74		29	—
1974–75		23	2
1975–76		34	1
1976–77		42	1
1977–78		36	3
1978–79		32	3
1979–80		22	—
1980–81		39	—
1981–82	Middlesbrough	27	1
1982–83		32	—
1983–84	Sheffield U	45	1
1984–85		34	—
1985–86		30	1

BOLTON, Tony

Born Newport 15.1.68. Ht 5 7 Wt 11 4
Midfield.

Season	Club	App	Goals
1984–85	Charlton Ath	—	—
1985–86		—	—

BOND, Kevin

Born London 22.6.57. Ht 6 0 Wt 12 4
Defender. From Bournemouth Apprentice.
England 'B'.

Season	Club	App	Goals
1974–75	Norwich C	—	—
1975–76		1	—
1976–77		3	—
1977–78		28	—
1978–79		42	2
1979–80		40	9
1980–81		28	1
From Seattle S			
1981–82	Manchester C	33	3

BONDS, Billy

Born Woolwich 17.9.46. Ht 6 0½ Wt 13 7
Defender. From Apprentice.
England Under-23.

Season	Club	App	Goals
1964–65	Charlton Ath	13	—
1965–66		40	—
1966–67		42	1
1967–68	West Ham U	37	1
1968–69		42	1
1969–70		42	3
1970–71		37	—
1971–72		42	3
1972–73		39	3
1973–74		40	13
1974–75		31	7
1975–76		18	1
1976–77		41	3
1977–78		29	1
1978–79		39	4
1979–80		34	1
1980–81		41	—
1981–82		29	1
1982–83		34	3
1983–84		27	—
1984–85		22	3
1985–86		—	—

BONNER, Pat

Born Donegal 25.5.60. Ht 6 2 Wt 13 1
Goalkeeper. From Keadie Rovers. Republic
of Ireland 10 full caps.

Season	Club	App	Goals
1978–79	Celtic	2	—
1979–80		—	—
1980–81		36	—
1981–82		36	—
1982–83		36	—
1983–84		33	—
1984–85		34	—
1985–86		30	—

All appearances include those as substitute

Season	Club	League Appearances/Goals		Season	Club	League Appearances/Goals	

BONNYMAN, Phil

Born Glasgow 6.2.54. Ht 5 10½ Wt 12 4
Midfield. From Anniesland W.

Season	Club	App	Goals
1971–72	Rangers	—	—
1972–73		—	—
1973–74	Hamilton A	13	—
1974–75		35	5
1975–76		23	2
1975–76	Carlisle U	9	—
1976–77		37	1
1977–78		33	8
1978–79		45	7
1979–80		28	10
1979–80	Chesterfield	11	3
1980–81		42	8
1981–82		46	14
1982–83	Grimsby T	40	1
1983–84		29	3
1984–85		37	8
1985–86		29	3
1985–86	*Stoke C*	7	—

BOOKER, Bob

Born Watford 25.1.58. Ht 6 2½ Wt 12 4
Forward. From Bedmond Sports.

Season	Club	App	Goals
1978–79	Brentford	3	—
1979–80		12	6
1980–81		26	7
1981–82		38	4
1982–83		39	6
1983–84		29	4
1984–85		38	7
1985–86		44	8

BOOTH, Dennis

Born Stanley 9.4.49. Ht 5 7½ Wt 11 3
Defender. From Apprentice.

Season	Club	App	Goals
1965–66	Charlton Ath	—	—
1966–67		3	—
1967–68		17	—
1968–69		21	5
1969–70		30	—
1970–71		6	—
1971–72	Blackpool	12	—
1971–72	Southend U	16	—
1972–73		43	—
1973–74		19	1
1973–74	Lincoln C	16	3
1974–75		46	2
1975–76		42	1
1976–77		45	2
1977–78		13	1
1977–78	Watford	31	—
1978–79		37	—
1979–80		32	2
1980–81	Hull C	37	—
1981–82		37	2
1982–83		34	—
1983–84		14	—
1984–85		1	—
1985–86		—	—

BOOTH, Paul

Born Bolton 7.12.65. Ht 5 11 Wt 11 6
Midfield. From Apprentice. England
Schools.

Season	Club	App	Goals
1983–84	Bolton W	—	—
1984–85		1	—
1985–86	Crewe Alex	27	—

BORROWS, Brian

Born Liverpool 20.12.60. Ht 5 10
Wt 10 12
Defender. From Amateur.

Season	Club	App	Goals
1979–80	Everton	—	—
1980–81		—	—
1981–82		15	—
1982–83		12	—
1982–83	Bolton W	9	—
1983–84		44	—
1984–85		42	—
1985–86	Coventry C	41	—

Season	Club	League Appearances/Goals		Season	Club	League Appearances/Goals	

BORTHWICK, John

Born Hartlepool 24.3.64.   Ht 5 10
Wt 10 12
Forward. Local.

1982–83	Hartlepool U	2	—
1983–84		10	—
1984–85		6	1
1985–86		32	8

BOTHAM, Ian

Born Heswell 24.11.55.   Ht 6 3   Wt 14 2
Defender. From Yeovil.

1980–81	Scunthorpe U	2	—
1981–82		4	—
1982–83		—	—
1983–84		3	—
1984–85		2	—
1985–86		—	—

BOULD, Stephen

Born Stoke 16.11.62.   Ht 6 3   Wt 12 8
Defender. From Apprentice.

1980–81	Stoke C	—	—
1981–82		2	—
1982–83		14	—
1982–83	*Torquay U*	9	—
1983–84	Stoke C	38	2
1984–85		38	3
1985–86		33	—

BOWDEN, John

Born Stockport 21.1.63.   Ht 6 0   Wt 11 7
Forward. From Local.

1979–80	Oldham Ath	—	—
1980–81		—	—
1981–82		5	2
1982–83		31	2
1983–84		31	1
1984–85		15	—
1985–86		—	—
1985–86	Port Vale	36	3

BOWEN, Keith

Born Northampton 26.2.58.   Ht 6 1
Wt 11 2
Forward. From Amateur. Wales Schools.

1976–77	Northampton T	1	—
1977–78		—	—
1978–79		5	—
1979–80		24	12
1980–81		32	13
1981–82		3	—
1981–82	Brentford	38	8
1982–83		13	1
1982–83	Colchester U.	13	4
1983–84		46	12
1984–85		42	17
1985–86		15	5

BOWEN, Mark

Born Neath 7.12.63.   Ht 5 8   Wt 11 13
Defender. From Apprentice.
Wales Youth, Under-21, 2 full caps.

1981–82	Tottenham H.	—	—
1982–83		—	—
1983–84		7	—
1984–85		6	—
1985–86		2	1

BOWMAN, David

Born Tunbridge Wells 10.3.60.   Ht 5 10
Wt 11 2
Midfield. From Salvesen BC. Scotland
Under-21.

1980–81	Hearts	17	1
1981–82		16	1
1982–83		39	5
1983–84		33	—
1984–85		11	1
1984–85	Coventry C	10	—
1985–86		30	2

BOWYER, Ian

Born Ellesmere Port 6.6.51.   Ht 5 10
Wt 11 11
Midfield. From Apprentice.

Season	Club	League Appearances/Goals		Season	Club	League Appearances/Goals	

Season	Club	Apps	Goals
1968–69	Manchester C	6	1
1969–70		34	12
1970–71		10	—
1971–72	Orient	42	14
1972–73		36	4
1973–74		—	—
1973–74	Nottingham F	28	6
1974–75		32	6
1975–76		40	13
1976–77		41	12
1977–78		29	4
1978–79		29	4
1979–80		19	1
1980–81		21	3
1980–81	Sunderland	9	1
1981–82		6	—
1981–82	Nottingham F	24	1
1982–83		40	4
1983–84		42	6
1984–85		39	2
1985–86		26	3

BOYCE, David

Born Sutton 17.8.66.   Ht 5 11   Wt 11 0
Forward.

Season	Club	Apps	Goals
1984–85	C. Palace	—	—
1985–86		—	—

BOYD, David

Born Glasgow 21.8.67.
Forward.

Season	Club	Apps	Goals
1984–85	Manchester C	—	—
1985–86		—	—

BOYD, Tom

Born Glasgow 24.11.65.   Ht 5 11   Wt 11 4
Defender. 'S' Form. Scotland Youth.

Season	Club	Apps	Goals
1983–84	Motherwell	13	—
1984–85		36	—
1985–86		31	—

BOYLE, Terry

Born Ammanford 29.10.58.   Ht 5 10
Wt 12 8
Defender. From Apprentice. Wales Schools,
2 full caps.

Season	Club	Apps	Goals
1975–76	Tottenham H	—	—
1976–77		—	—
1977–78		—	—
1977–78	Crystal Palace	1	—
1978–79		—	—
1979–80		5	—
1980–81		20	1
1981–82	*Wimbledon*	5	1
1981–82	Bristol C	23	—
1982–83		14	—
1982–83	Newport Co	29	—
1983–84		45	1
1984–85		46	3
1985–86		46	7

BOYS, Steve

Born Lambeth 1.10.67.
Forward. From Apprentice.

Season	Club	Apps	Goals
1985–86	C. Palace	—	—

BRACEWELL, Paul

Born Stoke 19.7.62.   Ht 5 8   Wt 10 9
Midfield. From Apprentice.
England Under-21, 3 full caps.

Season	Club	Apps	Goals
1979–80	Stoke C	6	—
1980–81		40	2
1981–82		42	1
1982–83		41	2
1983–84	Sunderland	38	4
1984–85	Everton	37	2
1985–86		38	3

BRADLEY, Darren

Born Birmingham 24.11.65.   Ht 5 10
Wt 11 4
Defender. From Apprentice. England
Youth.

All appearances include those as substitute

Season	Club	League Appearances/Goals

Season	Club	League Appearances/Goals

1983–84	Aston Villa	—	—
1984–85		2	—
1985–86		18	—
1985–86	WBA	10	—

BRADSHAW, Paul

Born Altrincham 28.4.56.   Ht 6 3   Wt 13 4
Goalkeeper. From Apprentice.
England Youth, Under-21.

1973–74	Blackburn R	18	—
1974–75		—	—
1975–76		12	—
1976–77		41	—
1977–78		7	—
1977–78	Wolverhampton W	34	—
1978–79		39	—
1979–80		37	—
1980–81		38	—
1981–82		42	—
1982–83			—
1983–84		10	—
From Vancouver W			
1984–85	WBA	—	—
1985–86		8	—

BRADY, Liam

Born Dublin 13.2.56.   Ht 5 7   Wt 10 7
Midfield. From Apprentice. Eire 57 full caps.

1973–74	Arsenal	13	1
1974–75		32	3
1975–76		42	5
1976–77		38	5
1977–78		39	9
1978–79		37	13
1979–80		34	7
1980–81	Juventus	28	8
1981–82		29	5
1982–83	Sampdoria	29	2
1983–84		28	4
1984–85	Internazionale	29	2
1985–86		29	3

BRAITHWAITE, Roderick

Born Isleworth 19.12.65.   Ht 5 9   Wt 10 8½
Midfield.

1984–85	Fulham	—	—
1985–86		2	1

BRAMHALL, John

Born Warrington 20.11.56.   Ht 6 2   Wt 13 6
Defender. From Amateur.

1976–77	Tranmere R	8	—
1977–78		10	—
1978–79		35	2
1979–80		45	1
1980–81		37	1
1981–82		35	3
1981–82	Bury	9	—
1982–83		46	6
1983–84		45	6
1984–85		42	4
1985–86		25	1
1985–86	*Chester C*	4	—

BRANAGAN, Jim

Born Barton 3.7.55.   Ht 5 11   Wt 11 10
Defender. From Amateur.

1973–74	Oldham Ath	—	—
1974–75		5	—
1975–76		13	—
1976–77		9	—
From Cape Town C.			
1977–78	Huddersfield T	24	—
1978–79		14	—
1979–80		—	—
1979–80	Blackburn R	31	1
1980–81		42	—
1981–82		40	1
1982–83		37	1
1983–84		41	—
1984–85		40	1
1985–86		33	—

BRANAGAN, Keith

Born Fulham 10.7.66.   Ht 6 0   Wt 11 10
Goalkeeper.

1983–84	Cambridge U	1	—
1984–85		19	—
1985–86		9	—

Season	Club	League Appearances/Goals

BRAY, Ian

Born Neath 6.12.62.   Ht 5 8   Wt 11 4½
Defender. From Apprentice.

Season	Club	Apps	Goals
1980–81	Hereford U	—	—
1981–82		16	2
1982–83		27	—
1983–84		23	1
1984–85		42	1
1985–86	Huddersfield T	32	1

BRAZIER, Colin

Born Solihull 6.6.57.   Ht 6 1   Wt 10 13
Defender. From Alvechurch.

Season	Club	Apps	Goals
1975–76	Wolverhampton W	—	—
1976–77		2	—
1977–78		13	—
1978–79		7	—
1979–80		20	1
1980–81		24	—
1981–82		12	1
1982–83	Birmingham C	11	1
1982–83	Lincoln C	9	—
1983–84	Walsall	45	2
1984–85		41	—
1985–86		27	2

BRAZIL, Alan

Born Glasgow 15.6.59.   Ht 6 0   Wt 12 4
Forward. From Apprentice.
Scotland Under-21, 13 full caps.

Season	Club	Apps	Goals
1977–78	Ipswich T	2	—
1978–79		19	9
1979–80		35	12
1980–81		35	17
1981–82		35	22
1982–83		28	10
1982–83	Tottenham H	12	6
1983–84		19	3
1984–85	Manchester U	20	5
1985–86		11	3
1985–86	Coventry C	15	2

BRAZIL, Ally

Born Currie 10.12.58.   Ht 5 11   Wt 11 3
Defender. From Currie Hearts. Scotland
Under-21.

Season	Club	Apps	Goals
1976–77	Hibernian	4	—
1977–78		25	2
1978–79		18	—
1979–80		32	—
1980–81		7	1
1981–82		24	—
1982–83		11	—
1983–84		29	1
1984–85		31	1
1985–86		23	2

BRAZIL, Derek

Born Dublin 14.12.68.   Ht 6 0   Wt 12 0
Defender. From Rivermount BC. Eire
Youth.

Season	Club	Apps	Goals
1985–86	Manchester U	—	—

BRAZIL, Gary

Born Tunbridge Wells 19.9.62.   Ht 5 11
Wt 9 12½
Forward. From Crystal Palace Apprentice.

Season	Club	Apps	Goals
1980–81	Sheffield U	3	—
1981–82		1	—
1982–83		33	5
1983–84		19	2
1984–85		6	2
1984–85	*Port Vale*	6	3
1984–85	Preston NE	17	3
1985–86		43	14

BREACKER, Tim

Born Bicester 2.7.65.   Ht 6 0   Wt 12 6
Defender. England Under-21.

Season	Club	Apps	Goals
1983–84	Luton T	2	—
1984–85		35	—
1985–86		36	—

All appearances include those as substitute

Season	Club	League Appearances/Goals	Season	Club	League Appearances/Goals

BREMNER, Des

Born Aberchider 7.9.52.   Ht 5 9½   Wt 11 11
Midfield. From Deveronvale.
Scotland Under-23, 1 full cap.

Season	Club	Apps	Goals
1972–73	Hibernian	11	—
1973–74		21	2
1974–75		30	2
1975–76		32	3
1976–77		36	4
1977–78		33	2
1978–79		31	5
1979–80		5	—
1979–80	Aston Villa	36	3
1980–81		42	2
1981–82		38	3
1982–83		37	—
1983–84		17	—
1984–85		4	1
1984–85	Birmingham C	30	—
1985–86		32	—

BREMNER, Kevin

Born Banff 7.10.57.   Ht 5 10   Wt 12 3½
Forward. From Keith.

Season	Club	Apps	Goals
1980–81	Colchester U	34	8
1981–82		46	21
1982–83		15	2
1982–83	*Birmingham C*	4	1
1982–83	*Wrexham*	4	1
1982–83	*Plymouth Arg*	5	1
1982–83	Millwall	17	6
1983–84		42	16
1984–85		37	11
1985–86	Reading	22	7

BRENNAN, Mark

Born Rossendale 4.10.65.   Ht 5 10
Wt 10 13
Midfield. From Apprentice. England Youth.

Season	Club	Apps	Goals
1982–83	Ipswich T	—	—
1983–84		19	1
1984–85		36	2
1985–86		40	3

BRENTANO, Stephen

Born Hull 9.11.61.   Ht 5 8   Wt 10 12
Defender. From Local.

Season	Club	Apps	Goals
1984–85	Hull C	2	—
1985–86		8	—

BRETT, David

Born Chester 8.4.61.   Ht 5 8   Wt 11 0
Midfield. Local.

Season	Club	Apps	Goals
1983–84	Chester	29	2
1984–85		31	4
1985–86		7	—

BRIGGS, Gary

Born Leeds 8.5.58.   Ht 6 3   Wt 12 10
Defender. From Apprentice.

Season	Club	Apps	Goals
1977–78	Middlesbrough	—	—
1977–78	Oxford U	20	2
1978–79		39	—
1979–80		46	1
1980–81		42	1
1981–82		45	1
1982–83		37	1
1983–84		38	3
1984–85		42	4
1985–86		38	—

BRIGHT, Mark

Born Stoke 6.6.62.   Ht 6 0   Wt 11 0
Forward. From Leek T.

Season	Club	Apps	Goals
1981–82	Port Vale	2	—
1982–83		1	1
1983–84		26	9
1984–85	Leicester C	16	—
1985–86		24	6

BRIGNULL, Phil

Born Scotland 2.10.60.   Ht 6 0   Wt 11 2
Defender. From Apprentice.
England Schools.

All appearances include those as substitute

Season	Club	League Appearances/Goals		Season	Club	League Appearances/Goals	
1978–79	West Ham U	1	—	1975–76		40	8
1979–80		—	—	1976–77		37	10
1980–81		—	—	1977–78		40	1
1981–82	Bournemouth	29	2	1978–79		13	—
1982–83		46	2	1979–80		41	10
1983–84		44	6	1980–81		28	1
1984–85		10	1	1981–82		18	—
1985–86		—	—	1982–83	Dundee U	10	1
1985–86	*Wrexham*	5	1	1983–84	Blackpool	30	9
1985–86	Cardiff C	15	—	1984–85		46	5
				1985–86		30	1

BRILEY, Les

Born Lambeth 2.10.56.   Ht 5 8   Wt 10 6
Midfield. From Apprentice.

Season	Club	Apps	Goals
1974–75	Chelsea	—	—
1975–76		—	—
1976–77	Hereford U	34	1
1977–78		27	1
1977–78	Wimbledon	14	1
1978–79		26	1
1979–80		21	—
1979–80	Aldershot	12	—
1980–81		44	—
1981–82		37	2
1982–83		28	—
1983–84		36	1
1984–85	Millwall	33	—
1985–86		39	1

BRIMACOMBE, John

Born Plymouth 25.11.58.
Defender. From Liskeard and Saltash.

Season	Club	Apps	Goals
1985–86	Plymouth Arg	1	1

BRITTON, Ian

Born Dundee 19.5.54.   Ht 5 5   Wt 9 7
Midfield. From Apprentice.

Season	Club	Apps	Goals
1971–72	Chelsea	—	—
1972–73		14	—
1973–74		17	2
1974–75		15	1

BROCK, Kevin

Born Middleton Stoney 9.9.62.   Ht 5 9
Wt 10 10
Midfield. From Apprentice.
England Schools, Under-21.

Season	Club	Apps	Goals
1979–80	Oxford U	19	2
1980–81		26	5
1981–82		28	5
1982–83		37	4
1983–84		45	3
1984–85		37	6
1985–86		23	—

BRODDLE, Julian

Born Laughton 1.11.64.   Ht 5 9   Wt 11 3
Midfield. From Apprentice.

Season	Club	Apps	Goals
1981–82	Sheffield U	1	—
1982–83		—	—
1983–84	Scunthorpe U	13	1
1984–85		45	14
1985–86		41	7

BRODIE, Colin

Born Glasgow 13.8.64.   Ht 6 1   Wt 13 0
Goalkeeper. From Clydebank Youths.

Season	Club	Apps	Goals
1981–82	Clydebank	—	—
1982–83		4	—
1983–84		—	—
1984–85		2	—
1985–86		1	—

Season	Club	League Appearances/Goals	Season	Club	League Appearances/Goals

BROLLY, Mike

Born Kilmarnock 6.10.54.   Ht 5 9   Wt 10 12
Forward. From Amateur. Scotland Schools.

Season	Club	App	Goals
1971–72	Chelsea	—	—
1972–73		7	1
1973–74		1	—
1974–75	Bristol C	15	1
1975–76		15	1
1976–77		—	—
1976–77	Grimsby T	41	3
1977–78		46	4
1978–79		44	9
1979–80		45	4
1980–81		40	4
1981–82		38	3
1982–83	Derby Co	42	4
1983–84	Scunthorpe U	41	4
1984–85		34	9
1985–86		20	2

BROMAGE, Russel

Born Stoke 9.11.59.   Ht 5 11   Wt 11 5
Defender. From Apprentice.

Season	Club	App	Goals
1977–78	Port Vale	6	—
1978–79		20	2
1979–80		29	1
1980–81		45	4
1981–82		45	—
1982–83		46	2
1983–84		38	1
1983–84	*Oldham Ath*	2	—
1984–85	Port Vale	37	1
1985–86		40	1

BROOKE, Gary

Born Bethnal Green 24.11.60.   Ht 5 6
Wt 10 5
Midfield. From Apprentice.

Season	Club	App	Goals
1978–79	Tottenham H	—	—
1979–80		—	—
1980–81		18	3
1981–82		16	4
1982–83		23	7
1983–84		12	—

Season	Club	App	Goals
1984–85		4	1
1985–86	Norwich C	13	2

BROOKS, Shaun

Born London 9.10.62.   Ht 5 7   Wt 11 0
Midfield. From Apprentice.
England Schools, Youth.

Season	Club	App	Goals
1979–80	Crystal Palace	1	—
1980–81		17	—
1981–82		25	2
1982–83		7	2
1983–84		4	—
1983–84	Orient	36	9
1984–85		29	5
1985–86		38	7

BROTHERSTON, Noel

Born Belfast 18.11.56.   Ht 5 8   Wt 11 5
Midfield. From Apprentice.
Northern Ireland Under-21, 27 full caps.

Season	Club	App	Goals
1973–74	Tottenham H	—	—
1974–75		—	—
1975–76		1	—
1976–77		—	—
1977–78	Blackburn R	40	11
1978–79		35	2
1979–80		41	7
1980–81		33	3
1981–82		38	2
1982–83		39	6
1983–84		21	1
1984–85		33	7
1985–86		19	1

BROWN, Alan

Born Easington 22.5.59.   Ht 5 11½   Wt 11 2
Forward. From Apprentice.

Season	Club	App	Goals
1976–77	Sunderland	11	—
1977–78		6	—
1978–79		22	6
1979–80		33	9
1980–81		34	5
1981–82		7	1
1981–82	*Newcastle U*	5	3
1982–83	Shrewsbury T	36	10

Season	Club	League Appearances/Goals		Season	Club	League Appearances/Goals	

1983–84	....	29	5
1983–84	Doncaster R	9	2
1984–85	....	4	4
1985–86	....	2	—

BROWN, Ally

Born Musselburgh 12.4.51.   Ht 6 0   Wt 11 0
Forward. From Amateur.

1967–68	Leicester C..................	—	—
1968–69	....	2	2
1969–70	....	31	8
1970–71	....	38	14
1971–72	....	30	7
1971–72	WBA	11	3
1972–73	....	29	3
1973–74	....	15	3
1974–75	....	4	—
1975–76	....	31	10
1976–77	....	22	6
1977–78	....	19	5
1978–79	....	41	18
1979–80	....	29	6
1980–81	....	36	10
1981–82	....	25	3
1982–83	....	16	5
1982–83	Crystal Palace	11	2
1983–84	Walsall.......................	38	13
1984–85	Port Vale	40	17
1985–86	....	27	5

BROWN, David

Born Hartlepool 28.1.57.   Ht 6 1   Wt 12 8
Goalkeeper. From Horden C.W.

1976–77	Middlesbrough.............	—	—
1977–78	....	10	—
1978–79	....	—	—
1979–80	....	—	—
1979–80	*Plymouth Arg*	5	—
1979–80	Oxford U	18	—
1980–81	....	3	—
1981–82	....	—	—
1981–82	Bury..........................	27	—
1982–83	....	45	—
1983–84	....	28	—
1984–85	....	46	—
1985–86	....	—	—

BROWN, Jim

Born Coatbridge 11.5.52.   Ht 5 11   Wt 12 4
Goalkeeper. From Bargeddie Amat.
Scotland Under-23, 1 full cap.

1970–71	Albion R	30	—
1971–72	....	33	—
1972–73	....	16	—
1972–73	Chesterfield..................	21	—
1973–74	....	26	—
1973–74	Sheffield U	10	—
1974–75	....	42	—
1975–76	....	37	—
1976–77	....	42	—
1977–78	....	39	—

From Detroit Express, Washington D and Chicago S

| 1982–83 | Cardiff C .... | 3 | — |

From Kettering T

1983–84	Chesterfield..................	40	1
1984–85	....	8	—
1985–86	....	14	—

BROWN, John

Born Stirling 26.1.62.   Ht 5 11   Wt 11 2
Midfield. From Blantyre Welfare.

1979–80	Hamilton A	19	—
1980–81	....	38	6
1981–82	....	28	5
1982–83	....	9	—
1983–84	....	39	—
1984–85	Dundee	34	7
1985–86	....	29	11

BROWN, John

Born Winsford 6.12.67.
Midfield. From Apprentice.

| 1985–86 | Liverpool.................... | — | — |

BROWN, Ken

Born Barking 11.7.67.   Ht 5 8   Wt 11 6
Defender. From Apprentice.

| 1984–85 | Norwich C.................. | — | — |
| 1985–86 | .... | — | — |

Season	Club	League Appearances/Goals	Season	Club	League Appearances/Goals

BROWN, Kevan

Born Andover 2.1.66.   Ht 5 9   Wt 11 8
Midfield.

Season	Club	App	Goals
1983–84	Southampton	—	—
1984–85		—	—
1985–86		—	—

BROWN, Malcolm

Born Salford 13.12.56.   Ht 6 2   Wt 13 0
Defender. From Apprentice.

Season	Club	App	Goals
1973–74	Bury	1	—
1974–75		—	—
1975–76		5	—
1976–77		5	—
1977–78	Huddersfield T	30	1
1978–79		42	—
1979–80		46	2
1980–81		46	3
1981–82		46	1
1982–83		46	9
1983–84	Newcastle U	—	—
1984–85		39	—
1985–86	Huddersfield T	37	—

BROWN, Mike

Born Birmingham 8.2.68.   Ht 5 9   Wt 10 12
Forward. From Apprentice.

Season	Club	App	Goals
1985–86	Shrewsbury T	—	—

BROWN, Nicky

Born Hull 16.10.66.   Ht 6 0   Wt 12 3
Forward. From Local.

Season	Club	App	Goals
1984–85	Hull C	—	—
1985–86		1	—

BROWN, Phil

Born Sheffield 16.1.66.   Ht 5 7   Wt 9 7
Forward. From Apprentice.

BROWN, Phil

Born South Shields 30.5.59.   Ht 5 11
Wt 11 6
Defender. Local.

Season	Club	App	Goals
1978–79	Hartlepool U	—	—
1979–80		10	—
1980–81		46	1
1981–82		44	4
1982–83		44	2
1983–84		31	—
1984–85		42	1
1985–86	Halifax T	45	2

BROWN, Richard

Born Nottingham 13.1.67.   Ht 5 9   Wt 11 9
Midfield. From Derby Co. Amateur and
Ilkeston T.

Season	Club	App	Goals
1984–85	Sheffield W	—	—
1985–86		—	—

BROWN, Roger

Born Tamworth 12.12.52.   Ht 6 1   Wt 14 2
Defender. From AP Leamington.

Season	Club	App	Goals
1977–78	Bournemouth	18	—
1978–79		45	3
1979–80	Norwich C	16	—
1979–80	Fulham	1	—
1980–81		39	2
1981–82		46	12
1982–83		42	4
1983–84		13	—
1983–84	Bournemouth	23	2
1984–85		26	2
1985–86		34	1

Season	Club	League Appearances/Goals	Season	Club	League Appearances/Goals

BROWN, Tony

Born Bradford 17.9.58.   Ht 6 2   Wt 12 10
Defender. From Thackley.

Season	Club	Apps	Goals
1982–83	Leeds U	1	—
1983–84		22	1
1984–85		1	—
1984–85	*Doncaster R*	14	—
1985–86	Doncaster R	38	2

BRUCE, Steve

Born Newcastle 31.12.60.   Ht 6 0½   Wt 12 6
Midfield. From Apprentice. England Youth.

Season	Club	Apps	Goals
1978–79	Gillingham	—	—
1979–80		40	6
1980–81		41	4
1981–82		45	6
1982–83		39	7
1983–84		40	6
1984–85	Norwich C	39	1
1985–86		42	8

BRUSH, Paul

Born Plaistow 22.2.58.   Ht 5 11   Wt 12 2
Defender. From Apprentice.

Season	Club	Apps	Goals
1976–77	West Ham U	—	—
1977–78		24	—
1978–79		42	—
1979–80		27	—
1980–81		11	—
1981–82		13	—
1982–83		6	—
1983–84		10	—
1984–85		18	1
1985–86		—	—
1985–86	C Palace	26	2

BRYANT, Richard

Born Bristol 20.6.63.   Ht 6 3   Wt 11 8
Defender. From Robinsons DRG.

Season	Club	Apps	Goals
1985–86	Bristol C	2	1

BUCKLEY, Gary

Born Manchester 3.3.61.   Ht 5 4   Wt 9 6
Midfield. From Apprentice.

Season	Club	Apps	Goals
1977–78	Manchester C	—	—
1978–79		—	—
1979–80		—	—
1980–81		6	—
1981–82		—	—
1981–82	Preston NE	22	2
1982–83		12	—
From Chorley			
1983–84	Bury	9	—
1984–85		19	1
1985–86		3	—

BUCKLEY, John

Born Glasgow 10.5.62.   Ht 5 9   Wt 10 7
Forward. From Queen's Park and Celtic.

Season	Club	Apps	Goals
1982–83	Partick T	8	1
1983–84		37	4
1984–85	Doncaster R	39	6
1985–86		45	5

BUCKLEY, Steve

Born Brinsley 16.10.53.   Ht 5 11   Wt 11 12
Defender. From Burton Albion.

Season	Club	Apps	Goals
1973–74	Luton T	—	—
1974–75		24	—
1975–76		33	2
1976–77		42	3
1977–78		24	4
1977–78	Derby Co	18	1
1978–79		42	4
1979–80		42	—
1980–81		32	1
1981–82		40	5
1982–83		26	2
1983–84		31	—
1984–85		46	7
1985–86		46	1

Season	Club	League Appearances/Goals	Season	Club	League Appearances/Goals

BUDD, Kevin

Born Hillingdon 20.3.62.
Defender. From Bournemouth Apprentice.

Season	Club	App	Goals
1979–80	Norwich C	—	—
1980–81		—	—
1980–81	Manchester C	—	—
From			
1985–86	Swansea C	1	—

BULL, Steve

Born Tipton 28.3.65.
Forward. From Apprentice.

Season	Club	App	Goals
1985–86	WBA	1	—

BULLIVANT, Terry

Born London 23.9.56.   Ht 5 7½   Wt 10 11
Midfield. From Apprentice.

Season	Club	App	Goals
1974–75	Fulham	1	—
1975–76		3	—
1976–77		19	1
1977–78		35	1
1978–79		28	—
1979–80		15	—
1979–80	Aston Villa	6	—
1980–81		—	—
1981–82		7	—
1982–83	Charlton Ath	30	3
1983–84	Brentford	24	1
1983–84	*Reading*	—	—
1984–85	Brentford	5	—
1985–86		8	1

BULLOCK, Steven

Born Stockport 5.10.66.   Ht 5 8   Wt 11 1
Midfield. From school.

Season	Club	App	Goals
1983–84	Oldham Ath	1	—
1984–85		9	—
1985–86		8	—

BUMSTEAD, John

Born Rotherhithe 27.11.58.   Ht 5 7   Wt 10 5
Midfield. From Apprentice.

Season	Club	App	Goals
1977–78	Chelsea	—	—
1978–79		8	1
1979–80		28	3
1980–81		41	1
1981–82		21	4
1982–83		36	4
1983–84		31	7
1984–85		25	3
1985–86		32	1

BUNCE, Paul

Born Coalville. 7.1.67.   Ht 5 7   Wt 10 7
Forward. From Apprentice.

Season	Club	App	Goals
1984–85	Leicester C	—	—
1985–86		—	—

BUNN, Frankie

Born Birmingham 6.11.62.   Ht 5 11   Wt 10 6
Forward. From Apprentice.

Season	Club	App	Goals
1980–81	Luton T	3	1
1981–82		2	—
1982–83		4	—
1983–84		30	3
1984–85		20	5
1985–86	Hull C	42	14

BURGESS, Dave

Born Liverpool .   Ht 5 10   Wt 11 2
Defender. Local.

Season	Club	App	Goals
1981–82	Tranmere R	46	1
1982–83		46	—
1983–84		44	—
1984–85		41	—
1985–86		41	—

BURKE, David

Born Liverpool 6.8.60.   Ht 5 10   Wt 11 1
Defender. From Apprentice.
England Youth.

Season	Club	League Appearances/Goals		Season	Club	League Appearances/Goals	

1977–78	Bolton W	—	—
1978–79		20	1
1979–80		27	—
1980–81		22	—
1981–82	Huddersfield T	41	1
1982–83		44	1
1983–84		42	—
1984–85		31	1
1985–86		—	—

BURKE, Steve

Born Nottingham 29.9.60.   Ht 5 10   Wt 11 7
Forward. From Apprentice.

1977–78	Nottingham F	—	—
1978–79		—	—
1979–80		—	—
1979–80	QPR	31	4
1980–81		14	1
1981–82		12	—
1982–83		5	—
1983–84		5	—
1983–84	*Millwall*	7	1
1984–85	QPR	—	—
1984–85	*Notts Co*	5	—
1985–86	QPR	—	—
1985–86	*Lincoln C*	5	—
1985–86	*Brentford*	10	1

BURLEY, George

Born Cumnock 3.6.56.   Ht 5 9½   Wt 11 0
Defender. From Apprentice. Scotland
Schools, Under-21, 11 full caps.

1973–74	Ipswich T	20	—
1974–75		31	—
1975–76		42	—
1976–77		40	2
1977–78		31	—
1978–79		38	1
1979–80		38	—
1980–81		23	—
1981–82		29	—
1982–83		31	1
1983–84		28	—
1984–85		37	—
1985–86		6	—
1985–86	Sunderland	27	—

BURMAN, Simon

Born Ipswich 26.11.65.   Ht 5 9½   Wt 11 2
Defender. From school.

1983–84	Colchester U	—	—
1984–85		9	—
1985–86		11	1

BURNS, Hugh

Born Lanark 13.12.65.   Ht 6 0   Wt 11 7
Defender. From Cambuslang Rangers.
Scotland Youth, Under-21.

1982–83	Rangers	—	—
1983–84		5	—
1984–85		15	—
1985–86		28	3

BURNS, Kenny

Born Glasgow 23.9.53.   Ht 5 10   Wt 11 0
Defender. From Apprentice.
Scotland Under-23, 20 full caps.

1971–72	Birmingham C	8	—
1972–73		14	3
1973–74		37	10
1974–75		39	8
1975–76		36	5
1976–77		36	19
1977–78	Nottingham F	41	4
1978–79		25	—
1979–80		34	3
1980–81		30	5
1981–82		7	1
1981–82	Leeds U	23	—
1982–83		20	2
1982–83	*Derby Co*	7	1
1983–84	Leeds U	13	—
1983–84	Derby Co	11	—
1984–85		20	1
1984–85	*Notts Co*	2	—
1985–86	Barnsley	22	—

Season	Club	League Appearances/Goals		Season	Club	League Appearances/Goals	

BURNS, Tommy

Born Glasgow 16.2.56.   Ht 5 11   Wt 11 3
Midfield. From Maryhill Juniors, Scotland
Under-21, 7 full caps.

Season	Club	App	Goals
1974–75	Celtic	1	—
1975–76		5	—
1976–77		22	1
1977–78		23	3
1978–79		29	3
1979–80		15	—
1980–81		33	4
1981–82		33	9
1982–83		17	7
1983–84		33	9
1984–85		27	7
1985–86		34	5

BURR, David

Born Hull 15.11.67.   Ht 5 4   Wt 10 7
Defender. From Apprentice.

Season	Club	App	Goals
1985–86	Hull C	—	—

BURRIDGE, John

Born Workington 3.12.51.   Ht 5 11
Wt 12 11
Goalkeeper. From Apprentice.

Season	Club	App	Goals
1968–69	Workington	1	—
1969–70		—	—
1970–71		26	—
1970–71	Blackpool	3	—
1971–72		34	—
1972–73		22	—
1973–74		30	—
1974–75		38	—
1975–76		7	—
1975–76	Aston Villa	30	—
1976–77		35	—
1977–78		—	—
1977–78	*Southend U*	6	—
1977–78	Crystal Palace	10	—
1978–79		42	—
1979–80		36	—
1980–81		—	—
1980–81	QPR	19	—

Season	Club	App	Goals
1981–82		20	—
1982–83	Wolverhampton W	42	—
1983–84		32	—
1984–85		—	—
1984–85	*Derby Co*	6	—
1984–85	Sheffield U	30	—
1985–86		42	—

BURROWS, Adrian

Born Sutton 16.1.59.   Ht 5 11   Wt 12 0
Defender. Local.

Season	Club	App	Goals
1979–80	Mansfield T	17	—
1980–81		20	3
1981–82		41	2
1982–83	Northampton T	43	4
1983–84		45	—
1984–85	Plymouth Arg	39	—
1985–86		7	2

BURROWS, David

Born Dudley 25.10.68.
Defender. From Apprentice.

Season	Club	App	Goals
1985–86	WBA	1	—

BURROWS, Paul

Born Swansea 2.10.67.
Midfield. From Apprentice. Wales Youth.

Season	Club	App	Goals
1985–86	Swansea C	3	—

BURVILL, Glen

Born Canning Town 26.10.62.   Ht 5 9
Wt 10 5
Forward. From Apprentice.

Season	Club	App	Goals
1980–81	West Ham U	—	—
1981–82		—	—
1982–83		—	—
1983–84	Aldershot	38	12
1984–85		27	3
1984–85	Reading	14	—
1985–86		16	—
1985–86	*Fulham*	9	2

Season	Club	League Appearances/Goals		Season	Club	League Appearances/Goals	

BUSHELL, Mark

Born Northampton 5.6.68. Ht 5 7½
Wt 10 12
Defender.

| 1984–85 | Northampton T | 1 | — |
| 1985–86 | | — | — |

BUTCHER, John

Born Newcastle 27.5.56. Ht 6 2   Wt 12 3
Goalkeeper. From Amateur.

1975–76	Blackburn R	—	—
1976–77		1	—
1977–78		35	—
1978–79		32	—
1979–80		8	—
1980–81		22	—
1981–82		6	—
1982–83	Oxford U	16	—
1982–83	*Halifax T*	5	—
1983–84		—	—
1983–84	*Bury*	11	—
1984–85	Chester C	33	—
1985–86		34	—
1985–86	*Bury*	5	—

BUTCHER, Terry

Born Singapore 28.12.58. Ht 6 4   Wt 14 0
Defender. From Amateur. England
Under-21 'B', 40 full caps.

1976–77	Ipswich T	—	—
1977–78		3	—
1978–79		21	2
1979–80		36	2
1980–81		40	4
1981–82		27	1
1982–83		42	—
1983–84		34	1
1984–85		41	2
1985–86		27	4

BUTLER, Barry

Born Farnworth 4.6.62.
Midfield. From Atherton T.

| 1985–86 | Chester C | 14 | — |

BUTLER, Brian

Born Salford 4.7.66. Ht 5 6   Wt 10 8
Midfield. From Apprentice.

| 1984–85 | Blackpool | — | — |
| 1985–86 | | 19 | 1 |

BUTLER, John

Born Liverpool 7.2.62. Ht 5 11   Wt 11 0
Midfield. From Prescot Cables.

1981–82	Wigan Ath	1	—
1982–83		40	5
1983–84		41	3
1984–85		45	3
1985–86		36	—

BUTLER, Martin

Born Hull 3.3.66. Ht 5 8   Wt 10 9
Forward. From YTS.

1984–85	York C	19	3
1985–86		14	—
1985–86	*Aldershot*	2	1

BUTLER, Paul

Born Stockton 9.6.64. Ht 5 7   Wt 10 0
Forward. From Apprentice.

1982–83	Wolverhampton W	8	—
1983–84		3	—
1983–84	*Hereford U*	16	2
1984–85	Wolves	18	2
1984–85	Hereford U	17	1
1985–86		21	—

Season	Club	League Appearances/Goals	Season	Club	League Appearances/Goals

BUTLER, Peter

Born Halifax 27.8.66.   Ht 5 9   Wt 11 1
Midfield. From Apprentice.

1984–85	Huddersfield T	4	—
1985–86	....	1	—
1985–86	*Cambridge U*	14	1

BUTLER, Steven

Born Birmingham 27.1.62.   Ht 6 2   Wt 13 1
Forward. From Wokingham.

| 1984–85 | Brentford | 3 | 1 |
| 1985–86 | .... | 18 | 2 |

BUTTERWORTH, Aidan

Born Leeds 7.11.61.   Ht 5 8   Wt 11 0
Forward. From Amateur. England Schools.

1980–81	Leeds U	1	—
1981–82	....	14	3
1982–83	....	38	11
1983–84	....	11	1
1984–85	Doncaster R	29	5
1985–86	....	21	—

BUTTERWORTH, Ian

Born Crewe 25.1.65.   Ht 6 1   Wt 12 6
Defender. From Apprentice. England
Under-21.

1981–82	Coventry C	14	—
1982–83	....	30	—
1983–84	....	24	—
1984–85	....	22	—
1985–86	Nottingham F	23	—

BUXTON, Steve

Born Birmingham 13.3.60.   Ht 5 5   Wt 11 2
Forward. From Amateur.

1977–78	Wrexham	1	—
1978–79	....	13	2
1979–80	....	13	1
1980–81	....	14	2

1981–82	....	9	3
1982–83	....	39	10
1983–84	....	20	3
1984–85	Stockport Co	18	1
1985–86	Torquay U	—	—
1985–86	Wrexham	5	3

BYRNE, David

Born London 5.3.61.   Ht 5 8   Wt 11 0
Forward. From Kingstonian.

| 1985–86 | Gillingham | 23 | 3 |

BYRNE, John

Born Manchester 1.2.61.   Ht 5 11   Wt 11 6
Forward. From Apprentice. Eire, 3 full caps.

1978–79	York C	—	—
1979–80	....	9	2
1980–81	....	38	6
1981–82	....	29	6
1982–83	....	43	12
1983–84	....	46	27
1984–85	....	10	2
1984–85	QPR	23	3
1985–86	....	36	12

BYRNE, Peter

Born Liverpool 24.9.67.
Defender. From Everton amateur.

| 1985–86 | Liverpool | — | — |

All appearances include those as substitute

| Season | Club | League Appearances/Goals | | Season | Club | League Appearances/Goals | |

CADETTE, Richard

Born Hammersmith 21.3.65.
Forward. From Wembley.

Season	Club	App	Goals
1984–85	Orient	21	4
1985–86	Southend U	44	25

CAESER, Gus

Born London 5.3.66.   Ht 6 0   Wt 12 0
Defender. From Apprentice.

Season	Club	App	Goals
1983–84	Arsenal	—	—
1984–85		—	—
1985–86		2	—

CALDERWOOD, Colin

Born Stranraer 20.1.65.   Ht 6 0   Wt 11 9
Defender. From Amateur.

Season	Club	App	Goals
1981–82	Mansfield T	1	—
1982–83		28	—
1983–84		30	1
1984–85		41	—
1985–86	Swindon T	46	2

CALDWELL, Dave

Born Aberdeen 31.7.60.   Ht 5 10   Wt 10 8
Forward. From Inverness Caley.

Season	Club	App	Goals
1979–80	Mansfield T	3	—
1980–81		28	8
1981–82		33	9
1982–83		35	10
1983–84		38	21
1984–85		20	9
1984–85	*Carlisle U*	4	—
1984–85	*Swindon T*	5	—
1985–86	Chesterfield	22	3

CALDWELL, Tony

Born Salford 21.3.58.   Ht 5 9   Wt 11 6
Forward. From Salford, Irlam, Hyde and
Horwich RMI.

Season	Club	App	Goals
1983–84	Bolton W	33	19
1984–85		31	18
1985–86		40	10

CALLACHAN, Ralph

Born Edinburgh 29.4.55.   Ht 5 11   Wt 11 6
Midfield. From Tynecastle B.C.

Season	Club	App	Goals
1971–72	Hearts	—	—
1972–73		—	—
1973–74		1	—
1974–75		28	5
1975–76		35	2
1976–77		13	2
1977–78	Newcastle U	9	—
1978–79	Hibernian	33	9
1979–80		30	2
1980–81		38	4
1981–82		29	4
1982–83		28	1
1983–84		33	4
1984–85		24	1
1985–86		5	1

CALLAGHAN, Aaron

Born Dublin 8.10.66.   Ht 5 11   Wt 11 2
Defender. From Apprentice. Eire Youth.

Season	Club	App	Goals
1984–85	Stoke C	5	—
1985–86		—	—
1985–86	*Crewe Alex*	8	—

CALLAGHAN, Nigel

Born Singapore 12.9.62.   Ht 5 9   Wt 10 9
Midfield. From Apprentice.
England Under-21.

Season	Club	App	Goals
1979–80	Watford	1	—
1980–81		21	2
1981–82		37	5
1982–83		41	9
1983–84		41	10
1984–85		38	8
1985–86		23	4

Season	Club	League Appearances/Goals	Season	Club	League Appearances/Goals

CAME, Mark

Born Exeter 14.9.61.　Ht 6 1　Wt 13 0
Defender. From Winsford U.

Season	Club	App	Goals
1983–84	Bolton W	—	—
1984–85		23	1
1985–86		35	1

CAMERON, Ian

Born Glasgow 24.8.66.　Ht 5 9　Wt 10 4
Midfield. 'S' Form. Scotland Schools, Youth.

Season	Club	App	Goals
1983–84	St Mirren	8	—
1984–85		9	1
1985–86		12	—

CAMMACK, Steve

Born Sheffield 20.3.54.　Ht 5 10　Wt 11 6
Forward. From Apprentice. England Youth.

Season	Club	App	Goals
1971–72	Sheffield U	1	—
1972–73		3	1
1973–74		7	1
1974–75		13	3
1975–76		12	—
1975–76	Chesterfield	20	5
1976–77		27	3
1977–78		44	9
1978–79		22	4
1979–80		—	—
1979–80	Scunthorpe U	38	12
1980–81		46	15
1981–82	Lincoln C	18	6
1981–82	Scunthorpe U	10	3
1982–83		41	25
1983–84		39	18
1984–85		34	24
1985–86		33	12
1985–86	*Port Vale*	3	—
1985–86	*Stockport Co*	4	1

CAMPBELL, Bobby

Born Belfast 13.9.56.　Ht 6 0　Wt 12 7
Forward. From Apprentice.
Northern Ireland Youth, 2 full caps.

Season	Club	App	Goals
1973–74	Aston Villa	3	1
1974–75		7	—
1974–75	*Halifax T*	15	—
1975–76	Huddersfield T	11	1
1976–77		20	8
1977–78	Sheffield U	37	11
1978–79		—	—
1978–79	Huddersfield T	7	3
1978–79	Halifax T	22	3
From Brisbane C			
1979–80	Bradford C	21	8
1980–81		42	19
1981–82		45	24
1982–83		40	25
1983–84	Derby Co	11	4
1983–84	Bradford C	32	9
1984–85		46	23
1985–86		41	10

CAMPBELL, David

Born Eglinton 2.6.65.　Ht 5 9　Wt 10 9
Midfield. From Oxford BC(NI); Northern
Ireland, 1 full cap.

Season	Club	App	Goals
1983–84	Nottingham F	—	—
1984–85		1	—
1985–86		18	3

CAMPBELL, Glen

Born Leyland 26.2.65.　Ht 5 11　Wt 11 7
Goalkeeper. From Apprentice.

Season	Club	App	Goals
1982–83	Preston NE	1	—
1983–84		—	—
1984–85		17	—
1985–86	Bolton W		

CAMPBELL, Greg

Born Portsmouth 13.7.65.　Ht 5 11　Wt 11 5
Forward. From Manchester U. Amateur
and West Ham U. Apprentice.

Season	Club	App	Goals
1982–83	West Ham U	—	—
1983–84		—	—
1984–85		2	—
1985–86		3	—

All appearances include those as substitute

Season	Club	League Appearances/Goals	Season	Club	League Appearances/Goals

CAMPBELL, Stephen

Born Dundee 20.11.67. Ht 5 9 Wt 11 2
Midfield. From Downfield B.C.

1985–86	Dundee	5	—

CAMPBELL, Winston

Born Sheffield 9.10.62. Ht 5 8 Wt 11 6
Midfield. From Apprentice.

1979–80	Barnsley	1	—
1980–81		1	—
1981–82		7	—
1982–83		17	3
1982–83	*Doncaster R*	3	—
1983–84	Barnsley	31	2
1984–85		38	3
1985–86		29	1

CANHAM, Tony

Born Leeds 8.6.60. Ht 5 8 Wt 10 7
Midfield. From Harrogate Railway.

1984–85	York C	3	1
1985–86		41	13

CANNON, Jim

Born Glasgow 2.10.53. Ht 6 0 Wt 13 0
Defender. From Apprentice.

1970–71	Crystal Palace	—	—
1971–72		—	—
1972–73		3	1
1973–74		14	1
1974–75		36	3
1975–76		40	2
1976–77		46	2
1977–78		39	2
1978–79		41	2
1979–80		42	4
1980–81		33	1
1981–82		42	1
1982–83		41	1
1983–84		30	2
1984–85		40	2
1985–86		42	1

CANOVILLE, Paul

Born Hillingdon 4.3.62. Ht 6 0 Wt 11 5
Forward. From Hillingdon Borough.

1981–82	Chelsea	3	—
1982–83		19	3
1983–84		20	6
1984–85		24	1
1985–86		13	1

CARNEY, Steve

Born Wallsend 22.9.57. Ht 5 10 Wt 11 5
Defender. From Blyth Spartans.

1979–80	Newcastle U	11	—
1980–81		27	—
1981–82		28	—
1982–83		29	—
1983–84		33	—
1984–85		6	1
1984–85	*Carlisle U*	6	—
1985–86	Darlington	12	—
1985–86	*Rochdale*	4	—
1985–86	Hartlepool U	7	—

CARPENTER, Steve

Born Torquay 23.9.60.
Midfield. From STC.

1985–86	Torquay U	2	—

CARR, Cliff

Born London 19.6.64. Ht 5 5½ Wt 10 4
Midfield. From Apprentice. England Under-21.

1982–83	Fulham	6	1
1983–84		41	4
1984–85		38	4
1985–86		35	4

CARR, Darren

Born Bristol 4.9.68.
Defender.

1985–86	Bristol R	1	—

Season	Club	League Appearances/Goals		Season	Club	League Appearances/Goals	

CARR, Franz

Born Preston 24.9.66. Ht 5 6 Wt 10 8½
Midfield. From Apprentice. England Youth.

| 1984–85 | Blackburn R | — | — |
| 1985–86 | Nottingham F | 23 | 3 |

CARR, Kevin

Born Ashington 6.11.58. Ht 6 2 Wt 13 6
Goalkeeper. From Burnley Apprentice.

1976–77	Newcastle U	—	—
1977–78		9	—
1978–79		8	—
1979–80		1	—
1980–81		38	—
1981–82		42	—
1982–83		32	—
1983–84		19	—
1984–85		24	—
1985–86	Carlisle U	15	—

CARROLL, Robert

Born Greenford 15.2.68.
Forward. From Apprentice.

| 1985–86 | Southampton | — | — |

CARTER, James

Born London 9.11.65. Ht 5 10 Wt 10 4
Midfield. From Apprentice.

1983–84	Crystal Palace	—	—
1984–85		—	—
1985–86	QPR	—	—

CARTER, Mike

Born Warrington 18.4.60. Ht 5 9 Wt 10 7
Forward. From Apprentice.

1977–78	Bolton W	—	—
1978–79		—	—
1978–79	*Mansfield T*	18	4
1979–80	Bolton W	22	5
1980–81		14	2

1981–82		13	1
1981–82	*Swindon T*	5	—
1982–83	Plymouth Arg	12	1
1982–83	*Hereford U*	10	—
1983–84	Hereford U	—	—
1984–85		28	—
1985–86		31	9

CARTER, Roy

Born Torpoint 19.2.54. Ht 6 0 Wt 11 0
Midfield. From Falmouth.

1974–75	Hereford U	1	—
1975–76		33	5
1976–77		24	3
1977–78		13	1
1977–78	Swindon T	24	2
1978–79		46	10
1979–80		41	3
1980–81		41	5
1981–82		45	13
1982–83		3	1
1982–83	*Torquay U*	6	5
1982–83	*Bristol R*	4	1
1982–83	Torquay U	16	3
1983–84		5	—
1983–84	Newport Co	39	4
1984–85		29	4
1985–86		42	7

CARTER, Tim

Born Bristol 5.10.67. Ht 6 1 Wt 12 0
Goalkeeper. From Apprentice. England
Youth.

| 1985–86 | Bristol R | 2 | — |

CARTWRIGHT, Ian

Born Brierley Hill 13.11.64. Ht 5 10
Wt 11 3
Midfield. From Apprentice.

1982–83	Wolves	9	1
1983–84		16	—
1984–85		23	1
1985–86		13	1

Season	Club	League Appearances/Goals	Season	Club	League Appearances/Goals

CARVER, John

Born Newcastle 16.1.65.   Ht 5 8   Wt 10 8
Defender. From Apprentice.

Season	Club	App	Goals
1982–83	Newcastle U	—	—
1983–84		—	—
1984–85		—	—
1985–86	Cardiff C	13	—

CASCARINO, Tony

Born St Paul's Cray 1.9.62.   Ht 6 1½
Wt 13 0
Forward. From Crockenhill. Eire 3 full caps.

Season	Club	App	Goals
1981–82	Gillingham	24	5
1982–83		38	15
1983–84		37	12
1984–85		43	16
1985–86		34	14

CASE, Jimmy

Born Liverpool 18.5.54.   Ht 5 9   Wt 12 7
Forward. From Sth Liverpool.
England Under-23.

Season	Club	App	Goals
1973–74	Liverpool	—	—
1974–75		1	—
1975–76		27	6
1976–77		27	1
1977–78		33	5
1978–79		37	7
1979–80		37	3
1980–81		24	1
1981–82	Brighton	33	3
1982–83		35	3
1983–84		35	4
1984–85		24	—
1984–85	Southampton	10	1
1985–86		36	2

CASHLEY, Ray

Born Bristol 23.10.51.   Ht 5 11   Wt 12 12
Goalkeeper. From Amateur.

Season	Club	App	Goals
1970–71	Bristol C	11	—
1971–72		29	—
1972–73		32	—
1973–74		27	1
1974–75		42	—
1975–76		42	—
1976–77		8	—
1977–78		—	—
1978–79		2	—
1979–80		14	—
1980–81		20	—
1980–81	*Hereford U*	20	—
1981–82	Bristol R	—	—
1982–83		—	—
1983–84		27	—
1984–85		26	—
1985–86	Chester C	9	—

CASSELLS, Keith

Born London 10.7.57.   Ht 5 10   Wt 11 12
Forward. From Wembley T.

Season	Club	App	Goals
1977–78	Watford	—	—
1978–79		3	—
1979–80		7	—
1979–80	*Peterborough U*	8	—
1980–81	Watford	2	—
1980–81	Oxford U	18	3
1981–82		27	10
1981–82	Southampton	6	2
1982–83		13	2
1982–83	Brentford	16	7
1983–84		30	9
1984–85		40	12
1985–86	Mansfield T	40	13

CASSIDY, Francis

Born Watford 20.8.64.   Ht 5 10   Wt 11 6
Midfield. From Apprentice.

Season	Club	App	Goals
1982–83	Watford	—	—
1983–84		—	—
1983–84	*Plymouth Arg*	1	—
1984–85	Peterborough U	31	7
1985–86		15	2

Season	Club	League Appearances/Goals

CASTLE, Steve

Born Barkingside 17.5.66.
Defender. From Apprentice.

Season	Club	App	Goals
1984–85	Orient	21	1
1985–86		23	4

CASWELL, Brian

Born Wednesbury 14.2.56.   Ht 5 10
Wt 10 7
Defender. From Apprentice.

Season	Club	App	Goals
1972–73	Walsall	4	—
1973–74		15	—
1974–75		22	1
1975–76		17	—
1976–77		38	2
1977–78		36	3
1978–79		42	1
1979–80		45	6
1980–81		34	1
1981–82		41	3
1982–83		39	—
1983–84		32	—
1984–85		35	—
1985–86	Doncaster R	15	2
1985–86	Leeds U	8	—

CATON, Tommy

Born Liverpool 6.10.62.   Ht 6 2   Wt 13 0
Defender. From Apprentice.
England Schools, Youth, Under-21.

Season	Club	App	Goals
1979–80	Manchester C	42	—
1980–81		30	—
1981–82		39	1
1982–83		38	5
1983–84		16	2
1983–84	Arsenal	26	—
1984–85		35	1
1985–86		20	1

CAVENER, Phil

Born Tynemouth 2.6.61.   Ht 5 8   Wt 10 7
Forward. From Apprentice.

Season	Club	App	Goals
1979–80	Burnley	14	2
1980–81		40	2
1981–82		9	—
1982–83		6	—
1982–83	*Bradford C*	9	2
1983–84	Gillingham	10	1
1984–85	Northampton T	28	7
1985–86		17	4
1985–86	Peterborough U	10	—

CECERE, Michele

Born Chester 4.1.68.   Ht 6 0   Wt 11 4
Forward. From Apprentice.

Season	Club	App	Goals
1985–86	Oldham Ath	—	—

CEGIELSKI, Wayne

Born Bedwelty 11.1.56.   Ht 6 0   Wt 12 0
Defender. From Apprentice.
Wales Under-21.

Season	Club	App	Goals
1973–74	Tottenham H	—	—
1974–75		—	—
1974–75	*Northampton T*	11	—
From Stuttgart			
1976–77	Wrexham	9	—
1977–78		9	—
1978–79		29	—
1979–80		3	—
1980–81		38	—
1981–82		35	—
1982–83	Port Vale	45	5
1983–84		39	—
1984–85		8	—
1984–85	Blackpool	6	1
1985–86	Hereford U	32	2

CHADWICK, Simon

Born Liverpool 15.3.68.   Ht 5 11   Wt 10 7
Forward. From school.

Season	Club	App	Goals
1985–86	Wrexham	2	—

CHALMERS, Paul

Born Glasgow 31.10.63.   Ht 5 10   Wt 10 3
Forward. From Eastercraigs. Scotland
Youth.

All appearances include those as substitute

Season	Club	League Appearances/Goals		Season	Club	League Appearances/Goals	
1980–81	Celtic	—	—	1983–84	*Plymouth Arg*	11	3
1981–82		—	—	1984–85	Newport Co	41	13
1982–83		—	—	1985–86	Mansfield T	40	16
1983–84		—	—				
1984–85		1	1				
1985–86		3	—				
1985–86	*Bradford C*	2	—				

CHAMBERLAIN, Alec

Born March 20.6.64.   Ht 6 2   Wt 11 11
Goalkeeper. From Ramsey T.

Season	Club	League Appearances/Goals	
1981–82	Ipswich T	—	—
1982–83	Colchester U	—	—
1983–84		46	—
1984–85		46	—
1985–86		46	—

CHAMBERLAIN, Mark

Born Stoke 19.11.61.   Ht 5 8½   Wt 10 7
Forward. From Apprentice.
England Schools, Under-21, 8 full caps.

Season	Club	League Appearances/Goals	
1978–79	Port Vale	8	—
1979–80		11	—
1980–81		31	9
1981–82		46	8
1982–83	Stoke C	37	6
1983–84		40	7
1984–85		28	1
1985–86		7	3
1985–86	Sheffield W	21	2

CHAMBERLAIN, Neville

Born Stoke 22.1.60.   Ht 5 7½   Wt 11 5
Forward. From Apprentice.

Season	Club	League Appearances/Goals	
1977–78	Port Vale	10	2
1978–79		26	7
1979–80		35	11
1980–81		35	9
1981–82		30	4
1982–83		5	—
1982–83	Stoke C	3	—
1983–84		3	—
1983–84	*Newport Co*	6	2

CHAMBERS, Phil

Born Barnsley 10.11.53.   Ht 5 8   Wt 11 1
Defender. From Apprentice.
England Schools.

Season	Club	League Appearances/Goals	
1970–71	Barnsley	3	—
1971–72		7	—
1972–73		46	1
1973–74		46	1
1974–75		46	2
1975–76		30	1
1976–77		9	1
1977–78		10	—
1978–79		45	1
1979–80		32	—
1980–81		43	—
1981–82		42	—
1982–83		40	—
1983–84		37	1
1984–85		7	—
1985–86	Rochdale	10	—
1985–86	Hartlepool U	29	—

CHANDLER, Jeff

Born Hammersmith 19.6.59.   Ht 5 6½
Wt 10 0
Midfield. From Apprentice.
Eire Under-21, 2 full caps.

Season	Club	League Appearances/Goals	
1976–77	Blackpool	—	—
1977–78		13	2
1978–79		24	5
1979–80		—	—
1979–80	Leeds U	17	2
1980–81		9	—
1981–82		—	—
1981–82	Bolton W	33	2
1982–83		37	4
1983–84		46	14
1984–85		41	16
1985–86	Derby Co	37	9

Season	Club	League Appearances/Goals	Season	Club	League Appearances/Goals

CHANDLER, Simon

Born Reading 4.12.67. Ht 5 7½ Wt 10 7
Forward. From Apprentice.

1985–86	Chelsea	—	—

CHANNON, Mick

Born Orcheston 28.11.48. Ht 6 0½
Wt 12 11
Forward. From Apprentice. England Under-23, 46 full caps, Football League.

1965–66	Southampton	3	1
1966–67		1	—
1967–68		28	7
1968–69		34	8
1969–70		39	15
1970–71		42	18
1971–72		42	14
1972–73		40	16
1973–74		41	21
1974–75		40	19
1975–76		42	19
1976–77		40	17
1977–78	Manchester C	34	12
1978–79		36	11
1979–80		2	1
1979–80	Southampton	37	10
1980–81		42	10
1981–82		40	7
From Hong Kong			
1982–83	Newcastle U	4	1
1982–83	Bristol R	9	—
1982–83	Norwich C	20	3
1983–84		37	5
1984–85		31	8
1985–86	Portsmouth	34	6

CHAPMAN, Campbell

Born Mansfield 28.6.63. Ht 5 8 Wt 10 7
Midfield. From Apprentice.

1981–82	Peterborough U	—	—
1982–83	Derby Co	—	—
1982–83	Crewe Alex	6	2

From Bilston
1984–85	Wolverhampton W	20	2
1985–86		33	2

CHAPMAN, Lee

Born Lincoln 5.12.59. Ht 6 1½ Wt 13 5
Forward. From Amateur.
England Under-21.

1978–79	Stoke C	—	—
1978–79	*Plymouth Arg*	4	—
1979–80	Stoke C	17	3
1980–81		41	15
1981–82		41	16
1982–83	Arsenal	19	3
1983–84		4	1
1983–84	Sunderland	15	3
1984–85	Sheffield W	40	15
1985–86		31	10

CHAPMAN, Les

Born Oldham 27.9.48. Ht 5 7 Wt 10 4
Midfield. From High Barn.

1966–67	Oldham Ath	16	—
1967–68		10	1
1968–69		41	7
1969–70		9	1
1969–70	Huddersfield T	10	—
1970–71		14	1
1971–72		39	3
1972–73		22	2
1973–74		33	1
1974–75		15	1
1974–75	Oldham Ath	24	—
1975–76		41	2
1976–77		42	2
1977–78		38	4
1978–79		42	3
1979–80	Stockport Co	32	1
1979–80	Bradford C	14	2
1980–81		45	—
1981–82		34	1
1982–83		46	—
1983–84	Rochdale	45	—
1984–85		43	—
1985–86	Stockport Co	38	3

Season	Club	League Appearances/Goals		Season	Club	League Appearances/Goals	

CHAPPLE, Phil

Born Norwich 26.11.66.   Ht 6 2   Wt 12 7
Defender. From Apprentice.

1984–85	Norwich C	—	—
1985–86		—	—

CHARD, Phil

Born Corby 16.10.60.   Ht 5 8   Wt 11 12
Midfield. From Nottingham F. Amateur.

1978–79	Peterborough U	6	1
1979–80		20	2
1980–81		—	—
1981–82		39	3
1982–83		44	4
1983–84		38	7
1984–85		25	1
1985–86	Northampton T	41	7

CHARLES, Jeremy

Born Swansea 26.9.59.   Ht 6 1¼   Wt 13 8½
Forward. From Apprentice. Wales Under-
21, 18 full caps.

1976–77	Swansea C	41	23
1977–78		33	4
1978–79		40	12
1979–80		40	5
1980–81		38	5
1981–82		13	2
1982–83		32	2
1983–84		10	—
1983–84	QPR	12	5
1984–85	Oxford U	11	4
1985–86		28	9

CHARLES, Steve

Born Sheffield 10.5.60.   Ht 5 9   Wt 10 7
Midfield. From Sheffield University.
England Schools.

1979–80	Sheffield U	14	1
1980–81		31	6
1981–82		30	1
1982–83		35	—

1983–84		11	1
1984–85		2	1
1984–85	Wrexham	32	7
1985–86		40	20

CHATTERTON, Nicky

Born Norwood 18.5.54.   Ht 5 9½   Wt 11 4
Midfield. From Amateur.

1973–74	Crystal Palace	7	—
1974–75		25	6
1975–76		37	7
1976–77		37	6
1977–78		32	9
1978–79		13	3
1978–79	Millwall	27	4
1979–80		43	10
1980–81		40	8
1981–82		45	12
1982–83		32	9
1983–84		27	6
1984–85		33	3
1985–86		17	4

CHERRY, Paul

Born Derby 14.10.64.   Ht 6 0   Wt 11 7
Defender. From Salvesen B.C.

1983–84	Hearts	—	—
1984–85		3	—
1985–86		5	—

CHERRY, Steve

Born Nottingham 5.8.60.   Ht 5 11   Wt 11 0
Goalkeeper. From Apprentice. England
Youth.

1977–78	Derby Co	—	—
1978–79		—	—
1979–80		4	—
1980–81	*Port Vale*	4	—
1981–82	Derby Co	4	—
1982–83		31	—
1983–84		38	—
1984–85	Walsall	41	—
1985–86		30	—

Season	Club	League Appearances/Goals	Season	Club	League Appearances/Goals

CHIEDOZIE, John

Born Nigeria 18.4.60.   Ht 5 7   Wt 10 10
Forward. From Apprentice. Nigeria full caps.

Season	Club	App	Goals
1976–77	Orient	15	—
1977–78		21	2
1978–79		36	6
1979–80		37	3
1980–81		36	9
1981–82	Notts Co	32	1
1982–83		39	5
1983–84		40	9
1984–85	Tottenham H	34	5
1985–86		18	7

CHILDS, Gary

Born Birmingham 19.4.64.   Ht 5 7   Wt 10 9
Midfield. From Apprentice. England Youth.

Season	Club	App	Goals
1981–82	WBA	2	—
1982–83		—	—
1983–84		1	—
1983–84	Walsall	30	2
1984–85		40	2
1985–86		33	5

CHILTON, Tony

Born Maryport 7.9.65.   Ht 5 7½   Wt 10 8½
Midfield. From Apprentice.

Season	Club	App	Goals
1983–84	Sunderland	—	—
1984–85	Burnley	1	—
1985–86	Hartlepool U	3	—

CHIPPENDALE, Brian

Born Bradford 29.10.64.   Ht 5 9   Wt 11 6
Midfield. From Bradford C.

Season	Club	App	Goals
1983–84	York C	4	—
1984–85		4	—
1984–85	*Halifax T*	2	—
1985–86	Burnley	8	—
1985–86	Preston NE	6	—

CHISHOLM, Gordon

Born Glasgow 8.4.60.   Ht 6 0¾   Wt 12 0
Defender. From Apprentice.

Season	Club	App	Goals
1977–78	Sunderland	—	—
1978–79		27	1
1979–80		13	—
1980–81		34	3
1981–82		22	—
1982–83		32	1
1983–84		36	4
1984–85		32	1
1985–86		1	—
1985–86	Hibernian	29	2

CHIVERS, Gary

Born Stockwell 15.5.60.   Ht 5 11   Wt 11 5
Defender. From Apprentice.

Season	Club	App	Goals
1978–79	Chelsea	5	—
1979–80		29	2
1980–81		40	2
1981–82		29	—
1982–83		30	—
1983–84	Swansea C	10	—
1983–84	QPR	—	—
1984–85		23	—
1985–86		14	—

CHRISTENSEN, Tommy

Born Denmark 20.7.61.
Forward. From Vejle and Elche.

Season	Club	App	Goals
1985–86	Leicester C	2	—
1985–86	Portsmouth	3	2

CHRISTIE, Derrick

Born Bletchley 15.3.57.   Ht 5 8   Wt 11 0
Forward. From Apprentice.

Season	Club	App	Goals
1973–74	Northampton T	3	—
1974–75		14	—
1975–76		19	1

All appearances include those as substitute

Season	Club	League Appearances/Goals		Season	Club	League Appearances/Goals	

Season	Club	App	Goals
1976–77	....	44	5
1977–78	....	43	9
1978–79	....	15	3
1978–79	Cambridge U	21	3
1979–80	....	31	5
1980–81	....	31	5
1981–82	....	15	1
1982–83	....	17	2
1983–84	....	23	3
1984–85	Reading	14	1
1985–86	....	—	—
1985–86	Cardiff C	19	2

CHRISTIE, Trevor

Born Newcastle 28.2.59. Ht 6 2 Wt 12 0
Forward. From Apprentice.

Season	Club	App	Goals
1976–77	Leicester C	—	—
1977–78	....	5	—
1978–79	....	26	8
1979–80	Notts Co	41	9
1980–81	....	39	14
1981–82	....	35	13
1982–83	....	33	9
1983–84	....	39	19
1984–85	Nottingham F	14	5
1984–85	Derby Co	20	7
1985–86	....	45	15

CLARIDGE, Steve

Born Portsmouth 10.4.66. Ht 5 11 Wt 11 8
Forward. From Fareham.

Season	Club	App	Goals
1984–85	Bournemouth	6	1
1985–86	....	1	—

CLARK, Billy

Born Christchurch 19.5.67. Ht 5 11
Wt 11 8
Defender. From Local.

Season	Club	App	Goals
1984–85	Bournemouth	1	—
1985–86	....	1	—

CLARK, Jim

Born Kilmarnock 14.8.52. Ht 5 6 Wt 10 2
Midfield. From Glenafton Athletic.

Season	Club	App	Goals
1972–73	Stirling Albion	12	1
1973–74	....	32	5
1974–75	....	32	2
1975–76	....	26	2
1976–77	....	39	5
1977–78	....	35	7
1978–79	Kilmarnock	32	3
1979–80	....	34	1
1980–81	....	27	—
1981–82	....	28	2
1982–83	....	36	2
1983–84	....	17	—
1984–85	....	—	—
1985–86	Motherwell	5	—
1985–86	Meadowbank T	9	1

CLARK, John

Born Edinburgh 22.9.64. Ht 6 0 Wt 13 1
Forward. 'S' Form. Scotland Youth.

Season	Club	App	Goals
1981–82	Dundee U	—	—
1982–83	....	1	—
1983–84	....	9	1
1984–85	....	10	3
1985–86	....	11	1

CLARK, Jonathan

Born Swansea 12.11.58. Ht 5 10 Wt 11 10
Midfield. From Apprentice.
Wales Schools, Under-21.

Season	Club	App	Goals
1975–76	Manchester U	—	—
1976–77	....	1	—
1977–78	....	—	—
1978–79	....	—	—
1978–79	Derby Co	17	—
1979–80	....	14	1
1980–81	....	22	2
1981–82	Preston NE	18	—
1982–83	....	3	—
1983–84	....	31	5
1984–85	....	40	5
1985–86	....	6	—

Season	Club	League Appearances/Goals	Season	Club	League Appearances/Goals

CLARK, Paul

Born Benfleet 14.9.58. Ht 5 10 Wt 12 12
Midfield. From Apprentice.
England Schools, Youth.

Season	Club	App	Goals
1976–77	Southend U	25	—
1977–78		8	1
1977–78	Brighton	26	3
1978–79		33	4
1979–80		11	2
1980–81		9	—
1981–82	*Reading*	2	—
1982–83	Southend U	31	1
1983–84		20	—
1984–85		29	1
1985–86		39	1

CLARK, Robert

Born Hamilton 4.11.62. Ht 6 0 Wt 11 11
Midfield. From Blantyre Victoria.

Season	Club	App	Goals
1980–81	Rangers	1	—
1981–82		—	—
1982–83	Kilmarnock	24	1
1983–84		37	11
1984–85		6	—
1984–85	Motherwell	10	1
1985–86		2	—

CLARK, Sandy

Born Airdrie 28.10.56. Ht 6 0 Wt 12 7
Forward. From Airdrie B.C.

Season	Club	App	Goals
1974–75	Airdrieonians	3	—
1975–76		20	7
1976–77		32	8
1977–78		38	7
1978–79		38	23
1979–80		37	22
1980–81		36	10
1981–82		30	15
1982–83	West Ham U	26	7
1982–83	Rangers	10	4
1983–84		30	9
1984–85		1	—
1984–85	Hearts	25	8
1985–86		33	12

CLARK, Steve

Born Baldock 20.9.64. Ht 5 11 Wt 11 2
Defender. From Apprentice.

Season	Club	App	Goals
1982–83	Cambridge U	—	—
1983–84		16	—
1984–85		22	—
1985–86		28	—

CLARKE, Colin

Born Newry 30.10.62. Ht 5 10 Wt 12 7
Forward. From Apprentice. Northern
Ireland, 3 full caps.

Season	Club	App	Goals
1980–81	Ipswich T	—	—
1981–82	Peterborough U	27	4
1982–83		37	9
1983–84		18	5
1983–84	*Gillingham*	8	1
1984–85	Tranmere R	45	22
1985–86	Bournemouth	46	26

CLARKE, David

Born Nottingham 3.12.64. Ht 5 10 Wt 11 0
Midfield. From Apprentice. England Youth.

Season	Club	App	Goals
1982–83	Notts Co	16	—
1983–84		20	—
1984–85		22	—
1985–86		42	1

CLARKE, Jeff

Born Pontefract 18.1.54. Ht 6 0½ Wt 13 8
Defender. Local.

Season	Club	App	Goals
1971–72	Manchester C	—	—
1972–73		—	—
1973–74		—	—
1974–75		13	—
1975–76	Sunderland	31	—
1976–77		27	—
1977–78		24	3

Season	Club	League Appearances/Goals		Season	Club	League Appearances/Goals	
1978–79	....	34	2				
1979–80	....	39	1				
1980–81	....	—	—				
1981–82	....	26	—				
1982–83	Newcastle U	39	1				
1983–84	....	14	—				
1984–85	....	23	—				
1984–85	*Brighton*	4	—				
1985–86	Newcastle U	41	3				

CLARKE, John

Born Dublin 4.1.69.
Midfield. From Apprentice. Eire Youth.

1985–86	Manchester C	—	—

CLARKE, Nicky

Born Walsall 20.8.67.   Ht 5 11   Wt 11 10
Defender. From Apprentice.

1984–85	Wolverhampton W........	—	—
1985–86	....	23	1

CLARKE, Paul

Born Liverpool 25.2.68.
Defender. From school.

1985–86	Liverpool....................	—	—

CLARKE, Stephen

Born Saltcoats 29.8.63.   Ht 5 10   Wt 10 2
Defender. From Beith Juniors. Scotland
Youth, Under–21.

1981–82	St Mirren	—	—
1982–83	....	31	—
1983–84	....	33	2
1984–85	....	33	—
1985–86	....	31	3

CLARKE, Wayne

Born Wolverhampton 28.2.61.   Ht 6 0
Wt 11 8
Forward. From Apprentice. England
Schools, Youth.

1977–78	Wolverhampton W........	1	—
1978–79	....	8	1
1979–80	....	16	2
1980–81	....	24	3
1981–82	....	29	6
1982–83	....	39	12
1983–84	....	31	6
1984–85	Birmingham C..............	40	17
1985–86	....	28	5

CLAYTON, John

Born Elgin 20.8.61.   Ht 5 11   Wt 11 7
Forward. From Apprentice.

1978–79	Derby C	1	—
1979–80	....	—	—
1980–81	....	9	1
1981–82	....	14	3
From Bulova, Hong Kong			
1983–84	Chesterfield.................	33	5
1984–85	Tranmere R..................	44	31
1985–86	....	3	4
1985–86	Plymouth Arg	36	12

CLAYTON, Paul

Born Dunstable 4.1.65.   Ht 5 11   Wt 11 3
Forward. From Apprentice.

1982–83	Norwich C....................	—	—
1983–84	....	7	—
1984–85	....	5	—
1985–86	....	1	—

CLEGG, Tony

Born Keighley 8.11.65.   Ht 6 0   Wt 11 5
Defender. From Apprentice.

1983–84	Bradford C....................	2	—
1984–85	....	7	—
1985–86	....	21	1

All appearances include those as substitute

Season	Club	League Appearances/Goals	Season	Club	League Appearances/Goals

CLEMENCE, Ray

Born Skegness 5.8.48.   Ht 5 11½   Wt 12 9
Goalkeeper. From Notts Co. and Scunthorpe
U Amateur. England Under-23, 61 full caps,
Football League.

Season	Club	Apps	Goals
1965–66	Scunthorpe U	4	—
1966–67		44	—
1967–68	Liverpool	—	—
1968–69		—	—
1969–70		14	—
1970–71		41	—
1971–72		42	—
1972–73		41	—
1973–74		42	—
1974–75		42	—
1975–76		42	—
1976–77		42	—
1977–78		40	—
1978–79		42	—
1979–80		41	—
1980–81		41	—
1981–82	Tottenham H	38	—
1982–83		41	—
1983–84		26	—
1984–85		42	—
1985–86		42	—

CLEMENT, Andy

Born Cardiff 12.11.67.   Ht 5 8   Wt 11 0
Defender. From Apprentice. Wales Youth.

Season	Club	Apps	Goals
1985–86	Wimbledon	—	—

CLEMENTS, Kenny

Born Manchester 9.4.55.   Ht 6 1   Wt 12 6
Defender. From Amateur.

Season	Club	Apps	Goals
1975–76	Manchester C	27	—
1976–77		35	—
1977–78		42	—
1978–79		15	—
1979–80		—	—
1979–80	Oldham Ath	36	1
1980–81		40	—
1981–82		27	1

Season	Club	Apps	Goals
1982–83		38	—
1983–84		41	—
1984–85		24	—
1984–85	*Manchester C*	12	1
1985–86	Manchester C	30	—

CLISS, Tony

Born March 22.9.59.   Ht 5 8   Wt 10 7
Forward. From Apprentice.

Season	Club	Apps	Goals
1977–78	Peterborough U	3	1
1978–79		19	2
1979–80		34	7
1980–81		22	1
1981–82		4	—
1982–83		3	—
1982–83	Crewe Alex	30	4
1983–84		37	3
1984–85		41	4
1985–86		—	—

CLOSE, Shaun

Born Islington 8.9.66.   Ht 5 8   Wt 10 1
Forward. From YTS.

Season	Club	Apps	Goals
1984–86	Tottenham H	—	—
1985–86		—	—

CLOUGH, Nigel

Born Sunderland 19.3.66.   Ht 5 9   Wt 11 4
Forward. From AC Hunters. England
Under-21.

Season	Club	Apps	Goals
1984–85	Nottingham F	9	1
1985–86		39	15

COADY, Mike

Born Dipton 1.10.58.   Ht 5 11   Wt 11 0
Defender. From Apprentice.

Season	Club	Apps	Goals
1976–77	Sunderland	2	—
1977–78		—	—
1978–79		3	—
1979–80		1	—

Season	Club	League Appearances/Goals			Season	Club	League Appearances/Goals	
1980–81	Carlisle U	45	1		1980–81	Tottenham H	—	—
1981–82		6	—		1981–82		—	—
From Sydney Olympic					1982–83		—	—
1984–85	Wolverhampton W	7	—		1983–84		2	—
1985–86		8	1		1984–85		—	—
					1985–86	Bristol R	1	—

COCHRANE, Terry

Born Killyleagh 23.1.53.   Ht 5 7½   Wt 10 9
Midfield. From Coleraine. Northern Ireland
26 full caps.

Season	Club	League Appearances/Goals	
1976–77	Burnley	21	4
1977–78		40	8
1978–79		6	1
1978–79	Middlesbrough	19	3
1979–80		29	1
1980–81		24	1
1981–82		25	1
1982–83		14	1
1983–84		—	—
1983–84	Gillingham	34	6
1984–85		35	6
1985–86		38	5

COCKERILL, Glenn

Born Grimsby 25.8.59.   Ht 6 0   Wt 12 3½
Midfield. From Louth U.

Season	Club	League Appearances/Goals	
1976–77	Lincoln C	4	—
1977–78		13	1
1978–79		35	6
1979–80		19	3
1979–80	Swindon T	10	1
1980–81		16	—
1981–82	Lincoln C	44	11
1982–83		38	8
1983–84		33	6
1983–84	Sheffield U	10	1
1984–85		40	7
1985–86		12	2
1985–86	Southampton	30	7

COCKRAM, Allan

Born Kensington 8.10.63.   Ht 5 7   Wt 10 0
Midfield. Local.

COGHIEL, Roy

Born Bolton 9.1.66.   Ht 5 7   Wt 11 0
Midfield.

Season	Club	League Appearances/Goals	
1984–85	Bolton W	—	—
1984–85	Norwich C	—	—
1985–86		—	—

COLE, David

Born Barnsley 28.9.62.   Ht 6 0   Wt 11 10
Defender. From Sunderland.

Season	Club	League Appearances/Goals	
1984–85	Swansea C	8	—
1984–85	Swindon T	20	—
1985–86		44	3

COLE, Michael

Born Stepney 3.9.66.   Ht 5 10½   Wt 11 3½
Forward. From Amateur.

Season	Club	League Appearances/Goals	
1983–84	Ipswich T	—	—
1984–85		2	—
1985–86		18	1

COLEMAN, David

Born Salisbury 8.4.67.   Ht 5 7   Wt 10 8
Midfield.

Season	Club	League Appearances/Goals	
1985–86	Bournemouth	1	—

COLEMAN, Nicky

Born Crayford 6.5.66.   Ht 5 8   Wt 11 7
Defender. From Apprentice.

Season	Club	League Appearances/Goals	
1983–84	Millwall	—	—
1984–85		1	—
1985–86		6	—
1985–86	*Swindon T*	13	4

Season	Club	League Appearances/Goals		Season	Club	League Appearances/Goals	

COLEMAN, Phil

Born Woolwich 8.9.60. Ht 5 11 Wt 11 9
Defender. From Apprentice.

1978–79	Millwall	2	—
1979–80		26	1
1980–81		8	—
1980–81	Colchester U	4	—
1981–82		37	4
1982–83		37	2
1983–84		8	—
1983–84	*Wrexham*	17	2
1984–85	Exeter C	6	—
1984–85	Aldershot	21	4
1985–86		24	1

COLEMAN, Simon

Born Worksop 13.3.68.
Midfield.

| 1985–86 | Mansfield T | — | — |

COLES, David

Born Wandsworth 15.6.64. Ht 6 0 Wt 11 0
Goalkeeper. From Apprentice.

1981–82	Birmingham C	—	—
1982–83		—	—
1982–83	Mansfield T	3	—
1983–84	Aldershot	45	—
1984–85		34	—
1985–86		29	—

COLLINS, Eamonn

Born Dublin 22.10.65. Ht 5 6½ Wt 8 13
Midfield. From Blackpool and Southampton
Apprentice. Eire Youth.

1982–83	Southampton	—	—
1983–84		—	—
1984–85		3	—
1985–86		—	—

COLLINS, Jimmy

Born Urmston 27.12.66. Ht 5 7½ Wt 10 2
Midfield.

1983–84	Oldham Ath	1	—
1984–85		—	—
1985–86		—	—

COLLINS, John

Born Galashiels 31.1.68. Ht 5 7 Wt 9 10
Midfield. From Hutchison Vale B.C.
Scotland Youth.

| 1984–85 | Hibernian | — | — |
| 1985–86 | | 19 | 1 |

COLLINS, Paul

Born West Ham 11.8.66. Ht 6 0 Wt 12 0
Midfield. From Apprentice.

| 1984–85 | Gillingham | 6 | 1 |
| 1985–86 | | 23 | 1 |

COLLINS, Rod

Born Dublin 7.8.62.
Forward. From Dundalk.

| 1985–86 | Mansfield T | 12 | — |

COLLINS, Steve

Born Stamford 21.3.62. Ht 5 8 Wt 12 4
Defender. From Apprentice.

1978–79	Peterborough U	5	—
1979–80		8	—
1980–81		1	—
1981–82		34	1
1982–83		46	—
1983–84	Southend U	36	—
1984–85		15	—
1984–85	*Lincoln C*	13	—
1985–86	Lincoln C	11	—
1985–86	Peterborough U	22	—

COLQUHOUN, John

Born Stirling 14.7.63. Ht 5 7 Wt 10 0
Forward. From Grangemouth Inter.

| 1980–81 | Stirling Albion | 13 | — |
| 1981–82 | | 37 | 13 |

Season	Club	League Appearances/Goals		Season	Club	League Appearances/Goals	
1982–83	....	39	21	1983–84	Wigan Ath	29	2
1983–84	....	15	11	1984–85	....	6	—
1983–84	Celtic.........................	12	2	1984–85	Wrexham....................	28	3
1984–85	....	20	2	1985–86	....	35	3
1985–86	Hearts........................	36	8				

COLVILLE, Robert

Born Nuneaton 27.4.63.   Ht 5 11   Wt 11 12
Forward. From Rhos.

Season	Club	League Appearances/Goals	
1983–84	Oldham Ath	4	1
1984–85	....	7	1
1985–86	....	17	2

COMFORT, Alan

Born Aldershot 8.12.64.   Ht 5 7   Wt 11 2
Midfield. From Apprentice. England Youth.

Season	Club	League Appearances/Goals	
1982–83	QPR............................	—	—
1983–84	....	—	—
1984–85	....	—	—
1984–85	Cambridge U	33	2
1985–86	....	30	3
1985–86	Orient.........................	15	5

COMPTON, Paul

Born Stroud 6.6.61.   Ht 6 1½   Wt 13 1
Defender. From Trowbridge T.

Season	Club	League Appearances/Goals	
1980–81	Bournemouth	31	—
1981–82	....	20	—
1982–83	....	13	—
1983–84	....	—	—
1983–84	Aldershot	13	—
1983–84	Torquay U	16	2
1984–85	....	22	1
1985–86	....	43	1

COMSTIVE, Paul

Born Southport 25.11.61.   Ht 5 11   Wt 11 6
Defender. From Amateur.

Season	Club	League Appearances/Goals	
1979–80	Blackburn R	—	—
1980–81	....	3	—
1981–82	....	2	—
1982–83	....	1	—
1982–83	*Rochdale*	9	2

CONEY, Dean

Born Dagenham 18.9.63.   Ht 6 0   Wt 13 4
Forward. From Apprentice. England Under-21.

Season	Club	League Appearances/Goals	
1980–81	Fulham	7	3
1981–82	....	42	13
1982–83	....	37	4
1983–84	....	27	7
1984–85	....	24	7
1985–86	....	37	12

CONNOR, Robert

Born Kilmarnock 4.8.60.   Ht 5 11   Wt 11 4
Midfield. From Ayr U B.C. Scotland Youth,
Under-21, 1 full cap.

Season	Club	League Appearances/Goals	
1977–78	Ayr U	9	—
1978–79	....	29	—
1979–80	....	38	9
1980–81	....	39	8
1981–82	....	30	—
1982–83	....	39	4
1983–84	....	39	7
1984–85	Dundee	34	7
1985–86	....	35	2

CONNOR, Terry

Born Leeds 9.11.62.   Ht 5 7   Wt 10 0
Forward. From Apprentice. England Youth.

Season	Club	League Appearances/Goals	
1979–80	Leeds U.......................	23	6
1980–81	....	27	4
1981–82	....	27	4
1982–83	....	19	5
1982–83	Brighton....................	7	1
1983–84	....	40	13
1984–85	....	38	14
1985–86	....	33	14

Season	Club	League Appearances/Goals		Season	Club	League Appearances/Goals	

CONROY, Brendan

Born Islington 27.10.67.
Midfield. From Apprentice.

1985–86	Tottenham H	—	—

CONROY, Michael

Born Glasgow 31.12.65.   Ht 6 0   Wt 11 0
Forward. From Apprentice.

1983–84	Coventry C	—	—
1983–84	Clydebank	2	—
1984–85		26	11
1985–86		28	7

CONROY, Mike

Born Johnstone 31.7.57.   Ht 5 9   Wt 11 3
Midfield. From Pt. Glasgow.

1977–78		5	2
1978–79		21	4
1979–80		18	2
1980–81		15	—
1981–82		8	1
1982–83	Hibernian	22	1
1983–84		9	1
1984–85	Blackpool	41	2
1985–86		25	—

CONROY, Steve

Born Chesterfield 19.12.56.   Ht 6 0¼
Wt 12 2½
Goalkeeper. From Apprentice. England
Schools.

1973–74	Sheffield U	—	—
1974–75		—	—
1975–76		—	—
1976–77		—	—
1977–78		3	—
1978–79		41	—
1979–80		20	—
1980–81		21	—
1981–82		1	—
1981–82	*Leeds U*	—	—

1982–83	Sheffield U	18	—
1982–83	Rotherham U	5	—
1983–84	Rochdale	46	—
1984–85		3	—
1984–85	Rotherham U	—	—
1985–86		—	—

CONWAY, Pat

Born Newcastle 19.9.68.
Forward.

1985–86	Cambridge U	1	—

COOK, Mitch

Born Scarborough 15.10.61.   Ht 5 10
Wt 12 0
Midfield. From Scarborough

1984–85	Darlington	31	3
1985–86		3	1
1985–86	Middlesbrough	6	—

COOK, Paul

Born Liverpool 22.2.67.   Ht 5 11   Wt 10 10
Midfield.

1984–85	Wigan Ath	2	—
1985–86		13	2

COOKE, Joe

Born Dominica 15.2.55.   Ht 6 1   Wt 13 0
Defender. From Apprentice.

1971–72	Bradford C	11	—
1972–73		3	—
1973–74		20	—
1974–75		34	8
1975–76		42	22
1976–77		40	17
1977–78		38	8
1978–79		16	7
1978–79	Peterborough U	18	5
1979–80	Oxford U	42	7
1980–81		30	6

Season	Club	League Appearances/Goals		Season	Club	League Appearances/Goals	

Season	Club	League Appearances/Goals	
1981–82	Exeter C	17	3
1981–82	Bradford C	22	1
1982–83		34	5
1983–84		6	—
1984–85	Rochdale	41	3
1985–86		34	1

COOKE, John

Born Salford 25.4.62. Ht 5 8   Wt 11 0
Forward. From Apprentice.

Season	Club	League Appearances/Goals	
1979–80	Sunderland	4	1
1980–81		17	1
1981–82		10	1
1982–83		14	1
1983–84		4	—
1984–85		6	—
1984–85	*Carlisle U*	6	2
1985–86	Sheffield W	—	—
1985–86	Carlisle U	33	4

COOKE, Richard

Born Islington 4.9.65.   Ht 5 6   Wt 9 0
Forward. From Apprentice. England Youth, Under-21.

Season	Club	League Appearances/Goals	
1982–83	Tottenham H	—	—
1983–84		9	1
1984–85		—	—
1985–86		2	1

COOKE, Robbie

Born Rotherham 16.2.57.   Ht 5 9   Wt 10 8
Forward. From Apprentice.

Season	Club	League Appearances/Goals	
1976–77	Mansfield T	9	1
1977–78		6	—
From Grantham T			
1980–81	Peterborough U	46	22
1981–82		46	24
1982–83		23	5
1982–83	*Luton T*	—	—
1982–83	Cambridge U	12	2
1983–84		37	6
1984–85		16	6
1984–85	Brentford	24	12
1985–86		44	17

COOMBES, Lee

Born Dinnington 5.7.66.
Midfield. From Apprentice.

Season	Club	League Appearances/Goals	
1984–85	Sheffield W	—	—
1985–86	Scunthorpe U	—	—

COOPER, Colin

Born Durham 28.2.67.
Midfield.

Season	Club	League Appearances/Goals	
1984–85	Middlesbrough	—	—
1985–86		11	—

COOPER, Davie

Born Hamilton 25.2.56.   Ht 5 8   Wt 12 5
Forward. From Hamilton Avondale.
Scotland Under-21. 14 full caps.

Season	Club	League Appearances/Goals	
1974–75	Clydebank	26	4
1975–76		26	13
1976–77		38	11
1977–78	Rangers	35	6
1978–79		30	5
1979–80		30	2
1980–81		25	3
1981–82		30	3
1982–83		31	5
1983–84		34	6
1984–85		32	5
1985–86		32	4

COOPER, Gary

Born London 20.11.65.   Ht 5 7   Wt 10 10
Midfield. From Apprentice.
England Schools, Youth.

Season	Club	League Appearances/Goals	
1983–84	QPR	—	—
1984–85		1	—
1985–86		—	—
1985–86	*Brentford*	10	—
1985–86	Torquay U	—	—

Season	Club	League Appearances/Goals		Season	Club	League Appearances/Goals	

COOPER, Graham

Born Bolton 18.11.65. Ht 5 10 Wt 10 9
Forward. From Amateur.

Season	Club	App	Goals
1983–84	Huddersfield T	3	1
1984–85		34	5
1985–86		—	—

COOPER, Leigh

Born Reading 7.5.61. Ht 5 8 Wt 10 9
Midfield. From Apprentice.

Season	Club	App	Goals
1979–80	Plymouth Arg	14	—
1980–81		28	3
1981–82		43	5
1982–83		45	4
1983–84		43	2
1984–85		21	—
1985–86		40	1

COOPER, Mark

Born Cambridge 5.4.67. Ht 6 1 Wt 13 0
Midfield. From Apprentice.

Season	Club	App	Goals
1983–84	Cambridge U	2	—
1984–85		18	3
1985–86		19	1

COOPER, Neale

Born India 24.11.63. Ht 6 1 Wt 12 3
Defender. From King St. Scotland Schools,
Youth, Under-21.

Season	Club	App	Goals
1979–80	Aberdeen	—	—
1980–81		5	—
1981–82		27	3
1982–83		31	2
1983–84		26	—
1984–85		20	1
1985–86		23	—

COOPER, Neil

Born Aberdeen 12.8.59. Ht 5 11 Wt 12 7
Defender. From Hilton Academy.
Scotland Schools, Youth.

Season	Club	App	Goals
1974–75	Aberdeen	1	—
1975–76		2	—
1976–77		—	—
1977–78		1	—
1978–79		7	1
1979–80		1	—
1979–80	Barnsley	20	3
1980–81		30	2
1981–82		10	1
1981–82	Grimsby T	16	1
1982–83		24	1
1983–84		7	—
1983–84	St Mirren	25	—
1984–85		10	—
1985–86		30	—

COOPER, Paul

Born Brierley Hill 21.12.53. Ht 5 11
Wt 13 10
Goalkeeper. From Apprentice.

Season	Club	App	Goals
1971–72	Birmingham C	12	—
1972–73		3	—
1973–74		2	—
1973–74	Ipswich T	1	—
1974–75		2	—
1975–76		40	—
1976–77		34	—
1977–78		40	—
1978–79		41	—
1979–80		40	—
1980–81		38	—
1981–82		32	—
1982–83		35	—
1983–84		36	—
1984–85		36	—
1985–86		36	—

COOPER, Richard

Born London 7.5.65. Ht 5 10 Wt 10 8
Midfield. From Amateur.

Season	Club	App	Goals
1982–83	Sheffield U	2	—
1983–84		—	—
1984–85		4	—
1985–86	Lincoln C	20	—

Season	Club	League Appearances/Goals	Season	Club	League Appearances/Goals

COOPER, Robert

Born Sutton Coldfield 3.9.66.   Ht 5 8½
Wt 10 7
Midfield.

1984–85	Leicester C	—	—
1985–86		—	—
1985–86	*Preston NE*	5	—

COOPER, Steve

Born Birmingham 22.6.64.   Ht 5 11½
Wt 10 12
Forward.

1983–84	Birmingham C	—	—
1983–84	*Halifax T*	7	1
1984–85	*Mansfield T*	—	—
1984–85	Newport Co	38	11
1985–86	Plymouth Arg	38	8

CORBETT, Pat

Born Hackney 12.2.63.   Ht 6 0   Wt 11 0
Defender. From Apprentice. England
Youth.

1980–81	Tottenham H	—	—
1981–82		4	1
1982–83		1	—
1983–84	Orient	43	1
1984–85		24	1
1985–86		10	—

CORDEN, Stephen

Born Eston 9.1.67.   Ht 5 8   Wt 11 2
Midfield. From Local.

| 1984–85 | Middlesbrough | — | — |
| 1985–86 | | 1 | — |

CORDER, Peter

Born Loughton 8.12.66.   Ht 6 0   Wt 12 7
Goalkeeper. From Apprentice.

1984–85	Tottenham H	—	—
1985–86		—	—
1985–86	*Peterborough U*	2	—

CORK, Alan

Born Derby 4.3.59.   Ht 6 0   Wt 12 0
Forward. From Amateur.

1977–78	Derby C	—	—
1977–78	*Lincoln C*	5	—
1977–78	Wimbledon	17	4
1978–79		45	22
1979–80		42	12
1980–81		41	23
1981–82		6	—
1982–83		7	5
1983–84		42	29
1984–85		28	11
1985–86		38	11

CORK, David

Born Doncaster 28.10.62.   Ht 5 9   Wt 11 8
Midfield. From Apprentice.

1980–81	Arsenal	—	—
1981–82		—	—
1982–83		—	—
1983–84		7	1
1984–85		—	—
1985–86	Huddersfield T	38	8

CORKAIN, Steve

Born Stockton-on-Tees 25.2.67.   Ht 5 9
Wt 10 8
Midfield. From Local.

| 1984–85 | Hull C | — | — |
| 1985–86 | | — | — |

CORNER, David

Born Sunderland 15.5.66.   Ht 6 2   Wt 12 7
Defender. From Apprentice.
England Youth.

1983–84	Sunderland	—	—
1984–85		3	—
1985–86		9	—
1985–86	*Cardiff C*	6	—

Season	Club	League Appearances/Goals	Season	Club	League Appearances/Goals

CORNFORTH, John

Born Whitley Bay 7.10.67.   Ht 6 1   Wt 11 5
Defender. From Apprentice.

1984–85	Sunderland	1	—
1985–86		—	—

CORNWELL, John

Born Bethnal Green 13.10.64.   Ht 6 0
Wt 12 0
Defender. From Apprentice.

1981–82	Orient	3	—
1982–83		31	3
1983–84		42	7
1984–85		36	10
1985–86		44	8

COTON, Tony

Born Tamworth 19.5.61.   Ht 6 1   Wt 11 8
Goalkeeper. From Mile Oak.

1978–79	Birmingham C	—	—
1979–80		—	—
1979–80	*Hereford U*	—	—
1980–81	Birmingham C	3	—
1981–82		15	—
1982–83		28	—
1983–84		41	—
1984–85		7	—
1984–85	Watford	33	—
1985–86		40	—

COTTEE, Tony

Born West Ham 11.7.65.   Ht 5 8   Wt 11 4
Forward. From Apprentice. England Youth,
Under-21.

1982–83	West Ham U	8	5
1983–84		39	15
1984–85		41	17
1985–86		42	20

COTTINGTON, Brian

Born London 14.2.65.   Ht 5 9   Wt 10 6
Midfield. From Apprentice.

1982–83	Fulham	—	—
1983–84		1	—
1984–85		7	—
1985–86		42	—

COUGHLIN, Russell

Born Swansea 15.2.60.   Ht 5 8   Wt 12 2
Midfield. From Apprentice.

1977–78	Manchester C	—	—
1978–79		—	—
1978–79	Blackburn R	11	—
1979–80		10	—
1980–81		3	—
1980–81	Carlisle U	25	3
1981–82		37	5
1982–83		38	2
1983–84		30	3
1984–85	Plymouth Arg	38	3
1985–86		45	10

COWAN, Steven

Born Paisley 17.2.63.   Ht 5 11   Wt 11 4
Forward. From Claremont H.S. Scotland
Youth.

1978–79	St Mirren	—	—
1979–80	Aberdeen	—	—
1980–81		5	1
1981–82		13	3
1982–83		3	—
1983–84		5	—
1984–85		16	5
1985–86	Hibernian	36	19

COWANS, Gordon

Born Durham 27.10.58.   Ht 5 7   Wt 9 8
Midfield. From Apprentice.
England Youth, Under-21 'B', 9 full caps.

Season	Club	League Appearances/Goals		Season	Club	League Appearances/Goals	

Season	Club	App	Goals
1975–76	Aston Villa	1	—
1976–77		18	3
1977–78		35	7
1978–79		34	4
1979–80		42	6
1980–81		42	5
1981–82		42	6
1982–83		42	10
1983–84		—	—
1984–85		30	1
1985–86	Bari	20	—

COWDRILL, Barry

Born Birmingham 3.1.57.   Ht 5 11   Wt 11 4
Defender. From Sutton Coldfield T.

Season	Club	App	Goals
1979–80	WBA	9	—
1980–81		10	—
1981–82		8	—
1982–83		2	—
1983–84		22	—
1984–85		9	—
1985–86		10	—
1985–86	Rotherham U	2	—

COWIE, George

Born Findochty 6.5.61.   Ht 5 9   Wt 10 7
Defender. From Buckie Rovers. Scotland
Youth.

Season	Club	App	Goals
1981–82	West Ham U	6	—
1982–83		2	—
1983–84	Hearts	35	1
1984–85		15	—
1985–86		8	—

COWLING, Chris

Born Scunthorpe 19.9.62.   Ht 6 1½
Wt 12 11
Forward. From Apprentice.

Season	Club	App	Goals
1979–80	Scunthorpe U	15	—
1980–81		2	—
1981–82		26	4
1982–83		42	9
1983–84		22	4
1984–85		27	9
1985–86		—	—

COWLING, David

Born Doncaster 27.11.58.   Ht 5 9   Wt 11 0
Forward. From Mansfield T. Apprentice.

Season	Club	App	Goals
1977–78	Huddersfield T	—	—
1978–79		26	1
1979–80		40	10
1980–81		43	4
1981–82		38	8
1982–83		41	7
1983–84		41	3
1984–85		32	4
1985–86		39	6

COX, Brian

Born Sheffield 7.5.61.   Ht 6 1   Wt 13 10
Goalkeeper. From Apprentice.

Season	Club	App	Goals
1978–79	Sheffield Wed	4	—
1979–80		15	—
1980–81		3	—
1981–82	Huddersfield T	14	—
1982–83		45	—
1983–84		23	—
1984–85		37	—
1985–86		37	—

COX, Graham

Born London 30.4.59.
Goalkeeper. From Apprentice.

Season	Club	App	Goals
1976–77	Brentford	3	—
1977–78		1	—
1978–79		—	—
1978–79	Cambridge U	—	—
From Hillingdon			
1984–85	Aldershot	12	—
1985–86		1	—
To Slough			

COY, Bob

Born Birmingham 30.11.61.   Ht 5 11
Wt 12 0
Defender. From Apprentice.

Season	Club	League Appearances/Goals	
1979–80	Wolverhampton W	—	—
1980–81		—	—
1981–82		20	—
1982–83		18	—
1983–84		5	—
1983–84	*Chester C*	14	—
1984–85	Chester C	35	1
1985–86		44	1

COYLE, Robert

Born Belfast 27.3.65.
Defender. From Linfield.

Season	Club	League Appearances/Goals	
1985–86	Everton	—	—

COYLE, Ronnie

Born Glasgow 19.8.61. Ht 5 10 Wt 11 0
Midfield. From Celtic B.C. Scotland Schools, Under-21.

Season	Club	League Appearances/Goals	
1981–82	Celtic	—	—
1982–83		—	—
1983–84		—	—
1984–85		—	—
1985–86		1	—

COYLE, Tony

Born Glasgow 17.1.60. Ht 5 10 Wt 11 2
Forward. From Avoco Amats.

Season	Club	League Appearances/Goals	
1977–78	Albion R	1	—
1978–79		30	1
1979–80		15	4
1979–80	Stockport Co	14	—
1980–81		34	1
1981–82		36	7
1982–83		34	5
1983–84		38	5
1984–85		38	6
1985–86		25	4

COYNE, Peter

Born Hartlepool 13.11.58. Ht 5 9 Wt 10 7
Forward. From Apprentice.

Season	Club	League Appearances/Goals	
1975–76	Manchester U	2	1
1976–77		—	—
From Ashton U			
1977–78	Crewe Alex	41	16
1978–79		36	16
1979–80		25	2
1980–81		32	13
From Hyde U			
1984–85	Swindon T	45	15
1985–86		31	10

COYNE, Tommy

Born Glasgow 14.11.62. Ht 6 0 Wt 10 7
Forward. From Hillwood B.C.

Season	Club	League Appearances/Goals	
1981–82	Clydebank	31	9
1982–83		38	18
1983–84		11	10
1983–84	Dundee U	18	3
1984–85		21	3
1985–86		13	2

CRABBE, John

Born Weymouth 20.10.54. Ht 5 8 Wt 10 6
Midfield. From Apprentice.

Season	Club	League Appearances/Goals	
1972–73	Southampton	—	—
1973–74		—	—
1974–75		9	—
1975–76		2	—
1976–77		1	—
1976–77	Gillingham	24	3
1977–78		41	4
1978–79		34	2
1979–80		46	2
1980–81		36	1
1981–82	Carlisle U	26	4
1982–83	Hereford U	16	2
1983–84	Crewe Alex	37	4
1984–85		34	3
1985–86		4	—
1985–86	Torquay U	29	2

CRAINIE, Danny

Born Kilsyth 24.5.62. Ht 5 8 Wt 10 7
Forward. From Celtic BC.

Season	Club	League Appearances/Goals		Season	Club	League Appearances/Goals	
1979–80	Celtic	—	—	1983–84		31	15
1980–81		—	—	1984–85		16	4
1981–82		16	7	1985–86	Exeter C	33	3
1982–83		7					
1983–84		1	—				

CRANE, Andy

Born Ipswich 3.1.67.   Ht 5 9   Wt 11 3
Midfield. From Apprentice. England Youth.

1983–84	Ipswich T	—	—
1984–85		—	—
1985–86		—	—

CRANSON, Ian

Born Easington 2.7.64.   Ht 5 11½   Wt 12 4
Defender. From Apprentice. England
Under-21.

1982–83	Ipswich T	—	—
1983–84		8	—
1984–85		20	1
1985–86		42	1

CRAWFORD, Alan

Born Rotherham 30.11.53.   Ht 5 8   Wt 9 10
Forward. From Apprentice.

1972–73	Rotherham U	—	—
1972–73	*Mansfield T*	2	—
1973–74	Rotherham U	32	3
1974–75		46	7
1975–76		46	7
1976–77		46	23
1977–78		28	7
1978–79		39	2
1979–80	Chesterfield	35	10
1980–81		18	5
1981–82		41	5
1982–83	Bristol C	45	7

Continued from left column:

1983–84	Wolverhampton W	28	3
1984–85		13	—
1984–85	*Blackpool*	6	—
1985–86	Wolverhampton W	23	1
1985–86	Dundee	3	—

CRIBLEY, Alex

Born Liverpool 1.4.57.   Ht 5 11   Wt 12 9
Defender. Local.

1978–79	Liverpool	—	—
1979–80		—	—
1980–81		—	—
1980–81	Wigan Ath	30	—
1981–82		31	—
1982–83		41	1
1983–84		44	1
1984–85		31	1
1985–86		38	2

CROFT, Brian

Born Chester 27.9.67.
Midfield.

1984–85	Chester	—	—
1985–86		1	—

CROMBIE, Dean

Born Lincoln 9.8.57.   Ht 6 0   Wt 11 12
Defender. From Ruston Sports.

1976–77	Lincoln C	13	—
1977–78		20	—
1978–79	Grimsby T	46	1
1979–80		39	—
1980–81		33	—
1981–82		38	—
1982–83		32	1
1983–84		40	—
1984–85		39	—
1985–86		34	1

CRONIN, Dennis

Born Manchester 30.10.67.   Ht 5 6   Wt 9 8
Forward. From Apprentice.

1985–86	Manchester U	—	—

All appearances include those as substitute

Season	Club	League Appearances/Goals

CROOK, Ian

Born Romford 18.1.63.   Ht 5 8   Wt 10 6
Midfield. From Apprentice.

Season	Club	App	Goals
1980–81	Tottenham H	—	—
1981–82		4	—
1982–83		4	—
1983–84		3	—
1984–85		5	1
1985–86		4	—

CROOKS, Garth

Born Stoke 10.3.58.   Ht 5 8   Wt 11 6
Forward. From Apprentice. England
Under-21.

Season	Club	App	Goals
1975–76	Stoke C	2	—
1976–77		23	6
1977–78		42	18
1978–79		40	12
1979–80		40	12
1980–81	Tottenham H	40	16
1981–82		27	13
1982–83		26	8
1983–84		10	1
1983–84	*Manchester U*	7	2
1984–85	Tottenham H	22	10
1985–86	WBA	19	5

CROSBY, Malcolm

Born South Shields 4.7.54.   Ht 5 9   Wt 11 3
Midfield. From Apprentice.

Season	Club	App	Goals
1971–72	Aldershot	1	—
1972–73		1	—
1973–74		7	—
1974–75		26	2
1975–76		39	2
1976–77		42	3
1977–78		45	5
1978–79		34	1
1979–80		41	6
1980–81		44	2
1981–82		14	2
1981–82	York C	23	2
1982–83		38	2

Season	Club	League Appearances/Goals
1983–84		31	—
1984–85		11	—
1984–85	*Wrexham*	6	—
1985–86	York C	—	—

CROSBY, Phil

Born Leeds 9.11.62.   Ht 5 9   Wt 10 8
Defender. From Apprentice. England
Youth.

Season	Club	App	Goals
1979–80	Grimsby T	4	—
1980–81		10	—
1981–82		15	1
1982–83		10	—
1983–84	Rotherham U	39	—
1984–85		33	—
1985–86		12	—

CROSS, David

Born Heywood 8.12.50.   Ht 6 1   Wt 12 2
Forward. From Amateur.

Season	Club	App	Goals
1969–70	Rochdale	16	3
1970–71		33	10
1971–72		10	8
1971–72	Norwich C	32	8
1972–73		37	11
1973–74		15	2
1973–74	Coventry C	26	8
1974–75		25	7
1975–76		38	14
1976–77		2	—
1976–77	WBA	27	12
1977–78		11	6
1977–78	West Ham	21	10
1978–79		40	17
1979–80		39	13
1980–81		41	22
1981–82		38	16
1982–83	Manchester C	31	12
1983–84	Oldham Ath	22	6
1984–85	WBA	16	2
1985–86	Bolton W	20	8
1985–86	Bury	13	—

Season	Club	League Appearances/Goals		Season	Club	League Appearances/Goals	

CROSS, Nicky

Born Birmingham 7.2.61.   Ht 5 9   Wt 11 1
Forward. From Apprentice.

Season	Club	App	Goals
1978–79	WBA	—	—
1979–80		—	—
1980–81		2	1
1981–82		22	2
1982–83		32	4
1983–84		25	3
1984–85		24	5
1985–86	Walsall	44	21

CROSS, Paul

Born Barnsley 31.10.65.   Ht 5 8   Wt 10 0
Midfield. From Apprentice.

Season	Club	App	Goals
1983–84	Barnsley	—	—
1984–85		1	—
1985–86		20	—

CROSS, Steve

Born Wolverhampton 22.12.59.   Ht 5 10
Wt 10 8
Defender. From Apprentice.

Season	Club	App	Goals
1976–77	Shrewsbury T	5	—
1977–78		1	—
1978–79		19	2
1979–80		19	—
1980–81		35	2
1981–82		34	3
1982–83		33	5
1983–84		41	9
1984–85		40	5
1985–86		35	8

CROWE, Mark

Born Southwold 21.1.65.   Ht 5 10   Wt 10 10
Defender. From Apprentice.

Season	Club	App	Goals
1982–83	Norwich C	1	—
1983–84		—	—
1984–85		—	—
1985–86	Torquay U	45	2

CROWN, David

Born Enfield 16.2.58.   Ht 5 10   Wt 11 4
Forward. From Walthamstow Ave.

Season	Club	App	Goals
1980–81	Brentford	38	6
1981–82		8	2
1981–82	Portsmouth	27	2
1982–83		1	—
1982–83	*Exeter C*	7	3
1983–84	Reading	45	7
1984–85		43	8
1985–86	Cambridge U	43	24

CRUDGINGTON, Geoff

Born Wolverhampton 14.2.52.   Ht 6 0
Wt 12 12
Goalkeeper. From Wolverhampton W.
Amateur. England Schools.

Season	Club	App	Goals
1969–70	Aston Villa	—	—
1970–71		3	—
1970–71	*Bradford C*	1	—
1971–72	Aston Villa	1	—
1971–72	Crewe Alex	14	—
1972–73		46	—
1973–74		20	—
1973–74	*Preston NE*	—	—
1974–75	Crewe Alex	46	—
1975–76		46	—
1976–77		32	—
1977–78		46	—
1978–79	Swansea C	46	—
1979–80		6	—
1979–80	Plymouth Arg	37	—
1980–81		46	—
1981–82		46	—
1982–83		44	—
1983–84		46	—
1984–85		33	—
1985–86		46	—

CRUMPTON, Dean

Born Stanford le Hope 9.11.67.
Defender. From Apprentice. England
Schools.

Season	Club	App	Goals
1985–86	West Ham U	—	—

Season	Club	League Appearances/Goals	Season	Club	League Appearances/Goals

CULPIN, Paul

Born Kirby Muxloe 8.2.62.
Forward.

1981–82	Leicester C	—	—
From Nuneaton			
1985–86	Coventry C	7	1

CULVERHOUSE, Ian

Born Bishop's Stortford 22.9.64. Ht 5 10
Wt 11 2
Defender. From Apprentice. England Youth

1982–83	Tottenham H	—	—
1983–84		2	—
1984–85		—	—
1985–86		—	—
1985–86	Norwich C	30	—

CUMMING, Bob

Born Airdrie 7.12.55. Ht 5 8   Wt 10 5
Midfield. From Baillieston Jnrs.

1973–74	Grimsby T	—	—
1974–75		5	—
1975–76		32	2
1976–77		41	—
1977–78		27	3
1978–79		34	9
1979–80		40	14
1980–81		32	11
1981–82		24	2
1982–83		33	7
1983–84		30	1
1984–85		20	5
1985–86		24	2

CUMMINS, Stan

Born Durham 6.12.58. Ht 5 6   Wt 9 1
Midfield. From Apprentice.

1976–77	Middlesbrough	2	—
1977–78		25	6
1978–79		12	1
1979–80		5	2

1979–80	Sunderland	26	12
1980–81		42	9
1981–82		35	4
1982–83		30	4
1983–84	Crystal Palace	18	4
1984–85		10	3
1984–85	Sunderland	17	—
1985–86		—	—

CUNNINGHAM, John

Born Londonderry 30.11.66. Ht 5 8   Wt 10 8
Forward. From N. Ireland Youth.

1984–85	Mansfield T	4	—
1985–86		—	—
1985–86	*Derry C*	Not known	

CUNNINGHAM, Laurie

Born Archway 8.3.56. Ht 5 8   Wt 10 13
Forward. From Apprentice. England Under-21 and 6 full caps.

1974–75	Orient	17	1
1975–76		34	8
1976–77		24	6
1976–77	WBA	13	6
1977–78		33	5
1978–79		40	9
From Real Madrid			
1982–83	Manchester U	5	1
From Marseille			
1985–86	Leicester C	15	—

CUNNINGHAM, Tommy

Born Bethnal Green 7.12.55. Ht 6 1
Wt 13 3
Defender. From Apprentice.

1973–74	Chelsea	—	—
1974–75		—	—
1975–76	QPR	—	—
1976–77		5	—
1977–78		16	2
1978–79		9	—

Season	Club	League Appearances	/Goals
1978–79	Wimbledon	15	3
1979–80	....	39	5
1980–81	....	43	4
1981–82	....	2	—
1981–82	Orient	18	1
1982–83	....	28	3
1983–84	....	36	6
1984–85	....	36	1
1985–86	....	13	2

Season	Club	League Appearances	/Goals
1979–80	Birmingham C	42	3
1980–81	....	29	6
1981–82	....	29	1
1982–83	....	30	1
1982–83	Aston Villa	7	—
1983–84	....	26	1
1984–85	....	3	—
1984–85	Charlton Ath	23	2
1985–86	....	30	4

CUNNINGHAM, Tony

Born Jamaica 12.11.57.   Ht 6 2   Wt 13 4
Forward. From Stourbridge.

Season	Club	League Appearances	/Goals
1979–80	Lincoln C	38	12
1980–81	....	34	6
1981–82	....	46	11
1982–83	....	5	3
1982–83	Barnsley	29	7
1983–84	....	13	4
1983–84	Sheffield W	28	5
1984–85	Manchester C	18	1
1984–85	Newcastle U	13	1
1985–86	....	17	1

CUNNINGTON, Shaun

Born Bourne 4.1.66.   Ht 5 8   Wt 10 4
Defender. From Bourne T.

Season	Club	League Appearances	/Goals
1982–83	Wrexham	4	—
1983–84	....	42	—
1984–85	....	41	6
1985–86	....	42	2

CURBISHLEY, Alan

Born Forest Gate 8.11.57.   Ht 5 10½
Wt 11 4
Midfield. From Apprentice.
England Schools, Youth, Under-21.

Season	Club	League Appearances	/Goals
1974–75	West Ham U	2	—
1975–76	....	14	2
1976–77	....	10	1
1977–78	....	32	1
1978–79	....	27	1

CURLE, Keith

Born Bristol 14.11.63.   Ht 6 0   Wt 11 9
Midfield. From Apprentice.

Season	Club	League Appearances	/Goals
1981–82	Bristol R	20	2
1982–83	....	12	2
1983–84	Bristol R	—	—
1983–84	Torquay U	16	5
1983–84	Bristol C	6	—
1984–85	....	40	—
1985–86	....	44	1

CURRAN, Terry

Born Kinsley 20.3.55.   Ht 5 10   Wt 12 4
Forward. From Kinsley FC.

Season	Club	League Appearances	/Goals
1973–74	Doncaster R.	22	2
1974–75	....	44	7
1975–76	....	2	2
1975–76	Nottingham F	33	6
1976–77	....	15	6
1977–78	....	—	—
1977–78	*Bury*	2	—
1977–78	Derby C	26	2
1978–79	Southampton	26	—
1978–79	Sheffield W	12	1
1979–80	....	41	22
1980–81	....	36	9
1981–82	....	36	3
1982–83	Sheffield U	33	3
1982–83	*Everton*	7	1
1983–84	Sheffield U	—	—
1983–84	Everton	8	—
1984–85	....	9	—
1985–86	Huddersfield T	34	7

Season	Club	League Appearances/Goals		Season	Club	League Appearances/Goals	

CURRIE, David

Born Stockton 27.11.62.   Ht 6 0   Wt 11 13
Forward. Local.

1981–82	Middlesbrough	1	—
1982–83		8	—
1983–84		39	15
1984–85		39	12
1985–86		26	4

CURRY, Sean

Born Liverpool 13.11.66.   Ht 5 8½   Wt 10 11
Forward. From Apprentice.

| 1984–85 | Liverpool | — | — |
| 1985–86 | | — | — |

CURTIS, Alan

Born Rhondda 16.4.54.   Ht 5 11   Wt 12 7½
Forward. From Amateur.
Wales Under-21, Under-23, 34 full caps.

1972–73	Swansea C	13	—
1973–74		38	4
1974–75		37	—
1975–76		41	9
1976–77		46	14
1977–78		39	32
1978–79		34	13
1979–80	Leeds U	22	4
1980–81		6	1
1980–81	Swansea C	20	6
1981–82		40	10
1982–83		21	4
1983–84		9	1
1983–84	Southampton	9	—
1984–85		30	4
1985–86		11	1
1985–86	*Stoke C*	3	—

CURTIS, Paul

Born London 1.7.63.   Ht 5 10   Wt 11 2
Defender. From Apprentice.

1981–82	Charlton Ath	—	—
1982–83		20	1
1983–84		24	3
1984–85		28	1
1985–86	Northampton T	27	1

CURTIS, Wayne

Born Port Talbot 22.2.67.   Ht 5 5   Wt 9 2
Defender. From Swansea C. Apprentice.

| 1984–85 | Cardiff C | — | — |
| 1985–86 | | 27 | 2 |

CUSACK, David

Born Thurcroft 6.6.56.   Ht 6 1   Wt 13 11
Defender. From Apprentice.

1975–76	Sheffield W	37	—
1976–77		27	—
1977–78		31	1
1978–79		—	—
1978–79	Southend U	37	1
1979–80		36	1
1980–81		42	6
1981–82		43	5
1982–83		28	4
1982–83	Millwall	14	1
1983–84		39	—
1984–85		45	8
1985–86	Doncaster R	43	2

CUTLER, Chris

Born Manchester 7.4.64.   Ht 5 11   Wt 11 0
Forward. From Amateur.

1981–82	Bury	2	—
1982–83		5	—
1983–84		12	2
1984–85		4	1
1985–86	Crewe Alex	28	6

Season	Club	League Appearances/Goals		Season	Club	League Appearances/Goals	

DALEY, Steve

Born Barnsley 15.4.53.   Ht 5 10   Wt 12 0
Midfield. From Apprentice. England Youth,
'B'.

Season	Club	App	Goals
1971–72	Wolverhampton W	10	2
1972–73		12	—
1973–74		15	1
1974–75		23	1
1975–76		31	6
1976–77		42	13
1977–78		39	8
1978–79		40	6
1979–80		—	—
1979–80	Manchester C	33	2
1980–81		15	2
From Seattle S			
1983–84	Burnley	23	4
From San Diego S			
1985–86	Walsall	28	1

DALEY, Tony

Born Birmingham 18.10.67.   Ht 5 9   Wt 10 5
Forward. From Apprentice. England Youth.

Season	Club	App	Goals
1984–85	Aston Villa	5	—
1985–86		23	2

DALGLISH, Kenny

Born Glasgow 4.3.51.   Ht 5 8   Wt 11 13
Forward. From Cumbernauld U. Scotland
Under-23, 100 full caps.

Season	Club	App	Goals
1969–70	Celtic	2	—
1970–71		3	—
1971–72		31	17
1972–73		32	23
1973–74		33	18
1974–75		33	16
1975–76		35	24
1976–77		35	14
1977–78	Liverpool	42	20
1978–79		42	21
1979–80		42	16
1980–81		34	8
1981–82		42	13

Season	Club	App	Goals
1982–83		42	18
1983–84		33	7
1984–85		36	6
1985–86		21	3

DALTON, Tim

Born Waterford 14.10.65.   Ht 5 11   Wt 11 8
Goalkeeper. From Apprentice.

Season	Club	App	Goals
1983–84	Coventry C	—	—
1983–84	*Bournemouth*	—	—
1984–85	Notts Co	—	—
1985–86		1	—

DALY, Gerry

Born Dublin 30.4.54.   Ht 5 8   Wt 11 4
Midfield. From Bohemians. Eire Under-21,
43 full caps.

Season	Club	App	Goals
1972–73	Manchester U	—	—
1973–74		16	1
1974–75		37	11
1975–76		41	7
1976–77		17	4
1976–77	Derby C	17	7
1977–78		37	10
1978–79		37	13
1979–80		21	1
1980–81	Coventry C	35	8
1981–82		19	4
1982–83		2	—
1982–83	*Leicester C*	17	1
1983–84	Coventry C	28	7
1984–85	Birmingham C	30	1
1985–86		2	—
1985–86	Shrewsbury T	27	4

DALZIEL, Ian

Born South Shields 24.10.62.   Ht 5 8
Wt 11 10
Midfield. From Apprentice.

Season	Club	App	Goals
1979–80	Derby Co	—	—
1980–81		—	—
1981–82		4	—
1982–83		18	4
1983–84	Hereford U	30	4
1984–85		26	—
1985–86		41	3

Season	Club	League Appearances/Goals	Season	Club	League Appearances/Goals

DANIEL, Peter

Born Hull 12.12.55.   Ht 5 9   Wt 11 4
Midfield. From Amateur. England Under-
21, Under-23.

1973–74	Hull C	—	—
1974–75		19	—
1975–76		27	2
1976–77		41	6
1977–78		26	1
1978–79	Wolverhampton W	40	5
1979–80		37	6
1980–81		28	—
1981–82		20	2
1982–83		13	—
1983–84		19	—
1984–85	Sunderland	25	—
1985–86		9	—
1985–86	Lincoln C	16	2

DANIEL, Ray

Born Luton 10.12.64.   Ht 5 10   Wt 11 0
Midfield. From Apprentice.

1982–83	Luton T	3	—
1983–84		7	2
1983–84	*Gillingham*	5	—
1984–85	Luton T	7	1
1985–86		5	1

DANSKIN, Jason

Born Winsford 28.12.67.   Ht 5 8   Wt 10 8
Midfield.

1984–85	Everton	1	—
1985–86		—	—

DARBY, Julian

Born Bolton 3.10.67.
Defender. England Schools.

1984–85	Bolton W	—	—
1985–86		2	—

DAVENPORT, Peter

Born Birkenhead 24.3.61.   Ht 5 11   Wt 11 3
Forward. From Everton Amateur; Cammell
Laird. England 1 full cap.

1981–82	Nottingham F	5	4
1982–83		18	6
1983–84		33	15
1984–85		35	16
1985–86		27	13
1985–86	Manchester U	11	1

DAVIDSON, Alan

Born Melbourne 1.6.60.
Defender. From South Melbourne and
Hellas FC.

1984–85	Nottingham Forest	3	—
1985–86		—	—

DAVIES, Alan

Born Manchester 5.12.61.   Ht 5 8   Wt 11 4
Midfield. From Apprentice. Wales Under-
21, 6 full caps.

1981–82	Manchester U	1	—
1982–83		3	—
1983–84		3	—
1984–85		—	—
1985–86	Newcastle U	14	1
1985–86	*Charlton Ath*	1	—

DAVIES, Gordon

Born Merthyr 3.8.55.   Ht 5 7   Wt 10 12
Forward. From Merthyr T. Wales 18 full caps.

1977–78	Fulham	5	1
1978–79		32	9
1979–80		39	15
1980–81		45	18
1981–82		41	24
1982–83		38	19
1983–84		36	22
1984–85		11	5
1984–85	Chelsea	12	6
1985–86		1	—
1985–86	Manchester C	26	9

| Season | Club | League Appearances/Goals | | Season | Club | League Appearances/Goals | |

DAVIES, Ian

Born Bristol 29.3.57.   Ht 5 8   Wt 10 8
Defender. From Apprentice.
Wales Under-21.

Season	Club		
1973–74	Norwich C	1	—
1974–75		—	—
1975–76		—	—
1976–77		2	—
1977–78		2	—
1978–79		27	2
1979–80	Newcastle U	37	1
1980–81		25	—
1981–82		13	2
1982–83	Manchester C	2	—
1982–83	*Bury*	14	—
1983–84	Manchester C	5	—
1983–84	*Brentford*	2	—
1983–84	*Cambridge U*	5	—
1983–84	Carlisle U	4	—
1984–85	Exeter C	5	—
1985–86	Bristol R	14	1
1985–86	Swansea C	11	—

DAVIES, John

Born Carmarthen 18.11.59. Ht 6 3 Wt 13 6
Goalkeeper. From Apprentice.

Season	Club		
1977–78	Cardiff C	—	—
1978–79		4	—
1979–80		3	—
1980–81	Hull C	4	—
1981–82		10	—
1982–83		10	—
1983–84		—	—
1984–85		—	—
1985–86		—	—
1985–86	*Notts Co*	10	—

DAVIES, John

Born Glasgow 25.9.66.   Ht 5 7   Wt 10 0
Midfield. From Anniesland United.

Season	Club		
1985–86	Clydebank	3	—

DAVIES, Kevin

Born Hereford 1.4.63.
Midfield. From Apprentice.

Season	Club		
1985–86	Hereford U	1	—

DAVIES, Michael

Born Stretford 19.1.66.   Ht 5 8   Wt 10 0
Midfield. From Apprentice.

Season	Club		
1983–84	Blackpool	3	—
1984–85		17	—
1985–86		36	5

DAVIS, Darren

Born Sutton-in-Ashfield 5.2.67.   Ht 6 0
Wt 11 0
Defender. From Apprentice. England
Youth.

Season	Club		
1983–84	Notts Co	1	—
1984–85		4	—
1985–86		22	1

DAVIS, Paul

Born London 9.12.61.   Ht 5 8   Wt 9 7
Midfield. From Apprentice. England
Under-21.

Season	Club		
1979–80	Arsenal	2	—
1980–81		10	1
1981–82		38	4
1982–83		41	4
1983–84		35	1
1984–85		24	1
1985–86		29	4

DAVIS, Paul

Born Newham 31.1.68.
Defender. From Apprentice.

Season	Club		
1985–86	QPR	—	—

Season	Club	League Appearances/Goals	Season	Club	League Appearances/Goals

DAVIS, Steve

Born Birmingham 26.7.65.   Ht 6 0
Wt 10 10
Defender. From Stoke C. Apprentice.
England Youth.

1983–84	Crewe Alex	24	—
1984–85		40	—
1985–86		45	1

DAVISON, Bob

Born S. Shields 17.7.59.   Ht 5 8   Wt 11 8
Forward. From Seaham C.W.

1980–81	Huddersfield T	2	—
1981–82	Halifax T	46	20
1982–83		17	9
1982–83	Derby Co	26	8
1983–84		40	14
1984–85		46	24
1985–86		41	17

D'AVRAY, Mich

Born Johannesburg 19.2.62.   Ht 6 1
Wt 13 2
Forward. From Apprentice. England Under-21.

1979–80	Ipswich	2	—
1980–81		5	1
1981–82		13	2
1982–83		17	2
1983–84		23	6
1984–85		33	6
1985–86		26	5

DAWES, Ian

Born Aldershot 5.1.65.   Ht 6 0   Wt 11 7
Defender. From school. England Schools.

1983–84	Newcastle U	—	—
1984–85		—	—
1985–86	Northampton T	5	—

DAWES, Ian

Born Croydon 22.2.63.   Ht 5 7   Wt 11 11
Defender. From Apprentice.
England Schools.

1980–81	QPR	—	—
1981–82		5	—
1982–83		42	—
1983–84		42	2
1984–85		42	—
1985–86		42	1

DAWKINS, Derek

Born Edmonton 29.11.59.   Ht 5 10   Wt 11 1
Defender. From Apprentice.

1977–78	Leicester C	3	—
1978–79		—	—
1978–79	Mansfield T	26	—
1979–80		35	—
1980–81		12	—
1981–82	Bournemouth	5	—
1982–83		3	—
1983–84	Torquay U	16	—
1984–85		46	—
1985–86		39	3

DAWS, Tony

Born Sheffield 10.9.66.   Ht 5 8   Wt 10 8
Midfield. From Apprentice. England Youth.

| 1984–85 | Notts Co | 7 | 1 |
| 1985–86 | | 1 | — |

DAWSON, Alistair

Born Glasgow 25.2.58.   Ht 5 10   Wt 11 10
Defender. From school.
Scotland Youth, Under-21, 5 full caps.

1975–76	Rangers	3	—
1976–77		1	—
1977–78		2	—
1978–79		23	1
1979–80		32	—
1980–81		22	2

Season	Club	League Appearances/Goals		Season	Club	League Appearances/Goals	
1981–82	....	25	1	1978–79	Aston Villa...................	—	—
1982–83	....	25	—	1979–80	....	3	—
1983–84	....	28	—	1980–81	....	9	—
1984–85	....	26	1	1981–82	....	4	—
1985–86	....	24	1	1982–83	....	4	1
				1983–84	....	13	—
				1983–84	*Derby Co*	5	—
				1984–85	Aston Villa...................	—	—
				1985–86	....	—	—

DAWSON, Richard

Born Sheffield 12.4.67.   Ht 6 0   Wt 12 0
Goalkeeper. From Stoke C.

1984–85	Grimsby T...................	1	—
1985–86	....	—	—

DAY, Keith

Born Grays 29.11.62.   Ht 6 1   Wt 13 0
Defender. From Aveley.

1984–85	Colchester U	45	4
1985–86	....	30	5

DAY, Mervyn

Born Chelmsford 26.6.55.   Ht 6 2   Wt 14 12
Goalkeeper. From Apprentice.
England Youth, Under-23.

1972–73	West Ham U................	—	—
1973–74	....	33	—
1974–75	....	42	—
1975–76	....	41	—
1976–77	....	42	—
1977–78	....	23	—
1978–79	....	13	—
1979–80	Orient........................	42	—
1980–81	....	40	—
1981–82	....	42	—
1982–83	....	46	—
1983–84	Aston Villa.................	14	—
1984–85	....	16	—
1984–85	Leeds U......................	18	—
1985–86	....	40	—

DEACY, Eamonn

Born Galway 1.10.58.   Ht 5 8½   Wt 10 8
Defender. From Galway Rovers. Eire
4 full caps.

DEAKIN, John

Born Wortley 29.9.66.
Midfield. From Barnsley Apprentice.

1985–86	Doncaster R	14	—

DEAKIN, Ray

Born Liverpool 19.6.59.   Ht 5 8   Wt 11 1
Defender. From Apprentice.

1977–78	Everton.......................	—	—
1978–79	....	—	—
1979–80	....	—	—
1980–81	....	—	—
1981–82	Port Vale	23	6
1982–83	Bolton W	30	1
1983–84	....	41	1
1984–85	....	34	—
1985–86	Burnley.......................	46	3

DEANE, Brian

Born Leeds 7.2.68.   Ht 6 3   Wt 12 7
Forward. From Apprentice.

1985–86	Doncaster R	3	—

DEANS, Ray

Born Glasgow 24.1.66.   Ht 6 2   Wt 13 4
Forward. Chelsea schoolboy. Scottish
Youth.

1983–84	Clyde..........................	31	7
1984–85	....	22	7
1984–85	Doncaster R	14	5
1985–86	....	5	—

All appearances include those as substitute

Season	Club	League Appearances/Goals	Season	Club	League Appearances/Goals

DEARLOVE, Mark

Born Kidderminster 31.5.67.
Midfield.

1985–86	WBA	— —

DEARY, John

Born Ormskirk 18.10.62.   Ht 5 10   Wt 11 11
Midfield. From Apprentice.

1979–80	Blackpool	— —
1980–81		10 —
1981–82		27 —
1982–83		45 6
1983–84		31 6
1984–85		32 13
1985–86		40 7

DEEHAN, John

Born Solihull 6.8.57.   Ht 6 0   Wt 11 3
Forward. From Apprentice. England Youth,
Under-21.

1974–75	Aston Villa	— —
1975–76		15 7
1976–77		27 13
1977–78		36 12
1978–79		26 10
1979–80		6 —
1979–80	WBA	28 3
1980–81		15 2
1981–82		4 —
1981–82	Norwich C	22 10
1982–83		40 20
1983–84		34 15
1984–85		40 13
1985–86		26 4

DELVE, John

Born Isleworth 27.9.53.   Ht 5 8   Wt 10 12
Midfield. From Apprentice.

1971–72	QPR	— —
1972–73		9 —
1973–74		6 —
1974–75	Plymouth Arg	42 5

1975–76		38 1
1976–77		32 —
1977–78		20 —
1977–78	Exeter C	11 1
1978–79		42 6
1979–80		42 1
1980–81		36 4
1981–82		40 3
1982–83		44 5
1983–84	Hereford U	36 3
1984–85		20 —
1985–86		38 6

DE MANGE, Ken

Born Dublin 3.9.64.   Ht 5 9½   Wt 11 10
Midfield. From Home Farm. Eire Youth.

1983–84	Liverpool	— —
1984–85		— —
1985–86		— —

DEMPSEY, Mark

Born Manchester 14.1.64.   Ht 5 7   Wt 9 4
Midfield. From Apprentice.

1981–82	Manchester U	— —
1982–83		— —
1983–84		— —
1984–85		— —
1984–85	*Swindon T*	5 —
1985–86	Manchester U	1 —

DENNIS, Mark

Born Streatham 2.5.61.   Ht 5 9   Wt 10 8
Defender. From Apprentice. England
Youth, Under-21.

1978–79	Birmingham C	31 —
1979–80		40 —
1980–81		19 —
1981–82		17 —
1982–83		23 1
1983–84		— —
1983–84	Southampton	20 —
1984–85		31 —
1985–86		24 —

Season	Club	League Appearances/Goals	Season	Club	League Appearances/Goals

DENNISON, Robert

Born Banbridge 30.4.63.
Forward. From Glenavon.

Season	Club	App	Goals
1985–86	WBA	12	1

DERRICK, Paul

Born Bristol 29.11.63.
Forward. From Local.

Season	Club	App	Goals
1984–85	Bristol C	—	—
1985–86		—	—

DEVINE, John

Born Dublin 11.11.58.   Ht 5 10½   Wt 12 1
Defender. From Apprentice. Eire Under-21,
12 full caps.

Season	Club	App	Goals
1976–77	Arsenal	—	—
1977–78		3	—
1978–79		7	—
1979–80		20	—
1980–81		39	—
1981–82		11	—
1982–83		9	—
1983–84	Norwich C	32	3
1984–85		21	—
1985–86		—	—
1985–86	Stoke C	15	1

DEVINE, Peter

Born Blackburn 25.5.60.   Ht 5 8   Wt 11 6
Forward. From Chorley and Vancouver
Whitecaps.

Season	Club	App	Goals
1981–82	Bristol C	21	1
1982–83	Blackburn R	1	—
1983–84		7	2
1984–85	Burnley	19	2
1985–86		37	2

DEVINE, Steve

Born Strabane 11.12.64.   Ht 5 9   Wt 10 7
Midfield. From Apprentice.

Season	Club	App	Goals
1982–83	Wolverhampton W	—	—
1983–84	Derby Co	10	—
1984–85		1	—
1985–86	Stockport Co	2	—
1985–86	Hereford U	11	1

DEVONSHIRE, Alan

Born London 13.4.56.   Ht 5 10½   Wt 11 0
Midfield. From Southall & Ealing Bor.
England 'B', 8 full caps.

Season	Club	App	Goals
1976–77	West Ham U	28	—
1977–78		34	3
1978–79		41	5
1979–80		34	5
1980–81		39	6
1981–82		35	1
1982–83		39	3
1983–84		22	1
1984–85		—	—
1985–86		38	3

DIAMOND, Barry

Born Dumbarton 20.2.60.   Ht 5 7   Wt 11 5
Forward. From Barrow.

Season	Club	App	Goals
1984–85	Rochdale	43	15
1985–86		9	1
1985–86	*Stockport Co*	6	—
1985–86	Halifax T	12	3

DIBBLE, Andy

Born Cwmbran 8.5.65.   Ht 6 0½   Wt 13 7
Goalkeeper. From Apprentice. Wales
Youth, Under-21, 2 full caps.

Season	Club	App	Goals
1981–82	Cardiff C	1	—
1982–83		20	—
1983–84		41	—
1984–85	Luton T	13	—
1985–86		7	—
1985–86	*Sunderland*	12	—

Season	Club	League Appearances/Goals	Season	Club	League Appearances/Goals

DICK, Alistair

Born Stirling 25.4.65.   Ht 5 9   Wt 10 7
Forward. From Apprentice.
Scotland Schools, Youth.

Season	Club	Apps	Goals
1981–82	Tottenham H	1	—
1982–83		2	—
1983–84		11	2
1984–85		2	—
1985–86		1	—

DICKENS, Alan

Born Plaistow 3.9.64.   Ht 5 11   Wt 12 1
Midfield. From Apprentice. England Youth,
Under-21.

Season	Club	Apps	Goals
1982–83	West Ham U	15	6
1983–84		10	—
1984–85		25	2
1985–86		41	4

DICKENSON, Kevin

Born London 24.11.62.   Ht 5 6   Wt 10 6
Defender. From Tottenham H. Apprentice.

Season	Club	Apps	Goals
1979–80	Charlton Ath	1	—
1980–81		—	—
1981–82		7	—
1982–83		12	—
1983–84		42	1
1984–85		13	—
1985–86	Orient	46	1

DICKINSON, Martin

Born Leeds 14.3.63.   Ht 5 10   Wt 11 0
Defender. From Apprentice.

Season	Club	Apps	Goals
1979–80	Leeds U	6	—
1980–81		1	—
1981–82		—	—
1982–83		31	—
1983–84		34	—
1984–85		12	1
1985–86		19	1
1985–86	WBA	7	—

DICKS, Julian

Born Bristol 8.8.68.
Midfield. From Apprentice.

Season	Club	Apps	Goals
1985–86	Birmingham C	23	—

DICKSON, Joe

Born Glasgow 24.3.65.   Ht 5 10   Wt 10 7
Defender. From Possil Y.M. Scotland
Youth.

Season	Club	Apps	Goals
1981–82	Clydebank	—	—
1982–83		7	—
1983–84		32	—
1984–85		35	—
1985–86		28	1

DIGBY, Fraser

Born Sheffield 23.4.67.   Ht 6 1½   Wt 12 12
Goalkeeper. From Apprentice. England
Youth.

Season	Club	Apps	Goals
1984–85	Manchester U	—	—
1985–86		—	—
1985–86	*Oldham Ath*	—	—
1985–86	*Swindon T*	—	—

DIGWEED, Perry

Born London 26.10.59.   Ht 6 0   Wt 11 4
Goalkeeper. From Apprentice.

Season	Club	Apps	Goals
1976–77	Fulham	1	—
1977–78		—	—
1978–79		2	—
1979–80		11	—
1980–81		1	—
1980–81	Brighton	15	—
1981–82		12	—
1982–83		15	—
1983–84		4	—
1983–84	*WBA*	—	—
1984–85	Brighton	—	—
1984–85	*Charlton Ath*	—	—
1985–86	Brighton	33	—

Season	Club	League Appearances/Goals	Season	Club	League Appearances/Goals

DILLON, Kevin

Born Sunderland 18.12.59.   Ht 5 11
Wt 10 13
Midfield. From Apprentice. England Youth,
Under-21.

Season	Club	App	Goals
1977–78	Birmingham C	17	1
1978–79	....	36	2
1979–80	....	31	6
1980–81	....	39	2
1981–82	....	36	1
1982–83	....	27	3
1982–83	Portsmouth	11	5
1983–84	....	36	9
1984–85	....	37	9
1985–86	....	31	5

DI PALMA, John

Born Wimbledon 15.2.66.
Defender.

Season	Club	App	Goals
1985–86	C. Palace	—	—

DIXON, Kerry

Born Luton 24.7.61.   Ht 6 0   Wt 13 0
Forward. From Tottenham H. Apprentice
and Dunstable. England Under-21. 6 full
caps.

Season	Club	App	Goals
1980–81	Reading	39	13
1981–82	....	42	12
1982–83	....	35	26
1983–84	Chelsea	42	28
1984–85	....	41	24
1985–86	....	38	14

DIXON, Kevin

Born Blackhill 27.7.60.   Ht 5 10   Wt 10 6
Forward. From Annfield Plain & Tow Law T.

Season	Club	App	Goals
1983–84	Carlisle U	9	—
1983–84	*Hartlepool U*	6	3
1984–85	Hartlepool U	42	12
1985–86	....	22	5
1985–86	*Scunthorpe U*	14	2

DIXON, Lee

Born Manchester 17.3.64.   Ht 5 9½
Wt 10 12
Defender. Local.

Season	Club	App	Goals
1982–83	Burnley	3	—
1983–84	....	1	—
1983–84	Chester	16	1
1984–85	....	41	—
1985–86	Bury	45	6

DOBBIN, Jim

Born Dunfermline 17.9.61.   Ht 5 8   Wt 10 7
Midfield. From Whitburn BC.

Season	Club	App	Goals
1980–81	Celtic	—	—
1981–82	....	—	—
1982–83	....	—	—
1983–84	....	2	—
1983–84	*Motherwell*	2	—
1983–84	Doncaster R	11	2
1984–85	....	17	1
1985–86	....	31	6

DOBSON, Martin

Born Blackburn 14.2.48.   Ht 5 9   Wt 11 7
Midfield. From Amateur.
England, 5 full caps, Football League.

Season	Club	App	Goals
1966–67	Bolton W	—	—
1967–68	Burnley	14	3
1968–69	....	23	4
1969–70	....	36	6
1970–71	....	25	4
1971–72	....	42	9
1972–73	....	41	12
1973–74	....	40	4
1974–75	....	3	1
1974–75	Everton	30	5
1975–76	....	42	5
1976–77	....	40	8
1977–78	....	38	7
1978–79	....	40	4
1979–80	Burnley	29	5

Season	Club	League Appearances/Goals		Season	Club	League Appearances/Goals	
1980–81	....	46	7				
1981–82	....	44	3				
1982–83	....	39	1				
1983–84	....	28	4				
1983–84	Bury..........................	10	—				
1984–85	....	38	—				
1985–86	....	13	4				

DOLAN, Pat

Born Chelmsford 20.9.67. Ht 5 11 Wt 11 11
Defender. From Apprentice. Eire Youth.

Season	Club	App	Goals
1985–86	Arsenal	—	—

DOBSON, Paul

Born Hartlepool 17.12.62. Ht 5 9 Wt 10 6
Forward. From Newcastle U. Amateur.

Season	Club	App	Goals
1981–82	Hartlepool U	5	—
1982–83	....	26	8
From Horden			
1983–84	....	27	12
1984–85	....	38	10
1985–86	....	15	2

DONACHIE, Willie

Born Glasgow 5.10.51. Ht 5 9 Wt 11 3
Defender. From juniors.
Scotland Under-23, 35 full caps.

Season	Club	App	Goals
1968–69	Manchester C................	—	—
1969–70	....	3	—
1970–71	....	11	—
1971–72	....	37	—
1972–73	....	40	1
1973–74	....	42	—
1974–75	....	40	1
1975–76	....	40	—
1976–77	....	42	—
1977–78	....	39	—
1978–79	....	38	—
1979–80	....	19	—
From Portland Timbers			
1981–82	Norwich C..................	11	—
From Portland Timbers			
1982–83	Burnley......................	23	—
1983–84	....	37	3
1984–85	Oldham Ath	39	—
1985–86	....	33	—

DODDS, Davie

Born Dundee 23.9.58. Ht 5 11 Wt 11 5
Forward. 'S' Form. Scotland Schools, Youth,
Under-21, 2 full caps.

Season	Club	App	Goals
1975–76	Dundee U	—	—
1976–77	....	—	—
1977–78	....	1	—
1977–78	*Arbroath*	6	1
1977–78	Dundee U	9	1
1978–79	....	27	10
1979–80	....	21	6
1980–81	....	24	14
1981–82	....	35	14
1982–83	....	36	22
1983–84	....	33	15
1984–85	....	26	8
1985–86	....	31	12

DONAGHY, Mal

Born Belfast 13.9.57. Ht 5 10 Wt 12 7
Defender. From Larne.
Northern Ireland Under-21, 42 full caps.

Season	Club	App	Goals
1978–79	Luton T......................	40	—
1979–80	....	42	1
1980–81	....	42	—
1981–82	....	42	9
1982–83	....	40	3
1983–84	....	40	1
1984–85	....	42	1
1985–86	....	42	—

DOLAN, Eamonn

Born Dagenham 20.9.67. Ht 5 10 Wt 12 3
Forward. From Apprentice. Eire Youth.

Season	Club	App	Goals
1984–85	West Ham U	—	—
1985–86	....	—	—

All appearances include those as substitute

Season	Club	League Appearances/Goals

DONALD, Warren

Born Hillingdon 7.10.64. Ht 5 7 Wt 10 3
Midfield. From Apprentice.
England Schools.

Season	Club	App	Goals
1982–83	West Ham U	—	—
1983–84		2	—
1984–85		—	—
1984–85	*Northampton T*	11	2
1985–86	West Ham U	—	—
1985–86	Northampton T	32	3

DONNELLAN, Leo

Born Brent 19.1.65. Ht 5 10 Wt 11 5
Midfield. From Apprentice.

Season	Club	App	Goals
1982–83	Chelsea	—	—
1983–84		—	—
1984–85		—	—
1984–85	*Orient*	6	—
1985–86	Fulham	23	—

DONOVAN, Terry

Born Liverpool 27.2.58. Ht 5 11 Wt 10 12
Forward. From Louth U.
Eire Under-21, 1 full cap.

Season	Club	App	Goals
1976–77	Grimsby T	21	6
1977–78		38	14
1978–79		5	3
1979–80	Aston Villa	9	2
1980–81		—	—
1981–82		8	4
1982–83	*Oxford U*	3	—
1982–83	Burnley	14	6
1983–84		1	—
1983–84	Rotherham U	6	—
1984–85		7	—
1984–85	*Blackpool*	2	—
1985–86	Rotherham U	—	—

DONOWA, Lou

Born Ipswich 24.9.64. Ht 5 9 Wt 11 0
Forward. From Apprentice. England
Under-21.

Season	Club	App	Goals
1982–83	Norwich C	1	—
1983–84		25	4
1984–85		34	7
1985–86		2	—
1985–86	*Stoke C*	4	1

DORIGO, Tony

Born Australia 31.12.65. Ht 5 8 Wt 9 11
Defender. From Apprentice.

Season	Club	App	Goals
1983–84	Aston Villa	1	—
1984–85		31	—
1985–86		38	1

DORNAN, Andy

Born Aberdeen 19.8.61. Ht 5 8 Wt 10 8
Defender. From King St. Scotland Youth.

Season	Club	App	Goals
1978–79	Aberdeen	—	—
1979–80		—	—
1980–81		2	—
1981–82		—	—
1982–83	Motherwell	19	—
1983–84		26	2
1984–85		21	1
1985–86		26	—

DOUGHERTY, Paul

Born Leamington 12.5.66. Ht 5 0 Wt 8 0
Midfield. From Apprentice.

Season	Club	App	Goals
1983–84	Wolverhampton W	5	—
1984–85		21	2
1984–85	*Torquay U*	5	—
1985–86	Wolverhampton W	11	1

DOUGLAS, Colin

Born Hurlford 9.9.62. Ht 6 1 Wt 11 0
Forward. From Celtic.

Season	Club	App	Goals
1981–82	Doncaster R	42	3
1982–83		38	7
1983–84		44	15
1984–85		46	10
1985–86		42	13

Season	Club	League Appearances/Goals	Season	Club	League Appearances/Goals

DOUGLAS, John

Born Stockton 13.3.61.
Defender.

| 1985–86 | Darlington | 3 — |

DOWMAN, Steve

Born Manor Park 15.4.58.   Ht 5 11   Wt 12 4
Defender. From Apprentice.

1975–76	Colchester U	— —
1976–77		36 12
1977–78		43 5
1978–79		38 2
1979–80		37 2
1980–81	Wrexham	4 —
1981–82		40 —
1982–83		43 2
1983–84	Charlton Ath	35 3
1984–85		26 2
1985–86	Newport Co	9 1
1985–86	Cambridge U	28 2

DOWNES, Wally

Born London 9.6.61.   Ht 5 10   Wt 10 11
Midfield. From Apprentice.

1978–79	Wimbledon	3 1
1979–80		26 3
1980–81		34 4
1981–82		42 —
1982–83		38 2
1983–84		33 5
1984–85		7 —
1985–86		9 —

DOWNING, Keith

Born Oldbury 23.7.65.   Ht 5 8   Wt 10 9
Forward. From Mile Oak R.

| 1984–85 | Notts Co | 12 — |
| 1985–86 | | 3 — |

DOWNS, Greg

Born Carlton 13.12.58.   Ht 5 9½   Wt 10 7
Defender. From Apprentice.

1976–77	Norwich C	— —
1977–78		1 —
1977–78	*Torquay U*	1 1
1978–79	Norwich C	3 —
1979–80		18 —
1980–81		29 2
1981–82		28 1
1982–83		28 —
1983–84		42 4
1984–85		20 —
1985–86	Coventry C	41 —

DOYLE, Bobby

Born Dumbarton 27.12.53.   Ht 6 0   Wt 11 2
Midfield. From Dumbarton.

1972–73	Barnsley	17 —
1973–74		43 4
1974–75		43 6
1975–76		46 6
1976–77	Peterborough U	43 5
1977–78		46 2
1978–79		41 3
1979–80	Blackpool	38 2
1980–81		11 —
1980–81	Portsmouth	25 4
1981–82		43 8
1982–83		44 1
1983–84		37 1
1984–85		27 2
1985–86		1 —
1985–86	Hull C	39 2

DOYLE, Jamie

Born Glasgow 1.10.61.   Ht 5 9   Wt 10 3
Midfield. From Auchengill B.C.

1978–79	Partick T	7 —
1979–80		33 1
1980–81		23 —
1981–82		33 2
1982–83		28 2

Season	Club	League Appearances/Goals		Season	Club	League Appearances/Goals	
1983–84	....	26	4				
1984–85	....	4	—				
1984–85	Motherwell	15	—				
1985–86	....	16	1				

DOYLE, Jeff

Born Dublin 25.2.67.
Midfield. From Apprentice.

Season	Club	App	Goals
1984–85	Coventry C..................	—	—
1985–86	....	—	—

DOYLE, Steve

Born Neath 2.6.58.   Ht 5 9½   Wt 11 1
Midfield. From Apprentice.
Wales Under-21.

Season	Club	App	Goals
1974–75	Preston NE	13	—
1975–76	....	24	1
1976–77	....	22	—
1977–78	....	32	1
1978–79	....	29	2
1979–80	....	14	—
1980–81	....	27	1
1981–82	....	36	3
1982–83	Huddersfield T	42	2
1983–84	....	36	2
1984–85	....	36	2
1985–86	....	42	—

DOZZELL, Jason

Born Ipswich 9.12.67.   Ht 6 1   Wt 11 4
Forward. From school. England Youth.

Season	Club	App	Goals
1983–84	Ipswich T	5	1
1984–85	....	14	2
1985–86	....	41	3

DREYER, John

Born Alnwick 11.6.63.
Defender. From Wallingford T

Season	Club	App	Goals
1984–85	Oxford U	—	—
1985–86	....	—	—
1985–86	*Torquay U*	5	—
1985–86	*Fulham*	12	2

DRINKELL, Kevin

Born Grimsby 18.6.60.   Ht 5 10½   Wt 12 6
Forward. From Apprentice.

Season	Club	App	Goals
1976–77	Grimsby T....................	4	2
1977–78	....	26	5
1978–79	....	28	7
1979–80	....	33	16
1980–81	....	41	7
1981–82	....	28	6
1982–83	....	39	17
1983–84	....	36	15
1984–85	....	35	14
1985–86	Norwich C...................	41	22

DROY, Micky

Born Highbury 7.5.51.   Ht 6 4½   Wt 14 5
Defender. From Slough T.

Season	Club	App	Goals
1970–71	Chelsea	4	—
1971–72	....	1	—
1972–73	....	15	—
1973–74	....	30	1
1974–75	....	26	2
1975–76	....	25	1
1976–77	....	8	1
1977–78	....	35	1
1978–79	....	14	—
1979–80	....	28	1
1980–81	....	30	1
1981–82	....	23	2
1982–83	....	31	3
1983–84	....	—	—
1984–85	....	2	—
1984–85	*Luton T*	2	—
1984–85	Crystal Palace	10	2
1985–86	....	27	4

DUBLIN, Keith

Born Wycombe 29.1.66.   Ht 5 11   Wt 11 9
Defender. From Apprentice. England
Youth.

Season	Club	App	Goals
1983–84	Chelsea	1	—
1984–85	....	11	—
1985–86	....	11	—

All appearances include those as substitute

Season	Club	League Appearances/Goals

DUCKWORTH, Alan

Born Cleethorpes 3.12.67. Ht 5 9½ Wt 10 7
Defender. From Apprentice.

1985–86	Grimsby T	—	—

DUFFY, Jim

Born Glasgow 27.4.59. Ht 5 10 Wt 11 0
Defender. From Maryhill Juniors.

1978–79	Celtic	—	—
1979–80		—	—
1980–81		—	—
1981–82	Morton	20	—
1982–83		27	—
1983–84		38	2
1984–85		34	1
1985–86	Dundee	36	—

DUGGAN, Andy

Born Bradford 19.9.67.
Defender.

1984–85	Barnsley	—	—
1985–86		—	—

DUNCAN, Cameron

Born Lanark 4.8.65. Ht 6 1 Wt 11 0
Goalkeeper. From Scotland Youth.

1983–84	Sunderland	—	—
1984–85		—	—
1985–86		1	—

DUNCAN, Colin

Born Wantage 5.8.57. Ht 5 10½ Wt 11 12
Midfield. From Apprentice.

1974–75	Oxford U	23	—
1975–76		5	—
1976–77		46	—
1977–78		45	3
1978–79		43	3
1979–80		27	—
1979–80	Gillingham	19	1
1980–81		32	—
1981–82		25	2

1982–83		8	2
1983–84		1	—
1983–84	Reading	33	2
1984–85		23	1
1985–86	Aldershot	15	—

DUNCAN, Donald

Born Stirling 29.8.67. Ht 5 7½ Wt 11 8
Defender.

1984–85	Burnley	—	—
1985–86		—	—

DUNGWORTH, John

Born Rotherham 30.3.55. Ht 6 0 Wt 12 1
Forward. From Apprentice.

1971–72	Huddersfield T	—	—
1972–73		16	1
1973–74		3	—
1974–75		4	—
1974–75	*Barnsley*	3	1
1974–75	Oldham Ath	—	—
1975–76		4	—
1976–77		—	—
1976–77	*Rochdale*	14	3
1977–78	Aldershot	45	23
1978–79		46	26
1979–80		14	9
1979–80	Shrewsbury T	28	7
1980–81		34	5
1981–82		24	5
1981–82	*Hereford U*	7	3
1982–83	Mansfield T	39	14
1983–84		17	2
1983–84	Rotherham U	22	3
1984–85		46	8
1985–86		46	2

DURHAM, Jonathan

Born Wombwell 12.6.65. Ht 5 10½ Wt 11 8
Forward. From Apprentice.

1983–84	Rotherham U	6	1
1984–85		—	—
1984–85	Torquay U	12	1
1985–86		12	1

Season	Club	League Appearances/Goals		Season	Club	League Appearances/Goals	

DURIE, Gordon

Born Paisley 6.12.65.   Ht 5 10   Wt 10 7
Forward. From Hill of Beath Hawthorn.

Season	Club	App	Goals
1981–82	East Fife	13	1
1982–83		25	2
1983–84		34	16
1984–85		9	7
1984–85	Hibernian	22	8
1985–86		25	6
1985–86	Chelsea	1	—

DURNIN, John

Born Bootle 18.8.65.
Forward. From Waterloo Dock.

Season	Club	App	Goals
1985–86	Liverpool	—	—

DURRANT, Iain

Born Glasgow 29.10.66.   Ht 5 8   Wt 9 7
Midfield. From Glasgow United. Scotland Youth.

Season	Club	App	Goals
1984–85	Rangers	5	—
1985–86		30	2

DUXBURY, Mike

Born Accrington 1.9.59.   Ht 5 10   Wt 10 12
Defender. From Apprentice.
England Under-21, 10 full caps.

Season	Club	App	Goals
1976–77	Manchester U.	—	—
1977–78		—	—
1978–79		—	—
1979–80		—	—
1980–81		33	2
1981–82		24	—
1982–83		42	1
1983–84		39	—
1984–85		30	1
1985–86		23	1

DYER, Alex

Born West Ham 14.11.65.   Ht 5 11
Wt 11 12
Midfield. From Watford Apprentice.

Season	Club	App	Goals
1983–84	Blackpool	9	—
1984–85		36	8
1985–86		39	8

DYSON, Paul

Born Birmingham 27.12.59.   Ht 6 2
Wt 13 6
Defender. From Apprentice.
England Under-21.

Season	Club	App	Goals
1977–78	Coventry C.	—	—
1978–79		2	—
1979–80		18	2
1980–81		41	2
1981–82		40	—
1982–83		39	1
1983–84	Stoke C	38	2
1984–85		37	3
1985–86		31	—
1985–86	WBA	11	—

All appearances include those as substitute

Season	Club	League Appearances/Goals		Season	Club	League Appearances/Goals

EARLE, Robbie

Born Newcastle, Staffs. 27.1.65.   Ht 5 9
Wt 10 10
Forward. From Stoke C.

Season	Club	Apps	Goals
1981–82	Port Vale	—	—
1982–83		8	1
1983–84		12	—
1984–85		46	15
1985–86		46	15

EASTOE, Peter

Born Tamworth 2.8.53.   Ht 5 9½   Wt 11 0
Forward. From Apprentice. England Youth.

Season	Club	Apps	Goals
1971–72	Wolverhampton W.	3	—
1972–73		2	—
1973–74		1	—
1973–74	Swindon T.	19	8
1974–75		46	26
1975–76		26	9
1975–76	QPR	—	—
1976–77		27	6
1977–78		19	6
1978–79		26	3
1978–79	Everton	8	—
1979–80		26	6
1980–81		42	15
1981–82		19	5
1982–83	WBA	31	8
1983–84		—	—
1983–84	*Leicester C*	5	1
1983–84	*Huddersfield T*	10	—
1984–85	WBA	—	—
1984–85	*Walsall*	6	1
1984–85	*Leicester C*	6	1
1984–85	*Wolverhampton W*	8	—
1985–86	WBA	—	—

EBANKS, Wayne

Born Birmingham 2.10.64.   Ht 5 10
Wt 11 5
Defender. From school.

Season	Club	Apps	Goals
1981–82	WBA	—	—
1982–83		—	—
1983–84		7	—

Season	Club	Apps	Goals
1984–85	*Stoke C*	10	—
1984–85	*Port Vale*	11	—
1985–86	Port Vale	12	—

ECKHARDT, Jeff

Born Sheffield 7.10.65.   Ht 5 11   Wt 11 6
Defender.

Season	Club	Apps	Goals
1984–85	Sheffield U	7	—
1985–86		33	2

EDGE, Declan

Born Malacca 18.9.65.   Ht 5 8   Wt 10 6
Forward. From Shrewsbury T Apprentice
and Gisborne C. New Zealand full caps.

Season	Club	Apps	Goals
1985–86	Notts Co	10	2

EDWARDS, Andy

Born Wrexham 28.3.65.   Ht 5 7   Wt 12 0
Midfield. Local. Wales Youth.

Season	Club	Apps	Goals
1982–83	Wrexham	14	—
1983–84		29	7
1984–85		37	11
1985–86		34	9

EDWARDS, Dean

Born Wolverhampton 25.2.62.   Ht 5 10
Wt 10 6
Forward. From Apprentice.

Season	Club	Apps	Goals
1979–80	Shrewsbury T	4	—
1980–81		6	1
1981–82		3	—
From Palloseura and Telford U			
1985–86	Wolverhampton W	23	7

EDWARDS, Keith

Born Stockton 16.7.57.   Ht 5 8   Wt 10 3
Forward.

Season	Club	Apps	Goals
1975–76	Sheffield U	3	—
1976–77		31	18

Season	Club	League Appearances/Goals		Season	Club	League Appearances/Goals	
1977–78	....	36	11	1980–81	....	12	—
1978–79	Hull C	46	24	1981–82	....	22	—
1979–80	....	41	19	1982–83	....	7	—
1980–81	....	40	13	1982–83	Crewe Alex	19	1
1981–82	....	5	1	1983–84	....	39	—
1981–82	Sheffield U	41	35	1984–85	Rochdale	4	—
1982–83	....	42	13	1984–85	Tranmere R.................	35	4
1983–84	....	44	33	1985–86	....	34	2
1984–85	....	29	13				
1985–86	....	35	20				

EDWARDS, Levi

Born St Lucia 10.9.61.   Ht 5 7   Wt 10 7
Midfield. From Manchester U.

1984–85	Oldham Ath	—	—
1985–86	Crewe Alex	13	—

EDWARDS, Neil

Born Liverpool 2.7.67.
Midfield. From Liverpool Apprentice.

1985–86	Burnley	1	—

EDWARDS, Neil

Born Rowley Regis 14.3.66.
Forward. From Oldswinford.

1985–86	Wolverhampton W........	13	7

EDWARDS, Sean

Born Hastings 29.10.67.
Defender. From Apprentice.

1985–86	Brighton & HA	—	—

EDWARDS, Steve

Born Birkenhead 11.1.58.   Ht 5 9   Wt 11 0
Defender. From Apprentice.

1975–76	Oldham Ath	—	—
1976–77	....	—	—
1977–78	....	5	—
1978–79	....	21	—
1979–80	....	13	—

ELEY, Kevin

Born Mexborough 4.3.68.   Ht 5 6   Wt 9 7
Midfield. From school.

1983–84	Rotherham U	1	—
1984–85	....	6	—
1985–86	....	5	—

ELI, Roger

Born Bradford 11.9.65.   Ht 5 11   Wt 11 3
Defender. From Apprentice.

1983–84	Leeds U.......................	—	—
1984–85	....	1	—
1985–86	....	1	—
1985–86	Wolverhampton W........	14	—

ELKINS, Gary

Born Wallingford 4.5.66.   Ht 5 8½   Wt 10 10
Midfield. From Apprentice. England Youth.

1983–84	Fulham	—	—
1984–85	....	21	—
1985–86	....	13	—

ELLIOTT, Paul

Born London 18.3.64.   Ht 6 2   Wt 11 11
Defender. From Apprentice. England
Youth, Under-21.

1980–81	Charlton Ath	—	—
1981–82	....	38	1
1982–83	....	25	—
1982–83	Luton T.......................	13	1
1983–84	....	38	2
1984–85	....	9	1
1985–86	....	6	—
1985–86	Aston Villa..................	23	2

Season	Club	League Appearances/Goals		Season	Club	League Appearances/Goals	

ELLIOTT, Shaun

Born Haltwistle 26.1.57.   Ht 6 0
Wt 11 6¼
Midfield. From Apprentice. England 'B'.

Season	Club	App	Goals
1974–75	Sunderland	—	—
1975–76		—	—
1976–77		19	1
1977–78		29	3
1978–79		41	1
1979–80		41	4
1980–81		38	—
1981–82		36	1
1982–83		20	—
1983–84		33	—
1984–85		32	—
1985–86		32	2

ELLIOTT, Steve

Born Haltwistle 15.9.58.   Ht 5 11½
Wt 11 10
Forward. From Apprentice.

Season	Club	App	Goals
1977–78	Nottingham F	—	—
1978–79		4	—
1978–79	Preston NE	7	—
1979–80		42	16
1980–81		35	9
1981–82		35	10
1982–83		45	19
1983–84		44	16
1984–85	Luton T	12	3
1984–85	Walsall	28	5
1985–86		41	16

ELLIS, Mark

Born Bradford 6.1.62.   Ht 5 9   Wt 10 9
Forward. Local.

Season	Club	App	Goals
1980–81	Bradford C	4	1
1981–82		18	—
1982–83		25	3
1983–84		37	8
1984–85		45	7
1985–86		25	3

ELSEY, Karl

Born Swansea 20.11.58.   Ht 5 10   Wt 12 6
Midfield. From Pembroke Boro.

Season	Club	App	Goals
1978–79	QPR	3	—
1979–80		4	—
1980–81	Newport C	34	2
1981–82		40	7
1982–83		42	5
1983–84		7	1
1983–84	Cardiff C	29	1
1984–85		30	4
1985–86	Gillingham	46	5

EMERSON, Dean

Born Salford 27.12.62.   Ht 5 8   Wt 10 8
Midfield. From Local.

Season	Club	App	Goals
1981–82	Stockport Co	23	1
1982–83		45	3
1983–84		44	1
1984–85		44	2
1985–86	Rotherham U	45	7

EMERY, Steve

Born Ledbury 7.2.56.   Ht 5 10   Wt 11 10
Midfield. From Apprentice.

Season	Club	App	Goals
1973–74	Hereford U	7	—
1974–75		44	—
1975–76		45	2
1976–77		19	—
1977–78		39	2
1978–79		44	5
1979–80		6	1
1979–80	Derby Co	27	2
1980–81		32	1
1981–82		16	1
1982–83	Newport Co	—	—
1983–84	Hereford U	34	1
1984–85		41	1
1985–86	Wrexham	9	—

| Season | Club | League Appearances/Goals | Season | Club | League Appearances/Goals |

EMMANUEL, Gary

Born Swansea 1.2.54.   Ht 5 9   Wt 11 0
Midfield. From Apprentice. Wales
Under-23.

Season	Club	App	Goals
1971–72	Birmingham C	—	—
1972–73		—	—
1973–74		—	—
1974–75		9	1
1975–76		11	1
1976–77		16	3
1977–78		22	1
1978–79		13	—
1978–79	Bristol R	21	—
1979–80		21	1
1980–81		23	1
1981–82	Swindon T	37	2
1982–83		32	2
1983–84		42	4
1984–85	Newport C	12	—
1985–86	Bristol C	2	—
1985–86	Swansea C	40	3

EMSON, Paul

Born Lincoln 22.10.58.   Ht 5 11   Wt 11 3
Forward. From Brigg T.

Season	Club	App	Goals
1978–79	Derby C	6	—
1979–80		26	4
1980–81		38	4
1981–82		41	5
1982–83		16	—
1983–84	Grimsby T	39	6
1984–85		35	4
1985–86		23	5

ENDERSBY, Scott

Born Lewisham 20.2.62.   Ht 5 10   Wt 12 4
Goalkeeper. From Kettering T. and Ipswich
T. Apprentice.

Season	Club	App	Goals
1978–79	Ipswich T	—	—
1979–80		—	—
1980–81		—	—
1981–82	Tranmere R	43	—
1982–83		36	—
1983–84	Swindon T	37	—
1984–85		46	—
1985–86		2	—
1985–86	Carlisle U	27	—

ENGLAND, Mike

Born Bristol 4.1.61.   Ht 6 0   Wt 11 2
Defender. From Apprentice.

Season	Club	App	Goals
1978–79	Bristol R	1	—
1979–80		—	—
1980–81		—	—
From Bath C. and Forest Green R.			
1985–86	Bristol R	17	—

ENGLISH, Tom

Born Cirencester 18.10.61.   Ht 5 9
Wt 11 6
Forward. From Apprentice. England Youth.

Season	Club	App	Goals
1979–80	Coventry C	30	10
1980–81		28	7
1981–82		8	—
1982–83		—	—
1982–83	Leicester C	28	3
1983–84		16	—
1984–85	Rochdale	3	1
1984–85	Plymouth Arg	4	1
1984–85	Colchester U	—	—
1985–86		23	8

ENGLISH, Tony

Born Luton 10.10.66.   Ht 5 11   Wt 11 2
Midfield. From Coventry C. Apprentice.
England Youth.

Season	Club	App	Goals
1984–85	Colchester U	22	3
1985–86		45	13

ENGWELL, Micky

Born Grays 27.9.66.   Ht 5 10½   Wt 11 0
Forward.

Season	Club	App	Goals
1984–85	Southend U	7	2
1985–86		2	1

All appearances include those as substitute

| Season | Club | League Appearances/Goals | | Season | Club | League Appearances/Goals | |

ENTWISTLE, Wayne

Born Bury 6.8.58. Ht 5 11 Wt 11 8
Forward. From Apprentice. England Youth.

Season	Club	App	Goals
1976–77	Bury	20	5
1977–78		11	2
1977–78	Sunderland	7	1
1978–79		36	11
1979–80		2	—
1979–80	Leeds U	11	2
1980–81		—	—
1980–81	Blackpool	20	3
1981–82		12	3
1981–82	Crewe Alex	11	—
1982–83	Wimbledon	9	3
From Grays Ath			
1983–84	Bury	38	11
1984–85		45	21
1985–86	Carlisle U	9	2
1985–86	Bolton W	8	—

EVANS, Allan

Born Dunfermline 12.10.56. Ht 6 1
Wt 12 12½
Defender. From Dunfermline U. Scotland,
4 full caps.

Season	Club	App	Goals
1973–74	Dunfermline Ath	9	—
1974–75		26	—
1975–76		26	1
1976–77		37	13
1977–78	Aston Villa	9	1
1978–79		37	6
1979–80		35	8
1980–81		39	7
1981–82		38	2
1982–83		40	4
1983–84		36	7
1984–85		38	6
1985–86		35	3

EVANS, Chris

Born Rhondda 13.10.62. Ht 5 10 Wt 11 2
Defender. From Apprentice.

Season	Club	App	Goals
1980–81	Arsenal	—	—
1981–82	Stoke C	—	—

Season	Club	App	Goals
1982–83	York C	46	—
1983–84		19	—
1984–85		24	—
1985–86		7	1
1985–86	Darlington	33	—

EVANS, Clive

Born Birkenhead 1.5.57. Ht 5 10 Wt 10 9
Midfield. From Apprentice.

Season	Club	App	Goals
1976–77	Tranmere R	3	—
1977–78		46	2
1978–79		46	11
1979–80		40	5
1980–81		43	9
1981–82	Wigan Ath	32	2
1982–83	Crewe Alex	28	7
1983–84	Stockport Co	31	7
1984–85		44	8
1985–86		35	1

EVANS, David

Born Chester 4.4.67. Ht 6 1 Wt 11 7
Defender. From school.

Season	Club	App	Goals
1983–84	Chester	10	—
1984–85		6	1
1985–86		—	—

EVANS, David

Born W. Bromwich 20.5.58. Ht 5 11
Wt 12 5
Defender. From Apprentice.

Season	Club	App	Goals
1975–76	Aston Villa	—	—
1976–77		—	—
1977–78		—	—
1978–79		2	—
1979–80	Halifax T	45	3
1980–81		39	1
1981–82		46	2
1982–83		42	1
1983–84		46	2
1984–85	Bradford C	45	1
1985–86		35	—

All appearances include those as substitute

Season	Club	League Appearances/Goals	Season	Club	League Appearances/Goals

EVANS, Gareth

Born Coventry 14.1.67.
Forward. From Apprentice.

Season	Club	App	Goals
1984–85	Coventry C	—	—
1985–86		6	—

EVANS, Stewart

Born Maltby 15.11.60.   Ht 6 4   Wt 11 5
Forward. From Rotherham U. Apprentice.

Season	Club	App	Goals
1978–79	Rotherham U	—	—
1979–80		—	—
From Gainsborough T			
1980–81	Sheffield U	—	—
1981–82	Wimbledon	18	4
1982–83		42	14
1983–84		45	12
1984–85		40	14
1985–86		30	6

EVANS, Terry

Born London 12.4.65.   Ht 6 4   Wt 12 7
Defender. From Hillingdon B.

Season	Club	App	Goals
1985–86	Brentford	19	1

EVANS, Tony

Born Liverpool 11.1.54.   Ht 5 8   Wt 11 7
Forward. From Formby.

Season	Club	App	Goals
1973–74	Blackpool	—	—
1974–75		6	—
1975–76	Cardiff C	45	21
1976–77		34	15
1977–78		14	4
1978–79		31	7
1979–80	Birmingham C	13	4
1980–81		17	7
1981–82		29	15
1982–83		7	2
1983–84	Crystal Palace	21	7
1984–85	Wolverhampton W	23	5
1984–85	*Bolton W*	4	—
1985–86	Swindon T	10	—

EVES, Mel

Born Wednesbury 10.9.56.   Ht 5 11
Wt 11 8
Forward. From Amateur. England 'B'

Season	Club	App	Goals
1975–76	Wolverhampton W	—	—
1976–77		—	—
1977–78		12	3
1978–79		19	2
1979–80		31	6
1980–81		36	5
1981–82		27	7
1982–83		40	18
1983–84		15	3
1983–84	*Huddersfield T*	7	4
1984–85	Sheffield U	17	9
1985–86		9	1

Season	Club	League Appearances/Goals	Season	Club	League Appearances/Goals

FACKERELL, Mark

Born London 1.9.67.
Goalkeeper. From YTS.

Season	Club	App	Goals
1984–85	Orient	—	—
1985–86		—	—

FADIDA, Aharon

Born Israel 20.9.61.
Forward. From Hapoel Haifa. Israel Youth.

Season	Club	App	Goals
1985–86	Aldershot	9	4

FAIRCLOUGH, Chris

Born Nottingham 12.4.64. Ht 5 11 Wt 11 2
Defender. From Apprentice. England Under-21.

Season	Club	App	Goals
1981–82	Nottingham F	—	—
1982–83		15	—
1983–84		31	—
1984–85		35	—
1985–86		—	—

FAIRBROTHER, Ian

Born Bootle 2.10.66. Ht 5 10 Wt 12 0
Midfield. From Apprentice.

Season	Club	App	Goals
1984–85	Liverpool	—	—
1985–86		—	—

FAIRCLOUGH, David

Born Liverpool 5.1.57. Ht 5 9 Wt 11 0
Forward. From Apprentice. England Under-21

Season	Club	App	Goals
1973–74	Liverpool	—	—
1974–75		—	—
1975–76		14	7
1976–77		20	3
1977–78		29	10
1978–79		4	2
1979–80		14	5
1980–81		9	4
1981–82		—	—
1982–83		8	3
From Lucerne			
1984–85	Norwich C	2	—
1985–86	Oldham Ath	17	1

FAIRCLOUGH, Wayne

Born Nottingham 27.4.68.
Defender. From Apprentice.

Season	Club	App	Goals
1985–86	Notts Co	5	—

FAIRWEATHER, Carlton

Born London 22.9.61. Ht 5 11 Wt 11 0
Forward. From Tooting & Mitcham.

Season	Club	App	Goals
1984–85	Wimbledon	13	2
1985–86		20	7

FALCO, Mark

Born Hackney 22.10.60. Ht 6 0 Wt 12 0
Forward. From Apprentice. England Youth.

Season	Club	App	Goals
1978–79	Tottenham H	1	1
1979–80		9	2
1980–81		3	1
1981–82		21	5
1982–83		16	5
1982–83	*Chelsea*	3	—
1983–84	Tottenham H	36	13
1984–85		42	22
1985–86		40	18

FALCONER, Willie

Born Aberdeen 5.4.66. Ht 6 1 Wt 11 9
Midfield. From Lewis United. Scotland
Schools, Youth.

Season	Club	App	Goals
1982–83	Aberdeen	1	—
1983–84		8	1
1984–85		16	4
1985–86		8	—

FALLON, Jim

Born Cambuslang 24.3.50. Ht 5 10 Wt 11 7
Defender. From school.

Season	Club	App	Goals
1967–68	Clydebank	—	—
1968–69		33	2
1969–70		31	—
1970–71		36	3
1971–72		36	6
1972–73		34	—

Season	Club	League Appearances/Goals		Season	Club	League Appearances/Goals	
1973–74	....	35	5				
1974–75		38	—				
1975–76		25	—				
1976–77		39	—				
1977–78		35	—				
1978–79		38	1				
1979–80		39	1				
1980–81		34	1				
1981–82		38	3				
1982–83		39	—				
1983–84		39	—				
1984–85		31	—				
1985–86		20	—				

FALLON, Steve

Born Whittlesey 3.8.56. Ht 6 1 Wt 12 7
Defender. From Kettering T.

1974–75	Cambridge U	8	—
1975–76		36	1
1976–77		43	4
1977–78		46	8
1978–79		42	—
1979–80		40	2
1980–81		40	3
1981–82		42	5
1982–83		41	1
1983–84		33	1
1984–85		23	1
1985–86		15	1

FARNABY, Craig

Born Hartlepool 8.8.67.
Forward.

1984–85	Hartlepool U	5	—
1985–86		—	—
1985–86	Middlesbrough	—	—

FARNWORTH, Simon

Born Chorley 28.10.63. Ht 5 11 Wt 10 11
Goalkeeper. From Apprentice.

1981–82	Bolton W	—	—
1982–83		—	—
1983–84		36	—
1984–85		46	—
1985–86		31	—

FARRELL, Andy

Born Colchester 7.10.65. Ht 5 11 Wt 11 7
Defender. From school.

1983–84	Colchester U	15	—
1984–85		38	—
1985–86		24	1

FARRELL, Peter

Born Liverpool 10.1.57. Ht 5 7 Wt 10 9
Midfield. Local.

1975–76	Bury	2	—
1976–77		32	4
1977–78		9	4
1978–79		11	1
1978–79	Port Vale	28	4
1979–80		32	5
1980–81		25	1
1981–82		4	—
1981–82	*Doncaster R*	—	—
1981–82	*Shrewsbury T*	—	—
1982–83	Rochdale	43	9
1983–84		25	8
1984–85		5	—
1984–85	Crewe Alex	8	1
1985–86		20	1

FARRINGTON, Mark

Born Liverpool 15.6.65. Ht 5 10 Wt 11 12
Forward. From Everton Apprentice.

1983–84	Norwich C	2	—
1984–85		12	2
1984–85	*Cambridge U*	10	1
1985–86	Cardiff C	31	3

FASHANU, John

Born Kensington 18.9.62. Ht 6 1 Wt 11 1
Forward. From Cambridge U. Amateur.

1979–80	Norwich C	—	—
1980–81		—	—
1981–82		5	1
1982–83		2	—
1983–84		—	—
1983–84	*Crystal Palace*	1	—

Season	Club	League Appearances/Goals		Season	Club	League Appearances/Goals	
1983–84	Lincoln C	26	7	1978–79	Hereford U	26	—
1984–85		10	4	1979–80		25	3
1984–85	Millwall	25	4	1979–80	*Chelsea*	—	—
1985–86		25	8	1980–81	Hereford U	—	—
1985–86	Wimbledon	9	4		From Trowbridge T		
				1983–84	Leicester C	3	—
				1984–85		35	—
				1985–86		26	—

FASHANU, Justin

Born Kensington 18.9.62.   Ht 6 1   Wt 13 1½
Forward. From Apprentice.
England Youth, Under-21, 'B'.

FELGATE, David

Born Blaenau Ffestiniog 4.3.60.   Ht 6 2
Wt 13 10
Goalkeeper. From Blaenau Ffestiniog.
Wales Schools, Under-21, 1 full cap.

Season	Club	App	Goals
1978–79	Norwich C	16	5
1979–80		34	11
1980–81		40	19
1981–82	Nottingham F	32	3
1982–83	*Southampton*	9	3
1982–83	Nottingham F	—	—
1982–83	Notts Co	15	7
1983–84		17	5
1984–85		32	8
1985–86	Brighton	16	2

Season	Club	App	Goals
1978–79	Bolton W	—	—
1978–79	*Rochdale*	35	—
1979–80	Bolton W	—	—
1979–80	*Bradford C*	—	—
1979–80	*Crewe Alex*	14	—
1979–80	*Rochdale*	12	—
1980–81	Bolton W	—	—
1980–81	Lincoln C	42	—
1981–82		43	—
1982–83		46	—
1983–84		46	—
1984–85		21	—
1984–85	*Cardiff C*	4	—
1984–85	*Grimsby T*	12	—
1985–86	Grimsby T	12	—
1985–86	Bolton W	15	—

FAZACKERLEY, Derek

Born Preston 5.11.51.   Ht 5 11   Wt 11 2
Defender. From Apprentice.

Season	Club	App	Goals
1970–71	Blackburn R	14	—
1971–72		39	—
1972–73		46	2
1973–74		46	2
1974–75		23	4
1975–76		42	1
1976–77		38	—
1977–78		28	—
1978–79		37	3
1979–80		46	1
1980–81		38	—
1981–82		39	1
1982–83		38	—
1983–84		39	4
1984–85		39	4
1985–86		37	1

FENWICK, Terry

Born Camden, Co. Durham 17.11.59.
Ht 5 11   Wt 11 1
Midfield. From Apprentice.
England Youth, Under-21, 15 full caps.

Season	Club	App	Goals
1976–77	Crystal Palace	—	—
1977–78		10	—
1978–79		24	—
1979–80		15	—
1980–81		21	—
1980–81	QPR	19	2
1981–82		36	5
1982–83		39	3

FEELEY, Andy

Born Hereford 30.9.61.   Ht 5 9   Wt 12 7
Midfield. From Apprentice.

Season	Club	League Appearances/Goals	Season	Club	League Appearances/Goals

Season	Club	Appearances	Goals
1983–84		41	0
1984–85		41	2
1985–86		37	7

FEREDAY, Wayne

Born Warley 16.6.63.   Ht 5 9   Wt 11 0
Midfield. From Apprentice. England
Under-21.

Season	Club	Appearances	Goals
1980–81	QPR	6	2
1981–82		4	—
1982–83		5	—
1983–84		17	4
1984–85		26	7
1985–86		34	2

FERGUSON, Brian

Born Irvine 14.12.60.   Ht 5 10   Wt 10 6
Midfield. From Mansfield T. Apprentice.

Season	Club	Appearances	Goals
1978–79	Newcastle U	—	—
1979–80		5	1
1980–81		—	—
1980–81	Hull C	13	—
1981–82		15	2
From Goole T			
1983–84	Southend U	29	5
1984–85		5	1
1984–85	Chesterfield	31	—
1985–86		—	—

FERGUSON, Derek

Born Glasgow 31.7.67.   Ht 5 8   Wt 10 11
Midfield. From Gartcosh United. Scotland
Schools, Youth.

Season	Club	Appearances	Goals
1983–84	Rangers	1	—
1984–85		8	—
1985–86		19	—

FERGUSON, Don

Born Toronto 2.1.63.
Goalkeeper. Canada 'B'.

Season	Club	Appearances	Goals
1985–86	Wrexham	20	—

FERGUSON, Eric

Born Kincardine, Fife 12.2.65.   Ht 6 0
Wt 10 12
Forward. From Gairdoch United. Scotland
Youth.

Season	Club	Appearances	Goals
1982–83	Rangers	—	—
1983–84		5	—
1984–85		9	1
1985–86		1	—
1985–86	Southampton	—	—

FERGUSON, Iain

Born Newarthill 4.8.62.   Ht 5 7   Wt 10 7
Forward. From Fir Park B.C. Scotland
Youth, Under-21.

Season	Club	Appearances	Goals
1979–80	Dundee	13	5
1980–81		11	1
1981–82		34	12
1982–83		29	9
1983–84		33	12
1984–85	Rangers	28	6
1985–86		4	—

FERGUSON, Mike

Born Newcastle 3.10.54.   Ht 6 1¼   Wt 12 8
Forward. From Apprentice.

Season	Club	Appearances	Goals
1971–72	Coventry C	—	—
1972–73		—	—
1973–74		—	—
1974–75		12	2
1975–76		15	3
1976–77		32	13
1977–78		30	17
1978–79		18	6
1979–80		17	10
1980–81		3	—
1981–82	Everton	8	4
1982–83	Birmingham C	20	8
1983–84	Birmingham C	—	—
1983–84	Coventry C	7	3
1984–85	Birmingham C	2	1
1984–85	Brighton	8	1
1985–86		9	5
1985–86	Colchester U	10	7

All appearances include those as substitute

Season	Club	League Appearances/Goals	Season	Club	League Appearances/Goals

FERNS, Phil

Born Liverpool 12.9.61. Ht 5 11 Wt 11 4
Defender. From Apprentice.

Season	Club	App	Goals
1978–79	Bournemouth	15	—
1979–80		42	1
1980–81		38	5
1981–82	Charlton Ath	28	—
1982–83		10	1
1982–83	*Wimbledon*	7	—
1983–84	Blackpool	38	—
1984–85		9	—
1985–86	Aldershot	24	2

FERRIS, Paul

Born Belfast 10.7.65. Ht 5 8 Wt 10 8
Forward. From Lisburn Juniors.

Season	Club	App	Goals
1981–82	Newcastle U	2	—
1982–83		5	—
1983–84		—	—
1984–85		4	—
1985–86		—	—

FERRY, Willie

Born Sunderland 21.11.66. Ht 6 2 Wt 12 2
Forward. From school.

Season	Club	App	Goals
1984–85	Scunthorpe U	1	—
1985–86		2	—

FIELDER, Colin

Born Winchester 5.1.64. Ht 5 8 Wt 10 7
Defender. From Apprentice.

Season	Club	App	Goals
1981–82	Aldershot	1	—
1982–83		7	—
1983–84		2	—
1984–85		17	—
1985–86		30	8

FILLERY, Mike

Born Mitcham 17.9.60. Ht 5 10 Wt 11 7
Midfield. From Apprentice.
England Schools, Youth.

Season	Club	App	Goals
1978–79	Chelsea	7	—
1979–80		41	11
1980–81		36	6
1981–82		40	6
1982–83		37	9
1983–84	QPR	30	1
1984–85		32	6
1985–86		17	—

FINDLAY, Jake

Born Blairgowrie 13.7.54. Ht 6 1 Wt 14 1
Goalkeeper. From Apprentice.

Season	Club	App	Goals
1972–73	Aston Villa	—	—
1973–74		1	—
1974–75		1	—
1975–76		5	—
1976–77		7	—
1977–78		—	—
1978–79		—	—
1978–79	Luton T	23	—
1979–80		41	—
1980–81		40	—
1981–82		34	—
1982–83		26	—
1983–84		—	—
1983–84	*Barnsley*	6	—
1983–84	*Derby Co*	1	—
1984–85	Luton T	3	—
1985–86	Swindon T	4	—
1985–86	Portsmouth	—	—
1985–86	Peterborough U	—	—

FINNEY, Shaun

Born Dinnington 5.10.66. Ht 5 5 Wt 10 2
Midfield. From Nottingham Forest
Apprentice.

Season	Club	App	Goals
1984–85	Scunthorpe U	2	—
1985–86		—	—

FINNEY, Tom

Born Belfast 6.11.52. Ht 5 10 Wt 11 8
Forward. From Crusaders.
Northern Ireland, 14 full caps.

All appearances include those as substitute

Season	Club	League Appearances/Goals	
1973–74	Luton T	14	5
1974–75	Sunderland	7	—
1975–76		8	1
1976–77	Cambridge U	41	16
1977–78		44	13
1978–79		42	8
1979–80		28	13
1980–81		33	3
1981–82		27	2
1982–83		31	1
1983–84		22	—
1983–84	Brentford	15	2
1984–85		5	—
1984–85	Cambridge U	26	3
1985–86		38	2

FINNIGAN, Tony

Born Wimbledon 17.10.62. Ht 6 0 Wt 12 0
Forward. Crystal Palace Apprentice.

Season	Club	League Appearances/Goals	
1980–81	Fulham	—	—
1981–82		—	—
1982–83		—	—
1983–84		—	—
1984–85	Crystal Palace	11	1
1985–86		36	3

FIORE, Garry

Born London 30.10.67. Ht 6 0 Wt 12 7
Midfield. From Apprentice.

Season	Club	League Appearances/Goals	
1985–86	Wimbledon	—	—

FIRM, Neil

Born Bradford 23.1.58. Ht 6 3 Wt 13 9
Defender. From Apprentice.

Season	Club	League Appearances/Goals	
1975–76	Leeds U	—	—
1976–77		—	—
1977–78		—	—
1978–79		—	—
1979–80		3	—
1980–81		6	—
1981–82		3	—
1981–82	*Oldham Ath*	9	—

Season	Club	League Appearances/Goals	
1982–83	Peterborough U	39	3
1983–84		25	—
1984–85		8	—
1985–86		—	—

FISHENDEN, Paul

Born Hillingdon 2.8.63. Ht 6 0 Wt 10 12
Forward. Local.

Season	Club	League Appearances/Goals	
1981–82	Wimbledon	5	1
1982–83		9	4
1983–84		23	8
1984–85		20	10
1985–86		18	2
1985–86	*Fulham*	3	—

FISHER, Bobby

Born Wembley 3.8.56. Ht 5 8 Wt 11 2
Defender. From Apprentice.

Season	Club	League Appearances/Goals	
1973–74	Orient	8	—
1974–75		42	—
1975–76		37	—
1976–77		32	—
1977–78		42	1
1978–79		37	—
1979–80		42	3
1980–81		41	—
1981–82		31	—
1982–83		2	—
1982–83	Cambridge U	25	—
1983–84		17	—
1983–84	Brentford	17	—
1984–85		28	—
1985–86		—	—

FITZPATRICK, Paul

Born Liverpool 5.10.65. Ht 6 4 Wt 11 10
Defender.

Season	Club	League Appearances/Goals	
1984–85	Tranmere R	—	—
1984–85	Liverpool	—	—
1984–85	Preston NE	—	—
1984–85	Bolton W	3	—
1985–86		11	—

Season	Club	League Appearances/Goals		Season	Club	League Appearances/Goals	

FITZPATRICK, Tony

Born Glasgow 3.3.56.   Ht 5 9   Wt 10 5
Midfield. From Possil Y.M.
Scotland Under-21.

1973–74	St Mirren	9	—
1974–75		20	2
1975–76		24	—
1976–77		37	2
1977–78		34	2
1978–79		36	3
1979–80	Bristol C	41	—
1980–81		34	1
1981–82	St Mirren	24	1
1982–83		26	3
1983–84		28	—
1984–85		30	1
1985–86		29	3

FLANAGAN, John

Born Liverpool 11.9.67.
Forward. From Apprentice.

1984–85	Liverpool	—	—
1985–86		—	—
1985–86	Tranmere R	—	—

FLANAGAN, Mike

Born Ilford 9.11.52.   Ht 5 9   Wt 12 5
Forward. From Tottenham H. Amateur.
England Youth, 'B'.

1971–72	Charlton Ath	18	—
1972–73		42	12
1973–74		42	11
1974–75		15	4
1975–76		38	6
1976–77		42	23
1977–78		32	16
1978–79		25	13
1979–80	Crystal Palace	36	5
1980–81		20	3
1980–81	QPR	14	3
1981–82		37	10
1982–83		22	7
1983–84		5	—

1983–84	Charlton Ath	18	2
1984–85		38	11
1985–86		37	11

FLECK, Robert

Born Glasgow 11.8.65.   Ht 5 7   Wt 10 8
Forward. From Possil Y.M. Scotland Youth.

1983–84	Partick T	2	1
1983–84	Rangers	1	—
1984–85		8	—
1985–86		15	3

FLEMING, Gary

Born Londonderry 17.2.67.   Ht 5 9½   Wt 11 1
Midfield. From Apprentice.

| 1984–85 | Nottingham F | 2 | — |
| 1985–86 | | 16 | — |

FLEMING, Paul

Born Halifax 6.9.67.
Defender.

| 1985–86 | Halifax T | 13 | — |

FLOUNDERS, Andy

Born Hull 13.12.63.   Ht 5 11   Wt 11 6
Forward. From Apprentice.

1980–81	Hull C	5	—
1981–82		13	5
1982–83		23	13
1983–84		30	9
1984–85		39	14
1985–86		25	10

FLOWERS, Tim

Born Kenilworth 3.2.67.   Ht 6 2   Wt 13 4
Goalkeeper. From Apprentice. England
Youth.

1984–85	Wolverhampton W	38	—
1985–86		25	—
1985–86	*Southampton*	—	—

Season	Club	League Appearances/Goals		Season	Club	League Appearances/Goals	

FLYNN, Brian

Born Port Talbot 12.10.55. Ht 5 4   Wt 12 0
Midfield. From Apprentice.
Wales Schools, Under-23, 66 full caps.

Season	Club	Apps	Goals
1972–73	Burnley	—	—
1973–74		2	—
1974–75		26	—
1975–76		39	4
1976–77		41	2
1977–78		12	2
1977–78	Leeds U	29	1
1978–79		41	3
1979–80		24	3
1980–81		41	3
1981–82		17	1
1981–82	*Burnley*	2	—
1982–83	Leeds U	2	—
1982–83	Burnley	28	1
1983–84		43	9
1984–85		9	1
1984–85	Cardiff C	22	—
1985–86		10	—
1985–86	Doncaster R	27	—

FOGG, Dave

Born Liverpool 28.5.51.   Ht 5 10½ Wt 11 5
Defender. Local.

Season	Club	Apps	Goals
1970–71	Wrexham	1	—
1971–72		14	—
1972–73		36	—
1973–74		46	—
1974–75		35	—
1975–76		29	—
1976–77	Oxford U	39	1
1977–78		46	2
1978–79		44	2
1979–80		36	2
1980–81		44	1
1981–82		46	3
1982–83		33	5
1983–84		3	—
1984–85		2	—
1985–86		—	—

FOLEY, Steve

Born Liverpool 4.10.62.   Ht 5 7   Wt 10 12
Forward. From Apprentice.

Season	Club	Apps	Goals
1980–81	Liverpool	—	—
1981–82		—	—
1982–83		—	—
1983–84		—	—
1983–84	*Fulham*	3	—
1984–85	Grimsby T	31	2
1985–86	Sheffield U	28	5

FOLEY, Will

Born Bellshill 25.6.60.   Ht 5 10   Wt 11 7
Forward. From Frickley Ath.

Season	Club	Apps	Goals
1985–86	Swansea C	5	2
1985–86	Cardiff C	7	1

FOLKES, Paul

Born Gt. Yarmouth 9.8.67.   Ht 5 8   Wt 10 6
Defender. From Apprentice.

Season	Club	Apps	Goals
1984–85	Norwich C	—	—
1985–86		—	—

FORBES, Graeme

Born Forfar 29.7.58.   Ht 5 11   Wt 11 0
Midfield. From Lochee United.

Season	Club	Apps	Goals
1980–81	Motherwell	28	4
1981–82		31	6
1982–83		26	1
1983–84		32	1
1984–85		36	4
1985–86		27	—

FORD, Francis

Born Bridgend 3.2.67.   Ht 5 10   Wt 10 12
Defender.

Season	Club	Apps	Goals
1984–85	Cardiff C	2	—
1985–86		—	—

Season	Club	League Appearances/Goals	Season	Club	League Appearances/Goals

FORD, Gary

Born York 8.2.61.   Ht 5 8   Wt 11 10
Midfield. From Apprentice.

1978–79	York C	33	4
1979–80		29	2
1980–81		43	4
1981–82		41	8
1982–83		45	11
1983–84		46	11
1984–85		44	5
1985–86		40	3

FORD, Mike

Born Bristol 9.2.66.   Ht 5 11½   Wt 11 0
Defender. From Apprentice.

1983–84	Leicester C	—	—
From Devizes			
1984–85	Cardiff C	20	1
1985–86		44	4

FORD, Tony

Born Grimsby 14.5.59.   Ht 5 9   Wt 12 8
Forward. From Apprentice.

1975–76	Grimsby T	14	—
1976–77		6	—
1977–78		34	2
1978–79		45	15
1979–80		37	5
1980–81		28	4
1981–82		35	7
1982–83		37	4
1983–84		42	8
1984–85		42	6
1985–86		34	3
1985–86	Sunderland	9	1

FORMAN, Matt

Born Evesham 8.9.67.
Midfield. From Apprentice.

| 1985–86 | Aston Villa | — | — |

FORREST, Craig

Born Vancouver 20.9.67.   Ht 6 4
Goalkeeper. From Apprentice.

| 1985–86 | Ipswich T | — | — |

FORREST, Gerry

Born Stockton 21.1.57.   Ht 5 10   Wt 10 11
Defender. From South Bank.

1976–77	Rotherham U	—	—
1977–78		44	—
1978–79		46	—
1979–80		43	4
1980–81		44	2
1981–82		35	1
1982–83		39	—
1983–84		45	—
1984–85		44	—
1985–86		17	—
1985–86	Southampton	22	—

FORSTER, Mark

Born Middlesbrough 1.11.64.   Ht 6 0
Wt 11 11
Forward. From Middlesbrough Amateur.

1983–84	Leicester C	—	—
1983–84	*Darlington*	12	4
1984–85	Darlington	25	9
1985–86		1	—

FORSTER, Stephen

Born Tynemouth 18.11.67.
Midfield. From Apprentice.

| 1985–86 | Newcastle U | — | — |

FORSYTH, Mike

Born Liverpool 20.3.66.   Ht 5 11   Wt 11 0
Defender. From Apprentice. England
Youth.

Season	Club	League Appearances/Goals		Season	Club	League Appearances/Goals	
1983–84	WBA	8	—	1978–79		28	—
1984–85		10	—	1979–80		46	—
1985–86		11	—	1980–81		46	—
1985–86	*Northampton T*	—	—	1981–82		10	—
1985–86	Derby Co	—	—	1981–82	*Exeter C*	28	—
				1982–83	Derby Co	30	—
				1983–84	Mansfield T	42	—
				1984–85		44	—
				1985–86		46	—

FORSYTH, Stewart

Born Insch 26.10.61.   Ht 6 0   Wt 11 0
Defender. From Middlefield B.C.

Season	Club	Apps	Goals
1977–78	Arbroath	—	—
1978–79		—	—
1979–80		12	—
1980–81		28	1
1981–82		27	1
1982–83		33	—
1983–84		35	4
1984–85	Dundee	13	—
1985–86		9	1

FOSTER, Nigel

Born Sutton-in-Ashfield 23.3.68.
Defender.

Season	Club	Apps	Goals
1984–85	Mansfield T	1	—
1985–86		—	—

FOSTER, Colin

Born Chislehurst 16.7.64.   Ht 6 4   Wt 13 10
Defender. From Apprentice.

Season	Club	Apps	Goals
1981–82	Orient	23	2
1982–83		43	2
1983–84		11	1
1984–85		42	1
1985–86		36	2

FOSTER, Steve

Born Portsmouth 24.9.57.   Ht 6 0   Wt 12 8
Defender. From Apprentice. England
Under-21, 3 full caps.

Season	Club	Apps	Goals
1975–76	Portsmouth	11	—
1976–77		31	1
1977–78		31	3
1978–79		36	2
1979–80	Brighton	38	1
1980–81		42	1
1981–82		40	2
1982–83		36	1
1983–84		16	1
1983–84	Aston Villa	7	1
1984–85		8	2
1984–85	Luton T	25	1
1985–86		35	3

FOSTER, Deane

Born Reading 22.8.66.   Ht 5 7   Wt 11 9
Defender. From Rotherham U. Schoolboy.

Season	Club	Apps	Goals
1984–85	Reading	—	—
1985–86		—	—

FOSTER, George

Born Plymouth 26.9.56.   Ht 5 10   Wt 11 2
Defender. From Apprentice.

Season	Club	Apps	Goals
1973–74	Plymouth Arg	5	—
1974–75		—	—
1975–76		16	1
1976–77		15	2
1976–77	*Torquay U*	6	3
1977–78	Plymouth Arg	46	3

FOSTER, Wayne

Born Leigh 11.9.63.   Ht 5 8½   Wt 11 0
Forward. From Apprentice. England Youth.

Season	Club	Apps	Goals
1981–82	Bolton W	23	2
1982–83		24	4
1983–84		30	3
1984–85		28	4
1985–86	Preston NE	31	3

Season	Club	League Appearances/Goals	Season	Club	League Appearances/Goals

FOWLER, Derek

Born Torquay 28.11.61.   Ht 5 10   Wt 11 7
Defender. From Local.

1983–84	Torquay U	8	1
1984–85		30	1
1985–86		35	2

FOWLER, Sean

Born Newcastle 17.12.67.   Ht 6 0   Wt 11 10
Defender. From Apprentice.

1985–86	Doncaster R	—	—

FOWLER, Tony

Born Birmingham 3.10.62.   Ht 6 0   Wt 12 3
Goalkeeper. From Foxhole U.

1984–85	Torquay U	1	—
1985–86		8	—

FOX, Peter

Born Scunthorpe 5.7.57.   Ht 5 10½
Wt 12 10
Goalkeeper. From Apprentice.

1972–73	Sheffield W	1	—
1973–74		—	—
1974–75		20	—
1975–76		27	—
1976–77		1	—
1976–77	West Ham	—	—
1977–78	Sheffield W		
1977–78	Barnsley	1	—
1977–78	Stoke C	—	—
1978–79		1	—
1979–80		23	—
1980–81		42	—
1981–82		38	—
1982–83		35	—
1983–84		42	—
1984–85		14	—
1985–86		37	—

FOX, Ruel

Born Ipswich 14.1.68.   Ht 5 6   Wt 10 0
Midfield. From Apprentice.

1985–86	Norwich C	—	—

FOX, Steve

Born Tamworth 17.2.58.   Ht 5 7½   Wt 11 8
Forward. From Apprentice.

1976–77	Birmingham C	4	1
1977–78		11	—
1978–79		14	—
1978–79	Wrexham	22	1
1979–80		38	2
1980–81		38	6
1981–82		38	1
1982–83		6	—
1982–83	Port Vale	34	3
1983–84		40	3
1984–85	Chester C	32	4
1985–86		1	—

FOYLE, Martin

Born Salisbury 2.5.63.   Ht 5 9¾   Wt 11 2
Forward. From Amateur.

1980–81	Southampton	—	—
1981–82		—	—
1982–83		7	1
1983–84		5	—
1983–84	Blackburn R	—	—
1984–85	Aldershot	44	15
1985–86		20	9

FRAIN, David

Born Sheffield 11.10.62.
Forward. From Rowlinson Y.C.

1985–86	Sheffield U	7	1

FRAIN, John

Born Birmingham 8.10.68.
Forward. From Apprentice.

1985–86	Birmingham C	3	—

Season	Club	League Appearances/Goals		Season	Club	League Appearances/Goals	

FRANCIS, Gerry

Born Chiswick 6.12.51.   Ht 5 10   Wt 12 2
Midfield. From Apprentice. England Under-23, 12 full caps.

Season	Club	App	Goals
1969–70	QPR	10	2
1970–71	....	37	5
1971–72	....	38	3
1972–73	....	42	9
1973–74	....	40	8
1974–75	....	35	7
1975–76	....	36	12
1976–77	....	11	3
1977–78	....	13	2
1978–79	....	31	2
1979–80	Crystal Palace	34	3
1980–81	....	25	4
1980–81	QPR	10	4
1981–82	....	7	—
1981–82	Coventry C	18	1
1982–83	....	32	1
1983–84	Exeter C	28	3
1984–85	Cardiff C	7	—
1984–85	Swansea C	3	—
1984–85	Portsmouth	3	—
1985–86	Wimbledon	—	—
1985–86	Bristol R	27	—

FRANCIS, Nick

Born Sussex 1.7.66.   Ht 6 0   Wt 12 6
Forward. From school.

Season	Club	App	Goals
1985–86	Charlton Ath	—	—

FRANCIS, Steve

Born Billericay 29.5.64.   Ht 5 11   Wt 11 5
Goalkeeper. From Apprentice. England Youth.

Season	Club	App	Goals
1981–82	Chelsea	29	—
1982–83	....	37	—
1983–84	....	—	—
1984–85	....	2	—
1985–86	....	3	—

FRANCIS, Trevor

Born Plymouth 19.4.54.   Ht 5 10   Wt 11 7
Forward. From Apprentice. England Youth, Under-23, 52 full caps.

Season	Club	App	Goals
1960–71	Birmingham C	22	15
1971–72	....	39	12
1972–73	....	31	6
1973–74	....	37	6
1974–75	....	23	13
1975–76	....	35	17
1976–77	....	42	21
1977–78	....	42	25
From Detroit E			
1978–79	Birmingham C	9	3
1978–79	Nottingham F	20	6
From Detroit E			
1979–80	Nottingham F	30	14
1980–81	....	18	6
1981–82	....	2	2
1981–82	Manchester C	26	12
1982–83	Sampdoria	14	7
1983–84	....	15	3
1984–85	....	24	6
1985–86	....	15	1

FRANKLIN, Paul

Born Hainault 5.10.63.   Ht 6 2   Wt 12 2
Defender. From Apprentice.

Season	Club	App	Goals
1981–82	Watford	—	—
1982–83	....	1	—
1983–84	....	24	—
1984–85	....	—	—
1985–86	....	4	—

FRASER, Cammy

Born Dundee 22.7.57.   Ht 5 10   Wt 11 7
Midfield. From Invergowrie B.C.

Season	Club	App	Goals
1973–74	Hearts	—	—
1974–75	....	3	—
1975–76	....	15	—
1976–77	....	22	—
1977–78	....	39	2
1978–79	....	36	3
1979–80	....	36	12
1980–81	....	1	1

All appearances include those as substitute

Season	Club	League Appearances/Goals		Season	Club	League Appearances/Goals	

1980–81	Dundee	30	5
1981–82		31	6
1982–83		34	5
1983–84		29	3
1984–85	Rangers	28	3
1985–86		8	2

FRENCH, Nigel

Born Swansea 24.3.68.
Midfield. From Apprentice.

| 1985–86 | Swansea C | 14 | 1 |

FRIAR, Paul

Born Glasgow 6.6.63.   Ht 5 8½   Wt 10 2
Defender. From Apprentice. Scotland Youth.

1980–81	Leicester C	15	—
1981–82		23	—
1982–83		20	—
1982–83	Rotherham U	15	—
1983–84		5	—
1983–84	*Motherwell*	2	—
1984–85	Charlton Ath	32	—
1985–86		4	—
1985–86	*Northampton T*	14	—

FRIDGE, Les

Born Inverness 27.8.68.   Ht 5 11   Wt 11 12
Goalkeeper. From Apprentice. Scotland Youth.

| 1985–86 | Chelsea | 1 | — |

FRY, David

Born Bournemouth 5.1.60.   Ht 6 1   Wt 12 7
Goalkeeper. From Apprentice.

1976–77	Crystal Palace	—	—
1977–78		1	—
1978–79		—	—
1979–80		6	—
1980–81		6	—
1981–82		2	—
1982–83		25	—
1983–84	Gillingham	38	—
1984–85		11	—
1985–86	Torquay U	30	—

FUCCILLO, Lil

Born Bedford 2.5.56.   Ht 5 11   Wt 11 4
Midfield. From Apprentice.

1974–75	Luton T	1	—
1975–76		14	3
1976–77		42	6
1977–78		42	5
1978–79		18	7
1979–80		—	—
1980–81		5	1
1981–82		29	2
1982–83		9	—
From Tulsa R			
1983–84	Southend U	23	2
1984–85		22	3
1985–86	Peterborough U	45	3

FULTON, Mark

Born Johnstone 16.9.59.   Ht 6 0   Wt 11 12
Defender. From Johnstone Burgh.
Scotland Schools, Youth, Under-21.

1977–78	St Mirren	—	—
1978–79		—	—
1979–80		28	—
1980–81		25	—
1981–82		29	—
1982–83		30	3
1983–84		30	1
1984–85		18	1
1985–86	Hibernian	30	—

FUTCHER, Paul

Born Chester 25.9.56.   Ht 6 2   Wt 12 2
Defender. From Apprentice. England Under-21.

1972–73	Chester	2	—
1973–74		18	—
1974–75	Luton T	19	—
1975–76		41	—
1976–77		40	1
1977–78		31	—
1978–79	Manchester C	24	—
1979–80		13	—

Season	Club	League Appearances/Goals	
1980–81	Oldham Ath	36	1
1981–82		37	—
1982–83		25	—
1982–83	Derby Co	17	—
1983–84		18	—
1983–84	Barnsley	10	—
1984–85		36	—
1985–86		37	—

FUTCHER, Ron

Born Chester 25.9.56. Ht 6 0 Wt 12 3
Forward. From Apprentice.

Season	Club	League Appearances/Goals	
1973–74	Chester	4	—
1974–75	Luton	17	7
1975–76		31	10
1976–77		33	13
1977–78		39	10
1978–79	Manchester C	17	7

From Minnesota K, Portland T, Tulsa R and NAC Breda

1984–85	Barnsley	19	6
1985–86	Oldham Ath	40	17

GABBIADINI, Marco

Born Nottingham 20.1.68. Ht 5 10 Wt 11 2
Forward. From Apprentice.

Season	Club	League Appearances/Goals	
1984–85	York C	1	—
1985–86		22	4

GAGE, Kevin

Born Chiswick 21.4.64. Ht 5 9 Wt 11 2
Midfield. From Apprentice. England Youth.

Season	Club	League Appearances/Goals	
1980–81	Wimbledon	1	—
1981–82		21	1
1982–83		26	4
1983–84		24	4
1984–85		37	2
1985–86		29	1

GAGE, Wakeley

Born Northampton 5.5.58. Ht 6 4 Wt 13 7
Defender. From Desborough T.

Season	Club	League Appearances/Goals	
1979–80	Northampton T	21	1
1980–81		31	1
1981–82		43	2
1982–83		40	3
1983–84		40	6
1984–85		43	4
1985–86	Chester C	17	1
1985–86	Peterborough U	27	—

GAHAGAN, John

Born Glasgow 24.8.58. Ht 5 9 Wt 10 7
Forward. From Shettleston Juniors.

Season	Club	League Appearances/Goals	
1977–78	Clydebank	5	—
1978–79		—	—
1979–80	Motherwell	17	3
1980–81		34	1
1981–82		39	7
1982–83		28	4
1983–84		30	7
1984–85		31	5
1985–86		21	3

All appearances include those as substitute

Season	Club	League Appearances/Goals		Season	Club	League Appearances/Goals	

GALE, Darren

Born Port Talbot 25.10.63.   Ht 5 10½
Wt 12 13
Forward. From Apprentice.
Wales Under-21.

Season	Club	App	Goals
1980–81	Swansea C	—	—
1981–82		1	—
1982–83		15	3
1983–84		20	3
1984–85		1	—
1985–86	Exeter C	18	5

GALE, Tony

Born London 19.11.59.   Ht 6 1½   Wt 13 10
Defender. From Apprentice. England
Under-21.

Season	Club	App	Goals
1977–78	Fulham	38	8
1978–79		36	2
1979–80		42	4
1980–81		40	1
1981–82		44	1
1982–83		42	2
1983–84		35	1
1984–85	West Ham U	37	—
1985–86		42	—

GALLACHER, Bernard

Born Johnstone 22.3.67.   Ht 5 8   Wt 11 2½
Defender. From Apprentice.

Season	Club	App	Goals
1984–85	Aston Villa	—	—
1985–86		—	—

GALLACHER, Kevin

Born Clydebank 23.11.66.   Ht 5 6   Wt 8 8
Forward. From Duntocher B.C. Scotland
Youth.

Season	Club	App	Goals
1983–84	Dundee U	—	—
1984–85		—	—
1985–86		20	3

GALLACHER, Jim

Born Clydebank 29.3.51.   Ht 6 0   Wt 12 0
Goalkeeper. From Yoker Athletic.

Season	Club	App	Goals
1969–70	Arbroath	7	—
1970–71		3	—
1971–72		23	—
1972–73	Clydebank	18	—
1973–74		35	—
1974–75		35	—
1975–76		—	—
1976–77		36	—
1977–78		30	—
1978–79		35	—
1979–80		39	—
1980–81		36	—
1981–82		39	—
1982–83		35	—
1983–84		39	—
1984–85		37	—
1985–86		35	—

GALLAGHER, Barry

Born Bradford 7.4.61.   Ht 5 10   Wt 12 3
Midfield. From Apprentice.

Season	Club	App	Goals
1977–78	Bradford C	2	—
1978–79		—	1
1979–80		1	1
1980–81		12	2
1981–82		42	16
1982–83		14	3
1982–83	*Mansfield T*	3	—
1982–83	Halifax T	10	—
1983–84		35	14
1984–85		45	8
1985–86		25	5

GALLAGHER, Brian

Born Glasgow 8.9.58.   Ht 5 9   Wt 11 1
Forward. From Radnor Park Juveniles.

Season	Club	App	Goals
1977–78	Dumbarton	34	10
1978–79		32	8

Season	Club	League Appearances/Goals		Season	Club	League Appearances/Goals	
1979–80	....	39	11				
1980–81		33	14				
1981–82	Kilmarnock	35	10				
1982–83		34	9				
1983–84		35	11				
1984–85	St Mirren	32	9				
1985–86		31	6				

GALLAGHER, Jackie

Born Wisbech 6.4.58. Ht 5 10½ Wt 12 9
Forward. From March T.

Season	Club	League Appearances/Goals	
1975–76	Lincoln C.....................	—	—·
1976–77	....	1	—
1977–78		—	—
From King's Lynn			
1979–80	Peterborough U............	1	—
1980–81		12	1
From Wisbech T			
1982–83	Torquay U	42	7
From Wisbech T			
1985–86	Peterborough U............	42	11

GALLAGHER, Joe

Born Liverpool 11.1.55. Ht 6 1 Wt 12 11
Defender. From Apprentice. England 'B'.

Season	Club	League Appearances/Goals	
1971–72	Birmingham C..............	—	—
1972–73		—	—
1973–74		26	2
1974–75		38	1
1975–76		41	3
1976–77		37	4
1977–78		21	3
1978–79		41	3
1979–80		41	1
1980–81		41	—
1981–82	Wolverhampton W........	28	—
1982–83		3	—
1982–83	West Ham U	9	—
1983–84	Burnley	1	—
1983–84	*Halifax T*	4	—
1984–85	Burnley	5	—
1985–86		—	—

GALLIERS, Steve

Born Fulwood 21.8.57. Ht 5 6 Wt 9 7
Midfield. From Chorley.

Season	Club	League Appearances/Goals	
1977–78	Wimbledon	27	1
1978–79		44	3
1979–80		36	2
1980–81		37	4
1981–82		11	—
1981–82	Crystal Palace	13	—
1982–83	Wimbledon	34	2
1983–84		36	1
1984–85		29	1
1985–86		32	1

GALLOWAY, Mick

Born Oswestry 30.5.65. Ht 5 11 Wt 11 7
Defender. From Amateur. Scotland Youth.

Season	Club	League Appearances/Goals	
1983–84	Mansfield T	17	—
1984–85		31	3
1985–86		6	—
1985–86	Halifax T	19	—

GALLOWAY, Steve

Born Hannover 13.2.63. Ht 6 0 Wt 12 0
Forward. From Sutton U.

Season	Club	League Appearances/Goals	
1984–85	C. Palace	4	1
1985–86		1	—
1985–86	*Cambridge U*	1	—

GALVIN, Tony

Born Huddersfield 12.7.56. Ht 5 9
Wt 11 5
Forward. From Goole T. Eire, 12 full caps.

Season	Club	League Appearances/Goals	
1977–78	Tottenham H	—	—
1978–79		1	—
1979–80		10	4
1980–81		17	1
1981–82		32	3
1982–83		26	2
1983–84		30	1
1984–85		38	4
1985–86		23	4

Season	Club	League Appearances/Goals	Season	Club	League Appearances/Goals

GAMBLE, Francis

Born Liverpool 21.8.61.   Ht 5 9   Wt 11 0
Midfield. From Burscough.

1981–82	Derby Co	2	—
1982–83	....	4	2
From Barrow			
1984–85	Rochdale	21	5
1985–86	....	25	4

GAMBLE, Simon

Born Cottam 5.3.68.
Forward. From Apprentice.

1985–86	Lincoln C	16	5

GAME, Kirk

Born Rochford 22.10.66.   Ht 6 2   Wt 12 0
Defender.

1984–85	Southend U	—	—
1985–86	Colchester U	4	—

GANNON, John

Born Wimbledon 18.12.66.
Forward. From Apprentice.

1984–85	Wimbledon	—	—
1985–86	....	1	1

GARDINER, John

Born Glasgow 2.4.58.   Ht 6 1   Wt 11 8
Goalkeeper. From Campsie Black Watch.

1976–77	Aberdeen	—	—
1977–78	....	—	—
1978–79	....	2	—
1979–80	....	—	—
1980–81	Dundee U	—	—
1980–81	*Airdrieonians*	10	—
1981–82	*Forfar Ath*	5	—
1982–83	Dundee U	—	—
1983–84	....	2	—
1984–85	Motherwell	24	—
1985–86	....	32	—

GARDINER, Mark

Born Cirencester 25.12.66.   Ht 5 10
Wt 10 7
Forward. From Apprentice.

1983–84	Swindon T	1	—
1984–85	....	4	—
1985–86	....	1	—

GARDNER, Paul

Born Southport 22.9.57.   Ht 5 9   Wt 12 6
Defender. From Apprentice.

1975–76	Blackpool	—	—
1976–77	....	22	—
1977–78	....	31	—
1978–79	....	23	—
1979–80	....	40	—
1980–81	....	24	1
1981–82	....	12	—
1982–83	Bury	46	—
1983–84	....	44	—
1984–85	....	—	—
1984–85	Swansea C	4	—
1984–85	Preston NE	—	—
1984–85	Wigan Ath	5	—
1985–86	Exeter C	—	—

GARNER, Andy

Born Chesterfield 8.3.66.   Ht 6 0   Wt 12 1
Forward. From Apprentice.

1983–84	Derby Co	13	5
1984–85	....	16	3
1985–86	....	16	5

GARNER, Paul

Born Doncaster 1.12.55.   Ht 5 8¾   Wt 10 8
Defender. From Apprentice.
England Youth.

1972–73	Huddersfield T	2	—
1973–74	....	43	—

Season	Club	League Appearances/Goals		Season	Club	League Appearances/Goals	
1974–75	....	35	2				
1975–76	....	16	—				
1975–76	Sheffield U	25	1				
1976–77	....	40	—				
1977–78	....	3	—				
1978–79	....	19	1				
1979–80	....	36	1				
1980–81	....	35	3				
1981–82	....	34	—				
1982–83	....	35	—				
1983–84	....	24	1				
1983–84	*Gillingham*	5	—				
1984–85	Sheffield U	—	—				
1984–85	Mansfield T	39	2				
1985–86	....	28	4				

GASCOIGNE, Paul

Born Gateshead 27.5.67.   Ht 5 10   Wt 11 7
Midfield. From Apprentice.

Season	Club	League Appearances/Goals	
1984–85	Newcastle U	2	—
1985–86	....	31	9

GARNER, Simon

Born Boston 23.11.59.   Ht 5 10   Wt 11 4
Forward. From Apprentice.

Season	Club	League Appearances/Goals	
1978–79	Blackburn R	25	8
1979–80	....	28	6
1980–81	....	33	7
1981–82	....	36	14
1982–83	....	41	22
1983–84	....	42	19
1984–85	....	37	12
1985–86	....	38	12

GATES, Eric

Born Ferryhill 28.6.55.   Ht 5 6   Wt 10 8
Forward. From Apprentice.
England, 2 full caps.

Season	Club	League Appearances/Goals	
1972–73	Ipswich T	—	—
1973–74	....	6	—
1974–75	....	6	—
1975–76	....	13	1
1976–77	....	12	1
1977–78	....	24	2
1978–79	....	22	7
1979–80	....	36	13
1980–81	....	37	11
1981–82	....	38	9
1982–83	....	24	3
1983–84	....	37	13
1984–85	....	41	13
1985–86	Sunderland	39	9

GARNER, Tim

Born Herts 30.3.61.
Goalkeeper. From Kidderminster H.

Season	Club	League Appearances/Goals	
1985–86	Northampton T	2	—

GARTON, Billy

Born Salford 15.3.65.   Ht 5 11   Wt 11 8
Defender. From Apprentice.

Season	Club	League Appearances/Goals	
1982–83	Manchester U	—	—
1983–84	....	—	—
1984–85	....	2	—
1985–86	....	10	—
1985–86	*Birmingham C*	5	—

GATTING, Steve

Born Park Royal 29.5.59.   Ht 5 11
Wt 11 11
Defender. From Apprentice.

Season	Club	League Appearances/Goals	
1976–77	Arsenal	—	—
1977–78	....	—	—
1978–79	....	21	1
1979–80	....	14	1
1980–81	....	23	3
1981–82	....	—	—
1981–82	Brighton......................	39	3
1982–83	....	40	4
1983–84	....	35	4
1984–85	....	8	—
1985–86	....	17	—

Season	Club	League Appearances/Goals	Season	Club	League Appearances/Goals

GAVIN, Mark

Born Bailleston 10.12.63.   Ht 5 7   Wt 10 8
Midfield. From Apprentice.

Season	Club	App	Goals
1981–82	Leeds U	—	—
1982–83		7	1
1983–84		12	1
1984–85		11	1
1984–85	*Hartlepool U*	7	—
1985–86	Carlisle U	13	1
1985–86	Bolton W	8	1

GAYLE, Brian

Born London 6.3.65.   Ht 6 1   Wt 12 7
Defender.

Season	Club	App	Goals
1984–85	Wimbledon	12	1
1985–86		13	—

GAYLE, Howard

Born Liverpool 18.5.58.   Ht 5 10   Wt 10 9
Midfield. Local. England Under-21.

Season	Club	App	Goals
1977–78	Liverpool	—	—
1978–79		—	—
1979–80		—	—
1979–80	*Fulham*	14	—
1980–81	Liverpool	4	1
1981–82		—	—
1982–83	Liverpool	—	—
1982–83	*Birmingham C*	13	1
1982–83	*Newcastle U*	8	2
1983–84	Birmingham C	33	8
1984–85	Sunderland	25	2
1985–86		23	2

GEDDES, Bobby

Born Inverness 12.8.60.   Ht 6 0   Wt 11 4
Goalkeeper. From Ross County. Scotland
Under-21.

Season	Club	App	Goals
1977–78	Dundee	—	—
1978–79		—	—
1979–80		—	—
1980–81		20	—
1981–82		28	—

Season	Club	App	Goals
1982–83		1	—
1983–84		24	—
1984–85		16	—
1985–86		36	—

GEDDIS, David

Born Carlisle 12.3.58.   Ht 5 10½   Wt 12 12
Forward. From Apprentice.
England Youth 'B'.

Season	Club	App	Goals
1975–76	Ipswich T	—	—
1976–77		2	—
1976–77	*Luton T*	13	4
1977–78	Ipswich T	26	4
1978–79		15	1
1979–80		—	—
1979–80	Aston Villa	20	2
1980–81		9	4
1981–82		14	6
1982–83		4	—
1982–83	*Luton T*	4	—
1983–84	Aston Villa	—	—
1983–84	Barnsley	31	14
1984–85		14	10
1984–85	Birmingham C	18	12
1985–86		26	6

GEE, Phil

Born Pelsall 19.12.64.   Ht 5 9   Wt 10 4
Forward. From Riley Sports and Gresley R.

Season	Club	App	Goals
1985–86	Derby Co	4	2

GEELAN, Ken

Born Sheffield 12.9.67.
Midfield. From Apprentice.

Season	Club	App	Goals
1985–86	Sheffield U	—	—

GENNOE, Terry

Born Shrewsbury 16.3.53.   Ht 6 2   Wt 13 1
Goalkeeper. From Bricklayers Sports.

Season	Club	League Appearances/Goals	
1972–73	Bury	1	—
1973–74		2	—
1973–74	*Blackburn R*	—	—
1974–75	Bury	—	—
1974–75	*Leeds U*	—	—
1975–76	Halifax T	26	—
1976–77		26	—
1977–78		26	—
1977–78	Southampton		
1978–79		23	—
1979–80		13	—
1980–81	*Everton*	—	—
1980–81	*Crystal Palace*	3	—
1981–82	Blackburn R	35	—
1982–83		33	—
1983–84		30	—
1984–85		37	—
1985–86		32	—

GERNON, Irvin

Born Birmingham 30.12.62.   Ht 6 2
Wt 12 1
Defender.   From   Apprentice.   England
Youth.

Season	Club	League Appearances/Goals	
1979–80	Ipswich T	—	—
1980–81		—	—
1981–82		4	—
1982–83		26	—
1983–84		19	—
1984–85		13	—
1985–86		11	—

GIBBINS, Roger

Born Enfield 6.9.55.   Ht 5 10½   Wt 11 9
Forward. From Apprentice. England Schools.

Season	Club	League Appearances/Goals	
1972–73	Tottenham H	—	—
1973–74		—	—
1974–75		—	—
1975–76	Oxford U	19	2
1976–77	Norwich C	20	5
1977–78		28	7
From New England Tea Men			
1979–80	Cambridge U	35	4
1980–81		30	4
1981–82		35	4
1982–83	Cardiff C	46	8

Season	Club	League Appearances/Goals	
1983–84		42	4
1984–85		40	5
1985–86		11	—
1985–86	Swansea C	35	6

GIBBS, Nigel

Born St Albans 20.11.65.   Ht 5 7   Wt 10 12
Midfield. From Apprentice. England Youth.

Season	Club	League Appearances/Goals	
1983–84	Watford	3	—
1984–85		12	—
1985–86		40	1

GIBSON, Charlie

Born Dumbarton 12.6.61.   Ht 5 10
Wt 10 10
Forward. From St Anthony's.

Season	Club	League Appearances/Goals	
1980–81	Shrewsbury T	—	—
1981–82		6	—
1982–83	East Stirling	37	6
1983–84		37	13
1984–85		14	9
1984–85	Clydebank	14	2
1985–86		17	1

GIBSON, Colin

Born Bridport 6.4.60.   Ht 5 8   Wt 10 8½
Defender. From Apprentice. England
Under-21.

Season	Club	League Appearances/Goals	
1977–78	Aston Villa	—	—
1978–79		12	—
1979–80		31	2
1980–81		21	—
1981–82		23	—
1982–83		23	1
1983–84		28	1
1984–85		40	4
1985–86		7	2
1985–86	Manchester U	18	5

GIBSON, Simon

Born Nottingham 10.12.64.   Ht 6 0
Wt 11 0
Defender. From Apprentice.

Season	Club	League Appearances/Goals		Season	Club	League Appearances/Goals	
1983–84	Chelsea	—	—	1976–77	Crystal Palace	—	—
1983–84	Swindon T	29	3	1977–78		18	—
1984–85		2	—	1978–79		41	1
1984–85	Preston NE	17	3	1979–80		40	1
1985–86		25	2	1980–81		39	—
				1981–82		31	—
				1982–83		34	—
				1983–84		34	1
				1984–85	Portsmouth	35	—
				1985–86		36	—

GIBSON, Terry

Born Walthamstow 23.12.62.   Ht 5 5
Wt 10 0
Forward. From Apprentice.
England Schools, Youth.

GILES, David

Season	Club	League Appearances/Goals	
1979–80	Tottenham H	1	—
1980–81		—	—
1981–82		1	—
1982–83		16	4
1983–84	Coventry C	36	17
1984–85		38	15
1985–86		24	11
1985–86	Manchester U	7	—

Born Cardiff 21.9.56.   Ht 5 7   Wt 10 4½
Forward. From Apprentice. Wales Schools,
Under-21, 12 full caps.

Season	Club	League Appearances/Goals	
1974–75	Cardiff C	4	—
1975–76		11	1
1976–77		12	1
1977–78		28	1
1978–79		4	—
1978–79	Wrexham	23	1
1979–80		15	1
1979–80	Swansea C	25	8
1980–81		27	5
1981–82		2	—
1981–82	*Orient*	3	2
1981–82	Crystal Palace	21	1
1982–83		38	—
1983–84		29	5
1984–85	Birmingham C	—	—
1984–85	Newport Co	32	1
1985–86	Cardiff C	34	—

GIDMAN, John

Born Liverpool 10.1.54.   Ht 5 11   Wt 12 2
Defender. From Liverpool Apprentice.
England Youth, Under-23, 'B', 1 full cap.

Season	Club	League Appearances/Goals	
1971–72	Aston Villa	—	—
1972–73		13	—
1973–74		30	—
1974–75		14	1
1975–76		39	—
1976–77		27	4
1977–78		34	1
1978–79		36	3
1979–80		4	—
1979–80	Everton	29	1
1980–81		35	1
1981–82	Manchester U	37	1
1982–83		3	—
1983–84		4	—
1984–85		27	3
1985–86		24	—

GILES, Mike

Born Leeds 3.6.64.   Ht 5 6   Wt 10 3
Defender. From Shamrock R and UCD.

Season	Club	League Appearances/Goals	
1984–85	WBA	—	—
1985–86	Bradford C	—	—

GILKES, Michael

Born Hackney 20.7.65.   Ht 5 8   Wt 10 2
Forward.

Season	Club	League Appearances/Goals	
1984–85	Reading	16	2
1985–86		9	2

GILBERT, Billy

Born Lewisham 10.11.59.   Ht 5 11   Wt 12 0
Defender. From Apprentice. England
Schools, Youth, Under-21.

Season	Club	League Appearances/Goals	Season	Club	League Appearances/Goals

GILL, Gary

Born Middlesbrough 28.11.64.   Ht 5 10
Wt 11 9
Defender. From Apprentice.

1982–83	Middlesbrough	—	—
1983–84		6	—
1983–84	*Hull C*	1	—
1984–85	Middlesbrough	14	—
1985–86		9	—

GILL, Ken

Born Swindon 5.11.55.
Midfield. From Forest Green R.

1985–86	Newport Co	19	1

GILL, Tony

Born Bradford 6.3.68.   Ht 5 9½   Wt 10 0
Defender. From Apprentice.

1985–86	Bradford C	—	—

GILLARD, Ian

Born Hammersmith 9.10.50.   Ht 6 2   Wt 13 3
Defender. From Apprentice. England
Under-23, 3 full caps.

1968–69	QPR	6	—
1969–70		15	1
1970–71		17	—
1971–72		24	—
1972–73		8	—
1973–74		23	—
1974–75		42	2
1975–76		41	—
1976–77		41	1
1977–78		38	—
1978–79		38	3
1979–80		38	1
1980–81		42	—
1981–82		35	1
1982–83	Aldershot	39	2
1983–84		26	—
1984–85		12	—
1985–86		6	—

GILLESPIE, Gary

Born Stirling 5.7.60.   Ht 6 2   Wt 12 7
Defender. From school. Scotland Under-21.

1977–78	Falkirk	22	—
1978–79	Coventry C	15	—
1979–80		38	1
1980–81		37	1
1981–82		40	2
1982–83		42	2
1983–84	Liverpool	—	—
1984–85		12	1
1985–86		14	3

GILLIGAN, Jimmy

Born London 24.1.64.   Ht 6 2   Wt 13 2
Forward. From Apprentice.

1981–82	Watford	1	—
1982–83		4	2
1982–83	*Lincoln C*	3	—
1983–84	Watford	12	4
1984–85		10	—
1985–86	Grimsby T	25	4

GITTENS, Jon

Born Moseley 22.1.64.
Defender. From Paget R.

1985–86	Southampton	4	—

GIVEN, Jim

Born Port Glasgow 12.6.55.   Ht 5 9
Wt 10 7
Midfield. From Johnstone Burgh.

1978–79	Clydebank	38	3
1979–80		38	2
1980–81		38	7
1981–82		39	6
1982–83		34	6
1983–84		35	9
1984–85		37	7
1985–86		30	—

Season	Club	League Appearances/Goals	Season	Club	League Appearances/Goals

GLAVIN, Ronnie

Born Glasgow 27.3.51.   Ht 5 10   Wt 12 6
Midfield. From Lochend Rovers.
Scotland 1 full cap.

Season	Club	Apps	Goals
1968–69	Partick T	—	—
1969–70		8	2
1970–71		14	9
1971–72		29	2
1972–73		33	9
1974–75		11	3
1974–75	Celtic	20	5
1975–76		10	—
1976–77		34	19
1977–78		28	9
1978–79		10	3
1979–80	Barnsley	42	20
1980–81		37	18
1981–82		27	7
1982–83		35	17
1983–84		35	11
From Belenenses			
1985–86	Barnsley	6	—

GLEASURE, Peter

Born Luton 8.10.60.   Ht 5 11   Wt 12 13
Goalkeeper. From Apprentice.

Season	Club	Apps	Goals
1978–79	Millwall	—	—
1979–80		—	—
1980–81		13	—
1981–82		38	—
1982–83		4	—
1982–83	*Northampton T*	11	—
1983–84	Northampton T	46	—
1984–85		43	—
1985–86		44	—

GLEGHORN, Nigel

Born Seaham 12.8.62.   Ht 6 0   Wt 12 13
Midfield. From Seaham Red Star.

Season	Club	Apps	Goals
1985–86	Ipswich T	21	2

GLENN, David

Born Wigan 30.11.62.   Ht 5 10   Wt 10 10
Defender. From Apprentice.

Season	Club	Apps	Goals
1980–81	Wigan Ath	11	2
1981–82		35	2
1982–83		26	—
1983–84	Blackburn R	22	—
1984–85		2	—
1985–86	Chester	33	1

GLENNIE, Bobby

Born Dundee 2.10.57.   Ht 5 11   Wt 11 4
Defender. From St Columba's B.C.

Season	Club	Apps	Goals
1974–75	Aberdeen	—	—
1975–76		—	—
1976–77		—	—
1977–78		3	—
1977–78	Dundee	13	1
1978–79		37	1
1979–80		35	—
1980–81		39	—
1981–82		35	—
1982–83		26	—
1983–84		27	2
1984–85		29	—
1985–86		33	2

GLOVER, Dean

Born West Bromwich 29.12.63.   Ht 5 9
Wt 11 2
Defender. From Apprentice.

Season	Club	Apps	Goals
1981–82	Aston Villa	—	—
1982–83		—	—
1983–84		—	—
1984–85		5	—
1985–86		18	—

GODDARD, Karl

Born Leeds 29.12.67.   Ht 5 6   Wt 10 1
Forward. From Apprentice. England
Schools.

Season	Club	Apps	Goals
1985–86	Manchester U	—	—

Season	Club	League Appearances/Goals		Season	Club	League Appearances/Goals	

GODDARD, Paul

Born Harlington 12.10.59.   Ht 5 8   Wt 12 0
Forward. From Apprentice.
England Under-21, 1 full cap.

1977–78	QPR	7	1
1978–79		23	6
1979–80		40	16
1980–81	West Ham U	37	17
1981–82		39	15
1982–83		39	10
1983–84		5	1
1984–85		40	9
1985–86		6	1

GODDEN, Tony

Born Gillingham 2.8.55.   Ht 6 1   Wt 12 4
Goalkeeper. From Ashford T.

1975–76	WBA	—	—
1976–77		6	—
1976–77	*Preston NE*	—	—
1977–78	WBA	42	—
1978–79		42	—
1979–80		42	—
1980–81		42	—
1981–82		19	—
1982–83		12	—
1982–83	*Luton T.*	12	—
1983–84	WBA	—	—
1983–84	*Walsall*	19	—
1984–85	WBA	41	—
1985–86		21	—
1985–86	*Chelsea*	8	—

GODFREY, Kevin

Born Kennington 24.2.60.   Ht 5 10
Wt 10 11
Forward. From Apprentice.

1976–77	Orient	—	—
1977–78		11	—
1978–79		6	—
1979–80		5	1

1980–81		9	2
1981–82		42	7
1982–83		45	11
1983–84		41	10
1984–85		40	10
1985–86		16	4
1985–86	*Plymouth Arg*	7	1

GODFREY, Peter

Born Falkirk 12.10.57.   Ht 6 0   Wt 11 7
Defender. From Linlithgow Rose.

1979–80	Stenhousemuir	2	—
1980–81	Meadowbank T	2	—
1981–82		30	6
1982–83		38	3
1983–84		37	3
1984–85		19	—
1984–85	St Mirren	15	1
1985–86		34	3

GOLAC, Ivan

Born Yugoslavia 15.6.50.   Ht 5 10   Wt 13 1
Defender. From Partizan Belgrade.
Yugoslavia full caps.

1978–79	Southampton	36	—
1979–80		31	2
1980–81		41	2
1981–82		36	—
1982–83	Bournemouth	9	—
From Bjelasica			
1983–84	Southampton	11	—
1984–85		4	—
1984–85	*Portsmouth*	8	—
1985–86	Southampton	9	—

GOLLOGLY, John

Born Bridlington 4.7.62.   Ht 6 0   Wt 12 3
Midfield.

1984–85	Hartlepool	7	1
1985–86		13	1

Season	Club	League Appearances/Goals		Season	Club	League Appearances/Goals	

GOODING, Mick

Born Newcastle 12.4.59.   Ht 5 7   Wt 10 8
Forward. From Bishop Auckland.

Season	Club		
1979–80	Rotherham U	34	3
1980–81		37	4
1981–82		22	2
1982–83		9	1
1982–83	Chesterfield	12	—
1983–84		—	—
1983–84	Rotherham U	26	7
1984–85		44	10
1985–86		40	8

GOODISON, Wayne

Born Wakefield 23.9.64.   Ht 5 8   Wt 11 7
Defender. From Apprentice.

Season	Club		
1982–83	Barnsley	3	—
1983–84		—	—
1984–85		12	—
1985–86		21	—

GOODMAN, Donald

Born Leeds 9.5.66.   Ht 5 10   Wt 11 0
Forward. From school.

Season	Club		
1983–84	Bradford C	2	—
1984–85		25	5
1985–86		20	4

GOODWIN, Mark

Born Sheffield 23.2.60.   Ht 5 10   Wt 10 9
Midfield. From Apprentice.

Season	Club		
1977–78	Leicester C	14	3
1978–79		28	1
1979–80		30	4
1980–81		19	—
1980–81	Notts Co	10	2
1981–82		38	4
1982–83		34	4
1983–84		29	—
1984–85		38	4
1985–86		43	6

GOODYEAR, Clive

Born Lincoln 15.1.61.   Ht 6 0   Wt 11 4
Defender. Local.

Season	Club		
1978–79	Luton T	—	—
1979–80		1	—
1980–81		5	1
1981–82		32	1
1982–83		35	2
1983–84		17	—
1984–85	Plymouth Arg	33	2
1985–86		41	2

GORAM, Andy

Born Bury 13.4.64.   Ht 5 11   Wt 11 6
Goalkeeper. From West Bromwich
Apprentice. Scotland 3 full caps.

Season	Club		
1981–82	Oldham Ath	3	—
1982–83		38	—
1983–84		22	—
1984–85		41	—
1985–86		41	—

GORDON, Colin

Born Stourbridge 17.1.63.   Ht 6 1   Wt 12 12
Forward. From Oldbury U.

Season	Club		
1984–85	Swindon T	33	17
1985–86		39	17

GORDON, Dale

Born Gt Yarmouth 9.1.67.   Ht 5 10
Wt 11 8
Forward. From Apprentice. England
Schools, Youth.

Season	Club		
1983–84	Norwich C	—	—
1984–85		23	3
1985–86		6	1

Season	Club	League Appearances/Goals	Season	Club	League Appearances/Goals

GORDON, Stuart

Born Glasgow 14.7.60.
Midfield. From Pollok Juniors.

1985–86	Clydebank	3 —

GORE, Shaun

Born London 21.9.68.
Defender.

1985–86	Fulham	5 —

GORMAN, Keith

Born Bishop Auckland 13.10.66. Ht 5 10
Wt 10 9½
Forward. From Apprentice.

1983–84	Ipswich T	— —
1984–85		— —
1985–86		— —

GORMAN, Paul

Born Dublin 6.8.63. Ht 5 10 Wt 11 8
Defender. From Apprentice.

1980–81	Arsenal	— —
1981–82		4 —
1982–83		— —
1983–84		2 —
1984–85	Birmingham C	6 —
1984–85	Carlisle U	7 1
1985–86		24 —

GORTON, Andy

Born Salford 23.9.66. Ht 5 11 Wt 11 4
Goalkeeper.

1984–85	Oldham Ath	— —
1985–86		1 —

GOSNEY, Andy

Born Southampton 8.11.63. Ht 6 4
Wt 13 5
Goalkeeper. From Apprentice.
England Youth.

1981–82	Portsmouth	1 —
1982–83		— —
1983–84		— —
1984–85		— —
1985–86		4 —

GOSS, Jeremy

Born Cyprus 11.5.65. Ht 5 9 Wt 10 9
Midfield. Amateur.

1982–83	Norwich C	— —
1983–84		1 —
1984–85		5 —
1985–86		— —

GOUGH, Richard

Born Stockholm 5.4.62. Ht 6 0 Wt 12 0
Defender. From Witz University. Scotland
Under–21, 23 full caps.

1980–81	Dundee U	4 —
1981–82		30 1
1982–83		34 8
1983–84		33 3
1984–85		33 6
1985–86		31 5

GRAHAM, Alastair

Born Glasgow 11.8.66. Ht 6 3 Wt 12 7
Forward. From Anniesland United.

1985–86	Clydebank	2 —

GRAHAM, Arthur

Born Glasgow 26.10.52. Ht 5 8 Wt 11 0
Forward. From Cambuslang R.
Scotland Under–23, 10 full caps.

All appearances include those as substitute

Season	Club	League Appearances/Goals		Season	Club	League Appearances/Goals	

Season	Club	League Appearances/Goals	
1969–70	Aberdeen	5	1
1970–71		31	5
1971–72		29	7
1972–73		23	—
1973–74		32	3
1974–75		34	11
1975–76		35	—
1976–77		35	5
1977–78	Leeds U	40	9
1978–79		39	8
1979–80		27	3
1980–81		40	3
1981–82		38	9
1982–83		39	5
1983–84	Manchester U	37	5
1984–85		—	—
1985–86	Bradford C	25	2

GRAHAM, Mike

Born Lancaster 24.2.59.   Ht 5 9½   Wt 11 7
Defender. From Apprentice.

Season	Club	League Appearances/Goals	
1976–77	Bolton W	—	—
1977–78		1	—
1978–79		9	—
1979–80		9	—
1980–81		27	—
1981–82	Swindon T	30	1
1982–83		46	—
1983–84		36	—
1984–85		29	—
1985–86	Mansfield T	45	—

GRAHAM, Milton

Born Tottenham 2.11.62.   Ht 5 10½
Wt 12 4
Forward. Local.

Season	Club	League Appearances/Goals	
1981–82	Bournemouth	5	3
1982–83		20	2
1983–84		30	4
1984–85		18	3
1985–86	Chester C	38	3

GRAHAM, Tommy

Born Glasgow 31.3.58.   Ht 5 9   Wt 11 9
Forward. From Arthurlie.

Season	Club	League Appearances/Goals	
1977–78	Aston Villa	—	—
1978–79		—	—
1978–79	Barnsley	27	12
1979–80		11	1
1980–81		—	—
1980–81	Halifax T	34	9
1981–82		37	8
1982–83	Doncaster R	11	2
1982–83	Scunthorpe U	13	3
1983–84		27	4
1984–85		38	9
1985–86		31	5

GRANGER, Keith

Born Southampton 5.10.68.
Goalkeeper. From Apprentice.

Season	Club	League Appearances/Goals	
1985–86	Southampton	2	—

GRANT, David

Born Sheffield 2.6.60.   Ht 6 0   Wt 12 9
Defender. From Apprentice.

Season	Club	League Appearances/Goals	
1977–78	Sheffield W	24	1
1978–79		27	1
1979–80		43	1
1980–81		35	1
1981–82		4	—
1982–83	Oxford U	20	1
1983–84		4	—
1983–84	*Chesterfield*	7	—
1983–84	Crystal Palace	—	—
1983–84	Cardiff C	12	—
1984–85		13	—
1984–85	Rochdale	14	—
1985–86		41	1

GRANT, Peter

Born Bellshill 30.8.65.   Ht 5 9   Wt 10 3
Midfield. From Celtic B.C. Scotland Schools,
Youth, Under-21.

All appearances include those as substitute

Season	Club	League Appearances/Goals		Season	Club	League Appearances/Goals	
1982–83	Celtic	—	—	1971–72	Leeds U	—	—
1983–84		3	—	1972–73		4	1
1984–85		20	4	1973–74		6	—
1985–86		30	1	1974–75		18	2
				1975–76		42	2
				1976–77		41	3
				1977–78		41	3
				1978–79		41	6
				1979–80	Nottingham F	41	2
				1980–81		40	3
				1981–82	Leeds U	37	—
				1982–83		42	5
				1983–84		24	4
				1984–85		39	1
				1985–86	Sunderland	34	4

GRANVILLE, John

Born Tobago 6.5.56.
Goalkeeper. From Slough. Trinidad full caps.

1985–86	Millwall	6	—

GRAY, Andy

Born Glasgow 30.11.55. Ht 5 11 Wt 11 10
Forward. From Clydebank Strollers.
Scotland Under-23, 20 full caps.

1973–74	Dundee U	26	16
1974–75		33	20
1975–76		3	—
1975–76	Aston Villa	30	10
1976–77		36	25
1977–78		32	13
1978–79		15	6
1979–80		—	—
1979–80	Wolverhampton W	35	12
1980–81		27	9
1981–82		29	5
1982–83		33	10
1983–84		9	2
1983–84	Everton	23	5
1984–85		26	9
1985–86	Aston Villa	35	5

GRAY, Andy

Born Lambeth 22.2.64. Ht 5 10 Wt 11 6
Forward. From Corinthian C. and Dulwich H.

1984–85	C. Palace	21	5
1985–86		30	10

GRAY, Frankie

Born Glasgow 27.10.54. Ht 5 10 Wt 11 10
Defender. From Apprentice. Scotland
Schools, Under-23, 32 full caps.

GRAY, Steven

Born Irvine 7.2.67. Ht 5 6 Wt 10 2
Midfield. From Kilmarnock B.C. Scotland
Youth.

1985–86	Aberdeen	13	1

GRAY, Stuart

Born Withernsea 19.4.60. Ht 5 10 Wt 10 9
Defender. Local.

1980–81	Nottingham F	14	1
1981–82		33	2
1982–83		2	—
1982–83	*Bolton W*	10	—
1983–84	Barnsley	17	8
1984–85		7	—
1985–86		36	2

GRAY, Terry

Born Bradford 3.6.54. Ht 5 5 Wt 10 2
Forward. From Chelsea Amateur and Ashley
Road. England Youth.

1972–73	Huddersfield T	—	—
1973–74		13	1
1974–75		32	3
1975–76		29	15
1976–77		18	6
1977–78		45	10

Season	Club	League Appearances/Goals		Season	Club	League Appearances/Goals	

1978–79	....	26	1
1979–80	Southend U	41	7
1980–81	....	46	17
1981–82	....	23	4
1982–83	Bradford C	38	8
1983–84	....	31	7
1984–85	....	7	—
1984–85	Preston NE	13	—
1985–86	....	27	1

GREALISH, Tony

Born Paddington 21.9.56.   Ht 5 7   Wt 11 7
Midfield. From Apprentice. Eire Youth,
44 full caps.

1974–75	Orient.........................	25	2
1975–76	....	38	1
1976–77	....	33	2
1977–78	....	36	—
1978–79	....	39	5
1979–80	Luton T	41	2
1980–81	....	37	—
1981–82	Brighton	37	1
1982–83	....	38	2
1983–84	....	25	3
1983–84	WBA	11	—
1984–85	....	38	4
1985–86	....	16	1

GREEN, John

Born Rotherham 7.8.58.   Ht 5 11   Wt 12 12
Defender. From Apprentice.

1975–76	Rotherham U	38	—
1976–77	....	1	—
1977–78	....	41	1
1978–79	....	46	1
1979–80	....	44	2
1980–81	....	—	—
1981–82	....	41	3
1982–83	....	36	1
1983–84	....	1	—
1983–84	Scunthorpe U	45	2
1984–85	....	46	1
1985–86	....	9	1
1985–86	Darlington	30	1

GREEN, Ron

Born Birmingham 3.10.56.   Ht 6 2½
Wt 13 12
Goalkeeper. From Alvechurch.

1977–78	Walsall.......................	1	—
1978–79	....	1	—
1979–80	....	39	—
1980–81	....	24	—
1981–82	....	46	—
1982–83	....	35	—
1983–84	....	17	—
1983–84	*WBA*	—	—
1984–85	Shrewsbury T...............	19	—
1984–85	*Bristol R*	18	—
1985–86	Bristol R.....................	38	—

GREENALL, Colin

Born Billinge 30.12.63.   Ht 5 10   Wt 11 6
Defender. From Apprentice.

1980–81	Blackpool	12	—
1981–82	....	18	—
1982–83	....	24	1
1983–84	....	39	4
1984–85	....	44	3
1985–86	....	43	1

GREENOUGH, Ricky

Born Mexborough 30.5.61.   Ht 6 1   Wt 13 4
Forward. From Boston and Alfreton T.

| 1984–85 | Chester .... | 24 | 3 |
| 1985–86 | .... | 33 | 5 |

GREENWOOD, Nigel

Born Preston 27.11.66.   Ht 5 11   Wt 12 0
Forward. From Apprentice.

| 1984–85 | Preston N.E. .... | 15 | 5 |
| 1985–86 | .... | 30 | 9 |

Season	Club	League Appearances/Goals		Season	Club	League Appearances/Goals

GREGORY, David

Born Peterborough 6.10.51.   Ht 5 9
Wt 11 6
Midfield. From Chatteris T.

Season	Club	App	Goals
1973–74	Peterborough U............	12	—
1974–75	....	41	9
1975–76	....	46	14
1976–77	....	43	9
1977–78	Stoke C	23	3
1978–79	....	—	—
1978–79	*Blackburn R*	5	3
1978–79	Bury............................	36	10
1979–80	....	16	3
1979–80	Portsmouth	21	5
1980–81	....	39	13
1981–82	....	14	—
1982–83	Wrexham.....................	41	4
1983–84	....	44	19
1984–85	....	30	5
1985–86	....	38	3

GREGORY, John

Born Scunthorpe 11.5.54.   Ht 6 1   Wt 11 0
Defender. From Apprentice. England 6 full
caps.

Season	Club	App	Goals
1972–73	Northampton T	9	—
1973–74	....	46	—
1974–75	....	41	1
1975–76	....	45	3
1976–77	....	46	4
1977–78	Aston Villa..................	26	3
1978–79	....	39	7
1979–80	Brighton.....................	33	—
1980–81	....	39	7
1981–82	QPR............................	34	9
1982–83	....	42	15
1983–84	....	37	7
1984–85	....	37	5
1985–86	....	11	—
1985–86	Derby Co.....................	22	4

GREGORY, Paul

Born Sheffield 26.7.61.   Ht 5 10   Wt 11 7
Goalkeeper. From Apprentice.

Season	Club	App	Goals
1979–80	Chesterfield.................	—	—
1980–81	....	2	—
1981–82	....	1	—
1982–83	....	14	—
1983–84	....	6	—
1983–84	Doncaster R	—	—
1984–85	....	1	—
1984–85	Scunthorpe U	32	—
1985–86	....	34	—

GREGORY, Tony

Born Doncaster 21.3.68.
Midfield. From Apprentice. England
Schools, Youth.

Season	Club	App	Goals
1985–86	Sheffield W	5	—

GRENFELL, Steven

Born Enfield 27.10.66.   Ht 5 9   Wt 10 11
Defender. From Apprentice.

Season	Club	App	Goals
1984–85	Tottenham H	—	—
1985–86	....	—	—

GREW, Mark

Born Bilston 15.2.58.   Ht 5 10   Wt 11 2
Goalkeeper. From Amateur.

Season	Club	App	Goals
1976–77	WBA............................	—	—
1977–78	....	—	—
1978–79	....	—	—
1978–79	*Wigan Ath*	4	—
1978–79	*Notts Co*	—	—
1979–80	WBA............................	—	—
1980–81	....	—	—
1981–82	....	23	—
1982–83	....	10	—
1983–84	Leicester C..................	5	—
1983–84	*Oldham Ath*	5	—
1983–84	Ipswich T	—	—
1984–85	....	6	—
1985–86	....	—	—
1985–86	*Fulham*	4	—
1985–86	*WBA*	1	—
1985–86	*Derby Co*	—	—

Season	Club	League Appearances/Goals	Season	Club	League Appearances/Goals

GREWCOCK, Neil

Born Leicester 26.4.62.   Ht 5 6   Wt 11 2
Forward. From Apprentice.

Season	Club	App	Goals
1979–80	Leicester C	1	1
1980–81		7	—
1981–82		—	—
1981–82	*Gillingham*	13	1
1982–83	Gillingham	21	3
From Shepshed C.			
1984–85	Burnley	46	6
1985–86		38	7

GREYGOOSE, Dean

Born Thetford 18.12.64.   Ht 5 11   Wt 11 5
Goalkeeper. From Apprentice. England
Youth.

Season	Club	App	Goals
1982–83	Cambridge U	—	—
1983–84		16	—
1984–85		10	—
1984–85	*Orient*	—	—
1985–86	Cambridge U	—	—
1985–86	*Lincoln C*	6	—
1985–86	Orient	1	—

GRIFFIN, Colin

Born Dudley 8.1.56.   Ht 60   Wt 11 2
Defender. From Apprentice.

Season	Club	App	Goals
1975–76	Derby Co	—	—
1975–76	Shrewsbury T	25	1
1976–77		44	2
1977–78		31	—
1978–79		46	2
1979–80		40	1
1980–81		41	—
1981–82		36	—
1982–83		34	—
1983–84		27	—
1984–85		41	1
1985–86		32	—

GRIFFIN, James

Born Hamilton 1.1.67.   Ht 5 8   Wt 11 4
Defender. From Fir Park B.C.

Season	Club	App	Goals
1985–86	Motherwell	1	—

GRIFFITHS, Ian

Born Birkenhead 17.4.60.   Ht 5 6   Wt 10 2
Midfield. From Amateur.

Season	Club	App	Goals
1978–79	Tranmere R	3	—
1979–80		2	—
1980–81		30	—
1981–82		38	1
1982–83		43	4
1983–84	Rochdale	41	5
1984–85		1	—
1984–85	Port Vale	12	—
1985–86	Wigan Ath	38	3

GRIFFITHS, Peter

Born Barnstaple 14.8.57.   Ht 5 6   Wt 10 8
Midfield. From Bideford.

Season	Club	App	Goals
1980–81	Stoke C	10	1
1981–82		31	3
1982–83		15	1
1983–84		4	—
1983–84	*Bradford C*	2	—
1984–85	Port Vale	31	3
1985–86		5	1

GRIMES, Ashley

Born Dublin 2.8.57.   Ht 60   Wt 11 0
Midfield. From Bohemians. Eire Under-21,
15 full caps.

Season	Club	App	Goals
1976–77	Manchester U	—	—
1977–78		13	2
1978–79		16	—
1979–80		26	3
1980–81		8	2
1981–82		11	1
1982–83		16	2
1983–84	Coventry C	32	1
1984–85	Luton T	9	—
1985–86		3	—

GRIMSHAW, Chris

Born Accrington 1.10.65.   Ht 5 7   Wt 10 6
Midfield. From Burnley Apprentice.

Season	Club	League Appearances/Goals		Season	Club	League Appearances/Goals	
1983–84	Burnley	—	—	1967–68	West Ham U	—	—
1983–84	Crewe Alex	3	—	1968–69		2	—
1984–85	Bury	1	—	1969–70		12	—
1985–86		2	—	1970–71		19	—
				1971–72		6	—
				1972–73		11	—
				1973–74		—	—

GRITT, Steve

Born Bournemouth 31.10.57.   Ht 5 9
Wt 10 10
Midfield. From Apprentice.

1976–77	Bournemouth	6	3	1973–74	*Cardiff C*	2	—
1977–78	Charlton Ath	34	3	1974–75	Lincoln C	46	—
1978–79		39	3	1975–76		46	—
1979–80		31	7	1976–77		44	—
1980–81		40	—	1977–78		44	—
1981–82		34	3	1978–79		32	—
1982–83		27	1	1979–80		21	—
1983–84		33	1	1979–80	Cardiff C	7	—
1984–85		35	1	1980–81		22	—
1985–86		11	2	1981–82		9	—
				1981–82	Grimsby T	—	—
				1982–83		4	—
				1983–84		—	—
				1984–85		6	—
				1985–86		—	—

GROBBELAAR, Bruce

Born Durban 6.10.57.   Ht 6 1   Wt 13 0
Goalkeeper. From Vancouver Whitecaps.
Zimbabwe full caps.

GROVES, Perry

Born London 19.4.65.   Ht 5 10   Wt 12 3
Midfield. From Apprentice.

1979–80	Crewe Alex	24	1	1981–82	Colchester U	9	—
From Vancouver Whitecaps				1982–83		17	2
1980–81	Liverpool	—	—	1983–84		42	2
1981–82		42	—	1984–85		44	10
1982–83		42	—	1985–86		43	12
1983–84		42	—				
1984–85		42	—				
1985–86		42	—				

GROCOCK, Chris

Born Grimsby 30.10.68.
Midfield. From School.

1985–86   Grimsby T 1   —

GUMMER, Jason

Born Tredegar 27.10.67.   Ht 5 9   Wt 11 0
Midfield. From Apprentice and YTS. Wales
Youth.

1985–86   Cardiff C 5   1

GROTIER, Peter

Born Stratford 18.10.50.   Ht 5 11   Wt 12 10
Goalkeeper. From Apprentice.

GUNN, Bryan

Born Thurso 22.12.63.   Ht 6 2   Wt 12 5
Goalkeeper. From Invergordon B.C.
Scotland Schools, Youth, Under-21.

Season	Club	League Appearances/Goals		Season	Club	League Appearances/Goals	

1980–81	Aberdeen	—	—
1981–82		—	—
1982–83		1	—
1983–84		—	—
1984–85		2	—
1985–86		10	—

GUNN, Bryn

Born Kettering 21.8.58.   Ht 6 2   Wt 13 7
Defender. From Apprentice.

1975–76	Nottingham F	11	—
1976–77		—	—
1977–78		—	—
1978–79		1	—
1979–80		2	—
1980–81		26	—
1981–82		37	—
1982–83		33	1
1983–84		4	—
1984–85		17	—
1985–86		—	—
1985–86	*Shrewsbury T*	9	—
1985–86	*Walsall*	6	—
1985–86	*Mansfield T*	5	—

GWINNETT, Mel

Born Worcester 14.5.63.   Ht 6 1½   Wt 11 5½
Goalkeeper. From Stourbridge.

1981–82	Peterborough U	—	—
1982–83	Hereford U	1	—
1983–84	Bradford C	—	—
1984–85		—	—
1985–86	Exeter C	2	—

GYMER, John

Born Romford 11.11.66.   Ht 5 10½   Wt 11 8
Forward. From Arsenal, West Ham U
schoolboy. Apprentice.

1983–84	Southend U	5	1
1984–85		19	5
1985–86		13	3

GYNN, Mick

Born Peterborough 19.8.61.   Ht 5 5
Wt 10 6
Midfield. From Apprentice.

1978–79	Peterborough U	11	2
1979–80		27	1
1980–81		29	7
1981–82		46	6
1982–83		43	17
1983–84	Coventry C	23	2
1984–85		39	4
1985–86		12	1

All appearances include those as substitute

Season	Club	League Appearances/Goals	Season	Club	League Appearances/Goals

HACKETT, Gary

Born Stourbridge 11.10.62.   Ht 5 8
Wt 10 13
Forward. From Bromsgrove R.

1983–84	Shrewsbury T	31	3
1984–85		38	5
1985–86		42	6

HADDOCK, Peter

Born Newcastle 9.12.61.   Ht 5 10   Wt 11 5
Defender. From Apprentice.

1979–80	Newcastle U	—	—
1980–81		—	—
1981–82		30	—
1982–83		17	—
1983–84		3	—
1984–85		1	—
1985–86		6	—
1985–86	*Burnley*	7	—

HAGAN, Jim

Born Monkstown 10.8.56.   Ht 5 10   Wt 10 9
Defender. From Larne.

1977–78	Coventry C	—	—
1978–79		13	—
1979–80		—	—
1979–80	*Torquay U*	7	—
From Detroit Express, Seiko, Hong Kong			
1981–82	Coventry C	3	—
1982–83	Birmingham C	32	—
1983–84		33	—
1984–85		29	—
1985–86		31	—

HAIGH, Paul

Born Scarborough 4.5.58.   Ht 5 10   Wt 12 8
Defender. From Apprentice.
England Under-21.

1974–75	Hull C	1	—
1975–76		7	—

1976–77		42	2
1977–78		38	1
1978–79		45	1
1979–80		29	2
1980–81		18	2
1980–81	Carlisle U	28	—
1981–82		23	—
1982–83		40	1
1983–84		34	—
1984–85		36	2
1985–86		28	—

HAIRE, Garry

Born Sedgefield 24.7.63.   Ht 5 6   Wt 10 4
Forward. From Apprentice.

1981–82	Oxford U	—	—
From Whitley Bay			
1983–84	Bradford C	43	13
1984–85		6	—
1984–85	Darlington	19	2
1985–86		6	—
1985–86	*Rochdale*	3	—

HAISTEAD, Tony

Born Croydon 18.12.66.
Midfield. From Apprentice.

1984–85	Crystal Palace	—	—
1985–86		—	—

HALES, Derek

Born Lower Halstow 15.12.51.   Ht 5 9
Wt 11 11
Forward. From Dartford.

1971–72	Luton T	—	—
1972–73		7	1
1973–74	Charlton Ath	29	8
1974–75		44	20
1975–76		40	28
1976–77		16	16
1976–77	Derby Co	18	4
1977–78		5	—
1977–78	West Ham	24	10
1978–79	Charlton Ath	20	8

Season	Club	League Appearances/Goals		Season	Club	League Appearances/Goals	

1979–80	....	23	8
1980–81	....	40	17
1981–82	....	35	11
1982–83	....	30	14
1983–84	....	29	10
1984–85	....	14	8
1984–85	Gillingham....................	11	1
1985–86	....	29	7

HALES, Kevin

Born Dartford 13.1.61.   Ht 5 7   Wt 10 4
Defender. From Apprentice.

1978–79	Chelsea	—	—
1979–80	....	7	—
1980–81	....	—	—
1981–82	....	10	2
1982–83	....	3	—
1983–84	Orient.......................	43	2
1984–85	....	33	—
1985–86	....	31	2

HALL, Derek

Born Manchester 5.1.65   Ht 5 8½   Wt 11 2
Midfield. From Apprentice.

1982–83	Coventry C..................	1	—
1983–84	....	—	—
1983–84	*Torquay U*	10	2
1984–85	Torquay U	45	4
1985–86	Swindon T..................	10	—

HALLIDAY, Bruce

Born Sunderland 3.1.61.   Ht 5 10   Wt 11 3
Defender. From Apprentice.

1978–79	Newcastle U	—	—
1979–80	....	—	—
1980–81	....	19	1
1981–82	....	13	—
1982–83	....	—	—
1982–83	*Darlington*	7	—
1982–83	Bury........................	29	—
1983–84	Bristol C....................	41	—
1984–85	....	12	—
1985–86	Hereford U	30	1

HALLWORTH, Jon

Born Stockport 26.10.65.   Ht 6 1   Wt 10 7
Goalkeeper. From school.

1983–84	Ipswich T...................	—	—
1984–85	....	—	—
1984–85	*Swindon T*..................	—	—
1984–85	*Fulham*	—	—
1984–85	*Bristol R*	2	—
1985–86	Ipswich T	6	—

HALPIN, John

Born Broxburn 15.11.61.   Ht 5 10   Wt 11 0
Midfield. From Celtic BC.

1981–82	Celtic.......................	3	—
1982–83	....	—	—
1983–84	....	4	—
1984–85	*Sunderland*.................	—	—
1984–85	Carlisle U	19	1
1985–86	....	33	5

HALSALL, Mick

Born Bootle 21.7.61.   Ht 5 10   Wt 11 4
Midfield. From Apprentice.

1979–80	Liverpool....................	—	—
1980–81	....	—	—
1981–82	....	—	—
1982–83	....	—	—
1982–83	Birmingham C..............	12	1
1983–84	....	21	2
1984–85	....	3	—
1984–85	Carlisle U	26	5
1985–86	....	41	4

HAMER, Kevin

Born Merthyr Tydfil 2.2.69.
Midfield.

| 1985–86 | Watford .... | — | — |
| 1985–86 | Newport Co................. | 1 | — |

Season	Club	League Appearances/Goals

HAMILL, Stewart

Born Glasgow 22.1.60.   Ht 5 9   Wt 10 8
Midfield. From Pollok.

Season	Club	App	Goals
1980–81	Leicester C	8	—
1981–82		2	2
1981–82	*Scunthorpe U*	4	—
From Local.			
1985–86	Northampton T	3	1

HAMILTON, Billy

Born Belfast 9.5.57.   Ht 6 1   Wt 12 0
Forward. From Linfield.
Northern Ireland Under-21, 38 full caps.

Season	Club	App	Goals
1977–78	QPR	—	—
1978–79		11	2
1979–80		1	—
1979–80	Burnley	25	7
1980–81		46	9
1981–82		44	11
1982–83		39	13
1983–84		46	18
1984–85	Oxford U	23	10
1985–86		8	3

HAMILTON, Brian

Born Paisley 5.8.67.   Ht 6 0   Wt 11 7
Defender. From Pollok United B.C.
Scotland Under-18 Schools.

Season	Club	App	Goals
1985–86	St Mirren	8	—

HAMILTON, David

Born South Shields 7.11.60.   Ht 5 7
Wt 10 0
Defender. From Apprentice.

Season	Club	App	Goals
1978–79	Sunderland	—	—
1979–80		—	—
1980–81		—	—
1980–81	Blackburn R	3	—
1981–82		17	—
1982–83		32	2

Season	Club	App	Goals
1983–84		26	2
1984–85		3	—
1984–85	*Cardiff C*	10	—
1985–86	Blackburn R	33	3

HAMILTON, Derek

Born Kilwinning 26.8.58.   Ht 5 8   Wt 10 10
Defender. From Beith Juniors.

Season	Club	App	Goals
1978–79	Aberdeen	10	—
1979–80		13	3
1980–81		8	—
1981–82		1	—
1982–83		2	—
1983–84	St Mirren	23	—
1984–85		13	—
1985–86		25	—

HAMILTON, Gary

Born Glasgow 27.12.65.   Ht 5 9   Wt 11 2
Forward. From Apprentice.

Season	Club	App	Goals
1982–83	Middlesbrough	9	2
1983–84		31	3
1984–85		36	—
1985–86		33	4

HAMILTON, Ian

Born Stevenage 14.12.67.
Forward. From Apprentice.

Season	Club	App	Goals
1985–86	Southampton	—	—

HAMMOND, Nicky

Born Essex 7.9.67.   Ht 5 8   Wt 11 8
Goalkeeper. From Apprentice.

Season	Club	App	Goals
1985–86	Arsenal	—	—

HAMPTON, Peter

Born Oldham 12.9.54.   Ht 5 7½   Wt 11 2
Defender. From Apprentice.
England Youth.

Season	Club	League Appearances/Goals		Season	Club	League Appearances/Goals	
1971–72	Leeds U	—	—	1979–80	Birmingham C	—	—
1972–73		2	—	1980–81		8	—
1973–74		—	—	1981–82		20	—
1974–75		2	—	1982–83		29	2
1975–76		1	1	1983–84		5	—
1976–77		31	1	1983–84	Walsall	18	4
1977–78		11	—	1984–85		38	4
1978–79		4	—	1985–86		10	3
1979–80		17	—	1985–86	Birmingham C	6	1
1980–81	Stoke C	33	2				
1981–82		33	—				
1982–83		40	1				
1983–84		32	1				
1984–85	Burnley	45	1				
1985–86		40	1				

HANKIN, Ray

Born Wallsend 2.2.56.   Ht 6 2   Wt 14 0
Forward. From Apprentice.
England Youth, Under-23.

HAMSON, Gary

Born Nottingham 24.8.59.   Ht 5 8   Wt 11 0
Midfield. From Apprentice.

Season	Club	League Appearances/Goals		Season	Club	League Appearances/Goals	
1976–77	Sheffield U	29	1	1972–73	Burnley	1	—
1977–78		38	3	1973–74		34	8
1978–79		41	4	1974–75		37	14
1979–80	Leeds U	19	1	1975–76		34	13
1980–81		11	—	1976–77		6	2
1981–82		18	2	1976–77	Leeds U	4	—
1982–83		—	—	1977–78		33	20
1983–84		25	—	1978–79		30	9
1984–85		31	—	1979–80		16	3
1985–86		30	—	From Vancouver Whitecaps			
				1982–83	Middlesbrough	21	1
				1983–84		—	—
				1983–84	Peterborough U	27	7
				1984–85		6	1
				1984–85	Wolves	10	1
				1985–86		—	—

HANDFORD, Phil

Born Chatham 18.7.64.   Ht 5 6½   Wt 10 4
Midfield. From Apprentice.

HANRAHAN, Joe

Born Limerick 21.3.64.   Ht 5 11½   Wt 13 0
Forward. From UCD. Eire Youth.

Season	Club	League Appearances/Goals	
1982–83	Gillingham	12	1
1983–84		20	—
1984–85	Wimbledon	7	—
1985–86		—	—
1985–86	*Crewe Alex*	9	—

Season	Club	League Appearances/Goals	
1985–86	Manchester U	—	—

HANDYSIDES, Ian

HANSBURY, Roger

Born Barnsley 26.1.55.   Ht 5 11   Wt 12 0
Goalkeeper. From Apprentice.

Born Jarrow 14.12.62.   Ht 5 8   Wt 10 9
Midfield. From Apprentice.

Season	Club	League Appearances/Goals	
1972–73	Norwich C	—	—
1973–74		—	—

All appearances include those as substitute

Season	Club	League Appearances/Goals	
1974–75	....	4	—
1975–76	....		
1976–77	....	4	—
1976–77	*Bolton W*	—	—
1977–78	Norwich C	14	—
1977–78	*Cambridge U*	11	—
1978–79	Norwich C	18	—
1978–79	*Orient*	—	—
1979–80	Norwich C	16	—
1980–81	....	22	—
1981–82	....	—	—
From Eastern, Hong Kong			
1983–84	Burnley	46	—
1984–85	....	37	—
1985–86	Cambridge U	37	—
1985–86	Birmingham C	—	—

HANSEN, Alan

Born Alloa 13.6.55.   Ht 6 1   Wt 13 0
Defender. From Sauchie BC.
Scotland Under-23, 23 full caps.

Season	Club	League Appearances/Goals	
1973–74	Partick T	1	—
1974–75	....	29	—
1975–76	....	21	2
1976–77	....	35	4
1976–77	Liverpool	—	—
1977–78	....	18	—
1978–79	....	34	1
1979–80	....	38	1
1980–81	....	36	1
1981–82	....	35	—
1982–83	....	34	—
1983–84	....	42	1
1984–85	....	41	—
1985–86	....	41	—

HARBACH, Peter

Born Carlisle 30.4.67.   Ht 5 6   Wt 10 5
Forward. From Apprentice.

Season	Club	League Appearances/Goals	
1984–85	Newcastle U	—	—
1985–86	....	—	—

HARBEY, Graham

Born Chesterfield 29.8.64.   Ht 5 8   Wt 10 8
Midfield. From Apprentice.

Season	Club	League Appearances/Goals	
1982–83	Derby Co	—	—
1983–84	....	19	—
1984–85	....	4	1
1985–86	....	3	—

HARBOTTLE, Mark

Born Nottingham 26.9.68.
Forward. From Apprentice. England Youth.

Season	Club	League Appearances/Goals	
1985–86	Notts Co	4	1

HARDWICK, Steve

Born Mansfield 6.9.56.   Ht 5 11   Wt 13 0
Goalkeeper. From Amateur.
England Youth.

Season	Club	League Appearances/Goals	
1974–75	Chesterfield	5	—
1975–76	....	12	—
1976–77	....	21	—
1976–77	Newcastle U	—	—
1977–78	....	9	—
1978–79	....	31	—
1979–80	....	41	—
1980–81	....	4	—
1981–82	....	—	—
1982–83	....	7	—
1982–83	Oxford U	18	—
1983–84	....	46	—
1984–85	....	42	—
1985–86	....	23	—
1985–86	*C Palace*	3	—

HARDYMAN, Paul

Born Portsmouth 11.3.64.   Ht 5 8½   Wt 11 4
Defender. Local. England Under-21.

Season	Club	League Appearances/Goals	
1983–84	Portsmouth	3	—
1984–85	....	15	—
1985–86	....	21	1

Season	Club	League Appearances/Goals		Season	Club	League Appearances/Goals	

HARE, Darren

Born Canterbury 2.4.67.
Forward.

1985–86	Gillingham	—	—
1985–86	*Dover*	Not known	

HARFORD, Mick

Born Sunderland 12.2.59.   Ht 6 2   Wt 12 9
Forward. From Lambton St BC.

1977–78	Lincoln C	27	9
1978–79		31	6
1979–80		36	16
1980–81		21	10
1980–81	Newcastle U	19	4
1981–82	Bristol C	30	11
1981–82	Birmingham C	12	9
1982–83		29	6
1983–84		39	8
1984–85		12	2
1984–85	Luton T	22	15
1985–86		37	22

HARKOUK, Rachid

Born Chelsea 19.5.56.   Ht 6 0½   Wt 12 5
Forward. From Feltham. Algeria full caps.

1976–77	Crystal Palace	28	12
1977–78		26	9
1978–79	QPR	15	3
1979–80		5	—
1980–81	Notts Co	25	4
1981–82		18	4
1982–83		14	3
1983–84		32	6
1984–85		35	15
1985–86		20	7

HARLE, David

Born Denaby 15.8.63.   Ht 5 9   Wt 10 7
Midfield. From Apprentice.

1979–80	Doncaster R	1	—
1980–81		34	1
1981–82		26	2

1982–83	Exeter C	37	6
1983–84		6	—
1983–84	Doncaster R	29	6
1984–85		37	9
1985–86		17	2
1985–86	Leeds U	3	—
1985–86	*Bristol C*	8	—

HARLEY, Lee

Born Crewe 7.7.67.
Forward.

1984–85	Chester	—	—
1985–86		1	—

HARLOW, David

Born Epsom 2.11.67.   Ht 5 10   Wt 9 5½
Defender. From Apprentice.

1985–86	Fulham	—	—

HARMSWORTH, Lee

Born Southwark 27.10.67.   Ht 5 10
Wt 11 13
Goalkeeper. From Apprentice.

1984–85	Charlton Ath	3	—
1985–86		—	—

HARPER, Alan

Born Liverpool 1.11.60.   Ht 5 8   Wt 10 9
Defender. From Apprentice.

1977–78	Liverpool	—	—
1978–79		—	—
1979–80		—	—
1980–81		—	—
1981–82		—	—
1982–83		—	—
1983–84	Everton	29	1
1984–85		13	—
1985–86		21	—

Season	Club	League Appearances/Goals	Season	Club	League Appearances/Goals

HARRINGTON, Phil

Born Bangor 20.11.63.   Ht 5 10   Wt 11 4
Goalkeeper. From Local. Wales Youth.

Season	Club	App	Goals
1981–82	Chester	10	—
1982–83		19	—
1983–84		41	—
1984–85		6	—
1984–85	*Oxford U*	—	—
1984–85	Blackpool	—	—
1985–86		—	—
1985–86	*Burnley*	2	—
1985–86	*Preston NE*	2	—

HARRIS, Carl

Born Neath 3.11.56.   Ht 5 9   Wt 11 0
Forward. From Apprentice.
Wales Schools, Under-23, 24 full caps.

Season	Club	App	Goals
1973–74	Leeds U	—	—
1974–75		3	1
1975–76		14	3
1976–77		16	3
1977–78		19	2
1978–79		31	3
1979–80		15	4
1980–81		37	10
1981–82		19	—
1982–83	Charlton Ath	42	5
1983–84		24	2
1984–85		10	—
1985–86	Leeds U	—	—
1985–86	Bury	18	3

HARRIS, Colin

Born Sanquhar 22.2.61.   Ht 5 11   Wt 10 10
Forward. From Exit Th.

Season	Club	App	Goals
1979–80	Raith R	3	—
1980–81		25	9
1981–82		22	1
1982–83		36	18
1983–84		20	4
1983–84	Dundee	14	2
1984–85		15	1
1984–85	Hibernian	7	2
1985–86		19	2

HARRISON, Chris

Born Launceston 17.10.56   Ht 5 9   Wt 11 0
Defender. From Apprentice.

Season	Club	App	Goals
1973–74	Plymouth Arg	—	—
1974–75		—	—
1975–76		1	—
1976–77		21	1
1977–78		31	1
1978–79		24	1
1979–80		41	1
1980–81		45	—
1981–82		43	1
1982–83		41	1
1983–84		44	—
1984–85		33	1
1985–86		—	—
1985–86	Swansea C	36	5

HARRISON, Frankie

Born Middlesbrough 19.9.63.
Forward.

Season	Club	App	Goals
1982–83	Middlesbrough	—	—
From Local.			
1985–86	Lincoln C	1	—

HARRISON, Richard

Born Bristol 17.12.67.
Defender.

Season	Club	App	Goals
1985–86	Bury	—	—

HARRISON, Wayne

Born Stockport 15.11.67.   Ht 5 8   Wt 10 7
Forward. From Apprentice.

Season	Club	App	Goals
1984–85	Oldham Ath	5	1
1984–85	Liverpool	—	—
1984–85	*Oldham Ath*	1	—
1985–86	Liverpool	—	—

HARROW, Andy

Born Kirkcaldy 6.11.56.   Ht 5 10   Wt 10 8
Forward. From Greigpark R.

All appearances include those as substitute

Season	Club	League Appearances/Goals		Season	Club	League Appearances/Goals	
1973–74	Cowdenbeath	25	5	1972–73		42	4
1974–75		38	6	1973–74	Blackpool	3	—
1975–76		24	7	1974–75		37	5
1976–77		8	—	1975–76		33	3
1976–77	Raith R	28	5	1976–77		42	6
1977–78		38	10	1977–78		28	3
1978–79		38	10	1977–78	Leeds U	12	—
1979–80		35	12	1978–79		40	5
1980–81	Luton T	4	—	1979–80		30	3
1980–81	Aberdeen	12	1	1980–81		38	4
1981–82		6	2	1981–82		32	1
1982–83	Motherwell	19	—	1982–83		39	3
1983–84		29	6	1983–84	Nottingham F	36	—
1984–85		37	9	1984–85		34	1
1985–86		20	2	1985–86	Sheffield W	34	1

HARROWER, Steven

Born Exeter 9.10.61.   Ht 5 8   Wt 11 1
Midfield. Local.

1983–84	Exeter C	13	1
1984–85		31	1
1985–86		38	6

HART, Nigel

Born Golborne 1.10.58.   Ht 6 0   Wt 12 3
Defender. Local.

1978–79	Wigan Ath	—	—
1979–80		1	—
1979–80	Leicester C	—	—
1980–81		—	—
1981–82	Blackpool	28	—
1982–83		9	—
1982–83	Crewe Alex	28	—
1983–84		37	3
1984–85		44	6
1985–86		23	—

HART, Paul

Born Manchester 4.5.53.   Ht 6 2   Wt 12 8
Defender. From Amateur.

1970–71	Stockport Co	10	1
1971–72		36	—

HART, Peter

Born Mexborough 14.8.57.   Ht 5 10
Wt 12 7
Defender. From Apprentice.

1973–74	Huddersfield T	1	—
1974–74		13	—
1975–76		19	1
1976–77		44	1
1977–78		41	—
1978–79		46	1
1979–80		46	4
1980–81	Walsall	45	5
1981–82		45	1
1982–83		45	—
1983–84		45	3
1984–85		46	—
1985–86		44	2

HARTFORD, Asa

Born Clydebank 24.10.50.   Ht 5 7   Wt 11 4
Midfield. From Amateur.
Scotland Under-21, Under-23, 50 full caps.

1967–68	WBA	6	1
1968–69		26	7
1969–70		34	1
1970–71		34	2
1971–72		39	1

All appearances include those as substitute

Season	Club	League Appearances/Goals	
1972–73	....	41	3
1973–74	....	33	3
1974–75	Manchester C	30	2
1975–76	....	39	9
1976–77	....	40	4
1977–78	....	37	4
1978–79	....	39	3
1979–80	Nottingham F	3	—
1979–80	Everton	35	1
1980–81	....	39	5
1981–82	....	7	—
1981–82	Manchester C	30	3
1982–83	....	38	3
1983–84	....	7	1
From Ft Lauderdale			
1984–85	Norwich C..................	28	2
1985–86	Bolton W	46	5

HARVEY, Graham

Born Musselburgh 23.4.61.   Ht 5 11
Wt 11 4
Forward. From Ormiston Primrose.

Season	Club	League Appearances/Goals	
1982–83	Hibernian	14	1
1983–84	....	16	2
1984–85	....	3	—
1984–85	Dundee......................	7	2
1985–86	....	30	5

HARVEY, Jimmy

Born Lurgan 2.5.58.   Ht 5 9½   Wt 11 4
Midfield. From Glenavon.

Season	Club	League Appearances/Goals	
1977–78	Arsenal	1	—
1978–79	....	2	—
1979–80	....	—	—
1979–80	*Hereford U*..................	11	—
1980–81	Hereford U	30	1
1981–82	....	42	5
1982–83	....	41	5
1983–84	....	44	9
1984–85	....	34	5
1985–86	....	42	9

HARVEY, Lee

Born Harlow 21.12.66.
Midfield. From Local. England Youth.

Season	Club	League Appearances/Goals	
1983–84	Orient........................	4	—
1984–85	....	4	—
1985–86	....	12	2

HASLEGRAVE, Sean

Born Stoke 7.6.51.   Ht 5 8   Wt 10 7
Midfield. From Amateur.

Season	Club	League Appearances/Goals	
1968–69	Stoke C	—	—
1969–70	....	—	—
1970–71	....	15	—
1971–72	....	18	—
1972–73	....	6	2
1973–74	....	27	1
1974–75	....	19	1
1975–76	....	28	1
1976–77	Nottingham F	7	1
1977–78	....	—	—
1977–78	Preston NE	38	—
1978–79	....	41	1
1979–80	....	25	—
1980–81	....	9	1
1981–82	Crewe Alex	40	1
1982–83	....	42	—
1983–84	York C	26	—
1984–85	....	42	—
1985–86	....	39	—

HATELEY, Mark

Born Liverpool 7.11.61.   Ht 6 1   Wt 11 7
Forward. From Apprentice.
England Youth, Under-21, 18 full caps.

Season	Club	League Appearances/Goals	
1978–79	Coventry C..................	1	—
1979–80	....	4	—
1980–81	....	19	3
1981–82	....	34	13
1982–83	....	35	9
1983–84	Portsmouth	38	22
1984–85	AC Milan..................	21	7
1985–86	....	22	8

All appearances include those as substitute

Season	Club	League Appearances/Goals		Season	Club	League Appearances/Goals	

HATTER, Steve

Born London 21.10.58. Ht 6 2 Wt 13 0
Defender. From Apprentice.

Season	Club	App	Goals
1976–77	Fulham	—	—
1977–78		5	—
1978–79		5	—
1979–80		6	—
1980–81		10	1
1981–82		—	—
1982–83		—	—
1982–83	*Exeter C*	11	1
1982–83	Wimbledon	28	1
1983–84		40	2
1984–85		16	1
1984–85	Southend U	18	—
1985–86		44	2

HAWKER, Phil

Born Solihull 7.12.62. Ht 6 1 Wt 11 7
Defender. From Apprentice.

Season	Club	App	Goals
1980–81	Birmingham C	11	—
1981–82		20	1
1982–83		4	—
1982–83	Walsall	5	—
1983–84		11	—
1984–85		20	—
1985–86		33	4

HAWLEY, John

Born Withernsea 8.5.54. Ht 6 0 Wt 13 12
Forward. From Amateur.

Season	Club	App	Goals
1972–73	Hull C	2	—
1973–74		19	3
1974–75		31	7
1975–76		22	3
1976–77		18	5
1977–78		22	4
1977–78	Leeds U	—	—
1978–79		32	16
1979–80		1	—
1979–80	Sunderland	9	4

Season	Club	App	Goals
1980–81		16	7
1981–82		—	—
1981–82	Arsenal	14	3
1982–83		6	—
1982–83	*Orient*	4	1
1982–83	*Hull C*	3	1
1983–84	Bradford C	42	22
1984–85		25	6
1985–86	Scunthorpe U	21	7

HAY, Alan

Born Dunfermline 28.11.58. Ht 5 11
Wt 11 3
Defender. From Bolton W. Amateur

Season	Club	App	Goals
1978–79	Bristol C	—	—
1979–80		4	—
1980–81		36	1
1981–82		34	—
1981–82	*St Mirren*	—	—
1982–83	York C	42	1
1983–84		42	1
1984–85		45	—
1985–86		21	1

HAYES, Martin

Born Walthamstow 21.3.66. Ht 6 0
Wt 11 8
Midfield. From Apprentice.

Season	Club	App	Goals
1983–84	Arsenal	—	—
1984–85		—	—
1985–86		11	2

HAYLOCK, Paul

Born Lowestoft 24.3.63. Ht 5 8 Wt 11 0
Defender. From Apprentice.

Season	Club	App	Goals
1980–81	Norwich C	—	—
1981–82		21	—
1982–83		42	1
1983–84		39	—
1984–85		41	1
1985–86		12	1

Season	Club	League Appearances/Goals		Season	Club	League Appearances/Goals	

HAYTOR, Tony

Born Castle Ward 7.2.67.　Ht 5 8　Wt 11 0
Midfield. From Apprentice.

1984–85	Newcastle U	—	—
1985–86		—	—

HAZARD, Mike

Born Sunderland 5.2.60.　Ht 5 7　Wt 10 5
Midfield. From Apprentice.

1977–78	Tottenham H	—	—
1978–79		—	—
1979–80		3	—
1980–81		4	—
1981–82		28	5
1982–83		18	1
1983–84		11	2
1984–85		23	4
1985–86		4	1
1985–86	Chelsea	18	1

HAZEL, Desmond

Born Bradford 15.7.67.
Forward. From Apprentice.

1985–86	Sheffield W	—	—

HAZEL, Ian

Born London 1.12.67.　Ht 5 10　Wt 10 4
Midfield. From Apprentice.

1985–86	Wimbledon	—	—

HAZELL, Bob

Born W Indies 14.6.59.　Ht 6 2　Wt 14 6
Defender. From Apprentice. England
Youth, Under-21, 'B'.

1977–78	Wolverhampton W	20	1
1978–79		13	—
1979–80		—	—
1979–80	QPR	29	1
1980–81		8	2

1981–82		24	2
1982–83		39	3
1983–84		6	—
1983–84	Leicester C	27	2
1984–85		14	—
1985–86		—	—
1985–86	*Wolverhampton W*	1	—

HEALEY, Jonathan

Born Oldham 30.12.66.　Ht 5 10　Wt 11 0
Forward.

1985–86	Oldham Ath	—	—

HEAP, Stuart

Born Barrowford 7.2.65.
Midfield.

1984–85	Tranmere R	3	—
1985–86		—	—

HEARD, Pat

Born Hull 17.3.60.　Ht 5 10　Wt 11 2
Midfield. From Apprentice. England Youth.

1977–78	Everton	—	—
1978–79		10	—
1979–80		1	—
1979–80	Aston Villa	9	—
1980–81		—	—
1981–82		8	2
1982–83		7	—
1982–83	Sheffield W	19	2
1983–84		5	1
1984–85		1	—
1984–85	Newcastle U	34	2
1985–86		—	—
1985–86	Middlesbrough	25	2
1985–86	*Hull C*	8	—

HEATH, Adrian

Born Stoke 11.1.61.　Ht 5 6　Wt 10 1
Midfield. From Apprentice.
England Under-21.

Season	Club	League Appearances/Goals		Season	Club	League Appearances/Goals	
1978–79	Stoke C	2	—	1981–82	Oxford U	15	2
1979–80		38	5	1982–83		39	10
1980–81		38	6	1983–84		46	11
1981–82		17	5	1984–85		42	6
1981–82	Everton	22	6	1985–86		41	3
1982–83		38	10				
1983–84		36	12				
1984–85		17	11				
1985–86		36	10				

HEATH, Philip

Born Stoke 24.11.64.   Ht 5 9   Wt 11 5
Forward. From Apprentice.

Season	Club	League Appearances/Goals	
1982–83	Stoke C	1	—
1983–84		4	1
1984–85		36	2
1985–86		38	5

HEATON, Paul

Born Hyde 24.1.61.   Ht 5 10   Wt 11 5
Midfield. From Apprentice.

Season	Club	League Appearances/Goals	
1977–78	Oldham Ath	3	1
1978–79		23	5
1979–80		21	3
1980–81		21	2
1981–82		39	12
1982–83		19	3
1983–84		10	2
1983–84	*Rochdale*	5	—
1984–85	Rochdale	41	5
1985–86		43	4

HEBBERD, Trevor

Born Winchester 19.6.58.   Ht 5 11½
Wt 11 4
Midfield. From Apprentice.

Season	Club	League Appearances/Goals	
1976–77	Southampton	12	2
1977–78		12	1
1978–79		22	2
1979–80		36	2
1980–81		11	—
1981–82		4	—
1981–82	*Bolton W*	6	—
1981–82	*Leicester C*	4	1

HEDMAN, Rudi

Born London 16.11.64.   Ht 6 3   Wt 12 1
Midfield. Local.

Season	Club	League Appearances/Goals	
1983–84	Colchester U	4	—
1984–85		30	2
1985–86		39	3

HEDWORTH, Chris

Born Newcastle 5.1.64.   Ht 6 1   Wt 10 11
Defender. From Apprentice.

Season	Club	League Appearances/Goals	
1981–82	Newcastle U	—	—
1982–83		4	—
1983–84		—	—
1984–85		1	—
1985–86		4	—

HEESOM, Darren

Born Warrington 8.5.68.   Ht 5 8   Wt 11 4
Defender. From Apprentice.

Season	Club	League Appearances/Goals	
1985–86	Burnley	25	1

HEFFERNAN, Tom

Born Dublin 30.4.55.   Ht 6 2   Wt 12 7
Defender. From Dunleary.

Season	Club	League Appearances/Goals	
1977–78	Tottenham H	—	—
1978–79		—	—
1979–80	Bournemouth	20	2
1980–81		46	2
1981–82		45	7
1982–83		43	10
1983–84	Sheffield U	42	2
1984–85		40	3
1985–86	Bournemouth	37	4

Season	Club	League Appearances/Goals	Season	Club	League Appearances/Goals

HEGARTY, Paul

Born Edinburgh 25.7.54. Ht 5 10 Wt 11 4
Defender. From Tynecastle B.C. Scotland 8
full caps.

Season	Club	App	Goals
1972–73	Hamilton A	36	7
1973–74	....	31	10
1974–75		12	5
1974–75	Dundee U	17	4
1975–76	....	33	8
1976–77	....	36	6
1977–78	....	36	4
1978–79	....	36	5
1979–80	....	27	—
1980–81	....	33	3
1981–82	....	36	2
1982–83	....	36	3
1983–84	....	36	4
1984–85	....	33	2
1985–86	....	36	5

HEGGARTY, Jim

Born Larne 4.8.65.
Defender.

Season	Club	App	Goals
1984–85	Brighton	—	—
1985–86	Burnley	36	1

HELLIN, Matthew

Born Merthyr Tydfil 12.9.66. Ht 5 11¾
Wt 11 7
Defender. From Apprentice.

Season	Club	App	Goals
1984–85	Aston Villa	—	—
1985–86	....	—	—

HEMMING, Chris

Born Newcastle 13.4.66. Ht 5 11 Wt 11 2
Defender. From school.

Season	Club	App	Goals
1983–84	Stoke C	3	—
1984–85	....	16	1
1985–86	....	24	—

HENCHER, Nick

Born Wrexham 24.8.61.
Midfield. From Juniors.

Season	Club	App	Goals
1978–79	Wrexham	—	—
	From Lex		
1985–86	Wrexham	25	4

HENDERSON, Mick

Born Gosforth 31.3.56. Ht 5 10 Wt 11 4
Defender. From Apprentice.

Season	Club	App	Goals
1973–74	Sunderland	—	—
1974–75	....	—	—
1975–76	....	13	1
1976–77	....	9	—
1977–78	....	32	1
1978–79	....	30	—
1979–80	....	—	—
1979–80	Watford	28	—
1980–81	....	19	—
1981–82	....	4	—
1981–82	Cardiff C	11	—
1982–83	Sheffield U	32	—
1983–84	....	22	—
1984–85	....	13	—
1984–85	Chesterfield	18	—
1985–86	....	43	5

HENDRIE, John

Born Lennoxtown 24.10.63. Ht 5 7
Wt 11 4
Forward. From Apprentice.

Season	Club	App	Goals
1981–82	Coventry C	6	—
1982–83	....	12	2
1983–84	....	3	—
1983–84	*Hereford U*	6	—
1984–85	Bradford C	46	9
1985–86	....	42	10

HENDRIE, Paul

Born Glasgow 27.3.54. Ht 5 6 Wt 10 3
Midfield. From Rob Roy. Scotland Schools.

Season	Club	League Appearances/Goals		Season	Club	League Appearances/Goals	
1971–72	Birmingham C	—	—	1974–75	Manchester C	—	—
1972–73		1	—	1975–76		—	—
1973–74		5	—	1976–77		2	—
1974–75		12	1	1977–78		1	—
1975–76		5	—	1978–79		15	—
From Portland Timbers				1979–80		32	4
1977–78	Bristol R	12	—	1980–81		27	2
1978–79		18	1	1981–82		2	—
1979–80	Halifax T	34	3	1981–82	Bolton W	39	13
1980–81		34	4	1982–83		31	9
1981–82		45	2	1982–83	Oldham Ath	11	1
1982–83		34	1	1983–84		42	4
1983–84		40	2	1984–85		40	3
1984–85	Stockport Co	42	4	1985–86		40	7
1985–86		36	1				

HENDRY, Colin

Born Keith 7.12.65.   Ht 6 2   Wt 12 4
Forward. From Islavale.

1983–84	Dundee	4	—
1984–85		4	—
1985–86		20	—

HENRY, Charlie

Born Acton 13.2.62.   Ht 5 11   Wt 12 8
Forward. From Apprentice.

1980–81	Swindon T	32	—
1981–82		42	3
1982–83		19	—
1983–84		29	—
1984–85		16	—
1985–86		38	18

HENRY, Gerry

Born Belshill 20.7.67.   Ht 5 7   Wt 10 8
Midfield. From Apprentice.

1985–86	Sunderland	—	—

HENRY, Tony

Born Newcastle 26.11.57.   Ht 5 11   Wt 12 0
Midfield. From Apprentice.

HENSHAW, Gary

Born Leeds 18.2.65.   Ht 5 9½   Wt 9 10
Midfield. From Apprentice.

1982–83	Grimsby T	—	—
1983–84		4	—
1984–85		7	1
1985–86		10	4

HERBERT, Ricki

Born Auckland 10.4.61.   Ht 6 0   Wt 12 4
Defender. New Zealand full caps.

1981–82	Southampton	—	—
From Sydney Olympic			
1984–85	Wolverhampton W	25	—
1985–86		20	—

HESFORD, Iain

Born Zambia 4.3.60.   Ht 6 2   Wt 14 6
Goalkeeper. From Apprentice. England
Youth, Under-21.

1977–78	Blackpool	14	—
1978–79		33	—
1979–80		30	—
1980–81		42	—
1981–82		39	—
1982–83		44	—

Season	Club	League Appearances/Goals		Season	Club	League Appearances/Goals	
1983–84	Sheffield W	—	—				
1984–85		—	—				
1984–85	*Fulham*	3	—				
1985–86	Sheffield W	—	—				
1985–86	*Notts Co*	10	—				

HETZKE, Steve

Born Marlborough 3.6.55. Ht 6 2   Wt 13 4
Defender. From Apprentice.

1971–72	Reading	4	—
1972–73		1	—
1973–74		22	1
1974–75		15	—
1975–76		17	1
1976–77		24	3
1977–78		16	—
1978–79		42	9
1979–80		43	2
1980–81		45	5
1981–82		32	2
1982–83	Blackpool	42	2
1983–84		45	7
1984–85		30	5
1985–86		23	4
1985–86	Sunderland	8	—

HEWITT, Jamie

Born Chesterfield 17.5.68.
Defender. From school.

1984–85	Chesterfield	—	—
1985–86		17	—

HEWITT, John

Born Aberdeen 9.2.63.   Ht 5 8   Wt 10 8
Forward. From Middlefield Wasps. Scotland
Schools, Youth, Under-21.

1979–80	Aberdeen	4	—
1980–81		21	2
1981–82		25	11
1982–83		16	4
1983–84		32	12
1984–85		21	3
1985–86		23	6

HEWITT, Martin

Born Hartlepool 24.7.65.
Midfield.

1985–86	Hartlepool U	1	—

HEYES, Darren

Born Swansea 11.1.67.   Ht 5 11   Wt 11 6
Goalkeeper. England Schools, Youth.

1984–85	Nottingham F	—	—
1985–86		—	—

HEYWOOD, David

Born Wolverhampton 25.7.67.
Defender. From Apprentice.

1984–85	Wolverhampton W	7	—
1985–86		—	—

HIBBITT, Kenny

Born Bradford 3.1.51.   Ht 5 10½   Wt 12 0
Midfield. From Apprentice.
England Under-23.

1967–68	Bradford PA	8	—
1968–69		7	—
1968–69	Wolverhampton W	1	—
1969–70		—	—
1970–71		31	2
1971–72		34	7
1972–73		31	6
1973–74		33	2
1974–75		41	17
1975–76		41	8
1976–77		41	16
1977–78		23	6
1978–79		37	6
1979–80		32	9
1980–81		33	3
1981–82		33	4
1982–83		31	2
1983–84		23	—
1984–85	Coventry C	33	3
1985–86		14	1

HICKS, Jim

Born Ipswich 16.9.60.
Defender. From Exeter Univ.

Season	Club	App	Goals
1983–84	Exeter C	3	—
1984–85	Oxford U	—	—
1985–86		—	—
1985–86	Fulham	10	—

HICKS, Keith

Born Oldham 9.8.54. Ht 6 0   Wt 13 2
Defender. From Apprentice. England
Youth.

Season	Club	App	Goals
1971–72	Oldham Ath	3	—
1972–73		46	1
1973–74		44	2
1974–75		32	—
1975–76		29	3
1976–77		24	1
1977–78		25	—
1978–79		34	4
1979–80		5	—
1980–81	Hereford U	39	1
1981–82		42	—
1982–83		39	—
1983–84		43	—
1984–85		38	1
1985–86	Rochdale	31	1

HICKS, Martin

Born Stratford-on-Avon 27.2.57.   Ht 6 3
Wt 13 6
Defender. From Stratford T.

Season	Club	App	Goals
1976–77	Charlton Ath	—	—
1977–78		—	—
1977–78	Reading	19	1
1978–79		46	1
1979–80		1	1
1980–81		27	2
1981–82		44	3
1982–83		32	1
1983–84		46	1
1984–85		40	2
1985–86		34	2

HIGGINBOTTOM, Andy

Born Chesterfield 22.10.64.   Ht 5 10
Wt 11 0
Midfield. From Apprentice.

Season	Club	App	Goals
1982–83	Chesterfield	3	—
1983–84	Everton	—	—
1984–85	Cambridge U	1	—
1985–86	C Palace	16	2

HIGGINS, Mark

Born Buxton 29.9.58.   Ht 6 1   Wt 13 5
Defender. From Apprentice. England
Schools, Youth.

Season	Club	App	Goals
1976–77	Everton	2	—
1977–78		26	1
1978–79		21	1
1979–80		19	—
1980–81		2	—
1981–82		29	3
1982–83		39	1
1983–84		14	—
Retired			
1985–86	Manchester U	6	—

HILAIRE, Vince

Born Forest Hill 10.10.59.   Ht 5 6   Wt 10 0
Forward. From Apprentice. England Youth,
Under-21, 'B'.

Season	Club	App	Goals
1976–77	Crystal Palace	3	—
1977–78		30	2
1978–79		31	6
1979–80		42	5
1980–81		31	4
1981–82		36	5
1982–83		42	5
1983–84		40	2
1984–85	Luton T	6	—
1984–85	Portsmouth	26	7
1985–86		41	8

HILDERSLEY, Ron

Born Fife 6.4.65.   Ht 5 4   Wt 9 2
Forward. From Apprentice.

Season	Club	League Appearances/Goals		Season	Club	League Appearances/Goals	
1982–83	Manchester C	1	—	1981–82	Arsenal	—	—
1983–84		—	—	1982–83		7	—
1983–84	*Chester*	9	—	1983–84		37	1
1984–85	Chester C	9	—	1984–85		2	—
1985–86	Rochdale	16	—	1985–86		—	—
				1985–86	*Brighton*	—	—

HILDITCH, Mark

Born Royton 20.8.60.   Ht 5 11   Wt 11 8
Forward. From Amateur.

1977–78	Rochdale	3	1
1978–79		27	3
1979–80		44	3
1980–81		44	12
1981–82		40	14
1982–83		39	7
1983–84	Tranmere R	39	8
1984–85		3	1
1985–86		7	3

HILL, Andy

Born Derbyshire 10.11.60.   Ht 6 1   Wt 11 8
Forward. From Kimberley.

1981–82	Derby Co	6	2
1982–83		15	—
1983–84		1	—
1983–84	Carlisle U	26	3
1984–85		29	4
1985–86		30	8

HILL, Andy

Born Maltby 20.1.65.   Ht 5 11   Wt 12 0
Defender. From Apprentice. England
Youth.

1982–83	Manchester U	—	—
1983–84		—	—
1984–85	Bury	43	3
1985–86		35	2

HILL, Colin

Born Hillingdon 12.11.63.   Ht 5 11
Wt 12 2
Defender. From Apprentice.

HILL, David

Born Nottingham 6.6.66.   Ht 5 9   Wt 10 3
Midfield. Local.

1983–84	Scunthorpe U	2	—
1984–85		29	2
1985–86		42	2

HILL, Jamie

Born Leamington 27.1.67.   Ht 5 9½
Wt 12 10
Midfield. From school.

1985–86	Charlton Ath	—	—

HILL, Ricky

Born London 5.3.59.   Ht 5 11   Wt 13 0
Midfield. From Apprentice.
England Youth, 3 full caps.

1975–76	Luton T	2	1
1976–77		11	4
1977–78		40	5
1978–79		38	3
1979–80		40	6
1980–81		42	7
1981–82		38	5
1982–83		42	9
1983–84		26	2
1984–85		39	2
1985–86		38	3

HILL, Ricky

Born Hinckley 20.9.63.   Ht 6 0   Wt 12 1
Forward.

1981–82	Leicester C	—	—
From Grankulla, Nuneaton			
1985–86	Northampton T	41	17

Season	Club	League Appearances/Goals	Season	Club	League Appearances/Goals

HILLYARD, Ron

Born Rotherham 31.3.53.   Ht 5 11   Wt 11 4
Goalkeeper. From Amateur.

1969–70	York C	3 —
1970–71		34 —
1971–72		17 —
1971–72	*Hartlepool U*	23 —
1972–73	York C	4 —
1973–74		3 —
1973–74	*Bury*	— —
1973–74	*Brighton*	— —
1974–75	Gillingham	46 —
1975–76		44 —
1976–77		25 —
1977–78		44 —
1978–79		46 —
1979–80		46 —
1980–81		37 —
1981–82		44 —
1982–83		42 —
1983–84		8 —
1984–85		25 —
1985–86		46 —

HILTON, Paul

Born Oldham 8.10.59.   Ht 6 1   Wt 11 6
Defender. From Amateur. England Schools.

1978–79	Bury	9 1
1979–80		28 5
1980–81		32 13
1981–82		41 7
1982–83		19 7
1983–84		19 6
1983–84	West Ham U	8 2
1984–85		9 1
1985–86		2 —

HINDMARCH, Rob

Born Stannington 27.4.61.   Ht 6 1½
Wt 13 4½
Defender. From Apprentice.
England Youth.

1977–78	Sunderland	2 —
1978–79		— —
1979–80		21 —
1980–81		29 —
1981–82		36 2
1982–83		14 —
1983–84		13 —
1983–84	*Portsmouth*	2 —
1984–85	Derby Co	22 1
1985–86		39 6

HINE, Mark

Born Middlesbrough 18.5.64.   Ht 5 8
Wt 9 11
Midfield. Local.

1983–84	Grimsby T	— —
1984–85		9 —
1985–86		13 1

HINNIGAN, Joe

Born Liverpool 3.12.55.   Ht 6 0¼   Wt 12 0
Defender. From South Liverpool.

1978–79	Wigan Ath	39 5
1979–80		27 5
1979–80	Sunderland	14 —
1980–81		16 4
1981–82		30 1
1982–83		3 —
1982–83	Preston NE	13 3
1983–84		39 5
1984–85	Gillingham	37 5
1985–86		39 2

HINSHELWOOD, Paul

Born Bristol 14.8.56.   Ht 6 0   Wt 12 6
Defender. From Apprentice.
England Under-21.

1973–74	Crystal Palace	4 1
1974–75		11 3
1975–76		5 —
1976–77		43 4
1977–78		40 2

Season	Club	League Appearances/Goals		Season	Club	League Appearances/Goals	

1978–79	....	31	1
1979–80	....	42	2
1980–81	....	38	1
1981–82	....	27	2
1982–83	....	35	7
1983–84	Oxford........................	43	—
1984–85	....	2	—
1984–85	Millwall......................	21	—
1985–86	....	36	2

HIRD, Kevin

Born Colne 11.2.55.   Ht 5 7   Wt 10 6
Defender. From Apprentice.

1972–73	Blackburn R................	—	—
1973–74	....	6	—
1974–75	....	2	—
1975–76	....	21	6
1976–77	....	39	1
1977–78	....	42	7
1978–79	....	22	6
1978–79	Leeds U......................	14	—
1979–80	....	39	8
1980–81	....	33	4
1981–82	....	38	2
1982–83	....	39	4
1983–84	....	18	1
1984–85	Burnley......................	44	16
1985–86	....	39	7

HIRST, David

Born Barnsley 7.12.67.
Forward. From Apprentice. England Youth.

| 1985–86 | Barnsley..................... | 28 | 9 |

HIRST, Martyn

Born Batley 26.10.61.   Ht 5 9   Wt 11 7
Midfield. From Bath C. England Schools.

1983–84	Bristol C.....................	24	1
1984–85	....	16	—
1985–86	....	1	—
1985–86	*Torquay U*	4	—

HITCHCOCK, Kevin

Born Custom House 5.10.62.   Ht 6 0
Wt 12 10
Goalkeeper. From Barking.

1983–84	Nottingham F	—	—
1983–84	*Mansfield T*	14	—
1984–85	Mansfield T	43	—
1985–86	....	46	—

HOBSON, Gordon

Born Sheffield 27.11.57.   Ht 5 9   Wt 10 7
Forward. From Sheffield RGRS.

1977–78	Lincoln C....................	5	2
1978–79	....	33	6
1979–80	....	43	10
1980–81	....	44	21
1981–82	....	32	7
1982–83	....	41	14
1983–84	....	36	6
1984–85	....	38	7
1985–86	Grimsby T...................	41	15

HOCKADAY, David

Born Billingham 9.11.57.   Ht 5 10   Wt 10 9
Forward. From Amateur.

1975–76	Blackpool	—	—
1976–77	....	5	—
1977–78	....	—	—
1978–79	....	18	4
1979–80	....	7	1
1980–81	....	36	4
1981–82	....	41	7
1982–83	....	40	8
1983–84	Swindon T...................	36	3
1984–85	....	22	1
1985–86	....	37	1

HODDLE, Glenn

Born Hayes 27.10.57.   Ht 6 0   Wt 11 6
Midfield. From Apprentice.
England Youth, Under-21 'B', 33 full caps.

All appearances include those as substitute

Season	Club	League Appearances/Goals	Season	Club	League Appearances/Goals
1974–75	Tottenham H	— —	1984–85		42 12
1975–76		7 1	1985–86		2 —
1976–77		39 4	1985–86	Aston Villa	36 8
1977–78		41 12			
1978–79		35 7			
1979–80		41 19			
1980–81		38 12			
1981–82		34 10			
1982–83		24 1			
1983–84		24 4			
1984–85		28 8			
1985–86		31 7			

HODDY, Kevin

Born Essex 6.1.68.   Ht 5 10¼   Wt 11 1
Midfield. From Apprentice.

Season	Club	League Appearances/Goals
1985–86	Fulham	— —

HODGE, Martin

Born Southport 4.2.59.   Ht 6 0   Wt 13 2
Goalkeeper. From Apprentice.

Season	Club	League Appearances/Goals
1976–77	Plymouth Arg	— —
1977–78		5 —
1978–79		38 —
1979–80	Everton	23 —
1980–81		2 —
1981–82	*Preston NE*	28 —
1982–83	*Oldham Ath*	4 —
1982–83	*Gillingham*	4 —
1982–83	*Preston NE*	16 —
1983–84	Sheffield W	42 —
1984–85		42 —
1985–86		42 —

HODGE, Stephen

Born Nottingham 25.10.62.   Ht 5 8   Wt 9 11
Midfield. From Apprentice.
England Under-21, 3 full caps.

Season	Club	League Appearances/Goals
1980–81	Nottingham F	— —
1981–82		1 —
1982–83		39 8
1983–84		39 10

HODGES, Glyn

Born Streatham 30.4.63.   Ht 6 0   Wt 12 3
Forward. From Apprentice. Wales Under-21, 2 full caps.

Season	Club	League Appearances/Goals
1980–81	Wimbledon	30 5
1981–82		34 2
1982–83		37 9
1983–84		42 15
1984–85		22 3
1985–86		30 6

HODGES, Kevin

Born Bridport 12.6.60.   Ht 5 8   Wt 10 0
Midfield. From Apprentice.

Season	Club	League Appearances/Goals
1977–78	Plymouth Arg	— —
1978–79		12 —
1979–80		44 5
1980–81		41 5
1981–82		46 11
1982–83		46 11
1983–84		43 4
1984–85		45 10
1985–86		46 16

HODGSON, Dave

Born Gateshead 1.11.60.   Ht 5 9   Wt 12 2
Forward. From Amateur.
England Under-21.

Season	Club	League Appearances/Goals
1978–79	Middlesbrough	19 1
1979–80		40 7
1980–81		32 5
1981–82		34 3
1982–83	Liverpool	23 4
1983–84		5 —
1984–85	Sunderland	25 4
1985–86		15 1

Season	Club	League Appearances/Goals	Season	Club	League Appearances/Goals

HODKINSON, Andrew

Born Ashton 4.11.65. Ht 5 6   Wt 10 10
Midfield. From Bolton W. Apprentice.
England Schools.

Season	Club	App	Goals
1983–84	Oldham Ath	4	1
1984–85		1	—
1985–86	Stockport Co	41	6

HODSON, Simeon

Born Lincoln 5.3.66. Ht 5 9   Wt 10 2
Defender. From Apprentice.

Season	Club	App	Goals
1983–84	Notts Co	13	—
1984–85		14	—
1984–85	Charlton Ath	5	—
1985–86		—	—
1985–86	Lincoln C	15	—

HOGAN, Roy

Born Hartlepool 24.9.60. Ht 5 8   Wt 10 6
Midfield. From Apprentice.

Season	Club	App	Goals
1977–78	Hartlepool U	3	—
1978–79		23	1
1979–80		8	—
1980–81		43	7
1981–82		39	4
1982–83		27	3
From Consett			
1983–84	Hartlepool U	27	2
1984–85		38	3
1985–86		38	8

HOGG, Graeme

Born Aberdeen 17.6.64. Ht 6 1   Wt 12 12
Defender. From Apprentice. Scotland
Under-21.

Season	Club	App	Goals
1982–83	Manchester U	—	—
1983–84		16	1
1984–85		29	—
1985–86		17	—

HOLDEN, Andrew

Born Flint 14.9.62. Ht 6 2   Wt 13 0
Defender. From Rhyl. Wales Under-21,
1 full cap.

Season	Club	App	Goals
1983–84	Chester	44	7
1984–85		38	6
1985–86		10	2

HOLDEN, Richard

Born Skipton 9.9.64.
Midfield.

Season	Club	App	Goals
1985–86	Burnley	1	—

HOLLAND, Robert

Born Willesden 18.8.65.
Defender. From Wimbledon.

Season	Club	App	Goals
1985–86	Crewe Alex	7	—

HOLLIFIELD, Mike

Born Middlesbrough 2.5.61. Ht 5 11   Wt 11 3
Midfield. From Apprentice.

Season	Club	App	Goals
1978–79	Wolverhampton W	—	—
1979–80		—	—
1980–81		16	—
1981–82		5	—
1982–83		—	—
1983–84	Hull C	33	1
1984–85		12	—
1985–86	Tranmere R	1	—

HOLLOWAY, Ian

Born Kingswood 12.3.63. Ht 5 7   Wt 9 12
Midfield. From Apprentice.

Season	Club	App	Goals
1980–81	Bristol R	1	—
1981–82		1	—
1982–83		31	7
1983–84		36	1
1984–85		42	6
1985–86	Wimbledon	19	2
1985–86	*Brentford*	13	2

All appearances include those as substitute

Season	Club	League Appearances/Goals		Season	Club	League Appearances/Goals

HOLMES, Jimmy

Born Dublin 11.11.53.   Ht 5 11   Wt 11 0
Defender. From Apprentice. Eire. 30 full
caps.

Season	Club	App	Goals
1970–71	Coventry C	—	—
1971–72		3	—
1972–73		1	—
1973–74		41	1
1974–75		22	6
1975–76		35	—
1976–77		26	—
1976–77	Tottenham H	10	1
1977–78		38	—
1978–79		33	1
1979–80		—	—
1980–81		—	—
From Vancouver W			
1982–83	Leicester C	2	—
1982–83	Brentford	4	—
1982–83	Torquay U	10	—
1983–84		15	3
1983–84	Peterborough U	21	2
1984–85		13	1
1985–86		15	4

HOLMES, Micky

Born Blackpool 9.9.65.   Ht 5 6   Wt 10 3
Midfield.

Season	Club	App	Goals
1984–85	Bradford C	5	—
1985–86	Burnley	—	—
1985–86	Wolverhampton W	26	3

HOLMES, Nick

Born Southampton 11.11.54.   Ht 5 11
Wt 12 1
Midfield. From Apprentice.

Season	Club	App	Goals
1972–73	Southampton	—	—
1973–74		2	—
1974–75		24	2
1975–76		39	11
1976–77		38	8
1977–78		39	6
1978–79		38	8

Season	Club	App	Goals
1979–80		41	5
1980–81		41	5
1981–82		40	—
1982–83		36	5
1983–84		42	3
1984–85		29	1
1985–86		26	—

HOLMES, Paul

Born Wortley 18.2.68.   Ht 5 10   Wt 11 0
Defender. From Apprentice.

Season	Club	App	Goals
1985–86	Doncaster R	5	1

HOLT, John

Born Dundee 21.11.56.   Ht 5 9   Wt 11 10
Midfield. 'S' Form. Scotland Youth.

Season	Club	App	Goals
1973–74	Dundee U	3	—
1974–75		—	—
1975–76		16	—
1976–77		8	—
1977–78		15	3
1978–79		27	3
1979–80		17	4
1980–81		24	—
1981–82		28	1
1982–83		26	4
1983–84		32	2
1984–85		25	—
1985–86		27	—

HONE, Mark

Born Croydon 31.3.68.
Defender.

Season	Club	App	Goals
1985–86	Crystal Palace	—	—

HONOR, Chris

Born Bristol 5.6.68.
Defender. From Apprentice.

Season	Club	App	Goals
1985–86	Bristol C	1	—

Season	Club	League Appearances/Goals		Season	Club	League Appearances/Goals	

HONOUR, Brian

Born Horden 16.2.64. Ht 5 7 Wt 12 5
Midfield. From Apprentice.

Season	Club	App	Goals
1981–82	Darlington	1	—
1982–83		32	3
1983–84		41	1
From Peterlee			
1984–85	Hartlepool U	17	—
1985–86		46	8

HOOD, Derek

Born Washington 17.12.58. Ht 5 11
Wt 12 8
Midfield. From Apprentice.

Season	Club	App	Goals
1976–77	WBA	—	—
1977–78	Hull	4	—
1978–79		17	—
1979–80		3	—
1979–80	York C	16	1
1980–81		42	—
1981–82		46	8
1982–83		46	7
1983–84		34	4
1984–85		30	4
1985–86		31	1

HOOKS, Paul

Born Wallsend 30.5.59. Ht 5 7 Wt 10 8
Forward. From Apprentice.

Season	Club	App	Goals
1976–77	Notts Co	1	—
1977–78		19	4
1978–79		38	10
1979–80		34	5
1980–81		36	5
1981–82		28	3
1982–83		17	3
1982–83	Derby Co	8	2
1983–84		17	1
1984–85		23	1
1985–86	Mansfield T	—	—

HOOLICKIN, Gary

Born Middleton 29.10.57. Ht 5 11 Wt 11 1
Defender. From Apprentice.

Season	Club	App	Goals
1975–76	Oldham Ath	—	—
1976–77		1	—
1977–78		17	—
1978–79		1	1
1979–80		4	—
1980–81		14	—
1981–82		28	—
1982–83		31	—
1983–84		34	1
1984–85		31	—
1985–86		32	—

HOOPER, Michael

Born Bristol 10.2.64. Ht 6 1 Wt 13 0
Goalkeeper.

Season	Club	App	Goals
1983–84	Bristol C	—	—
1984–85		1	—
1984–85	*Wrexham*	20	—
1985–86	Wrexham	14	—
1985–86	Liverpool	—	—

HOPKINS, Jeff

Born Swansea 14.4.64. Ht 6 1 Wt 11 11
Defender. From Apprentice.
Wales Under-21, 14 full caps.

Season	Club	App	Goals
1980–81	Fulham	1	—
1981–82		35	—
1982–83		41	1
1983–84		33	—
1984–85		40	2
1985–86		23	—

HOPKINS, Robert

Born Birmingham 25.10.61. Ht 5 7 Wt 10 5
Midfield. From Apprentice.

Season	Club	App	Goals
1979–80	Aston Villa	2	1
1980–81		—	—
1981–82		—	—
1982–83		1	—
1982–83	Birmingham C	11	2
1983–84		32	5
1984–85		39	9
1985–86		38	4

Season	Club	League Appearances/Goals	Season	Club	League Appearances/Goals

HORNE, Barry

Born St. Asaph 18.5.62.   Ht 5 9   Wt 11 4
Midfield. From Rhyl.

Season	Club	App	Goals
1984–85	Wrexham	44	6
1985–86		46	3

HORNE, Brian

Born Billericay 5.10.67.   Ht 5 10½   Wt 12 4
Goalkeeper. From Apprentice. England
Youth.

Season	Club	App	Goals
1985–86	Millwall	—	—

HORNER, Philip

Born Leeds 10.11.66.   Ht 6 1½   Wt 12 7
Forward. From Lincoln C. Schoolboy.

Season	Club	App	Goals
1984–85	Leicester C	—	—
1985–86		—	—
1985–86	*Rotherham U*	4	—

HORNBY, Steven

Born Blackpool 2.1.68.
Forward. From Apprentice.

Season	Club	App	Goals
1985–86	Blackpool	—	—

HORRIX, Dean

Born Taplow 21.11.61.   Ht 5 10   Wt 10 10
Forward. From Apprentice.

Season	Club	App	Goals
1978–79	Millwall	—	—
1979–80		—	—
1980–81		13	4
1981–82		44	15
1982–83		15	—
1982–83	Gillingham	14	—
1983–84	Reading	43	8
1984–85		43	19
1985–86		41	6

HORTON, Brian

Born Hednesford 4.2.49.   Ht 5 10   Wt 11 4
Midfield. From Hednesford T.

Season	Club	App	Goals
1970–71	Port Vale	39	1
1971–72		42	5
1972–73		39	6
1973–74		41	4
1974–75		44	13
1975–76		31	4
1975–76	Brighton	11	—
1976–77		45	9
1977–78		42	8
1978–79		40	11
1979–80		42	4
1980–81		38	1
1981–82	Luton T	41	1
1982–83		40	4
1983–84		37	3
1984–85	Hull C	22	—
1985–86		10	—

HOSKIN, Ashley

Born Accrington 27.3.68.   Ht 5 2   Wt 8 5
Midfield. From Apprentice.

Season	Club	App	Goals
1985–86	Burnley	19	2

HOSKIN, Mick

Born Chesterfield 3.11.66.   Ht 5 8   Wt 10 6
Midfield. Local.

Season	Club	App	Goals
1983–84	Chesterfield	1	—
1984–85		1	—
1985–86		—	—

HOTTE, Tim

Born Bradford 4.10.63.
Forward. From Arsenal Apprentice.

Season	Club	App	Goals
1981–82	Huddersfield T	14	4
1982–83		2	—
From Finland			
1985–86	Halifax T	4	—

Season	Club	League Appearances/Goals	Season	Club	League Appearances/Goals

HOUCHEN, Keith

Born Middlesbrough 25.7.60.   Ht 6 2
Wt 12 8
Forward. From Chesterfield Amateur.

Season	Club	Apps	Goals
1977–78	Hartlepool U	13	4
1978–79		39	12
1979–80		41	14
1980–81		45	17
1981–82		32	18
1981–82	Orient	14	1
1982–83		32	10
1983–84		30	9
1983–84	York C	7	1
1984–85		35	12
1985–86		25	6
1985–86	Scunthorpe U	9	2

HOUGH, David

Born Crewe 20.2.66.   Ht 5 10½   Wt 11 2
Midfield. From Apprentice. Wales Youth.

Season	Club	Apps	Goals
1983–84	Swansea C	2	—
1984–85		25	2
1985–86		31	3

HOUGHTON, Peter

Born Liverpool 30.11.54.   Ht 5 11   Wt 12 7
Forward. From South Liverpool.

Season	Club	Apps	Goals
1978–79	Wigan Ath	26	13
1979–80		41	15
1980–81		32	6
1981–82		46	15
1982–83		34	12
1983–84		6	1
1983–84	Preston NE	32	10
1984–85		24	6
1984–85	*Wrexham*	5	2
1985–86	Chester	37	10

HOUGHTON, Ray

Born Glasgow 9.1.62.   Ht 5 7   Wt 10 10
Midfield. Amateur. Eire 2 caps.

Season	Club	Apps	Goals
1979–80	West Ham U	—	—
1980–81		—	—
1981–82		1	—
1982–83	Fulham	42	5
1983–84		40	3
1984–85		42	8
1985–86		5	—
1985–86	Oxford U	35	4

HOUSTON, Graham

Born Gibraltar 24.2.60.   Ht 5 8   Wt 11 4
Forward. From Amateur.

Season	Club	Apps	Goals
1977–78	Preston NE	—	—
1978–79		—	—
1979–80		1	—
1980–81		17	1
1981–82		18	—
1982–83		20	2
1983–84		41	3
1984–85		31	5
1985–86		—	—
1985–86	Burnley	—	—
1985–86	Preston NE	—	—

HOUSTON, Stewart

Born Dunoon 20.8.49.   Ht 5 11   Wt 12 3
Defender. From Port Glasgow.
Scotland Under-23, 1 full cap.

Season	Club	Apps	Goals
1967–68	Chelsea	1	—
1968–69		2	—
1969–70		6	—
1970–71		—	—
1971–72		—	—
1971–72	Brentford	15	2
1972–73		39	6
1973–74		23	1
1973–74	Manchester U	20	2
1974–75		40	6
1975–76		42	2
1976–77		36	3
1977–78		31	—
1978–79		22	—
1979–80		14	—
1980–81	Sheffield U	32	—
1981–82		27	—

Season	Club	League Appearances/Goals		Season	Club	League Appearances/Goals	
1982–83	....	35	1				
1983–84	Colchester U	42	4				
1984–85	....	29	1				
1985–86	....	36	—				

HUBBICK, Dave

Born South Shields 16.3.60. Ht 5 7½
Wt 10 10
Forward. From Apprentice.

HOWARD, Terence

Born Stepney 26.2.66. Ht 6 1 Wt 11 7
Defender. From Apprentice. England Youth.

1983–84	Chelsea	—	—
1984–85	....	4	—
1985–86	....	1	—
1985–86	*C Palace*	4	—

HOWELL, Peter

Born Birmingham 5.6.67. Ht 5 9 Wt 11 2½
Forward. From Apprentice.

| 1985–86 | Aston Villa.................. | — | — |

HOWELLS, David

Born Guildford 15.12.67. Ht 5 11 Wt 11 1
Forward. From YTS. England Youth.

| 1984–85 | Tottenham H .... | — | — |
| 1985–86 | .... | 1 | 1 |

HOWLETT, Gary

Born Dublin 2.4.63. Ht 5 8 Wt 10 4
Midfield. From Home Farm. Eire Youth, 1
full cap.

1980–81	Coventry C..................	—	—
1981–82	....	—	—
1982–83	Brighton......................	9	1
1983–84	....	17	—
1984–85	....	6	1
1984–85	Bournemouth	17	2
1985–86	....	20	2

HOYLAND, Jamie

Born Sheffield 23.1.66. Ht 6 0 Wt 12 8½
Forward. From Apprentice. England Youth.

1983–84	Manchester C	1	—
1984–85	....	1	—
1985–86	....	—	—

HUBBICK, Dave

Born South Shields 16.3.60. Ht 5 7½
Wt 10 10
Forward. From Apprentice.

1977–78	Ipswich T	—	—
1978–79	....	—	—
1979–80	....	—	—
1980–81	....	—	—
1980–81	Wimbledon	22	4
1981–82	....	4	2
From Dagenham			
1983–84	Colchester U	10	—
1984–85	....	5	1
1985–86	....	—	—

HUCKER, Peter

Born London 28.10.59. Ht 6 2 Wt 12 12
Goalkeeper. From Apprentice. England
Under-21.

1977–78	QPR............................	—	—
1977–78	*Cambridge U*	—	—
1978–79	QPR............................	—	—
1979–80	....	—	—
1980–81	....	1	—
1981–82	....	22	—
1982–83	....	42	—
1983–84	....	42	—
1984–85	....	42	—
1985–86	....	11	—

HUDSON, Alan

Born Chelsea 21.6.51. Ht 5 10 Wt 11 12
Midfield. From Apprentice. England Under-
23, 2 full caps.

1968–69	Chelsea	1	—
1969–70	....	29	3
1970–71	....	34	3
1971–72	....	36	2
1972–73	....	26	—
1973–74	....	19	2
1973–74	Stoke C	18	3
1974–75	....	42	4
1975–76	....	34	—
1976–77	....	11	—

Season	Club	League Appearances/Goals		Season	Club	League Appearances/Goals	
1976–77	Arsenal	19	—				
1977–78		17	—				

From Seattle S

Season	Club	League Appearances/Goals	
1983–84	Chelsea	—	—
1983–84	*Stoke C*	16	—
1984–85	Stoke C	17	—
1985–86		6	—

HUDSON, John

Born Middleton 25.11.64.   Ht 5 9   Wt 11 1
Midfield. From Manchester C.

1982–83	Oldham Ath	7	—
1983–84		13	—
1984–85		—	—
1985–86		—	—

HUGHES, Darren

Born Prescot 6.10.65.   Ht 5 11   Wt 10 11½
Defender. From Apprentice.

1983–84	Everton	1	—
1984–85		2	—
1985–86	Shrewsbury T	31	1

HUGHES, Ken

Born Barmouth 9.1.66.
Goalkeeper.

1985–86	Crystal Palace	—	—

HUGHES, Mark

Born Port Talbot 3.2.62.   Ht 5 11   Wt 11 8
Defender. From Apprentice. Wales Youth.

1979–80	Bristol R	1	—
1980–81		38	1
1981–82		22	2
1982–83		4	—
1982–83	*Torquay U*	9	1
1983–84	Bristol R	9	—
1984–85	Swansea C	12	—
1984–85	Bristol C	20	—
1985–86		2	—
1985–86	Tranmere R	32	—

HUGHES, Mark

Born Wrexham 1.11.63.   Ht 5 9   Wt 11 12
Forward. From Apprentice.
Wales Under-21, 12 full caps.

1980–81	Manchester U	—	—
1981–82		—	—
1982–83		—	—
1983–84		11	4
1984–85		38	16
1985–86		40	17

HUGHES, Mark

Born Swindon 17.7.67.   Ht 5 9   Wt 11 0
Midfield. From Apprentice.

1983–84	Swindon T	1	—
1984–85		—	—
1985–86		—	—

HUGHES, Martin

Born Glasgow 20.1.62.   Ht 5 9   Wt 10 0
Midfield. From Clydebank B.C.

1980–81	Clydebank	—	—
1981–82		16	1
1982–83		39	4
1983–84		39	3
1984–85		38	8
1985–86		27	2

HUGHES, Mike

Born Bridgend 19.8.64.   Ht 5 10½   Wt 11 3
Goalkeeper. From Apprentice.
Wales Youth.

1982–83	Swansea C	—	—
1983–84		21	—
1984–85		13	—
1985–86		27	—

HUGHES, Philip

Born Manchester 19.11.64.   Ht 5 11   Wt 12 7
Goalkeeper. From Manchester U.
Apprentice. Northern Ireland Youth.

Season	Club	League Appearances/Goals	Season	Club	League Appearances/Goals

1982–83	Leeds U	— —
1983–84		2 —
1984–85		4 —
1985–86	Bury	41 —

HUGHTON, Chris

Born West Ham 11.12.58.   Ht 5 7¼   Wt 11 5
Defender. From Amateur.
Eire Under-21, 29 full caps.

1977–78	Tottenham H	— —
1978–79		— —
1979–80		39 1
1980–81		34 1
1981–82		37 2
1982–83		38 3
1983–84		34 3
1984–85		31 1
1985–86		33 1

HUGHTON, Henry

Born Stratford 18.11.59.   Ht 5 8½   Wt 11 10
Midfield. From Apprentice.

1976–77	Orient	— —
1977–78		— —
1978–79		33 2
1979–80		40 —
1980–81		11 —
1981–82		27 —
1982–83	Crystal Palace	40 1
1983–84		35 —
1984–85		32 —
1985–86		11 —

HULL, Jeff

Born Rochford 25.8.60.   Ht 5 6   Wt 9 11
Midfield. From Apprentice.

1978–79	Southend U	1 —
1979–80		9 —
1980–81		5 1
From Basildon U
1982–83	Colchester U	27 4
1983–84		33 1
1984–85		18 5
1985–86		5 —

HUMES, Anthony

Born Blyth 19.3.66.   Ht 5 11   Wt 10 10
Defender. From Apprentice.

1983–84	Ipswich T	— —
1984–85		— —
1985–86		— —

HUMPHREY, John

Born Paddington 31.1.61   Ht 5 10   Wt 11 1
Defender. From Apprentice.

1978–79	Wolverhampton W	— —
1979–80		2 —
1980–81		12 —
1981–82		23 —
1982–83		42 3
1983–84		28 —
1984–85		42 —
1985–86	Charlton Ath	39 2

HUMPHRIES, Glenn

Born Hull 11.8.64.   Ht 6 0   Wt 12 0
Midfield. From Apprentice. England Youth.

1980–81	Doncaster R	1 —
1981–82		14 —
1982–83		40 5
1983–84		44 2
1984–85		27 —
1985–86		29 —

HUNT, David

Born Leicester 17.4.59.   Ht 5 11   Wt 11 0
Midfield. From Apprentice.

1977–78	Derby Co	5 —
1977–78	Notts Co	12 —
1978–79		37 2
1979–80		38 4
1980–81		42 3
1981–82		30 3
1982–83		37 1
1983–84		39 2
1984–85		37 3
1985–86		34 8

Season	Club	League Appearances/Goals		Season	Club	League Appearances/Goals	

HUNT, Robert

Born Newcastle 20.9.66.
Goalkeeper. From Barnsley Amateur.

Season	Club	App	Goals
1984–85	Halifax T	3	—
1985–86		—	—

HUNT, Steve

Born Birmingham 4.8.56.   Ht 5 9   Wt 11 4
Forward. From Apprentice. England 2 full caps.

Season	Club	App	Goals
1973–74	Aston Villa	—	—
1974–75		2	—
1975–76		4	1
1976–77		1	—
From New York Cosmos			
1978–79	Coventry C	24	5
1979–80		35	1
1980–81		40	6
1981–82		36	9
1982–83		35	4
1983–84		15	1
1983–84	WBA	12	2
1984–85		37	9
1985–86		19	4
1985–86	Aston Villa	12	2

HUNTER, Geoff

Born Hull 27.10.59.   Ht 5 10   Wt 10 12
Defender. From Apprentice.

Season	Club	App	Goals
1976–77	Manchester U	—	—
1977–78		—	—
1978–79		—	—
1979–80	Crewe Alex	41	4
1980–81		46	4
1981–82	Port Vale	41	3
1982–83		46	4
1983–84		42	1
1984–85		42	2
1985–86		45	5

HUNTER, Gordon

Born Wallyford 3.5.67.   Ht 5 10   Wt 10 5
Midfield. From Musselburgh Windsor.
Scotland Youth.

Season	Club	App	Goals
1983–84	Hibernian	1	—
1984–85		6	—
1985–86		25	—

HUNTER, Les

Born Middlesbrough 15.1.58.   Ht 6 2
Wt 12 5
Defender. From Apprentice.

Season	Club	App	Goals
1975–76	Chesterfield	45	2
1976–77		16	—
1977–78		17	2
1978–79		40	—
1979–80		22	1
1980–81		13	2
1981–82		12	1
1982–83	Scunthorpe U	46	8
1983–84		15	—
1983–84	Chesterfield	21	2
1984–85		46	3
1985–86		32	4
1985–86	·Scunthorpe U	12	1

HUNTLEY, John

Born Great Lumley 5.11.67.
Defender.

Season	Club	App	Goals
1985–86	Darlington	6	—

HURLOCK, Terry

Born Hackney 22.9.58.   Ht 5 9   Wt 13 2
Midfield. From Leytonstone and Ilford.

Season	Club	App	Goals
1980–81	Brentford	42	4
1981–82		40	2
1982–83		39	3
1983–84		32	4
1984–85		40	3
1985–86		27	2
1985–86	Reading	16	—

Season	Club	League Appearances/Goals	Season	Club	League Appearances/Goals

HURST, Graham

Born Oldham 23.11.67.   Ht 5 7
Midfield. From YTS.

Season	Club	App	Goals
1984–85	Rochdale	1	—
1985–86		—	—

HUTCHINGS, Chris

Born Winchester 5.7.57.   Ht 5 10   Wt 11 0
Defender. From Harrow Bor.

Season	Club	App	Goals
1980–81	Chelsea	12	1
1981–82		35	1
1982–83		36	—
1983–84		4	1
1983–84	Brighton	26	1
1984–85		42	1
1985–86		29	1

HUTCHINSON, Bobby

Born Glasgow 19.6.53.   Ht 5 9   Wt 11 4
Forward. From Aberdeen LCU.

Season	Club	App	Goals
1971–72	Montrose	3	—
1972–73		10	1
1973–74		28	7
1974–75	Dundee	23	7
1975–76		21	5
1976–77		35	12
1977–78		9	1
1977–78	Hibernian	20	6
1978–79		22	4
1979–80		25	3
1980–81	Wigan Ath	35	3
1981–82	Tranmere R	29	4
1982–83		6	2
1982–83	Mansfield T	25	3
1983–84		10	—
1983–84	Tranmere R	21	4
1984–85	Bristol C	31	4
1985–86		42	4

HUTCHISON, Tommy

Born Cardenden 22.9.47.   Ht 5 11½
Wt 11 2
Midfield. From Dundonald Bluebell.
Scotland 17 full caps.

Season	Club	App	Goals
1965–66	Alloa	16	1
1966–67		29	2
1967–68		23	1
1967–68	Blackpool	9	—
1968–69		32	2
1969–70		41	2
1970–71		38	1
1971–72		35	2
1972–73		10	3
1972–73	Coventry C	30	2
1973–74		41	3
1974–75		42	4
1975–76		42	1
1976–77		33	3
1977–78		40	3
1978–79		42	6
1979–80		40	1
1980–81		4	1
1980–81	Manchester C	24	3
1981–82		22	1
From Bulova, Hong Kong			
1983–84	Burnley	46	4
1984–85		46	—
1985–86	Swansea C	41	3

Season	Club	League Appearances/Goals	Season	Club	League Appearances/Goals

IBBOTSON, Danny

Born Morecambe 5.10.86.
Midfield.

1985–86	Preston NE	1	—

ILES, Robert

Born Bristol 21.5.67.
Defender.

1985–86	Bristol R	1	—

IMPEY, John

Born Exeter 11.8.54.   Ht 5 11   Wt 11 12
Defender. From Apprentice. England
Schools, Youth.

1972–73	Cardiff C	1	—
1973–74		11	—
1974–75		9	—
1975–76	Bournemouth	9	—
1976–77		40	1
1977–78		43	3
1978–79		38	1
1979–80		43	—
1980–81		41	—
1981–82		43	2
1982–83		27	—
1983–84	Torquay U	41	—
1984–85		31	—
1985–86	Exeter C	26	—

INCE, Paul

Born Ilford 21.10.67.
Forward. From YTS.

1985–86	West Ham U	—	—

IRVINE, Alan

Born Glasgow 12.7.58.   Ht 5 8   Wt 11 4
Forward. From Glasgow BC.

1977–78	Queen's Park	4	—
1978–79		8	—

1979–80		38	5
1980–81		38	4
1981–82	Everton	25	3
1982–83		14	1
1983–84		21	—
1984–85	Crystal Palace	35	5
1985–86		41	3

IRVINE, Brian

Born Bellshill 24.5.65.   Ht 6 2   Wt 13 0
Defender. From Victoria Park.

1983–84	Falkirk	3	—
1984–85		35	—
1985–86	Aberdeen	1	—

IRVINE, Willie

Born Whitburn 26.5.56.   Ht 5 10   Wt 11 7
Forward. From Fauldhouse United.

1977–78	Alloa	24	4
1978–79		30	13
1978–79	Motherwell	9	4
1979–80		37	13
1980–81		34	12
1981–82		39	20
1982–83		1	—
1982–83	Hibernian	24	4
1983–84		36	19
1984–85		25	3
1985–86		3	—

IRVING, Russell

Born Wallsend 4.1.64.   Ht 5 8   Wt 11 2½
Forward. From Apprentice.

1980–81	Ipswich T	—	—
1981–82		—	—
1982–83		—	—
1983–84		—	—
1984–85	Colchester U	41	9
1985–86		9	—

All appearances include those as substitute

Season	Club	League Appearances/Goals		Season	Club	League Appearances/Goals	

IRWIN, Dennis

Born Cork 31.10.65. Ht 5 8 Wt 11 0
Defender. From Apprentice. Eire Youth.

1983–84	Leeds U	12	—
1984–85		41	1
1985–86		19	—

ISAAC, Robert

Born Hackney 30.11.65. Ht 5 11 Wt 12 7
Defender. From Apprentice. England
Youth.

1983–84	Chelsea	—	—
1984–85		1	—
1985–86		3	—

JACK, Ross

Born Inverness 21.3.59. Ht 5 10 Wt 11 2
Forward. From Apprentice.

1976–77	Everton	—	—
1977–78		—	—
1978–79		1	1
1979–80		—	—
1979–80	*Cardiff C*	—	—
1979–80	Norwich C	—	—
1980–81		11	—
1981–82		35	10
1982–83		10	—
1983–84	Lincoln C	36	9
1984–85		24	7
1985–86	Dundee	6	—

JACKETT, Kenny

Born Watford 5.1.62. Ht 5 10½ Wt 11 2
Defender. From Apprentice.
Wales Under-21, 25 full caps.

1979–80	Watford	2	—
1980–81		42	3
1981–82		18	2
1982–83		41	4
1983–84		31	1
1984–85		36	4
1985–86		41	4

JACKSON, Craig

Born Rennishaw 17.1.69.
Midfield. From YTS.

1985–86	Notts Co	1	—

JACKSON, Gary

Born Swinton 30.9.64. Ht 5 6 Wt 10 3
Midfield. From Apprentice.

1981–82	Manchester C	8	—
1982–83		—	—
1983–84		—	—
1984–85		—	—
1985–86	Exeter C	32	2

Season	Club	League Appearances/Goals		Season	Club	League Appearances/Goals	

JACKSON, Mike

Born Lancaster 3.8.67.
Forward.

| 1985–86 | Newcastle U | — | — |

JACKSON, Peter

Born Bradford 6.4.61. Ht 6 1 Wt 12 6
Defender. From Apprentice.

1978–79	Bradford C	9	1
1979–80		12	—
1980–81		45	1
1981–82		32	8
1982–83		41	3
1983–84		42	3
1984–85		45	8
1985–86		42	—

JACOBS, Steve

Born West Ham 5.7.61. Ht 5 8 Wt 12 2
Defender. From Apprentice.

1978–79	Coventry C	—	—
1979–80		1	—
1980–81		11	—
1981–82		39	—
1982–83		32	—
1983–84		18	—
1984–85	Brighton	18	2
1985–86		30	1

JAKUB, Joe

Born Falkirk 7.12.56. Ht 5 6 Wt 9 6
Midfield. From Apprentice.

1973–74	Burnley	—	—
1974–75		—	—
1975–76		1	—
1976–77		5	—
1977–78		—	—
1978–79		13	—
1979–80		23	—
1980–81		—	—
1980–81	Bury	33	1
1981–82		46	2
1982–83		46	3
1983–84		46	11
1984–85		40	3
1985–86		44	6

JAMES, Leighton

Born Llwchwr 16.2.53. Ht 5 9½ Wt 12 5½
Forward. From Apprentice.
Wales Schools, Under-23, 54 full caps.

1969–70	Burnley	—	—
1970–71		4	—
1971–72		36	8
1972–73		42	10
1973–74		40	7
1974–75		42	16
1975–76		17	3
1975–76	Derby Co	22	6
1976–77		39	9
1977–78		7	—
1977–78	QPR	27	4
1978–79		1	—
1978–79	Burnley	37	3
1979–80		39	6
1979–80	Swansea C	1	1
1980–81		40	15
1981–82		38	9
1982–83		19	2
1982–83	Sunderland	18	2
1983–84		34	2
1984–85	Bury	46	5
1985–86	Newport Co	28	2

JAMES, Robbie

Born Swansea 23.3.57. Ht 5 11 Wt 13 0
Forward. From Apprentice. Wales Under-21, 40 full caps.

1972–73	Swansea C	1	—
1973–74		29	2
1974–75		42	8
1975–76		45	8
1976–77		46	14
1977–78		42	16
1978–79		43	14
1979–80		29	6
1980–81		35	8
1981–82		42	14
1982–83		40	9
1983–84	Stoke C	40	6
1984–85		8	—
1984–85	QPR	20	2
1985–86		28	1

Season	Club	League Appearances/Goals			Season	Club	League Appearances/Goals	

JARDINE, Iain

Born Irvine 17.2.55.   Ht 5 10   Wt 12 0
Midfield. From Irvine Victoria. Scotland
Under-21.

Season	Club	Apps	Goals
1976–77	Kilmarnock	12	—
1977–78		36	2
1978–79		29	2
1979–80		4	1
1979–80	Partick T.	17	1
1980–81		26	1
1981–82		24	4
1982–83		17	4
1983–84		32	2
1984–85	Anorthosis	Not known	
1985–86	Hearts	22	7

JARDINE, Sandy

Born Edinburgh 31.12.48.   Ht 5 9   Wt 11 5
Defender. From Edinburgh Athletic.
Scotland Youth, Under–23, 38 full caps.

Season	Club	Apps	Goals
1965–66	Rangers	—	—
1966–67		14	2
1967–68		10	—
1968–69		18	4
1969–70		10	7
1970–71		32	1
1971–72		31	5
1972–73		34	2
1973–74		34	3
1974–75		34	9
1975–76		25	2
1976–77		36	2
1977–78		32	5
1978–79		35	—
1979–80		35	3
1980–81		31	3
1981–82		36	
1982–83	Hearts	39	2
1983–84		33	—
1984–85		34	—
1985–86		35	—

JARVIE, Drew

Born Annathill 5.10.48.   Ht 5 10   Wt 11 6
Forward. From Kilsyth Rangers. Scotland
Under-23, 3 full caps.

Season	Club	Apps	Goals
1967–68	Airdrieonians	19	6
1968–69		27	5
1969–70		33	17
1970–71		34	16
1971–72		28	9
1972–73	Aberdeen	34	15
1973–74		32	13
1974–75		32	9
1975–76		32	4
1976–77		20	9
1977–78		35	12
1978–79		26	4
1979–80		30	12
1980–81		23	5
1981–82		10	2
1982–83	Airdrieonians	22	4
1983–84		6	1
1983–84	St Mirren	13	2
1984–85		1	—
1985–86		2	1

JARVIS, Antony

Born Radcliffe 18.3.64.
Forward. From Irlam T.

Season	Club	Apps	Goals
1985–86	Oldham Ath	—	—

JASPER, Dale

Born Croydon 14.1.64.   Ht 6 0   Wt 11 7
Defender. From Amateur.

Season	Club	Apps	Goals
1981–82	Chelsea	—	—
1982–83		—	—
1983–84		3	—
1984–85		7	—
1985–86		—	—

JEFFELS, Simon

Born Darton 18.1.66.   Ht 6 1   Wt 11 8
Defender. From Apprentice.
England Youth.

Season	Club	Apps	Goals
1983–84	Barnsley	3	—
1984–85		18	—
1985–86		11	—

Season	Club	League Appearances/Goals		Season	Club	League Appearances/Goals	

JEMSON, Nigel

Born Preston 10.8.69.
Midfield. From YTS.

1985–86	Preston NE	1	—

JENKINS, Lee

Born West Bromwich 17.3.61. Ht 5 10
Wt 12 0
Forward. From Apprentice. England Youth.

1978–79	Aston Villa	2	—
1979–80		1	—
1980–81		—	—
1980–81	Port Vale	1	—
From Roveniemi			
1985–86	Birmingham C	1	—

JENNINGS, Pat

Born Newry 12.6.45. Ht 6 0 Wt 12 6
Goalkeeper. From Newry T. Northern
Ireland Youth, Under-23, 116 full caps.

1962–63	Watford	2	—
1963–64		46	—
1964–65	Tottenham H	23	—
1965–66		22	—
1966–67		41	—
1967–68		42	—
1968–69		42	—
1969–70		41	—
1970–71		40	—
1971–72		41	—
1972–73		40	—
1973–74		36	—
1974–75		41	—
1975–76		40	—
1976–77		23	—
1977–78	Arsenal	42	—
1978–79		39	—
1979–80		37	—
1980–81		31	—
1981–82		16	—
1982–83		19	—
1983–84		38	—
1984–85		15	—
1985–86	Tottenham H	—	—

JEWELL, Paul

Born Liverpool 28.9.64. Ht 5 8 Wt 10 8
Forward. From Apprentice.

1982–83	Liverpool	—	—
1983–84		—	—
1984–85	Wigan Ath	26	9
1985–86		29	6

JOBLING, Kevin

Born Sunderland 1.1.68.
Midfield. From Apprentice.

1985–86	Leicester C	—	—

JOBSON, Richard

Born Hull 9.5.63. Ht 6 2 Wt 12 5
Forward. From Burton A.

1982–83	Watford	13	1
1983–84		13	2
1984–85		2	1
1984–85	Hull C	8	—
1985–86		36	7

JOHN, Stephen

Born Brentwood 22.12.66.
Midfield. From Apprentice.

1984–85	Orient	—	—
1985–86		8	—

JOHNS, Nicky

Born Bristol 8.6.57. Ht 6 2 Wt 11 5
Goalkeeper. From Minehead.

1975–76	Millwall	—	—
1976–77		16	—
1977–78		34	—
From Tampa Bay R			
1978–79	*Sheffield U*	1	—
1978–79	Charlton Ath	10	—

Season	Club	League Appearances/Goals		Season	Club	League Appearances/Goals

1979–80	....	34	—
1980–81	....	37	—
1981–82	....	40	—
1982–83	....	42	—
1983–84	....	36	—
1984–85	....	30	—
1985–86	....	38	—

JOHNSON, Bob

Born Bedford 22.2.62.   Ht 5 6   Wt 9 12
Midfield. From Apprentice.

1979–80	Luton T.......................	—	—
1980–81	....	—	—
1981–82	....	—	—
1982–83	....	—	—
1983–84	....	2	—
1983–84	*Lincoln C*.....................	4	—
1984–85	Luton T.......................	—	—
1985–86	....	15	—

JOHNSON, David

Born Gloucester 26.12.63.   Ht 5 8   Wt 11 0
Forward. From Redhill.

1981–82	Watford	1	—
1982–83	....	4	—
1983–84	....	2	—
1984–85	Peterborough U............	30	4
1985–86	....	5	—

JOHNSON, Gary

Born Peckham 14.9.59.   Ht 5 11   Wt 11 7
Forward. From Apprentice.

1978–79	Chelsea	1	1
1978–79	*C. Palace*	—	—
1979–80	Chelsea	15	7
1980–81	....	3	1
1980–81	Brentford	22	5
1981–82	....	30	8
From PG Rangers			
1985–86	Aldershot	43	15

JOHNSON, Ian

Born Oldham 11.11.60.   Ht 6 0
Defender. From Chadderton.

| 1984–85 | Rochdale .... | 8 | — |
| 1985–86 | .... | 39 | — |

JOHNSON, Jeff

Born Cardiff 26.11.53.   Ht 5 8   Wt 11 12
Midfield. From Apprentice. Wales Schools.

1970–71	Manchester C	5	—
1971–72	....	1	—
1972–73	....	—	—
1972–73	*Swansea C*....................	39	4
1973–74	....	—	—
1973–74	Crystal Palace	22	2
1974–75	....	36	1
1975–76	....	29	1
1976–77	Sheffield W	34	1
1977–78	....	39	1
1978–79	....	38	3
1979–80	....	35	1
1980–81	....	34	—
1981–82	Newport Co.................	34	2
1982–83	....	—	—
1982–83	Gillingham..................	31	2
1983–84	....	32	2
1984–85	....	25	—
1985–86	Port Vale	10	1

JOHNSON, Nigel

Born Rotherham 23.6.64.   Ht 6 2½   Wt 12 8
Defender. From Apprentice.

1982–83	Rotherham U	11	—
1983–84	....	43	1
1983–84	*Nottingham F*...............	—	—
1984–85	Rotherham U	35	—
1985–86	Manchester C	4	—

JOHNSON, Paul

Born Stoke 25.5.59.   Ht 5 9   Wt 11 3
Defender. From Apprentice.

All appearances include those as substitute

Season	Club	League Appearances/Goals		Season	Club	League Appearances/Goals	
1977–78	Stoke C	—	—	1981–82		31	13
1978–79		8	—	1982–83		34	10
1979–80		25	—	1983–84	Rochdale	19	7
1980–81		1	—	1983–84	Wigan Ath	21	7
1981–82	Shrewsbury T	41	1	1984–85		30	11
1982–83		33	1	1984–85	Bristol C	8	3
1983–84		18	—	1985–86		13	—
1984–85		36	1	1985–86	*Rochdale*	6	1
1985–86		13	—	1985–86	*Chester C*	10	6

JOHNSON, Paul

Born Scunthorpe 10.5.63.   Ht 5 11½   Wt 11 1
Goalkeeper. From Apprentice.

1981–82	Scunthorpe U	2	—
From Local			
1985–86	Scunthorpe U	12	—

JOHNSON, Peter

Born Harrogate 5.10.58.   Ht 5 9½   Wt 11 0
Defender. From Apprentice.

1976–77	Middlesbrough	—	—
1977–78		4	—
1978–79		21	—
1979–80		18	—
1980–81	Newcastle U	16	—
1981–82		—	—
1982–83		—	—
1982–83	*Bristol C*	20	—
1982–83	Doncaster R	12	—
1983–84	Darlington	44	1
1984–85		45	1
1985–86	Crewe Alex	8	—
1985–86	Exeter C	5	—

JOHNSON, Steve

Born Liverpool 23.6.57.   Ht 6 0   Wt 12 9
Forward. From Altrincham.

1977–78	Bury	11	1
1978–79		8	1
1979–80		27	9
1980–81		43	18

JOHNSTON, Craig

Born S. Africa 8.12.60.   Ht 5 8½   Wt 10 13
Midfield. From Lake McQuarrie, Sydney C
and Apprentice. England Under-21.

1977–78	Middlesbrough	5	1
1978–79		2	—
1979–80		30	5
1980–81		27	10
1980–81	Liverpool	—	—
1981–82		18	6
1982–83		33	7
1983–84		29	2
1984–85		11	—
1985–86		41	7

JOHNSTON, Mo

Born Glasgow 30.4.63.   Ht 5 9   Wt 10 6
Forward. From Milton Battlefield
Scotland Under-21, 9 full caps.

1980–81	Partick T	—	—
1981–82		32	9
1982–83		39	22
1983–84		14	10
1983–84	Watford	29	20
1984–85		9	3
1984–85	Celtic	27	14
1985–86		32	15

JOHNSTONE, Derek

Born Dundee 4.11.53.   Ht 6 0   Wt 13 2
Forward. From St Columba's.
Scotland Schools, Under-23, 14 full caps.

1970–71	Rangers	16	5
1971–72		17	11
1972–73		31	4

All appearances include those as substitute

Season	Club	League Appearances/Goals		Season	Club	League Appearances/Goals	
1973–74	....	31	1	1982–83	Crystal Palace	18	3
1974–75	....	27	15	1983–84	Charlton Ath	23	2
1975–76	....	33	15	1984–85	Orient..........................	36	4
1976–77	....	27	15	1985–86	....	41	9
1977–78	....	33	25				
1978–79	....	31	9				
1979–80	....	33	14				

JONES, Frank

Born Llandudno 3.10.60. Ht 5 11 Wt 11 0
Defender. From Juniors. Wales Under-21.

1980–81	....	26	4	1978–79	Wrexham....................	2	—
1981–82	....	28	9	1979–80	....	2	—
1982–83	....	16	6	1980–81	....	4	—
1983–84	Chelsea	—	—		From Local		
1983–84	*Dundee U*	4	—	1984–85	Wrexham....................	2	—
1984–85	Chelsea	2	—	1985–86	....	28	—
1984–85	Rangers....................	11	1				
1985–86	....	8	—				

JONES, Alex

Born Blackburn 27.11.64. Ht 6 0 Wt 11 6
Defender. From Apprentice.

1982–83	Oldham Ath	2	—
1983–84	....	2	—
1984–85	....	5	—
1984–85	*Stockport Co*..............	3	—
1985–86	Oldham Ath	—	—

JONES, Andy

Born Wrexham 9.1.63. Ht 5 10 Wt 12 7
Forward. From Rhyl.

1985–86	Port Vale	41	12

JONES, Chris

Born Jersey 18.4.56. Ht 5 11 Wt 10 7
Forward. From Apprentice.
England Under-21.

1973–74	Tottenham H	—	—
1974–75	....	16	1
1975–76	....	34	5
1976–77	....	31	9
1977–78	....	20	8
1978–79	....	19	5
1979–80	....	37	9
1980–81	....	—	—
1981–82	....	7	—
1982–83	Manchester C	3	—

JONES, Joey

Born Llandudno 4.3.55. Ht 5 10 Wt 11 7
Defender. From Amateur.
Wales Under-23, 72 full caps.

1972–73	Wrexham....................	17	—
1973–74	....	41	—
1974–75	....	40	2
1975–76	Liverpool....................	13	—
1976–77	....	39	3
1977–78	....	20	—
1978–79	....	—	—
1978–79	Wrexham....................	30	2
1979–80	....	36	3
1980–81	....	37	1
1981–82	....	36	—
1982–83	....	7	—
1982–83	Chelsea	28	1
1983–84	....	34	1
1984–85	....	16	—
1985–86	Huddersfield T	38	1

JONES, Keith

Born Dulwich 14.10.65. Ht 5 6½ Wt 10 9
Midfield. From Apprentice. England
Schools, Youth.

1982–83	Chelsea	2	—
1983–84	....	—	—
1984–85	....	19	2
1985–86	....	14	2

Season	Club	League Appearances/Goals	Season	Club	League Appearances/Goals

JONES, Linden

Born Tredegar 5.3.61.   Ht 5 6   Wt 11 2
Defender. From Apprentice. Wales
Under-21.

1978–79	Cardiff C	14	—
1979–80		17	1
1980–81		29	1
1981–82		36	—
1982–83		43	—
1983–84		6	—
1983–84	Newport Co	32	—
1984–85		44	4
1985–86		31	1

JONES, Mark

Born Warley 22.10.61.   Ht 5 6   Wt 10 5½
Defender. From Apprentice.

1979–80	Aston Villa	—	—
1980–81		—	—
1981–82		2	—
1982–83		17	—
1983–84		5	—
1983–84	Brighton	6	—
1984–85		3	—
1984–85	Birmingham C	10	—
1985–86		19	—

JONES, Mark

Born Berinsfield 26.9.61.   Ht 5 8   Wt 9 12
Forward. From Apprentice.

1979–80	Oxford U	2	—
1980–81		36	1
1981–82		21	3
1982–83		26	1
1983–84		20	2
1984–85		18	—
1985–86		6	—

JONES, Mark

Born Liverpool 16.9.60.   Ht 5 10½   Wt 11 10
Defender. From Local.

1983–84	Preston NE	4	—
1984–85		35	2
1985–86		37	1

JONES, Mark

Born Walsall 4.1.68.   Ht 5 8   Wt 10 1
Forward. From Apprentice.

| 1985–86 | Walsall | — | — |

JONES, Paul

Born Ellesmere Port 13.5.53.   Ht 6 1
Wt 12 9
Defender. From Apprentice.

1970–71	Bolton W	3	—
1971–72		38	1
1972–73		46	7
1973–74		38	—
1974–75		42	5
1975–76		41	6
1976–77		42	10
1977–78		21	4
1978–79		32	1
1979–80		32	1
1980–81		35	—
1981–82		41	1
1982–83		33	1
1983–84	Huddersfield T	36	7
1984–85		23	1
1985–86		14	—
1985–86	Oldham Ath	18	1

JONES, Paul

Born Walsall 6.9.65.   Ht 5 9   Wt 10 4
Midfield. From Apprentice.

1982–83	Walsall	2	—
1983–84		4	—
1984–85		22	—
1985–86		26	1

Season	Club	League Appearances/Goals	Season	Club	League Appearances/Goals

JONES, Peter

Born Caerphilly 22.9.57.
Defender. From Merthyr T.

1985–86	Newport Co	36	1

JONES, Robert

Born Coventry 17.11.64.   Ht 5 6½   Wt 10 1
Forward. From Manchester C. Apprentice.
Wales Youth.

1982–83	Leicester C	2	1
1983–84		8	2
1984–85		2	—
1985–86		3	—

JONES, Steven

Born Newport 17.11.67.   Ht 5 11   Wt 11 0
Midfield.

1984–85	Sunderland	—	—
1985–86		—	—

JONES, Vaughan

Born Tonyrefail 2.9.59.   Ht 5 8   Wt 12 0
Defender. From Apprentice.
Wales Under-21.

1976–77	Bristol R	1	—
1977–78		—	—
1978–79		22	1
1979–80		23	1
1980–81		21	1
1981–82		34	—
1982–83	Newport Co	43	—
1983–84		25	4
1984–85	Cardiff C	11	—
1984–85	Bristol R	20	—
1985–86		32	—

JONSSON, Siggi

Born Akranes 27.9.66.   Ht 5 11   Wt 11 11
Midfield. From I A Akranes. Iceland full caps.

1984–85	Sheffield W.	3	—
1985–86		10	2
1985–86	*Barnsley*	5	—

JORDAN, Joe

Born Carlisle 15.12.51.   Ht 6 0¼   Wt 12 3
Forward.

1968–69	Morton	5	1
1969–70		5	1
1970–71		2	—
1970–71	Leeds U	—	—
1971–72		12	—
1972–73		26	9
1973–74		33	7
1974–75		29	4
1975–76		17	2
1976–77		32	10
1977–78		20	3
1977–78	Manchester U	14	3
1978–79		30	6
1979–80		32	13
1980–81		33	15
1981–82	AC Milan	22	2
1982–83		30	10
1983–84	Verona	12	1
1984–85	Southampton	34	12
1985–86		12	—

JOSEPH, Francis

Born Kilburn 6.3.60.   Ht 5 10   Wt 12 0
Forward. From Hillingdon Bor.

1980–81	Wimbledon	11	1
1981–82		40	13
1982–83	Brentford	43	24
1983–84		43	18
1984–85		3	—
1985–86		8	1

JOSEPH, Roger

Born Paddington 24.12.65.   Ht 6 0   Wt 12 0
Defender. From Juniors.

1984–85	Brentford	1	—
1985–86		28	1

Season	Club	League Appearances/Goals	Season	Club	League Appearances/Goals

JOYCE, Joe

Born Consett 18.3.61.   Ht 5 9   Wt 10 5
Defender. From school.

Season	Club	App	Goals
1979–80	Barnsley	8	—
1980–81		33	—
1981–82		20	—
1982–83		32	1
1983–84		40	1
1984–85		41	—
1985–86		40	—

JOYCE, Sean

Born Doncaster 15.2.67.
Midfield.

Season	Club	App	Goals
1985–86	Doncaster R	15	1

JOYCE, Warren

Born Oldham 20.1.65.   Ht 5 8½   Wt 11 5
Midfield. Local.

Season	Club	App	Goals
1982–83	Bolton W	8	—
1983–84		45	3
1984–85		45	5
1985–86		31	4

JUDGE, Alan

Born Kingsbury 14.5.60.   Ht 5 11   Wt 11 5½
Goalkeeper. From Amateur.

Season	Club	App	Goals
1977–78	Luton T	—	—
1978–79		—	—
1979–80		1	—
1980–81		2	—
1981–82		4	—
1982–83		4	—
1982–83	*Reading*	33	—
1983–84	Reading	41	—
1984–85		3	—
1984–85	Oxford U	—	—
1985–86		19	—
1985–86	*Lincoln C*	2	—

JUKES, Stuart

Born London 10.3.68.   Ht 5 8¼   Wt 9 13½
Forward. From Apprentice.

Season	Club	App	Goals
1985–86	Fulham	—	—

JURYEFF, Ian

Born Gosport 24.11.62.   Ht 5 11   Wt 12 0
Forward. From Apprentice.

Season	Club	App	Goals
1980–81	Southampton	—	—
1981–82		—	—
1982–83		—	—
From Sweden			
1983–84	Southampton	2	—
1983–84	*Mansfield T*	12	5
1984–85	Southampton	—	—
1984–85	*Reading*	7	1
1984–85	Orient	19	7
1985–86		27	10

Season	Club	League Appearances/Goals		Season	Club	League Appearances/Goals	

KAMARA, Chris

Born Middlesbrough 25.12.57.   Ht 6 1
Wt 12 0
Midfield. From Apprentice.

1975–76	Portsmouth	24	4
1976–77		39	3
1977–78	Swindon T	40	10
1978–79		28	2
1979–80		34	5
1980–81		45	4
1981–82	Portsmouth	11	—
1981–82	Brentford	31	5
1982–83		44	11
1983–84		38	6
1984–85		39	6
1985–86	Swindon T	20	1

KANE, Paul

Born Edinburgh 20.6.65.   Ht 5 8   Wt 9 9
Midfield. From Salvesen B.C. Scotland
Youth.

1982–83	Hibernian	—	—
1983–84		13	1
1984–85		34	8
1985–86		32	5

KARAA, Roch

Born Tunisia 3.4.64.   Ht 5 11   Wt 11 10
Goalkeeper.

| 1984–85 | Darlington | 1 | — |
| 1985–86 | | — | — |

KAY, John

Born Sunderland 29.1.64.   Ht 5 10   Wt 11 6
Defender. From Apprentice.

1981–82	Arsenal	—	—
1982–83		7	—
1983–84		7	—
1984–85	Wimbledon	21	1
1984–85	*Middlesbrough*	8	—
1985–86	Wimbledon	26	1

KAYE, David

Born Huddersfield 14.11.59.   Ht 6 1
Wt 12 4
Goalkeeper.

| 1984–85 | Chester C | 7 | — |
| 1985–86 | | 3 | — |

KEANE, Tommy

Born Galway. 16.9.68.   Ht 5 6½   Wt 10 4
Forward. From Apprentice. Eire Youth.

| 1985–86 | | 1 | — |

KEANEY, Paul

Born Chelmsford 21.2.67.   Ht 6 1   Wt 12 4
Defender.

| 1984–85 | Colchester U | — | — |
| 1985–86 | | — | — |

KEARNEY, Mark

Born Ormskirk 12.6.62.   Ht 5 10   Wt 11 0
Defender. From Marine.

1981–82	Everton	—	—
1982–83		—	—
1982–83	Mansfield T	11	1
1983–84		17	2
1984–85		38	4
1985–86		31	7

KEARNS, Mike

Born Banbury 26.11.50.   Ht 6 4½   Wt 14 0
Goalkeeper. From Apprentice.
Eire, 18 full caps.

1968–69	Oxford U	—	—
1969–70		3	—
1970–71		42	—
1971–72		22	—
1972–73		—	—
1972–73	*Plymouth Arg*	1	—
1972–73	*Charlton Ath*	4	—

Season	Club	League Appearances/Goals	
1973–74	Walsall	45	—
1974–75		46	—
1975–76		46	—
1976–77		46	—
1977–78		42	—
1978–79		24	—
1979–80	Wolverhampton W	5	—
1980–81		4	—
1981–82		—	—
1982–83	Walsall	11	—
1983–84		10	—
1984–85		5	—
1985–86		—	—

KEARNS, Ollie

Born Banbury 12.6.56. Ht 6 0 Wt 12 0
Forward. From Banbury U.

Season	Club	League Appearances/Goals	
1976–77	Reading	5	2
1977–78		27	16
1978–79		27	11
1979–80		27	11
1980–81		—	—
1981–82	Oxford U	18	4
1982–83	Walsall	38	11
1983–84	Hereford U	41	10
1984–85		45	18
1985–86		33	13

KEAY, Jack

Born Glasgow 14.6.60. Ht 6 0 Wt 11 6
Defender. From Glasgow Celtic.

Season	Club	League Appearances/Goals	
1977–78	Shrewsbury T	21	1
1978–79		28	2
1979–80		42	9
1980–81		40	8
1981–82		24	—
1982–83		—	—
1982–83	Wrexham	37	2
1983–84		38	3
1984–85		41	4
1985–86		40	—

KEE, Paul

Born Londonderry 21.2.67. Ht 5 9 Wt 10 0
Midfield. From Apprentice.
Northern Ireland Youth.

Season	Club	League Appearances/Goals	
1983–84	Mansfield T	1	—
1984–85		—	—
1984–85	Nottingham F	—	—
1985–86		—	—

KEELEY, Glenn

Born Barking 1.9.54. Ht 6 2 Wt 13 1
Defender. From Apprentice.
England Youth.

Season	Club	League Appearances/Goals	
1972–73	Ipswich T	1	—
1973–74		3	—
1974–75	Newcastle U	39	2
1975–76		5	—
1976–77	Blackburn R	33	—
1977–78		27	—
1978–79		26	—
1979–80		45	3
1980–81		42	2
1981–82		41	3
1982–83		14	4
1982–83	*Everton*	1	—
1983–84	Blackburn R	35	4
1984–85		41	2
1985–86		31	4

KEEN, John

Born Barrow 16.3.67.
Midfield.

Season	Club	League Appearances/Goals	
1984–85	Burnley	—	—
1985–86		—	—

KEEN, Kevin

Born Amersham 25.2.67. Ht 5 7 Wt 10 4
Midfield. From Wycombe W and
Apprentice. England Schools, Youth.

Season	Club	League Appearances/Goals	
1983–84	West Ham U	—	—
1984–85		—	—
1985–86		—	—

Season	Club	League Appearances/Goals

KEEN, Mike

Born Wrexham 12.2.63.
Goalkeeper. From Chester and Lex. Wales
Schools.

Season	Club	App	Goals
1985–86	Wrexham	5	—

KEEN, Nigel

Born Barrow 23.10.61.   Ht 5 8   Wt 11 3
Midfield. From Barrow.

Season	Club	App	Goals
1978–79	Manchester U	—	—
1979–80		—	—
1980–81		—	—
From South Africa			
1985–86	Preston NE	24	—

KELLOCK, Billy

Born Glasgow 7.2.54.   Ht 5 10   Wt 11 10
Midfield. From Aston Villa. Apprentice.
Scotland Schools.

Season	Club	App	Goals
1971–72	Cardiff C	6	—
1972–73		29	2
1973–74	Norwich C	3	—
1974–75	Millwall	—	—
From Chelmsford C and Kettering T			
1979–80	Peterborough U	45	19
1980–81		46	13
1981–82		43	11
1982–83	Luton T	7	—
1982–83	Wolverhampton W	9	3
1983–84		3	—
1983–84	Southend U	40	6
1984–85		13	3
1984–85	Port Vale	11	4
1985–86	Halifax T	43	17

KELLOW, Tony

Born Falmouth 1.5.52.   Ht 5 10   Wt 12 7
Forward. From Falmouth T.

Season	Club	App	Goals
1976–77	Exeter C	44	19
1977–78		46	14
1978–79		17	7
1978–79	Blackpool	25	11
1979–80		32	12
1979–80	Exeter C	10	5

Season	Club	App	Goals
1980–81		46	25
1981–82		46	21
1982–83		33	10
1983–84		8	—
1983–84	Plymouth Arg	10	2
1984–85	Swansea C	1	—
1984–85	Newport Co	20	8
1985–86	Exeter C	33	9

KELLY, Alan

Born Preston 11.8.68. Ht 6 2   Wt 12 5
Goalkeeper. Eire Youth.

Season	Club	App	Goals
1985–86	Preston NE	13	—

KELLY, David

Born Birmingham 25.11.65.   Ht 5 11
Wt 11 1
Forward. From Alvechurch.

Season	Club	App	Goals
1983–84	Walsall	6	3
1984–85		32	7
1985–86		28	10

KELLY, Eddie

Born Glasgow 7.2.51.   Ht 5 10   Wt 12 8
Midfield. From Amateur. Scottish Under-23.

Season	Club	App	Goals
1969–70	Arsenal	16	2
1970–71		23	4
1971–72		23	2
1972–73		27	1
1973–74		37	1
1974–75		32	1
1975–76		17	2
1976–77		—	—
1976–77	QPR	28	1
1977–78	Leicester C	24	1
1978–79		27	—
1979–80		34	3
1980–81	Notts Co	27	1
1981–82	Bournemouth	13	—
1981–82	Leicester C	14	—
1982–83		20	—
From Melton T			
1984–85	Torquay U	22	—
1985–86		13	1

Season	Club	League Appearances/Goals		Season	Club	League Appearances/Goals	

KELLY, Errington

Born St. Vincent 8.4.58. Ht 5 8   Wt 11 8
Forward. From Ledbury T.

Season	Club	App	Goals
1981–82	Bristol R	5	—
1982–83		13	3
1982–83	Lincoln C	2	—
1982–83	Bristol C	5	1
1983–84	Coventry C	—	—
1983–84	*Peterborough U*	11	7
1984–85	Peterborough U	40	11
1985–86		21	4

KELLY, Gary

Born Fulwood 3.8.66. Ht 5 10½   Wt 12 3
Goalkeeper. From Apprentice.

Season	Club	App	Goals
1984–85	Newcastle U	—	—
1985–86		—	—

KELLY, John

Born Bebbington 20.10.60.   Ht 5 10
Wt 10 9
Forward. From Cammell Laird.

Season	Club	App	Goals
1979–80	Tranmere R	28	4
1980–81		29	5
1981–82		7	—
1981–82	Preston NE	30	5
1982–83		29	2
1983–84		34	13
1984–85		37	7
1985–86	Chester C	43	8

KELLY, Mark

Born Blackpool 7.10.66.
Midfield.

Season	Club	App	Goals
1985–86	Shrewsbury T	—	—

KELLY, Robert

Born Birmingham 21.12.64.   Ht 5 9½
Wt 10 10
Midfield. From Apprentice.

Season	Club	App	Goals
1982–83	Leicester C	—	—
1983–84		1	—
1984–85		—	—
1984–85	*Tranmere R*	5	2
1985–86	Leicester C	9	—

KELLY, Tom

Born Bellshill 28.3.64.   Ht 5 10   Wt 11 10
Defender. From Hibs.

Season	Club	App	Goals
1985–86	Hartlepool U	15	—

KELLY, Tony

Born Prescot 1.10.64.   Ht 5 10   Wt 12 7
Defender. From Liverpool Apprentice.

Season	Club	App	Goals
1983–84	Derby Co	—	—
1983–84	Wigan Ath	29	2
1984–85		40	4
1985–86		32	9
1985–86	Stoke C	1	—

KENDAL, Steve

Born Birtley 4.8.61.   Ht 6 0   Wt 11 2
Midfield. From Apprentice.

Season	Club	App	Goals
1981–82	Nottingham F	1	—
1982–83		—	—
1982–83	Chesterfield	22	—
1983–84		43	9
1984–85		45	5
1985–86		9	—

KENDALL, Mark

Born Blackwood 20.9.58.   Ht 6 0   Wt 13 9
Goalkeeper. From Apprentice. Wales
Schools, Under-21.

Season	Club	App	Goals
1976–77	Tottenham H	—	—
1977–78		—	—
1978–79		23	—
1979–80		2	—
1979–80	*Chesterfield*	9	—
1980–81	Tottenham H	4	—

Season	Club	League Appearances/Goals		Season	Club	League Appearances/Goals	

Season	Club	Apps	Goals
1980–81	Newport Co	28	—
1981–82		46	—
1982–83		44	—
1983–84		43	—
1984–85		44	—
1985–86		46	—

KENDALL, Paul

Born Halifax 19.10.64.   Ht 6 0   Wt 12 6
Defender. From Apprentice.

Season	Club	Apps	Goals
1981–82	Halifax T	13	—
1982–83		10	—
1983–84		39	2
1984–85		23	—
1985–86		21	2

KENNEDY, Alan

Born Sunderland 31.8.54.   Ht 5 9   Wt 10 7
Defender. From Apprentice. England
Under-23, 'B', 2 full caps.

Season	Club	Apps	Goals
1972–73	Newcastle U	2	—
1973–74		18	—
1974–75		28	3
1975–76		42	1
1976–77		42	2
1977–78		26	3
1978–79	Liverpool	37	3
1979–80		37	1
1980–81		19	2
1981–82		34	3
1982–83		42	3
1983–84		42	2
1984–85		32	1
1985–86		8	—
1985–86	Sunderland	32	2

KENNEDY, Alex

Born Irvine 25.6.63.   Ht 6 0   Wt 11 7
Defender. From Craigmark Juniors.

Season	Club	Apps	Goals
1982–83	Motherwell	—	—
1983–84		11	—
1984–85		16	2
1985–86		20	1

KENNEDY, Andy

Born Stirling 8.10.64.
Forward. From Sauchie Ath.

Season	Club	Apps	Goals
1983–84	Rangers	13	3
1984–85		2	—
1984–85	Birmingham C	7	4
1985–86		32	6

KENNEDY, Mick

Born Salford 9.4.61.   Ht 5 10   Wt 10 6
Midfield. From Apprentice.

Season	Club	Apps	Goals
1978–79	Halifax T	30	—
1979–80		46	4
1980–81	Huddersfield T	42	2
1981–82		39	7
1982–83	Middlesbrough	38	5
1983–84		30	—
1984–85	Portsmouth	37	—
1985–86		39	2

KENNEDY, Stephen

Born Audenshaw 22.7.65.   Ht 5 11½
Wt 11 6
Defender. From Apprentice.

Season	Club	Apps	Goals
1983–84	Burnley	7	—
1984–85		8	—
1985–86		—	—

KENT, Kevin

Born Stoke 19.3.65.   Ht 5 10½   Wt 11 0
Forward. From Apprentice.

Season	Club	Apps	Goals
1982–83	WBA	—	—
1983–84		2	—
1984–85	Newport Co	33	1
1985–86	Mansfield T	34	8

KENWORTHY, Tony

Born Leeds 30.10.58.   Ht 5 10   Wt 10 7
Defender. From Apprentice. England
Youth.

Season	Club	League Appearances/Goals		Season	Club	League Appearances/Goals	

Season	Club	App	Goals
1975–76	Sheffield U	6	—
1976–77		37	1
1977–78		20	1
1978–79		37	3
1979–80		41	3
1980–81		37	7
1981–82		45	15
1982–83		23	3
1983–84		8	1
1984–85		19	—
1985–86		13	—
1985–86	*Mansfield T*	13	—

KEOUGH, Danny

Born Rawtenstall 31.1.63. Ht 5 7½ Wt 9 9
Midfield. From Apprentice.

Season	Club	App	Goals
1979–80	Manchester U	—	—
1980–81		—	—
1981–82		—	—
1982–83		—	—
1983–84		—	—
1984–85	Preston NE	—	—
1984–85	Burnley	—	—
1984–85	Bury	—	—
1985–86	Exeter C	32	—

KEOWN, Martin

Born Oxford 24.7.66. Ht 6 1 Wt 12 4
Defender. From Apprentice. England
Youth.

Season	Club	App	Goals
1983–84	Arsenal	—	—
1984–85		—	—
1984–85	*Brighton*	16	—
1985–86	Arsenal	22	—
1985–86	*Brighton*	7	1

KERNAGHAN, Alan

Born Otley 25.4.67. Ht 6 1 Wt 12 12½
Forward. From Apprentice.

Season	Club	App	Goals
1984–85	Middlesbrough	8	1
1985–86		6	—

KERR, Andy

Born West Bromwich 7.4.66. Ht 6 0
Wt 11 4
Defender.

Season	Club	App	Goals
1983–84	Shrewsbury T	—	—
1984–85		1	—
1985–86		9	—
1985–86	*Port Vale*	—	—

KERR, John

Born Birkenhead 23.11.59. Ht 6 1 Wt 12 5
Forward. From Apprentice.

Season	Club	App	Goals
1978–79	Tranmere R	25	6
1979–80		30	6
1980–81		26	5
1981–82		40	13
1982–83		33	8
1983–84	Bristol City	14	4
1983–84	Stockport Co	21	6
1984–85		26	10
1984–85	Bury	8	—
1985–86		23	4

KERR, Paul

Born Portsmouth 9.6.64. Ht 5 8 Wt 11 11
Forward. From Apprentice.

Season	Club	App	Goals
1982–83	Aston Villa	—	—
1983–84		2	—
1984–85		10	—
1985–86		6	1

KERRINS, Wayne

Born Essex 5.8.65. Ht 5 8½ Wt 11 2
Forward. From Apprentice.

Season	Club	App	Goals
1983–84	Fulham	—	—
1984–85		2	—
1984–85	*Port Vale*	7	—
1985–86	Fulham	16	—

Season	Club	League Appearances/Goals		Season	Club	League Appearances/Goals	

KERSLAKE, David

Born London 19.6.66.   Ht 5 8   Wt 11 4
Midfield. From Apprentice. England
Schools, Youth, Under-21.

Season	Club	App	Goals
1983–84	QPR	—	—
1984–85		1	—
1985–86		14	1

KETTERIDGE, Steve

Born Stevenage 7.11.59.   Ht 5 8½   Wt 10 7
Midfield. From Derby Co. Apprentice.

Season	Club	App	Goals
1977–78	Wimbledon	—	—
1978–79		17	1
1979–80		34	6
1980–81		39	1
1981–82		36	7
1982–83		39	6
1983–84		43	7
1984–85		29	4
1985–86	Crystal Palace	33	4

KEVAN, David

Born Wigtown 31.8.68.
Midfield. From Apprentice.

Season	Club	App	Goals
1985–86	Notts Co	3	—

KEY, Richard

Born Coventry 13.4.56.   Ht 6 0   Wt 12 4
Goalkeeper. From Coventry C. Amateur.

Season	Club	App	Goals
1975–76	Exeter C	37	—
1976–77		31	—
1977–78		41	—
1978–79	Cambridge U	1	—
1979–80			—
1980–81		30	—
1981–82		18	—
1982–83		3	—
1982–83	*Northampton T*	2	—
1983–84	Orient	42	—
1984–85	Brentford	1	—
1984–85	Sunderland	—	—

Season	Club	App	Goals
1984–85	Cambridge U	13	—
1985–86	Brentford	3	—
1985–86	Swindon T	—	—

KIDD, Albert

Born Dundee 16.10.57.   Ht 5 7   Wt 10 4
Midfield. From Carnoustie Panmure.

Season	Club	App	Goals
1976–77	Brechin C		—
1977–78	Arbroath	39	5
1978–79		36	8
1979–80		20	6
1979–80	Motherwell	16	5
1980–81		37	13
1981–82	Dundee	30	2
1982–83		19	4
1983–84		25	1
1984–85		23	3
1985–86		13	2

KIDD, Walter

Born Edinburgh 10.3.58.   Ht 5 11   Wt 12 3
Defender. From Newtongrange Star.

Season	Club	App	Goals
1977–78	Hearts	23	—
1978–79		30	—
1979–80		34	2
1980–81		25	1
1981–82		30	—
1982–83		37	—
1983–84		31	1
1984–85		33	1
1985–86		28	—

KILCLINE, Brian

Born Nottingham 7.5.62.   Ht 6 2   Wt 12 0
Defender. From Apprentice. England
Under-21.

Season	Club	App	Goals
1979–80	Notts Co	16	1
1980–81		42	1
1981–82		36	3
1982–83		40	3
1983–84		24	1
1984–85	Coventry C	26	2
1985–86		32	7

Season	Club	League Appearances/Goals	Season	Club	League Appearances/Goals

KILFORD, Brian

Born Jarrow 1.2.67.   Ht 5 8½   Wt 10 6
Defender.

Season	Club	App	Goals
1984–85	Newcastle U	—	—
1985–86		—	—

KILMORE, Kevin

Born Scunthorpe 11.11.59.   Ht 5 9
Wt 11 10
Forward. From Amateur. England Youth.

Season	Club	App	Goals
1976–77	Scunthorpe U	19	3
1977–78		32	8
1978–79		46	17
1979–80		5	—
1979–80	Grimsby T	30	15
1980–81		24	2
1981–82		30	6
1982–83		18	4
1983–84	Rotherham U	45	13
1984–85		39	7
1985–86	Lincoln C	18	4

KILNER, Andy

Born Bolton 11.10.66.
Midfield. From Apprentice.

Season	Club	App	Goals
1984–85	Burnley	—	—
1985–86		5	—

KIMBLE, Alan

Born Poole 6.8.66.
Defender.

Season	Club	App	Goals
1984–85	Charlton Ath	6	—
1985–86		—	—
1985–86	*Exeter C*	1	—

KIMBLE, Garry

Born Poole 6.8.66.
Forward.

Season	Club	App	Goals
1984–85	Charlton Ath	9	1
1985–86		—	—
1985–86	*Exeter C*	1	—

KING, Andy

Born Luton 14.8.56.   Ht 5 9   Wt 10 10
Midfield. From Apprentice. England Under-21.

Season	Club	App	Goals
1974–75	Luton T	1	—
1975–76		32	9
1975–76	Everton	3	2
1976–77		37	7
1977–78		42	8
1978–79		40	12
1979–80		29	9
1980–81		—	—
1980–81	QPR	26	6
1981–82		4	3
1981–82	WBA	25	4
1982–83	Everton	24	9
1983–84		20	2
From Cambuur			
1984–85	Wolverhampton W	8	—
1985–86		20	10
1985–86	Luton T	3	—

KING, Jake

Born Glasgow 29.1.55.   Ht 5 10   Wt 11 0
Defender. From Apprentice.

Season	Club	App	Goals
1972–73	Shrewsbury T	2	—
1973–74		28	—
1974–75		45	—
1975–76		31	1
1976–77		44	—
1977–78		37	—
1978–79		39	6
1979–80		36	7
1980–81		42	6
1981–82		2	—
1982–83	Wrexham	34	1
1983–84		44	4
1984–85		14	—
1984–85	Cardiff C	23	—
1985–86		7	—

KING, Jamie

Born Rogerstone 2.8.67.
Forward.

Season	Club	App	Goals
1984–85	Cardiff C	—	—
1985–86		—	—

Season	Club	League Appearances/Goals	Season	Club	League Appearances/Goals

KING, Phil

Born Bristol 28.12.67.   Ht 5 9   Wt 11 0
Defender. From Apprentice.

1984–85	Exeter C.	16	—
1985–86		11	—

KING, Simon

Born Ebbw Vale 19.7.64.   Ht 5 9   Wt 10 6
Defender. From Cwmbran T.

1984–85	Newport Co.	1	—
1985–86		—	—

KINSELLA, Tony

Born Orsett 30.10.61.   Ht 5 8   Wt 10 9
Midfield. From Apprentice. Eire Under-21.

1978–79	Millwall	1	—
1979–80		26	—
1980–81		34	1
From Tampa Bay R			
1981–82	Ipswich T	—	—
1982–83		4	—
1983–84		5	—
1984–85	Millwall	8	—
1985–86		14	1

KINSEY, Steve

Born Manchester 2.1.63.   Ht 5 7   Wt 9 9
Forward. From Apprentice.

1979–80	Manchester C	—	—
1980–81		1	—
1981–82		16	—
1982–83		13	1
1982–83	*Chester*	3	1
1982–83	*Chesterfield*	3	—
1983–84	Manchester C	23	7
1984–85		35	7
1985–86		13	—

KIRKUP, Graeme

Born Newcastle 31.5.65.   Ht 6 0   Wt 12 4
Defender. From Apprentice.

1981–82	Exeter C	8	—
1982–83		17	—
1983–84		36	1
1984–85		38	—
1985–86		8	—

KIRKWOOD, Billy

Born Edinburgh 1.9.58.   Ht 5 10   Wt 11 0
Midfield. 'S' Form. Scotland Schools.

1976–77	Dundee U	4	1
1977–78		27	4
1978–79		34	9
1979–80		28	3
1980–81		29	10
1981–82		32	2
1982–83		31	3
1983–84		26	9
1984–85		23	1
1985–86		15	1

KITE, Phil

Born Bristol 26.10.62.   Ht 6 1½   Wt 14 7
Goalkeeper. From Apprentice. England
Youth.

1980–81	Bristol R	4	—
1981–82		27	—
1982–83		46	—
1983–84		19	—
1983–84	*Tottenham H*	—	—
1984–85	Southampton	1	—
1985–86		3	—
1985–86	*Middlesbrough*	2	—

KIWOMYA, Andy

Born Huddersfield 1.10.67.
Forward. From YTS. England Youth.

1984–85	Barnsley	—	—
1985–86		1	—

Season	Club	League Appearances/Goals		Season	Club	League Appearances/Goals	

KNIGHT, Alan

Born Balham 3.7.61. Ht 6 1 Wt 13 1½
Goalkeeper. From Apprentice.
England Youth, Under-21.

Season	Club	App	Goals
1977–78	Portsmouth	1	—
1978–79		—	—
1979–80		8	—
1980–81		1	—
1981–82		45	—
1982–83		46	—
1983–84		42	—
1984–85		42	—
1985–86		38	—

KNIGHT, Ian

Born Hartlepool 26.10.66. Ht 6 2 Wt 12 4
Defender. From Apprentice.

Season	Club	App	Goals
1984–85	Barnsley	—	—
1985–86	Sheffield W	4	—

KNILL, Alan

Born Slough 8.10.64. Ht 6 2½ Wt 10 9
Defender. From Apprentice. Wales Youth.

Season	Club	App	Goals
1982–83	Southampton	—	—
1983–84		—	—
1984–85	Halifax T	44	1
1985–86		33	2

KNOWLES, Jim

Born Wigan 25.4.59. Ht 5 9 Wt 11 8
Defender. From Bangor.

Season	Club	App	Goals
1984–85	Wigan Ath	20	1
1985–86		45	—

KOWALSKI, Andy

Born Mansfield 26.2.53. Ht 5 10 Wt 11 0
Midfield. From Worksop T.

Season	Club	App	Goals
1972–73	Chesterfield	10	—
1973–74		21	3
1974–75		45	8
1975–76		31	1
1976–77		43	4
1977–78		39	1
1978–79		44	5
1979–80		28	2
1980–81		25	3
1981–82		37	2
1982–83		42	1
1983–84	Doncaster R	32	1
1984–85		20	—
1985–86	Peterborough U	35	4

KRAAY, Hans

Born Utrecht 22.12.59. Ht 5 11 Wt 11 12
Defender. From Edmonton, San Jose,
Excelsior and NAC Breda.

Season	Club	App	Goals
1983–84	Brighton	5	—
1984–85		18	3
1985–86		—	—

KUHL, Martin

Born Frimley 10.1.65. Ht 5 11 Wt 11 13
Midfield. From Apprentice.

Season	Club	App	Goals
1982–83	Birmingham C	2	—
1983–84		22	1
1984–85		27	2
1985–86		37	1

All appearances include those as substitute

Season	Club	League Appearances/Goals	Season	Club	League Appearances/Goals

LAKE, Trevor

Born Orpington 2.1.68.
Goalkeeper. From Apprentice. England Schools.

1985–86	West Ham U	— —

LAMBERT, Martin

Born Southampton 24.9.65.   Ht 5 10½ Wt 13 0
Forward. From Apprentice. England Schools, Youth.

1983–84	Brighton	3 —
1984–85		— —
1985–86	Torquay U	6 2

LAMBERT, Paul

Born Glasgow 7.8.69.   Ht 5 8   Wt 9 8
Midfield. From Linwood Rangers B.C.

1985–86	St Mirren	1 —

LAMPARD, Frank

Born West Ham 20.9.48.   Ht 5 11   Wt 12 13
Defender. From Apprentice.
England Youth, Under-23, 2 full caps.

1965–66	West Ham U	— —
1966–67		— —
1967–68		19 —
1968–69		1 —
1969–70		30 —
1970–71		41 1
1971–72		39 1
1972–73		38 —
1973–74		42 2
1974–75		40 4
1975–76		37 3
1976–77		36 1
1977–78		40 —
1978–79		29 3
1979–80		36 —
1980–81		39 1

1981–82		28 —
1982–83		37 2
1983–84		18 —
1984–85		1 —
1985–86	Southend U	34 1

LANE, Martin

Born Altrincham 12.4.61.   Ht 5 9   Wt 11 3
Defender. From Amateur.

1979–80	Manchester U	— —
1980–81		— —
1981–82		— —
1982–83	Chester	41 2
1983–84		38 —
1984–85		31 —
1985–86		44 1

LANGAN, David

Born Dublin 15.2.57.   Ht 5 10   Wt 11 2
Defender. From Apprentice. Eire, 19 full caps.

1976–77	Derby Co	21 —
1977–78		42 —
1978–79		40 —
1979–80		40 1
1980–81	Birmingham C	42 —
1981–82		36 1
1982–83		14 2
1983–84		— —
1984–85	Oxford U	39 1
1985–86		34 —

LANGE, Tony

Born London 10.12.64.   Ht 6 0   Wt 12 9
Goalkeeper. From Apprentice.

1982–83	Charlton Ath	— —
1983–84		6 —
1984–85		2 —
1985–86		4 —
1985–86	*Aldershot*	7 —

Season	Club	League Appearances/Goals		Season	Club	League Appearances/Goals	

LANGLEY, Kevin

Born St. Helens 24.5.64. Ht 6 1 Wt 10 5
Defender. From Apprentice.

Season	Club	Apps	Goals
1981–82	Wigan Ath	2	—
1982–83		28	2
1983–84		44	1
1984–85		43	1
1985–86		43	2

LARNACH, Michael

Born Lybster 9.11.52. Ht 5 10 Wt 11 0
Forward. From Campsie Black Watch.

Season	Club	Apps	Goals
1971–72	East Stirling	2	—
1972–73	Clydebank	35	17
1973–74		20	3
1974–75		30	7
1975–76		26	7
1976–77		39	25
1977–78		17	4
1977–78	Newcastle U	14	—
1978–79	Motherwell	32	4
1979–80		20	3
1980–81		6	—
1980–81	Ayr U	13	1
1981–82		14	—
1982–83		22	7
1983–84	Stenhousemuir	12	2
1983–84	Clydebank	26	7
1984–85		37	10
1985–86		23	3

LATCHFORD, Bob

Born Birmingham 18.1.51. Ht 6 0 Wt 13 6
Forward. From Apprentice. England Youth,
Under-23, 12 full caps, Football League.

Season	Club	Apps	Goals
1968–69	Birmingham C	3	2
1969–70		10	1
1970–71		36	13
1971–72		42	23
1972–73		42	19
1973–74		26	10
1973–74	Everton	13	7
1974–75		36	17
1975–76		31	12

Season	Club	Apps	Goals
1976–77		36	17
1977–78		39	30
1978–79		36	11
1979–80		26	6
1980–81		19	6
1981–82	Swansea C	31	12
1982–83		38	20
1983–84		18	3
To NAC Breda			
1984–85	Coventry C	12	2
1985–86	Lincoln C	15	2
1985–86	Newport Co	20	5

LATCHFORD, Peter

Born Birmingham 27.9.52. Ht 6 0 Wt 14 2
Goalkeeper. From Apprentice.

Season	Club	Apps	Goals
1971–72	WBA	—	—
1972–73		26	—
1973–74		42	—
1974–75		13	—
1974–75	Celtic	10	—
1975–76		35	—
1976–77		31	—
1977–78		36	—
1978–79		27	—
1979–80		36	—
1980–81		—	—
1981–82		—	—
1982–83		—	—
1983–84		3	—
1984–85		2	—
1985–86		6	—

LAW, Nicky

Born London 8.9.61. Ht 6 0 Wt 13 5
Defender. From Apprentice.

Season	Club	Apps	Goals
1979–80	Arsenal	—	—
1980–81		—	—
1981–82	Barnsley	19	—
1982–83		28	—
1983–84		31	1
1984–85		35	—
1985–86		1	—
1985–86	Blackpool	39	1

All appearances include those as substitute

Season	Club	League Appearances/Goals

LAWRENCE, George

Born London 14.9.62. Ht 5 10 Wt 12 2
Forward. From Apprentice.

Season	Club	App	Goals
1980–81	Southampton	—	—
1981–82		4	—
1981–82	*Oxford U*	15	4
1982–83	Southampton	6	1
1982–83	Oxford U	22	9
1983–84		34	9
1984–85		7	3
1984–85	Southampton	11	1
1985–86		21	2

LAWRENCE, Les

Born Wolverhampton 18.5.57. Ht 6 3
Wt 11 1
Forward. From Stourbridge.

Season	Club	App	Goals
1974–75	Shrewsbury T	—	—
1975–76		5	—
1976–77		9	2
From Telford U			
1977–78	Torquay U	34	5
1978–79		45	17
1979–80		42	14
1980–81		26	5
1981–82		42	4
1982–83	Port Vale	8	—
1983–84	Aldershot	39	23
1984–85	Rochdale	15	4
1984–85	Burnley	10	2
1985–86		21	6

LAWRENSON, Mark

Born Preston 2.6.57. Ht 6 0 Wt 11 7
Defender. From Amateur. Eire, 34 full caps.

Season	Club	App	Goals
1974–75	Preston NE	3	—
1975–76		24	—
1976–77		46	2
1977–78	Brighton	40	1
1978–79		39	2
1979–80		33	1
1980–81		40	1
1981–82	Liverpool	39	2
1982–83		40	5
1983–84		42	—
1984–85		33	1
1985–86		38	3

LAWS, Brian

Born Wallsend 14.10.61. Ht 5 8 Wt 11 0
Defender. From Apprentice.

Season	Club	App	Goals
1979–80	Burnley	1	—
1980–81		42	2
1981–82		44	6
1982–83		38	4
1983–84	Huddersfield T	31	—
1984–85		25	1
1984–85	Middlesbrough	11	1
1985–86		42	2

LEADBITTER, Chris

Born Middlesbrough 17.10.67. Ht 5 9
Wt 10 7
Forward. From Apprentice.

Season	Club	App	Goals
1985–86	Grimsby T	—	—

LEANING, Andy

Born York 18.5.63. Ht 6 0 Wt 13 0
Goalkeeper. From Rowntree Mackintosh.

Season	Club	App	Goals
1984–85	York C	—	—
1985–86		30	—

LEE, Andy

Born Liverpool 14.9.62.
Defender. From Liverpool Apprentice and
New Zealand.

Season	Club	App	Goals
1984–85	Tranmere R	18	—
1985–86	Cambridge U	9	—

Season	Club	League Appearances/Goals	Season	Club	League Appearances/Goals

LEE, Colin

Born Plymouth 12.6.56.   Ht 6 1   Wt 11 9
Forward. From Apprentice.

Season	Club	App	Goals
1974–75	Bristol C	—	—
1974–75	*Hereford U*	9	—
1975–76		—	—
1976–77		—	—
1976–77	Torquay U	23	10
1977–78		12	4
1977–78	Tottenham H	25	11
1978–79		27	7
1979–80		10	—
1979–80	Chelsea	5	1
1980–81		35	15
1981–82		40	11
1982–83		35	5
1983–84		33	3
1984–85		22	1
1985–86		13	—

LEE, Dave

Born Manchester 5.11.67.
Midfield. From Blackburn schools.

Season	Club	App	Goals
1984–85	Bury	—	—
1985–86		1	—

LEE, Robert

Born West Ham 1.2.66.   Ht 5 8   Wt 10 12
Forward. From ABTA.

Season	Club	App	Goals
1983–84	Charlton Ath	11	4
1984–85		39	10
1985–86		35	8

LEE, Sammy

Born Liverpool 7.2.59.   Ht 5 7   Wt 10 1
Midfield. From Apprentice.
England Youth, Under-21, 14 full caps.

Season	Club	App	Goals
1976–77	Liverpool	—	—
1977–78		2	1
1978–79		2	—

Season	Club	App	Goals
1979–80		7	—
1980–81		37	4
1981–82		35	3
1982–83		40	3
1983–84		42	2
1984–85		17	—
1985–86		15	—

LEIGH, Ian

Born Ilfracombe 1.6.62.   Ht 5 11   Wt 12 3
Goalkeeper. From Swaythling.

Season	Club	App	Goals
1979–80	Bournemouth	—	—
1980–81		—	—
1981–82		36	—
1982–83		28	—
1983–84		41	—
1984–85		6	—
1984–85	*Bristol C*	1	—
1985–86	Bournemouth	12	—
1985–86	*Torquay U*	4	—

LEIGHTON, Jim

Born Johnstone 24.7.58.   Ht 6 1   Wt 11 9
Goalkeeper. From Dalry Thistle.
Scotland Under-21, 26 full caps.

Season	Club	App	Goals
1978–79	Aberdeen	11	—
1979–80		1	—
1980–81		35	—
1981–82		36	—
1982–83		35	—
1983–84		36	—
1984–85		34	—
1985–86		26	—

LEMON, Paul

Born Middlesbrough 3.6.66.   Ht 5 10
Wt 11 11
Forward. From Apprentice.

Season	Club	App	Goals
1984–85	Sunderland	11	—
1984–85	*Carlisle U*	2	—
1985–86	Sunderland	5	—

All appearances include those as substitute

Season	Club	League Appearances/Goals	Season	Club	League Appearances/Goals

LEONARD, Carleton

Born Oswestry 3.2.58. Ht 5 9 Wt 10 3
Defender. From Amateur.

Season	Club	App	Goals
1975–76	Shrewsbury T	18	—
1976–77		45	1
1977–78		37	—
1978–79		26	—
1979–80		27	—
1980–81		32	—
1981–82		26	—
1982–83		16	—
1983–84	Hereford T	25	—
1984–85		5	—
1985–86	Cardiff C	4	—

LEONARD, Gary

Born Newcastle 28.11.65. Ht 5 9 Wt 10 12
Defender. From Apprentice.

Season	Club	App	Goals
1983–84	WBA	—	—
1984–85		—	—
1985–86	Shrewsbury T	21	1

LEONARD, Mark

Born St Helens 27.9.62. Ht 5 11 Wt 11 10
Forward. From Witton Albion.

Season	Club	App	Goals
1981–82	Everton	—	—
1982–83		—	—
1982–83	*Tranmere R*	7	—
1983–84	Crewe Alex	38	10
1984–85		16	5
1984–85	Stockport Co	23	4
1985–86		44	19

LEONARD, Mick

Born Carshalton 9.5.59. Ht 5 11 Wt 11 0
Goalkeeper. From Epsom & Ewell.

Season	Club	App	Goals
1976–77	Halifax T	19	—
1977–78		20	—
1978–79		25	—
1979–80		5	—

Season	Club	App	Goals
1979–80	Notts Co	9	—
1980–81		4	—
1981–82		—	—
1982–83		6	—
1983–84		18	—
1984–85		31	—
1985–86		23	—

LESLIE, John

Born London 25.10.55. Ht 5 8 Wt 11 2
Forward. From Dulwich H.

Season	Club	App	Goals
1977–78	Wimbledon	41	13
1978–79		45	19
1979–80		43	11
1980–81		44	11
1981–82		38	9
1982–83		42	23
1983–84	Gillingham	45	9
1984–85		20	3
1985–86	Millwall	16	1

LESTER, Mike

Born Manchester 4.8.54. Ht 5 10 Wt 11 7
Midfield. From Apprentice.

Season	Club	App	Goals
1972–73	Oldham Ath	16	1
1973–74		11	—
1973–74	Manchester C	1	—
1974–75		—	—
1975–76		—	—
1975–76	*Stockport Co*	9	1
1976–77	Manchester C	1	—
From Washington D			
1977–78	Grimsby T	16	3
1978–79		30	7
1979–80		2	—
1979–80	Barnsley	33	6
1980–81		31	5
1981–82	Exeter C	19	6
1981–82	Bradford C	18	1
1982–83		31	1
1982–83	Scunthorpe U	11	3
1983–84		33	3
1984–85		44	3
1985–86		18	—
1985–86	*Hartlepool U*	11	1

Season	Club	League Appearances/Goals	Season	Club	League Appearances/Goals

LEVEIN, Craig

Born Dunfermline 22.10.64.   Ht 6 0   Wt 11 4
Defender. From Lochore Welfare.
Scotland Youth, Under-21.

1981–82	Cowdenbeath	15	—
1982–83		30	—
1983–84		15	—
1983–84	Hearts	22	—
1984–85		36	1
1985–86		33	2

LEWINGTON, Ray

Born Lambeth 7.9.56.   Ht 5 6   Wt 11 8
Midfield. From Apprentice.

1973–74	Chelsea	—	—
1974–75		—	—
1975–76		9	—
1976–77		42	2
1977–78		24	2
1978–79		10	—
From Vancouver Whitecaps			
1979–80	*Wimbledon*	23	—
1979–80	Fulham	10	1
1980–81		20	—
1981–82		31	4
1982–83		42	10
1983–84		33	—
1984–85		38	5
1985–86	Sheffield U	36	—

LEWIS, Dudley

Born Swansea 17.11.62.   Ht 5 10¼   Wt 10 9
Defender. From Apprentice. Wales Schools,
Under-21, 1 full cap.

1979–80	Swansea C	—	—
1980–81		12	—
1981–82		1	—
1982–83		23	1
1983–84		37	—
1984–85		43	1
1985–86		24	—

LEWIS, John

Born Tredegar 15.10.55.   Ht 5 10   Wt 11 10
Midfield. From Pontllanfraith.

1978–79	Cardiff C	16	—
1979–80		28	2
1980–81		32	1
1981–82		19	1
1982–83		39	5
1983–84		6	—
1983–84	Newport Co	25	1
1984–85		33	2
1985–86		44	1

LEWIS, John

Born Hexham 30.11.67.   Ht 5 10   Wt 10 10
Defender. From Apprentice.

| 1985–86 | Sunderland | — | — |

LEWIS, Mickey

Born Birmingham 15.2.65.   Ht 5 6   Wt 10 6
Midfield. From school. England Youth.

1981–82	WBA	4	—
1982–83		5	—
1983–84		14	—
1984–85		1	—
1984–85	Derby Co	22	—
1985–86		5	1

LEWIS, Morgan

Born Bournemouth 8.9.65.   Ht 5 8½
Wt 11 0
Midfield. From school.

1983–84	Bournemouth	1	—
1984–85		4	—
1985–86		4	—

Season	Club	League Appearances/Goals		Season	Club	League Appearances/Goals	

LEWIS, Russell

Born Neath 15.9.56. Ht 5 10½ Wt 12 12
Defender. From Everwarm.

Season	Club	App	Goals
1976–77	Swindon T	4	—
1977–78		2	—
1978–79		9	—
1979–80		43	3
1980–81		37	2
1981–82		43	1
1982–83		43	1
1983–84	Northampton T	45	4
1984–85		44	2
1985–86		43	—

LEWORTHY, David

Born Portsmouth 22.10.62. Ht 5 8½
Wt 11 11
Forward. From Apprentice.

Season	Club	App	Goals
1980–81	Portsmouth	—	—
1981–82		1	—
From Fareham T			
1984–85	Tottenham H	6	3
1985–86		5	—
1985–86	Oxford U	7	4

LIDDLE, Mark

Born Willington Quay 6.1.68. Ht 6 2
Wt 12 6
Defender. From Apprentice.

Season	Club	App	Goals
1985–86	Sunderland	—	—

LILLIS, Mark

Born Manchester 17.1.60. Ht 6 0 Wt 12 12
Forward. Local.

Season	Club	App	Goals
1978–79	Huddersfield T	12	—
1979–80		—	—
1980–81		34	7
1981–82		42	5

Season	Club	App	Goals
1982–83		46	20
1983–84		37	11
1984–85		35	13
1985–86	Manchester C	39	11

LIM, Harvey

Born Halesworth 30.8.67. Ht 6 0 Wt 13 7
Goalkeeper. From Apprentice.

Season	Club	App	Goals
1984–85	Norwich C	—	—
1985–86		—	—
1985–86	*Plymouth Arg*	—	—

LINDSAY, David

Born Havering 17.5.66. Ht 5 7½ Wt 10 7
Midfield. From Apprentice.

Season	Club	App	Goals
1983–84	Crystal Palace	1	—
1984–85		11	—
1985–86		9	—

LINEKER, Gary

Born Leicester 30.11.60. Ht 5 9¾
Wt 11 10½
Forward. From Apprentice. England
13 full caps.

Season	Club	App	Goals
1978–79	Leicester C	7	1
1979–80		19	3
1980–81		9	2
1981–82		39	17
1982–83		40	26
1983–84		39	22
1984–85		41	24
1985–86	Everton	41	30

LING, Martin

Born West Ham 15.7.66. Ht 5 7 Wt 9 12
Forward. From Apprentice.

Season	Club	League Appearances/Goals		Season	Club	League Appearances/Goals	

1983–84	Exeter C	29	—
1984–85		42	6
1985–86		45	8

LINIGHAN, Andy

Born Hartlepool 18.6.62. Ht 6 2½ Wt 12 6
Defender. From Smiths B.C.

1980–81	Hartlepool U	6	—
1981–82		17	—
1982–83		45	3
1983–84		42	1
1984–85	Leeds U	42	2
1985–86		24	1
1985–86	Oldham Ath	15	1

LINIGHAN, David

Born Hartlepool 9.1.65. Ht 6 2 Wt 10 12
Defender. Local.

1981–82	Hartlepool U	6	—
1982–83		6	1
1983–84		23	1
1984–85		17	2
1984–85	*Leeds U*	—	—
1985–86	Hartlepool U	39	1

LISTER, Steve

Born Doncaster 18.11.61. Ht 6 1 Wt 11 0
Midfield. From Apprentice.

1978–79	Doncaster R	9	—
1979–80		40	12
1980–81		39	3
1981–82		41	7
1982–83		41	4
1983–84		31	2
1984–85		36	2
1985–86	Scunthorpe U	37	2

LITCHFIELD, Peter

Born Manchester 27.7.56. Ht 6 1 Wt 12 12
Goalkeeper. From Manchester C and
Droylsden.

1978–79	Preston NE	—	—
1979–80		—	—
1980–81		3	—
1981–82		18	—
1982–83		23	—
1983–84		45	—
1984–85		18	—
1985–86	Bradford C	42	—

LITTLE, Alan

Born Newcastle 5.2.55. Ht 5 11 Wt 11 7
Midfield. From Apprentice.

1972–73	Aston Villa	—	—
1973–74		—	—
1974–75		3	—
1974–75	Southend U	24	1
1975–76		45	6
1976–77		34	5
1977–78	Barnsley	44	7
1978–79		40	7
1979–80		7	—
1979–80	Doncaster R	22	2
1980–81		37	7
1981–82		20	2
1982–83		6	—
1982–83	Torquay	37	3
1983–84		14	1
1983–84	Halifax T	27	3
1984–85		41	3
1985–86	Hartlepool U	12	1

LITTLEJOHNS, Colin

Born 8.9.68.
Midfield. From YTS.

| 1985–86 | Cambridge U | 1 | — |

Season	Club	League Appearances/Goals	Season	Club	League Appearances/Goals

LLEWELLYN, Andy

Born Bristol 26.2.66.   Ht 5 7   Wt 11 12
Midfield. From Apprentice. England Youth.

1983–84	Bristol C	—	—
1984–85		22	—
1985–86		38	1

LLOYD, David

Born Glasgow 18.10.60.   Ht 6 0   Wt 11 4
Forward. From Lesmahagow Juniors

1981–82	Alloa	2	—
1982–83		35	6
1983–84		32	10
1984–85		36	16
1985–86	Clydebank	18	7

LLOYD, Philip

Born Hemsworth 26.12.64.   Ht 6 0
Wt 11 13
Defender. From Apprentice.

1982–83	Middlesbrough	—	—
1983–84	Barnsley	—	—
1983–84	Darlington	14	—
1984–85		41	2
1985–86		29	—

LOCK, Kevin

Born Plaistow 27.12.53.   Ht 6 0   Wt 12 5
Defender. From Apprentice. England Youth, Under-23.

1971–72	West Ham U	3	—
1972–73		18	1
1973–74		11	—
1974–75		42	—
1975–76		26	—
1976–77		26	—
1977–78		6	1
1978–79	Fulham	39	3
1979–80		38	5
1980–81		29	5
1981–82		26	5

1982–83		34	2
1983–84		15	2
1984–85		30	5
1985–86	Southend U	10	—

LOCKE, Gary

Born Kingsbury 12.7.54.   Ht 5 11   Wt 11 5
Defender. From Apprentice. England Youth.

1971–72	Chelsea	—	—
1972–73		18	—
1973–74		31	—
1974–75		41	1
1975–76		23	1
1976–77		42	—
1977–78		18	—
1978–79		8	—
1979–80		32	—
1980–81		22	—
1981–82		31	1
1982–83		6	—
1982–83	Crystal Palace	13	—
1983–84		36	1
1984–85		25	—
1985–86		10	—

LOCKHART, Keith

Born Wallsend 19.7.64.   Ht 6 0   Wt 11 5
Midfield. From Apprentice.

1981–82	Cambridge U	2	—
1982–83		13	2
1983–84		15	3
1984–85		19	1
1985–86		9	2
1985–86	Wolverhampton W	12	2

LODGE, Paul

Born Liverpool 13.2.61.   Ht 5 8½   Wt 10 11
Midfield. From Apprentice. England Schools.

1978–79	Everton	—	—
1979–80		—	—

Season	Club	League Appearances/Goals	
1980–81	....	11	—
1981–82	....	13	—
1982–83	....	—	—
1982–83	*Wigan Ath*	5	1
1982–83	*Rotherham U*	4	—
1982–83	Preston NE	19	—
1983–84	....	19	—
1984–85	Bolton W	4	—
1984–85	*Port Vale*	3	—
1984–85	*Stockport Co*	12	2
1985–86	Stockport Co	1	—

LOGAN, David

Born Middlesbrough 5.12.63.   Ht 5 9
Wt 10 9
Defender. From Whitby.

Season	Club	League Appearances/Goals	
1984–85	Mansfield T	17	—
1985–86	....	24	1

LOHMAN, Jan

Born Hook 18.2.59.   Ht 5 10   Wt 11 7½
Forward. From Lokeren. Holland Under-21.

Season	Club	League Appearances/Goals	
1981–82	Watford	26	2
1982–83	....	19	1
1983–84	....	7	2
1984–85	....	7	—
1985–86	....	4	1

LOMAX, Geoff

Born Manchester 6.7.64.   Ht 5 8   Wt 11 5
Defender. Local.

Season	Club	League Appearances/Goals	
1981–82	Manchester C	—	—
1982–83	....	1	—
1983–84	....	17	1
1984–85	....	7	—
1985–86	....	—	—
1985–86	*Wolverhampton W*	5	—
1985–86	Carlisle U	13	—

LONGDEN, Paul

Born Wakefield 28.9.62.   Ht 5 7   Wt 10 3
Defender. From Apprentice.

Season	Club	League Appearances/Goals	
1981–82	Barnsley.....................	4	—
1982–83	....	1	—
1983–84	Scunthorpe U	43	—
1984–85	....	14	—
1985–86	....	31	—

LONGHURST, David

Born Northampton 15.1.65   Ht 5 8
Wt 10 12
Forward. From Apprentice.

Season	Club	League Appearances/Goals	
1982–83	Nottingham F	—	—
1983–84	....	—	—
1984–85	....	—	—
1985–86	Halifax T	44	14

LONGLEY, Nick

Born Mexborough 21.5.61.   Ht 6 1   Wt 13 0
Goalkeeper.

Season	Club	League Appearances/Goals	
1981–82	Crewe Alex	3	—
1982–83	....	—	—
1983–84	....	—	—
1984–85	....	17	—
1985–86	....	3	—

LORAM, Mike

Born Brixham 13.8.67.   Ht 6 0   Wt 12 0
Midfield. From Brixham.

Season	Club	League Appearances/Goals	
1984–85	Torquay U	14	2
1985–86	....	38	6
1985–86	*QPR*...........................	—	—

LORIMER, Peter

Born Dundee 14.12.46.   Ht 5 10   Wt 12 12
Midfield. From school. Scotland schools,
Youth, amateur, Under-23, 21 full caps.

Season	Club	League Appearances/Goals		Season	Club	League Appearances/Goals	
1962–63	Leeds U	1	—	1979–80	Swansea C	2	—
1963–64		—	—	1980–81		1	—
1964–65		1	—	1981–82		1	—
1965–66		33	13	1982–83		17	1
1966–67		30	9	1983–84		18	2
1967–68		37	17	1984–85		8	1
1968–69		28	8	1985–86	Charlton Ath	6	—
1969–70		39	14				
1970–71		38	12				
1971–72		42	23				
1972–73		41	15				
1973–74		37	12				
1974–75		36	9				
1975–76		29	10				
1976–77		26	3				
1977–78		28	6				
1978–79		3	—				
1979–80	York C	29	8				

From Toronto Blizzard

1983–84	Leeds U	22	4
1984–85		40	9
1985–86		14	4

To Israel

LOVELL, Steve

Born Swansea 16.7.60.   Ht 5 9   Wt 11 2
Midfield. From Apprentice. Wales 6 full caps.

1977–78	Crystal Palace	—	—
1978–79		—	—
1979–80		—	—
1979–80	Stockport Co	12	—
1980–81	Crystal Palace	25	2
1981–82		30	1
1982–83		19	—
1982–83	Millwall	17	1
1983–84		46	7
1984–85		41	22
1985–86		42	14

LOVERIDGE, Jimmy

Born Swansea 19.10.62.   Ht 5 8¼   Wt 11 1½
Midfield. From Apprentice. Wales Schools, Under-21.

LOWE, David

Born Liverpool 30.8.65.   Ht 5 10   Wt 9 3
Forward. From Apprentice. England Youth.

1982–83	Wigan Ath	28	6
1983–84		40	8
1984–85		29	5
1985–86		46	5

LOWE, Gary

Born Prescot 21.2.67.
Midfield.

1985–86	Bury	4	—

LOWE, Simon

Born London 26.12.62.   Ht 5 10½   Wt 12 3
Forward.

1983–84	Barnsley	2	—
1984–85	Halifax T	42	12
1985–86		35	7

LOWERY, Tony

Born Wallsend 6.7.61.   Ht 5 9   Wt 11 1
Midfield. From Ashington.

1980–81	WBA	—	—
1981–82		1	—
1981–82	Walsall	6	1
1982–83		—	—
1982–83	Mansfield T	1	—
1983–84		45	6
1984–85		45	3
1985–86		40	5

Season	Club	League Appearances/Goals	Season	Club	League Appearances/Goals

LOWEY, John

Born Manchester 7.3.58.   Ht 6 0   Wt 12 6
Midfield. From Apprentice.

Season	Club	Apps	Goals
1974–75	Manchester U	—	—
1975–76		—	—
1976–77		—	—
From Chicago Stings			
1977–78	Blackburn	—	—
1977–78	Port Vale	—	—
From California S			
1978–79	Sheffield W	29	3
1979–80		13	1
1980–81		—	—
1980–81	Blackburn R	19	2
1981–82		14	1
1982–83		22	5
1983–84		42	—
1984–85		21	3
1985–86		23	3

LOWNDES, Steve

Born Cwmbran 17.6.60.   Ht 5 10   Wt 11 0
Forward. From Amateur. Wales Under-21,
8 full caps.

Season	Club	Apps	Goals
1977–78	Newport Co	5	—
1978–79		43	8
1979–80		46	7
1980–81		40	9
1981–82		31	3
1982–83		43	12
1983–84	Millwall	20	3
1984–85		37	7
1985–86		39	6

LUKE, Noel

Born Birmingham 28.12.64.   Ht 5 11
Wt 10 11
Midfield. From school.

Season	Club	Apps	Goals
1981–82	WBA	—	—
1982–83		1	—

Season	Club	Apps	Goals
1983–84		8	1
1984–85	Mansfield T	36	6
1985–86		14	3

LUKIC, John

Born Chesterfield 11.12.60.   Ht 6 4
Wt 13 7
Goalkeeper. From Apprentice. England
Youth, Under-21.

Season	Club	Apps	Goals
1978–79	Leeds U	—	—
1979–80		33	—
1980–81		42	—
1981–82		42	—
1982–83		29	—
1983–84	Arsenal	4	—
1984–85		27	—
1985–86		40	—

LUND, Gary

Born Grimsby 13.9.64.   Ht 5 11   Wt 11 0
Forward. From school. England Youth,
Under-21.

Season	Club	Apps	Goals
1983–84	Grimsby T	7	4
1984–85		24	12
1985–86		29	8

LUNN, Grant

Born Guildford 26.8.67.
Goalkeeper. From Chelsea Apprentice
and Farnborough.

Season	Club	Apps	Goals
1985–86	Aldershot	9	

LYNCH, Tony

Born Paddington 20.1.66.   Ht 5 8   Wt 10 8
Forward.

Season	Club	League Appearances/Goals		Season	Club	League Appearances/Goals	

1983–84	Brentford	2	—
1984–85		10	—
1985–86		33	6

LYNEX, Steve

Born West Bromwich 23.1.58.   Ht 5 9
Wt 11 5
Forward. From Apprentice.

1975–76	WBA	—	—
1976–77		—	—
From Shamrock R			
1978–79	Birmingham C	2	1
1979–80		30	8
1980–81		14	1
1980–81	Leicester C	12	5
1981–82		41	10
1982–83		38	9
1983–84		40	12
1984–85		42	13
1985–86		30	8

LYONS, Mick

Born Liverpool 8.12.51.   Ht 6 0   Wt 12 2
Defender. From Apprentice. England
Under-23, 'B'.

1969–70	Everton	—	—
1970–71		2	1
1971–72		24	3
1972–73		25	2
1973–74		41	9
1974–75		38	8
1975–76		42	5
1976–77		40	4
1977–78		42	5
1978–79		37	6
1979–80		39	—
1980–81		33	2
1981–82		27	3
1982–83	Sheffield W	39	3
1983–84		42	5
1984–85		37	3
1985–86		11	1
1985–86	Grimsby T	24	4

MACARI, Lou

Born Aberdeen 4.6.49.   Ht 5 5½.   Wt 11 4
Forward. From St Michaels.
Scotland Under-23, 24 full caps.

1968–69	Celtic	1	1
1969–70		13	8
1970–71		11	5
1971–72		20	15
1972–73		11	3
1972–73	Manchester U	16	5
1973–74		35	5
1974–75		38	11
1975–76		36	12
1976–77		38	9
1977–78		32	8
1978–79		32	6
1979–80		39	9
1980–81		38	9
1981–82		11	2
1982–83		9	2
1983–84		5	—
1984–85	Swindon T	27	3
1985–86		9	—

MacDONALD, Alex

Born Glasgow 17.3.48.   Ht 5 6   Wt 10 10
Midfield. From Glasgow United. Scotland
Under-23, 1 full cap.

1965–66	St Johnstone	8	3
1966–67		17	3
1967–68		30	9
1968–69		11	2
1968–69	Rangers	8	1
1969–70		15	3
1970–71		33	5
1971–72		32	11
1972–73		29	3
1973–74		30	3
1974–75		30	2
1975–76		35	4
1976–77		30	9
1977–78		34	3
1978–79		33	5
1979–80		26	1

Season	Club	League Appearances/Goals	
1980–81	Hearts	28	3
1981–82		16	1
1982–83		31	5
1983–84		24	1
1984–85		22	2
1985–86		1	—

MACDONALD, Gary

Born Middlesbrough 26.3.62.   Ht 6 0
Wt 12 1
Forward. From Apprentice.

Season	Club	League Appearances/Goals	
1979–80	Middlesbrough	—	—
1980–81		7	—
1981–82		8	1
1982–83		9	1
1983–84		29	3
1984–85	Carlisle U	9	—
1984–85	Darlington	33	4
1985–86		36	16

MacDONALD, John

Born Glasgow 15.4.61.   Ht 5 8
Wt 10 1
Forward. From Clydebank Strollers.
Scotland Schools, Youth, Under-21.

Season	Club	League Appearances/Goals	
1978–79	Rangers	2	—
1979–80		26	5
1980–81		30	11
1981–82		34	14
1982–83		30	10
1983–84		18	1
1984–85		18	3
1985–86		2	—

MACDONALD, Kevin

Born Inverness 22.12.60.   Ht 6 0¼
Wt 11 11¼
Midfield. From Inverness Caley.

Season	Club	League Appearances/Goals	
1980–81	Leicester C	20	2
1981–82		25	1
1982–83		42	4

Season	Club	League Appearances/Goals	
1983–84		38	1
1984–85		13	—
1984–85	Liverpool	13	—
1985–86		17	1

MacDONALD, Roddy

Born Dingwall 30.8.54.   Ht 6 1   Wt 12 9
Defender. From Brora Rangers.
Scotland Under-23.

Season	Club	League Appearances/Goals	
1972–73	Celtic	—	—
1973–74		2	—
1974–75		15	—
1975–76		27	—
1976–77		24	2
1977–78		36	7
1978–79		18	2
1979–80		29	6
1980–81		14	2
1981–82	Hearts	35	6
1982–83		39	3
1983–84		34	2
1984–85		28	1
1985–86		10	2

MACKAY, Billy

Born Glenrothes 27.10.60.   Ht 5 7
Wt 10 0
Forward. From Glenrothes. Scotland
Schools, Youth.

Season	Club	League Appearances/Goals	
1977–78	Rangers	1	—
1978–79		1	—
1979–80		2	—
1980–81		6	—
1981–82		7	1
1982–83		4	—
1983–84		2	—
1984–85		—	—
1985–86	Hearts	3	—

MACKAY, Gary

Born Edinburgh 23.1.64.   Ht 5 9   Wt 10 5
Midfield. From Salvesen B.C. Scotland
Schools, Youth.

Season	Club	League Appearances/Goals		Season	Club	League Appearances/Goals	
1980–81	Hearts	12	—	1976–77	Dundee	4	—
1981–82		17	2	1977–78		25	3
1982–83		34	6	1978–79		1	—
1983–84		31	4	1978–79	Partick T	35	—
1984–85		17	2	1979–80		30	—
1985–86		32	4	1980–81		8	—
				1981–82		26	—

MACKENZIE, Steve

Born Romford 23.11.61. Ht 5 10 Wt 11 4
Midfield. From Apprentice. England Youth,
Under-21, 'B'.

				1982–83	Rangers	31	1
				1983–84		17	—
				1984–85		30	—
				1985–86		24	—

Season	Club	App	Goals
1979–80	Crystal Palace	—	—
1979–80	Manchester C	19	2
1980–81		39	6
1981–82	WBA	37	5
1982–83		1	—
1983–84		19	4
1984–85		38	8
1985–86		31	4

MacLAREN, Ross

Born Edinburgh 14.4.62. Ht 5 10 Wt 12 7
Midfield. From Glasgow Rangers.

Season	Club	App	Goals
1980–81	Shrewsbury T	4	—
1981–82		35	—
1982–83		40	5
1983–84		40	7
1984–85		42	6
1985–86	Derby Co	46	4

MACKIE, Peter

Born Glasgow 17.1.58. Ht 5 7 Wt 10 7
Forward. From Celtic B.C.

Season	Club	App	Goals
1974–75	Celtic	—	—
1975–76		—	—
1976–77		—	—
1977–78		1	—
1978–79		2	—
1979–80	Dundee	22	2
1980–81		34	5
1981–82		32	4
1982–83		36	5
1983–84		26	3
1984–85	St Mirren	21	2
1985–86		24	2

MACOWAT, Ian

Born Oxford 19.11.65. Ht 5 9½ Wt 11 10
Forward. From Apprentice. England
Schools, Youth.

Season	Club	App	Goals
1983–84	Everton	—	—
1984–85		—	—
1984–85	Gillingham	2	—
1985–86		3	—

MacPHAIL, John

Born Dundee 7.12.55. Ht 6 0 Wt 12 3
Defender. From St. Columba's.

Season	Club	App	Goals
1975–76	Dundee	6	—
1976–77		25	—
1977–78		34	—
1978–79		3	—
1978–79	Sheffield U	15	1
1979–80		44	5
1980–81		39	—
1981–82		26	1
1982–83		11	—

MacKINNON, Dave

Born Glasgow 23.5.56. Ht 5 9 Wt 11 13
Defender. From Apprentice.

Season	Club	App	Goals
1973–74	Arsenal	—	—
1974–75		—	—
1975–76		—	—

All appearances include those as substitute

Season	Club	League Appearances/Goals		Season	Club	League Appearances/Goals	

Season	Club	Appearances	Goals
1982–83	York C	12	2
1983–84	....	46	10
1984–85	....	42	5
1985–86	....	42	7

McADAM, Colin

Born Glasgow 28.8.51.   Ht 6 2   Wt 13 4
Forward. From Clydebank Juveniles.

Season	Club	Appearances	Goals
1969–70	Dumbarton	8	—
1970–71	....	7	3
1971–72	....	12	—
1972–73	....	4	—
1973–74	....	22	5
1974–75	....	19	6
1975–76	Motherwell	24	—
1976–77	....	28	—
1977–78	....	10	3
1977–78	Partick T	12	3
1978–79	....	26	4
1979–80	....	32	17
1980–81	Rangers	31	12
1981–82	....	22	2
1982–83	....	4	—
1983–84	....	8	1
From Adelaide City			
1985–86	Hearts	6	—

McADAM, Tom

Born Glasgow 9.4.54.   Ht 6 0   Wt 12 9
Defender. From Glasgow schools.

Season	Club	Appearances	Goals
1971–72	Dumbarton	—	—
1972–73	....	17	9
1973–74	....	19	5
1974–75	....	33	11
1975–76	....	6	4
1975–76	Dundee U	26	12
1976–77	....	33	9
1977–78	....	2	—
1977–78	Celtic	33	8
1978–79	....	28	7
1979–80	....	34	8
1980–81	....	35	4
1981–82	....	34	5
1982–83	....	35	3

Season	Club	Appearances	Goals
1983–84	....	28	1
1984–85	....	26	—
1985–86	....	5	—

McALLISTER, Gary

Born Motherwell 25.12.64.   Ht 5 10   Wt 9 6
Midfield. From Fir Park B.C.

Season	Club	Appearances	Goals
1981–82	Motherwell	1	—
1982–83	....	1	—
1983–84	....	21	—
1984–85	....	35	6
1985–86	....	1	—
1985–86	Leicester C	31	7

McALLISTER, Kevin

Born Falkirk 8.11.62.   Ht 5 5   Wt 11 0
Forward.

Season	Club	Appearances	Goals
1983–84	Falkirk	35	11
1984–85	....	29	7
1985–86	Chelsea	20	—

McALISTER, Tom

Born Clydebank 10.12.52.   Ht 6 1
Wt 12 13
Goalkeeper. From Apprentice.

Season	Club	Appearances	Goals
1970–71	Sheffield U	—	—
1971–72	....	4	—
1972–73	....	42	—
1973–74	....	12	—
1974–75	....	—	—
1975–76	....	5	—
1975–76	Rotherham U	22	—
1976–77	....	46	—
1977–78	....	46	—
1978–79	....	45	—
1979–80	Blackpool	16	—
1980–81	Swindon T	1	—
1980–81	*Bristol R*	13	—
1981–82	West Ham U	3	—
1982–83	....	—	—
1983–84	....	—	—
1984–85	....	32	—
1985–86	....	—	—

Season	Club	League Appearances/Goals	Season	Club	League Appearances/Goals

McALPINE, Hamish

Born Kilspindie 21.1.48. Ht 5 11 Wt 12 6
Goalkeeper. From Dundee N.E. Scotland
Under-21.

Season	Club	App	Goals
1966–67	Dundee	—	—
1967–68	*Montrose*	25	—
1968–69	Dundee U	1	—
1969–70		—	—
1970–71		24	—
1971–72		29	—
1972–73		24	—
1973–74		19	—
1974–75		34	—
1975–76		36	1
1976–77		36	2
1977–78		35	—
1978–79		36	—
1979–80		29	—
1980–81		36	—
1981–82		35	—
1982–83		36	—
1983–84		34	—
1984–85		25	—
1985–86		8	—

McANDREW, Tony

Born Glasgow 11.4.56. Ht 5 10 Wt 12 6
Defender. From Apprentice.

Season	Club	App	Goals
1973–74	Middlesbrough	1	—
1974–75		1	—
1975–76		12	3
1976–77		39	1
1977–78		41	—
1978–79		38	1
1979–80		39	1
1980–81		37	3
1981–82		39	4
1982–83			
1982–83	Chelsea	7	—
1983–84		13	4
1984–85		—	—
1984–85	Middlesbrough	32	—
1985–86		34	2

McATEER, Andy

Born Preston 24.4.61. Ht 5 10 Wt 11 3
Defender. From Apprentice.

Season	Club	App	Goals
1978–79	Preston NE	—	—
1979–80		21	—
1980–81		20	—
1981–82		41	—
1982–83		44	5
1983–84		34	—
1984–85		33	2
1985–86		29	—

McAUGHTRIE, David

Born Cumnock 30.1.63. Ht 6 2¼ Wt 12 3
Defender. From Apprentice.

Season	Club	App	Goals
1980–81	Stoke C	1	—
1981–82		13	—
1982–83		20	1
1983–84		17	—
1984–85	Carlisle U	28	1
1985–86	York C	41	1

McAVENNIE, Frank

Born Glasgow 22.11.59. Ht 5 9 Wt 11 0
Forward. From Johnstone Borough and
Partick T trialist. Scotland Under-21, 2 full
caps.

Season	Club	App	Goals
1981–82	St Mirren	31	13
1982–83		36	9
1983–84		34	12
1984–85		34	16
1985–86	West Ham U	41	26

McBRIDE, Andy

Born Glasgow 12.8.68. Ht 5 5 Wt 8 6½
Midfield. From Apprentice.

Season	Club	App	Goals
1985–86	Manchester U	—	—

All appearances include those as substitute

Season	Club	League Appearances/Goals		Season	Club	League Appearances/Goals	

McBRIDE, Joe

Born Glasgow 17.8.60. Ht 5 8   Wt 11 2
Forward. From Apprentice.
Scotland Schools, Youth, Under-21.

Season	Club	App	Goals
1978–79	Everton	—	—
1979–80		18	1
1980–81		31	7
1981–82		8	1
1982–83	Rotherham U	42	11
1983–84		3	1
1983–84	Oldham Ath	25	4
1984–85		11	1
1984–85	Hibernian	12	2
1985–86		14	1

McBRIDE, Martin

Born Bellshill 28.11.67. Ht 5 8   Wt 10 0
Forward. From Wishaw Juniors.

Season	Club	App	Goals
1984–85	Motherwell	—	—
1985–86		1	—

McCABE, Gerry

Born Hamilton 26.9.56. Ht 5 10   Wt 10 7
Forward. From Windsor All-Stars.

Season	Club	App	Goals
1977–78	Clyde	20	3
1978–79		37	3
1979–80		39	8
1980–81	Clydebank	38	1
1981–82		37	8
1982–83		37	4
1983–84		37	4
1984–85		33	4
1985–86		24	—

McCAFFERY, Aiden

Born Newcastle 30.8.57. Ht 5 11   Wt 11 5
Defender. From Apprentice.
England Youth.

Season	Club	App	Goals
1974–75	Newcastle U	3	—
1975–76		4	—
1976–77		38	3
1977–78		14	1

Season	Club	App	Goals
1978–79	Derby C	6	—
1979–80		31	4
1980–81	Bristol R	38	5
1981–82		25	3
1981–82	*Bristol C*	6	1
1981–82	Bristol R	4	—
1982–83		45	3
1983–84		45	—
1984–85		27	—
1984–85	*Torquay U*	6	—
1985–86	Exeter C	33	—

McCALL, Steve

Born Carlisle 15.10.60. Ht 5 11   Wt 11 3
Midfield. From Apprentice.
England Youth, Under-21.

Season	Club	App	Goals
1978–79	Ipswich T	—	—
1979–80		10	—
1980–81		31	1
1981–82		42	1
1982–83		42	4
1983–84		42	1
1984–85		31	—
1985–86		33	—

McCALL, Stuart

Born Leeds 10.6.64. Ht 5 6   Wt 10 1
Midfield. From Apprentice.

Season	Club	App	Goals
1982–83	Bradford C	28	4
1983–84		46	5
1984–85		46	8
1985–86		38	4

McCALL, Walker

Born Irvine 29.3.54. Ht 6 2   Wt 13 1
Forward. From Hurlford United.

Season	Club	App	Goals
1973–74	Aberdeen	6	2
1974–75		14	6
1975–76		1	—
1976–77	Ayr U	33	16
1977–78		35	12
1978–79	St Johnstone	5	—
1979–80		—	—

Season	Club	League Appearances/Goals		Season	Club	League Appearances/Goals	

Season	Club	App	Goals
1980–81	Aberdeen	17	10
1981–82		8	4
1982–83		3	—
1983–84	Dundee	31	13
1984–85		24	1
1985–86		2	—

McCARRICK, Mark

Born Liverpool 4.2.62.   Ht 5 8   Wt 10 8
Defender. From Witton Albion.

Season	Club	App	Goals
1983–84	Birmingham C	15	—
1984–85	Lincoln C	30	—
1985–86		14	—
1985–86	Crewe Alex	11	—

McCART, Chris

Born Motherwell 17.4.67.   Ht 5 9   Wt 10 5
Midfield. From Fir Park B.C.

Season	Club	App	Goals
1984–85	Motherwell	—	—
1985–86		13	—

McCARTHY, Mike

Born Barnsley 7.2.59.   Ht 6 1½   Wt 13 3
Defender. From Apprentice. Eire 13 full caps.

Season	Club	App	Goals
1977–78	Barnsley	46	1
1978–79		46	2
1979–80		44	1
1980–81		43	1
1981–82		42	1
1982–83		39	1
1983–84		12	—
1983–84	Manchester C	24	1
1984–85		39	—
1985–86		38	—

McCARTHY, Sean

Born Bridgend 12.9.67.
Forward.

Season	Club	App	Goals
1985–86	Swansea C	22	3

McCARTNEY, Mike

Born Edinburgh 28.9.54.   Ht 5 7   Wt 10 12
Defender. From Apprentice.
Scotland Schools.

Season	Club	App	Goals
1971–72	WBA	—	—
1972–73		—	—
1973–74	Carlisle U	4	—
1974–75		2	—
1975–76		14	3
1976–77		20	1
1977–78		46	6
1978–79		44	5
1979–80		26	2
1980–81	Southampton	22	1
1981–82	Plymouth Arg	16	—
1982–83		33	5
1982–83	Carlisle U	9	—
1983–84		21	—
1984–85		40	5
1985–86		40	2

McCLAIR, Brian

Born Bellshill 8.12.63.   Ht 5 10   Wt 10 6
Forward. From Apprentice. Scotland
Under-21.

Season	Club	App	Goals
1980–81	Aston Villa	—	—
1981–82	Motherwell	11	4
1982–83		28	11
1983–84	Celtic	35	23
1984–85		32	19
1985–86		34	22

McCLAREN, Steve

Born Fulford 3.5.61.   Ht 5 9   Wt 10 7
Midfield. From Apprentice.

Season	Club	App	Goals
1978–79	Hull C	—	—
1979–80		1	—
1980–81		20	1
1981–82		37	4
1982–83		40	4
1983–84		40	3
1984–85		40	4
1985–86	Derby Co	23	—

Season	Club	League Appearances/Goals		Season	Club	League Appearances/Goals	

McCLELLAND, John

Born Belfast 7.12.55.   Ht 6 1   Wt 11 4
Defender. From Portadown. Northern
Ireland 38 full caps.

Season	Club	App	Goals
1973–74	Cardiff C	—	—
1974–75		4	1
From Bangor			
1978–79	Mansfield T	36	1
1979–80		43	1
1980–81		46	6
1981–82	Rangers	14	—
1982–83		35	2
1983–84		36	2
1984–85		11	—
1984–85	Watford	29	1
1985–86		31	1

McCLOY, Peter

Born Girvan 16.11.46.   Ht 6 4   Wt 14 8
Goalkeeper. Scotland Youth, 4 full caps.

Season	Club	App	Goals
1964–65	Motherwell	5	—
1965–66		32	—
1966–67		32	—
1967–68		34	—
1968–69		19	—
1969–70		15	—
1969–70	Rangers	7	—
1970–71		31	—
1971–72		34	—
1972–73		33	—
1973–74		30	—
1974–75		—	—
1975–76		24	—
1976–77		5	—
1977–78		14	—
1978–79		36	—
1979–80		34	—
1980–81		26	—
1981–82		10	—
1982–83		17	—
1983–84		26	—
1984–85		21	—
1985–86		2	—

McCLURE, Doug

Born London 6.9.64.   Ht 5 8   Wt 11 4
Defender. From Apprentice.
England Schools, Youth.

Season	Club	App	Goals
1982–83	QPR	—	—
1983–84		—	—
1984–85	Exeter C	1	—
1984–85	Torquay U	4	—
1984–85	Wimbledon	2	—
1985–86	Peterborough U	4	—
1985–86	Wimbledon	—	—
1985–86	Crewe Alex	3	—
1985–86	Wimbledon	—	—

McCLUSKEY, George

Born Hamilton 19.9.57.   Ht 6 1   Wt 12 1
Forward. From Celtic Boys Club.
Scotland Under-21.

Season	Club	App	Goals
1975–76	Celtic	4	—
1976–77		—	—
1977–78		15	6
1978–79		21	5
1979–80		23	10
1980–81		22	10
1981–82		35	21
1982–83		10	2
1983–84	Leeds U	32	8
1984–85		19	5
1985–86		22	3

McCLUSKIE, Jim

Born Rossendale 29.9.66.
Forward. Local.

Season	Club	App	Goals
1983–84	Rochdale	5	—
1984–85		—	—
1985–86		14	—

McCOIST, Ally

Born Bellshill 24.9.62.   Ht 5 10   Wt 12 0
Forward. From Fir Park B.C. Scotland
Youth, Under-21, 1 full cap.

Season	Club	League Appearances/Goals		Season	Club	League Appearances/Goals	
1978–79	St Johnstone	4	—	1978–79	Arsenal	2	—
1979–80		15	—	1979–80		1	—
1980–81		38	22	1980–81		23	5
1981–82	Sunderland	28	2	1981–82		13	1
1982–83		28	6	1982–83		9	4
1983–84	Rangers	30	9	1982–83	*Fulham*	3	—
1984–85		25	12	1983–84	Arsenal	13	2
1985–86		33	24	1984–85	Oxford U	18	2
				1985–86		4	—

McCORMACK, John

Born Glasgow 25.4.55.   Ht 5 10   Wt 11 7
Defender. From St Roch's.

Season	Club	App	Goals
1976–77	Clydebank	3	—
1977–78		34	5
1978–79		39	10
1979–80		38	9
1980–81	St Mirren	29	3
1981–82		25	—
1982–83		19	—
1983–84		36	3
1984–85	Dundee	34	7
1985–86		27	2

McCREERY, David

Born Belfast 16.9.57.   Ht 5 6   Wt 9 7
Midfield. From Apprentice. Northern
Ireland Schools, Under-21, 53 full caps.

Season	Club	App	Goals
1974–75	Manchester U	2	—
1975–76		28	4
1976–77		25	2
1977–78		17	1
1978–79		15	—
1979–80	QPR	42	4
1980–81		15	—
From Tulsa R			
1982–83	Newcastle U	26	—
1983–84		40	—
1984–85		35	1
1985–86		41	—

McDERMOTT, Brian

Born Slough 8.4.61.   Ht 5 8   Wt 9 12
Forward. From Apprentice. England Youth.

McDONAGH, Jim (Seamus)

Born Rotherham 6.10.52.   Ht 6 0   Wt 13 9
Goalkeeper. From Apprentice.
Eire Youth, 24 full caps.

Season	Club	App	Goals
1970–71	Rotherham U	4	—
1971–72		9	—
1972–73		23	—
1972–73	*Manchester U*	—	—
1973–74	Rotherham U	22	—
1974–75		46	—
1975–76		17	—
1976–77	Bolton W	35	—
1977–78		42	—
1978–79		42	—
1979–80		42	—
1980–81	Everton	40	—
1981–82	Bolton W	39	—
1982–83		42	1
1983–84	Notts Co	24	—
1984–85		11	—
1984–85	*Birmingham C*	1	—
1984–85	*Gillingham*	10	—
1985–86	Notts Co	—	—
1985–86	*Sunderland*	7	—

McDONALD, Alan

Born Belfast 12.10.63.   Ht 6 2½   Wt 12 7
Defender. From Apprentice.
Northern Ireland Youth, 5 full caps.

Season	Club	App	Goals
1981–82	QPR	—	—
1982–83		—	—
1982–83	*Charlton Ath*	9	—
1983–84	QPR	5	—
1984–85		16	1
1985–86		42	—

| Season | Club | League Appearances/Goals | Season | Club | League Appearances/Goals |

McDONALD, Bobby

Born Aberdeen 13.4.55. Ht 5 10 Wt 12 5
Defender. From Apprentice.

Season	Club	App	Goals
1972–73	Aston Villa	4	—
1973–74		4	—
1974–75		18	1
1975–76		13	2
1976–77	Coventry C	39	1
1977–78		42	5
1978–79		42	4
1979–80		37	4
1980–81		1	—
1980–81	Manchester C	28	4
1981–82		36	4
1982–83		32	3
1983–84	Oxford U	39	4
1984–85		34	7
1985–86		14	3

McDONALD, Ian

Born Barrow 10.5.53. Ht 5 7 Wt 10 5
Midfield. From Apprentice.

Season	Club	App	Goals
1970–71	Barrow	12	—
1971–72		23	2
1972–73			
1972–73	Workington	16	2
1973–74		26	2
1973–74	Liverpool	—	—
1974–75		—	—
1974–75	Colchester U	5	2
1975–76	Mansfield T	34	4
1976–77		22	—
1977–78		—	—
1977–78	York City	30	2
1978–79		43	6
1979–80		46	8
1980–81		46	11
1981–82		10	2
1981–82	Aldershot	31	3
1982–83		46	5
1983–84		46	11
1984–85		41	10
1985–86		46	2

McDONALD, Neil

Born Wallsend 2.11.65. Ht 5 11 Wt 11 4
Midfield. From Wallsend BC.
England Schools, Youth.

Season	Club	App	Goals
1982–83	Newcastle U	24	4
1983–84		12	—
1984–85		36	6
1985–86		28	4

McDONOUGH, Darron

Born Antwerp 7.11.62. Ht 5 11 Wt 11 7
Forward. From Apprentice.

Season	Club	App	Goals
1979–80	Oldham Ath	—	—
1980–81		15	3
1981–82		36	1
1982–83		38	10
1983–84		38	—
1984–85		32	—
1985–86		20	—

McDONOUGH, Roy

Born Solihull 16.10.58. Ht 6 1 Wt 11 11
Forward. From Apprentice.

Season	Club	App	Goals
1976–77	Birmingham C	2	1
1977–78		—	—
1978–79		—	—
1978–79	Walsall	34	7
1979–80		42	7
1980–81		6	1
1980–81	Chelsea	—	—
1980–81	Colchester U	12	2
1981–82		40	14
1982–83		41	8
1983–84	Southend U	22	4
1983–84	Exeter C	16	—
1984–85		4	1
1984–85	Cambridge U	32	5
1985–86	Southend U	38	7

Season	Club	League Appearances/Goals		Season	Club	League Appearances/Goals	

McDOUGALL, Frank

Born Glasgow 21.2.58 Ht 5 9 Wt 11 9
Forward. From Glasgow Perthshire.

1978–79	Clydebank	38	25
1979–80	St Mirren	16	5
1980–81	....	23	10
1981–82	....	18	7
1982–83	....	29	9
1983–84	....	29	12
1984–85	Aberdeen	28	22
1985–86	....	25	14

McDOWALL, Kenny

Born Glasgow 29.7.63 Ht 5 10 Wt 10 3
Forward. From Drumchapel Amateurs.

1980–81	Partick T	—	—
1981–82	....	1	—
1982–83	....	24	5
1983–84	....	36	13
1984–85	....	6	1
1984–85	St Mirren	23	3
1985–86	....	12	1

McELHINNEY, Gerry

Born Londonderry 19.9.56. Ht 6 2
Wt 13 0
Defender. From Distillery. Northern Ireland
6 full caps.

1980–81	Bolton W	17	—
1981–82	....	19	1
1982–83	....	16	—
1982–83	*Rochdale*	20	1
1983–84	Bolton W	43	1
1984–85	....	14	—
1984–85	Plymouth Arg	21	—
1985–86	....	44	2

McEVOY, Richard

Born Gibraltar 6.8.67.
Midfield. From Apprentice. Eire Youth.

| 1985–86 | Luton T | — | — |

McEWAN, Stan

Born Cambusrethan 8.6.57. Ht 6 0
Wt 12 7
Forward. From Apprentice.

1974–75	Blackpool	1	—
1975–76	....	17	—
1976–77	....	11	—
1977–78	....	39	1
1978–79	....	46	5
1979–80	....	39	12
1980–81	....	36	1
1981–82	....	25	5
1982–83	Exeter C	37	6
1983–84	....	28	9
1983–84	Hull C	16	1
1984–85	....	37	11
1985–86	....	42	10

McFADDEN, Paul

Born Glasgow 14.9.65. Ht 5 9 Wt 10 7
Forward. From Duntocher B.C. Scotland
Youth.

1982–83	Motherwell	—	—
1983–84	....	—	—
1984–85	....	8	2
1985–86	....	1	—

McGARVEY, Frank

Born Glasgow 17.3.56. Ht 5 10 Wt 11 0
Forward. From Kilsyth Rangers. Scotland
Under-21, 7 full caps.

1974–75	St Mirren	1	—
1975–76	....	25	5
1976–77	....	38	17
1977–78	....	35	17
1978–79	....	33	13
1979–80	Liverpool	—	—
1979–80	Celtic	12	2
1980–81	....	34	23
1981–82	....	26	10
1982–83	....	34	17
1983–84	....	30	10
1984–85	....	33	15
1985–86	St Mirren	35	6

Season	Club	League Appearances/Goals	Season	Club	League Appearances/Goals

McGARVEY, Scott

Born Glasgow 22.4.63.   Ht 6 0½   Wt 11 5
Forward. From Apprentice. Scotland
Under-21

Season	Club	App	Goals
1979–80	Manchester U	—	—
1980–81		2	—
1981–82		16	2
1982–83		7	1
1983–84		—	—
1983–84	*Wolverhampton W*	13	2
1984–85	Portsmouth	18	5
1985–86		5	1
1985–86	*Carlisle U*	10	3

McGEACHIE, George

Born Skinflats 5.2.59.   Ht 5 11   Wt 11 4
Defender. From Bo'ness United.

Season	Club	App	Goals
1977–78	Dundee	15	2
1978–79		5	—
1979–80		28	1
1980–81		30	2
1981–82		29	3
1982–83		22	—
1983–84		23	—
1984–85		35	1
1985–86		2	—

McGEENEY, Pat

Born Sheffield 31.10.66.   Ht 5 10½   Wt 11 0
Defender. From Apprentice.

Season	Club	App	Goals
1984–85	Sheffield U	10	—
1985–86		6	—

McGHEE, Mark

Born Glasgow 25.5.57.   Ht 5 10   Wt 12 0
Forward. From Apprentice. Scotland Under-
21, 4 full caps.

Season	Club	App	Goals
1974–75	Bristol C	—	—
1975–76	Morton	5	1
1976–77		39	20
1977–78		20	16
1977–78	Newcastle U	18	3
1978–79		10	2
1978–79	Aberdeen	11	4
1979–80		21	6
1980–81		36	13
1981–82		31	8
1982–83		32	16
1983–84		33	16
1984–85	SV Hamburg	26	6
1985–86		4	1
1985–86	Celtic	18	4

McGHIE, William

Born Glasgow 13.11.61.   Ht 5 10   Wt 10 7
Defender. From Clydebank B.C.

Season	Club	App	Goals
1979–80	Clydebank	—	—
1980–81		—	—
1981–82		35	—
1982–83		39	4
1983–84		39	7
1984–85		35	2
1985–86		15	—

McGINLAY, Pat

Born Glasgow 30.5.67.
Midfield. Scottish Junior.

Season	Club	App	Goals
1985–86	Blackpool	—	—

McGINLEY, John

Born Rowlands Gill 11.6.59.   Ht 6 2   Wt 13 8
Forward. From Gateshead.

Season	Club	App	Goals
1981–82	Sunderland	3	—
From Charleroi and Nairn Co			
1984–85	Lincoln C	40	4
1985–86		29	7

McGINNIS, Gary

Born Dundee 21.10.63.   Ht 5 11   Wt 10 3
Defender. From Dundee B.C. Scotland
Schools, Youth, Under-21.

Season	Club	League Appearances/Goals		Season	Club	League Appearances/Goals	

1981–82	Dundee U	—	—
1982–83		—	—
1983–84		4	—
1984–85		10	—
1985–86		4	—

McGONIGAL, John

Born Coatbridge 9.6.67.   Ht 5 9   Wt 9 10
Forward. From Apprentice.

| 1985–86 | Sunderland | — | — |

McGRAIN, Danny

Born Glasgow 1.5.50.   Ht 5 9   Wt 12 1
Defender. From Maryhill Juniors. Scotland
Under-23, 62 full caps.

1967–68	Celtic	—	—
1968–69		—	—
1969–70		—	—
1970–71		7	—
1971–72		3	—
1972–73		30	—
1973–74		30	1
1974–75		30	—
1975–76		35	—
1976–77		36	—
1977–78		7	—
1978–79		18	3
1979–80		34	—
1980–81		33	—
1981–82		27	—
1982–83		33	1
1983–84		33	—
1984–85		30	—
1985–86		28	—

McGRATH, Lloyd

Born Birmingham 24.2.65.   Ht 5 9   Wt 11 6
Defender. From Apprentice. England
Youth, Under-21.

1982–83	Coventry C	—	—
1983–84		1	—
1984–85		23	—
1985–86		32	—

McGRATH, Paul

Born Greenford 4.12.59.   Ht 6 0½   Wt 13 2
Defender. From St Patrick's Ath. Eire 8 full
caps.

1981–82	Manchester U	—	—
1982–83		14	3
1983–84		9	1
1984–85		23	—
1985–86		40	3

McGREGOR, John

Born Airdrie 5.1.63.   Ht 5 11   Wt 12 0
Defender. From school.

1979–80	Queen's Park	30	2
1980–81		38	13
1981–82		37	4
1982–83	Liverpool	—	—
1983–84		—	—
1983–84	*St Mirren*	5	1
1984–85	Liverpool	—	—
1985–86		—	—
1985–86	*Leeds U*	5	—

McGUGAN, Paul

Born Glasgow 17.7.64.   Ht 6 2   Wt 12 0
Defender. From Eastercraigs.

1980–81	Celtic	—	—
1981–82		—	—
1982–83		—	—
1983–84		1	—
1984–85		3	—
1985–86		21	2

McGUINNESS, Paul

Born Manchester 2.3.66.   Ht 5 7   Wt 11 5½
Midfield. From Local.

| 1984–85 | Manchester U | — | — |
| 1985–86 | | — | — |

All appearances include those as substitute

Season	Club	League Appearances/Goals		Season	Club	League Appearances/Goals	

McGUIRE, Mick

Born Blackpool 4.9.52.　Ht 5 7　Wt 10 12
Midfield. From Amateur. England Youth.

Season	Club	App	Goals
1969–70	Coventry C	—	—
1970–71		—	—
1971–72		26	1
1972–73		17	—
1973–74		24	—
1974–75		5	—
1974–75	Norwich C	16	2
1975–76		30	2
1976–77		—	—
1977–78		11	—
1978–79		24	—
1979–80		19	2
1980–81		28	3
1981–82		39	2
1982–83		15	—
1982–83	Barnsley	7	1
1983–84		36	5
1984–85		4	—
1984–85	Oldham Ath	20	1
1985–86		40	2

McHALE, Ray

Born Sheffield 12.8.50.　Ht 5 8　Wt 12 6
Midfield. Local.

Season	Club	App	Goals
1971–72	Chesterfield	35	6
1972–73		36	10
1973–74		44	8
1974–75		9	3
1974–75	Halifax T	36	7
1975–76		46	12
1976–77		4	2
1976–77	Swindon T	41	10
1977–78		45	10
1978–79		46	5
1979–80		41	8
1980–81	Brighton	11	—
1980–81	Barnsley	13	1
1981–82		40	—
1982–83	Sheffield U	12	—
1982–83	*Bury*	6	—
1983–84	Sheffield U	42	1

Season	Club	App	Goals
1984–85		13	1
1984–85	Swansea C	19	—
1985–86		28	1

McILROY, Sammy

Born Belfast 2.8.54.　Ht 5 10　Wt 11 8
Midfield. From Apprentice.
Northern Ireland 84 full caps.

Season	Club	App	Goals
1971–72	Manchester U	16	4
1972–73		10	—
1973–74		29	6
1974–75		42	7
1975–76		41	10
1976–77		40	2
1977–78		39	9
1978–79		40	5
1979–80		41	6
1980–81		32	5
1981–82		12	3
1981–82	Stoke C	18	3
1982–83		41	8
1983–84		40	1
1984–85		34	2
1985–86	Manchester C	12	1

McINALLY, Alan

Born Ayr 10.2.63.　Ht 6 1　Wt 11 6
Forward. From Ayr U B.C.

Season	Club	App	Goals
1980–81	Ayr U	6	—
1981–82		17	9
1982–83		35	7
1983–84		35	16
1984–85	Celtic	11	1
1985–86		16	1

McINALLY, Jim

Born Glasgow 19.2.64.　Ht 6 0　Wt 12 0
Midfield. From Celtic BC. Scottish Youth.

Season	Club	App	Goals
1982–83	Celtic	1	—
1983–84		—	—
1984–85	Nottingham F	24	—
1985–86		12	—
1985–86	Coventry C	5	—

Season	Club	League Appearances/Goals

McINNES, Ian

Born Hamilton 22.3.57.   Ht 5 8
Forward. From Apprentice.

1983–84	Rotherham U	2	—
1984–85		7	—
1985–86		—	—
1985–86	Lincoln C	21	2

McINTYRE, Tommy

Born Bellshill 26.12.63.   Ht 6 0   Wt 10 10
Defender. From Fir Park B.C.

1981–82	Aberdeen	—	—
1982–83		—	—
1983–84		10	—
1984–85		—	—
1985–86		5	—

McKEE, Kevin

Born Edinburgh 10.6.66.   Ht 5 9   Wt 11 4
Defender. From Whitburn B.C.

1982–83	Hibernian	4	—
1983–84		16	—
1984–85		17	—
1985–86		2	—

McKELLAR, David

Born Ardrossan 22.5.56.   Ht 6 0   Wt 11 8
Goalkeeper. From Apprentice.

1973–74	Ipswich T	—	—
1974–75		—	—
1974–75	Colchester U	—	—
1975–76	Ipswich T	—	—
1975–76	Peterborough U	—	—
From Ardrossan			
1977–78	Derby Co	—	—
1978–79		16	—
1979–80		25	—
1980–81		—	—
1980–81	Brentford	39	—
1981–82		45	—
1982–83		—	—
1983–84	Carlisle U	42	—
1984–85		40	—

1985–86	Hibernian	—	—
1985–86	Manchester C	—	—
1985–86	Newcastle U	10	—

McKENZIE, Ian

Born Wallsend 22.8.66.
Midfield. From Apprentice.

| 1985–86 | Barnsley | 1 | — |

McKENZIE, Stuart

Born Hull 19.9.67.   Ht 5 11   Wt 11 0
Defender. From juniors.

| 1985–86 | York C | 4 | — |

McKERNON, Paul

Born Gloucester 23.2.68.   Ht 5 9   Wt 11 0
Midfield. From Apprentice.

| 1984–85 | Mansfield T | 2 | — |
| 1985–86 | | 11 | — |

McKIMMIE, Stuart

Born Aberdeen 27.10.62   Ht 5 8   Wt 10 7
Defender. From Banks o' Dee. Scotland
Under-21.

1980–81	Dundee	17	—
1981–82		16	—
1982–83		31	—
1983–84		16	—
1983–84	Aberdeen	18	1
1984–85		34	3
1985–86		34	3

McKINLAY, Tosh

Born Glasgow 3.12.64.   Ht 5 7   Wt 10 3
Defender. From Celtic B.C. Scotland Youth,
Under-21.

1981–82	Dundee	—	—
1982–83		1	—
1983–84		36	3
1984–85		34	3
1985–86		22	—

Season	Club	League Appearances/Goals		Season	Club	League Appearances/Goals	

McKINNON, Rob

Born Glasgow 31.7.66.   Ht 5 11   Wt 11 1
Defender. From Rutherglen Glencairn.

| 1984–85 | Newcastle U | — | — |
| 1985–86 | | 1 | — |

McLAUGHLIN, Joe

Born Greenock 2.6.60.   Ht 6 1   Wt 12 0
Defender. From school. Scotland Under-21.

1977–78	Morton	—	—
1978–79		—	—
1979–80		30	2
1980–81		34	1
1981–82		36	—
1982–83		34	—
1983–84	Chelsea	41	—
1984–85		36	1
1985–86		40	1

McLEAN, David

Born Newcastle 24.11.57.   Ht 5 8   Wt 11 0
Midfield. From Apprentice. England
Schools.

1975–76	Newcastle U	2	—
1976–77		—	—
1977–78		7	—
1977–78	Carlisle U	6	—
1978–79		9	—
1979–80	Darlington	36	4
1980–81		41	4
1981–82		46	7
1982–83		46	9
1983–84		43	3
1984–85		44	10
1985–86		38	9

McLEARY, Alan

Born London 6.10.64.   Ht 5 10½   Wt 10 10
Midfield. From Apprentice. England Youth.

1981–82	Millwall	—	—
1982–83		3	1
1983–84		30	—
1984–85		21	—
1985–86		35	3

McLEISH, Alex

Born Glasgow 21.1.59.   Ht 6 1   Wt 12 4
Defender. From Glasgow United. Scotland
Under-21, 43 full caps.

1977–78	Aberdeen	1	—
1978–79		19	1
1979–80		35	2
1980–81		32	3
1981–82		32	5
1982–83		34	2
1983–84		32	2
1984–85		30	1
1985–86		34	3

McLEOD, Gordon

Born Edinburgh 2.10.67.   Ht 5 8   Wt 10 4
Midfield. From Hutchison Vale B.C.
Scotland Schools, Youth.

1983–84	Dundee U	—	—
1984–85		3	—
1985–86		3	—

MacLEOD, Ian

Born Glasgow 19.11.59.   Ht 5 11   Wt 11 6
Defender. From Claremont B.C.

1977–78	Motherwell	5	—
1978–79		25	—
1979–80		24	—
1980–81		25	1
1981–82		37	—
1982–83		30	1
1983–84		29	—
1984–85		38	—
1985–86		29	1

Season	Club	League Appearances/Goals		Season	Club	League Appearances/Goals	

MacLEOD, Murdo

Born Glasgow 24.9.58   Ht 5 8   Wt 12 0
Midfield. From Glasgow Amateurs. Scotland
Under-21, 1 full cap.

Season	Club		
1974–75	Dumbarton	—	—
1975–76		7	—
1976–77		27	7
1977–78		39	1
1978–79		14	1
1978–79	Celtic	23	3
1979–80		36	7
1980–81		18	8
1981–82		36	10
1982–83		35	11
1983–84		34	7
1984–85		31	3
1985–86		30	3

McLOUGHLIN, Alan

Born Manchester 20.4.67.   Ht 5 8½   Wt 10 0
Defender. From Local.

Season	Club		
1984–85	Manchester U	—	—
1985–86		—	—

McLOUGHLIN, Paul

Born Bristol 23.12.63.   Ht 5 10   Wt 10 7
Forward. From Bristol C and Gisborne C.

Season	Club		
1984–85	Cardiff C	17	—
1985–86		32	4

McMAHON, Ian

Born Wells 7.10.64.   Ht 6 0   Wt 12 0
Defender. From Apprentice.

Season	Club		
1982–83	Oldham Ath	2	—
1983–84		—	—
1983–84	Rochdale	21	1
1984–85		38	4
1985–86		32	3

McMAHON, Steve

Born Liverpool 20.8.61.   Ht 5 7   Wt 10 9
Midfield. From Apprentice.
England Under-21.

Season	Club		
1979–80	Everton	—	—
1980–81		34	5
1981–82		32	2
1982–83		34	4
1983–84	Aston Villa	37	5
1984–85		35	2
1985–86		3	—
1985–86	Liverpool	23	6

McMANUS, Eric

Born Limavady 14.11.50.   Ht 6 1   Wt 13 0
Goalkeeper. From Coleraine. Northern
Ireland Amateur.

Season	Club		
1968–69	Coventry C	—	—
1969–70		2	—
1970–71		2	—
1971–72		2	—
1972–73	Notts Co	4	—
1973–74		34	—
1974–75		25	—
1975–76		40	—
1976–77		42	—
1977–78		42	—
1978–79		42	—
1979–80		—	—
1979–80	Stoke C	—	—
1979–80	*Lincoln C*	21	—
1980–81	Stoke C	—	—
1981–82		4	—
1982–83	Bradford C	27	—
1983–84		46	—
1984–85		40	—
1985–86		—	—
1985–86	*Middlesbrough*	2	—
1985–86	*Peterborough U*	18	—

McMANUS, Stuart

Born Falkirk 19.3.65.   Ht 5 11   Wt 12 7
Forward. From Local.

Season	Club		
1984–85	Southampton	—	—
1985–86		2	1
1985–86	*Newport Co*	5	—

Season	Club	League Appearances/Goals		Season	Club	League Appearances/Goals	

McMASTER, John

Born Greenock 23.2.55.   Ht 5 8   Wt 11 12
Midfield. From Port Glasgow.

Season	Club	App	Goals
1972–73	Aberdeen	—	—
1973–74		—	—
1974–75		1	—
1975–76		21	3
1976–77		2	—
1977–78		32	4
1978–79		26	3
1979–80		33	4
1980–81		10	2
1981–82		31	1
1982–83		24	2
1983–84		12	—
1984–85		1	—
1985–86		7	1

McMENEMY, Paul

Born Farnborough 5.11.66.   Ht 5 10
Wt 11 12
Forward. From Apprentice.

Season	Club	App	Goals
1984–85	West Ham U	—	—
1985–86		—	—
1985–86	*Aldershot*	10	5

McMINN, Ted

Born Castle Douglas 28.9.62.   Ht 5 11
Wt 11 2
Forward. From Glenafton Athletic.

Season	Club	App	Goals
1982–83	Queen of the S	22	1
1983–84		32	3
1984–85		8	1
1984–85	Rangers	20	1
1985–86		28	2

McNAB, Neil

Born Greenock 4.6.57.   Ht 5 7   Wt 10 10
Midfield. Scotland Schools. Under-21.

Season	Club	App	Goals
1972–73	Morton	3	—
1973–74		11	—

Season	Club	App	Goals
1973–74	Tottenham H	1	—
1974–75		2	—
1975–76		15	—
1976–77		10	—
1977–78		42	3
1978–79		2	—
1978–79	Bolton W	23	3
1979–80		12	1
1979–80	Brighton	16	—
1980–81		33	1
1981–82		40	3
1982–83		14	—
1982–83	*Leeds U*	5	—
1982–83	*Portsmouth*	—	—
1983–84	Manchester C	33	1
1984–85		18	—
1985–86		37	4

McNALLY, Bernard

Born Shrewsbury 17.2.63.   Ht 5 7   Wt 9 11
Forward. From Apprentice. Northern
Ireland 1 full cap.

Season	Club	App	Goals
1980–81	Shrewsbury T	1	—
1981–82		33	1
1982–83		25	1
1983–84		41	4
1984–85		42	2
1985–86		35	6

McNAUGHT, John

Born Glasgow 19.6.64.   Ht 5 11   Wt 11 12
Defender. From Auchengill B.C.

Season	Club	App	Goals
1982–83	Hamilton A	27	1
1983–84		28	3
1984–85		27	4
1985–86		24	11
1985–86	Chelsea	1	—

McNAUGHT, Ken

Born Kirkcaldy 11.1.55.   Ht 6 2   Wt 13 11½
Defender. From Apprentice.

Season	Club	League Appearances/Goals		Season	Club	League Appearances/Goals	
1972–73	Everton	—	—				
1973–74		—	—				
1974–75		4	—				
1975–76		20	—				
1976–77		42	3				
1977–78	Aston Villa	40	2				
1978–79		32	1				
1979–80		30	1				
1980–81		42	—				
1981–82		22	2				
1982–83		41	2				
1983–84	WBA	42	1				
1984–85		—	—				
1984–85	*Manchester C*	7	—				
1985–86	Sheffield U	34	5				

McNAUGHTON, Brian

Born Edinburgh 22.1.63.   Ht 5 10   Wt 10 12
Forward. From Broxburn Athletic.

1984–85	Hearts	8	2
1985–86		4	—

McNEIL, Bobby

Born Hamilton 1.11.62.   Ht 5 9   Wt 10 12
Defender. From Apprentice.

1980–81	Hull C	14	—
1981–82		21	—
1982–83		33	—
1983–84		46	3
1984–85		24	—
1985–86	Lincoln C	4	—
1985–86	Preston NE	19	—

McNEIL, Mark

Born Forest Gate 3.12.62.   Ht 5 10   Wt 10 5
Forward. From Apprentice.

1979–80	Orient	—	—
1980–81		—	—
1981–82		24	3
1982–83		18	6
1983–84		39	4
1984–85		8	—
1984–85	Aldershot	19	2
1985–86		6	—

McNICHOL, Jim

Born Glasgow 9.6.58.   Ht 6 0   Wt 12 10
Defender. From Ipswich T Apprentice.
Scotland Under-21.

1976–77	Luton T	2	—
1977–78		12	—
1978–79		1	—
1978–79	Brentford	32	4
1979–80		31	8
1980–81		14	—
1981–82		26	3
1982–83		32	3
1983–84		20	4
1984–85	Exeter C	42	5
1985–86		45	5

McPARLAND, Ian

Born Edinburgh 4.10.61.   Ht 5 8   Wt 10 8
Midfield. From Ormiston Primrose.

1980–81	Notts Co	2	—
1981–82		12	—
1982–83		11	1
1983–84		21	2
1984–85		20	—
1985–86		44	15

McPHERSON, David

Born Paisley 28.1.64.   Ht 6 3   Wt 11 11
Defender. From Gartcosh United. Scotland
Youth, Under-21.

1980–81	Rangers	—	—
1981–82		—	—
1982–83		18	1
1983–84		36	2
1984–85		31	—
1985–86		34	5

McPHERSON, Keith

Born Greenwich 11.9.63.   Ht 5 11
Wt 10 11
Defender. From Apprentice.

Season	Club	League Appearances/Goals		Season	Club	League Appearances/Goals

Season	Club	Apps	Goals
1981–82	West Ham U	—	—
1982–83		—	—
1983–84		—	—
1984–85		1	—
1985–86		—	—
1985–86	*Cambridge U*	11	1
1985–86	Northampton T	20	—

McQUEEN, Eric

Born Johnstone 31.12.63.   Ht 5 8   Wt 10 0
Midfield. From Beith Juniors.

Season	Club	Apps	Goals
1985–86	St Mirren	3	—

McQUEEN, Tommy

Born Bellshill 1.4.63.   Ht 5 11   Wt 11 0
Defender. From Gartcosh United.

Season	Club	Apps	Goals
1981–82	Clyde	39	—
1982–83		35	—
1983–84		38	1
1984–85	Aberdeen	35	3
1985–86		17	1

McQUILLAN, Pat

Born Belfast 27.6.61   Ht 5 11   Wt 11 0
Defender. From Pembroke B.

Season	Club	Apps	Goals
1979–80	Swansea C	—	—
1980–81		—	—
1981–82		—	—
1982–83		—	—
From Pembroke B.			
1983–84	Swansea C	19	—
1984–85		7	1
1985–86		—	—

McSTAY, John

Born Larkhall 24.12.65.   Ht 5 9   Wt 10 12
Defender. From Gartcosh United

Season	Club	Apps	Goals
1982–83	Motherwell	—	—
1983–84		1	—
1984–85		6	1
1985–86		10	—

McSTAY, Paul

Born Hamilton 22.10.64.   Ht 5 10   Wt 10 7
Midfield. From Celtic B.C. Scotland Schools,
Youth, Under-21, 13 full caps.

Season	Club	Apps	Goals
1981–82	Celtic	10	1
1982–83		36	6
1983–84		34	3
1984–85		32	4
1985–86		34	8

McSTAY, Willie

Born Hamilton 26.11.61.   Ht 5 11   Wt 10 7
Defender. From Celtic B.C. Scotland
Schools, Youth.

Season	Club	Apps	Goals
1979–80	Celtic	—	—
1980–81		—	—
1981–82		—	—
1982–83		1	—
1983–84		19	1
1984–85		14	1
1985–86		18	—

McVICAR, Don

Born Perth 6.11.62.
Midfield.

Season	Club	Apps	Goals
1985–86	Tranmere R	7	—

McWILLIAMS, Derek

Born Broxburn 16.1.66.   Ht 5 10   Wt 11 7
Forward. From Broxburn Athletic.

Season	Club	Apps	Goals
1984–85	Dundee	16	2
1985–86		11	1

MABBUTT, Gary

Born Bristol 23.8.61.   Ht 5 9   Wt 10 10
Midfield. From Apprentice.
England Youth, Under-21, 9 full caps.

Season	Club	League Appearances/Goals		Season	Club	League Appearances/Goals	
1978–79	Bristol R	11	—	1981–82		7	2
1979–80		33	—	1981–82	Millwall	10	—
1980–81		42	5	1982–83		37	2
1981–82		45	5	1983–84	Sheffield W	38	1
1982–83	Tottenham H	38	10	1984–85		19	—
1983–84		21	2	1985–86		25	—
1984–85		25	2				
1985–86		32	3				

MADDEN, Craig

Born Manchester 25.9.58. Ht 5 8   Wt 10 2
Forward. From Northern Nomads.

1977–78	Bury	4	—
1978–79		13	1
1979–80		35	10
1980–81		30	10
1981–82		46	35
1982–83		43	20
1983–84		46	17
1984–85		46	22
1985–86		34	14
1985–86	WBA	9	2

MADDEN, David

Born London 6.1.63. Ht 6 0   Wt 11 3
Defender. From Apprentice.

1980–81	Southampton	—	—
1981–82		—	—
1982–83		—	—
1982–83	*Bournemouth*	5	—
1983–84	Arsenal	2	—
1984–85	Charlton Ath	20	1
1985–86		—	—

MADDEN, Lawrie

Born London 28.9.55. Ht 6 0   Wt 12 6
Defender. From Arsenal Amateur.

1974–75	Mansfield T	7	—
1975–76		3	—
From Manchester Univ			
1977–78	Charlton Athletic	4	—
1978–79		38	3
1979–80		36	1
1980–81		28	1

MADDIX, Danny

Born Ashford 11.10.67.
Forward. From Apprentice.

1985–86	Tottenham H	—	—

MADDY, Paul

Born Cwmcarn 17.8.62. Ht 5 10   Wt 9 10½
Midfield. From Apprentice. Wales
Under-21.

1980–81	Cardiff C	8	2
1981–82		27	1
1982–83		8	—
1982–83	*Stoke C*	—	—
1982–83	*Hereford U*	9	1
1983–84	Swansea C	20	3
1983–84	Hereford U	10	1
1984–85		34	8
1985–86		33	7

MAGUIRE, Gavin

Born Hammersmith 24.11.67.
Midfield. From Apprentice.

1985–86	QPR	—	—

MAGUIRE, Paul

Born Glasgow 21.8.56. Ht 5 8   Wt 11 3
Forward. From Kilbirnie Ladeside.

1976–77	Shrewsbury T	42	5
1977–78		41	8
1978–79		40	13
1979–80		28	9
1980–81		—	—
1980–81	Stoke C	15	3

Season	Club	League Appearances/Goals		Season	Club	League Appearances/Goals

Season	Club	Apps	Goals
1981–82	....	35	7
1982–83	....	24	5
1983–84	....	33	9
From Tacoma			
1985–86	Port Vale	45	10

MAHAN, Tony

Born Ipswich 25.10.67.
Midfield. From Apprentice.

Season	Club	Apps	Goals
1985–86	Coventry C.................	—	—

MAHER, John

Born Glasgow 18.12.66. Ht 5 11 Wt 11 7
Defender. From Anniesland United.

Season	Club	Apps	Goals
1984–85	Clydebank	8	—
1985–86	....	24	—

MAIL, David

Born Bristol 12.9.62. Ht 5 10 Wt 11 4
Defender. From Apprentice.

Season	Club	Apps	Goals
1980–81	Aston Villa.................	—	—
1981–82	Blackburn R	—	—
1982–83	....	34	—
1983–84	....	11	1
1984–85	....	4	—
1985–86	....	18	1

MAIR, Gordon

Born Coatbridge 18.12.58. Ht 5 9 Wt 10 6
Midfield. From Apprentice. Scotland
Schools.

Season	Club	Apps	Goals
1976–77	Notts Co	5	—
1977–78	....	—	—
1978–79	....	4	1
1979–80	....	42	5
1980–81	....	4	—
1981–82	....	34	9
1982–83	....	25	4
1983–84	....	17	—
1984–85	Lincoln C....................	31	—
1985–86	....	26	3

MALCOLM, Paul

Born Dulwich 8.2.68.
Forward. From Apprentice.

Season	Club	Apps	Goals
1985–86	Millwall......................	—	—

MALCOLM, Paul

Born Heworth 11.12.64. Ht 6 4
Goalkeeper. From Newcastle U. Apprentice
and Durham C.

Season	Club	Apps	Goals
1984–85	Rochdale	24	—
1985–86	Shrewsbury T...............	—	—

MALLEY, Phillip

Born Felling 1.11.65. Ht 5 7½ Wt 11 2
Midfield. From Sunderland Apprentice.

Season	Club	Apps	Goals
1983–84	Hartlepool U	1	—
1983–84	Berwick R...................	1	—
1983–84	Burnley......................	2	—
1984–85	....	9	—
1984–85	*Stockport Co*	3	—
1985–86	Burnley......................	43	2

MALONEY, Sean

Born Lincoln 19.9.67. Ht 5 8½ Wt 11 0
Defender. From Apprentice.

Season	Club	Apps	Goals
1985–86	Grimsby T...................	—	—

MALPAS, Maurice

Born Dunfermline 3.8.62. Ht 5 8 Wt 10 11
Defender. 'S' Form. Scotland Schools,
Youth, Under-21, 10 full caps.

Season	Club	Apps	Goals
1979–80	Dundee U	—	—
1980–81	....	—	—
1981–82	....	19	—
1982–83	....	34	1
1983–84	....	34	2
1984–85	....	35	2
1985–86	....	36	2

All appearances include those as substitute

Season	Club	League Appearances/Goals		Season	Club	League Appearances/Goals	

MANN, Adrian

Born Northampton 12.7.67. Ht 5 4   Wt 9 0
Midfield. From Local.

1983–84	Northampton T	2	—
1984–85		38	2
1985–86		32	2

MARDENBOROUGH, Steve

Born Birmingham 11.9.64. Ht 5 8   Wt 11 0
Forward. From Apprentice.

1982–83	Coventry C	—	—
1983–84	Wolves	9	1
1983–84	*Cambridge U*	6	—
1984–85	Swansea C	36	7
1985–86	Newport Co	39	7

MARINER, Paul

Born Bolton 22.5.53. Ht 6 0   Wt 12 6
Forward. From Chorley.
England 'B', 35 full caps.

1973–74	Plymouth Arg	41	14
1974–75		46	20
1975–76		38	15
1976–77		10	7
1976–77	Ipswich T	28	10
1977–78		37	11
1978–79		33	13
1979–80		41	17
1980–81		36	13
1981–82		25	8
1982–83		37	13
1983–84		23	12
1983–84	Arsenal	15	7
1984–85		36	7
1985–86		9	—

MARKER, Nick

Born Exeter 3.5.65. Ht 6 1   Wt 13 0
Defender. From Apprentice.

| 1981–82 | Exeter C | 14 | 1 |
| 1982–83 | | 18 | 1 |

1983–84		31	—
1984–85		45	—
1985–86		40	—

MARPLES, Chris

Born Chesterfield 3.8.64. Ht 5 11
Wt 11 12
Goalkeeper. From Sutton T and Goole

| 1984–85 | Chesterfield | 38 | — |
| 1985–86 | | 32 | — |

MARRIOTT, Brian

Born Oldham 4.10.62. Ht 5 9   Wt 11 2
Defender. From Chadderton.

| 1984–85 | Oldham Ath | — | — |
| 1985–86 | | — | — |

MARSHALL, Gary

Born Bristol 20.4.64. Ht 5 11½   Wt 10 10
Forward. From Shepton Mallet.

1983–84	Bristol C	1	—
1984–85		5	2
1984–85	*Torquay U*	7	1
1985–86	Bristol C	19	2

MARSHALL, Ian

Born Oxford 20.3.66. Ht 6 1   Wt 12 12
Defender. From Apprentice.

1983–84	Everton	—	—
1984–85		—	—
1985–86		9	—

MARSHALL, John

Born Surrey 18.8.64. Ht 5 10   Wt 11 5
Defender. From Apprentice.

1982–83	Fulham	—	—
1983–84		25	—
1984–85		32	1
1985–86		42	3

Season	Club	League Appearances/Goals		Season	Club	League Appearances/Goals	

MARTIN, Alvin

Born Bootle 29.7.58.   Ht 6 1   Wt 13 3
Defender. From Apprentice.
England Youth, Under-21, 'B', 15 full caps.

Season	Club	App	Goals
1976–77	West Ham U	—	—
1977–78		7	1
1978–79		22	1
1979–80		40	2
1980–81		41	1
1981–82		28	4
1982–83		38	3
1983–84		29	3
1984–85		40	1
1985–86		40	4

MARTIN, David

Born East Ham 25.4.63.   Ht 6 1   Wt 11 8
Midfield. From Apprentice. England Youth.

Season	Club	App	Goals
1979–80	Millwall	3	—
1980–81		33	1
1981–82		38	1
1982–83		33	1
1983–84		31	3
1984–85		2	—
1984–85	Wimbledon	20	2
1985–86		15	1

MARTIN, Dean

Born Halifax 9.9.67.   Ht 5 10   Wt 10 2
Midfield. From Local.

Season	Club	App	Goals
1984–85	Halifax T	—	—
1985–86		—	—

MARTIN, Mick

Born Dublin 9.7.51.   Ht 5 10   Wt 10 11
Midfield. From Bohemians.
Eire Amateur, 51 full caps.

Season	Club	App	Goals
1972–73	Manchester U	16	2
1973–74		16	—
1974–75		8	—

Season	Club	App	Goals
1975–76		—	—
1975–76	WBA	34	5
1976–77		34	6
1977–78		20	—
1978–79		1	—
1978–79	Newcastle U	23	1
1979–80		19	—
1980–81		31	1
1981–82		39	—
1982–83		35	3
1983–84	Wolverhampton W	—	—
1984–85	Cardiff C	7	—
1984–85	Peterborough U	12	—
1985–86	Rotherham U	5	—
1985–86	Preston NE	35	—

MARUSTIK, Chris

Born Swansea 10.8.61.   Ht 5 8½   Wt 11 5½
Midfield. From Apprentice. Wales Schools,
Under-21, 6 full caps.

Season	Club	App	Goals
1978–79	Swansea C	4	—
1979–80		12	—
1980–81		3	—
1981–82		22	1
1982–83		23	1
1983–84		38	4
1984–85		42	5
1985–86		8	—
1985–86	Cardiff C	26	1

MARWOOD, Brian

Born Seaham Harbour 5.2.60.   Ht 5 7½
Wt 10 10
Midfield. From Apprentice.

Season	Club	App	Goals
1977–78	Hull C	—	—
1978–79		—	—
1979–80		6	—
1980–81		31	4
1981–82		42	12
1982–83		40	19
1983–84		39	16
1984–85	Sheffield W	41	7
1985–86		37	13

Season	Club	League Appearances/Goals		Season	Club	League Appearances/Goals	

MASKELL, Craig

Born Aldershot 10.4.68.
Midfield. From Apprentice.

1985–86	Southampton	2	1

MASKERY, Chris

Born Stoke 25.9.64.   Ht 5 7½   Wt 10 8
Midfield. From Apprentice.

1982–83	Stoke C	7	—
1983–84		19	—
1984–85		34	—
1985–86		19	3

MASON, Keith

Born Leicester 19.7.58.   Ht 6 1   Wt 13 7
Goalkeeper.

1982–83	Huddersfield T	1	—
1983–84		19	—
1984–85		5	—
1985–86		5	—

MASSEY, Andy

Born London 20.10.61. Ht 5 10   Wt 11 6
Midfield. From Eire Youth. Amateur.

1978–79	Millwall	—	—
1979–80		—	—
1980–81		21	—
1981–82		29	2
1982–83		25	5
1983–84		13	1
1983–84	*Port Vale*	4	1
1984–85	Aldershot	32	1
1985–86		39	2

MASSEY, Kevin

Born Gainsborough 30.11.65.   Ht 5 6½   Wt 9 5
Midfield. From Apprentice.

1983–84	Cambridge U	1	—
1984–85		12	—
1985–86		3	1

MASSEY, Richard

Born Seisdon 11.10.68.
Defender. From YTS.

1985–86	Exeter C	2	—

MASSEY, Steve

Born Denton 28.3.58.   Ht 5 11   Wt 11 5
Forward. From Apprentice.

1974–75	Stockport Co	8	2
1975–76		35	5
1976–77		22	2
1977–78		36	11
1978–79	Bournemouth	36	6
1979–80		30	9
1980–81		31	9
1981–82	Peterborough U	18	2
1981–82	Northampton T	18	5
1982–83		42	21
1983–84	Hull C	13	4
1984–85		29	5
1985–86	Cambridge U	31	11

MASSIMO, Franco

Born Horsham 23.9.68.
Forward. From Apprentice.

1985–86	Brighton	1	—

MATTHEWS, John

Born London 1.11.55.   Ht 6 0   Wt 12 6
Defender. From Apprentice.

1973–74	Arsenal	—	—
1974–75		20	—
1975–76		1	—
1976–77		17	2
1977–78		7	—
1978–79	Sheffield U	32	5
1979–80		32	5
1980–81		14	1
1981–82		25	3

Season	Club	League Appearances/Goals	
1982–83	Mansfield T	40	3
1983–84		32	3
1984–85	Chesterfield	38	1
1985–86	Plymouth Arg	31	1

MATTHEWS, Mike

Born Hull 25.9.60.   Ht 5 8   Wt 11 3
Forward. From Apprentice.

Season	Club	League Appearances/Goals	
1978–79	Wolverhampton W	—	—
1979–80		—	—
1980–81		1	—
1981–82		32	2
1982–83		40	5
1983–84		3	—
1983–84	Scunthorpe U	25	1
1984–85		22	3
1985–86		11	1

MATTHEWS, Neil

Born Manchester 3.12.67.
Defender. From Apprentice.

Season	Club	League Appearances/Goals	
1985–86	Blackpool	1	—

MATTHEWS, Neil

Born Grimsby 19.9.66.
Forward.

Season	Club	League Appearances/Goals	
1984–85	Grimsby T	4	1
1985–86		4	—
1985–86	*Scunthorpe U*	1	—

MATTHEWSON, Trevor

Born Sheffield 12.2.63.   Ht 6 1   Wt 12 5
Defender. From Apprentice.

Season	Club	League Appearances/Goals	
1980–81	Sheffield W	1	—
1981–82		1	—
1982–83		1	—
1983–84		—	—
1983–84	Newport Co	32	—
1984–85		43	—
1985–86	Stockport Co	35	—

MAUCHLEN, Alister

Born Kilwinning 29.6.60   Ht 5 7   Wt 10 5
Midfield. From Irvine Meadow.

Season	Club	League Appearances/Goals	
1978–79	Kilmarnock	20	—
1979–80		30	2
1980–81		31	3
1981–82		37	4
1982–83		2	1
1982–83	Motherwell	25	3
1983–84		20	—
1984–85		30	1
1985–86		1	—
1985–86	Leicester C	37	2

MAXWELL, Alistair

Born Hamilton 29.6.60   Ht 5 7   Wt 10 5
Goalkeeper. From Fir Park B.C.

Season	Club	League Appearances/Goals	
1981–82	Motherwell	—	—
1982–83		—	—
1983–84		4	—
1984–85		15	—
1985–86		4	—

MAY, Andy

Born Bury 26.2.64.   Ht 5 8   Wt 10 10
Defender. From Apprentice. England
Under-21.

Season	Club	League Appearances/Goals	
1980–81	Manchester C	1	—
1981–82		6	—
1982–83		8	—
1983–84		42	5
1984–85		39	3
1985–86		37	—

MAY, Edward

Born Edinburgh 30.8.67   Ht 5 7   Wt 10 3
Forward. From Hutchison Vale B.C.
Scotland Youth.

Season	Club	League Appearances/Goals	
1983–84	Dundee U	—	—
1984–85		—	—
1984–85	Hibernian	—	—
1985–86		19	1

Season	Club	League Appearances/Goals		Season	Club	League Appearances/Goals	

MAY, Larry

Born Sutton Coldfield 26.12.58. Ht 6 0¼
Wt 12 6
Defender. From Apprentice.

1976–77	Leicester C	1	—
1977–78		5	—
1978–79		36	4
1979–80		42	4
1980–81		34	—
1981–82		34	3
1982–83		35	1
1983–84	Barnsley	41	1
1984–85		23	1
1985–86		36	—

MAY, Warren

Born Rochford 31.12.64. Ht 5 10 Wt 11 8
Defender. From Apprentice.

1982–83	Southend U	14	1
1983–84		22	2
1984–85		29	1
1985–86		25	—

MAYES, Alan

Born London 11.12.53. Ht 5 7 Wt 10 10
Forward. From Apprentice.

1971–72	QPR	—	—
1972–73		—	—
1973–74		—	—
1974–75		—	—
1974–75	Watford	22	2
1975–76		14	—
1975–76	*Northampton*	10	4
1976–77	Watford	43	14
1977–78		41	15
1978–79		13	—
1978–79	Swindon T	21	11
1979–80		44	19
1980–81		24	8
1980–81	Chelsea	13	4
1981–82		39	12

1982–83		14	2
1983–84	Swindon T	39	17
1984–85		23	10
1985–86	Carlisle U	10	2
1985–86	Newport Co	3	1

MAYES, Bobby

Born Ipswich 18.12.67.
Midfield. From YTS. England Youth.

| 1985–86 | West Ham U | — | — |

MAZZON, Giorgio

Born Cheshunt 4.9.60. Ht 5 10 Wt 11 5
Defender. From Hertford T.

1978–79	Tottenham H	—	—
1979–80		—	—
1980–81		2	—
1981–82		—	—
1982–83		—	—
1983–84	Aldershot	45	3
1984–85		33	1
1985–86		44	—

MEACOCK, Kevin

Born Bristol 15.9.63 Ht 5 10 Wt 11 0
Forward. From Paulton R. England Youth.

1983–84	Bristol C	—	—
From Gisborne C			
1984–85	Cardiff C	21	3
1985–86		4	—

MEADE, Raphael

Born Islington 22.11.62. Ht 5 10 Wt 11 9
Forward. From Apprentice.

1980–81	Arsenal	—	—
1981–82		16	4
1982–83		4	2
1983–84		13	5
1984–85		8	3
To Sporting Lisbon			

All appearances include those as substitute

Season	Club	League Appearances/Goals		Season	Club	League Appearances/Goals	

MEASHAM, Ian

Born Barnsley 14.12.64.   Ht 5 11   Wt 11 1
Defender. From Apprentice.

1982–83	Huddersfield T	—	—
1983–84		—	—
1984–85		17	—
1985–86		—	—
1985–86	*Lincoln C*	6	—
1985–86	*Rochdale*	12	—

MEGSON, Gary

Born Manchester 2.5.59.   Ht 5 10   Wt 11 6
Midfield. From Apprentice.

1977–78	Plymouth Arg	24	2
1978–79		42	8
1979–80		12	—
1979–80	Everton	12	1
1980–81		10	1
1981–82	Sheffield W	40	5
1982–83		41	4
1983–84		42	4
1984–85	Nottingham F	—	—
1984–85	Newcastle U	20	1
1985–86		4	—
1985–86	Sheffield W	20	3

MEHEW, David

Born Camberley 29.10.67.   Ht 5 11   Wt 11 7
Forward.

1984–85	Leeds U	—	—
1985–86	Bristol R	4	—

MEHMET, Dave

Born London 2.12.60.   Ht 5 9½   Wt 11 10
Midfield. From Apprentice.

1976–77	Millwall	1	—
1977–78		14	4
1978–79		33	4
1979–80		36	4
1980–81		30	3

From Tampa Bay R

1981–82	Charlton Ath	16	1
1982–83		13	2
1982–83	Gillingham	13	3
1983–84		43	16
1984–85		45	13
1985–86		31	7

MELROSE, Jim

Born Glasgow 7.10.58.   Ht 5 8½   Wt 11 2
Forward. Scottish Under 21, Scottish
League. From Eastercraigs.

1975–76	Partick T	2	—
1976–77		27	8
1977–78		25	4
1978–79		33	10
1979–80		35	9
1980–81	Leicester C	32	9
1981–82		35	11
1982–83		5	1
1982–83	Coventry C	24	8
1983–84	Celtic	29	7
1984–85		—	—
1984–85	*Wolverhampton W*	7	2
1984–85	Manchester C	24	7
1985–86		10	1
1985–86	Charlton Ath	11	5

MELVILLE, Andy

Born Swansea 29.11.68.
Defender. From school.

1985–86	Swansea C	5	—

MENDHAM, Peter

Born Kings Lynn 9.4.60.   Ht 5 10   Wt 11 6
Midfield. From Apprentice.

1977–78	Norwich C	—	—
1978–79		8	—
1979–80		20	2
1980–81		13	—
1981–82		29	6
1982–83		26	2

Season	Club	League Appearances/Goals		Season	Club	League Appearances/Goals	
1983–84	....	41	1	1976–77	....	39	—
1984–85	....	36	4	1977–78	....	39	2
1985–86	....	35	8	1978–79	....	39	11
				1979–80	Wigan Ath	35	2
				1980–81	....	46	2
				1981–82	....	46	9
				1982–83	....	44	1
				1983–84	....	39	—
				1984–85	....	43	—
				1985–86	....	43	7

MENNIE, Vince

Born Dortmund 19.5.64.   Ht 5 9   Wt 11 4
Forward. From Borussia Lippstadt.

1983–84	Cologne	17	1
1984–85	....	7	1
1985–86	....	5	—
1985–86	Dundee	11	1

MERSON, Paul

Born London 20.3.68.   Ht 5 10   Wt 11 9
Forward. From Apprentice.

1985–86	Arsenal	—	—

METCALF, Mark

Born Norwich 25.9.65.   Ht 5 10   Wt 10 0
Midfield. From Apprentice. England
Schools, Youth.

1983–84	Norwich C	—	—
1984–85	....	—	—
1985–86	....	—	—

METGOD, Johnny

Born Amsterdam 27.2.58.   Ht 6 4
Wt 13 6½
Midfield. From DWS, Haarlem, AZ '67 and
Real Madrid. Holland full caps.

1984–85	Nottingham F	40	6
1985–86	....	39	6

METHVEN, Colin

Born India 10.12.55.   Ht 6 2   Wt 12 7
Defender. From Leven Royals.

1974–75	East Fife	1	—
1975–76	....	26	1

MICALLEF, 'Tarki'

Born Cardiff 24.1.61.   Ht 5 6   Wt 10 10
Forward. From Apprentice. Wales Schools,
Under-21.

1978–79	Cardiff C	2	—
1979–80	....	8	1
1980–81	....	18	1
1981–82	....	33	8
1982–83	....	20	1
1983–84	Newport Co	24	2
1984–85	Gillingham	2	—
1984–85	Cardiff C	12	1
1985–86	....	28	—

MICKLEWHITE, Gary

Born Southwark 21.3.61.   Ht 5 7   Wt 10 4
Forward. From Apprentice.

1977–78	Manchester U	—	—
1978–79	....	—	—
1979–80	QPR	—	—
1980–81	....	1	—
1981–82	....	26	2
1982–83	....	34	6
1983–84	....	30	2
1984–85	....	15	1
1984–85	Derby Co	19	4
1985–86	....	46	11

MILES, Andy

Born Tredegar 25.5.61.
Forward. From Ebbw Vale.

1985–86	Newport Co	4	2

All appearances include those as substitute

Season	Club	League Appearances/Goals	Season	Club	League Appearances/Goals

MILLAR, John

Born Lanark 8.12.66.
Defender.

Season	Club	App	Goals
1984–85	Chelsea	—	—
1985–86		7	—

MILLEN, Keith

Born Croydon 26.9.66. Ht 6 1 Wt 12 5
Defender. From Juniors.

Season	Club	App	Goals
1984–85	Brentford	17	—
1985–86		32	2

MILLER, Colin

Born Lanark 4.10.64. Ht 5 8 Wt 11 7
Defender. From Toronto INEX. Canada full caps.

Season	Club	App	Goals
1985–86	Rangers	2	—

MILLER, David

Born Burnley 8.1.64. Ht 5 10½ Wt 10 3
Midfield. From Apprentice.

Season	Club	App	Goals
1981–82	Burnley	—	—
1982–83		1	—
1982–83	*Crewe Alex*	3	—
1983–84	Burnley	17	2
1984–85		14	1
1985–86	Tranmere R	29	1

MILLER, Ian

Born Perth 13.5.55. Ht 5 9 Wt 11 7
Forward.

Season	Club	App	Goals
1973–74	Bury	15	—
1974–75		—	—
1974–75	Nottingham F	—	—
1975–76	Doncaster R	43	9
1976–77		46	5
1977–78		35	—
1978–79	Swindon T	44	3
1979–80		40	2
1980–81		43	4

Season	Club	App	Goals
1981–82	Blackburn R	42	3
1982–83		32	4
1983–84		36	3
1984–85		38	4
1985–86		38	1

MILLER, Joe

Born Glasgow 8.12.67. Ht 5 8 Wt 9 12
Forward. 'S' Form. Scotland Schools, Youth.

Season	Club	App	Goals
1984–85	Aberdeen	1	—
1985–86		18	3

MILLER, Paul

Born London 11.10.59. Ht 6 1 Wt 12 2
Defender. From Apprentice.

Season	Club	App	Goals
1977–78	Tottenham H	—	—
1978–79		7	—
1979–80		27	2
1980–81		25	2
1981–82		35	—
1982–83		23	1
1983–84		21	—
1984–85		39	—
1985–86		29	2

MILLER, Willie

Born Glasgow 2.5.55. Ht 5 10 Wt 11 8
Defender. From Eastercraigs. Scotland
Youth, Under-21, Under-23, 48 full caps.

Season	Club	App	Goals
1971–72	Aberdeen	—	—
1972–73		—	—
1973–74		31	1
1974–75		34	1
1975–76		36	—
1976–77		36	—
1977–78		36	2
1978–79		34	—
1979–80		31	1
1980–81		33	2
1981–82		36	—
1982–83		36	2
1983–84		34	2
1984–85		34	3
1985–86		33	1

Season	Club	League Appearances/Goals	Season	Club	League Appearances/Goals

MILLIGAN, Mike

Born Manchester 20.2.67. Ht 5 8 Wt 11 0
Midfield.

1984–85	Oldham Ath	—	—
1985–86		5	1

MILLIGAN, Terry

Born Manchester 10.1.66. Ht 5 10 Wt 9 5
Midfield. From Apprentice. Northern
Ireland Youth.

1983–84	Manchester C	—	—
From New Zealand			
1985–86	Oldham Ath	—	—

MILLS, David

Born Whitby 6.12.51. Ht 5 9½ Wt 10 10
Midfield. From Apprentice. England
Under-23, 'B'.

1968–69	Middlesbrough	1	—
1969–70		5	2
1970–71		18	1
1971–72		27	8
1972–73		37	5
1973–74		39	11
1974–75		36	8
1975–76		38	10
1976–77		42	15
1977–78		35	10
1978–79		17	6
1978–79	WBA	18	3
1979–80		17	—
1980–81		10	—
1981–82		11	2
1981–82	*Newcastle U*	23	4
1982–83	WBA	3	1
1982–83	Sheffield W	15	3
1983–84	Newcastle U	16	5
1984–85	Middlesbrough	32	15
1985–86		—	—

MILLS, Gary

Born Northampton 11.11.61. Ht 5 11
Wt 11 5
Forward. From Apprentice. England
Schools, Youth, Under-21.

1978–79	Nottingham F	4	1
1979–80		13	1
1980–81		27	5
1981–82		14	1
From Seattle S			
1982–83	Derby Co	18	1
From Seattle S			
1983–84	Nottingham F	7	—
1984–85		26	4
1985–86		14	—

MILLS, Mick

Born Godalming 4.1.49. Ht 5 7½ Wt 11 11
Defender. From Portsmouth Apprentice.
England Youth, Under-23, 42 full caps,
Football League.

1965–66	Ipswich T	2	—
1966–67		22	—
1967–68		10	—
1968–69		36	2
1969–70		40	3
1970–71		42	1
1971–72		35	—
1972–73		42	—
1973–74		42	2
1974–75		41	1
1975–76		42	1
1976–77		37	—
1977–78		34	6
1978–79		42	2
1979–80		37	1
1980–81		33	—
1981–82		42	3
1982–83		11	—
1982–83	Southampton	27	1
1983–84		34	2
1984–85		42	—
1985–86	Stoke C	31	—

Season	Club	League Appearances/Goals		Season	Club	League Appearances/Goals	

MILLS, Simon

Born Sheffield 16.8.64.   Ht 5 11   Wt 10 12
Midfield. From Apprentice. England Youth.

1982–83	Sheffield W	1	—
1983–84		2	—
1984–85		2	—
1985–86	York C	36	2

MILNE, Callum

Born Edinburgh 27.8.65.   Ht 5 8   Wt 10 7
Defender. From Salvesen B.C.

1983–84	Hibernian	—	—
1984–85		1	—
1985–86		7	—

MILNE, Ralph

Born Dundee 13.5.61.   Ht 5 8   Wt 11 10
Forward. 'S' Form. Scotland Youth, Under-21.

1977–78	Dundee U	—	—
1978–79		—	—
1979–80		13	2
1980–81		21	7
1981–82		35	8
1982–83		34	16
1983–84		25	5
1984–85		19	4
1985–86		18	1

MIMMS, Bobby

Born York 12.10.63.   Ht 6 2½   Wt 12 13
Goalkeeper. From Halifax T Apprentice.
England Under-21.

1981–82	Rotherham U	2	—
1982–83		13	—
1983–84		22	—
1984–85		46	—
1985–86	Everton	10	—
1985–86	*Notts Co*	2	—

MITCHELL, Bobby

Born South Shields 4.1.55.   Ht 5 10   Wt 11 0
Midfield. From Apprentice.

1971–72	Sunderland	—	—
1972–73		—	—
1973–74		2	—
1974–75		—	—
1975–76		1	—
1976–77	Blackburn R	21	6
1977–78		8	—
1978–79	Grimsby T	24	2
1979–80		46	2
1980–81		42	—
1981–82		30	2
1982–83	Carlisle U	2	—
1982–83	Rotherham U	10	—
1983–84		43	2
1984–85		42	—
1985–86	Lincoln C	14	—

MITCHELL, Brian

Born Stonehaven 16.7.63.   Ht 6 1   Wt 13 1
Defender. From King St. Scotland Schools.

1981–82	Aberdeen	1	—
1982–83		1	—
1983–84		9	—
1984–85		14	1
1985–86		23	—

MITCHELL, Jimmy

Born Liverpool 13.6.67.   Ht 5 9   Wt 11 5
Defender. From Apprentice.

| 1984–85 | Wigan Ath | 2 | — |
| 1985–86 | | — | — |

MOLBY, Jan

Born Kolding 4.7.63.   Ht 6 1   Wt 14 7
Midfield. From Kolding, Ajax. Denmark full caps.

| 1984–85 | Liverpool | 22 | 1 |
| 1985–86 | | 39 | 13 |

Season	Club	League Appearances/Goals		Season	Club	League Appearances/Goals	

MONCUR, John

Born Stepney 22.9.66. Ht 5 7 Wt 9 10
Defender. From Apprentice.

| 1984–85 | Tottenham H | — | — |
| 1985–86 | | — | — |

MONEY, Campbell

Born Maybole 31.8.60. Ht 5 11 Wt 12 3
Goalkeeper. From Dailly Ams. Scotland
Youth.

1978–79	St Mirren	—	—
1979–80		—	—
1980–81		—	—
1981–82		1	—
1982–83		1	—
1983–84		6	—
1984–85		30	—
1985–86		33	—

MONEY, Richard

Born Lowestoft 13.10.55.   Ht 5 11½
Wt 11 5
Defender. From Lowestoft T.
England 'B'.

1973–74	Scunthorpe U	29	1
1974–75		43	—
1975–76		45	3
1976–77		38	—
1977–78		18	—
1977–78	Fulham	23	2
1978–79		42	1
1979–80		41	—
1979–80	Liverpool	—	—
1980–81		14	—
1981–82		—	—
1981–82	*Derby Co*	5	—
1981–82	Luton T	13	1
1982–83		31	—
1983–84	Portsmouth	16	—
1984–85		—	—
1985–86		1	—
1985–86	Scunthorpe U	25	—

MOONEY, Brian

Born Dublin 2.2.66. Ht 5 10½ Wt 11 2
Midfield. From Home Farm. Eire Youth.

1983–84	Liverpool	—	—
1984–85		—	—
1985–86		—	—
1985–86	*Wrexham*	9	2

MOORE, Andy

Born Grimsby 14.11.65. Ht 6 1 Wt 12 10
Defender. From Apprentice.

1983–84	Grimsby T	9	—
1984–85		13	—
1985–86		33	1

MOORE, David

Born Grimsby 17.12.59. Ht 5 10 Wt 12 13
Defender. From Apprentice.

1977–78	Grimsby T	—	—
1978–79		30	—
1979–80		29	—
1980–81		5	—
1981–82		34	2
1982–83		38	—
1983–84	Carlisle U	13	1
1983–84	Blackpool	28	1
1984–85		44	—
1985–86		41	—

MOORE, Gordon

Born Greenock 27.6.68.
Midfield. From school.

| 1985–86 | Bristol C | 1 | — |

MOORE, John

Born Consett 1.10.66. Ht 6 0 Wt 11 11
Forward. From Apprentice.

| 1984–85 | Sunderland | 4 | 1 |

To St Patrick's

| 1985–86 | Sunderland | — | — |
| 1985–86 | *Newport Co* | 2 | — |

Season	Club	League Appearances/Goals		Season	Club	League Appearances/Goals	

MOORE, Kevin

Born Grimsby 29.4.58. Ht 5 11 Wt 11 2
Defender. Local. England Schools.

Season	Club	App	Goals
1976–77	Grimsby T	28	—
1977–78		42	—
1978–79		46	6
1979–80		41	4
1980–81		41	1
1981–82		36	4
1982–83		38	—
1983–84		41	1
1984–85		31	4
1985–86		31	2

MOORE, Ronnie

Born Liverpool 29.1.53. Ht 6 0 Wt 13 12
Forward. From Amateur.

Season	Club	App	Goals
1971–72	Tranmere R	2	—
1972–73		—	—
1973–74		46	2
1974–75		44	2
1975–76		46	34
1976–77		42	9
1977–78		43	17
1978–79		26	8
1979–80	Cardiff C	18	3
1979–80		38	3
1980–81	Rotherham U	45	23
1981–82		40	21
1982–83		36	5
1983–84		4	2
1983–84	Charlton Ath	28	8
1984–85		34	5
1985–86	Rochdale	43	9

MOORE, Vincent

Born Scunthorpe 21.8.64. Ht 5 11 Wt 12 0
Midfield. From Campsie Black Watch.

Season	Club	App	Goals
1984–85	Clydebank	3	—
1985–86		23	2

MORAN, Kevin

Born Dublin 29.4.56. Ht 5 10½ Wt 12 9
Defender. From Pegasus-Eire Gaelic
Football. Eire, 18 full caps.

Season	Club	App	Goals
1977–78	Manchester U	—	—
1978–79		1	—
1979–80		9	1
1980–81		32	—
1981–82		30	7
1982–83		29	2
1983–84		38	7
1984–85		19	4
1985–86		19	—

MORAN, Paul

Born Enfield 22.5.68.
Forward. From YTS.

Season	Club	App	Goals
1984–85	Tottenham H	—	—
1985–86		—	—

MORAN, Steve

Born Croydon 10.1.61. Ht 5 8 Wt 10 11
Forward. From Amateur. England Under-21.

Season	Club	App	Goals
1979–80	Southampton	1	1
1980–81		31	18
1981–82		18	9
1982–83		36	10
1983–84		34	21
1984–85		32	11
1985–86		28	8

MORGAN, Darren

Born Camberwell 5.11.67. Ht 5 6½ Wt 9 5
Defender. From Apprentice. Wales Youth.

Season	Club	App	Goals
1985–86	Millwall	—	—

MORGAN, Gary

Born Consett 1.4.61. Ht 5 8 Wt 12 0
Defender. From Consett.

Season	Club	League Appearances/Goals		Season	Club	League Appearances/Goals	
1983–84	Berwick R	37	3	1980–81	Bournemouth	42	10
1984–85		30	1	1981–82		11	3
1985–86	Darlington	41	1	1981–82	Mansfield T	12	6
				1981–82	Bournemouth	14	4
				1982–83		45	16
				1983–84		29	13
				1983–84	Bristol C	15	5
				1984–85		17	3
				1984–85	Exeter C	26	9
				1985–86		4	—
				1985–86	Bristol R	36	16

MORGAN, Nick

Born East Ham 30.10.59.   Ht 5 10   Wt 12 8
Forward. From Apprentice.

Season	Club	League Appearances/Goals	
1977–78	West Ham U	—	—
1978–79		2	—
1979–80		6	1
1980–81		6	1
1981–82		—	—
1982–83		7	—
1982–83	Portsmouth	6	1
1983–84		25	9
1984–85		30	8
1985–86		30	14

MORGAN, Russell

Born Caerphilly 23.1.68.   Ht 6 3   Wt 12 9
Goalkeeper. From Birmingham C. Wales
Youth.

Season	Club	League Appearances/Goals	
1985–86	Cardiff C	—	—

MORGAN, Simon

Born Birmingham 5.9.66.   Ht 5 11   Wt 12 7
Defender.

Season	Club	League Appearances/Goals	
1984–85	Leicester C	—	—
1985–86		30	—

MORGAN, Steve

Born Oldham 19.9.68.   Ht 5 11   Wt 12 0
Defender. From Apprentice.

Season	Club	League Appearances/Goals	
1985–86	Blackpool	5	—

MORGAN, Trevor

Born Forest Gate 30.9.56.   Ht 6 1   Wt 13 1
Forward. From Leytonstone and Ilford.

MORLEY, Tony

Born Ormskirk 26.8.54.   Ht 5 8½   Wt 11 8½
Forward. From Apprentice. England Youth,
Under-23, 'B', 6 full caps.

Season	Club	League Appearances/Goals	
1972–73	Preston NE	4	—
1973–74		10	—
1974–75		45	10
1975–76		25	5
1975–76	Burnley	9	—
1976–77		34	2
1977–78		29	1
1978–79		19	2
1979–80	Aston Villa	18	3
1980–81		42	10
1981–82		37	6
1982–83		33	5
1983–84		7	1
1983–84	WBA	26	4
1984–85		7	—
1984–85	*Birmingham C*	4	3
1985–86	WBA	—	—

MORLEY, Trevor

Born Nottingham 20.3.61.   Ht 5 11
Wt 12 1
Forward. From Derby Co., Corby T,
Nuneaton.

Season	Club	League Appearances/Goals	
1985–86	Northampton T	43	13

Season	Club	League Appearances/Goals	Season	Club	League Appearances/Goals

MORRELL, Paul

Born Poole 23.3.61.   Ht 5 11   Wt 13 7
Defender. From Poole, Bath & Weymouth.

Season	Club	Apps	Goals
1983–84	Bournemouth	22	2
1984–85		44	1
1985–86		38	1

MORRIS, Andy

Born Sheffield 17.11.67.   Ht 6 5
Forward.

Season	Club	Apps	Goals
1984–85	Rotherham U	1	—
1985–86		—	—

MORRIS, Chris

Born Newquay 24.12.63.   Ht 5 10   Wt 10 8
Midfield. England Schools.

Season	Club	Apps	Goals
1982–83	Sheffield W	—	—
1983–84		13	1
1984–85		14	—
1985–86		30	—

MORRIS, Colin

Born Blyth 22.8.53.   Ht 5 7   Wt 10 5½
Forward. From Apprentice.

Season	Club	Apps	Goals
1971–72	Burnley	—	—
1972–73		—	—
1973–74		—	—
1974–75		2	—
1975–76		8	—
1976–77		—	—
1976–77	Southend U	23	3
1977–78		46	11
1978–79		44	7
1979–80		20	4
1979–80	Blackpool	21	4
1980–81		44	12
1981–82		22	10
1981–82	Sheffield U	23	4
1982–83		41	14
1983–84		42	20
1984–85		32	8
1985–86		40	10

MORRIS, Mark

Born Morden 26.9.62.   Ht 6 0   Wt 11 10
Defender. From Apprentice.

Season	Club	Apps	Goals
1980–81	Wimbledon	—	—
1981–82		33	1
1982–83		26	3
1983–84		39	3
1984–85		29	1
1985–86		20	1
1985–86	*Aldershot*	14	—

MORRIS, Mark

Born Chester 1.8.68.
Goalkeeper.

Season	Club	Apps	Goals
1985–86	Wrexham	3	—

MORRISON, Frank

Born Glasgow 17.4.67.   Ht 5 8   Wt 10 0
Defender. From Duntocher B.C.

Season	Club	Apps	Goals
1984–85	St Mirren	—	—
1985–86		1	—

MORRISSEY, John

Born Liverpool 8.3.65.   Ht 5 5   Wt 9 11
Midfield. From Apprentice. England Youth.

Season	Club	Apps	Goals
1982–83	Everton	—	—
1983–84		—	—
1984–85		1	—
1985–86	Wolverhampton W	10	1
1985–86	Tranmere R	32	5

MORTIMER, Dennis

Born Liverpool 5.4.52.   Ht 5 10   Wt 12 3
Midfield. From Apprentice.
England Youth, Under-23, 'B'.

Season	Club	Apps	Goals
1969–70	Coventry C	9	—
1970–71		27	—
1971–72		34	4
1972–73		39	1
1973–74		33	1

Season	Club	League Appearances/Goals		Season	Club	League Appearances/Goals	
1974–75	....	29	3	1978–79	WBA........................	—	—
1975–76	....	22	1	1979–80	....	18	1
1975–76	Aston Villa................	14	—	1980–81	....	41	4
1976–77	....	41	4	1981–82	....	4	—
1977–78	....	42	3	1981–82	Manchester U	21	2
1978–79	....	38	3	1982–83	....	29	—
1979–80	....	26	6	1983–84	....	35	2
1980–81	....	42	4	1984–85	....	26	3
1981–82	....	32	2	1985–86	....	4	—
1982–83	....	39	4				
1983–84	....	37	5				
1984–85	....	6	—				
1984–85	*Sheffield U*	7	—				
1985–86	Brighton......................	40	2				

MOSELEY, Graham

Born Manchester 16.11.53.   Ht 6 0   Wt 11 8
Goalkeeper. From Apprentice.
England Youth.

Season	Club	Apps	Goals
1971–72	Blackburn R	—	—
1971–72	Derby C	—	—
1972–73	....	2	—
1973–74	....	—	—
1974–75	....	—	—
1974–75	*Aston Villa*	3	—
1975–76	Derby Co......................	18	—
1976–77	....	12	—
1977–78	....	—	—
1977–78	*Walsall*	3	—
1977–78	Brighton......................	4	—
1978–79	....	17	—
1979–80	....	33	—
1980–81	....	26	—
1981–82	....	30	—
1982–83	....	27	—
1983–84	....	1	—
1983–84	*Ipswich T*	—	—
1984–85	Brighton......................	42	—
1985–86	....	9	—

MOSES, Remi

Born Manchester 14.11.60.   Ht 5 7
Wt 10 10
Midfield. From Apprentice.
England Under-21.

MOSS, David

Born Witney 18.3.52.   Ht 5 9   Wt 11 7
Forward. From Witney T.

Season	Club	Apps	Goals
1969–70	Swindon T....................	—	—
1970–71	....	—	—
1971–72	....	5	—
1972–73	....	16	4
1973–74	....	40	6
1974–75	....	41	14
1975–76	....	39	6
1976–77	....	44	14
1977–78	....	45	16
1978–79	Luton T......................	30	13
1979–80	....	40	24
1980–81	....	41	16
1981–82	....	36	15
1982–83	....	39	9
1983–84	....	16	4
1984–85	....	19	7
1985–86	Swindon T....................	4	—

MOSS, Ernie

Born Chesterfield 19.10.49.   Ht 6 1½
Wt 13 2
Forward. From Chesterfield Tube Wks.

Season	Club	Apps	Goals
1968–69	Chesterfield.................	17	—
1969–70	....	44	20
1970–71	....	44	16
1971–72	....	40	9
1972–73	....	16	7
1973–74	....	43	17
1974–75	....	46	20
1975–76	....	21	5
1975–76	Peterborough U............	21	6
1976–77	....	14	3

Season	Club	League Appearances/Goals		Season	Club	League Appearances/Goals	

1976–77	Mansfield T	29	13
1977–78		15	6
1978–79		13	2
1978–79	Chesterfield	23	5
1979–80		45	14
1980–81		39	14
1981–82	Port Vale	44	13
1982–83		30	10
1982–83	Lincoln C	11	2
1983–84	Doncaster R	44	15
1984–85	Chesterfield	33	12
1985–86		39	14

MOSSMAN, David

Born Sheffield 27.7.64.   Ht 6 1   Wt 12 2
Forward. England Schools.

1982–83	Sheffield W	—	—
1983–84		—	—
1984–85		—	—
1984–85	*Bradford C*	3	1
1985–86		—	—
1985–86	*Stockport Co*	9	4
1985–86	Rochdale	8	—
1985–86	Stockport Co	8	1

MOULDEN, Paul

Born Farnworth 6.9.67.   Ht 5 10   Wt 11 0
Forward. From Apprentice. England Youth.

| 1984–85 | Manchester C | — | — |
| 1985–86 | | 2 | — |

MOUNTFIELD, Derek

Born Liverpool 2.11.62.   Ht 6 1   Wt 12 7
Defender. From Apprentice. England
Under-21.

1980–81	Tranmere R	5	—
1981–82		21	1
1982–83	Everton	1	—
1983–84		31	3
1984–85		37	10
1985–86		15	3

MOUNTFORD, Eric

Born Stoke 19.3.67.   Ht 6 2   Wt 12 7
Defender. From Apprentice.

| 1984–85 | Port Vale | — | — |
| 1985–86 | | — | — |

MOUNTFORD, Peter

Born Stoke 9.4.60.   Ht 5 10   Wt 10 6
Midfield. From Apprentice.

1978–79	Norwich C	—	—
1979–80		—	—
1980–81		—	—
1981–82		2	—
1982–83		2	—
1983–84	Charlton Ath	11	1
1984–85	Orient	16	1
1985–86		15	1

MOWBRAY, Tony

Born Saltburn 22.11.63.   Ht 6 1   Wt 12 2
Defender. From Apprentice.

1981–82	Middlesbrough	—	—
1982–83		26	—
1983–84		35	1
1984–85		40	2
1985–86		35	4

MOWER, Ken

Born Walsall 1.12.60.   Ht 6 0   Wt 12 2
Defender. From Apprentice.

1978–79	Walsall	1	—
1979–80		44	1
1980–81		33	2
1981–82		34	—
1982–83		45	1
1983–84		44	1
1984–85		41	1
1985–86		43	1

Season	Club	League Appearances/Goals		Season	Club	League Appearances/Goals	

MOYES, David

Born Blythswood 25.4.63. Ht 6 0 Wt 12 3
Defender. From Drumchapel A.

Season	Club	App	Goals
1980–81	Celtic	—	—
1981–82		19	—
1982–83		5	—
1983–84		—	—
1983–84	Cambridge U	30	—
1984–85		40	1
1985–86		9	—
1985–86	Bristol C	27	2

MUIR, Ian

Born Coventry 5.5.63. Ht 5 7 Wt 10 9
Forward. From Apprentice. England Youth.

Season	Club	App	Goals
1980–81	QPR	2	2
1981–82		—	—
1982–83		—	—
1982–83	*Burnley*	2	1
1983–84	Birmingham C.	1	—
1983–84	Brighton	2	—
1984–85		2	—
1984–85	*Swindon T.*	2	—
1985–86	Tranmere R.	32	13

MULDOON, John

Born Clatterbridge 21.11.64. Ht 5 6
Wt 10 5
Midfield. From school.

Season	Club	App	Goals
1982–83	Wrexham	25	4
1983–84		32	4
1984–85		15	3
1985–86		11	—

MULLEN, Jimmy

Born Jarrow 8.11.52. Ht 5 10 Wt 12 12
Defender. From Apprentice.

Season	Club	App	Goals
1970–71	Sheffield W	7	—
1971–72		3	—
1972–73		24	1
1973–74		21	2
1974–75		16	—
1975–76		41	—
1976–77		27	—
1977–78		41	4
1978–79		35	1
1979–80		15	2
1980–81	Rotherham U	43	1
1981–82		6	—
1981–82	*Preston NE*	1	—
1982–83	*Cardiff C*	12	1
1982–83	Cardiff C	39	1
1983–84		12	—
1984–85		26	2
1985–86		44	8

MULLEN, Richard

Born Llantrisant 4.6.64. Ht 5 11 Wt 13 2½
Goalkeeper. From Crystal Palace
Apprentice.

Season	Club	App	Goals
1983–84	Hereford U	—	—
1984–85		—	—
1985–86		—	—

MULVANEY, Frank

Born Chapelhall 5.4.62. Ht 5 9 Wt 11 7
Forward. From Plains B.C.

Season	Club	App	Goals
1980–81	Albion R	18	4
From Forth Wanderers			
1985–86	Motherwell	5	—

MULVIHILL, Jim

Born Liverpool 26.2.68.
Defender. From Apprentice.

Season	Club	App	Goals
1985–86	Liverpool	—	—

MUNDEE, Brian

Born London 12.1.64. Ht 5 10 Wt 10 12
Forward. From Hungerford T.

Season	Club	League Appearances/Goals		Season	Club	League Appearances/Goals	

1981–82	Bournemouth	—	—
1982–83		4	—
1983–84	Northampton T	36	1
1984–85		33	2
1985–86		31	—
1985–86	Cambridge U	11	1

MUNGALL, Steve

Born Bellshill 22.5.58.   Ht 5 8   Wt 11 2
Defender.

1976–77	Motherwell	3	—
1977–78		13	—
1978–79		4	—
1979–80	Tranmere R	24	—
1980–81		38	3
1981–82		44	1
1982–83		31	1
1983–84		26	—
1984–85		23	—
1985–86		46	1

MUNRO, Iain

Born Uddingston 24.8.51.   Ht 5 7½   Wt 10 5
Defender. From Drumchapel Amateurs.
Scotland Youth, 7 full caps.

1969–70	St. Mirren	5	—
1970–71		31	3
1971–72		36	6
1972–73		32	9
1973–74	Hibernian	14	2
1974–75		30	8
1975–76		17	1
1976–77	Rangers	5	—
1977–78	St Mirren	24	3
1978–79		33	—
1979–80		32	—
1980–81	Stoke C	32	1
1981–82	Sunderland	34	—
1982–83		37	—
1983–84		9	—
1983–84	Dundee U	9	—
1984–85		5	—
1984–85	Hibernian	6	—
1985–86		27	—

MUNRO, Stuart

Born Falkirk 15.9.62   Ht 5 8   Wt 10 5
Defender. From Bo'ness United.

1980–81	St Mirren	1	—
1981–82		—	—
1982–83	Alloa	39	5
1983–84		21	1
1983–84	Rangers	5	—
1984–85		13	—
1985–86		29	—

MURPHY, Aidan

Born Manchester 17.9.67   Ht 5 10½
Wt 10 10
Midfield. From Apprentice. England
Schools, Youth.

| 1984–85 | Manchester U | — | — |
| 1985–86 | | — | — |

MURPHY, Colin

Born Birmingham 1.5.68.
Midfield. From Apprentice.

| 1985–86 | Nottingham F | — | — |

MURPHY, Jerry

Born Stepney 23.9.59.   Ht 5 9   Wt 11 10
Midfield. From Apprentice.
England Schools. Eire 3 full caps.

1976–77	Crystal Palace	1	—
1977–78		8	—
1978–79		41	5
1979–80		37	3
1980–81		19	2
1981–82		25	2
1982–83		30	2
1983–84		32	3
1984–85		36	3
1985–86	Chelsea	21	3

Season	Club	League Appearances/Goals	Season	Club	League Appearances/Goals

MURPHY, Nick

Born Tadcaster 22.10.66.   Ht 5 10   Wt 11 7
Defender.

1985–86	York C	— —

MURRAY, David

Born Chorley 30.9.67.
Forward. From Chorley.

1984–85	Wigan Ath	— —
1985–86	Chester	6 1

MURRAY, Derek

Born Dunfermline 26.11.60.   Ht 5 8   Wt 10 8
Defender. From Oakley.

1977–78	Dundee U	— —
1978–79		— —
1979–80		— —
1980–81		1 —
1981–82		12 —
1982–83		1 —
1983–84		2 —
1984–85	Motherwell	34 5
1985–86		25 —

MURRAY, Jamie

Born Glasgow 27.12.58.   Ht 5 9   Wt 10 12
Forward. From Rivet Sports.

1976–77	Cambridge U	1 —
1977–78		20 1
1978–79		26 1
1979–80		34 1
1980–81		40 —
1981–82		42 —
1982–83		42 —
1983–84		24 —
1983–84	*Sunderland*	1 —
1984–85	Brentford	46 —
1985–86		45 3

MURRAY, Steven

Born Kilmarnock 1.12.67.   Ht 5 7½
Wt 10 13
Midfield. From Apprentice. Scotland Youth.

1984–85	Nottingham F	— —
1985–86		— —

MUSKER, Russell

Born Liverpool 10.7.62.   Ht 5 8½   Wt 11 9
Midfield. From Apprentice.

1979–80	Bristol C	— —
1980–81		4 —
1981–82		33 —
1982–83		6 1
1983–84		3 —
1983–84	*Exeter C*	6 —
1983–84	Gillingham	27 5
1984–85		28 1
1985–86		9 1

MUTCH, Andy

Born Liverpool 28.12.63.   Ht 5 10½
Wt 11 0
Forward. From Southport.

1985–86	Wolverhampton W	15 7

Season	Club	League Appearances/Goals		Season	Club	League Appearances/Goals

NAREY, Dave

Born Dundee 21.6.56. Ht 6 0 Wt 12 6
Defender. 'S' Form. Scotland Youth, Under-21, Under–23, 28 full caps.

Season	Club	App	Goals
1973–74	Dundee U	12	—
1974–75		31	6
1975–76		33	—
1976–77		32	2
1977–78		35	—
1978–79		36	5
1979–80		35	1
1980–81		32	—
1981–82		34	1
1982–83		36	5
1983–84		34	1
1984–85		29	1
1985–86		35	—

NARDIELLO, Gerry

Born Warley 5.5.66. Ht 5 10 Wt 10 8
Midfield. From Apprentice.

Season	Club	App	Goals
1982–83	Shrewsbury T	1	—
1983–84		11	5
1984–85		4	1
1985–86		22	5
1985–86	*Cardiff C*	7	4

NATTRASS, Irving

Born Fishburn 12.12.52. Ht 5 11 Wt 12 0
Defender. From Apprentice.
England Under-23.

Season	Club	App	Goals
1970–71	Newcastle U	4	—
1971–72		24	1
1972–73		25	3
1973–74		14	2
1974–75		33	—
1975–76		39	3
1976–77		40	2
1977–78		38	3
1978–79		21	2
1979–80	Middlesbrough	13	—
1980–81		31	1
1981–82		27	—

1982–83		29	1
1983–84		42	—
1984–85		30	—
1985–86		19	—

NATTRESS, Clive

Born Durham 24.5.51. Ht 6 0 Wt 12 4½
Defender. From Consett.

Season	Club	App	Goals
1970–71	Blackpool	—	—
1971–72		—	—
1972–73	Darlington	26	—
1973–74		43	—
1974–75		28	2
1975–76		46	2
1976–77		46	4
1977–78		26	2
1978–79		45	1
1979–80		42	4
1980–81	Halifax T	37	5
From Local			
1984–85	Darlington	—	—
1985–86		1	—

NAUGHTON, Willie

Born Catrine 20.3.62. Ht 6 0 Wt 12 8
Forward. From Apprentice.

Season	Club	App	Goals
1979–80	Preston NE	3	—
1980–81		10	2
1981–82		33	3
1982–83		41	1
1983–84		42	3
1984–85		33	1
1984–85	Walsall	13	—
1985–86		39	5

NAYLOR, Stuart

Born Wetherby 6.12.62. Ht 6 4 Wt 12 10
Goalkeeper. From Yorkshire A. England
Youth.

Season	Club	App	Goals
1980–81	Lincoln C	—	—
1981–82		3	—

231

Season	Club	League Appearances/Goals		Season	Club	League Appearances/Goals

Season	Club	Apps	Goals
1982–83		1	—
1982–83	*Peterborough U*	8	—
1983–84	Lincoln C	—	—
1983–84	*Crewe Alex*	38	—
1984–85	*Crewe Alex*	17	—
1984–85	Lincoln C	25	—
1985–86		20	—
1985–86	WBA	12	—

NEAL, Dean

Born Edmonton 5.1.61.   Ht 5 10½   Wt 12 1½
Forward. From Apprentice.

Season	Club	Apps	Goals
1979–80	QPR	7	—
1980–81		16	8
From Tulsa R			
1981–82	Millwall	22	4
1982–83		40	18
1983–84		34	13
1984–85		24	7
1985–86		—	—
1985–86	Southend U	11	3

NEAL, Phil

Born Irchester 20.2.51.   Ht 5 11   Wt 12 2
Defender. From Apprentice.
England, 50 full caps.

Season	Club	Apps	Goals
1968–69	Northampton T	21	4
1969–70		13	1
1970–71		17	2
1971–72		41	2
1972–73		38	9
1973–74		46	9
1974–75		10	2
1974–75	Liverpool	23	—
1975–76		42	6
1976–77		42	7
1977–78		42	4
1978–79		42	5
1979–80		42	1
1980–81		42	2
1981–82		42	2
1982–83		42	8
1983–84		41	1
1984–85		42	4
1985–86		13	1
1985–86	Bolton W	20	2

NEBBELING, Gavin

Born Johannesburg 15.5.63.   Ht 6 0
Wt 12 4
Defender. From Arcadia Shepherds.

Season	Club	Apps	Goals
1981–82	Crystal Palace	1	—
1982–83		28	1
1983–84		16	—
1984–85		16	—
1985–86		14	—
1985–86	*Northampton T*	11	—

NEENAN, Joe

Born Manchester 17.3.59.   Ht 6 3
Wt 12 10
Goalkeeper. From Apprentice.

Season	Club	Apps	Goals
1976–77	York C	6	—
1977–78		13	—
1978–79		22	—
1979–80		15	—
1979–80	Scunthorpe U	2	—
1980–81		44	—
1981–82		44	—
1982–83		46	—
1983–84		41	—
1984–85		14	—
1984–85	*Burnley*	9	—
1985–86	Burnley	36	—

NEILL, Warren

Born Acton 21.11.62.   Ht 5 8   Wt 11 10
Defender. From Apprentice. England
Schools.

Season	Club	Apps	Goals
1980–81	QPR	4	—
1981–82		11	—
1982–83		39	2
1983–84		41	1
1984–85		18	—
1985–86		16	—

NELSON, Gary

Born Braintree 16.1.61.   Ht 5 10   .Wt 11 4
Forward. From Amateur.

Season	Club	League Appearances/Goals		Season	Club	League Appearances/Goals	
1979–80	Southend U	22	2	1981–82	Clyde	34	12
1980–81		22	3	1982–83		39	5
1981–82		40	4	1983–84	Chelsea	38	14
1982–83		45	8	1984–85		41	4
1983–84	Swindon T	36	4	1985–86		40	7
1984–85		43	3				
1985–86	Plymouth Arg	42	13				

NESBIT, Tony

Born Sunderland 26.1.68.
From Apprentice. England Schools.

1985–86	Newcastle U	—	—

NESBITT, Mike

Born Doncaster 8.1.69. Ht 5 10 Wt 11 7
Forward. From Apprentice. England Youth.

1985–86	Doncaster R	5	1

NEVILLE, Steve

Born Walthamstow 18.9.57. Ht 5 9
Wt 11 0
Forward. From Apprentice.

1975–76	Southampton	—	—
1976–77		—	—
1977–78		5	1
1978–79		—	—
1978–79	Exeter C	36	9
1979–80		43	8
1980–81		14	5
1980–81	Sheffield U	19	2
1981–82		30	4
1982–83	*Exeter C*	33	17
1983–84	Exeter C	43	9
1984–85		16	1
1984–85	Bristol C	28	8
1985–86		46	19

NEVIN, Pat

Born Glasgow 6.9.63. Ht 5 6 Wt 10 0
Forward. From Gartcosh U. Scotland
Under-21, 2 full caps.

NEWELL, Mike

Born Liverpool 27.1.65. Ht 6 0 Wt 12 0
Forward. From Liverpool Amateur. England
Under-21.

1983–84	Crewe Alex	3	—
1983–84	Wigan Ath	9	—
1984–85		39	9
1985–86		24	16
1985–86	Luton T	16	6

NEWMAN, Darren

Born Brighton 14.8.68.
Defender. From Apprentice.

1985–86	Brighton	1	—

NEWMAN, Rob

Born Bradford-on-Avon 13.12.63.
Ht 6 0½ Wt 12 0
Defender. From Apprentice.

1981–82	Bristol C	21	3
1982–83		43	3
1983–84		30	1
1984–85		34	3
1985–86		39	3

NEWSON, Mark

Born Stepney 7.12.60. Ht 5 10 Wt 12 6
Midfield. From Apprentice.

1979–80	Charlton Ath	—	—

From Maidstone U.

1985–86	Bournemouth	46	5

NEWTON, Bob

Born Chesterfield 23.11.56. Ht 5 11
Wt 14 2
Forward. From Apprentice.

Season	Club	League Appearances/Goals		Season	Club	League Appearances/Goals	
1973–74	Huddersfield T	4	—				
1974–75		3	—				
1975–76		18	5				
1976–77		17	2				
1977–78	*York C*	—	—				
1977–78	Hartlepool U	30	3				
1978–79		23	8				
1979–80		33	12				
1980–81		27	10				
1981–82		34	15				
1982–83		3	—				
1982–83	Port Vale	41	20				
1983–84		7	2				
1983–84	Chesterfield	33	14				
1984–85		45	15				
1985–86	Hartlepool U	11	2				
1985–86	*Stockport Co*	6	1				

NICHOLAS, Charlie

Born Glasgow 30.12.61. Ht 5 10 Wt 11 0
Forward. From Celtic BC. Scotland Youth.
Under-21, 15 full caps.

Season	Club	App	Goals
1980–81	Celtic	29	16
1981–82		10	3
1982–83		35	29
1983–84	Arsenal	41	11
1984–85		38	9
1985–86		41	10

NICHOLAS, Peter

Born Newport 10.11.59. Ht 5 8½ Wt 11 8
Midfield. From Apprentice.
Wales Under-21, 45 full caps.

Season	Club	App	Goals
1976–77	Crystal Palace	—	—
1977–78		23	1
1978–79		37	3
1979–80		39	2
1980–81		28	1
1980–81	Arsenal	8	1
1981–82		31	—
1982–83		21	—
1983–84		—	—
1983–84	*Crystal Palace*	25	3
1984–85	Crystal Palace	22	4
1984–85	Luton T	19	—
1985–86		41	—

NICHOLL, Jimmy

Born Canada 28.2.56. Ht 5 9½ Wt 11 8
Defender. From Apprentice. Northern
Ireland Under-21, 70 full caps.

Season	Club	App	Goals
1973–74	Manchester U	—	—
1974–75		1	—
1975–76		20	—
1976–77		30	—
1977–78		37	2
1978–79		21	—
1979–80		42	—
1980–81		36	1
1981–82		1	—
1981–82	Sunderland	3	—
From Toronto B.			
1982–83	Sunderland	29	—
From Toronto B.			
1983–84	Rangers	17	—
1984–85	WBA	27	—
1985–86		29	—

NICHOLSON, Gary

Born Newcastle 4.11.60. Ht 5 7½ Wt 9 11
Forward. From Apprentice.

Season	Club	App	Goals
1978–79	Newcastle U	8	—
1979–80		2	—
1980–81		2	—
1981–82	Mansfield T	38	3
1982–83		39	8
1983–84		41	8
1984–85	York C	24	4
1985–86	Halifax T	44	3

NICOL, Steve

Born Irvine 11.12.61. Ht 5 10 Wt 12 0
Midfield. From Ayr U.BC.
Scotland Under-21, 8 full caps.

Season	Club	App	Goals
1979–80	Ayr U	20	2
1980–81		39	3
1981–82		11	2
1981–82	Liverpool	—	—
1982–83		4	—
1983–84		23	5

Season	Club	League Appearances/Goals		Season	Club	League Appearances/Goals	
1984–85		31	5	1973–74		34	—
1985–86		34	4	1974–75		41	—
				1975–76		6	—
				1976–77		—	—

NIEDZWIECKI, Eddie

Born Bangor 3.5.59. Ht 6 0 Wt 11 0
Goalkeeper. From Amateur. Wales Schools,
1 full cap.

Season	Club	League Appearances/Goals	
1976–77	Wrexham	—	—
1977–78		15	—
1978–79		6	—
1979–80		6	—
1980–81		—	—
1981–82		42	—
1982–83		42	—
1983–84	Chelsea	42	—
1984–85		40	—
1985–86		30	—

NIGHTINGALE, Mark

Born Salisbury 1.2.57. Ht 5 10 Wt 10 7
Defender. From Apprentice.
England Youth.

Season	Club	League Appearances/Goals	
1974–75	Bournemouth	13	—
1975–76		36	4
1976–77	Crystal Palace	—	—
1977–78	Norwich C	1	—
1978–79		—	—
1979–80		9	—
1980–81		16	—
1981–82		9	—
1982–83	Bournemouth	26	2
1983–84		46	2
1984–85		46	—
1985–86		32	—

NISBET, Gordon

Born Wallsend 18.9.51. Ht 5 10 Wt 12 2
Defender. From Amateur.
England Under-23.

Season	Club	League Appearances/Goals	
1968–69	WBA	—	—
1969–70		1	—
1970–71		—	—
1971–72		21	—
1972–73		33	—

Season	Club	League Appearances/Goals	
1976–77	Hull C	38	—
1977–78		39	—
1978–79		46	1
1979–80		46	—
1980–81		24	—
1980–81	Plymouth Arg	19	—
1981–82		45	3
1982–83		46	2
1983–84		44	4
1984–85		46	2
1985–86		46	—

NISBET, Scott

Born Edinburgh 30.1.68. Ht 6 1 Wt 11 8
Defender. From Salvesen B.C. Scotland
Schools, Youth.

Season	Club	League Appearances/Goals	
1985–86	Rangers	5	—

NIXON, Eric

Born Manchester 4.10.62. Ht 6 2½ Wt 14 3
Goalkeeper. From Curzon Ashton.

Season	Club	League Appearances/Goals	
1983–84	Manchester C	—	—
1984–85		—	—
1985–86		28	—

NOBBS, Keith

Born Bishop Auckland 19.9.61. Ht 5 10
Wt 11 10
Defender. From Apprentice.

Season	Club	League Appearances/Goals	
1979–80	Middlesbrough	—	—
1980–81		1	—
1981–82		—	—
1982–83	Halifax T	46	1
1983–84		41	—
From Bishop Auckland			
1985–86	Hartlepool U	39	1

Season	Club	League Appearances/Goals	Season	Club	League Appearances/Goals

NOBLE, Wayne

Born Bristol 11.6.67.   Ht 5 9   Wt 11 8
Defender. From Apprentice.

Season	Club	Apps	Goals
1984–85	Bristol R	—	—
1985–86		7	—

NOHILLY, Ged

Born Leeds 17.8.65. Ht 5 10 Wt 11 13
Midfield. From Sheppey U.

Season	Club	Apps	Goals
1985–86	Northampton T	—	—

NORMAN, Sean

Born Lowestoft 27.11.66.   Ht 5 6   Wt 10 8
Defender. From Lowestoft T.

Season	Club	Apps	Goals
1984–85	Colchester U	—	—
1985–86		—	—

NORMAN, Tony

Born Mancot 24.2.58.   Ht 6 1¾   Wt 12 8
Goalkeeper. From Amateur. Wales 3 full caps.

Season	Club	Apps	Goals
1976–77	Burnley	—	—
1977–78		—	—
1978–79		—	—
1979–80		—	—
1979–80	Hull C	17	—
1980–81		42	—
1981–82		36	—
1982–83		36	—
1983–84		46	—
1984–85		46	—
1985–86		42	—

NORTH, Mark

Born Ware 29.5.66.   Ht 5 11   Wt 11 0
Forward. From Apprentice.

Season	Club	Apps	Goals
1983–84	Luton T	—	—
1984–85		—	—
1984–85	Lincoln C	4	—
1985–86	Luton T	13	3

NORTH, Stacey

Born Luton 25.11.64.   Ht 6 0   Wt 12 0
Defender. From Apprentice. England Youth.

Season	Club	Apps	Goals
1982–83	Luton T	—	—
1983–84		1	—
1984–85		7	—
1985–86		2	—
1985–86	Wolverhampton W	3	—

NORTON, David

Born Cannock 3.3.65.   Ht 5 7½   Wt 10 12
Midfield. From Apprentice. England Youth.

Season	Club	Apps	Goals
1982–83	Aston Villa	—	—
1983–84		—	—
1984–85		2	—
1985–86		20	2

NUTTELL, Mike

Born Boston 22.11.68.
Forward. From YTS.

Season	Club	Apps	Goals
1985–86	Peterborough U	3	—

NUTTON, Micky

Born St Johns Wood 3.10.59.   Ht 6 0   Wt 12 4½
Defender. From Apprentice.

Season	Club	Apps	Goals
1978–79	Chelsea	15	—
1979–80		19	—
1980–81		18	—
1981–82		19	—
1982–83		8	—
1982–83	Reading	6	—
1982–83	Millwall	10	—
1983–84		43	2
1984–85		7	—
1985–86		22	1

NWAJIOBI, Chukwuemeka

Born Nigeria 25.5 59.   Ht 5 9¼   Wt 12 6
Forward. From Dulwich Hamlet.

Season	Club	Apps	Goals
1983–84	Luton T	4	1
1984–85		29	9
1985–86		21	5

Season	Club	League Appearances/Goals		Season	Club	League Appearances/Goals	

OAKES, Keith

Born Bedworth 3.7.56. Ht 6 1   Wt 13 1
Defender. From Apprentice.

Season	Club	Apps	Goals
1972–73	Peterborough U	4	—
1973–74	"	4	—
1974–75	"	12	—
1975–76	"	9	1
1976–77	"	23	1
1977–78	"	10	—
1978–79	"	—	—
1978–79	Newport Co	34	5
1979–80	"	45	11
1980–81	"	43	8
1981–82	"	45	1
1982–83	"	28	1
1983–84	"	37	1
1984–85	Gillingham	45	5
1985–86	"	40	2

OBI, Anthony

Born Birmingham 15.9.65. Ht 5 5   Wt 8 13
Forward. From Apprentice. England Youth.

Season	Club	Apps	Goals
1983–84	Aston Villa	—	—
1984–85	"	—	—
1984–85	*Walsall*	2	—
1984–85	*Plymouth Arg*	5	—
1985–86	Bristol R	1	—

O'BRIEN, Jon

Born Rochford 2.11.61. Ht 5 10½   Wt 12 2
Goalkeeper. From Maldon T. and Tilbury.

Season	Club	Apps	Goals
1984–85	Southend U	11	—
1985–86	"	—	—

O'CALLAGHAN, Brendan

Born Bradford 23.7.55. Ht 6 2½   Wt 13 7
Forward. From Amateur.
Eire Under-21, 7 full caps.

Season	Club	Apps	Goals
1973–74	Doncaster R	38	10
1974–75	"	31	11
1975–76	"	42	22
1976–77	"	46	15
1977–78	"	30	7
1977–78	Stoke C	15	6
1978–79	"	41	16
1979–80	"	36	5
1980–81	"	37	7
1981–82	"	41	5
1982–83	"	37	5
1983–84	"	38	1
1984–85	"	20	—
1984–85	Oldham Ath	9	—
1985–86	"	1	—

O'CALLAGHAN, Kevin

Born London 19.10.61. Ht 5 8½   Wt 11 4
Forward. From Apprentice. Eire, 19 full
caps.

Season	Club	Apps	Goals
1978–79	Millwall	10	—
1979–80	"	10	3
1979–80	Ipswich T	4	—
1980–81	"	24	—
1981–82	"	19	1
1982–83	"	28	—
1983–84	"	25	2
1984–85	"	15	—
1984–85	Portsmouth	15	2
1985–86	"	39	11

O'CONNELL, Brendan

Born London 12.11.66. Ht 5 10   Wt 10 9
Forward.

Season	Club	Apps	Goals
1984–85	Portsmouth	—	—
1985–86	"	—	—

O'CONNOR, Mark

Born Rochdale 10.3.63. Ht 5 7   Wt 10 2
Midfield. From Apprentice.

Season	Club	Apps	Goals
1980–81	QPR	—	—
1981–82	"	1	—
1982–83	"	2	—
1983–84	"	—	—
1983–84	*Exeter C*	38	1
1984–85	Bristol R	46	8
1985–86	"	34	2
1985–86	Bournemouth	9	1

Season	Club	League Appearances/Goals	Season	Club	League Appearances/Goals

O'CONNOR, Tim

Born Neath 3.10.67.   Ht 5 11   Wt 11 4
Forward. From Afon Lido. Wales Youth.

| 1984–85 | Cardiff C | — — |
| 1985–86 | | 2 — |

O'DOHERTY, Ken

Born Dublin 30.3.63.
Forward. From UCD.

| 1984–85 | Crystal Palace | — — |
| 1985–86 | | 13 — |

O'DONNELL, Chris

Born Newcastle 26.5.68.   Ht 5 9   Wt 12 0
Defender. From Apprentice.

| 1985–86 | Ipswich T | — — |

O'DRISCOLL, Sean

Born Wolverhampton 1.7.57.   Ht 5 8
Wt 11 3
Midfield. From Alvechurch. Eire, 3 full caps.

1979–80	Fulham	10	1
1980–81		42	2
1981–82		42	7
1982–83		42	3
1983–84		12	—
1983–84	*Bournemouth*	19	1
1984–85	Bournemouth	44	1
1985–86		46	5

OGHANI, George

Born Manchester 2.9.60.   Ht 5 10   Wt 12 0
Forward. From Hyde.

1983–84	Bolton W	3	—
1984–85		41	16
1985–86		36	7

OGLEY, Mark

Born Barnsley 10.3.67.
Defender. From Apprentice.

| 1984–85 | Barnsley | — — |
| 1985–86 | | 2 — |

OGRIZOVIC, Steve

Born Mansfield 12.9.57.   Ht 6 3   Wt 14 0
Goalkeeper. From O.N.R.Y.C.

1977–78	Chesterfield	16	—
1977–78	Liverpool	2	—
1978–79		—	—
1979–80		1	—
1980–81		1	—
1981–82		—	—
1982–83	Shrewsbury T	42	—
1983–84		42	—
1984–85	Coventry C	42	—
1985–86		42	—

O'HANLON, Kelham

Born Saltburn 16.5.62.   Ht 6 0   Wt 12 0
Goalkeeper. From Apprentice.

1980–81	Middlesbrough	— —
1981–82		— —
1982–83		19 —
1983–84		30 —
1984–85		38 —
1985–86	Rotherham U	46 —

O'KEEFE, Eamon

Born Manchester 13.10.53.   Ht 5 7   Wt 11 5
Forward. From Stalybridge C.
Eire, 5 full caps.

1973–74	Plymouth Arg	— —
From Hyde U/S Arabia/Mossley		
1979–80	Everton	4	—
1980–81		25	3
1981–82		11	3
1981–82	Wigan Ath	22	9

Season	Club	League Appearances/Goals		Season	Club	League Appearances/Goals	
1982–83	....	36	16				
1983–84	Port Vale	37	10				
1984–85	....	22	7				
1984–85	Blackpool	12	6				
1985–86	....	22	17				

OLDROYD, Darren

Born Ormskirk 1.11.66.   Ht 5 8   Wt 10 6
Defender. From Apprentice.

Season	Club	App	Goals
1984–85	Everton	1	—
1985–86	....	—	—

O'KEEFE, Pat

Born Peterborough 17.7.67.
Midfield. From YTS.

Season	Club	App	Goals
1984–85	Peterborough U............	1	—
1985–86	....	—	—

O'KEEFE, Vince

Born Birmingham 2.4.57.   Ht 6 1½
Wt 12 10
Goalkeeper. Local.

Season	Club	App	Goals
1975–76	Birmingham C............	—	—
1975–76	*Peterborough U*	—	—
1976–77	Walsall......................	—	—
From AP Leamington			
1978–79	Exeter C....................	33	—
1979–80	....	20	—
1979–80	Torquay U	16	—
1980–81	....	46	—
1981–82	....	46	—
1982–83	Blackburn R	9	—
1983–84	....	12	—
1983–84	*Bury*............................	2	—
1984–85	Blackburn R	5	—
1985–86	....	10	—

O'LEARY, David

Born London 2.5.58.   Ht 5 11   Wt 11 3
Defender. From Apprentice.
Eire, 40 full caps.

Season	Club	App	Goals
1975–76	Arsenal	27	—
1976–77	....	33	2
1977–78	....	41	1
1978–79	....	37	2
1979–80	....	34	1
1980–81	....	24	1
1981–82	....	40	1
1982–83	....	36	1
1983–84	....	36	—
1984–85	....	36	—
1985–86	....	35	—

O'LEARY, Pierce

Born Dublin 5.11.59.   Ht 5 11   Wt 11 2
Defender. From Shamrock Rovers and
Vancouver W.
Republic of Ireland 7 full caps.

Season	Club	App	Goals
1984–85	Celtic........................	11	—
1985–86	....	13	—

O'KELLY, Richard

Born West Bromwich 8.1.57.   Ht 5 10
Wt 11 0
Midfield. From Alvechurch.

Season	Club	App	Goals
1979–80	Walsall......................	—	—
1980–81	....	38	7
1981–82	....	29	6
1982–83	....	35	7
1983–84	....	40	12
1984–85	....	34	16
1985–86	....	28	7

OLIVER, Gavin

Born Felling 6.9.62.   Ht 5 11   Wt 13 2
Defender. From Apprentice.

Season	Club	App	Goals
1980–81	Sheffield W	2	—
1981–82	....	—	—
1982–83	....	2	—
1982–83	*Tranmere R*	17	1
1983–84	Sheffield W	6	—
1984–85	....	10	—
1985–86	....	—	—
1985–86	*Brighton*	16	—
1985–86	Bradford C..................	27	1

Season	Club	League Appearances/Goals			Season	Club	League Appearances/Goals		

OLIVER, Steve

Born London 12.5.67.
Goalkeeper.

1985–86	Southend U	—	—

OLSEN, Jesper

Born Fakse 20.3.61. Ht 5 6 Wt 9 9
Forward. From Naestved and Ajax.
Denmark full caps.

1984–85	Manchester U	36	5
1985–86		28	11

OLSSON, Paul

Born Hull 24.12.65. Ht 5 8 Wt 10 11
Midfield. From Apprentice.

1983–84	Hull C	—	—
1984–85		—	—
1985–86		—	—

O'NEILL, John

Born Derry 11.3.58. Ht 5 11¾ Wt 13 3
Defender. From Derry ABC.
Northern Ireland Under-21, 36 full caps.

1978–79	Leicester C	23	—
1979–80		33	—
1980–81		32	2
1981–82		41	—
1982–83		41	2
1983–84		31	2
1984–85		42	2
1985–86		41	—

O'NEILL, Martin

Born Kilrea 1.3.52. Ht 5 10 Wt 11 3
Midfield. From Distillery.
Northern Ireland, 64 full caps.

1971–72	Nottingham F	17	2
1972–73		35	6

1973–74		27	1
1974–75		16	1
1975–76		30	5
1976–77		40	9
1977–78		40	8
1978–79		28	10
1979–80		28	3
1980–81		24	3
1980–81	Norwich C	11	1
1981–82	Manchester C	13	—
1981–82	Norwich C	20	6
1982–83		35	5
1983–84	Notts Co	38	4
1984–85		26	1
1985–86	Fulham	—	—

O'NEILL, Shaun

Born Belfast 24.2.52. Ht 5 9 Wt 12 2
Defender. From Apprentice.

1969–70	Leeds U	—	—
1970–71		—	—
1971–72		—	—
1972–73		—	—
1973–74		—	—
1974–75	Chesterfield	38	1
1975–76		41	2
1976–77		44	—
1977–78		40	—
1978–79		24	—
1979–80		46	—
1980–81		29	—
1981–82		42	—
1982–83		20	—
1983–84		34	2
1984–85		41	1
1985–86		43	—

O'REGAN, Kieran

Born Cork 9.11.63. Ht 5 8 Wt 10 11
Defender. From Tramore Ath.
Eire, 4 full caps.

1982–83	Brighton	1	—
1983–84		31	1
1984–85		15	—
1985–86		15	1

All appearances include those as substitute

Season	Club	League Appearances/Goals

O'REILLY, Gary

Born Isleworth 21.3.61.   Ht 5 11   Wt 12 0
Defender. From Amateur. Eire Youth.

Season	Club	League Appearances/Goals	
1979–80	Tottenham H.	—	—
1980–81		2	—
1981–82		5	—
1982–83		26	—
1983–84		12	—
1984–85	Brighton	36	3
1985–86		35	—

O'RIORDAN, Don

Born Dublin 14.5.57.   Ht 6 0   Wt 11 12
Defender. From Apprentice. Eire Under-21.

Season	Club	League Appearances/Goals	
1975–76	Derby Co	—	—
1976–77		1	—
1977–78		5	1
1977–78	*Doncaster R*	2	—
From Tulsa			
1978–79	Preston NE	32	—
1979–80		18	—
1980–81		21	—
1981–82		46	4
1982–83		41	4
1983–84	Carlisle U	42	8
1984–85		42	10
1985–86	Middlesbrough	41	2

ORMONDROYD, Ian

Born Bradford 22.9.64.
Forward. From Thackley.

Season	Club	League Appearances/Goals	
1985–86	Bradford C	12	3

ORMSBY, Brendan

Born Birmingham 1.10.60.   Ht 5 11
Wt 11 9½
Defender. From Apprentice.
England Schools, Youth.

Season	Club	League Appearances/Goals	
1978–79	Aston Villa	2	—
1979–80		23	—
1980–81		—	—

1981–82		12	—
1982–83		—	—
1983–84		34	2
1984–85		32	2
1985–86		14	—
1985–86	Leeds U	12	1

ORR, Neil

Born Airdrie 13.5.59.   Ht 5 10   Wt 12 2
Defender. From Morton. 186 Apps. 1 gl.

Season	Club	League Appearances/Goals	
1981–82	West Ham U	24	1
1982–83		14	—
1983–84		29	—
1984–85		20	—
1985–86		36	2

O'ROURKE, Billy

Born Nottingham 2.4.60.   Ht 6 0   Wt 12 7
Goalkeeper. From Apprentice.

Season	Club	League Appearances/Goals	
1977–78	Burnley	—	—
1978–79		—	—
1979–80		2	—
1980–81		2	—
1981–82	*Newport Co*	—	—
1982–83	Burnley	10	—
1983–84		—	—
1983–84	*Blackpool*	6	—
1983–84	Chester	5	—
1984–85	Blackpool	46	—
1985–86		46	—

OSBORNE, Lawrence

Born London 20.10.67.   Ht 5 10   Wt 11 7
Forward. From Apprentice.

Season	Club	League Appearances/Goals	
1985–86	Arsenal	—	—

OSBORNE, Roger

Born Otley 9.3.50.   Ht 5 9   Wt 10 11
Midfield. From Grundisburgh.

Season	Club	League Appearances/Goals	
1972–73	Ipswich T	—	—
1973–74		9	—
1974–75		12	3
1975–76		36	2
1976–77		34	3
1977–78		26	1
1978–79		—	—
1979–80		6	—
1980–81		1	—
1980–81	Colchester U	12	—
1981–82		39	5
1982–83		45	2
1983–84		36	1
1984–85		40	2
1985–86		34	1

OSGOOD, Keith

Born Isleworth 8.5.55. Ht 6 1 Wt 12 7
Defender. From Apprentice. England
Schools, Youth.

Season	Club	League Appearances/Goals	
1972–73	Tottenham H	—	—
1973–74		1	—
1974–75		10	—
1975–76		42	3
1976–77		42	7
1977–78		18	3
1977–78	Coventry C	14	1
1978–79		11	—
1979–80		—	—
1979–80	Derby Co	32	3
1980–81		30	4
1981–82		7	3
1981–82	Orient	6	—
1982–83		18	—
1983–84		12	—
1984–85	Cambridge U	33	1
1985–86		2	—

O'SHAUGHNESSY, Steve

Born Wrexham 13.10.67.
Defender. Wales Youth.

Season	Club	League Appearances/Goals	
1984–85	Leeds U	—	—
1985–86		—	—
1985–86	Bradford C	—	—

O'SHEA, Danny

Born Kennington 26.3.63. Ht 6 0 Wt 12 8
Defender. From Apprentice.

Season	Club	League Appearances/Goals	
1980–81	Arsenal	—	—
1981–82		—	—
1982–83		6	—
1983–84		—	—
1983–84	*Charlton Ath*	9	—
1984–85	Exeter C	45	2
1985–86	Southend U	35	9

O'SHEA, Tim

Born London 12.11.66. Ht 5 11 Wt 11 4
Defender. From Arsenal Schoolboy. Eire
Youth.

Season	Club	League Appearances/Goals	
1984–85	Tottenham H	—	—
1985–86		—	—

OSMAN, Russell

Born Repton 14.2.59. Ht 6 0 Wt 11 10
Defender. From Apprentice.
England Under-21, 'B', 11 full caps.

Season	Club	League Appearances/Goals	
1975–76	Ipswich	—	—
1976–77		—	—
1977–78		28	—
1978–79		39	2
1979–80		42	2
1980–81		42	1
1981–82		39	2
1982–83		38	4
1983–84		37	3
1984–85		29	3
1985–86	Leicester C	40	—

OTULAKOWSKI, Anton

Born Dewsbury 29.1.56. Ht 5 9 Wt 10 12½
Midfield. From Ossett T.

Season	Club	League Appearances/Goals	
1974–75	Barnsley	1	—
1975–76		31	2
1976–77		10	—
1976–77	West Ham U	12	—
1977–78		5	—

Season	Club	League Appearances/Goals		Season	Club	League Appearances/Goals	
1978–79	....	—	—				
1978–79	Southend U	9	—				
1979–80	....	42	—				
1980–81	....	43	2				
1981–82	....	38	1				
1982–83	....	31	5				
1982–83	Millwall.....................	14	2				
1983–84	....	33	7				
1984–85	....	44	5				
1985–86	....	23	—				

OUTTERSIDE, Mark

Born Hexham 13.1.67.   Ht 5 11½   Wt 11 8½
Defender. From Apprentice.

1984–85	Sunderland	—	—
1985–86	....	—	—
1985–86	*Blackburn R*	—	—

OVERSON, Vince

Born Kettering 15.5.62.   Ht 6 0   Wt 13 0
Defender. From Apprentice.

1979–80	Burnley.....................	22	—
1980–81	....	39	1
1981–82	....	36	4
1982–83	....	6	—
1983–84	....	38	—
1984–85	....	42	1
1985–86	....	28	—

OWEN, Gary

Born St. Helens 7.7.58.   Ht 5 9   Wt 11 2
Midfield. From Apprentice. England Youth,
Under-21, 'B'.

1975–76	Manchester C	4	—
1976–77	....	31	1
1977–78	....	33	7
1978–79	....	35	11
1979–80	WBA.........................	37	5
1980–81	....	34	6
1981–82	....	39	3
1982–83	....	38	4
1983–84	....	20	1
1984–85	....	15	2
1985–86	....	4	—

OWEN, Gordon

Born Barnsley 14.6.59.   Ht 5 8   Wt 10 1
Forward. From Amateur.

1976–77	Sheffield W	1	—
1977–78	....	2	—
1978–79	....	22	3
1979–80	....	4	1
1979–80	*Rotherham U*	9	—
1980–81	Sheffield W	6	—
1981–82	....	6	—
1982–83	....	7	1
1982–83	*Doncaster R*..................	9	—
1982–83	*Chesterfield*	6	2
1983–84	Cardiff C	39	14
1984–85	Barnsley.....................	36	14
1985–86	....	32	11

PAGE, Jim

Born Dundee 29.10.64.   Ht 5 11   Wt 10 11
Forward. From Celtic B.C. Scotland Youth.

Season	Club	Apps	Goals
1981–82	Dundee U	—	—
1982–83		—	—
1983–84		1	—
1984–85		—	—
1985–86		4	—

PAINTER, Ian

Born Wombourne 28.12.64.   Ht 5 7
Wt 10 2
Forward. From Apprentice. England Youth,
Under-21.

Season	Club	Apps	Goals
1982–83	Stoke C	22	4
1983–84		34	9
1984–85		38	6
1985–86		19	1

PALGRAVE, Brian

Born Birmingham 12.7.66.   Ht 5 9   Wt 10 7
Forward. From Alvechurch.

Season	Club	Apps	Goals
1984–85	Walsall	4	—
1985–86		2	1

PALIN, Leigh

Born Worcester 12.9.65.   Ht 5 9½   Wt 10 3
Midfield. From Apprentice. England Youth.

Season	Club	Apps	Goals
1983–84	Aston Villa	—	—
1984–85		—	—
1984–85	*Shrewsbury T*	2	—
1985–86	Aston Villa	—	—
1985–86	Nottingham F	—	—

PALLISTER, Gary

Born Ramsgate 30.6.65.   Ht 6 4
Wt 13 0
Defender.

Season	Club	Apps	Goals
1984–85	Middlesbrough	—	—
1985–86		28	—
1985–86	*Darlington*	7	—

PALMER, Carlton

Born West Bromwich 5.12.65.   Ht 5 10
Wt 11 0
Defender. From YTS.

Season	Club	Apps	Goals
1984–85	WBA	—	—
1985–86		20	—

PALMER, Charlie

Born Aylesbury 10.7.63   Ht 5 11   Wt 12 3
Defender. From Apprentice.

Season	Club	Apps	Goals
1981–82	Watford	—	—
1982–83		—	—
1983–84		10	1
1984–85	Derby Co	33	2
1985–86		18	—

PALMER, Geoff

Born Cannock 11.7.54.   Ht 5 11   Wt 12 2
Defender. From Apprentice.
England Under-23.

Season	Club	Apps	Goals
1972–73	Wolverhampton W	—	—
1973–74		29	1
1974–75		31	1
1975–76		26	1
1976–77		42	1
1977–78		38	—
1978–79		41	—
1979–80		40	1
1980–81		34	1
1981–82		34	1
1982–83		41	5
1983–84		30	1
1984–85		8	—
1984–85	Burnley	23	—
1985–86		11	—
1985–86	Wolverhampton W	21	—

Season	Club	League Appearances/Goals	Season	Club	League Appearances/Goals

PALMER, Roger

Born Manchester 30.1.59.   Ht 5 10
Wt 10 10
Forward. From Apprentice.

Season	Club	App	Goals
1976–77	Manchester C	—	—
1977–78		5	3
1978–79		14	4
1979–80		7	1
1980–81		5	1
1980–81	Oldham Ath	21	6
1981–82		37	7
1982–83		42	15
1983–84		42	13
1984–85		36	9
1985–86		41	15

PARIS, Alan

Born Slough 15.8.64.   Ht 5 11   Wt 10 12
Midfield. From Slough T.

Season	Club	App	Goals
1982–83	Watford	—	—
1983–84		—	—
1984–85		—	—
1985–86	Peterborough U	46	—

PARKER, Derrick

Born Wallsend 7.2.57.   Ht 5 10   Wt 11 6
Forward. From Apprentice.

Season	Club	App	Goals
1973–74	Burnley	—	—
1974–75		5	1
1975–76		1	1
1976–77		—	—
1976–77	Southend U	21	6
1977–78		46	19
1978–79		43	10
1979–80		19	8
1979–80	Barnsley	19	4
1980–81		38	11
1981–82		18	6
1982–83		32	11
1983–84	Oldham Ath	25	2
1984–85		32	9
1984–85	*Doncaster R*	5	1
1985–86	Oldham Ath	—	—
1985–86	Burnley	19	5

PARKER, Garry

Born Oxford 7.9.65.   Ht 5 8   Wt 11 0
Midfield. From Apprentice. England Youth,
Under-21.

Season	Club	App	Goals
1982–83	Luton T	1	—
1983–84		13	2
1984–85		20	1
1985–86		8	—
1985–86	Hull C	12	—

PARKER, Paul

Born Essex 4.4.64.   Ht 5 7   Wt 10 9
Defender. From Apprentice. England
Under-21.

Season	Club	App	Goals
1980–81	Fulham	1	—
1981–82		5	—
1982–83		16	—
1983–84		34	—
1984–85		36	—
1985–86		30	—

PARKES, Phil

Born Sedgeley 8.8.50.   Ht 6 3   Wt 15 1
Goalkeeper. From Amateur.
England Under-21, Under-23, 'B', 1 full cap.

Season	Club	App	Goals
1967–68	Walsall	—	—
1968–69		8	—
1969–70		44	—
1970–71	QPR	41	—
1971–72		42	—
1972–73		41	—
1973–74		42	—
1974–75		41	—
1975–76		42	—
1976–77		40	—
1977–78		31	—
1978–79		24	—
1978–79	West Ham	18	—
1979–80		40	—
1980–81		42	—
1981–82		39	—
1982–83		42	—
1983–84		42	—
1984–85		10	—
1985–86		42	—

All appearances include those as substitute

Season	Club	League Appearances/Goals	Season	Club	League Appearances/Goals

PARKIN, Brian

Born Birkenhead 12.10.65.   Ht 6 1   Wt 12 0
Goalkeeper. Local.

Season	Club	App	Goals
1982–83	Oldham Ath	—	—
1983–84		5	—
1984–85		1	—
1984–85	*Crewe Alex*	12	—
1985–86	Crewe Alex	39	—

PARKIN, Steve

Born Mansfield 7.11.65.   Ht 5 6   Wt 10 7
Defender. From Apprentice. England
Schools, Youth.

Season	Club	App	Goals
1982–83	Stoke C	2	—
1983–84		1	—
1984–85		13	1
1985–86		12	1

PARKIN, Tim

Born Penrith 31.12.57.   Ht 6 2   Wt 13 3
Defender. From Apprentice.

Season	Club	App	Goals
1976–77	Blackburn R	1	—
1977–78		—	—
1978–79		12	—
1979–80			
From Malmo and Almondsbury Greenway			
1981–82	Bristol R	40	2
1982–83		41	3
1983–84		39	2
1984–85		43	3
1985–86		43	2

PARKIN, Tommy

Born Gateshead 1.2.56.   Ht 5 7   Wt 10 4
Midfield. From Apprentice.

Season	Club	App	Goals
1973–74	Ipswich T	—	—
1974–75		—	—
1975–76		—	—
1975–76	*Grimsby T*	6	—
1976–77	Ipswich T	—	—
1976–77	*Peterborough U*	3	—

Season	Club	App	Goals
1977–78	Ipswich T	1	—
1978–79		4	—
1979–80		—	—
1980–81		4	—
1981–82		6	—
1982–83		6	—
1983–84		21	—
1984–85		11	—
1985–86		14	—

PARKINSON, Gary

Born Middlesbrough 10.1.68.
Defender. From Everton Amateur.

Season	Club	App	Goals
1985–86	Middlesbrough	—	—

PARKINSON, Noel

Born Hull 16.11.59.   Ht 5 8   Wt 10 7
Midfield. From Apprentice.

Season	Club	App	Goals
1976–77	Ipswich T	—	—
1977–78		—	—
1978–79		—	—
1979–80		—	—
1979–80	*Bristol R*	5	1
1979–80	*Brentford*	10	—
1980–81	Mansfield T	35	4
1981–82		35	9
1982–83	Scunthorpe U	31	6
1983–84		10	1
1984–85	Colchester U	44	6
1985–86		35	7

PARKINSON, Philip

Born Chorley 1.12.67.
Midfield. From Apprentice.

Season	Club	App	Goals
1985–86	Southampton	—	—

PARKS, Tony

Born Hackney 26.1.63.   Ht 5 10½   Wt 10 8
Goalkeeper. From Apprentice.

Season	Club	League Appearances/Goals		Season	Club	League Appearances/Goals	
1980–81	Tottenham H	—	—	1977–78		6	—
1981–82		2	—	1978–79	Blackpool	35	—
1982–83		1	—	1979–80		44	3
1983–84		16	—	1980–81		30	—
1984–85		—	—	1981–82		46	1
1985–86		—	—	1982–83		46	3
				1983–84	Bury	40	—
				1984–85		29	1
				1985–86		39	1

PARR, Andy

Born Reading 8.10.66. Ht 5 8 Wt 11 7
Midfield. From Apprentice.

1984–85	West Ham U	—	—
1985–86		—	—

PARRIS, George

Born Ilford 11.9.64. Ht 5 9 Wt 12 0
Midfield. From Apprentice. England
Schools.

1982–83	West Ham U	—	—
1983–84		—	—
1984–85		1	—
1985–86		26	1

PASCOE, Colin

Born Port Talbot 9.4.65. Ht 5 9½ Wt 10 0
Forward. From Apprentice. Wales Youth,
Under-21, 2 full caps.

1982–83	Swansea C	7	1
1983–84		32	2
1984–85		41	9
1985–86		19	3

PASHLEY, Terry

Born Chesterfield 11.10.56. Ht 5 8
Wt 12 0
Defender. From Apprentice.
England Schools.

1973–74	Burnley	—	—
1974–75		—	—
1975–76		1	—
1976–77		11	—

PATERSON, Craig

Born South Queensferry 2.10.59. Ht 6 2
Wt 12 12
Defender. From Bonnyrigg Rose.
Scotland Under-21.

1978–79	Hibernian	—	—
1979–80		30	—
1980–81		38	3
1981–82		36	1
1982–83	Rangers	20	—
1983–84		21	1
1984–85		22	2
1985–86		18	1

PATES, Colin

Born Mitcham 10.8.61. Ht 5 11 Wt 11 0
Defender. From Apprentice. England
Youth.

1979–80	Chelsea	16	—
1980–81		15	—
1981–82		42	1
1982–83		35	4
1983–84		42	—
1984–85		36	1
1985–86		35	1

PATTERSON, Mark

Born Darwen 24.5.65. Ht 5 8 Wt 11 3
Forward. From Apprentice.

1983–84	Blackburn R	29	7
1984–85		9	—
1985–86		26	10

Season	Club	League Appearances/Goals

PAYNE, Steven

Born London 17.1.67.
Forward.

1985–86	Wimbledon	—	—

PEACOCK, Darren

Born Bristol 3.2.68.   Ht 6 2   Wt 12 6
Defender. From Apprentice.

1984–85	Newport Co	—	—
1985–86		18	—

PEACOCK, Dennis

Born Lincoln 19.4.53.   Ht 6 2   Wt 14 1
Goalkeeper. From Apprentice.

1972–73	Nottingham F	1	—
1972–73	*Walsall*	10	—
1973–74	Nottingham F	7	—
1974–75		14	—
1975–76	Doncaster R	33	—
1976–77		46	—
1977–78		44	—
1978–79		46	—
1979–80		30	—
1979–80	Bolton W	—	—
1980–81		13	—
1981–82		3	—
1982–83	Doncaster R	39	—
1983–84		38	—
1984–85		44	—
1985–86		9	—
1985–86	*Burnley*	8	—

PEACOCK, Gavin

Born Kent 18.11.67.   Ht 5 7
Forward. England Schools, Youth.

1984–85	QPR	—	—
1985–86		—	—

PEAKE, Andy

Born Mkt Harborough 1.11.61.   Ht 5 9½
Wt 11 2½
Midfield. From Apprentice. England Youth.

1978–79	Leicester C	18	2
1979–80		25	3
1980–81		24	1
1981–82		31	2
1982–83		4	—
1983–84		24	4
1984–85		21	1
1985–86	Grimsby T	36	4

PEAKE, Trevor

Born Nuneaton 10.2.57.   Ht 6 0   Wt 12 9
Defender. From Nuneaton Bor.

1979–80	Lincoln C	45	1
1980–81		43	1
1981–82		37	4
1982–83		46	1
1983–84	Coventry C	33	3
1984–85		35	1
1985–86		37	1

PEARCE, Alan

Born Middlesbrough 25.10.65.   Ht 5 8
Wt 10 12
Midfield. From Apprentice.

1983–84	York C	18	5
1984–85		23	4
1985–86		7	—

PEARCE, Chris

Born Newport 7.8.61.   Ht 6 0   Wt 11 4
Goalkeeper. From Wolverhampton W.
Apprentice. Wales Schools.

1979–80	Blackburn R	—	—
1980–81	*Rochdale*	5	—
1981–82	*Barnsley*	—	—
1982–83	Rochdale	36	—
1983–84	Port Vale	7	—
1984–85		36	—
1985–86		5	—

Season	Club	League Appearances/Goals		Season	Club	League Appearances/Goals

PEARCE, Graham

Born Hammersmith 8.7.59.   Ht 5 9   Wt 11 0
Defender. From Barnet.

Season	Club	App	Goals
1981–82	Brighton	—	—
1982–83		14	—
1983–84		18	1
1984–85		24	—
1985–86		32	1

PEARCE, Stuart

Born London 24.4.62.   Ht 5 10   Wt 11 2
Defender. From Wealdstone.

Season	Club	App	Goals
1983–84	Coventry C	23	—
1984–85		28	4
1985–86	Nottingham F	30	1

PEARS, Steve

Born Brandon 22.1.62.   Ht 5 11½   Wt 12 2
Goalkeeper. From Apprentice.

Season	Club	App	Goals
1978–79	Manchester U	—	—
1979–80		—	—
1980–81		—	—
1981–82		—	—
1982–83		—	—
1983–84		—	—
1983–84	*Middlesbrough*	12	—
1984–85	Manchester U	4	—
1985–86	Middlesbrough	38	—

PEARSON, John

Born Sheffield 1.9.63.   Ht 6 2   Wt 13 1
Forward. From Apprentice.

Season	Club	App	Goals
1980–81	Sheffield W	15	4
1981–82		24	7
1982–83		30	7
1983–84		27	4
1984–85		9	2
1985–86	Charlton Ath	42	14

PEARSON, Jonathan

Born Birmingham 12.10.66.   Ht 5 7   Wt 10 0
Midfield.

Season	Club	App	Goals
1984–85	Leicester C	—	—
1985–86		—	—

PEARSON, Lawrie

Born Wallsend 2.7.65.   Ht 6 0   Wt 11 12
Defender. From Manchester U. Apprentice.

Season	Club	App	Goals
1984–85	Hull C	31	—
1985–86		20	—

PEARSON, Nigel

Born Nottingham 21.8.63.   Ht 6 0
Wt 12 10
Defender. From Heanor T.

Season	Club	App	Goals
1981–82	Shrewsbury T	—	—
1982–83		39	1
1983–84		26	—
1984–85		—	—
1985–86		35	1

PEATTIE, Don

Born Wharfdale 5.4.63.   Ht 6 0   Wt 12 0
Forward. From Gretna Green.

Season	Club	App	Goals
1984–85	Sheffield U	5	—
1985–86		—	—
1985–86	*Doncaster R*	4	—

PEJIC, Mel

Born Chesterton 27.4.59.   Ht 5 7½   Wt 10 6
Defender. Local.

Season	Club	App	Goals
1977–78	Stoke C	—	—
1978–79		—	—
1979–80		1	—
1980–81	Hereford U	13	—
1981–82		27	—
1982–83		45	1
1983–84		44	—
1984–85		46	1
1985–86		45	1

Season	Club	League Appearances/Goals	Season	Club	League Appearances/Goals

PEMBERTON, John

Born Oldham 18.11.64. Ht 5 11 Wt 11 9
Defender. From Chadderton.

Season	Club	App	Goals
1984–85	Rochdale	1	—
1984–85	Crewe Alex	6	—
1985–86		41	—

PENDER, John

Born Luton 19.11.63. Ht 6 0 Wt 12 7
Defender. From Apprentice. Eire Youth,
Under-21.

Season	Club	App	Goals
1981–82	Wolverhampton W	8	—
1982–83		39	1
1983–84		34	1
1984–85		36	1
1985–86	Charlton Ath	38	—

PENNEY, David

Born Wakefield 17.8.64. Ht 5 8 Wt 10 7
Forward. From Pontefract.

Season	Club	App	Goals
1985–86	Derby Co	—	—

PENNEY, Steve

Born Ballymena 16.1.64. Ht 5 8 Wt 10 1
Midfield. From Ballymena U. Northern
Ireland 7 full caps.

Season	Club	App	Goals
1983–84	Brighton	25	1
1984–85		26	4
1985–86		37	3

PENNYFATHER, Glenn

Born Billericay 11.2.63. Ht 5 8 Wt 10 10
Midfield. From Apprentice.

Season	Club	App	Goals
1980–81	Southend U	1	—
1981–82		33	4
1982–83		34	1
1983–84		33	4
1984–85		41	7
1985–86		41	7

PENRICE, Gary

Born Bristol 23.3.64. Ht 5 7 Wt 10 0
Forward. From Bristol C. Apprentice.

Season	Club	App	Goals
1984–85	Bristol R	5	1
1985–86		39	5

PEPPER, Nigel

Born Rotherham 25.4.68. Ht 5 10 Wt 10 3
Midfield. From Apprentice.

Season	Club	App	Goals
1985–86	Rotherham U	7	—

PERKS, Steve

Born Bridgnorth 19.4.63. Ht 6 0 Wt 11 0
Goalkeeper. From Apprentice.

Season	Club	App	Goals
1980–81	Shrewsbury T	—	—
1981–82		—	—
1982–83		—	—
1983–84		—	—
1984–85		23	—
1985–86		42	—

PERRY, Dave

Born Sheffield 17.5.67.
Midfield.

Season	Club	App	Goals
1984–85	Chesterfield	—	—
1985–86		2	—

PERRY, Mick

Born Wimbledon 4.4.64. Ht 5 10 Wt 11 4
Forward. From Apprentice.

Season	Club	App	Goals
1981–82	WBA	—	—
1982–83		7	1
1983–84		13	4
1984–85		—	—
1984–85	*Northampton T*	4	—
1984–85	Torquay U	20	3
1985–86		3	—

Season	Club	League Appearances/Goals		Season	Club	League Appearances/Goals	

PERRYMAN, Steve

Born Ealing 21.12.51.   Ht 5 8   Wt 10 10
Defender. From Apprentice. England
Schools, Youth, Under-23, 1 full cap.

Season	Club	App	Goals
1968–69	Tottenham H	—	—
1969–70		23	1
1970–71		42	3
1971–72		39	1
1972–73		41	2
1973–74		39	1
1974–75		42	6
1975–76		40	6
1976–77		42	1
1977–78		42	1
1978–79		42	1
1979–80		40	1
1980–81		42	2
1981–82		42	1
1982–83		33	1
1983–84		41	1
1984–85		42	1
1985–86		23	1
1985–86	Oxford U	9	—

PETERS, Gary

Born Carshalton 3.8.54.   Ht 5 11   Wt 11 12
Defender. From Aldershot Apprentice and
Guildford C.

Season	Club	App	Goals
1975–76	Reading	30	2
1976–77		35	2
1977–78		46	2
1978–79		45	1
1979–80	Fulham	29	—
1980–81		34	2
1981–82		1	—
1982–83	Wimbledon	46	4
1983–84		37	3
1984–85	Aldershot	17	1
1984–85	Reading	18	—
1985–86		41	2

PETTS, Paul

Born Hackney 27.9.61.   Ht 5 10   Wt 11 2
Forward. From Apprentice. England Youth.

Season	Club	App	Goals
1978–79	Bristol R	10	—
1979–80		3	—
1980–81	Shrewsbury T	24	—
1981–82		21	1
1982–83		37	5
1983–84		35	8
1984–85		32	2
1985–86		—	—

PEYTON, Gerry

Born Birmingham 20.5.56.   Ht 6 2   Wt 13 9
Goalkeeper. From Atherstone T.
Eire 22 full caps.

Season	Club	App	Goals
1975–76	Burnley	20	—
1976–77		10	—
1976–77	Fulham	23	—
1977–78		42	—
1978–79		40	—
1979–80		31	—
1980–81		28	—
1981–82		44	—
1982–83		42	—
1983–84		27	—
1983–84	Southend U	10	—
1984–85	Fulham	32	—
1985–86		36	—

PHELAN, Mike

Born Nelson 24.9.62.   Ht 5 10½   Wt 11 1½
Defender. From Apprentice.

Season	Club	App	Goals
1980–81	Burnley	16	2
1981–82		23	1
1982–83		42	3
1983–84		44	2
1984–85		43	1
1985–86	Norwich C	42	3

PHELAN, Terry

Born Manchester 16.3.67.
Defender. Eire Youth.

Season	Club	App	Goals
1984–85	Leeds U	—	—
1985–86		14	—

Season	Club	League Appearances/Goals		Season	Club	League Appearances/Goals	

PHILLIBEN, John

Born Stirling 14.3.64.   Ht 5 10   Wt 11 0
Defender. From Gairdoch U. Scotland
Youth.

Season	Club	App	Goals
1980–81	Stirling A	15	—
1981–82		37	1
1982–83		34	—
1983–**84**		23	—
1983–84	Doncaster R	12	—
1984–85		36	1
1985–86		22	—
1985–86	*Cambridge U*	6	—

PHILLIPS, David

Born Wegberg 29.7.63.   Ht 5 10   Wt 11 2
Midfield. From Apprentice.
Wales Under-21, 13 full caps.

Season	Club	App	Goals
1981–82	Plymouth Arg	8	1
1982–83		23	8
1983–84		42	6
1984–85	Manchester C	42	12
1985–86		39	1

PHILLIPS, Gary

Born St. Albans 20.9.61.   Ht 5 11   Wt 14 0
Goalkeeper.

Season	Club	App	Goals
1979–80	WBA	—	—
1980–81		—	—
From Barnet			
1984–85	Brentford	21	—
1985–86		43	—

PHILLIPS, Ian

Born Edinburgh 23.4.59.   Ht 5 10   Wt 12 0
Defender. From Ipswich T. Apprentice.

Season	Club	App	Goals
1977–78	Mansfield T	18	—
1978–79		5	—
1979–80	Peterborough U	39	1
1980–81		41	—
1981–82		17	2

Season	Club	App	Goals
1982–83	Northampton T	42	1
1983–84		—	—
1983–84	Colchester U	43	5
1984–85		37	1
1985–86		37	2

PHILLIPS, James

Born Bolton 8.2.66.   Ht 6 0   Wt 12 0
Forward. From Apprentice.

Season	Club	App	Goals
1983–84	Bolton W	1	—
1984–85		40	1
1985–86		33	1

PHILLIPS, Les

Born Lambeth 7.1.63.   Ht 5 8   Wt 10 6
Midfield. From Apprentice.

Season	Club	App	Goals
1980–81	Birmingham C	—	—
1981–82		11	1
1982–83		13	2
1983–84		20	—
1983–84	Oxford U	6	—
1984–85		3	—
1985–86		28	2

PHILLIPS, Steve

Born Edmonton 4.8.54.   Ht 5 6   Wt 10 13
Forward. From Apprentice. England Youth.

Season	Club	App	Goals
1971–72	Birmingham C	7	—
1972–73		3	—
1973–74		4	1
1974–75		2	—
1974–75	*Torquay U*	6	—
1975–76	Birmingham C	4	—
1975–76	Northampton T	34	6
1976–77		17	2
1976–77	Brentford	19	7
1977–78		46	32
1978–79		46	14
1979–80		46	12
1980–81	Northampton T	45	19
1981–82		30	10
1981–82	Southend U	18	10

Season	Club	League Appearances/Goals			Season	Club	League Appearances/Goals	

1982–83	....	43	17
1983–84	....	41	16
1984–85	....	43	21
1985–86	....	13	2
1985–86	Torquay U	23	8

PHILLIPS, Stewart

Born Halifax 30.12.61.　Ht 6 0½　Wt 11 7
Forward. From Amateur.

1977–78	Hereford U.	1	—
1978–79	....	8	—
1979–80	....	11	2
1980–81	....	8	1
1981–82	....	43	12
1982–83	....	41	13
1983–84	....	46	17
1984–85	....	46	19
1985–86	....	20	5

PHILLISKIRK, Tony

Born Sunderland 10.2.65.　Ht 6 1　Wt 11 3
Forward. From Amateur. England Schools.

1983–84	Sheffield U	21	8
1984–85	....	23	2
1985–86	....	4	—

PHILP, Dave

Born Fowey 8.7.60.　Ht 5 10　Wt 11 0
Goalkeeper. From Newquay.

| 1984–85 | Plymouth Arg .... | 7 | — |
| 1985–86 | .... | — | — |

PICKERING, Mike

Born Huddersfield 29.9.56.　Ht 5 11　Wt 12 6
Defender. Local.

1974–75	Barnsley	14	—
1975–76	....	41	—
1976–77	....	45	1
1977–78	Southampton	41	—
1978–79	....	3	—

1978–79	Sheffield W	35	—
1979–80	....	32	—
1980–81	....	15	—
1981–82	....	24	1
1982–83	....	4	—
1983–84	....	—	—
1983–84	*Norwich C*....................	1	—
1983–84	*Bradford C*..................	4	—
1983–84	*Barnsley*	3	—
1983–84	Rotherham U	24	—
1984–85	....	32	1
1985–86	....	46	—

PICKERING, Nick

Born Newcastle 4.8.63.　Ht 6 0　Wt 11 10
Defender. From Apprentice.
England Youth, Under-21, 1 full cap.

1981–82	Sunderland	37	3
1982–83	....	39	7
1983–84	....	42	1
1984–85	....	37	2
1985–86	....	24	5
1985–86	Coventry C...................	15	4

PIKE, Chris

Born Cardiff 19.10.61.
Forward. From Barry T.

| 1984–85 | Fulham .... | — | — |
| 1985–86 | .... | 26 | 4 |

PIKE, Geoff

Born Clapton 28.9.56.　Ht 5 6　Wt 11 0
Midfield. From Apprentice.

1975–76	West Ham U	3	—
1976–77	....	20	6
1977–78	....	28	2
1978–79	....	14	2
1979–80	....	31	4
1980–81	....	42	6
1981–82	....	34	2
1982–83	....	40	6
1983–84	....	28	2
1984–85	....	30	2
1985–86	....	10	—

Season	Club	League Appearances/Goals	Season	Club	League Appearances/Goals

PIKE, Martin

Born South Shields 21.10.64. Ht 5 9
Wt 11 4
Midfield. From Apprentice.

Season	Club	App	Goals
1982–83	WBA	—	—
1983–84	Peterborough U	35	2
1984–85	....	45	4
1985–86	....	46	2

PILE, Chris

Born Liverpool 4.4.67. Ht 5 9½ Wt 10 4
Goalkeeper. From Local.

Season	Club	App	Goals
1984–85	Liverpool	—	—
1985–86	....	—	—

PILLING, Andy

Born Wigan 30.6.69.
Defender. From YTS.

Season	Club	App	Goals
1985–86	Preston NE	1	—

PLATNAUER, Nicky

Born Leicester 10.6.61. Ht 5 11 Wt 12 10
Forward. From Northampton T Amateur and
Bedford T.

Season	Club	App	Goals
1982–83	Bristol R	24	7
1983–84	Coventry C	34	6
1984–85	....	10	—
1984–85	Birmingham C	11	1
1985–86	....	17	1
1985–86	*Reading*	7	—

PLATT, David

Born Chadderton 10.6.66. Ht 5 11 Wt 11 7
Forward. From Chadderton.

Season	Club	App	Goals
1984–85	Manchester U	—	—
1984–85	Crewe Alex	22	5
1985–86	....	43	9

PLATT, John

Born Ashton 22.8.54. Ht 5 10 Wt 11 7
Goalkeeper. From Ashton U.

Season	Club	App	Goals
1973–74	Oldham Ath	—	—
1974–75		—	—
1975–76		24	—
1976–77		27	—
1977–78		30	—
1978–79		—	—
1979–80		8	—
1980–81		20	—
1981–82	Bury	19	—
1982–83		1	—
1983–84	Bolton W	10	—
1984–85		—	—
1984–85	*Tranmere R*	8	—
1984–85	*Preston NE*	7	—
1985–86	Preston NE	31	—

PLUMMER, Calvin

Born Nottingham 14.2.63. Ht 5 9 Wt 9 10
Forward. From Apprentice.

Season	Club	App	Goals
1980–81	Nottingham F	—	—
1981–82		9	2
1982–83		3	—
1982–83	Chesterfield	28	7
1983–84	Derby Co	27	3
1983–84	Barnsley	2	1
1984–85		26	2
1985–86		23	3

PODD, Cec

Born St Kitts 7.8.52. Ht 5 10 Wt 10 6
Defender.

Season	Club	App	Goals
1970–71	Bradford C	19	—
1971–72		10	—
1972–73		41	—
1973–74		37	—
1974–75		44	—
1975–76		45	—
1976–77		43	—
1977–78		37	—
1978–79		39	—
1979–80		39	1

Season	Club	League Appearances/Goals		Season	Club	League Appearances/Goals	
1980–81	....	35	—				
1981–82	....	46	—				
1982–83	....	37	1				
1983–84	....	30	—				
1984–85	Halifax T	41	—				
1985–86	....	16	—				

POINTON, Neil

Born Church Warsop 28.11.64.   Ht 5 10
Wt 10 10
Defender. From Apprentice.

1981–82	Scunthorpe U	5	—
1982–83	....	46	1
1983–84	....	45	1
1984–85	....	46	—
1985–86	....	17	—
1985–86	Everton	15	—

POLLARD, Gary

Born Staveley 30.12.59.   Ht 6 1   Wt 11 10
Forward. From Amateur.

1977–78	Chesterfield..................	19	—
1978–79	....	1	—
1979–80	....	1	—
1980–81	....	17	—
1981–82	....	17	—
1982–83	....	32	1
1983–84	Port Vale	18	—
1984–85	Mansfield T	18	—
1985–86	....	35	1

POLSTON, John

Born London 10.6.68.
Defender. From Apprentice. England Youth.

1985–86	Tottenham H	—	—

POOLE, Gary

Born Stratford 11.9.67.
Defender. From Arsenal Schoolboys.

1984–85	Tottenham H	—	—
1985–86	....	—	—

POOLE, Kevin

Born Bromsgrove 21.7.63.   Ht 5 10½
Wt 11 6
Goalkeeper. From Apprentice.

1981–82	Aston Villa..................	—	—
1982–83	....	—	—
1983–84	....	—	—
1984–85	....	7	—
1984–85	*Northampton T.............*	3	—
1985–86	Aston Villa..................	11	—

PORTCH, Lee

Born Bristol 22.10.66.   Ht 5 11   Wt 12 7
Defender. From Apprentice.

1985–86	Bristol R......................	—	—

PORTEOUS, Ian

Born Glasgow 21.11.64.   Ht 5 9   Wt 10 3
Midfield. From Eastercraigs. Scotland Youth.

1981–82	Aberdeen	—	—
1982–83	....	1	—
1983–84	....	14	3
1984–85	....	13	1
1985–86	....	6	—

PORTER, Gary

Born Sunderland 6.3.66.   Ht 5 6½   Wt 9 10
Midfield. From Apprentice. England Youth.

1983–84	Watford	2	—
1984–85	....	9	—
1985–86	....	8	1

POSKETT, Malcolm

Born Middlesbrough 19.7.53.   Ht 6 0
Wt 12 1
Forward. From South Bank.

1972–73	Middlesbrough.............	—	—
1973–74	....	1	—
1974–75	Hartlepool U	—	—

Season	Club	League Appearances/Goals		Season	Club	League Appearances/Goals	

From Whitby T

Season	Club	Apps	Goals
1976–77	Hartlepool U	30	10
1977–78		21	10
1977–78	Brighton	13	6
1978–79		29	9
1979–80		3	1
1979–80	Watford	16	3
1980–81		40	13
1981–82		7	1
1982–83	Carlisle U	36	14
1983–84		41	17
1984–85		33	9
1985–86	Darlington	21	4
1985–86	Stockport Co	8	1
1985–86	*Hartlepool U*	5	—

POTTS, Steven

Born Hartford (USA) 7.5.67. Ht 5 8
Wt 10 5
Defender. From Apprentice. England
Youth.

Season	Club	Apps	Goals
1984–85	West Ham U	1	—
1985–86		1	—

POWELL, Barry

Born Kenilworth 29.1.54. Ht 5 7½ Wt 10 0
Midfield. From Apprentice.

Season	Club	Apps	Goals
1971–72	Wolverhampton W	—	—
1972–73		11	1
1973–74		27	4
1974–75		26	2
1975–76		—	—
1975–76	Coventry C	34	7
1976–77		40	4
1977–78		42	4
1978–79		38	9
1979–80		10	4
1979–80	Derby Co	23	3
1980–81		29	2
1981–82		32	2

From Hong Kong

Season	Club	Apps	Goals
1984–85	Burnley	11	—
1984–85	Swansea C	8	—
1985–86		—	—

POWELL, Cliff

Born Watford 21.2.68. Ht 5 11½ Wt 11 3
Defender. From Apprentice.

Season	Club	Apps	Goals
1985–86	Watford	—	—

POWELL, Steve

Born Derby 20.9.55. Ht 5 10 Wt 12 2
Midfield. From Apprentice.
England Schools, Youth, Under-23.

Season	Club	Apps	Goals
1971–72	Derby C	3	—
1972–73		22	2
1973–74		30	1
1974–75		15	2
1975–76		20	3
1976–77		29	4
1977–78		35	2
1978–79		41	3
1979–80		20	—
1980–81		36	—
1981–82		16	1
1982–83		23	—
1983–84		36	1
1984–85		28	1
1985–86		—	—

POWER, Mike

Born Stockport 3.10.61. Ht 6 0 Wt 12 0
Forward. From Amateur.

Season	Club	Apps	Goals
1980–81	Stockport Co	5	—
1981–82		22	6
1982–83		30	9
1983–84		5	—
1984–85		8	1
1985–86		1	—

POWER, Paul

Born Manchester 30.10.53. Ht 5 10
Wt 11 7
Midfield. From Amateur. England 'B'.

Season	Club	League Appearances/Goals		Season	Club	League Appearances/Goals	
1975–76	Manchester C	19	1				
1976–77		29	2				
1977–78		29	3				
1978–79		32	3				
1979–80		41	7				
1980–81		42	4				
1981–82		25	1				
1982–83		33	1				
1983–84		37	2				
1984–85		42	1				
1985–86		36	1				

POWER, Philip

Born Salford 25.7.66. Ht 5 7 Wt 10 0
Forward. From Northwich V and Witton
Alb.

1985–86	Crewe Alex	11	2

POWNER, Rob

Born Newcastle (Staffs.) 2.7.67.
Goalkeeper.

1985–86	Crewe Alex	4	—

PRATLEY, Dick

Born Banbury 12.1.63. Ht 6 2 Wt 14 2
Defender. From Banbury U.

1983–84	Derby Co	2	—
1983–84	*Scunthorpe U*	10	—
1984–85	Derby Co	13	1
1985–86		7	—

PRATT, Ray

Born Burry Port 11.11.53. Ht 5 10 Wt 12 0
Forward. From Merthyr T. Wales Youth.

1979–80	Exeter C	7	2
1980–81		17	4
1981–82		30	9
1982–83		31	9
1983–84		36	16
1984–85		34	20
1985–86		18	2

PREECE, David

Born Bridgnorth 28.5.63. Ht 5 6 Wt 10 10
Midfield. From Apprentice.

1980–81	Walsall	8	—
1981–82		8	—
1982–83		42	2
1983–84		41	3
1984–85		12	—
1984–85	Luton T	21	2
1985–86		41	2

PRESSMAN, Kevin

Born Fareham 6.11.67.
Goalkeeper. From Apprentice. England
Schools, Youth.

1985–86	Sheffield W	—	—

PRICE, Allen

Born Gelligser 24.3.68.
Defender. Wales Youth.

1984–85	Newport Co	—	—
1985–86	Cardiff C	2	—

PRICE, Chris

Born Hereford 30.3.60. Ht 5 7 Wt 10 2
Defender. From Apprentice. England
Youth.

1976–77	Hereford U	2	—
1977–78		13	—
1978–79		29	—
1979–80		42	—
1980–81		42	2
1981–82		41	10
1982–83		42	5
1983–84		37	1
1984–85		41	5
1985–86		41	4

Season	Club	League Appearances/Goals	Season	Club	League Appearances/Goals

PRICE, Neil

Born Hemel Hempstead 15.2.64.   Ht 5 9
Wt 11 6
Defender. From Apprentice.

Season	Club	App	Goals
1981–82	Watford	—	—
1982–83		—	—
1983–84		8	—
1983–84	*Plymouth Arg*	1	—
1984–85	Watford	—	—
1984–85	Blackpool	13	—
1985–86		—	—
1985–86	Swansea C	2	—

PRICE, Paul

Born St Albans 23.3.54.   Ht 5 11   Wt 12 0
Defender. From Amateur.
Wales Under-21, 25 full caps.

Season	Club	App	Goals
1971–72	Luton T	—	—
1972–73		1	—
1973–74		—	—
1974–75		—	—
1975–76		8	1
1976–77		41	1
1977–78		40	2
1978–79		34	2
1979–80		42	—
1980–81		41	2
1981–82	Tottenham H	21	—
1982–83		16	—
1983–84		2	—
1984–85	Swansea C	21	—
1985–86		41	1

PRIEST, Philip

Born Warley 9.9.66.   Ht 5 7½   Wt 10 6
Forward. From school. England Schools,
Youth.

Season	Club	App	Goals
1983–84	Chelsea	—	—
1984–85		—	—
1985–86		—	—

PRITCHARD, Howard

Born Cardiff 18.10.58.   Ht 5 10   Wt 12 0
Forward. From Apprentice. Wales Youth, 1
full cap.

Season	Club	App	Goals
1976–77	Bristol C	—	—
1977–78		—	—
1978–79		1	—
1979–80		16	—
1980–81		21	2
1981–82	Swindon T	28	1
1982–83		37	10
1983–84	Bristol C	46	10
1984–85		39	6
1985–86		34	6

PRITCHARD, Steve

Born Acton 5.12.67.   Ht 5 11   Wt 13 0
Defender. From Apprentice.

Season	Club	App	Goals
1985–86	Norwich C	—	—

PROCTOR, Mark

Born Middlesbrough 30.1.61.   Ht 5 9
Wt 11 10
Midfield. From Apprentice.
England Youth, Under-21.

Season	Club	App	Goals
1978–79	Middlesbrough	33	9
1979–80		38	2
1980–81		38	1
1981–82	Nottingham F	37	1
1982–83		27	4
1982–83	*Sunderland*	5	—
1983–84	Sunderland	41	2
1984–85		17	2
1985–86		19	7

PROUDLOCK, Paul

Born Hartlepool 25.10.65.   Ht 5 9   Wt 10 5
Forward. From Local.

Season	Club	App	Goals
1984–85	Hartlepool U	14	—
1985–86		1	—

Season	Club	League Appearances/Goals	Season	Club	League Appearances/Goals

PROVAN, Davie

Born Gourock 8.5.56.   Ht 5 10   Wt 11 4
Forward. From Port Glasgow Juniors.
Scotland Under-21, 10 full caps.

Season	Club	App	Goals
1974–75	Kilmarnock	22	1
1975–76		24	3
1976–77		34	1
1977–78		36	3
1978–79		4	1
1978–79	Celtic	30	4
1979–80		35	1
1980–81		33	7
1981–82		20	4
1982–83		33	5
1983–84		18	2
1984–85		25	2
1985–86		12	2

PRUDHOE, Mark

Born Washington 8.11.63.   Ht 6 0   Wt 12 12
Goalkeeper. From Apprentice.

Season	Club	App	Goals
1981–82	Sunderland	—	—
1982–83		7	—
1983–84		—	—
1983–84	*Hartlepool U*	3	—
1984–85	Sunderland	—	—
1984–85	Birmingham	1	—
1985–86		—	—
1985–86	Walsall	16	—

PRYER, Terry

Born London 4.12.67.
Defender.

Season	Club	App	Goals
1985–86	Southend U	2	—

PUCKETT, David

Born Southampton 29.10.60.   Ht 5 7   Wt 10 4
Forward. From Apprentice.

Season	Club	App	Goals
1978–79	Southampton	—	—
1979–80		—	—
1980–81		7	—
1981–82		17	3
1982–83		25	3
1983–84		18	3
1983–84	*Nottingham F*	—	—
1984–85	Southampton	13	1
1985–86		15	4

PUGH, Daral

Born Crynant 5.6.61.   Ht 5 8   Wt 10 5
Midfield. From Apprentice. Wales
Under-21.

Season	Club	App	Goals
1978–79	Doncaster R	21	1
1979–80		40	5
1980–81		42	3
1981–82		45	6
1982–83		6	—
1982–83	Huddersfield T	27	2
1983–84		29	4
1984–85		28	1
1985–86	Rotherham U	37	2

PUGH, Stephen

Born Wolverhampton 1.2.65.   Ht 5 10
Wt 11 3
Defender. From Wolves Apprentice.

Season	Club	App	Goals
1983–84	Torquay U	38	1
1984–85		37	—
1985–86		45	3

PULIS, Tony

Born Newport 16.1.58.   Ht 5 10   Wt 11 8
Midfield. From Apprentice.

Season	Club	App	Goals
1975–76	Bristol R	4	—
1976–77		9	—
1977–78		23	—
1978–79		7	—
1979–80		34	3
1980–81		8	—
From Happy Valley, Hong Kong			
1982–83	Bristol R	17	—
1983–84		28	2
1984–85	Newport C	37	—
1985–86		40	—

Season	Club	League Appearances/Goals	Season	Club	League Appearances/Goals

PULLAR, David

Born London 13.2.59.   Ht 5 11   Wt 11 4
Midfield. From Apprentice.

Season	Club	Apps	Goals
1975–76	Portsmouth	1	—
1976–77		30	2
1977–78		24	1
1978–79		38	1
1979–80	Exeter C	43	10
1980–81		25	5
1981–82		30	2
1982–83		32	5
1983–84	Crewe Alex	34	6
1984–85		39	—
1985–86		33	—

PYLE, Steve

Born Newcastle 28.9.63.   Ht 5 7   Wt 10 2
Midfield. From Apprentice.

Season	Club	Apps	Goals
1980–81	Cambridge U	1	—
1981–82		—	—
1982–83		5	—
1983–84		19	2
1984–85		30	2
1985–86		14	4
1985–86	Torquay U	14	2

PURDIE, Jon

Born Corby 22.2.67.   Ht 5 9   Wt 11 12
Forward. From Apprentice. England
Schools.

Season	Club	Apps	Goals
1984–85	Arsenal	—	—
1985–86	Wolverhampton W	42	6

PURNELL, Philip

Born Bristol 16.9.64.
Forward.

Season	Club	Apps	Goals
1985–86	Bristol R	11	2

PUTNEY, Trevor

Born Harold Hill 11.2.61.   Ht 5 7   Wt 10 11
Midfield. From Brentwood & W.

Season	Club	Apps	Goals
1980–81	Ipswich T	—	—
1981–82		—	—
1982–83		20	3
1983–84		35	2
1984–85		27	2
1985–86		21	1

Season	Club	League Appearances/Goals	Season	Club	League Appearances/Goals

QUINN, Jimmy

Born Belfast 18.11.59. Ht 6 1 Wt 12 0
Forward. From Oswestry T. Northern
Ireland 11 full caps.

1981–82	Swindon T	4	—
1982–83		13	3
1983–84		32	7
1984–85	Blackburn R	25	10
1985–86		31	4

QUINN, Mike

Born Liverpool 2.5.62. Ht 5 9½ Wt 12 0
Forward. From Derby Co Apprentice.

1979–80	Wigan Ath	4	1
1980–81		36	14
1981–82		29	4
1982–83	Stockport Co	39	24
1983–84		24	15
1983–84	Oldham Ath	14	5
1984–85		40	18
1985–86		26	11
1985–86	Portsmouth	11	6

QUINN, Niall

Born Dublin 6.10.66. Ht 6 4 Wt 12 4
Forward. From Eire Youth.

1983–84	Arsenal	—	—
1984–85		—	—
1985–86		12	1

QUOW, Trevor

Born Peterborough 28.9.60. Ht 5 7 Wt 10 12
Forward. From Apprentice.

1978–79	Peterborough U	8	—
1979–80		29	3
1980–81		44	4
1981–82		10	1
1982–83		18	1
1983–84		28	4
1984–85		36	1
1985–86		30	3

RAE, Gordon

Born Edinburgh 3.5.58. Ht 6 0 Wt 13 5
Defender. From Whitehill Welfare.

1977–78	Hibernian	2	1
1978–79		27	7
1979–80		33	4
1980–81		34	13
1981–82		29	11
1982–83		31	6
1983–84		16	—
1984–85		34	—
1985–86		32	2

RAFFERTY, Stuart

Born Port Glasgow 6.3.61. Ht 5 10 Wt 11 0
Midfield. From Port Glasgow. Scotland
Youth.

1978–79	Motherwell	5	—
1979–80		7	2
1980–81		5	2
1981–82		13	5
1982–83		33	4
1983–84		26	4
1984–85	Dundee	36	4
1985–86		29	3

RAJKOVIC, Ante

Born Yugoslavia 17.8.52. Ht 5 11¼
Wt 12 13
Midfield. From Sarajevo. Yugoslavia full
caps.

1980–81	Swansea C	2	—
1981–82		40	1
1982–83		33	1
From Sarajevo
1983–84	Swansea C	3	—
1984–85		2	—
1985–86		—	—

RAMSEY, Chris

Born Birmingham 28.4.62. Ht 5 9
Wt 10 12
Defender. From Bristol C. Amateur.

Season	Club	League Appearances/Goals		Season	Club	League Appearances/Goals	

Season	Club	Apps	Goals
1980–81	Brighton	3	—
1981–82		—	—
1982–83		23	—
1983–84		4	—
1984–85	Swindon T	32	1
1985–86		43	3

RAMSEY, Paul

Born Londonderry 3.9.62. Ht 5 10
Wt 12 0
Defender. From Apprentice. Northern
Ireland 9 full caps.

Season	Club	Apps	Goals
1970–80	Leicester C	—	—
1980–81		3	—
1981–82		10	—
1982–83		40	1
1983–84		33	1
1984–85		39	—
1985–86		13	1

RANDALL, Adrian

Born Amesbury 10.11.68. Ht 5 11
Wt 10 11
Forward. From Apprentice. England Youth.

Season	Club	Apps	Goals
1985–86	Bournemouth	2	—

RANDALL, Paul

Born Liverpool 16.2.58. Ht 5 11 Wt 12 12
Forward. From Frome T.

Season	Club	Apps	Goals
1977–78	Bristol R	31	20
1978–79		21	13
1978–79	Stoke C	20	5
1979–80		16	—
1980–81		10	2
1980–81	Bristol R	15	3
1981–82		37	12
1982–83		40	20
1983–84		32	6
1984–85		43	18
1985–86		17	2

RANDELL, Colin

Born Skewen 12.12.52. Ht 5 8 Wt 11 6
Midfield. From Apprentice. Wales Schools,
Under-23.

Season	Club	Apps	Goals
1970–71	Coventry C	—	—
1971–72		—	—
1972–73		—	—
1973–74		—	—
1973–74	Plymouth Arg	32	1
1974–75		36	4
1975–76		36	4
1976–77		35	—
1977–78		—	—
1977–78	Exeter C	40	1
1978–79		38	3
1979–80	Plymouth Arg	42	5
1980–81		30	—
1981–82		38	3
1982–83	Blackburn R	32	2
1983–84		11	2
1983–84	*Newport Co*	15	—
1984–85	Blackburn R	30	3
1985–86	Swansea C	19	1

RANSON, Ray

Born St. Helens 12.6.60. Ht 5 9 Wt 11 13
Defender. From Apprentice.
England Schools, Under-21.

Season	Club	Apps	Goals
1978–79	Manchester C	8	—
1979–80		40	—
1980–81		33	1
1981–82		36	—
1982–83		40	—
1983–84		26	—
1984–85		—	—
1984–85	Birmingham C	28	—
1985–86		37	—

RATCLIFFE, Kevin

Born Mancot 12.11.60. Ht 5 11 Wt 12 7
Defender. From Apprentice.
Wales Schools, Under-21, 36 full caps.

Season	Club	League Appearances/Goals		Season	Club	League Appearances/Goals	

Season	Club	App	Goals
1978–79	Everton	—	—
1979–80		2	—
1980–81		21	—
1981–82		25	—
1982–83		29	1
1983–84		38	—
1984–85		40	—
1985–86		39	1

RATCLIFFE, Simon

Born Davyhulme 8.2.67.   Ht 5 11   Wt 11 9
Defender. From Apprentice. England
Schools, Youth.

Season	Club	App	Goals
1984–85	Manchester U	—	—
1985–86		—	—

RATHBONE, Mike

Born Birmingham 6.11.58.   Ht 5 10
Wt 11 4
Defender. From Apprentice.
England Youth.

Season	Club	App	Goals
1976–77	Birmingham C	16	—
1977–78		2	—
1978–79		2	—
1978–79	Blackburn R	15	—
1979–80		28	1
1980–81		27	—
1981–82		41	1
1982–83		42	—
1983–84		11	—
1984–85		42	—
1985–86		42	—

RAWSTRON, Mark

Born Littleborough 21.1.67.   Ht 5 6   Wt 9 9
Midfield. From Apprentice.

Season	Club	App	Goals
1984–85	Burnley	—	—
1985–86		—	—

RAYMENT, Patrick

Born Peterborough 11.4.65.   Ht 5 11
Wt 12 0
Defender. From Apprentice.

Season	Club	App	Goals
1981–82	Peterborough U	2	—
1982–83		14	2
1983–84		13	1
1984–85		1	—
1984–85	Cambridge U	31	1
1985–86		13	1

RAYNES, Willie

Born Sheffield 30.10.64.   Ht 5 7   Wt 10 5
Midfield. From Heanor T.

Season	Club	App	Goals
1983–84	Rotherham U	14	1
1983–84	*Luton T*	—	—
1984–85	Rotherham U	6	1
1984–85	*Stockport Co*	2	—
1985–86	Rotherham U	—	—
1985–86	Wolverhampton W	7	—

RAYNOR, Paul

Born Nottingham 29.4.66.   Ht 6 0   Wt 11 4½
Forward. From Apprentice.

Season	Club	App	Goals
1983–84	Nottingham F	—	—
1984–85		3	—
1984–85	*Bristol R*	8	—
1985–86	Huddersfield T	30	5

RECK, Sean

Born Oxford 5.5.67.   Ht 5 10   Wt 12 7
Midfield. From Apprentice.

Season	Club	App	Goals
1984–85	Oxford U	—	—
1985–86		—	—
1985–86	*Newport Co*	15	—
1985–86	*Reading*	1	—

REDFEARN, Neil

Born Dewsbury 20.6.65.   Ht 5 10   Wt 11 6
Midfield. From Nottingham F. Apprentice.

Season	Club	League Appearances/Goals		Season	Club	League Appearances/Goals	
1982–83	Bolton W	10	—	1978–79	Barnsley	1	—
1983–84		25	1	1979–80		2	—
1983–84	*Lincoln C*	10	1	From Frickley Ath			
1984–85	Lincoln C	45	4	1985–86	Northampton T	36	1
1985–86		45	8				

REDFERN, David

Born Sheffield 8.11.62.   Ht 6 1   Wt 13 8
Goalkeeper. From school.

1981–82	Sheffield W	—	—
1982–83		—	—
1983–84		—	—
1984–85		—	—
1984–85	*Doncaster R*	—	—
1984–85	*Rochdale*	19	—
1985–86	Rochdale	46	—

REDFORD, Ian

Born Perth 5.4.60.   Ht 5 11   Wt 11 10
Midfield. From Errol Rovers.
Scotland Youth, Under-21.

1976–77	Dundee	1	—
1977–78		34	10
1978–79		37	15
1979–80		13	9
1979–80	Rangers	13	—
1980–81		35	9
1981–82		32	2
1982–83		34	3
1983–84		32	4
1984–85		26	5
1985–86	Dundee U	30	4

REDMOND, Steven

Born Liverpool 2.11.67.
Defender. From Apprentice. England
Youth.

1984–85	Manchester C	—	—
1985–86		9	—

REED, Graham

Born Doncaster 24.6.61.   Ht 5 11   Wt 12 7
Forward. From Apprentice.

REES, Mark

Born Smethwick 13.10.61.   Ht 5 10   Wt 11 10
Forward. From Apprentice.
England Schools.

1978–79	Walsall	10	—
1979–80		18	3
1980–81		25	6
1981–82		39	6
1982–83		18	3
1983–84		33	6
1984–85		27	9
1985–86		19	2

REES, Mel

Born Cardiff 25.1.67.   Ht 6 2   Wt 12 12
Goalkeeper. From Plymouth Arg. Schoolboy
and YTS. Wales Youth.

1984–85	Cardiff C	1	—
1985–86		9	—

REES, Tony

Born Merthyr Tydfil 1.8.64.   Ht 5 9   Wt 11 13
Forward. From Apprentice. Wales Youth,
Under-21, 1 full cap.

1982–83	Aston Villa	—	—
1983–84	Birmingham C	25	2
1984–85		9	2
1985–86		8	—
1985–86	*Peterborough U*	5	2
1985–86	*Shrewsbury T*	2	—

REEVES, John

Born London 8.7.63.   Ht 5 7   Wt 9 12
Midfield. From Apprentice.

1981–82	Fulham	7	—
1982–83		2	—

Season	Club	League Appearances/Goals		Season	Club	League Appearances/Goals	
1983–84	....	3	—				
1984–85	....	2	—				
1985–86	Colchester U	24	4				

REID, Paul

Born Warley 19.1.68.
Forward. From Apprentice.

1985–86	Leicester C.................	—	—

REGIS, Cyrille

Born French Guyana 9.2.58.   Ht 6 0
Wt 13 5
Forward. From Hayes.
England Under-21 'B', 4 full caps.

1977–78	WBA.........................	34	10
1978–79	....	39	13
1979–80	....	26	8
1980–81	....	38	14
1981–82	....	37	17
1982–83	....	26	9
1983–84	....	30	10
1984–85	....	7	1
1984–85	Coventry C..................	31	5
1985–86	....	34	5

REID, Mark

Born Kilwinning 15.9.61.   Ht 5 8   Wt 11 5
Defender. From Celtic B.C.

1980–81	Celtic.........................	22	—
1981–82	....	36	2
1982–83	....	26	1
1983–84	....	24	2
1984–85	....	16	—
1985–86	Charlton Ath	42	8

REID, Nicky

Born Ormston 30.10.60.   Ht 5 9   Wt 12 1
Defender. From Apprentice.
England, Under-21.

1978–79	Manchester C	8	—
1979–80	....	23	—
1980–81	....	37	—
1981–82	....	36	—
1982–83	....	25	—
1983–84	....	19	2
1984–85	....	32	—
1985–86	....	30	—

REID, Peter

Born Huyton 20.6.56.   Ht 5 8   Wt 10 7
Midfield. From Apprentice.
England Under-21, 6 full caps.

1974–75	Bolton W	27	—
1975–76	....	42	2
1976–77	....	42	5
1977–78	....	38	9
1978–79	....	14	—
1979–80	....	17	3
1980–81	....	18	2
1981–82	....	12	1
1982–83	....	15	1
1982–83	Everton	7	—
1983–84	....	35	2
1984–85	....	36	2
1985–86	....	15	1

REID, Shaun

Born Huyton 13.10.65.
Midfield. Local.

1983–84	Rochdale	17	—
1984–85	....	21	1
1985–86	....	8	—
1985–86	*Preston NE*..................	3	—

REID, Tony

Born Nottingham 9.5.63.   Ht 5 9   Wt 10 10
Midfield. From Apprentice.

1980–81	Derby Co.....................	15	1
1981–82	....	12	—
1982–83	....	3	—
1982–83	*Scunthorpe U*	6	—
1982–83	Newport Co..................	4	—
1983–84	....	37	6
1984–85	....	35	6
1985–86	Chesterfield.................	28	4

Season	Club	League Appearances/Goals		Season	Club	League Appearances/Goals	

REILLY, George

Born Bellshill 14.9.57.   Ht 6 3   Wt 13 5
Forward. From Corby T.

Season	Club	Apps	Goals
1976–77	Northampton T	22	2
1977–78		44	22
1978–79		43	19
1979–80		18	3
1979–80	Cambridge U	25	11
1980–81		37	8
1981–82		37	7
1982–83		39	10
1983–84	Watford	27	8
1984–85		21	6
1984–85	Newcastle U	14	3
1985–86		17	7
1985–86	WBA	20	4

REILLY, John

Born Dundee 21.3.62.   Ht 5 7   Wt 10 1
Forward. 'S' Form. Scotland Youth.

Season	Club	Apps	Goals
1979–80	Dundee U	—	—
1980–81		1	—
1981–82		8	1
1982–83		17	7
1983–84		19	7
1984–85		10	4
1985–86	Motherwell	30	9

RELISH, John

Born Liverpool 5.10.53.   Ht 5 9   Wt 12 0
Defender. From Apprentice.

Season	Club	Apps	Goals
1972–73	Chester	8	1
1973–74		3	—
1973–74	*Bury*	—	—
1974–75	Newport Co	22	—
1975–76		8	—
1976–77		26	4
1977–78		41	1
1978–79		27	—
1979–80		39	1
1980–81		33	—
1981–82		28	—
1982–83		44	1
1983–84		34	—
1984–85		18	—
1985–86		14	2

RENNIE, Allan

Born Glasgow 26.10.60   Ht 5 11   Wt 10 6
Midfield. From Celtic B.C.

Season	Club	Apps	Goals
1977–78	Queen's Park	—	—
1978–79		5	—
1979–80		17	—
1980–81		33	—
1981–82		28	—
1982–83		28	—
1983–84		13	—
1984–85		5	—
1985–86	Clydebank	3	—

RENNIE, David

Born Edinburgh 29.8.64.   Ht 5 11¾
Wt 11 12
Defender. From Apprentice.
Scotland Youth.

Season	Club	Apps	Goals
1982–83	Leicester C	—	—
1983–84		15	—
1984–85		3	1
1985–86		3	—
1985–86	Leeds U	16	2

REYNOLDS, Jamie

Born Swindon 27.10.67.
Forward. From Apprentice. England Youth.

Season	Club	Apps	Goals
1984–85	Swindon T	1	—
1985–86		—	—

RHOADES-BROWN, Peter

Born Hampton 2.1.62.   Ht 5 9   Wt 11 4
Forward. From Apprentice.

Season	Club	Apps	Goals
1979–80	Chelsea	4	—
1980–81		34	1
1981–82		27	1
1982–83		25	1
1983–84		6	1
1983–84	Oxford U	20	4
1984–85		31	4
1985–86		17	3

All appearances include those as substitute

Season	Club	League Appearances/Goals

RHODES, Andy

Born Doncaster 23.8.64.   Ht 6 0   Wt 12 0
Goalkeeper. From Apprentice.

Season	Club	League Appearances/Goals	
1982–83	Barnsley	—	—
1983–84		31	—
1984–85		5	—
1985–86		—	—
1985–86	Doncaster R	30	—

RHODES, Mark

Born Sheffield 26.8.57.   Ht 5 8   Wt 11 7
Midfield. From Apprentice.

Season	Club	League Appearances/Goals	
1975–76	Rotherham U	28	3
1976–77		19	—
1977–78		33	3
1978–79		20	1
1979–80		39	3
1980–81		38	1
1981–82		25	—
1982–83	*Darlington*	14	—
1982–83	*Mansfield T*	4	—
1983–84	Rotherham U	36	2
1984–85		20	—
1984–85	*Burnley*	9	—
1985–86	Burnley	4	—

RICE, Brian

Born Glasgow 11.10.63.   Ht 6 0   Wt 11 10
Midfield. From Whitburn Central. Scotland
Youth, Under-21.

Season	Club	League Appearances/Goals	
1980–81	Hibernian	1	—
1981–82		1	—
1982–83		22	2
1983–84		25	5
1984–85		35	4
1985–86	Nottingham F	19	3

RICHARDS, Gary

Born Swansea 2.8.63.   Ht 5 8½   Wt 11 1½
Defender. From Apprentice.

Season	Club	League Appearances/Goals	
1981–82	Swansea C	1	—
1982–83		15	—
1983–84		34	1
1984–85		16	—
1985–86	Lincoln C	7	—
1985–86	Cambridge U	8	—

RICHARDS, Steve

Born Dundee 24.10.61.   Ht 6 0   Wt 12 0
Defender. From Apprentice.

Season	Club	League Appearances/Goals	
1979–80	Hull C	1	—
1980–81		25	1
1981–82		29	1
1982–83		3	—
From Gainsborough T.			
1984–85	York C	7	—
1985–86	Lincoln C	21	—
1985–86	Cambridge U	4	2

RICHARDS, Pedro

Born Edmonton 1.11.56.   Ht 5 8   Wt 10 8
Defender. From Apprentice.

Season	Club	League Appearances/Goals	
1974–75	Notts Co	7	—
1975–76		32	—
1976–77		41	1
1977–78		36	—
1978–79		40	—
1979–80		32	1
1980–81		40	—
1981–82		40	1
1982–83		42	—
1983–84		34	1
1984–85		35	1
1985–86		20	—

RICHARDSON, Ian

Born Ely 9.5.64.   Ht 5 8   Wt 10 2
Forward. From Apprentice.

Season	Club	League Appearances/Goals	
1981–82	Watford	—	—
1982–83		—	—
1982–83	*Blackpool*	5	2
1983–84	Watford	7	2

Season	Club	League Appearances/Goals		Season	Club	League Appearances/Goals	

Season	Club	App	Goals
1984–85	....	1	—
1984–85	*Rotherham U*	5	2
1985–86	Watford	—	—
1985–86	Chester C....................	27	10

RICHARDSON, Kevin

Born Newcastle 4.12.62.   Ht 5 7   Wt 10 2
Midfield. From Apprentice.

Season	Club	App	Goals
1980–81	Everton........................	—	—
1981–82	....	18	2
1982–83	....	29	3
1983–84	....	28	4
1984–85	....	15	4
1985–86	....	18	3

RICHARDSON, Paul

Born Hucknall 7.11.62.   Ht 6 0   Wt 11 5
Midfield. From Nuneaton.

Season	Club	App	Goals
1984–85	Derby Co.....................	14	—
1985–86	....	—	—

RICHARDSON, Steve

Born Slough 11.2.62.   Ht 5 5   Wt 10 3
Defender. From Apprentice.

Season	Club	App	Goals
1979–80	Southampton...............	—	—
1980–81	....	—	—
1981–82	....	—	—
1982–83	Reading	40	1
1983–84	....	34	—
1984–85	....	43	—
1985–86	....	32	—

RIDEOUT, Paul

Born Bournemouth 14.8.64.   Ht 5 11½
Wt 12 1
Forward. From Apprentice. England
Schools, Youth, Under-21.

Season	Club	App	Goals
1980–81	Swindon T....................	16	4
1981–82	....	35	14
1982–83	....	44	20
1983–84	Aston Villa..................	25	5
1984–85	....	29	14
1985–86	Bari...........................	28	6

RIDLEY, John

Born Consett 27.4.52.   Ht 6 1½   Wt 11 13
Defender. From Sheffield Univ.

Season	Club	App	Goals
1973–74	Port Vale	10	1
1974–75	....	18	—
1975–76	....	46	1
1976–77	....	35	1
1977–78	....	40	—
1978–79	....	7	—
1978–79	Leicester C..................	24	—
1979–80	Chesterfield.................	46	3
1980–81	....	40	1
1981–82	....	38	4
1982–83	Port Vale	41	3
1983–84	....	30	2
1984–85	....	43	—
1985–86	....	—	—

RIGBY, Jon

Born Bury St. Edmunds 31.1.65.   Ht 6 1½
Wt 11 2
Forward. From Apprentice.

Season	Club	App	Goals
1982–83	Norwich C....................	—	—
1983–84	....	5	—
1984–85	....	5	—
1985–86	....	—	—
1985–86	Aldershot	1	—

RILEY, David

Born Northampton 8.12.60.   Ht 5 7   Wt 10 10
Forward. From Keyworth U.

Season	Club	App	Goals
1983–84	Nottingham F	1	—
1984–85	....	10	2
1985–86	....	—	—

RILEY, Glyn

Born Barnsley 24.7.58.   Ht 5 9¼   Wt 13 3¾
Forward. From Apprentice.

Season	Club	App	Goals
1974–75	Barnsley	2	1
1975–76	....	3	—
1976–77	....	—	—

Season	Club	League Appearances/Goals		Season	Club	League Appearances/Goals	
1977–78	....	10	1				
1978–79	....	41	3				
1979–80	....	27	4				
1979–80	*Doncaster R*.................	8	2				
1980–81	Barnsley	32	7				
1981–82	....	15	—				
1982–83	Bristol C.....................	44	16				
1983–84	....	42	16				
1984–85	....	44	18				
1985–86	....	41	10				

RIMMER, Stuart

Born Southport 12.10.64.   Ht 5 7   Wt 9 4
Forward. From Apprentice. England Youth.

Season	Club	App	Goals
1981–82	Everton.....................	2	—
1982–83	....	—	—
1983–84	....	1	—
1984–85	....	—	—
1984–85	Chester C...................	24	14
1985–86	....	18	16

RIMMER, Jimmy

Born Southport 10.2.48.   Ht 6 0½   Wt 13 4½
Goalkeeper. From Apprentice. England,
1 full cap.

Season	Club	App	Goals
1965–66	Manchester U	—	—
1966–67	....	—	—
1967–68	....	1	—
1968–69	....	4	—
1969–70	....	5	—
1970–71	....	20	—
1971–72	....	—	—
1972–73	....	4	—
1973–74	....	—	—
1973–74	*Swansea C*	17	—
1973–74	Arsenal	1	—
1974–75	....	40	—
1975–76	....	41	—
1976–77	....	42	—
1977–78	Aston Villa..................	42	—
1978–79	....	42	—
1979–80	....	41	—
1980–81	....	42	—
1981–82	....	42	—
1982–83	....	20	—
1983–84	Swansea C	14	—
1984–85	....	33	—
1985–86	....	19	—

RING, Mike

Born Brighton 13.2.61.   Ht 5 10   Wt 10 6
Forward. From Apprentice.

Season	Club	App	Goals
1978–79	Brighton.....................	—	—
1979–80	....	—	—
1980–81	....	—	—
1981–82	....	1	—
1982–83	....	1	—
1983–84	....	3	—
1984–85	Hull C.......................	15	1
1985–86	....	9	1
1985–86	*Bolton W*	3	—

RIMMER, Neill

Born Liverpool 13.11.67.   Ht 5 6½   Wt 10 3
Midfield. From Apprentice. England
Schools, Youth.

Season	Club	App	Goals
1984–85	Everton.....................	1	—
1985–86	Ipswich T	2	—

RIPLEY, Stuart

Born Middlesbrough 20.11.67.
Forward. From Apprentice. England Youth.

Season	Club	App	Goals
1984–85	Middlesbrough.............	1	—
1985–86	....	8	—
1985–86	*Bolton W*	5	1

RITCHIE, Andy

Born Manchester 28.11.60.   Ht 5 10   Wt 11 7
Forward. From Apprentice.
England Schools, Under-21.

Season	Club	App	Goals
1977–78	Manchester U	4	—
1978–79	....	17	10
1979–80	....	8	3
1980–81	....	4	—

Season	Club	League Appearances/Goals		Season	Club	League Appearances/Goals	
1980–81	Brighton	26	5	1978–79		17	—
1981–82		39	13	1979–80		14	—
1982–83		24	5	1980–81		42	—
1982–83	Leeds U	10	3	1981–82		34	—
1983–84		38	7	1982–83		38	1
1984–85		28	12	1983–84		30	—
1985–86		29	11	1983–84	Birmingham C	11	—
				1984–85		41	—
				1985–86		33	—

RIX, Graham

Born Doncaster 23.10.57.   Ht 5 9   Wt 11 0
Midfield. From Apprentice.
England Under-21, 17 full caps.

1974–75	Arsenal	—	—
1975–76		—	—
1976–77		7	1
1977–78		39	2
1978–79		39	3
1979–80		38	4
1980–81		35	5
1981–82		39	9
1982–83		36	6
1983–84		34	4
1984–85		18	2
1985–86		38	3

ROBERTS, Alan

Born Newcastle 8.12.64.   Ht 5 9   Wt 10 0
Midfield. From Apprentice.

1982–83	Middlesbrough	1	—
1983–84		7	1
1984–85		29	1
1985–86		1	—
1985–86	Darlington	38	4

ROBERTS, Brian

Born Manchester 6.11.55.   Ht 5 8   Wt 11 7
Defender. From Apprentice.

1974–75	Coventry C	—	—
1974–75	*Hereford U*	5	—
1975–76	Coventry C	2	—
1976–77		12	—
1977–78		26	—

ROBERTS, Brian

Born Windsor 3.2.67.
Forward. From Local.

1984–85	Reading	4	—
1985–86		1	—

ROBERTS, Dean

Born Mexborough 12.1.67.   Ht 5 10½
Wt 10 6
Forward. From Apprentice.

1984–85	Bolton W	—	—
1985–86		—	—

ROBERTS, Iwan

Born Bangor 26.6.68.
Forward. Wales Youth.

1985–86	Watford	4	—

ROBERTS, Garreth

Born Hull 15.11.60.   Ht 5 5   Wt 10 8
Midfield. From Apprentice. Wales Under-21.

1978–79	Hull C	19	3
1979–80		44	2
1980–81		20	3
1981–82		29	6
1982–83		44	6
1983–84		38	9
1984–85		29	3
1985–86		33	4

Season	Club	League Appearances/Goals		Season	Club	League Appearances/Goals	

ROBERTS, Gary

Born Rhyl 5.4.60.   Ht 6 0   Wt 11 6
Forward. From Wembley T.

1980–81	Brentford	19	3
1981–82		40	8
1982–83		45	12
1983–84		41	10
1984–85		39	11
1985–86		3	1

ROBERTS, Graham

Born Southampton 3.7.59.   Ht 5 10   Wt 12 12
Defender. From Southampton, Sholing,
Bournemouth, Portsmouth, Dorchester T
and Weymouth. England, 6 full caps.

1980–81	Tottenham H	24	—
1981–82		37	6
1982–83		24	2
1983–84		35	6
1984–85		40	7
1985–86		32	1

ROBERTS, Jeremy

Born Middlesbrough 24.11.66.   Ht 6 0
Wt 13 0
Goalkeeper. From school. England Youth.

1983–84	Hartlepool U	1	—
1984–85	Leicester C	—	—
1985–86		3	—

ROBERTS, Paul

Born London 27.4.62.   Ht 5 9   Wt 11 13
Defender. From Apprentice.

1978–79	Millwall	2	—
1979–80		27	—
1980–81		45	—
1981–82		41	—
1982–83		31	—
1983–84		—	—
1983–84	Brentford	34	—
1984–85		28	—
1985–86	Swindon T	27	—

ROBERTS, Stuart

Born Chirk 25.3.67.   Ht 6 2   Wt 14 0
Goalkeeper. From Oswestry. Wales Youth.

1984–85	Stoke C	3	—
1985–86		—	—

ROBERTSON, Alistair

Born Philipstown 9.9.52.   Ht 5 10   Wt 12 1
Defender. From Apprentice.
Scotland Schools.

1969–70	WBA	10	—
1970–71		4	—
1971–72		31	—
1972–73		36	1
1973–74		40	—
1974–75		21	1
1975–76		42	1
1976–77		42	—
1977–78		42	1
1978–79		39	—
1979–80		38	1
1980–81		28	—
1981–82		33	1
1982–83		37	2
1983–84		6	—
1984–85		37	—
1985–86		20	—

ROBERTSON, Ian

Born Inverness 14.10.66.   Ht 5 9   Wt 10 10
Midfield. 'S' Form. Scotland Youth.

1983–84	Aberdeen	—	—
1984–85		—	—
1985–86		4	—

ROBERTSON, John

Born Uddingston 20.1.53.   Ht 5 8   Wt 10 9
Midfield. From Apprentice.
Scotland Schools, Youth, 28 full caps.

Season	Club	League Appearances/Goals		Season	Club	League Appearances/Goals	
1970–71	Nottingham F	2	—				
1971–72		13	—				
1972–73		32	4				
1973–74		5	—				
1974–75		20	—				
1975–76		39	5				
1976–77		41	6				
1977–78		42	12				
1978–79		42	9				
1979–80		42	11				
1980–81		38	6				
1981–82		36	2				
1982–83		34	6				
1983–84	Derby Co	31	2				
1984–85		41	1				
1985–86	Nottingham F	11	—				

ROBERTSON, John

Born Edinburgh 2.10.64.   Ht 5 6   Wt 10 3
Forward. From Edina Hibs.
Scotland Under-21.

Season	Club	App	Goals
1980–81	Hearts	—	—
1981–82		1	—
1982–83		23	19
1983–84		35	15
1984–85		33	8
1985–86		35	20

ROBINSON, Andy

Born Oldham 10.3.66.   Ht 5 10   Wt 12 4
Defender. From Apprentice.

Season	Club	App	Goals
1983–84	Manchester U	—	—
1984–85		—	—
1985–86		—	—
1985–86	*Burnley*	5	1
1985–86	Bury	10	—

ROBINSON, Colin

Born Birmingham 15.5.60.   Ht 5 10
Wt 10 12
Forward. From Mile Oak Rovers.

Season	Club	App	Goals
1982–83	Shrewsbury T	12	3
1983–84		30	4
1984–85		42	14
1985–86		42	10

ROBINSON, David

Born Cleveland 14.1.65.   Ht 6 0   Wt 12 3
Defender.

Season	Club	App	Goals
1983–84	Hartlepool U	7	—
1984–85		38	—
1985–86		21	1

ROBINSON, Les

Born Mansfield 1.3.67.
Forward. From Local.

Season	Club	App	Goals
1984–85	Mansfield T	6	—
1985–86		7	—

ROBINSON, Liam

Born Bradford 29.12.65.   Ht 5 6   Wt 11 4
Forward. From Nottingham F schoolboy.

Season	Club	App	Goals
1983–84	Huddersfield T	5	1
1984–85		15	1
1985–86		1	—
1985–86	*Tranmere R*	4	3

ROBINSON, Mark

Born Basford 26.11.60.   Ht 6 0   Wt 11 7
Forward. From Ilkeston T.

Season	Club	App	Goals
1984–85	Notts Co	14	—
1985–86		12	1

ROBINSON, Mark

Born Manchester 21.11.68.
Midfield. From YTS.

Season	Club	App	Goals
1985–86	WBA	1	—

ROBINSON, Martin

Born Ilford 17.7.57.   Ht 5 8½   Wt 11 2
Forward. From Apprentice.

Season	Club	App	Goals
1975–76	Tottenham H	2	1
1976–77		—	—
1977–78		4	1
1977–78	Charlton Ath	16	7
1978–79		35	15

Season	Club	League Appearances/Goals		Season	Club	League Appearances/Goals

Season	Club	App	Goals
1979–80	....	33	7
1980–81	....	40	10
1981–82	....	39	5
1982–83	....	32	4
1982–83	*Reading*........................	6	2
1983–84	Charlton Ath	27	8
1984–85	....	6	2
1984–85	Gillingham..................	33	10
1985–86	....	33	10

ROBINSON, Michael

Born Leicester 12.7.58.   Ht 6 0   Wt 13 4
Forward. From Apprentice. Eire
22 full caps.

Season	Club	App	Goals
1975–76	Preston NE	2	—
1976–77	....	—	—
1977–78	....	10	2
1978–79	....	36	13
1979–80	Manchester C	30	8
1980–81	Brighton......................	42	19
1981–82	....	35	11
1982–83	....	36	7
1983–84	Liverpool.....................	24	6
1984–85	....	6	—
1984–85	QPR............................	11	1
1985–86	....	26	5

ROBINSON, Neil

Born Liverpool 20.4.57.   Ht 5 8   Wt 10 6
Defender. From Apprentice.

Season	Club	App	Goals
1974–75	Everton.......................	—	—
1975–76	....	1	—
1976–77	....	4	—
1977–78	....	4	1
1978–79	....	7	—
1979–80	....	—	—
1979–80	Swansea C	16	—
1980–81	....	36	6
1981–82	....	29	1
1982–83	....	18	—
1983–84	....	19	—
1984–85	....	5	—
1984–85	Grimsby T...................	17	—
1985–86	....	22	—

ROBINSON, Paul

Born Hampstead 5.1.63.   Ht 5 10   Wt 11 8
Defender. From Apprentice. England
Schools, Youth.

Season	Club	App	Goals
1979–80	Millwall......................	1	—
1980–81	....	7	—
1981–82	....	5	—
1982–83	....	13	—
1983–84	....	33	2
1984–85	....	—	—
1985–86	....	—	—

ROBINSON, Peter

Born Ashington 4.9.57.   Ht 6 1   Wt 12 6
Defender.

Season	Club	App	Goals
1976–77	Burnley	20	1
1977–78	....	18	1
1978–79	....	13	1
1979–80	....	4	—
From Sparta Rotterdam			
1984–85	Rochdale	12	—
1985–86	Darlington	29	1
1985–86	*Halifax T*	5	—

ROBINSON, Philip

Born Stafford 6.1.67.   Ht 5 9   Wt 10 10
Defender. From Apprentice.

Season	Club	App	Goals
1984–85	Aston Villa.................	—	—
1985–86	....	—	—

ROBINSON, Ron

Born Sunderland 22.10.66.   Ht 5 9   Wt 11 0
Defender.

Season	Club	App	Goals
1984–85	Ipswich T....................	—	—
From Vaux Breweries			
1985–86	Leeds U......................	16	—

ROBSON, Bryan

Born Chester-le-Street 11.1.57.   Ht 5 10½
Wt 11 12
Midfield. From Apprentice.
England Youth, Under-21, 'B', 51 full caps.

All appearances include those as substitute

Season	Club	League Appearances/Goals		Season	Club	League Appearances/Goals	
1974–75	WBA	3	2	1980–81		12	3
1975–76		16	1	1980–81	Carlisle U	9	6
1976–77		23	8	1981–82		39	15
1977–78		35	3	1982–83	Chelsea	15	3
1978–79		41	7	1982–83	*Carlisle U*	11	4
1979–80		34	8	1983–84	Sunderland	12	3
1980–81		40	10	1984–85	Carlisle U	11	1
1981–82		5	—	1985–86		2	—
1981–82	Manchester U	32	5				
1982–83		33	10				
1983–84		33	12				
1984–85		33	9				
1985–86		21	7				

ROBSON, Gary

Born Durham 6.7.65.   Ht 5 5   Wt 10 7
Midfield. From Apprentice.

Season	Club	App	Goals
1982–83	WBA	2	—
1983–84		7	—
1984–85		11	—
1985–86		14	—

ROBSON, 'Pop'

Born Sunderland 11.11.45.   Ht 5 7   Wt 11 8
Forward. From Amateur.
England Under-23, Football League.

Season	Club	App	Goals
1962–63	Newcastle U	—	—
1963–64		—	—
1964–65		20	7
1965–66		23	9
1966–67		37	9
1967–68		13	4
1968–69		42	21
1969–70		42	22
1970–71		29	9
1970–71	West Ham	14	3
1971–72		42	9
1972–73		42	28
1973–74		22	7
1974–75	Sunderland	42	19
1975–76		40	13
1976–77		8	2
1976–77	West Ham	30	14
1977–78		37	9
1978–79		40	24
1979–80	Sunderland	40	20

ROBSON, Stewart

Born Billericay 6.11.64.   Ht 5 11   Wt 11 13
Defender. From Apprentice.
England Youth, Under-21.

Season	Club	App	Goals
1981–82	Arsenal	20	2
1982–83		31	2
1983–84		28	6
1984–85		40	2
1985–86		27	4

ROCASTLE, David

Born Lewisham 2.5.67.   Ht 5 9   Wt 11 1
Forward. From Apprentice.

Season	Club	App	Goals
1984–85	Arsenal	—	—
1985–86		16	1

ROCHE, Paddy

Born Dublin 4.1.51.   Ht 6 1½   Wt 11 4
Goalkeeper. From Shelbourne.
Eire, 7 full caps.

Season	Club	App	Goals
1973–74	Manchester U	—	—
1974–75		2	—
1975–76		4	—
1976–77		2	—
1977–78		19	—
1978–79		14	—
1979–80		—	—
1980–81		2	—
1981–82		3	—
1982–83	Brentford	46	—
1983–84		25	—
1984–85	Halifax T	43	—
1985–86		46	—

Season	Club	League Appearances/Goals	Season	Club	League Appearances/Goals

RODAWAY, Billy

Born Liverpool 26.9.54.   Ht 5 10   Wt 13 2
Defender. From Apprentice. England
Schools.

Season	Club	App	Goals
1971–72	Burnley	2	—
1972–73		—	—
1973–74		9	—
1974–75		29	1
1975–76		15	—
1976–77		42	—
1977–78		33	—
1978–79		39	—
1979–80		29	—
1980–81		5	—
1981–82	Peterborough U	42	—
1982–83		39	—
1983–84	Blackpool	41	—
1984–85	Tranmere R	19	1
1985–86		39	4

RODGER, Graham

Born Glasgow 1.4.67.
Defender. From Apprentice.

Season	Club	App	Goals
1983–84	Wolverhampton W	1	—
1984–85	Coventry C	—	—
1985–86		10	—

RODGERS, Mark

Born Broxburn 20.9.67.
Midfield.

Season	Club	App	Goals
1985–86	Preston NE	1	—

RODGERSON, Ian

Born Hereford 9.4.66.   Ht 5 8   Wt 10 7
Midfield. From Pegasus Juniors.

Season	Club	App	Goals
1984–85	Hereford U	—	—
1985–86		19	2

ROEDER, Glenn

Born Woodford 13.12.55.   Ht 6 0   Wt 12 13
Defender. From Apprentice. England 'B'.

Season	Club	App	Goals
1974–75	Orient	6	—
1975–76		25	2
1976–77		42	2
1977–78		42	—
1978–79	QPR	27	4
1979–80		40	9
1980–81		39	2
1981–82		41	2
1982–83		9	—
1983–84		1	—
1983–84	*Notts Co*	4	—
1983–84	Newcastle U	23	—
1984–85		36	—
1985–86		42	6

ROFFEY, Bill

Born Stepney 6.2.54.   Ht 5 11   Wt 12 13
Defender. From Apprentice.

Season	Club	App	Goals
1972–73	Crystal Palace	19	—
1973–74		5	—
1973–74	Orient	21	1
1974–75		6	—
1975–76		14	—
1976–77		35	2
1977–78		42	1
1978–79		39	—
1979–80		40	1
1980–81		42	—
1981–82		18	—
1982–83		42	3
1983–84		29	—
1983–84	*Brentford*	13	1
1984–85	Millwall	25	1
1985–86		12	1

ROGERS, Alan

Born Plymouth 6.7.54.   Ht 5 10   Wt 10 7
Forward. From Apprentice.

Season	Club	App	Goals
1973–74	Plymouth Arg	30	1
1974–75		1	—

Season	Club	League Appearances/Goals		Season	Club	League Appearances/Goals	
1975–76	....	—	—				
1976–77	....	19	1				
1977–78	....	29	2				
1978–79	....	38	1				
1979–80	Portsmouth	42	9				
1980–81	....	45	3				
1981–82	....	18	—				
1982–83	....	42	2				
1983–84	....	14	—				
1983–84	Southend U	13	—				
1984–85	....	42	3				
1985–86	....	32	1				

ROGERS, Andy

Born Chatteris 1.12.56.   Ht 5 8   Wt 10 0
Forward. From Chatteris T.

Season	Club		
1975–76	Peterborough U............	5	—
1976–77	....	22	1
1977–78	....	2	—
From Hampton			
1979–80	Southampton	2	—
1980–81	....	1	—
1981–82	....	2	—
1981–82	Plymouth Arg	40	4
1982–83	....	44	5
1983–84	....	37	4
1984–85	....	42	1
1985–86	Reading	40	5

ROGERS, Graham

Born Newport 5.9.55.
Defender.

Season	Club		
1974–75	Newport Co.................	4	—
From Forest Green R.			
1985–86	Newport Co.................	7	—

ROGERS, Lee

Born Bristol 8.4.67.   Ht 5 11   Wt 12 7
Defender. From Apprentice.

Season	Club		
1984–85	Bristol C.....................	6	—
1985–86	....	21	—

RONALD, Gerry

Born Glasgow 31.12.58.   Ht 5 10   Wt 10 7
Forward. From Glasgow United.

Season	Club		
1976–77	Clydebank	11	—
1977–78	....	14	—
1978–79	....	—	—
1979–80	....	34	9
1980–81	....	30	—
1981–82	....	35	5
1982–83	....	33	6
1983–84	....	36	6
1984–85	....	24	2
1985–86	....	19	—

RONSON, Billy

Born Fleetwood 22.1.57.   Ht 5 5   Wt 9 5
Midfield. From Apprentice.

Season	Club		
1973–74	Blackpool	—	—
1974–75	....	2	—
1975–76	....	19	2
1976–77	....	41	4
1977–78	....	34	3
1978–79	....	32	3
1979–80	Cardiff C	41	2
1980–81	....	42	1
1981–82	....	7	1
1981–82	Wrexham.....................	32	1
1982–83	Barnsley	39	1
1983–84	....	32	2
1984–85	....	40	—
1985–86	....	2	—
1985–86	*Birmingham C*............	2	—
1985–86	Blackpool	3	—

ROONEY, Jim

Born Glasgow 1.1.56.   Ht 5 9   Wt 10 12
Midfield. From Queen's Park Youth.

Season	Club		
1974–75	Queen's Park	18	4
1975–76	....	24	1
1976–77	....	37	4
1977–78	....	39	3
1978–79	Morton	28	1
1979–80	....	17	1

Season	Club	League Appearances/Goals		Season	Club	League Appearances/Goals	
1980–81	....	36	5	1974–75	Arsenal	2	—
1981–82	....	33	4	1975–76	....	17	1
1982–83	....	36	7	1976–77	....	29	4
1983–84	....	36	8	1977–78	....	10	—
1984–85	St Mirren	27	2	1977–78	Everton	20	4
1985–86	....	32	6	1978–79	....	27	6
				1979–80	....	32	3
				1980–81	....	17	2

ROSARIO, Robert

Born Hammersmith 4.3.66.   Ht 6 3
Wt 12 1
Forward. From Hillingdon Bor. England
Youth.

Season	Club	App	Goals
1983–84	Norwich C....................	8	1
1984–85	....	4	1
1985–86	....	8	2
1985–86	*Wolverhampton W*	2	1

Season	Club	App	Goals
1981–82	....	28	1
1982–83	....	2	—
1982–83	*Portsmouth*	5	—
1982–83	*Sheffield U*	4	—
From AEK Athens			
1983–84	Sheffield U	4	—
1984–85	Bury............................	45	6
1985–86	....	31	3

ROSE, Kevin

Born Evesham 23.11.60.   Ht 6 1   Wt 13 6
Goalkeeper. From Ledbury T.

Season	Club	App	Goals
1979–80	Lincoln C.....................	—	—
1980–81	....	—	—
From Ledbury T			
1982–83	Hereford U.	15	—
1983–84	....	46	—
1984–85	....	46	—
1985–86	....	46	—

ROSTRON, Wilf

Born Sunderland 29.9.56.   Ht 5 7   Wt 11 1½
Midfield. From Apprentice.
England Schools.

Season	Club	App	Goals
1973–74	Arsenal	—	—
1974–75	....	6	2
1975–76	....	5	—
1976–77	....	6	—
1977–78	Sunderland	34	6
1978–79	....	34	11
1979–80	....	8	—
1979–80	Watford	31	3
1980–81	....	27	1
1981–82	....	27	2
1982–83	....	42	3
1983–84	....	39	4
1984–85	....	38	3
1985–86	....	30	5

ROSENIOR, Leroy

Born London 24.3.64.   Ht 6 1   Wt 11 10
Forward. From School. England Schools.

Season	Club	App	Goals
1982–83	Fulham	1	—
1983–84	....	23	8
1984–85	....	30	8
1985–86	QRP............................	18	3

ROUGH, Alan

Born Glasgow 25.11.51.   Ht 6 1   Wt 13 5
Goalkeeper. From Sighthill Amateurs.
Scotland Youth, Under-23, 53 full caps.

Season	Club	App	Goals
1969–70	Partick T.....................	2	—
1970–71	....	36	—
1971–72	....	34	—
1972–73	....	34	—

ROSS, Trevor

Born Ashton-Under-Lyne 16.1.57.   Ht 5 9½
Wt 11 10
Midfield. From Apprentice. England
Schools. Scotland Under-21

Season	Club	League Appearances/Goals		Season	Club	League Appearances/Goals	
1973–74	....	34	—				
1974–75	....	19	—				
1975–76	....	26	—				
1976–77	....	36	—				
1977–78	....	36	—				
1978–79	....	35	—				
1979–80	....	34	—				
1980–81	....	33	—				
1981–82	....	36	—				
1982–83	....	15	—				
1982–83	Hibernian	24	—				
1983–84	....	27	—				
1984–85	....	35	—				
1985–86	....	36	—				

ROUGVIE, Doug

Born Ballingry 24.5.56. Ht 6 2 Wt 13 8
Defender. Scotland, 1 full cap.

Season	Club	Apps	Goals
1976–77	Aberdeen	6	1
1977–78	....	1	—
1978–79	....	20	—
1979–80	....	25	2
1980–81	....	28	3
1981–82	....	28	6
1982–83	....	35	3
1983–84	....	35	4
1984–85	Chelsea	27	1
1985–86	....	34	2

ROWBOTHAM, Darren

Born Cardiff 22.10.66. Ht 5 10 Wt 11 5
Midfield. From YTS.

Season	Club	Apps	Goals
1984–85	Plymouth Arg	7	—
1985–86	....	14	1

ROWBOTHAM, Mike

Born Sheffield 2.9.65. Ht 5 11
Wt 11 11
Midfield. From Apprentice.

Season	Club	Apps	Goals
1983–84	Manchester U.	—	—
1984–85	Grimsby T.	4	—
1985–86	....	—	—

ROWELL, Gary

Born Seaham 6.6.57. Ht 5 10 Wt 11 3
Forward. From Apprentice.
England Under-21.

Season	Club	Apps	Goals
1974–75	Sunderland	—	—
1975–76	....	4	1
1976–77	....	32	5
1977–78	....	39	18
1978–79	....	32	21
1979–80	....	17	—
1980–81	....	31	10
1981–82	....	30	9
1982–83	....	35	16
1983–84	....	34	8
1984–85	Norwich C.	6	1
1985–86	Middlesbrough	27	10

ROWLAND, Andy

Born Derby 8.9.54. Ht 5 10½ Wt 12 0
Forward. From Derby Co. Amateur.
England Youth.

Season	Club	Apps	Goals
1974–75	Bury	35	10
1975–76	....	46	16
1976–77	....	45	17
1977–78	....	41	14
1978–79	....	7	1
1978–79	Swindon T.	28	13
1979–80	....	44	20
1980–81	....	42	12
1981–82	....	27	8
1982–83	....	45	16
1983–84	....	37	6
1984–85	....	46	5
1985–86	....	18	—

RUDDOCK, Neil

Born London 9.5.68. Ht 6 2 Wt 12 6
Defender. From Apprentice. England
Youth.

Season	Club	Apps	Goals
1985–86	Millwall	—	—
1985–86	Tottenham H	—	—

Season	Club	League Appearances/Goals		Season	Club	League Appearances/Goals	

RUDGE, Dale

Born Wolverhampton 9.9.63.   Ht 5 8½
Wt 10 3
Midfield. From Apprentice.

Season	Club	Apps	Goals
1981–82	Wolverhampton W	—	—
1982–83		8	—
1983–84		19	—
1984–85	Preston NE	24	2
1985–86		23	—

RUDGE, Simon

Born Warrington 30.12.64.   Ht 5 6½
Wt 10 6
Forward. From Apprentice.

Season	Club	Apps	Goals
1982–83	Bolton W	23	3
1983–84		32	7
1984–85		20	2
1985–86		16	2

RUSH, Ian

Born St. Asaph 20.10.61.   Ht 6 0½   Wt 12 6
Forward. From Apprentice.
Wales Schools, Under-21, 28 full caps.

Season	Club	Apps	Goals
1978–79	Chester	1	—
1979–80		33	14
1979–80	Liverpool	—	—
1980–81		7	—
1981–82		32	17
1982–83		34	24
1983–84		41	32
1984–85		28	14
1985–86		40	23

RUSHBURY, David

Born Wolverhampton 20.2.56.   Ht 5 10
Wt 10 12
Defender. From Apprentice.

Season	Club	Apps	Goals
1974–75	WBA	26	—
1975–76		2	—
1976–77		—	—
1976–77	Sheffield W	30	2
1977–78		45	4
1978–79		37	1
1979–80	Swansea C	40	—
1980–81		12	—
1981–82	Carlisle U	45	—
1982–83		35	—
1983–84		28	1
1984–85		21	—
1984–85	Gillingham	12	—
1985–86	Doncaster R	45	—

RUSSELL, Billy

Born Glasgow 14.9.59.   Ht 5 10   Wt 11 4
Defender. From Apprentice. Scotland
Youth.

Season	Club	Apps	Goals
1977–78	Everton	—	—
From Glasgow Celtic			
1979–80	Doncaster R	42	—
1980–81		46	1
1981–82		37	3
1982–83		40	5
1983–84		41	6
1984–85		38	—
1985–86	Scunthorpe U	42	—

RUSSELL, Bobby

Born Glasgow 11.2.57.   Ht 5 8   Wt 10 3
Midfield. From Shettleston.
Scotland Under-21.

Season	Club	Apps	Goals
1976–77	Rangers	—	—
1977–78		33	3
1978–79		36	4
1979–80		23	7
1980–81		28	6
1981–82		32	6
1982–83		21	4
1983–84		31	4
1984–85		18	—
1985–86		27	—

Season	Club	League Appearances/Goals		Season	Club	League Appearances/Goals	

RUSSELL, Colin

Born Liverpool 21.1.61.   Ht 5 7   Wt 10 7
Forward. From Apprentice.

1977–78	Liverpool	—	—
1978–79		—	—
1979–80		—	—
1980–81		1	—
1981–82		—	—
1982–83		—	—
1982–83	Huddersfield T	41	16
1983–84		25	7
1983–84	*Stoke C*	11	2
1984–85	Bournemouth	36	6
1985–86		32	8

RUSSELL, Guy

Born Shirley 28.9.67.
Forward. From YTS.

1984–85	Birmingham C	1	—
1985–86		1	—

RUSSELL, Kevin

Born Portsmouth 6.12.66.
Midfield. From Brighton Apprentice.
England Youth.

1984–85	Portsmouth	—	—
1985–86		1	—

RUSSELL, Martin

Born Dublin 27.4.67.   Ht 5 10   Wt 11 0
Midfield. From Apprentice. Eire Youth.

1984–85	Manchester U	—	—
1985–86		—	—

RUSSO, Donato

Born Bedford 28.11.67.   Ht 5 7   Wt 10 10
Defender.

1984–85	Arsenal	—	—
1985–86		—	—

RUTTER, John

Born Warrington 13.9.52.   Ht 5 9   Wt 10 10
Defender. From Apprentice.

1970–71	Wolverhampton W	—	—
1971–72		—	—
1972–73		—	—
1973–74	Bournemouth	4	—
1974–75	Exeter C	31	1
1975–76		1	—
1976–77	Stockport Co	46	1
1977–78		46	4
1978–79		45	—
1979–80		42	1
1980–81		46	2
1981–82		39	—
1982–83		44	1
1983–84		41	1
1984–85		38	—
1985–86		17	—

RYAN, Derek

Born Dublin 2.1.67.   Ht 5 10   Wt 10 4
Forward. From Apprentice.

1984–85	Wolverhampton W	10	1
1985–86		20	4

RYAN, Gerry

Born Dublin 4.10.55.   Ht 5 10   Wt 10 12
Forward. From Bohemians. Eire, 16 full
caps.

1977–78	Derby Co	24	4
1978–79		6	—
1978–79	Brighton	35	9
1979–80		35	5
1980–81		10	—
1981–82		20	1
1982–83		26	6
1983–84		24	6
1984–85		22	5
1985–86		—	—

Season	Club	League Appearances/Goals		Season	Club	League Appearances/Goals	

RYAN, John

Born Ashton 18.2.62.   Ht 5 10   Wt 11 6
Defender. From Apprentice.

Season	Club	App	Goals
1979–80	Oldham Ath	—	—
1980–81		—	—
1981–82		37	—
1982–83		40	8
1983–84	Newcastle U	22	1
1984–85		6	—
1984–85	Sheffield W	8	1
1985–86	Oldham Ath	22	—

SADDINGTON, Nigel

Born Sunderland 9.12.65.   Ht 6 1   Wt 12 6
Defender.

Season	Club	App	Goals
1984–85	Doncaster R	6	—
1985–86		—	—
1985–86	Sunderland	—	—

SAGE, Mel

Born Gillingham 24.3.64. Ht 5 8½ Wt 10 10
Defender. From Apprentice.

Season	Club	App	Goals
1981–82	Gillingham	1	—
1982–83		9	—
1983–84		40	2
1984–85		36	1
1985–86		46	2

SALATHIEL, Neil

Born Wrexham 19.11.62.   Ht 5 7   Wt 12 0
Defender. From Sheffield W. Amateur.
Wales Schools.

Season	Club	App	Goals
1980–81	Wrexham	4	—
1981–82	Crewe Alex.	44	—
1982–83		21	—
From Arcadia Shepherds			
1983–84	Wrexham	29	—
1984–85		36	—
1985–86		42	1

SALMAN, Danis

Born Cyprus 12.3.60.   Ht 5 10   Wt 11 8
Defender. From Apprentice. England Youth.

Season	Club	App	Goals
1975–76	Brentford	6	—
1976–77		18	1
1977–78		37	—
1978–79		40	1
1979–80		41	3
1980–81		38	—
1981–82		40	—
1982–83		1	—
1983–84		21	—
1984–85		43	3
1985–86		40	—

Season	Club	League Appearances/Goals	Season	Club	League Appearances/Goals

SALMON, Mike

Born Leyland 14.7.64.   Ht 6 2   Wt 13 0
Goalkeeper. Local.

Season	Club	App	Goals
1981–82	Blackburn R	1	—
1982–83		—	—
1982–83	*Chester*	16	—
1983–84	Stockport Co	46	—
1984–85		46	—
1985–86		26	—

SAMWAYS, Vince

Born Bethnal Green 27.10.68.
Midfield. From Apprentice. England Youth.

Season	Club	App	Goals
1985–86	Tottenham H	—	—

SANCHEZ, Lawrie

Born Lambeth 22.10.59.   Ht 5 11   Wt 11 7
Midfield. From Amateur.

Season	Club	App	Goals
1977–78	Reading	8	1
1978–79		39	4
1979–80		46	5
1980–81		37	2
1981–82		35	3
1982–83		37	1
1983–84		45	10
1984–85		15	2
1984–85	Wimbledon	20	5
1985–86		42	9

SANDER, Chris

Born Swansea 11.11.62.   Ht 5 11   Wt 10 4
Goalkeeper. From Apprentice.

Season	Club	App	Goals
1979–80	Swansea C	—	—
1980–81		—	—
1981–82		1	—
1982–83		12	—
1983–84		7	—
1984–85		—	—
1984–85	*Wrexham*	5	—
1985–86	Cardiff C	13	—

SANDERSON, Michael

Born Germany 26.10.66.
Midfield.

Season	Club	App	Goals
1985–86	Darlington	1	—

SANDERSON, Paul

Born Blackpool 16.12.66.   Ht 6 1   Wt 12 0
Forward. From Fleetwood T.

Season	Club	App	Goals
1983–84	Manchester C	—	—
1983–84	Chester	24	3
1984–85	Halifax T	33	1
1985–86		28	2

SANDFORD, Lee

Born Basingstoke 22.4.68.   Ht 6 1   Wt 12 2
Defender. From Apprentice. England
Youth.

Season	Club	App	Goals
1985–86	Portsmouth	7	—

SANDISON, James

Born Edinburgh 22.6.65.   Ht 6 0   Wt 11 2
Midfield. From Edinburgh Emmet.

Season	Club	App	Goals
1983–84	Hearts	—	—
1984–85		3	—
1985–86		3	—

SANKEY, Iain

Born Telford 13.5.67.   Ht 5 8   Wt 11 6
Midfield. From Apprentice.

Season	Club	App	Goals
1984–85	Ipswich T	—	—
1985–86		—	—

SANSOM, Kenny

Born Camberwell 26.9.58.   Ht 5 6   Wt 11 8
Defender. From Apprentice. England
Schools, Youth, Under-21, 'B', 65 full caps.

Season	Club	League Appearances/Goals		Season	Club	League Appearances/Goals	

1974–75	Crystal Palace	1	—
1975–76		6	—
1976–77		46	—
1977–78		41	2
1978–79		42	—
1979–80		36	1
1980–81	Arsenal	42	3
1981–82		42	—
1982–83		40	—
1983–84		40	1
1984–85		39	1
1985–86		42	—

SANSOME, Paul

Born N. Addington 6.10.61.   Ht 6 0   Wt 12 6½
Goalkeeper. From Crystal Palace.
Apprentice.

1979–80	Millwall	—	—
1980–81		—	—
1981–82		8	—
1982–83		24	—
1983–84		31	—
1984–85		46	—
1985–86		36	—

SAUNDERS, Carl

Born Marston Green 26.11.64.   Ht 5 8
Wt 10 12
Forward. Local.

1982–83	Stoke C	1	—
1983–84		—	—
1984–85		23	2
1985–86		37	2

SAUNDERS, Dean

Born Swansea 21.6.64.   Ht 5 8½   Wt 10 0
Forward. From Apprentice. Wales 3 full
caps.

1982–83	Swansea C	—	—
1983–84		19	3
1984–85		30	9
1984–85	*Cardiff C*	4	—
1985–86	Brighton	42	14

SAUNDERS, Steve

Born Warrington 21.9.64.   Ht 5 7½
Wt 10 6.
Forward. From Apprentice.

1982–83	Bolton W	—	—
1983–84		3	—
1984–85		—	—
1985–86	Crewe Alex	22	1

SAUNDERS, Wes

Born Sunderland 23.2.63.   Ht 6 0   Wt 11 11
Defender. From school.

1981–82	Newcastle U	29	—
1982–83		13	—
1983–84		16	—
1984–85		21	—
1984–85	*Bradford C*	4	—
1985–86	Carlisle U	35	3

SAVAGE, Bob

Born Liverpool 8.1.60.   Ht 5 7   Wt 11 1
Midfield. From Apprentice.

1977–78	Liverpool	—	—
1978–79		—	—
1979–80		—	—
1980–81		—	—
1981–82		—	—
1982–83		—	—
1982–83	*Wrexham*	27	10
1983–84	Stoke C	7	—
1983–84	Bournemouth	23	5
1984–85		43	9
1985–86		—	—

SAVILLE, Andrew

Born Hull 12.12.64.   Ht 6 0   Wt 12 0
Forward. From local.

1983–84	Hull C	1	—
1984–85		4	1
1985–86		9	1

Season	Club	League Appearances/Goals		Season	Club	League Appearances/Goals	

SAWYERS, Stokley

Born Willesden 3.9.66.
Forward. From Apprentice.

1984–85	Chelsea	—	—
1985–86		—	—

SAXBY, Mick

Born Mansfield 12.8.57. Ht 6 0 Wt 13 10
Defender. From Apprentice.

1974–75	Mansfield T	—	—
1975–76		2	1
1976–77		10	—
1977–78		21	—
1978–79		46	4
1979–80	Luton T	39	4
1980–81		31	1
1981–82		12	1
1982–83		—	—
1982–83	*Grimsby T*	10	—
1983–84	Luton T	—	—
1983–84	*Lincoln C*	10	1
1984–85	Newport Co	6	—
1984–85	Middlesbrough	15	—
1985–86		—	—

SAYER, Andy

Born Brent 6.6.66. Ht 5 9 Wt 10 12
Forward. From Apprentice.

1983–84	Wimbledon	2	—
1984–85		20	8
1985–86		7	—

SBRAGIA, Ricky

Born Lennoxtown 26.5.56. Ht 6 0 Wt 11 0
Defender. From Apprentice.

1974–75	Birmingham C	1	—
1975–76			
1975–76	*Morton*	4	—
1976–77	Birmingham C	9	—
1977–78		5	1
1978–79			
1978–79	Walsall	32	3
1979–80		45	1

1980–81	Blackpool	23	1
1981–82		3	—
1982–83	York C	46	1
1983–84		45	4
1984–85		25	2
1985–86		7	—
1985–86	*Darlington*	6	—

SCALES, John

Born Harrogate 4.7.66. Ht 6 0 Wt 12 2
Defender.

1984–85	Leeds U	—	—
1985–86	Bristol R	29	1

SCANLON, Ian

Born Uddingston 13.7.52. Ht 5 10 Wt 11 3
Forward. From Viewpark B.C.

1970–71	East Stirling	18	3
1971–72		27	15
1972–73	Notts Co	4	—
1973–74		2	—
1974–75		32	14
1975–76		38	12
1976–77		31	5
1977–78		4	—
1977–78	Aberdeen	1	1
1978–79		28	2
1979–80		29	4
1980–81		34	6
1981–82	St Mirren	25	5
1982–83		21	7
1983–84		30	12
1984–85		21	4
1985–86		1	—

SCHIAVI, Mark

Born London 1.5.64. Ht 5 8 Wt 10 9
Forward. From Apprentice. England Youth.

1981–82	West Ham U	—	—
1982–83		—	—
1983–84		—	—
1983–84	*Bournemouth*	10	—
1984–85	Bournemouth	19	—
1985–86	Northampton T	34	5

Season	Club	League Appearances/Goals		Season	Club	League Appearances/Goals	

SCHOFIELD, Mark

Born Wigan 10.10.66.
Midfield. From school.

1983–84	Wigan Ath	1	—
1984–85		1	—
1985–86		—	—

SCONCE, Mark

Born Wrexham 18.2.68.
Defender.

| 1984–85 | Chester | — | — |
| 1985–86 | | 2 | — |

SCOTT, Bob

Born Liverpool 22.2.53.   Ht 6 2½   Wt 13 4
Defender. From Amateur.

1970–71	Wrexham	1	—
1971–72		—	—
1972–73		6	—
1973–74		4	—
1974–75		5	—
1974–75	*Reading*	5	—
1975–76		3	—
1976–77	Hartlepool U	37	—
1977–78	Rochdale	40	1
1978–79		31	2
1979–80	Crewe Alex	43	2
1980–81		45	2
1981–82		46	3
1982–83		45	2
1983–84		46	6
1984–85		13	—
1985–86		1	—
1985–86	Wrexham	3	—

SCOTT, Derek

Born Gateshead 8.2.58.   Ht 5 8   Wt 11 12
Defender. From Apprentice.
England Schools.

| 1974–75 | Burnley | 2 | — |
| 1975–76 | | 17 | 2 |

1976–77		14	—
1977–78		26	1
1978–79		35	1
1979–80		28	2
1980–81		29	9
1981–82		30	2
1982–83		36	2
1983–84		40	4
1984–85		28	1
1985–86	Bolton W	43	—

SCOTT, Geoff

Born Birmingham 31.10.56.   Ht 5 11
Wt 11 12
Defender. From Highgate U.

1976–77	Stoke C	—	—
1977–78		24	2
1978–79		38	—
1979–80		16	1
1979–80	Leicester C	11	—
1980–81		21	—
1981–82		7	—
1981–82	Birmingham C	15	—
1982–83		4	—
1982–83	Charlton Ath	2	—
1983–84		—	—
1984–85	Middlesbrough	2	—
1984–85	Northampton T	17	—
1985–86	Cambridge U	19	—

SCOTT, Ian

Born Radcliffe 20.9.67.
Forward. From Apprentice. England
Schools.

| 1985–86 | Manchester C | — | — |

SCOTT, Kevin

Born Easington 17.12.66.   Ht 6 2   Wt 11 6
Defender.

| 1984–85 | Newcastle U | — | — |
| 1985–86 | | — | — |

Season	Club	League Appearances/Goals		Season	Club	League Appearances/Goals	

SCOTT, Martin

Born Sheffield 7.1.68. Ht 5 8 Wt 9 10
Midfield. From Apprentice.

1984–85	Rotherham U	3	—
1985–86		—	—

SCOTT, Peter

Born London 1.10.63. Ht 5 8 Wt 10 10
Midfield. From Apprentice.

1981–82	Fulham	1	—
1982–83		—	—
1983–84		32	4
1984–85		19	1
1985–86		32	5

SCRIMGEOUR, Brian

Born Dundee 11.8.59. Ht 5 11 Wt 11 3
Midfield. From St Columba's BC.

1976–77	Dundee	—	—
1977–78		—	—
1978–79		3	—
1979–80		—	—
1980–81		21	5
1981–82		12	—
1982–83		22	2
1983–84	Chesterfield	41	3
1984–85		15	—
1985–86		45	9

SEADEN, John

Born Rochford 4.6.67. Ht 5 8 Wt 11 4
Midfield. From Apprentice.

1984–85	Southend U	15	—
1985–86		5	—

SEAGRAVES, Mark

Born Bootle 22.10.66. Ht 6 0½ Wt 12 10
Defender. From England Schools, Youth.

1983–84	Liverpool	—	—
1984–85		—	—
1985–86		—	—

SEALEY, Les

Born Bethnal Green 29.9.57. Ht 6 1
Wt 12 8
Goalkeeper. From Apprentice.

1975–76	Coventry C	—	—
1976–77		11	—
1977–78		2	—
1978–79		36	—
1979–80		20	—
1980–81		35	—
1981–82		15	—
1982–83		39	—
1983–84	Luton T	42	—
1984–85		26	—
1984–85	*Plymouth Arg*	6	—
1985–86	Luton T	35	—

SEALY, Tony

Born London 7.5.59. Ht 5 8 Wt 11 8
Forward. From Apprentice.

1977–78	Southampton	2	—
1978–79		5	—
1978–79	Crystal Palace	5	—
1979–80		—	—
1979–80	*Port Vale*	17	6
1980–81	Crystal Palace	19	5
1980–81	QPR	8	2
1981–82		7	—
1981–82	*Port Vale*	6	4
1982–83	QPR	40	16
1983–84		8	—
1983–84	*Fulham*	5	1
1984–85	QPR	—	—
1984–85	Fulham	13	6
1985–86		7	3
1985–86	Leicester C	21	6

SEAMAN, David

Born Rotherham 19.9.63. Ht 6 3 Wt 13 0
Goalkeeper. From Apprentice. England
Under-21.

1981–82	Leeds U	—	—
1982–83	Peterborough U	38	—

Season	Club	League Appearances/Goals		Season	Club	League Appearances/Goals	

1983–84		45	—
1984–85		8	—
1984–85	Birmingham C	33	—
1985–86		42	—

SEASMAN, John

Born Liverpool 21.2.55.   Ht 5 9   Wt 11 7
Forward. From Apprentice.

1972–73	Tranmere R	2	—
1973–74		6	—
1974–75		9	—
1974–75	Luton T	2	1
1975–76		6	1
1975–76	Millwall	16	4
1976–77		36	14
1977–78		37	7
1978–79		35	9
1979–80		34	1
1980–81	Rotherham U	34	6
1981–82		25	10
1982–83		33	9
1983–84		8	—
1984–85	Cardiff C	12	2
1984–85	*Rochdale*	8	—
1984–85	Chesterfield	10	1
1985–86	Rochdale	30	2

SEGERS, Hans

Born Eindhoven 30.10.61.   Ht 5 11
Wt 12 7½
Goalkeeper. From PSV Eindhoven.

| 1984–85 | Nottingham F | 28 | — |
| 1985–86 | | 11 | — |

SELLARS, Scott

Born Sheffield 27.11.65.   Ht 5 6   Wt 10 0
Midfield. From Apprentice.

1982–83	Leeds U	1	—
1983–84		19	3
1984–85		39	7
1985–86		17	2

SEMLEY, Alan

Born Barnsley 21.2.66.   Ht 6 0½   Wt 11 0
Forward. From Apprentice.

1983–84	Barnsley	4	—
1984–85		—	—
1985–86		—	—

SENDALL, Richard

Born Stamford 10.7.67.   Ht 5 10   Wt 11 6
Forward. From Watford Apprentice.

| 1985–86 | Blackpool | 8 | — |

SENIOR, Steve

Born Sheffield 15.5.63.   Ht 5 8½   Wt 11 4
Defender. From Apprentice.

1980–81	York C	3	—
1981–82		17	1
1982–83		10	1
1983–84		39	1
1984–85		28	—
1984–85	*Darlington*	5	—
1985–86	York C	34	3

SENIOR, Trevor

Born Dorchester 28.11.61.   Ht 6 1½
Wt 12 8
Forward. From Dorchester T.

1981–82	Portsmouth	9	2
1982–83		2	—
1982–83	*Aldershot*	10	7
1983–84	Reading	45	36
1984–85		31	22
1985–86		46	27

SHAKESPEARE, Craig

Born Birmingham 26.10.63.   Ht 5 10
Wt 10 8
Forward. From Apprentice.

All appearances include those as substitute

Season	Club	League Appearances/Goals		Season	Club	League Appearances/Goals	
1981–82	Walsall	—	—	1980–81		4	—
1982–83		31	4	1981–82		29	15
1983–84		46	6	1982–83		41	15
1984–85		41	9	1983–84		28	7
1985–86		32	4	1984–85		36	21
				1985–86		37	19

SHANKLAND, Andy

Born Stoke 8.4.64. Ht 5 8 Wt 9 0
Defender. From Apprentice.

Season	Club	App	Goals
1981–82	Port Vale	12	1
1982–83		4	—
1983–84		7	—
1984–85		—	—
1985–86		2	1

SHANKS, David

Born Bellshill 18.4.62 Ht 6 0 Wt 11 7
Midfield. From Broxburn Athletic.

Season	Club	App	Goals
1982–83	Cowdenbeath	2	1
1983–84		29	2
1983–84	Clydebank	3	1
1984–85		34	2
1985–86		30	3

SHANNON, Rab

Born Bellshill 20.4.66. Ht 5 11 Wt 11 8
Defender. From St Columba's B.C. Scotland
Youth.

Season	Club	App	Goals
1982–83	Dundee	—	—
1983–84		6	—
1984–85		3	—
1985–86		33	—

SHARP, Graeme

Born Glasgow 16.10.60. Ht 6 1 Wt 11 8
Forward. From Eastercraigs.
Scotland 6 full caps.

Season	Club	App	Goals
1978–79	Dumbarton	6	1
1979–80		34	16
1979–80	Everton	2	—

SHARPE, John

Born Portsmouth 9.10.57. Ht 5 10½
Wt 11 12
Defender. From Apprentice.

Season	Club	App	Goals
1975–76	Southampton	—	—
1976–77		11	—
1977–78		10	—
1978–79		—	—
1978–79	Gillingham	37	—
1979–80		36	1
1980–81		26	—
1981–82		39	1
1982–83		39	—
1983–84		16	—
1984–85		1	—
1984–85	Southampton	—	—
1985–86	Swansea C	5	—

SHAW, Adrian

Born Easington 13.4.66. Ht 5 9 Wt 11 3
Forward. From Apprentice.

Season	Club	App	Goals
1983–84	Nottingham F	—	—
1984–85	Halifax T	21	1
1985–86		34	—

SHAW, Chris

Born Bournemouth 23.8.65. Ht 5 6 Wt 9 8
Forward. From Amateur.

Season	Club	App	Goals
1982–83	Bournemouth	2	—
1983–84		3	—
1983–84	*Weymouth*	Not known	
1984–85	Bournemouth	12	—
1985–86		8	2

Season	Club	League Appearances/Goals		Season	Club	League Appearances/Goals	

SHAW, Gary

Born Birmingham 21.1.61.   Ht 5 10
Wt 11 13½
Forward. From Apprentice.
England Under-21.

1978–79	Aston Villa	3	—
1979–80		28	9
1980–81		40	18
1981–82		26	9
1982–83		39	17
1983–84		12	5
1984–85		—	—
1985–86		12	1

SHAW, Graham

Born Stoke 7.6.67.   Ht 5 7   Wt 10 3
Forward. From Apprentice.

| 1985–86 | Stoke C | 20 | 5 |

SHAW, John

Born Stirling 4.2.54.   Ht 6 1¾   Wt 13 13¾
Goalkeeper. From Apprentice.

1970–71	Leeds U	—	—
1971–72		—	—
1972–73		—	—
1973–74		—	—
1974–75	Bristol C	—	—
1975–76		—	—
1976–77		32	—
1977–78		42	—
1978–79		40	—
1979–80		28	—
1980–81		5	—
1981–82		15	—
1982–83		46	—
1983–84		46	—
1984–85		41	—
1985–86	Exeter C	44	—

SHAW, Peter

Born Northolt 9.1.56.   Ht 6 2   Wt 13 8
Defender. From Staines T.

1977–78	Charlton Ath	7	—
1978–79		34	1
1979–80		28	3
1980–81		36	1
1981–82		—	—
1981–82	*Exeter C*	3	—
1981–82	Gillingham	16	—
1982–83		29	—
1983–84		33	1
1984–85		41	1
1985–86		24	—

SHEARER, David

Born Inverness 16.10.58.   Ht 5 10   Wt 12 0
Forward. From Inverness Clachnacuddin.

1977–78	Middlesbrough	4	2
1978–79		5	1
1979–80		5	1
1979–80	*Wigan Ath*	11	9
1980–81	Middlesbrough	30	7
1981–82		24	3
1982–83		29	9
1983–84	Grimsby T	4	—
1984–85	Gillingham	23	12
1985–86		23	9

SHEARER, Duncan

Born Fort William 28.8.62.   Ht 5 10
Wt 10 9
Forward. From Inverness Clach.

1983–84	Chelsea	—	—
1984–85		—	—
1985–86		2	1
1985–86	Huddersfield T	8	7

SHEARER, Peter

Born Birmingham 4.2.67.   Ht 6 0   Wt 11 6
Midfield. From Apprentice.

| 1984–85 | Birmingham C | 4 | — |
| 1985–86 | | — | — |

Season	Club	League Appearances/Goals		Season	Club	League Appearances/Goals	

SHEEDY, Kevin

Born Builth Wells 21.10.59.   Ht 5 9
Wt 10 11
Midfield. From Apprentice.
Eire Under-21, 8 full caps.

Season	Club	App	Goals
1975–76	Hereford U	1	—
1976–77		16	1
1977–78		34	3
1978–79	Liverpool	—	—
1979–80		—	—
1980–81		1	—
1981–82		2	—
1982–83	Everton	40	11
1983–84		28	4
1984–85		29	11
1985–86		31	5

SHELTON, Gary

Born Nottingham 21.3.58.   Ht 5 7   Wt 100
Midfield. From Apprentice.
England Under-21.

Season	Club	App	Goals
1975–76	Walsall	2	—
1976–77		10	—
1977–78		12	—
1977–78	Aston Villa	—	—
1978–79		19	7
1979–80		4	—
1979–80	*Notts Co*	8	—
1980–81	Aston Villa	—	—
1981–82		1	—
1981–82	Sheffield W	9	1
1982–83		40	4
1983–84		40	5
1984–85		41	4
1985–86		31	1

SHEPHERD, Greig

Born Edinburgh 29.9.60.   Ht 6 1   Wt 120
Forward. From Musselburgh Windsor.

Season	Club	App	Goals
1978–79	Norwich C	—	—
1979–80		1	—
1980–81		—	—
1981–82		15	2
1982–83		—	—

From Eastern, Hong Kong

Season	Club	App	Goals
1983–84	Southend U	39	8
1984–85		14	3
1984–85	Peterborough U	27	7
1985–86		25	6

SHEPHERD, Tony

Born Glasgow 16.11.66.   Ht 5 9   Wt 107
Midfield. From Celtic B.C. Scotland Schools,
Youth.

Season	Club	App	Goals
1983–84	Celtic	—	—
1984–85		—	—
1985–86		1	—

SHERIDAN, John

Born Manchester 1.10.64.   Ht 5 9   Wt 10 8
Midfield. Local. Eire Youth.

Season	Club	App	Goals
1981–82	Leeds U	—	—
1982–83		27	2
1983–84		11	1
1984–85		42	6
1985–86		32	4

SHERLOCK, Steve

Born Birmingham 10.5.59.   Ht 5 9   Wt 11 8
Defender. From Manchester C. Apprentice.

Season	Club	App	Goals
1978–79	Luton T	2	—
1979–80	Stockport Co	39	2
1980–81		41	2
1981–82		46	3
1982–83		35	—
1983–84		26	—
1984–85		33	—
1985–86		25	—

SHERINGHAM, Teddy

Born Highams Park 2.4.66.   Ht 5 8   Wt 11 7
Forward. From Apprentice. England Youth.

Season	Club	App	Goals
1983–84	Millwall	7	1
1984–85		—	—
1984–85	*Aldershot*	5	—
1985–86	Millwall	18	4

Season	Club	League Appearances/Goals		Season	Club	League Appearances/Goals	

SHERWOOD, Steve

Born Selby 10.12.53.   Ht 6 4   Wt 14 7
Goalkeeper. From Apprentice.

1970–71	Chelsea	—	—
1971–72		1	—
1972–73		3	—
1973–74		—	—
1973–74	*Brighton*	—	—
1973–74	*Millwall*	1	—
1973–74	*Brentford*	16	—
1974–75	Chelsea	—	—
1974–75	*Brentford*	46	—
1975–76	Chelsea	12	—
1976–77		—	—
1976–77	Watford	8	—
1977–78		16	—
1978–79		16	—
1979–80		4	—
1980–81		22	—
1981–82		41	—
1982–83		42	—
1983–84		40	1
1984–85		9	—
1985–86		2	—

SHILTON, Peter

Born Leicester 18.9.49.   Ht 6 0   Wt 14 0
Goalkeeper. From Apprentice. England
Schools, Youth, Under-23, 81 full caps.
Football League.

1965–66	Leicester C	1	—
1966–67		4	—
1967–68		35	1
1968–69		42	—
1969–70		39	—
1970–71		40	—
1971–72		37	—
1972–73		41	—
1973–74		42	—
1974–75		5	—
1974–75	Stoke C	25	—
1975–76		42	—
1976–77		40	—
1977–78		3	—
1977–78	Nottingham F	37	—
1978–79		42	—

1979–80		42	—
1980–81		40	—
1981–82		41	—
1982–83	Southampton	39	—
1983–84		42	—
1984–85		41	—
1985–86		37	—

SHINNERS, Paul

Born Westminster 8.1.59.
Forward, From Fisher Ath.

1984–85	Gillingham	4	—
1984–85	*Colchester U*	6	1
1985–86	Orient	34	16

SHIPLEY, George

Born Newcastle 7.3.59.   Ht 5 8   Wt 10 8
Midfield. From Apprentice.

1976–77	Southampton	—	—
1977–78		—	—
1978–79		—	—
1978–79	*Reading*	12	1
1979–80	Southampton	3	—
1979–80	*Blackpool*	—	—
1979–80	Lincoln C	23	2
1980–81		46	8
1981–82		43	11
1982–83		38	7
1983–84		42	4
1984–85		31	7
1985–86	Charlton Ath	37	4

SHIRTLIFF, Peter

Born Barnsley 6.4.61.   Ht 5 11   Wt 12 2
Defender. From Apprentice.

1978–79	Sheffield W	26	1
1979–80		3	—
1980–81		28	—
1981–82		31	2
1982–83		8	—
1983–84		36	1
1984–85		35	—
1985–86		21	—

Season	Club	League Appearances/Goals		Season	Club	League Appearances/Goals	

SHOTTON, Malcolm

Born Newcastle 16.2.57.   Ht 6 3   Wt 13 12
Defender. From Apprentice.

Season	Club	App	Goals
1974–75	Leicester C	—	—
1975–76		—	—
From Nuneaton Bor			
1980–81	Oxford U	38	5
1981–82		40	4
1982–83		46	1
1983–84		43	1
1984–85		42	1
1985–86		42	

SHOULDER, Alan

Born Bishop Auckland 4.2.53.   Ht 5 5½
Wt 10 5
Forward. From Blyth Spartans.

Season	Club	App	Goals
1978–79	Newcastle U	24	11
1979–80		41	20
1980–81		32	4
1981–82		10	—
1982–83	Carlisle U	42	21
1983–84		40	8
1984–85		30	3
1985–86	Hartlepool U	36	17

SHRUBB, Paul

Born Guildford 1.8.55.   Ht 5 8   Wt 10 4
Defender. From Apprentice.

Season	Club	App	Goals
1972–73	Fulham	1	—
1973–74		—	—
1974–75		—	—
From Hellenic, South Africa			
1976–77	Brentford	13	2
1977–78		45	1
1978–79		39	2
1979–80		39	1
1980–81		42	2
1981–82		4	—
1982–83	Aldershot	39	1
1983–84		33	
1984–85		44	2
1985–86		38	1

SHUTE, Phil

Born Darlington 15.12.53.
Defender. From Shildon.

Season	Club	App	Goals
1984–85	Darlington	—	—
1985–86		2	—

SHUTT, Carl

Born Sheffield 10.10.61.   Ht 5 10   Wt 11 10
Forward. From Spalding U.

Season	Club	App	Goals
1984–85	Sheffield W	—	—
1985–86		19	9

SHUTT, Steve

Born Barnsley 29.11.64.   Ht 5 10   Wt 10 4
Midfield. From Apprentice.

Season	Club	App	Goals
1982–83	Barnsley	1	—
1983–84		—	—
1984–85	Scunthorpe U	2	1
1985–86		—	—

SIDDALL, Barry

Born Ellesmere Port 12.9.54.   Ht 6 1   Wt 14 2
Goalkeeper. From Apprentice.
England Youth.

Season	Club	App	Goals
1971–72	Bolton W	—	—
1972–73		4	—
1973–74		42	—
1974–75		42	—
1975–76		42	—
1976–77		7	—
1976–77	Sunderland	34	—
1977–78		42	—
1978–79		41	—
1979–80		12	—
1980–81		15	—
1980–81	*Darlington*	8	—
1981–82	Sunderland	23	—
1982–83	Port Vale	33	—
1983–84		39	—
1983–84	*Blackpool*	7	—
1984–85	Port Vale	9	—

Season	Club	League Appearances/Goals		Season	Club	League Appearances/Goals

Season	Club	App	Goals
1984–85	Stoke C	15	—
1985–86		5	—
1985–86	*Tranmere R*	12	—
1985–86	*Manchester C*	6	—

SILKMAN, Barry

Born London 29.6.52.   Ht 5 8   Wt 10 13
Midfield. From Barnet.

Season	Club	App	Goals
1974–75	Hereford U	15	1
1975–76		22	1
1976–77	Crystal Palace	23	5
1977–78		24	2
1978–79		1	—
1978–79	Plymouth Arg	14	2
1978–79	*Luton T*	3	—
1978–79	Manchester C	12	3
1979–80		7	—
1980–81	Brentford	14	1
1980–81	QPR	23	2
1981–82		—	—
1981–82	Orient	35	5
1982–83		22	2
1983–84		41	4
1984–85		42	3
1985–86	Southend U	40	1

SIMMONITE, Gordon

Born Sheffield 25.4.57.   Ht 5 9   Wt 11 4
Defender. Local.

Season	Club	App	Goals
1976–77	Sheffield W	1	—
1977–78		—	—
From Boston U			
1980–81	Blackpool	18	—
1981–82		29	1
1982–83		16	—
1982–83	Lincoln C	25	—
1983–84		35	—
1984–85		12	—
1985–86		—	—

SIMMONDS, Lyndon

Born Pontypool 11.11.66.   Ht 5 4   Wt 9 10
Forward. From Apprentice. Wales Youth.

Season	Club	App	Goals
1984–85	Leeds U	1	—
1985–86		8	3

SIMMONS, Tony

Born Sheffield 9.2.65.   Ht 5 11   Wt 10 8
Forward. From Apprentice. England Youth.

Season	Club	App	Goals
1981–82	Sheffield W	1	—
1982–83		3	—
1983–84		—	—
1983–84	QPR	—	—
1983–84	*Rotherham U*	18	8
1984–85	Rotherham U	38	12
1985–86		38	7

SIMPSON, Neil

Born London 15.11.61   Ht 5 10   Wt 11 6
Midfield. From Middlefield Wasps.
Scotland Youth, Under-21, 2 full caps.

Season	Club	App	Goals
1978–79	Aberdeen	—	—
1979–80		—	—
1980–81		16	2
1981–82		29	4
1982–83		33	5
1983–84		24	2
1984–85		33	4
1985–86		22	1

SIMPSON, Paul

Born Carlisle 26.7.66.   Ht 5 6   Wt 11 2½
Forward. From Apprentice. England Youth,
Under-21.

Season	Club	App	Goals
1983–84	Manchester C	—	—
1984–85		10	6
1985–86		37	8

SIMS, Steve

Born Lincoln 2.7.57.   Ht 6 1½   Wt 13 9
Defender. From Apprentice. England
Under-21, 'B'.

Season	Club	App	Goals
1974–75	Leicester C	—	—
1975–76		10	—
1976–77		32	1
1977–78		29	2
1978–79		8	–
1978–79	Watford	14	1
1979–80		34	2
1980–81		37	1

Season	Club	League Appearances/Goals		Season	Club	League Appearances/Goals	

1981–82	....	17	—
1982–83	....	28	—
1983–84	....	22	—
1984–85	....	—	—
1984–85	Notts Co	34	2
1985–86	....	41	—

SINCLAIR, Nick

Born Manchester 3.1.60.   Ht 5 11   Wt 11 6
Defender. Local.

1978–79	Oldham Ath	1	—
1979–80	....	—	—
1980–81	....	22	—
1981–82	....	9	—
1982–83	....	24	1
1983–84	....	18	—
1984–85	....	1	—
1984–85	*Wolverhampton W*	1	—
1984–85	Rochdale	—	—
1984–85	Tranmere R	16	—
1985–86	....	6	1

SINCLAIR, Ron

Born Stirling 19.11.64.   Ht 5 10   Wt 11 9
Goalkeeper. From Apprentice.

1982–83	Nottingham F	—	—
1983–84	....	—	—
1983–84	*Wrexham*	11	—
1984–85	Nottingham F	—	—
1984–85	*Derby Co*	—	—
1985–86	Nottingham F	—	—
1985–86	*Sheffield U*	—	—
1985–86	*Leeds U*	—	—

SINGLETON, Martin

Born Banbury 2.8.63.   Ht 5 8   Wt 10 12
Midfield. From Apprentice. England Youth.

1980–81	Coventry C	—	—
1981–82	....	3	1
1982–83	....	5	—
1983–84	....	13	—
1984–85	....	2	—
1984–85	Bradford C	17	—
1985–86	....	36	2

SINNOTT, Lee

Born Pelsall 12.7.65.   Ht 6 1   Wt 11 9
Defender. From Apprentice. England
Youth, Under-21.

1981–82	Walsall	4	—
1982–83	....	32	2
1983–84	....	4	—
1983–84	Watford	20	—
1984–85	....	30	—
1985–86	....	18	2

SINTON, Andy

Born Newcastle. 19.3.66.   Ht 5 7   Wt 10 7
Midfield. From Apprentice. England
Schools.

1982–83	Cambridge U	13	5
1983–84	....	34	6
1984–85	....	26	2
1985–86	....	20	—
1985–86	Brentford	26	3

SITTON John

Born Hackney 21.10.59.   Ht 6 0½   Wt 12 2
Defender. From Apprentice.

1978–79	Chelsea	12	—
1979–80	....	1	—
1979–80	Millwall	13	1
1980–81	....	32	—
1981–82	....	—	—
1981–82	Gillingham	30	2
1982–83	....	30	—
1983–84	....	42	3
1984–85	....	5	—
1985–86	Orient	39	—

SIVEBAEK, John

Born Vejle 25.10.61.
Midfield. From Vejle. Denmark full caps.

| 1985–86 | Manchester U .... | 3 | — |

Season	Club	League Appearances/Goals		

SKIPPER, Peter

Born Hull 11.4.58.　Ht 5 11　Wt 12 5
Defender. Local.

1978–79	Hull C	17	2
1979–80		6	—
1979–80	*Scunthorpe U*	1	—
1980–81	Darlington	46	2
1981–82		45	2
1982–83	Hull C	46	4
1983–84		46	1
1984–85		46	5
1985–86		40	1

SLACK, Trevor

Born Peterborough 26.9.62.　Ht 6 1　Wt 13 0
Defender. From Apprentice.

1980–81	Peterborough U	35	4
1981–82		7	2
1982–83		40	1
1983–84		39	3
1984–85		41	3
1985–86		40	5

SLATTER, Neil

Born Cardiff 30.5.64.　Ht 5 11　Wt 10 9
Defender. From Apprentice.
Wales Under-21, 14 full caps.

1980–81	Bristol R	4	—
1981–82		28	1
1982–83		36	—
1983–84		43	1
1984–85		37	2
1985–86	Oxford U	22	2

SLAVEN, Bernie

Born Paisley 13.11.60.　Ht 5 10　Wt 10 10
Forward.

1981–82	Morton	13	1
1982–83		9	—
1983–84	Airdrie	2	—

1983–84	Queen of the South	2	—
1983–84	Albion R	3	—
1984–85		39	27
1985–86	Middlesbrough	32	8

SMALLEY, Mark

Born Newark 2.1.65.　Ht 5 11　Wt 11 6
Defender. From Apprentice. England
Youth.

1982–83	Nottingham F	1	—
1983–84		1	—
1984–85		1	—
1985–86		—	—
1985–86	*Birmingham C*	7	—

SMALLEY, Paul

Born Nottingham 17.11.66.　Ht 5 11　Wt 11 0
Defender. From Apprentice.

| 1984–85 | Notts Co | — | — |
| 1985–86 | | 26 | — |

SMALLWOOD, Neil

Born York 3.12.66.　Ht 6 1　Wt 11 10
Goalkeeper.

| 1985–86 | York C | — | — |

SMART, Gary

Born Bristol 8.12.63.
Midfield.

| 1985–86 | Bristol R | 3 | — |

SMART, Jason

Born Rochdale 15.2.69.
Defender. From YTS.

| 1985–86 | Rochdale | 1 | — |

Season	Club	League Appearances/Goals		Season	Club	League Appearances/Goals

SMELT, Lee

Born Edmonton 13.3.58. Ht 6 1   Wt 13 3
Goalkeeper. From Amateur.

Season	Club	App	Goals
1975–76	Colchester U	—	—
From Thanet U and Gravesend & N			
1980–81	Nottingham F	1	—
1981–82	Peterborough U	5	—
1981–82	Halifax T	34	—
1982–83		41	—
1983–84		44	—
1984–85	Cardiff C	13	—
1984–85	Exeter C	13	—
1985–86	Cardiff C	24	—

SMEULDERS, John

Born Hackney 28.3.57. Ht 5 10   Wt 13 0
Goalkeeper. From Appentice.
England Youth.

Season	Club	App	Goals
1974–75	Orient	—	—
1975–76		—	—
1976–77		—	—
1977–78		—	—
1978–79		—	—
1979–80	Bournemouth	12	—
1980–81		2	—
From Trowbridge and Weymouth			
1983–84	Bournemouth	1	—
1984–85		40	—
1985–86		34	—

SMILLIE, Neil

Born Barnsley 19.7.58. Ht 5 6   Wt 10 7
Forward. From Apprentice.

Season	Club	App	Goals
1975–76	Crystal Palace	—	—
1976–77		1	—
1976–77	Brentford	3	—
1977–78	Crystal Palace	1	—
1978–79		8	1
1979–80		8	1
1980–81		24	2
1981–82		41	3
1982–83	Brighton	25	—
1983–84		26	2
1984–85		24	—
1985–86	Watford	16	3

SMITH, Alan

Born Birmingham 21.11.62. Ht 6 2½
Wt 12 10
Forward. From Alvechurch.

Season	Club	App	Goals
1982–83	Leicester C	39	13
1983–84		40	15
1984–85		39	12
1985–86		40	19

SMITH, Alan

Born Sheffield 7.12.66. Ht 6 0   Wt 11 2
Defender. From Apprentice.

Season	Club	App	Goals
1984–85	Sheffield W	—	—
1985–86		—	—

SMITH, Bobby

Born Dalkeith 21.12.53. Ht 5 7   Wt 11 7¾
Midfield. From Musselburgh W.

Season	Club	App	Goals
1971–72	Hibernian	—	—
1972–73		9	—
1973–74		11	2
1974–75		21	3
1975–76		23	6
1976–77		36	8
1977–78		35	—
1978–79		17	—
1978–79	Leicester C	17	6
1979–80		35	12
1980–81		19	1
1981–82		4	—
1981–82	Peterborough U	5	—
1982–83		26	1
1982–83	Hibernian	5	1
1983–84	Leicester C	36	—
1984–85		30	—
1985–86		14	1

SMITH, Brian

Born Sheffield 27.10.66. Ht 5 9½   Wt 11 2
Defender. Local.

Season	Club	App	Goals
1984–85	Sheffield U	6	—
1985–86		8	—

All appearances include those as substitute

Season	Club	League Appearances/Goals		Season	Club	League Appearances/Goals	

SMITH, Colin

Born Ruddington 3.11.58.   Ht 6 0
Wt 12 10
Defender. Local.

1981–82	Nottingham F	—	—
1982–83	Norwich C	4	—
From Sea Bee, Hong Kong			
1983–84	Cardiff C	34	2
1984–85		16	1
1984–85	Aldershot	17	—
1985–86		34	1

SMITH, Chris

Born Hampshire 28.3.66.
Defender.

1984–85	Bristol R	1	—
1985–86		—	—

SMITH, David

Born Glasgow 28.10.65.   Ht 6 0   Wt 11 0
Defender. From Leven Valley.

1984–85	Clydebank	9	1
1985–86		1	—

SMITH, Gary

Born Harlow 3.12.68.
Midfield. From Apprentice.

1985–86	Fulham	1	—

SMITH, Gordon

Born Ayr 29.12.54.   Ht 5 11   Wt 12 0
Forward. Local. Scotland Under-21.

1972–73	Kilmarnock	34	4
1973–74		35	11
1974–75		33	5
1975–76		25	9
1976–77		35	7
1977–78		1	—

1977–78	Rangers	35	20
1978–79		33	11
1979–80		30	4
1980–81	Brighton	38	10
1981–82		27	2
1982–83		29	6
1982–83	*Rangers*	2	—
1983–84	Brighton	15	4
1983–84	Manchester C	9	1
1984–85		32	12
1985–86		1	—
1985–86	Oldham Ath	15	—

SMITH, Henry

Born Lanark 10.3.56.   Ht 6 2   Wt 12 0
Goalkeeper. From school.

1978–79	Leeds U	—	—
1979–80		—	—
1980–81		—	—
1981–82	Hearts	33	—
1982–83		39	—
1983–84		36	—
1984–85		36	—
1985–86		36	—

SMITH, Jim

Born Elderslie 14.5.61.   Ht 6 1   Wt 11 4
Defender. From Greenock Juniors.

1980–81	Dundee	—	—
1981–82		17	1
1982–83		36	1
1983–84		34	—
1984–85		23	1
1985–86		32	—

SMITH, Kevan

Born Eaglescliffe 13.12.59.   Ht 6 3   Wt 11 9
Defender. From Stockton.

1979–80	Darlington	35	1
1980–81		39	2
1981–82		45	1
1982–83		46	3
1983–84		44	2
1984–85		36	2
1985–86	Rotherham U	43	3

Season	Club	League Appearances/Goals		Season	Club	League Appearances/Goals	

SMITH, Kevin

Born Wallsend 20.4.65.   Ht 5 8   Wt 11 5
Forward. From Apprentice.

Season	Club	App	Goals
1982–83	Cambridge U	11	2
1983–84		25	2
1984–85		2	—
1984–85	Exeter C	26	2
1985–86	Torquay U	23	1

SMITH, Lindsay

Born Enfield 18.9.54.   Ht 5 11   Wt 12 0
Defender. From Apprentice.

Season	Club	App	Goals
1970–71	Colchester U	1	—
1971–72		17	3
1972–73		31	1
1973–74		34	1
1974–75		43	1
1975–76		41	4
1976–77		45	6
1977–78		—	—
1977–78	*Charlton Ath*	1	—
1977–78	*Millwall*	5	—
1977–78	Cambridge U	27	1
1978–79		40	—
1979–80		35	2
1980–81		39	2
1981–82		28	2
1981–82	*Lincoln C*	5	—
1982–83	Cambridge U	5	—
1982–83	Plymouth Arg	34	1
1983–84		42	4
1984–85	Millwall	41	5
1985–86		14	—

SMITH, Mark

Born Sheffield 21.3.60.   Ht 6 1   Wt 12 2
Defender. From Apprentice.
England Under-21.

Season	Club	App	Goals
1977–78	Sheffield W	2	—
1978–79		21	—
1979–80		44	9

Season	Club	App	Goals
1980–81		41	1
1981–82		41	—
1982–83		41	2
1983–84		27	2
1984–85		36	2
1985–86		13	—

SMITH, Mark

Born Sheffield 19.12.61.   Ht 5 9   Wt 12 0
Forward.

Season	Club	App	Goals
1979–80	Sheffield U	—	—
1980–81		—	—
1981–82		—	—
From Local			
1985–86	Scunthorpe U	1	—

SMITH, Mick

Born Sunderland 28.10.58.   Ht 6 0½
Wt 11 9
Defender. From Lambton St. BC.

Season	Club	App	Goals
1977–78	Lincoln C	5	—
1978–79		20	—
1979–80		—	—
1979–80	Wimbledon	20	—
1980–81		45	2
1981–82		39	2
1982–83		24	4
1983–84		24	3
1984–85		23	—
1984–85	*Aldershot*	7	—
1985–86	Wimbledon	24	3

SMITH, Nigel

Born Bath 12.1.66.   Ht 6 0   Wt 10 9
Forward. From Apprentice.

Season	Club	App	Goals
1983–84	Bristol C	—	—
1984–85		—	—
1984–85	*Exeter C*	—	—
1985–86	Bristol C	—	—

Season	Club	League Appearances/Goals		Season	Club	League Appearances/Goals	

SMITH, Nigel

Born Manchester 22.4.59.   Ht 6 0   Wt 11 2
Midfield. From Blackburn R. Amateur.

Season	Club	App	Goals
1979–80	Stockport Co	—	—
1980–81		2	—
1981–82		31	—
1982–83		40	1
1983–84		20	—
1984–85		27	—
1985–86		3	—

SMITH, Paul

Born Rotherham 9.11.64.   Ht 5 10½
Wt 10 9
Forward. From Apprentice.

Season	Club	App	Goals
1982–83	Sheffield U	7	—
1983–84		3	—
1984–85		8	1
1985–86		18	—
1985–86	*Stockport Co*	7	5

SMITH, Paul

Born London 5.10.67.   Ht 5 8   Wt 9 9
Forward. From Apprentice.

Season	Club	App	Goals
1985–86	Arsenal	—	—

SMITH, Richard

Born Reading 22.10.67.   Ht 5 7   Wt 10 7
Defender. From Apprentice.

Season	Club	App	Goals
1984–85	Wolverhampton W	—	—
1985–86		1	—

SMITH, Tony

Born Sunderland 20.2.57.   Ht 5 10   Wt 12 1
Defender. From Amateur.

Season	Club	App	Goals
1975–76	Newcastle U	—	—
1976–77		—	—
1977–78		2	—

Season	Club	App	Goals
1978–79		—	—
1978–79	Peterborough U	15	2
1979–80		9	—
1980–81		5	—
1981–82		39	3
1982–83	Halifax T	44	2
1983–84		39	1
1984–85	Hartlepool U	44	2
1985–86		46	3

SNEDDON, Alan

Born Baillieston 12.3.58.   Ht 5 11   Wt 12 3
Defender. From Larkhall Thistle.
Scotland Under-21.

Season	Club	App	Goals
1977–78	Celtic	15	—
1978–79		4	—
1979–80		32	1
1980–81		15	—
1980–81	Hibernian	14	—
1981–82		36	—
1982–83		36	—
1983–84		35	1
1984–85		36	2
1985–86		31	2

SNODIN, Glynn

Born Rotherham 14.2.60.   Ht 5 6   Wt 9 5
Forward. From Apprentice.

Season	Club	App	Goals
1976–77	Doncaster R	4	—
1977–78		22	2
1978–79		34	3
1979–80		41	1
1980–81		44	3
1981–82		40	7
1982–83		38	14
1983–84		43	13
1984–85		43	18
1985–86	Sheffield W	28	1

SNODIN, Ian

Born Rotherham 15.8.63.   Ht 5 7   Wt 8 11½
Midfield. From Apprentice. England Youth,
Under-21.

All appearances include those as substitute

Season	Club	League Appearances/Goals

1979–80	Doncaster R	9	1
1980–81		32	2
1981–82		33	2
1982–83		34	3
1983–84		39	9
1984–85		41	8
1985–86	Leeds U	37	5

SOUNESS, Graeme

Born Edinburgh 6.5.53.   Ht 5 11   Wt 12 13
Midfield. From Apprentice.
Scotland Schools, Under-23, 52 full caps.

1970–71	Tottenham H	—	—
1971–72		—	—
1972–73		—	—
1972–73	Middlesbrough	11	—
1973–74		35	7
1974–75		38	7
1975–76		35	3
1976–77		38	2
1977–78		19	3
1977–78	Liverpool	15	2
1978–79		41	8
1979–80		41	1
1980–81		37	6
1981–82		35	5
1982–83		41	9
1983–84		37	7
1984–85	Sampdoria	28	5
1985–86		28	3

SOUTHALL, Neville

Born Llandudno 16.9.58.   Ht 6 1   Wt 12 1
Goalkeeper. From Winsford.
Wales Under-21, 27 full caps.

1980–81	Bury	39	—
1981–82	Everton	26	—
1982–83		17	—
1982–83	*Port Vale*	9	—
1983–84	Everton	35	—
1984–85		42	—
1985–86		32	—

SPACKMAN, Nigel

Born Romsey 2.12.60.   Ht 6 1   Wt 12 4
Midfield. From Andover.

1980–81	Bournemouth	44	3
1981–82		35	3
1982–83		40	4
1983–84	Chelsea	40	3
1984–85		42	1
1985–86		39	7

SPARROW, Brian

Born London 24.6.62.   Ht 5 7   Wt 10 2
Forward. From Apprentice.

1979–80	Arsenal	—	—
1980–81		—	—
1981–82		—	—
1982–83		—	—
1982–83	*Wimbledon*	17	1
1983–84	Arsenal	2	—
1983–84	*Millwall*	5	2
1983–84	*Gillingham*	5	1
1984–85	Crystal Palace	38	2
1985–86		12	—

SPEARING, Tony

Born Romford 7.10.64.   Ht 5 9½   Wt 10 12
Defender. From Apprentice. England
Youth.

1982–83	Norwich C	—	—
1983–84		4	—
1984–85		—	—
1984–85	*Stoke C*	9	—
1984–85	*Oxford U*	5	—
1985–86	Norwich C	8	—

SPEEDIE, David

Born Glenrothes 20.2.60.   Ht 5 7   Wt 11 0
Midfield. From Amateur. Scotland Under-
21, 5 full caps.

Season	Club	League Appearances/Goals	
1978–79	Barnsley	10	—
1979–80		13	—
1980–81	Darlington	44	4
1981–82		44	17
1982–83	Chelsea	34	7
1983–84		37	13
1984–85		35	10
1985–86		34	14

SPEIGHT, Mick

Born Upton 1.11.51.   Ht 5 10   Wt 12 12
Midfield. From Apprentice. England 'B'.

Season	Club	League Appearances/Goals	
1969–70	Sheffield U	—	—
1970–71		—	—
1971–72		4	—
1972–73		9	—
1973–74		24	1
1974–75		33	2
1975–76		19	—
1976–77		3	—
1977–78		33	3
1978–79		39	2
1979–80		35	6
1980–81	Blackburn R	38	4
1981–82		13	—
1982–83	Grimsby T	13	—
1982–83	*Bury*	—	—
1983–84	Grimsby T	25	2
1984–85	Chester C	30	1
1985–86		10	—

SPEIRS, Gardner

Born Airdrie 14.4.63   Ht 5 8   Wt 10 0
Forward. From St Mirren B.C. Scotland Youth.

Season	Club	League Appearances/Goals	
1979–80	St Mirren	—	—
1980–81		2	—
1981–82		3	—
1982–83		1	—
1983–84		10	—
1984–85		17	6
1985–86		31	7

SPIERS, Alan

Born Oxford 2.10.66.   Ht 5 9   Wt 10 11
Defender. From Apprentice.

Season	Club	League Appearances/Goals	
1984–85	West Ham U	—	—
1985–86		—	—

SPINK, Nigel

Born Chelmsford 8.8.58.   Ht 6 1   Wt 13 10
Goalkeeper. From Chelmsford C.
England, 1 full cap.

Season	Club	League Appearances/Goals	
1976–77	Aston Villa	—	—
1977–78		—	—
1978–79		—	—
1979–80		1	—
1980–81		—	—
1981–82		—	—
1982–83		22	—
1983–84		28	—
1984–85		19	—
1985–86		31	—

SPOONER, Steve

Born London 25.1.61.   Ht 5 11   Wt 12 3
Midfield. From Apprentice.

Season	Club	League Appearances/Goals	
1978–79	Derby Co	1	—
1979–80		1	—
1980–81		2	—
1981–82		4	—
1981–82	Halifax T	29	2
1982–83		43	11
1983–84	Chesterfield	20	3
1984–85		41	6
1985–86		32	5

SPRIGGS, Steve

Born Doncaster 16.2.56.   Ht 5 3   Wt 10 2
Midfield. From Apprentice.

Season	Club	League Appearances/Goals	
1972–73	Huddersfield T	—	—
1973–74		—	—
1974–75		4	—

Season	Club	League Appearances/Goals		Season	Club	League Appearances/Goals	

1975–76	Cambridge U	45	4
1976–77		41	9
1977–78		38	5
1978–79		40	2
1979–80		40	7
1980–81		41	9
1981–82		33	7
1982–83		18	1
1983–84		28	2
1984–85		29	2
1985–86		29	5

SPRING, Andy

Born Newcastle 17.11.65.   Ht 5 10½
Wt 12 4
Defender. From Apprentice.

1983–84	Coventry C	1	—
1984–85		4	—
1985–86	Bristol R	19	—
1985–86	*Cardiff C*	1	—

SPROSON, Phil

Born Trent Vale 13.10.59.   Ht 6 0   Wt 12 0
Defender. From Amateur.

1977–78	Port Vale	2	—
1978–79		23	—
1979–80		39	3
1980–81		44	1
1981–82		42	6
1982–83		42	4
1983–84		38	2
1984–85		44	3
1985–86		44	4

STAFF, Paul

Born Durham 30.8.62.   Ht 5 9   Wt 10 12
Forward. From Apprentice.

1979–80	Hartlepool U	6	—
1980–81		3	—
1981–82		27	5
1982–83		29	4
1983–84		33	5
1984–85	Aldershot	16	5
1985–86		21	6

STAINROD, Simon

Born Sheffield 1.2.59.   Ht 5 10   Wt 12 9
Forward. From Apprentice. England Youth.

1975–76	Sheffield U	7	2
1976–77		21	3
1977–78		25	6
1978–79		14	3
1978–79	Oldham Ath	14	5
1979–80		37	11
1980–81		18	5
1980–81	QPR	15	4
1981–82		39	17
1982–83		31	9
1983–84		41	13
1984–85		19	5
1984–85	Sheffield W	9	1
1985–86		6	1
1985–86	Aston Villa	30	10

STANCLIFFE, Paul

Born Sheffield 5.5.58.   Ht 6 2   Wt 12 13
Defender. From Apprentice.

1975–76	Rotherham U	42	2
1976–77		46	—
1977–78		32	3
1978–79		33	—
1979–80		33	1
1980–81		44	—
1981–82		42	2
1982–83		13	—
1983–84	Sheffield U	43	1
1984–85		33	1
1985–86		40	1

STANIFORTH, Gordon

Born Hull 23.3.57.   Ht 5 7   Wt 10 7
Forward. From Apprentice.
England Schools.

1973–74	Hull C	1	—
1974–75		2	1
1975–76		4	—
1976–77		5	1

Season	Club	League Appearances/Goals	
1976–77	York C.	28	3
1977–78		46	12
1978–79		45	15
1979–80		9	3
1979–80	Carlisle U	21	4
1980–81		42	16
1981–82		37	11
1982–83		26	2
1982–83	Plymouth Arg	11	1
1983–84		39	11
1984–85		41	8
1985–86	Newport Co	45	9

STANLEY, Gary

Born Burton 4.3.54. Ht 5 9   Wt 12 6
Midfield. From Apprentice.

Season	Club	League Appearances/Goals	
1972–73	Chelsea	—	—
1973–74		—	—
1974–75		—	—
1975–76		29	3
1976–77		33	6
1977–78		11	1
1978–79		36	5
1979–80	Everton	24	1
1980–81		28	—
1981–82		—	—
1981–82	Swansea C	29	3
1982–83		28	—
1983–84		15	1
1983–84	Portsmouth	12	—
1984–85		29	1
1985–86		6	—

STANNARD, Jim

Born London 6.10.62. Ht 6 0   Wt 13 6
Goalkeeper. Local.

Season	Club	League Appearances/Goals	
1980–81	Fulham	17	—
1981–82		2	—
1982–83		—	—
1983–84		15	—
1984–85		7	—
1984–85	*Charlton Ath*	1	—
1984–85	*Southend U*	17	—
1985–86	Southend U	46	—

STANTON, Brian

Born Liverpool 7.2.56. Ht 5 7   Wt 10 12
Midfield. Local.

Season	Club	League Appearances/Goals	
1976–77	Bury	2	—
1977–78		42	10
1978–79		39	4
1979–80		—	—
1979–80	Huddersfield T	41	9
1980–81		44	12
1981–82		31	3
1982–83		44	13
1983–84		33	6
1984–85		3	1
1985–86		13	1
1985–86	*Wrexham*	8	—

STAPLETON, Frank

Born Dublin 10.7.56. Ht 5 11   Wt 13 2
Forward. From Apprentice.
Eire Youth, 49 full caps.

Season	Club	League Appearances/Goals	
1973–74	Arsenal	—	—
1974–75		1	—
1975–76		25	4
1976–77		40	13
1977–78		39	13
1978–79		41	17
1979–80		39	14
1980–81		40	14
1981–82	Manchester U.	41	13
1982–83		41	14
1983–84		42	13
1984–85		24	6
1985–86		41	7

STARK, Billy

Born Glasgow 1.12.56. Ht 6 1   Wt 11 4
Midfield. From Anniesland W. Scotland
Under-21.

Season	Club	League Appearances/Goals	
1975–76	St Mirren	21	6
1976–77		35	11
1977–78		33	7
1978–79		32	9
1979–80		36	8

All appearances include those as substitute

Season	Club	League Appearances/Goals		Season	Club	League Appearances/Goals	

1980–81	....	34	5
1981–82	....	33	10
1982–83	....	31	4
1983–84	Aberdeen	14	6
1984–85	....	32	15
1985–86	....	30	8

STATHAM, Derek

Born Wolverhampton 24.3.59.   Ht 5 5½
Wt 11 0
Defender. From Apprentice.
England Youth, Under-21, 'B', 3 full caps.

1976–77	WBA.........................	16	1
1977–78	....	40	—
1978–79	....	39	1
1979–80	....	16	—
1980–81	....	31	—
1981–82	....	35	—
1982–83	....	32	2
1983–84	....	16	—
1984–85	....	30	4
1985–86	....	37	—

STEAD, Mickey

Born West Ham 28.2.57.   Ht 5 7   Wt 11 8
Defender. From Apprentice.

1974–75	Tottenham H	—	—
1975–76	....	4	—
1976–77	....	8	—
1976–77	Swansea C...................	5	1
1977–78	Tottenham H	3	—
1978–79	....	—	—
1978–79	Southend U	38	2
1979–80	....	42	2
1980–81	....	35	—
1981–82	....	39	—
1982–83	....	45	—
1983–84	....	44	1
1984–85	....	37	—
1985–86	....	17	—
1985–86	Doncaster R	20	—

STEBBING, Gary

Born Croydon 11.8.65.   Ht 5 9   Wt 11 0
Midfield. From Apprentice.
England Youth.

1983–84	Crystal Palace	31	2
1984–85	....	24	1
1985–86	....	3	—
1985–86	Southend U	5	—

STEEL, Jim

Born Dumfries 4.12.59.   Ht 6 3   Wt 14 0
Forward. From Apprentice.

1978–79	Oldham Ath	7	4
1979–80	....	33	10
1980–81	....	24	3
1981–82	....	37	7
1982–83	....	7	—
1982–83	Wigan Ath	2	2
1982–83	Wrexham	9	6
1982–83	Port Vale	13	3
1983–84	....	15	3
1983–84	Wrexham	21	—
1984–85	....	45	14
1985–86	....	43	14

STEELE, Tim

Born Coventry 1.2.67.   Ht 5 9   Wt 11 0
Forward. From Apprentice.

| 1985–86 | Shrewsbury T............... | 2 | — |

STEELE, Eric

Born Newcastle 14.5.54.   Ht 6 0   Wt 12 8½
Goalkeeper. From Amateur.

1972–73	Newcastle U	—	—
1973–74	....	—	—
1973–74	Peterborough U............	20	—
1974–75	....	46	—
1975–76	....	46	—
1976–77	....	12	—
1976–77	Brighton.....................	15	—
1977–78	....	38	—
1978–79	....	25	—
1979–80	....	9	—

Season	Club	League Appearances/Goals		Season	Club	League Appearances/Goals

Season	Club	Apps	Goals
1979–80	Watford	28	—
1980–81		20	—
1981–82		1	—
1982–83	*Cardiff C*	7	—
1983–84	Watford	2	—
1984–85	Derby Co	26	—
1985–86		13	—

STEGGLES, Kevin

Born Ditchingham 19.3.61.   Ht 6 0   Wt 12 7
Defender. From Apprentice.

Season	Club	Apps	Goals
1978–79	Ipswich T	—	—
1979–80		—	—
1980–81		6	—
1981–82		18	1
1982–83		9	—
1983–84		5	—
1983–84	*Southend U*	3	—
1984–85	Ipswich T	6	—
1985–86		6	—
1985–86	*Everton*	—	—

STEIN, Brian

Born S. Africa 19.10.57.   Ht 5 10   Wt 11 8
Forward. From Edgware T.
England Under–21, 1 full cap.

Season	Club	Apps	Goals
1977–78	Luton T	24	3
1978–79		34	10
1979–80		42	8
1980–81		42	18
1981–82		42	21
1982–83		21	15
1983–84		42	9
1984–85		42	9
1985–86		33	14

STEIN, Mark

Born S. Africa 28.1.66.   Ht 5 6   Wt 10 0
Midfield. England Youth.

Season	Club	Apps	Goals
1983–84	Luton T	1	—
1984–85		1	—
1985–86		6	—
1985–86	*Aldershot*	2	1

STEPHEN, Ray

Born Aberdeen 9.12.62.   Ht 5 7   Wt 10 4
Forward. From Deeside. Scotland Youth,
Under–21.

Season	Club	Apps	Goals
1980–81	Dundee	23	8
1981–82		24	4
1982–83		29	5
1983–84		20	3
1984–85		35	8
1985–86		33	14

STEPHENS, Archie

Born Liverpool 19.5.54.   Ht 5 11   Wt 12 8
Forward. From Melksham.

Season	Club	Apps	Goals
1981–82	Bristol R	39	11
1982–83		30	6
1983–84		34	13
1984–85		24	10
1984–85	Middlesbrough	9	2
1985–86		28	4

STEPHENS, Kirk

Born Coventry 27.2.55.   Ht 5 9   Wt 11 8
Defender. From Nuneaton Bor.

Season	Club	Apps	Goals
1978–79	Luton T	25	—
1979–80		40	1
1980–81		40	1
1981–82		42	—
1982–83		40	—
1983–84		40	—
1984–85	Coventry C	32	2
1985–86		2	—

STEPHENSON, Paul

Born Wallsend 2.1.68.   Ht 5 10   Wt 10 9
Forward. From Apprentice. England Youth.

Season	Club	Apps	Goals
1985–86	Newcastle U	22	1

Season	Club	League Appearances/Goals	Season	Club	League Appearances/Goals

STERLAND, Mel

Born Sheffield 1.10.61.   Ht 6 0   Wt 13 2
Defender. From Apprentice.
England Under-21.

Season	Club	Apps	Goals
1978–79	Sheffield W	2	1
1979–80		2	—
1980–81		22	2
1981–82		27	—
1982–83		35	—
1983–84		39	8
1984–85		24	2
1985–86		38	8

STERLING, Worrell

Born Bethnal Green 8.6.65.   Ht 5 6½
Wt 10 11
Midfield. From Apprentice.

Season	Club	Apps	Goals
1982–83	Watford	3	—
1983–84		10	1
1984–85		15	4
1985–86		24	3

STEVEN, Trevor

Born Berwick 21.9.63.   Ht 5 8½   Wt 10 9
Midfield. From Apprentice. England Under-21, 10 full caps.

Season	Club	Apps	Goals
1980–81	Burnley	1	—
1981–82		36	3
1982–83		39	8
1983–84	Everton	27	1
1984–85		40	12
1985–86		41	9

STEVENS, Gary

Born Hillingdon 30.3.62.   Ht 6 0   Wt 12 0
Defender. From Apprentice.
England Under-21, 5 full caps.

Season	Club	Apps	Goals
1979–80	Brighton	26	1
1980–81		34	1
1981–82		32	—
1982–83		41	—
1983–84	Tottenham H	40	4
1984–85		28	—
1985–86		29	2

STEVENS, Gary

Born Barrow 27.3.63.   Ht 5 11   Wt 10 11
Defender. From Apprentice. England 9 full caps.

Season	Club	Apps	Goals
1980–81	Everton	—	—
1981–82		19	1
1982–83		28	—
1983–84		27	1
1984–85		37	3
1985–86		41	1

STEVENS, Gary

Born Birmingham 30.8.54.   Ht 6 1   Wt 12 4
Forward. From Evesham.

Season	Club	Apps	Goals
1978–79	Cardiff C	34	13
1979–80		38	11
1980–81		40	7
1981–82		38	13
1982–83		—	—
1982–83	Shrewsbury T	35	4
1983–84		38	1
1984–85		39	20
1985–86		38	4

STEVENS, Ian

Born Malta 21.10.66.   Ht 5 11   Wt 12 0
Forward. From YTS.

Season	Club	Apps	Goals
1984–85	Preston NE	4	1
1985–86		7	1

STEVENS, Keith

Born Merton 21.6.64.   Ht 5 11¾   Wt 12 5½
Defender. From Apprentice.

Season	Club	Apps	Goals
1980–81	Millwall	1	—
1981–82		7	—
1982–83		26	—
1983–84		17	—
1984–85		41	—
1985–86		33	1

All appearances include those as substitute

Season	Club	League Appearances/Goals	Season	Club	League Appearances/Goals

STEVENSON, Alan

Born Staveley 6.11.50.   Ht 6 1   Wt 12 2
Goalkeeper. From Amateur.
England Under-23.

Season	Club	Apps	Goals
1969–70	Chesterfield	35	—
1970–71		46	—
1971–72		23	—
1971–72	Burnley	17	—
1972–73		42	—
1973–74		40	—
1974–75		39	—
1975–76		22	—
1976–77		32	—
1977–78		42	—
1978–79		42	—
1979–80		40	—
1980–81		44	—
1981–82		46	—
1982–83		32	—
1983–84	Rotherham U	24	—
1984–85		—	—
1984–85	Hartlepool U	35	—
1985–86		—	—

STEVENSON, Andy

Born Scunthorpe 29.9.67.   Ht 6 0   Wt 12 3
Midfield. From school.

Season	Club	Apps	Goals
1985–86	Scunthorpe U	2	—

STEVENSON, Byron

Born Llanelli 7.9.56.   Ht 6 1   Wt 11 0
Defender. From Apprentice.
Wales Under-21, 15 full caps.

Season	Club	Apps	Goals
1973–74	Leeds U	—	—
1974–75		1	—
1975–76		1	—
1976–77		10	—
1977–78		5	—
1978–79		15	1
1979–80		26	—
1980–81		18	2
1981–82		19	1
1981–82	Birmingham C	12	—

Season	Club	Apps	Goals
1982–83		31	1
1983–84		25	2
1984–85		6	—
1985–86	Bristol R	31	3

STEVENSON, Nigel

Born Swansea 2.11.58.   Ht 6 2   Wt 12 10
Defender. From Apprentice.
Wales, 4 full caps.

Season	Club	Apps	Goals
1975–76	Swansea C	2	—
1976–77		—	—
1977–78		—	—
1978–79		39	2
1979–80		34	3
1980–81		40	5
1981–82		20	—
1982–83		26	1
1983–84		37	3
1984–85		34	1
1985–86		12	—
1985–86	*Cardiff C*	14	—
1985–86	*Reading*	3	—

STEWART, Billy

Born Liverpool 1.1.65.   Ht 5 11   Wt 11 7
Goalkeeper. From Apprentice.

Season	Club	Apps	Goals
1982–83	Liverpool	—	—
1983–84		—	—
1984–85	Wigan Ath	6	—
1985–86		8	—

STEWART, Ian

Born Belfast 10.9.61.   Ht 5 7   Wt 10 9
Forward. From juniors. Northern Ireland,
26 full caps.

Season	Club	Apps	Goals
1980–81	QPR	1	—
1981–82		3	—
1982–83		19	—
1982–83	*Millwall*	11	3
1983–84	QPR	31	2
1984–85		13	—
1985–86	Newcastle U	28	2

Season	Club	League Appearances/Goals		Season	Club	League Appearances/Goals	

STEWART, Jim

Born Kilwinning 9.3.54.　Ht 6 2　Wt 13 4
Goalkeeper. From Troon. Scotland Youth,
Under–23, Under–21, 2 full caps.

Season	Club	App	Goals
1970–71	Kilmarnock	—	—
1971–72		—	—
1972–73		22	—
1973–74		35	—
1974–75		18	—
1975–76		26	—
1976–77		35	—
1977–78		39	—
1978–79	Middlesbrough	27	—
1979–80		5	—
1980–81		2	—
1980–81	Rangers	10	—
1981–82		26	—
1982–83		18	—
1983–84		2	—
1983–84	*Dumbarton*	2	—
1984–85	St Mirren	6	—
1985–86		3	—

STEWART, Paul

Born Manchester 7.10.64.　Ht 5 11
Wt 11 10
Forward. From Apprentice.
England Youth.

Season	Club	App	Goals
1981–82	Blackpool	14	3
1982–83		38	7
1983–84		44	10
1984–85		31	7
1985–86		42	8

STEWART, Rab

Born Airdrie 3.1.62.　Ht 5 8　Wt 11 0
Forward. From Whitburn Bluebells.

Season	Club	App	Goals
1981–82	Dumfermline Ath	26	7
1982–83		24	6
1983–84		28	4
1984–85	Motherwell	26	9
1985–86		7	1
1985–86	Falkirk	8	—

STEWART, Ray

Born Perth 7.9.59.　Ht 5 11　Wt 11 11
Defender. From Errol Rovers.
Scotland Schools, Under–21, 7 full caps.

Season	Club	App	Goals
1975–76	Dundee U	—	—
1976–77		1	—
1977–78		6	1
1978–79		34	4
1979–80		3	—
1979–80	West Ham U	38	10
1980–81		41	5
1981–82		42	10
1982–83		39	8
1983–84		42	7
1984–85		37	6
1985–86		39	6

STILES, John

Born Manchester 6.5.64.　Ht 5 9½　Wt 10 12
Midfield. From Vancouver W.

Season	Club	App	Goals
1984–85	Leeds U	1	—
1985–86		12	1

STIMSON, Mark

Born Plaistow 27.12.67.
Defender. From YTS.

Season	Club	App	Goals
1984–85	Tottenham H	—	—
1985–86		—	—

STOBART, Sean

Born Wolverhampton 31.7.66.　Ht 5 10
Wt 12 7
Defender.

Season	Club	App	Goals
1984–85	Scunthorpe U	2	1
1985–86		—	—

STOCKWELL, Mike

Born Chelmsford 14.2.65.　Ht 5 6½　Wt 10 2
Midfield. From Apprentice.

Season	Club	League Appearances/Goals		
1982–83	Ipswich T	—	—
1983–84		—	—
1984–85		—	—
1985–86		8	—

STONEHOUSE, Kevin

Born Bishop Auckland 20.9.59.   Ht 5 11
Wt 11 1
Forward. From Shildon.

1979–80	Blackburn R	7	2
1980–81		26	10
1981–82		37	11
1982–83		15	4
1982–83	Huddersfield T	5	—
1983–84		17	4
1983–84	Blackpool	13	5
1984–85		26	11
1985–86		16	3

STORER, Stuart

Born Harborough 16.1.67.
Forward. Local.

1983–84	Mansfield T	1	—
1984–85	Birmingham C	—	—
1985–86		2	—

STORR, Kevin

Born Cleethorpes 4.9.67.   Ht 5 10   Wt 10 5
Forward. From Apprentice.

1985–86	Grimsby T	—	—

STOUTT, Stephen

Born Halifax 5.4.64.
Defender. Local.

1983–84	Huddersfield T	3	—
1984–85		3	—
1984–85	Wolverhampton W	—	—
1985–86		28	—

STOWELL, Mike

Born Preston 19.4.65.
Goalkeeper. From Leyland Motors.

1984–85	Preston NE	—	—
1985–86		—	—
1985–86	Everton	—	—

STRACHAN, Gordon

Born Edinburgh 9.2.57.   Ht 5 6   Wt 10 3
Midfield. Scotland 34 full caps.

1974–75	Dundee	1	—
1975–76		23	6
1976–77		36	7
1977–78	Aberdeen	12	2
1978–79		31	5
1979–80		33	10
1980–81		20	6
1981–82		30	7
1982–83		32	12
1983–84		25	13
1984–85	Manchester U	41	15
1985–86		28	5

STREETE, Floyd

Born W. Indies 5.5.59.   Ht 6 1   Wt 12 8
Defender. From Rivet Sports.

1976–77	Cambridge U	3	1
1977–78		21	3
1978–79		13	1
1979–80		21	1
1980–81		22	4
1981–82		31	5
1982–83		14	4
From Utrecht and SC Cambuur.			
1984–85	Derby Co	30	—
1985–86		5	—
1985–86	Wolverhampton W	25	1

STRINGFELLOW, Ian

Born Nottingham 8.5.69.
Midfield. From Apprentice.

1985–86	Mansfield T	3	—

Season	Club	League Appearances/Goals	Season	Club	League Appearances/Goals

STRODDER, Gary

Born Leeds 1.4.65.   Ht 6 1   Wt 11 3½
Defender. From Apprentice.

Season	Club	App	Goals
1982–83	Lincoln C	8	—
1983–84		22	1
1984–85		26	2
1985–86		43	1

STRONG, Andy

Born Hartlepool 17.9.66.   Ht 6 2   Wt 10 3
Defender. From Apprentice.

Season	Club	App	Goals
1984–85	Middlesbrough	6	—
1985–86		—	—

STUART, Mark

Born Hammersmith 15.12.66.   Ht 5 8½
Wt 11 2
Forward. From Q.P.R. Schoolboy.

Season	Club	App	Goals
1984–85	Charlton Ath.	6	1
1985–86		30	12

STURROCK, Paul

Born Ellon 10.10.56.   Ht 5 8   Wt 10 4
Forward. From Bankfoot. Scotland Youth,
Under-21, 17 full caps.

Season	Club	App	Goals
1974–75	Dundee U	12	6
1975–76		17	3
1976–77		36	15
1977–78		33	3
1978–79		33	6
1979–80		33	4
1980–81		35	13
1981–82		31	15
1982–83		28	8
1983–84		17	4
1984–85		30	14
1985–86		31	8

SUCKLING, Perry

Born Leyton 12.10.55.   Ht 6 0½   Wt 12 1
Goalkeeper. From Apprentice.
England Youth.

Season	Club	App	Goals
1982–83	Coventry C	3	—
1983–84		24	—
1984–85		—	—
1985–86		—	—

SUGRUE, Paul

Born Coventry 6.11.60   Ht 5 7   Wt 9 10
Midfield. From Nuneaton Bor.

Season	Club	App	Goals
1979–80	Manchester C	1	—
1980–81		5	—
1981–82	Cardiff C	5	—
From Kansas			
1982–83	Middlesbrough	22	3
1983–84		40	3
1984–85		7	—
1984–85	Portsmouth	1	—
1985–86		3	—
1985–86	Northampton T	8	2

SULLEY, Chris

Born Camberwell 3.12.59.   Ht 5 8   Wt 10 0
Forward. From Apprentice.

Season	Club	App	Goals
1978–79	Chelsea	—	—
1979–80		—	—
1980–81		—	—
1980–81	Bournemouth	8	—
1981–82		46	—
1982–83		46	1
1983–84		46	2
1984–85		23	—
1985–86		37	—

SULLIVAN, Colin

Born Saltash 24.6.51.   Ht 5 7   Wt 11 3
Defender. From Apprentice.
England Youth, Under-23.

All appearances include those as substitute

Season	Club	League Appearances/Goals		Season	Club	League Appearances/Goals	
1967–68	Plymouth Arg	11	—	1971–72	Wolverhampton W	8	—
1968–69		19	—	1972–73		16	5
1969–70		39	1	1973–74		34	7
1970–71		31	1	1974–75		17	—
1971–72		39	3	1975–76		29	—
1972–73		46	1	1976–77		41	15
1973–74		45	1	1977–78		13	2
1974–75	Norwich C	36	1	1977–78	Arsenal	23	4
1975–76		31	1	1978–79		37	9
1976–77		39	1	1979–80		37	14
1977–78		41	—	1980–81		34	7
1978–79		10	—	1981–82		38	11
1978–79	Cardiff C	19	1	1982–83		25	6
1979–80		30	—	1983–84		12	4
1980–81		7	—	1983–84	*Ipswich T*	15	3
1981–82		7	—	1984–85	Ipswich T	26	7
1981–82	Hereford U	8	—	1985–86		17	1
1981–82	Portsmouth	18	—				
1982–83		46	—				
1983–84		30	—				
1984–85		—	—				
1984–85	Swansea C	12	—				
1985–86		41	—				

SUMMERFIELD, Kevin

Born Walsall 7.1.59. Ht 5 11 Wt 11 0
Forward. From Apprentice.

Season	Club	League Appearances/Goals	
1976–77	WBA	—	—
1977–78		—	—
1978–79		2	1
1979–80		3	1
1980–81		—	—
1981–82		4	2
1982–83	Birmingham C	5	1
1982–83	Walsall	21	9
1983–84		33	8
1984–85	Cardiff C	10	1
1984–85	Plymouth Arg	17	2
1985–86		26	7

SUNDERLAND, Alan

Born Mexborough 1.7.53. Ht 5 9 Wt 11 6¼
Forward. From Apprentice.
England Under-21, Under-23, 'B', 1 full cap.

SUSSEX, Andy

Born Enfield 23.11.64. Ht 6 0 Wt 11 6
Forward. From Apprentice.

Season	Club	League Appearances/Goals	
1981–82	Orient	8	1
1982–83		24	2
1983–84		29	6
1984–85		19	2
1985–86		36	4

SUTCLIFFE, Mark

Born Canterbury 6.3.68.
Midfield. From Apprentice.

Season	Club	League Appearances/Goals	
1985–86	Crystal Palace	—	—

SUTTON, David

Born Tarleton 21.1.57. Ht 6 1 Wt 12 8
Defender. From Apprentice.

Season	Club	League Appearances/Goals	
1973–74	Plymouth Arg	2	—
1974–75		2	—
1975–76		22	—
1976–77		34	—
1977–78		1	—
1977–78	*Reading*	9	—
1977–78	Huddersfield T	14	—
1978–79		39	1
1979–80		46	6

Season	Club	League Appearances/Goals		Season	Club	League Appearances/Goals	
1980–81	....	39	1				

Season	Club	Apps	Goals
1980–81	....	39	1
1981–82	....	29	—
1982–83	....	41	2
1983–84	....	34	1
1984–85	....	—	—
1985–86	Bolton W	32	2

SUTTON, Steve

Born Hartington 16.4.61.   Ht 6 0   Wt 12 12
Goalkeeper. From Apprentice.

Season	Club	Apps	Goals
1980–81	Nottingham F	1	—
1980–81	*Mansfield T*	8	—
1981–82	Nottingham F	1	—
1982–83	....	17	—
1983–84	....	6	—
1984–85	....	14	—
1984–85	*Derby Co*	14	—
1985–86	Nottingham F	31	—

SWAIN, Kenny

Born Birkenhead 28.1.52.   Ht 5 9   Wt 11 7
Defender. From Wycombe W.

Season	Club	Apps	Goals
1973–74	Chelsea	7	1
1974–75	....	—	—
1975–76	....	25	4
1976–77	....	36	13
1977–78	....	36	4
1978–79	....	15	4
1978–79	Aston Villa...................	24	2
1979–80	....	41	—
1980–81	....	42	—
1981–82	....	39	—
1982–83	....	2	—
1982–83	Nottingham F	32	1
1983–84	....	41	1
1984–85	....	39	—
1985–86	Portsmouth	39	—

SWAN, Peter

Born Leeds 28.9.66.   Ht 6 0   Wt 11 12
Forward. Local.

Season	Club	Apps	Goals
1984–85	Leeds U......................	—	—
1985–86	....	16	3

SWANN, Gary

Born York 11.4.62.   Ht 5 9½   Wt 11 2
Defender. From Apprentice.

Season	Club	Apps	Goals
1980–81	Hull C......................	20	2
1981–82	....	20	—
1982–83	....	25	—
1983–84	....	41	2
1984–85	....	32	3
1985–86	....	39	2

SWINBURNE, Trevor

Born E. Rainton 20.6.53.   Ht 6 0   Wt 14 7
Goalkeeper. From Apprentice.

Season	Club	Apps	Goals
1970–71	Sunderland	—	—
1971–72	....	—	—
1972–73	....	1	—
1973–74	....	1	—
1974–75	....	2	—
1975–76	....	4	—
1976–77	....	2	—
1976–77	*Sheffield U*	—	—
1977–78	Carlisle U	31	—
1978–79	....	45	—
1979–80	....	46	—
1980–81	....	38	—
1981–82	....	46	—
1982–83	....	42	—
1983–84	Brentford	21	—
1984–85	....	24	—
1985–86	Leeds U......................	2	—
1985–86	*Doncaster R*.................	4	—
1985–86	Lincoln C...................	18	—

SWINDLEHURST, Dave

Born Edgware 6.1.56.   Ht 6 2   Wt 13 3
Forward. From Apprentice.
England Youth, Under-21.

Season	Club	Apps	Goals
1972–73	Crystal Palace	—	—
1973–74	....	9	—
1974–75	....	38	14
1975–76	....	43	16

All appearances include those as substitute

Season	Club	League Appearances/Goals	
1976–77	....	42	10
1977–78	....	40	12
1978–79	....	40	14
1979–80	....	25	7
1979–80	Derby Co...................	12	4
1980–81	....	34	11
1981–82	....	36	6
1982–83	....	28	8
1982–83	West Ham U................	9	3
1983–84	....	36	13
1984–85	....	16	—
1985–86	Sunderland	25	5

SWORD, Tommy

Born Newcastle 12.11.57.   Ht 6 2   Wt 14 0
Defender. From Bishop Auckland.

Season	Club	League Appearances/Goals	
1979–80	Stockport Co	25	8
1980–81	....	43	5
1981–82	....	16	3
1982–83	....	25	1
1983–84	....	45	10
1984–85	....	44	12
1985–86	....	40	12

TAIT, Mick

Born Wallsend 30.9.56.   Ht 5 11   Wt 12 5
Midfield. From Apprentice.

Season	Club	League Appearances/Goals	
1974–75	Oxford U	4	—
1975–76	....	37	12
1976–77	....	23	11
1976–77	Carlisle U	13	3
1977–78	....	43	10
1978–79	....	46	7
1979–80	....	4	—
1979–80	Hull C........................	33	3
1980–81	Portsmouth	38	8
1981–82	....	35	9
1982–83	....	44	6
1983–84	....	36	3
1984–85	....	33	1
1985–86	....	26	2

TALBOT, Brian

Born Ipswich 21.7.53.   Ht 5 10   Wt 12 0
Midfield. From Apprentice.
England Under-21, 'B', 6 full caps.

Season	Club	League Appearances/Goals	
1972–73	Ipswich T....................	—	—
1973–74	....	15	3
1974–75	....	40	8
1975–76	....	19	2
1976–77	....	42	5
1977–78	....	40	4
1978–79	....	21	3
1978–79	Arsenal	20	—
1979–80	....	42	1
1980–81	....	40	7
1981–82	....	42	7
1982–83	....	42	9
1983–84	....	27	6
1984–85	....	41	10
1985–86	Watford	41	7

TANKARD, Allen

Born Fleet 21.5.69.
Defender. From YTS. England Youth.

Season	Club	League Appearances/Goals	
1985–86	Southampton...............	3	—

Season	Club	League Appearances/Goals	Season	Club	League Appearances/Goals

TANNER, Micky

Born Bristol 28.10.64.   Ht 5 11   Wt 11 8
Forward. Local.

1984–85	Bristol C	— —
1985–86		2 —

TANNER, Nick

Born Bristol 24.5.65.   Ht 6 2   Wt 13 7
Defender. From Mangotsfield.

1984–85	Bristol R	— —
1985–86		37 2

TAYLOR, Alan

Born Hinckley 14.11.53.   Ht 5 9   Wt 10 6
Forward. From Morecambe.

1973–74	Rochdale	36	1
1974–75		19	6
1974–75	West Ham U	14	2
1975–76		35	13
1976–77		25	5
1977–78		11	2
1978–79		13	3
1979–80	Norwich C	24	5
From Vancouver Whitecaps			
1980–81	Cambridge U	8	2
From Vancouver Whitecaps			
1983–84	Hull C.	14	3
1984–85	Burnley	19	7
1985–86		45	16

TAYLOR, Andy

Born Chesterfield 30.12.67.
Forward.

1984–85	Chesterfield	— —
1985–86		— —

TAYLOR, Bob

Born Horden 3.2.67.   Ht 5 10   Wt 11 2
Forward. From Horden CW.

1985–86	Leeds U	2 —

TAYLOR, Kevin

Born Wakefield 22.1.61.   Ht 5 8   Wt 11 11
Midfield. From Apprentice.

1978–79	Sheffield W	5	—
1979–80		21	6
1980–81		30	5
1981–82		35	7
1982–83		29	3
1983–84		5	—
1984–85	Derby Co	22	2
1984–85	Crystal Palace	13	—
1985–86		31	6

TAYLOR, Les

Born North Shields 4.12.56.   Ht 5 8   Wt 11 7
Midfield. From Apprentice.

1974–75	Oxford U	5	—
1975–76		35	—
1976–77		32	2
1977–78		46	6
1978–79		46	1
1979–80		36	6
1980–81		19	—
1980–81	Watford	24	1
1981–82		42	4
1982–83		39	5
1983–84		27	—
1984–85		39	3
1985–86		1	—

TAYLOR, Mark

Born Hartlepool 20.11.64.   Ht 5 7   Wt 10 0
Midfield. Local.

1982–83	Hartlepool U	— —
1983–84		6 —
1984–85		36 4
1985–86		5 —
1985–86	*Crewe Alex*	3 —

TAYLOR, Mark

Born Walsall 22.2.66.   Ht 5 10   Wt 11 0
Midfield. Local.

All appearances include those as substitute

Season	Club	League Appearances/Goals		Season	Club	League Appearances/Goals	
1984–85	Walsall	4	—				
1985–86		18	2				

TAYLOR, Steve

Born Royton 18.10.55. Ht 5 10 Wt 10 8
Forward. From Apprentice.

Season	Club	App	Goals
1974–75	Bolton W	5	—
1975–76		3	—
1975–76	*Port Vale*	4	2
1976–77	Bolton W	31	16
1977–78		1	—
1977–78	Oldham Ath	32	20
1978–79		15	5
1978–79	Luton T	20	1
1979–80	Mansfield T	37	7
1980–81	Burnley ...,	38	16
1981–82		22	9
1982–83		26	12
1983–84	Wigan Ath	30	7
1983–84	Stockport Co	12	6
1984–85		14	2
1984–85	Rochdale	30	12
1985–86		45	25

TEMPEST, Dale

Born Leeds 30.12.63. Ht 5 11 Wt 12 4
Forward. From Apprentice.

Season	Club	App	Goals
1980–81	Fulham	1	—
1981–82		14	2
1982–83		4	—
1983–84		15	4
1984–85	Huddersfield T	35	15
1985–86		30	12
1985–86	*Gillingham*	9	4

TERRY, Steve

Born Clapton 14.6.62. Ht 6 1½ Wt 13 3
Defender. From Apprentice.

Season	Club	App	Goals
1979–80	Watford	2	—
1980–81		5	—
1981–82		26	2
1982–83		7	1
1983–84		17	1
1984–85		38	4
1985–86		41	4

TESTER, Paul

Born Stroud 10.3.59. Ht 5 9 Wt 10 10
Forward. From Cheltenham T.

Season	Club	App	Goals
1983–84	Shrewsbury T	8	—
1984–85		23	5
1984–85	*Hereford U*	4	—
1985–86	Shrewsbury T	9	1

THACKERAY, Andy

Born Huddersfield 13.2.68.
Midfield.

Season	Club	App	Goals
1985–86	Manchester C	—	—

THOMAS, Andy

Born Oxford 16.12.62. Ht 6 0 Wt 10 10
Forward. From Apprentice.

Season	Club	App	Goals
1980–81	Oxford U	9	1
1981–82		39	14
1982–83		24	7
1982–83	*Fulham*	4	2
1982–83	*Derby Co*	1	—
1983–84	Oxford U	23	7
1984–85		4	1
1985–86		17	2

THOMAS, Danny

Born Worksop 12.11.61. Ht 5 7 Wt 10 2
Defender. From Apprentice. England
Schools, Under-21, 2 full caps.

Season	Club	App	Goals
1978–79	Coventry C	—	—
1979–80		3	—
1980–81		25	1
1981–82		39	1
1982–83		41	3
1983–84	Tottenham H	27	—
1984–85		16	—
1985–86		27	1

Season	Club	League Appearances/Goals		Season	Club	League Appearances/Goals	

THOMAS, Dave

Born Kirkby-in-Ashfield 5.10.50.   Ht 5 8
Wt 10 10
Forward. From Apprentice. England
Schools, Youth, Under-23, 8 full caps.

Season	Club	App	Goals
1966–67	Burnley	1	—
1967–68		3	—
1968–69		39	4
1969–70		36	4
1970–71		34	3
1971–72		33	4
1972–73		11	—
1972–73	QPR	28	6
1973–74		41	6
1974–75		41	7
1975–76		41	9
1976–77		31	1
1977–78	Everton	38	2
1978–79		33	2
1979–80		—	—
1979–80	Wolverhampton W	10	—
1980–81		—	—
From Vancouver Whitecaps			
1981–82	Middlesbrough	13	1
1982–83	Portsmouth	13	—
1983–84		14	—
1984–85		3	—
1985–86		—	—

THOMAS, Geoff

Born Manchester 5.8.64.   Ht 5 10   Wt 10 7
Midfield. Local.

Season	Club	App	Goals
1981–82	Rochdale	—	—
1982–83		1	—
1983–84		10	1
1983–84	Crewe Alex	8	1
1984–85		40	4
1985–86		37	6

THOMAS, Glen

Born Hackney 6.10.67.   Ht 6 0½   Wt 11 6
Defender. From Apprentice.

Season	Club	App	Goals
1985–86	Fulham	—	—

THOMAS, Gwyn

Born Swansea 26.9.57.   Ht 5 8   Wt 11 0
Forward. From Apprentice.
Wales Under-21.

Season	Club	App	Goals
1974–75	Leeds U	1	—
1975–76		—	—
1976–77		7	1
1977–78		3	1
1978–79		2	—
1979–80		3	—
1980–81		2	—
1981–82		15	—
1982–83		39	1
1983–84		17	—
1983–84	Barnsley	13	—
1984–85		40	1
1985–86		39	5

THOMAS, John

Born Wednesbury 5.8.58.   Ht 5 8   Wt 11 3
Forward.

Season	Club	App	Goals
1978–79	Everton	—	—
1978–79	*Tranmere R*	11	2
1979–80	Everton	—	—
1979–80	*Halifax T*	5	—
1980–81	Bolton W	17	5
1981–82		5	1
1982–83	Chester	44	20
1983–84	Lincoln C	37	13
1984–85		30	5
1985–86	Preston NE	40	17

THOMAS, Martin

Born Caerphilly 28.11.59.   Ht 6 1   Wt 13 0
Goalkeeper. From Apprentice. Wales
Under-21.

Season	Club	App	Goals
1976–77	Bristol R	1	—
1977–78		37	—
1978–79		42	—
1979–80		38	—
1980–81		25	—
1981–82		19	—
1982–83	*Cardiff C*	15	—
1982–83	*Tottenham H*	—	—

Season	Club	League Appearances/Goals		Season	Club	League Appearances/Goals	
1982–83	*Southend U*	6	—	1982–83	Luton T	4	—
1982–83	*Newcastle U*	3	—	1983–84		26	—
1983–84	Newcastle U	23	—	1984–85		36	—
1984–85		18	—	1985–86		41	1
1984–85	*Middlesbrough*	4	—				
1985–86	Newcastle U	32	—				

THOMAS, Mickey

Born Mochdre 7.7.54.   Ht 5 6   Wt 10 7
Midfield. From Amateur.
Wales Under-23, 51 full caps.

Season	Club	League Appearances/Goals	
1971–72	Wrexham	20	3
1972–73		26	—
1973–74		19	4
1974–75		31	5
1975–76		30	2
1976–77		45	6
1977–78		43	7
1978–79		16	6
1978–79	Manchester U	25	1
1979–80		35	8
1980–81		30	2
1981–82	Everton	10	—
1981–82	Brighton	20	—
1982–83	Stoke C	41	11
1983–84		16	3
1983–84	Chelsea	17	4
1984–85		27	5
1985–86		—	—
1985–86	WBA	20	—
1985–86	*Derby Co*	9	—

THOMAS, Mike

Born Lambeth 24.8.67.   Ht 5 10   Wt 12 4
Defender. From Apprentice. England
Schools, Youth.

Season	Club	League Appearances/Goals	
1985–86	Arsenal	—	—

THOMAS, Mitchell

Born Luton 2.10.64.   Ht 6 0   Wt 12 0
Defender. From Apprentice. England
Youth, Under-21.

THOMPSON, Andy

Born Carnock 9.11.67.
Midfield. From Apprentice.

Season	Club	League Appearances/Goals	
1985–86	WBA	15	1

THOMPSON, Chris

Born Walsall 24.1.60.   Ht 5 10   Wt 11 10
Forward. From Apprentice. England Youth.

Season	Club	League Appearances/Goals	
1977–78	Bolton W	—	—
1978–79		—	—
1979–80		15	1
1980–81		6	1
1981–82		36	12
1982–83		16	4
1982–83	*Lincoln C*	6	—
1983–84	Blackburn R	33	8
1984–85		35	15
1985–86		17	1

THOMPSON, David

Born Manchester 27.5.62.   Ht 5 10½
Wt 12 4
Forward. Local.

Season	Club	League Appearances/Goals	
1981–82	Rochdale	2	—
1982–83		46	5
1983–84		40	4
1984–85		40	2
1985–86		27	2
1985–86	*Manchester U*		

THOMPSON, Garry

Born Birmingham 7.10.59.   Ht 6 0   Wt 12 8
Forward. From Apprentice.
England Under-21.

Season	Club	League Appearances/Goals	
1977–78	Coventry C	6	2
1978–79		20	8

Season	Club	League Appearances/Goals		Season	Club	League Appearances/Goals	
1979–80	....	17	6	1970–71	Liverpool....................	—	—
1980–81	....	35	8	1971–72	....	1	—
1981–82	....	36	10	1972–73	....	14	—
1982–83	....	20	4	1973–74	....	35	2
1982–83	WBA....................................	12	7	1974–75	....	32	—
1983–84	....	37	13	1975–76	....	41	—
1984–85	....	42	19	1976–77	....	26	2
1985–86	Sheffield W	36	6	1977–78	....	27	3
				1978–79	....	39	—
				1979–80	....	42	—
				1980–81	....	25	—
				1981–82	....	34	—
				1982–83	....	24	—
				1983–84	....	—	—
				1984–85	....	—	—
				1984–85	Sheffield U	10	—
				1985–86	....	27	—

THOMPSON, Ian

Born Dartford 8.6.58. Ht 6 1   Wt 13 0
Forward. From Salisbury.

1983–84	Bournemouth	44	12
1984–85	....	44	13
1985–86	....	33	5

THOMPSON, Keith

Born Birmingham 24.4.65. Ht 5 9   Wt 11 2
Forward. From Apprentice. England Youth.

1982–83	Coventry C....................	5	—
1983–84	....	6	—
1983–84	*Wimbledon*	3	—
1984–85	Coventry C....................	1	—
1984–85	*Northampton T*.............	10	1
1985–86	Coventry C....................	—	—

THOMPSON, Nigel

Born Leeds 1.3.67. Ht 5 7   Wt 10 12
Defender. From Apprentice

1983–84	Leeds U......................	1	—
1984–85	....	—	—
1985–86	....	1	—

THOMPSON, Phil

Born Liverpool 21.1.54. Ht 6 0   Wt 11 8
Defender. From Apprentice. England
Under-23, 'B', 42 full caps. Football League.

THOMPSON, Steve

Born Oldham 2.11.64. Ht 5 8½   Wt 11 0
Midfield. From Apprentice.

1982–83	Bolton W....................	3	—
1983–84	....	40	3
1984–85	....	34	4
1985–86	....	35	8

THOMPSON, Steve

Born Sheffield 28.7.55. Ht 6 1   Wt 14 4
Midfield. From Boston U.

1979–80	Lincoln C....................	—	—
1980–81	....	31	2
1981–82	....	30	2
1982–83	....	36	2
1983–84	....	16	1
1984–85	....	41	1
1985–86	Charlton Ath	38	—

THOMSON, Billy

Born Linwood 10.2.58. Ht 6 2   Wt 12 3
Goalkeeper. From Glasgow United.
Scotland Under-21, 7 full caps.

All appearances include those as substitute

Season	Club	League Appearances/Goals		Season	Club	League Appearances/Goals	
1975–76	Partick T	—	—				
1976–77		—	—				
1977–78		—	—				
1978–79	St Mirren	34	—				
1979–80		36	—				
1980–81		36	—				
1981–82		35	—				
1982–83		35	—				
1983–84		30	—				
1984–85	Dundee U	11	—				
1985–86		28	—				

THORPE, Adrian

Born Chesterfield 20.11.63.
Forward. From Heanor T.

Season	Club	League Appearances/Goals	
1984–85	Bradford C	—	—
1985–86		10	1

THOMSON, Bobby

Born Glasgow 21.3.55.   Ht 5 10   Wt 11 6
Forward.

Season	Club	League Appearances/Goals	
1973–74	St Johnstone	6	—
1974–75		14	—
1975–76		26	3
1976–77		36	7
1977–78		36	7
1978–79	Morton	30	11
1979–80		27	11
1980–81		29	2
1981–82		4	1
1981–82	Middlesbrough	20	2
1982–83	Hibernian	30	6
1983–84		16	4
1984–85		16	3
1984–85	Morton	11	2
1985–86	Hibs	—	—
1985–86	Blackpool	16	2

THORPE, Andy

Born Stockport 15.9.60.   Ht 5 11   Wt 12 0
Defender. From Amateur.

Season	Club	League Appearances/Goals	
1977–78	Stockport Co	4	—
1978–79		38	—
1979–80		36	1
1980–81		38	1
1981–82		46	—
1982–83		46	—
1983–84		45	1
1984–85		31	—
1985–86		30	—

THORN, Andy

Born Carshalton 12.11.66.   Ht 6 0   Wt 11 5
Defender. From Apprentice.

Season	Club	League Appearances/Goals	
1984–85	Wimbledon	10	—
1985–86		28	—

TINNION, Brian

Born Stanley 23.2.68.
Defender. From Apprentice.

Season	Club	League Appearances/Goals	
1985–86	Newcastle U	—	—

TOALE, Ian

Born Liverpool 28.8.67.   Ht 5 8½   Wt 10 0
Defender. From Apprentice.

Season	Club	League Appearances/Goals	
1984–85	Liverpool	—	—
1985–86		—	—

THORNBER, Stephen

Born Dewsbury 11.10.65. Ht 5 9   Wt 10 11
Forward. Local.

Season	Club	League Appearances/Goals	
1983–84	Halifax T	4	1
1984–85		31	3
1985–86		18	—

TODD, Mark

Born Belfast 4.12.67.   Ht 5 5½   Wt 8 3½
Midfield. From YTS.

Season	Club	League Appearances/Goals	
1985–86	Manchester U	—	—

All appearances include those as substitute

Season	Club	League Appearances/Goals		Season	Club	League Appearances/Goals	

TOLMIE, Jim

Born Glasgow 20.11.60.   Ht 5 6   Wt 10 3.
Forward. From Auchengill Star BC.

Season	Club	App	Goals
1977–78	Morton	—	—
1978–79		10	3
1979–80		28	2
1980–81		34	5
From Lokeren			
1983–84	Manchester C	41	13
1984–85		17	2
1985–86		3	—
1985–86	*Carlisle U*	8	1

TOMAN, Andy

Born Northallerton 7.3.62.
Midfield. From Bishop Auckland.

Season	Club	App	Goals
1985–86	Lincoln C	24	4

TOMLINSON, Andy

Born Hull 18.9.66.   Ht 5 9   Wt 11 4
Midfield. From Apprentice.

Season	Club	App	Goals
1984–85	Hull C	—	—
1985–86		—	—

TOMLINSON, Paul

Born Brierley Hill 22.2.64.   Ht 6 2
Wt 12 10
Goalkeeper. From Middlewood R.

Season	Club	App	Goals
1983–84	Sheffield U	30	—
1984–85		2	—
1985–86		—	—

TONG, David

Born Blackpool 21.9.55.   Ht 5 9   Wt 11 7
Midfield. From Apprentice.

Season	Club	App	Goals
1973–74	Blackpool	—	—
1974–75		27	2
1975–76		15	2

Season	Club	App	Goals
1976–77		13	—
1977–78		21	3
1978–79		2	—
1978–79	Shrewsbury T	37	5
1979–80		41	1
1980–81		42	1
1981–82		40	1
1982–83	Cardiff C	44	2
1983–84		42	—
1984–85		33	1
1985–86		1	—
1985–86	Rochdale	2	—
1985–86	Bristol C	19	—
1985–86	Gillingham	5	—

TOPLISS, Kevin

Born Grimsby 5.4.67.   Ht 5 6   Wt 8 4
Forward. From Apprentice.

Season	Club	App	Goals
1984–85	Grimsby T	—	—
1985–86		—	—

TORRANCE, George

Born Isle of Bute 17.9.57.   Ht 5 10   Wt 11 7
Forward. From Wokingham.

Season	Club	App	Goals
1984–85	Brentford	13	1
1985–86		21	—

TORTOLANO, Joe

Born Stirling 6.4.66.   Ht 5 8   Wt 11 2
Forward. From Apprentice.

Season	Club	App	Goals
1983–84	W.B.A.	—	—
1984–85		—	—
1985–86	Hibernian	20	3

TOTTOH, Mel

Born Manchester 26.7.56.
Forward. From Lytham.

Season	Club	App	Goals
1984–85	Preston NE	—	—
1985–86		1	—

Season	Club	League Appearances/Goals		Season	Club	League Appearances/Goals	

TOWNER, Tony

Born Brighton 2.5.55.   Ht 5 8   Wt 10 4
Forward. From Apprentice.

1972–73	Brighton	14	2
1973–74		23	2
1974–75		41	10
1975–76		29	2
1976–77		23	6
1977–78		26	2
1978–79		6	—
1978–79	Millwall	25	1
1979–80		43	12
1980–81	Rotherham U	36	7
1981–82		42	4
1982–83		30	1
1982–83	*Sheffield U*	10	1
1983–84	Wolverhampton W	31	2
1984–85		—	—
1984–85	Charlton Ath	26	2
1985–86		1	—
1985–86	Rochdale	5	—
1985–86	Cambridge U	6	—

TOWNSEND, Andy

Born Maidstone 23.7.63.   Ht 5 10½   Wt 12 7
Midfield. From Welling and Weymouth.

| 1984–85 | Southampton | 5 | — |
| 1985–86 | | 27 | 1 |

TRACEY, Simon

Born Woolwich 9.12.67.   Ht 6 0   Wt 12 0
Goalkeeper. From Apprentice.

| 1985–86 | Wimbledon | — | — |

TRAIN, Ray

Born Nuneaton 10.2.51.   Ht 5 5   Wt 10 5
Midfield. From Apprentice.

1968–69	Walsall	18	4
1969–70		18	3
1970–71		24	3
1971–72		13	1
1971–72	Carlisle U	20	—
1972–73		42	1

1973–74		27	3
1974–75		42	2
1975–76		24	2
1975–76	Sunderland	12	—
1976–77		20	1
1976–77	Bolton W	14	—
1977–78		32	—
1978–79		5	—
1978–79	Watford	21	1
1979–80		42	1
1980–81		29	1
1981–82		—	—
1981–82	Oxford U	15	—
1982–83		34	—
1983–84		1	—
1983–84	*Bournemouth*	7	—
1983–84	*Northampton T*	—	—
1984–85	Northampton T	46	1
1985–86	Tranmere R	36	—

TRAVIS, David

Born Doncaster 4.7.64.   Ht 5 10   Wt 10 7
Midfield. From Pilkingtons and Hatfield
Main.

1984–85	Doncaster R	10	—
1985–86		2	—
1985–86	Scunthorpe U	12	1

TREANOR, Mark

Born Glasgow 1.4.63.   Ht 6 0   Wt 11 0
Defender. From Eastercraigs.

1979–80	Clydebank	1	—
1980–81		16	—
1981–82		35	—
1982–83		36	3
1983–84		18	1
1984–85		38	1
1985–86		32	—

TREWICK, John

Born Bedlington 3.6.57.   Ht 5 10   Wt 10 13
Midfield. From Apprentice. England
Schools, Youth.

Season	Club	League Appearances/Goals		Season	Club	League Appearances/Goals	
1974–75	WBA	3	—	1970–71		11	—
1975–76		11	1	1971–72		42	—
1976–77		7	1	1972–73		37	—
1977–78		18	3	1973–74		23	—
1978–79		21	3	1973–74	*Ipswich T*	—	—
1979–80		21	2	1974–75	Rotherham U	24	—
1980–81		15	1	1974–75	*Newcastle U*		
1980–81	Newcastle U.	21	1	1974–75	Preston NE	27	—
1981–82		40	6	1975–76		43	—
1982–83		1	—	1976–77		38	—
1983–84		16	1	1977–78		46	—
1983–84	*Oxford U*	3	—	1978–79		42	—
1984–85	Oxford U	42	—	1979–80		42	—
1985–86		35	3	1980–81		39	—
				1981–82	Wigan Ath	31	—
				1982–83		46	—
				1983–84		42	—
				1984–85		40	—
				1985–86		38	—

TRUSSON, Mike

Born Northolt 26.5.59. Ht 5 10   Wt 12 4
Forward. From Apprentice.

1976–77	Plymouth Arg	4	—
1977–78		15	2
1978–79		27	5
1978–79	*Stoke C*	—	—
1979–80	Plymouth Arg	27	8
1980–81	Sheffield U	39	8
1981–82		44	11
1982–83		32	9
1983–84		11	3
1983–84	Rotherham U	25	2
1984–85		45	7
1985–86		37	6

TUITE, Marcus

Born Dublin 11.5.68 Ht 5 6   Wt 9 1
Midfield. From Apprentice. Eire Youth.

1985–86	Luton T	—	—

TUNKS, Roy

Born W. Germany 21.1.51.   Ht 6 1
Wt 13 11
Goalkeeper. From Apprentice.

1967–68	Rotherham U	—	—
1968–69		1	—
1968–69	*York C*	4	—
1969–70	Rotherham U	—	—

TUPLING, Steve

Born Wensleydale 11.7.64.   Ht 6 0   Wt 11 3
Midfield. From Apprentice.

1982–83	Middlesbrough	—	—
1983–84		—	—
1984–85	Carlisle U	1	—
1984–85	Darlington	39	4
1985–86		40	4

TURLEY, Russell

Born Walsall 20.8.67.
Midfield. From Apprentice.

1984–85	Nottingham F	—	—
1985–86		—	—
1985–86	Wolverhampton W	—	—

TURNBULL, Lee

Born Teesside 27.9.67.
Forward. Local.

1985–86	Middlesbrough	2	—

All appearances include those as substitute

Season	Club	League Appearances/Goals

TURNER, Chris

Born Sheffield 15.9.58. Ht 5 10½ Wt 11 11
Goalkeeper. From Apprentice.
England Youth.

Season	Club	League Appearances/Goals	
1976–77	Sheffield W	45	—
1977–78		23	—
1978–79		23	—
1978–79	*Lincoln C*	5	—
1979–80	Sunderland	30	—
1980–81		27	—
1981–82		19	—
1982–83		35	—
1983–84		42	—
1984–85		42	—
1985–86	Manchester U	17	—

TURNER, John

Born Peterlee 23.12.54. Ht 5 11 Wt 12 8
Goalkeeper. From Apprentice.

Season	Club	League Appearances/Goals	
1973–74	Derby Co	—	—
1973–74	*Doncaster R*	4	—
1973–74	*Brighton*	—	—
1974–75	Derby Co	—	—
1974–75	*Peterborough U*	—	—
1974–75	*Huddersfield T*	1	—
1975–76	Reading	14	—
1976–77		4	—
1977–78		13	—
1978–79	Torquay U	46	—
1979–80		30	—
1979–80	Chesterfield	12	—
1980–81		43	—
1981–82		45	—
1982–83		32	—
1983–84	Torquay U	34	—
1984–85	Burnley	—	—
1984–85	Peterborough U	38	—
1985–86		22	—

TURNER, Phil

Born Sheffield 12.2.62. Ht 5 8 Wt 10 13
Midfield. From Apprentice.

Season	Club	League Appearances/Goals	
1979–80	Lincoln C	14	1
1980–81		38	4
1981–82		28	1
1982–83		40	3
1983–84		42	3
1984–85		36	3
1985–86		43	4

TURNER, Robert

Born Durham 18.9.66. Ht 6 3½ Wt 14 1
Forward. From Apprentice.

Season	Club	League Appearances/Goals	
1984–85	Huddersfield T	1	—
1985–86	Cardiff C	34	7

TURNER, Robin

Born Carlisle 10.9.55. Ht 5 9 Wt 11 4
Forward. From Apprentice. England Youth.

Season	Club	League Appearances/Goals	
1972–73	Ipswich T	—	—
1973–74		—	—
1974–75		—	—
1975–76		1	—
1976–77		4	—
1977–78		14	—
1978–79		—	—
1979–80		7	—
1980–81		4	—
1981–82		3	—
1982–83		5	1
1982–83	*Beerschot and MVV Maastricht*	Not known	
1983–84	Ipswich T	10	1
1984–85		—	—
1984–85	Swansea C	11	5
1985–86		9	3
1985–86	*Colchester U*	11	—

TURNER, Wayne

Born Luton 9.3.61. Ht 5 9 Wt 11 5
Defender. From Apprentice.

Season	Club	League Appearances/Goals	
1977–78	Luton T	—	—
1978–79		1	—
1979–80		2	—
1980–81		1	—

Season	Club	League Appearances/Goals		Season	Club	League Appearances/Goals	
1981–82	....	7	1				
1981–82	*Lincoln C*	16	—				
1982–83	Luton T	30	1				
1983–84	....	19	—				
1984–85	....	24	—				
1985–86	Coventry C	15	1				

UNDERHILL, Graeme

Born Bristol 10.4.68.
Midfield. From Apprentice.

1985–86	Bristol C	1	—

TWENTYMAN, Geoff

Born Liverpool 10.3.59.   Ht 6 1   Wt 12 10
Defender. From Southport, Maghull,
Formby and Chorley.

1983–84	Preston NE	28	2
1984–85	....	44	2
1985–86	....	26	—

UZZELL, John

Born Plymouth 31.3.59.   Ht 5 10   Wt 11 3
Defender. From Apprentice.

1976–77	Plymouth Arg	—	—
1977–78	....	44	1
1978–79	....	21	—
1979–80	....	1	—
1980–81	....	16	—
1981–82	....	35	2
1982–83	....	42	1
1983–84	....	42	—
1984–85	....	29	1
1985–86	....	8	—

TYLER, Simon

Born Monmouth 1.5.62.   Ht 6 1   Wt 12 0
Forward. From Monmouth T.

1984–85	Newport Co	2	—
1985–86	....	2	—

TYNAN, Tommy

Born Liverpool 17.11.55.   Ht 5 10½
Wt 11 11
Forward. From Apprentice.

1972–73	Liverpool	—	—
1973–74	....	—	—
1974–75	....	—	—
1975–76	....	—	—
1975–76	*Swansea C*	6	2
1976–77	Liverpool	—	—
1976–77	Sheffield W	39	14
1977–78	....	44	16
1978–79	....	8	1
1978–79	Lincoln C	9	1
1978–79	Newport Co	20	7
1979–80	....	34	8
1980–81	....	45	13
1981–82	....	38	13
1982–83	....	46	25
1983–84	Plymouth Arg	35	12
1984–85	....	45	31
1985–86	Rotherham U	30	13
1985–86	*Plymouth Arg*	9	9

| Season | Club | League Appearances/Goals | | Season | Club | League Appearances/Goals | |

VALENTINE, Carl

Born Manchester 4.7.58.   Ht 5 8   Wt 11 2
Forward. Canada full caps.

Season	Club	App	Goals
1975–76	Oldham Ath	—	—
1976–77		16	2
1977–78		34	4
1978–79		11	1
1979–80		21	1
From Vancouver W			
1984–85	WBA	29	4
1985–86		15	2

VALENTINE, Peter

Born Huddersfield 16.6.63.   Ht 5 11
Wt 10 10
Midfield. From Apprentice.

Season	Club	App	Goals
1980–81	Huddersfield T	—	—
1981–82		14	1
1982–83		5	—
1983–84	Bolton W	42	1
1984–85		26	—
1985–86	Bury	46	3

VAN DEN HAUWE, Pat

Born Dendermonde 16.12.60.   Ht 6 0
Wt 10 8
Defender. From Apprentice.
Wales 3 full caps.

Season	Club	App	Goals
1978–79	Birmingham C	8	—
1979–80		1	—
1980–81		4	—
1981–82		31	—
1982–83		31	1
1983–84		42	—
1984–85		6	—
1984–85	Everton	31	—
1985–86		40	1

VAN WYK, Dennis

Born Oostzaan 16.12.62.   Ht 5 9½   Wt 11 2
Midfield. From Ajax.

Season	Club	App	Goals
1982–83	Norwich C	23	2
1983–84		33	—
1984–85		33	—
1985–86		29	1

VARADI, Imre

Born Paddington 8.7.59.   Ht 5 8½   Wt 11 1
Forward. From Letchworth G.C.

Season	Club	App	Goals
1977–78	Sheffield U	—	—
1978–79		10	4
1978–79	Everton	—	—
1979–80		4	—
1980–81		22	6
1981–82	Newcastle U	42	18
1982–83		39	21
1983–84	Sheffield W	38	17
1984–85		38	16
1985–86	WBA	32	9

VAUGHAN, John

Born Isleworth 26.6.64.   Ht 5 10   Wt 13 1
Goalkeeper. From Apprentice.

Season	Club	App	Goals
1981–82	West Ham U	—	—
1982–83		—	—
1983–84		—	—
1984–85		—	—
1984–85	Charlton Ath	6	—
1985–86		—	—
1985–86	Bristol R	6	—
1985–86	Wrexham	4	—
1985–86	Bristol C	2	—

VAUGHAN, Nigel

Born Caerleon 20.5.59.   Ht 5 5   Wt 8 9
Midfield. From Apprentice. Wales, 10 full
caps.

Season	Club	App	Goals
1976–77	Newport Co	1	—
1977–78		11	—
1978–79		27	4
1979–80		46	12
1980–81		45	1
1981–82		44	3

All appearances include those as substitute

Season	Club	League Appearances/Goals	Season	Club	League Appearances/Goals
1982–83	....	43	7	1983–84	....	42	—
1983–84	....	7	5	1984–85	....	45	1
1983–84	Cardiff C	36	8	1985–86	....	45	2
1984–85	....	38	16				
1985–86	....	43	12				

VENISON, Barry

Born Consett 16.8.64.   Ht 5 9   Wt 11 9
Midfield. From Apprentice.
England Youth, Under-21.

1981–82	Sunderland	20	1
1982–83	....	37	—
1983–84	....	41	—
1984–85	....	39	1
1985–86	....	36	—

VENUS, Mark

Born Hartlepool 6.4.67.
Defender.

1984–85	Hartlepool U	4	—
1985–86	Leicester C..................	1	—

VICKERS, Steve

Born Bishop Auckland 13.10.67.   Ht 6 2
Wt 12 0
Defender. From Spennymoor U.

1985–86	Tranmere R.................	3	—

VINEY, Keith

Born Portsmouth 26.10.57.   Ht 5 11
Wt 11 11
Defender. From Apprentice.

1975–76	Portsmouth	7	—
1976–77	....	35	1
1977–78	....	4	—
1978–79	....	39	2
1979–80	....	16	—
1980–81	....	41	—
1981–82	....	24	—
1982–83	Exeter C....................	44	4

VINTER, Mick

Born Boston 23.5.54.   Ht 5 9   Wt 11 0
Forward. From Boston U.

1971–72	Notts Co	—	—
1972–73	....	4	1
1973–74	....	6	1
1974–75	....	20	4
1975–76	....	20	5
1976–77	....	36	12
1977–78	....	39	18
1978–79	....	41	12
1979–80	Wrexham....................	35	11
1980–81	....	37	9
1981–82	....	30	5
1982–83	Oxford U	43	10
1983–84	....	26	11
1984–85	Mansfield T	33	3
1985–86	....	21	4

All appearances include those as substitute

Season	Club	League Appearances/Goals		Season	Club	League Appearances/Goals	

WADDELL, John

Born Watford 23.3.66. Ht 6 3   Wt 12 6
Forward. From Apprentice.

Season	Club	App	Goals
1983–84	Norwich C	—	—
1984–85		—	—
1984–85	Dundee	3	—
1985–86		2	—

WADDLE, Alan

Born Wallsend 9.6.54.   Ht 6 3   Wt 13 0
Forward.

Season	Club	App	Goals
1971–72	Halifax T	9	1
1972–73		30	3
1973–74	Liverpool	11	1
1974–75		5	—
1975–76		—	—
1976–77		—	—
1977–78		—	—
1977–78	Leicester C	11	1
1978–79	Swansea C	42	19
1979–80		34	8
1980–81		14	7
1980–81	Newport Co	9	4
1981–82		18	4
1982–83	Mansfield T	14	4
1983–84	Hartlepool U	12	2
1983–84	Peterborough U	33	12
1984–85		3	—
1984–85	Hartlepool U	4	—
1984–85	Swansea C	12	5
1985–86		28	5

WADDLE, Chris

Born Hepworth 14.12.60.   Ht 6 0   Wt 11 5
Forward. From Tow Law T. England
Under-21, 16 full caps.

Season	Club	App	Goals
1980–81	Newcastle U	13	1
1981–82		42	7
1982–83		37	7
1983–84		42	18
1984–85		36	13
1985–86	Tottenham H	39	11

WADDOCK, Gary

Born Kingsbury 17.3.62.   Ht 5 9½   Wt 11 0
Midfield. From Apprentice.
Eire Under-21, 18 full caps.

Season	Club	App	Goals
1979–80	QPR	16	1
1980–81		33	3
1981–82		35	—
1982–83		33	—
1983–84		36	3
1984–85		31	1
1985–86		15	—

WADE, Bryan

Born Bath 25.6.63.   Ht 5 8   Wt 11 5
Forward. From Trowbridge T.

Season	Club	App	Goals
1985–86	Swindon T	34	10

WADSWORTH, Ian

Born Huddersfield 24.9.66.   Ht 5 10   Wt 10 0
Forward. From Apprentice.

Season	Club	App	Goals
1984–85	Huddersfield T	1	—
1985–86	Doncaster R	2	—
1985–86	Burnley	—	—

WAITT, Mick

Born Newcastle 25.6.60.   Ht 6 4   Wt 13 7
Forward. From Keyworth U. and Arnold
Kingswell.

Season	Club	App	Goals
1984–85	Notts Co	13	1
1985–86		37	14

WAKENSHAW, Robbie

Born Northumberland 22.12.65.   Ht 5 10
Wt 11 10
Forward. From Apprentice. England Youth.

Season	Club	App	Goals
1983–84	Everton	1	1
1984–85		2	—
1985–86		—	—
1985–86	Carlisle U	8	2
1985–86	*Doncaster R*	8	3

All appearances include those as substitute

| Season | Club | League Appearances/Goals | | Season | Club | League Appearances/Goals | |

WALDRON, Malcolm

Born Emsworth 6.9.56. Ht 6 0½ Wt 12 4
Defender. From Apprentice. England 'B'.

Season	Club	Apps	Goals
1974–75	Southampton	3	—
1975–76		2	—
1976–77		32	—
1977–78		25	—
1978–79		42	6
1979–80		30	2
1980–81		7	—
1981–82		34	2
1982–83		3	—
1983–84	Burnley	16	—
1983–84	Portsmouth	12	—
1984–85		11	1
1985–86		—	—

WALFORD, Steve

Born Highgagte 5.1.58. Ht 6 1 Wt 11 7
Defender. From Apprentice. England
Youth.

Season	Club	Apps	Goals
1974–75	Tottenham H	—	—
1975–76		2	—
1976–77		—	—
1977–78	Arsenal	5	—
1978–79		33	2
1979–80		19	1
1980–81		20	—
1980–81	Norwich C	10	—
1981–82		42	1
1982–83		41	1
1983–84	West Ham U	41	2
1984–85		33	—
1985–86		27	—

WALKER, Alan

Born Mossley 17.12.59. Ht 6 1 Wt 12 7
Defender. From Stockport Co. and
Telford U.

Season	Club	Apps	Goals
1983–84	Lincoln C	33	2
1984–85		42	2
1985–86	Millwall	26	3

WALKER, Andy

Born Glasgow 6.4.65. Ht 5 8 Wt 10 7
Forward. From Baillieston Juniors.

Season	Club	Apps	Goals
1984–85	Motherwell	11	3
1985–86		22	4

WALKER, Clive

Born Oxford 26.5.57. Ht 5 8½ Wt 11 4
Forward. From Apprentice.
England Schools.

Season	Club	Apps	Goals
1974–75	Chelsea	—	—
1975–76		—	—
1976–77		1	—
1977–78		23	7
1978–79		30	4
1979–80		36	13
1980–81		37	11
1981–82		36	16
1982–83		29	6
1983–84		6	3
1984–85	Sunderland	38	10
1985–86		12	—
1985–86	QPR	5	1

WALKER, Colin

Born Rotherham 1.5.58. Ht 5 8 Wt 11 8
Forward. From Matlock T and Gisborne C.
New Zealand full caps.

Season	Club	Apps	Goals
1980–81	Barnsley	2	—
1981–82		19	11
1982–83		3	—
1982–83	Doncaster R	12	5
From Gisborne C.			
1985–86	Doncaster R	5	—
1985–86	Cambridge U	3	1

WALKER, Des

Born Hackney 26.11.65. Ht 5 11 Wt 11 3
Defender. From Apprentice. England
Under-21.

Season	Club	Apps	Goals
1983–84	Nottingham F	4	—
1984–85		3	—
1985–86		39	—

Season	Club	League Appearances/Goals		Season	Club	League Appearances/Goals	

WALKER, Gary

Born Manchester 11.10.63.
Goalkeeper. From Ashton T.

1985–86	Stockport Co	20	—

WALKER, Kevin

Born Cardiff 18.12.67.   Ht 6 1   Wt 12 7
Forward. From Gabalfa Draconians. Wales Youth.

1985–86	Cardiff C	—	—

WALKER, Nicky

Born Aberdeen 29.9.62.   Ht 6 2   Wt 11 12
Goalkeeper. From Elgin C. Scotland Youth.

1980–81	Leicester C	—	—
1981–82		6	—
1982–83	Motherwell	16	—
1983–84		15	—
1983–84	Rangers	8	—
1984–85		14	—
1985–86		34	—

WALKER, Nigel

Born Gateshead 7.4.59.   Ht 5 10   Wt 11 11
Forward. Local.

1977–78	Newcastle U	14	—
1978–79		20	2
1979–80		13	—
1980–81		18	1
1981–82		5	—
1981–82	*Plymouth Arg*	—	—
From San Diego S			
1982–83	Crewe Alex.	20	5
1983–84	Sunderland	1	—
1983–84	*Blackpool*	10	3
1984–85	Chester C	41	9
1985–86	Hartlepool U	45	5

WALKER, Phil

Born Kirkby 27.1.57.   Ht 6 1   Wt 12 11
Forward. From O.N.R.Y.C.

1977–78	Chesterfield	10	2
1978–79		40	9
1979–80		45	13
1980–81		33	5
1981–82		25	4
1982–83		13	5
1982–83	Rotherham U	10	2
1983–84		15	1
1983–84	*Cardiff C*	2	—
1984–85	Rotherham U	—	—
1984–85	Chesterfield	18	4
1985–86		20	5

WALKER, Ray

Born North Shields 28.9.63.   Ht 5 10
Wt 11 9
Defender. From Apprentice.

1981–82	Aston Villa	—	—
1982–83		1	—
1983–84		8	—
1984–85		7	—
1984–85	*Port Vale*	15	1
1985–86	Aston Villa	7	—

WALKER, Roger

Born Bolton 15.11.66.
Forward.

1984–85	Bolton W	1	1
1985–86		11	—

WALLACE, Danny

Born London 21.1.64.   Ht 5 4½   Wt 9 10
Forward. From Apprentice.
England Under-21, 1 full cap.

Season	Club	League Appearances/Goals		Season	Club	League Appearances/Goals	
1980–81	Southampton	2	—	1972–73		1	—
1981–82		7	—	1973–74		—	—
1982–83		35	12	1974–75		30	—
1983–84		41	11	1975–76		42	—
1984–85		35	7	1976–77		42	—
1985–86		35	8	1977–78		42	—
				1978–79		42	—
				1979–80		42	—
				1980–81		42	—
				1981–82		36	—
				1982–83		42	—
				1983–84		35	—
				1984–85		11	—
				1985–86	Derby Co	33	—

WALLACE, Ian

Born Glasgow 23.5.56.   Ht 5 8   Wt 11 8
Forward. From Yoker Ath.
Scotland Under-21, 3 full caps.

1974–75	Dumbarton	8	2
1975–76		26	9
1976–77	Coventry C	26	9
1977–78		41	20
1978–79		38	15
1979–80		25	13
1980–81	Nottingham F	37	11
1981–82		29	9
1982–83		41	13
1983–84		27	3
From Brest			
1984–85	Sunderland	15	3
1985–86		19	3

WALLER, David

Born Urmston 20.12.63.   Ht 5 10   Wt 10 0
Forward. Local.

1981–82	Crewe Alex.	1	—
1982–83		37	17
1983–84		42	10
1984–85		44	15
1985–86		44	13

WALLINGTON, Mark

Born Sleaford 17.9.52.   Ht 6 1   Wt 14 2½
Goalkeeper. England Youth, Under-23.

1971–72	Walsall	11	—
1971–72	Leicester C	5	—

WALSH, Alan

Born Darlington 9.12.56.   Ht 6 0   Wt 11 0
Forward. From Horden C.W.

1976–77	Middlesbrough	—	—
1977–78		3	—
1978–79		—	—
1978–79	Darlington	33	9
1979–80		43	15
1980–81		46	22
1981–82		45	13
1982–83		46	18
1983–84		38	10
1984–85	Bristol C	45	20
1985–86		44	18

WALSH, Colin

Born Hamilton 22.7.62.   Ht 5 9   Wt 10 11
Midfield. From Apprentice. Scotland
Under-21.

1979–80	Nottingham F	—	—
1980–81		16	4
1981–82		15	3
1982–83		37	5
1983–84		38	13
1984–85		13	1
1985–86		20	6

Season	Club	League Appearances/Goals	Season	Club	League Appearances/Goals

WALSH, Derek

Born Hamilton 24.10.67.   Ht 5 7   Wt 10 1
Midfield. From Apprentice.

Season	Club	App	Goals
1984–85	Everton	1	—
1985–86		—	—

WALSH, Gary

Born Wigan 21.3.68.   Ht 6 1   Wt 12 12
Goalkeeper.

Season	Club	App	Goals
1984–85	Manchester U	—	—
1985–86		—	—

WALSH, Ian

Born St. Davids 4.9.58.   Ht 5 9½   Wt 11 6
Forward. From Apprentice.
Wales Schools, Under-21, 18 full caps.

Season	Club	App	Goals
1975–76	Crystal Palace	—	—
1976–77		1	—
1977–78		16	2
1978–79		33	8
1979–80		29	6
1980–81		25	5
1981–82		13	2
1981–82	Swansea C	5	2
1982–83		8	3
1983–84		24	6
1984–85	Barnsley	16	—
1985–86		33	15

WALSH, Mario

Born Paddington 19.1.66.   Ht 6 1   Wt 11 12
Forward. From Apprentice.

Season	Club	App	Goals
1983–84	Portsmouth	—	—
1984–85		—	—
1984–85	Torquay U	21	5
1985–86		41	7

WALSH, Mark

Born Preston 7.10.62.   Ht 5 19   Wt 10 0
Midfield. From Apprentice.

Season	Club	App	Goals
1980–81	Preston NE	—	—
1981–82		10	1
1982–83		27	1
1983–84		25	—
From New Zealand			
1985–86	Exeter C	1	—

WALSH, Mick

Born Manchester 20.6.56.   Ht 6 0   Wt 12 0
Defender. Eire, 4 full caps.

Season	Club	App	Goals
1974–75	Bolton W	5	—
1975–76		9	—
1976–77		8	—
1977–78		41	1
1978–79		42	1
1979–80		42	1
1980–81		30	1
1981–82	Everton	18	—
1982–83		2	—
1982–83	*Norwich C*	5	—
1982–83	*Burnley*	3	—
From Ft. Lauderdale			
1983–84	Manchester C	4	—
1983–84	Blackpool	20	1
1984–85		35	1
1985–86		25	1

WALSH, Paul

Born Plumstead 1.10.62.   Ht 5 7   Wt 10 8
Forward. From Apprentice.
England Youth, Under-21, 5 full caps.

Season	Club	App	Goals
1979–80	Charlton Ath	9	—
1980–81		40	11
1981–82		38	13
1982–83	Luton T	41	13
1983–84		39	11
1984–85	Liverpool	26	8
1985–86		20	11

Season	Club	League Appearances/Goals		Season	Club	League Appearances/Goals	

WALSH, Steve

Born Fulwood 3.11.64.   Ht 6 2   Wt 14 0
Defender. Local.

1982–83	Wigan Ath	31	—
1983–84		42	1
1984–85		40	2
1985–86		13	1

WALSHAW, Lee

Born Sheffield 20.1.67.   Ht 5 9   Wt 11 5
Midfield. From Apprentice.

1984–85	Sheffield U	3	—
1985–86		4	1

WALTERS, Mark

Born Birmingham 12.1.61.   Ht 5 9
Wt 10 12
Forward. From Apprentice. England Youth,
Under-21.

1981–82	Aston Villa	1	—
1982–83		22	1
1983–84		37	8
1984–85		36	10
1985–86		40	10

WALWYN, Keith

Born W. Indies 17.2.56.   Ht 6 1   Wt 13 2
Forward. From Winterton.

1979–80	Chesterfield	—	—
1980–81		3	2
1981–82	York C	44	23
1982–83		41	21
1983–84		45	25
1984–85		27	9
1985–86		46	22

WARBURTON, Ray

Born Rotherham 7.10.67.   Ht 6 0   Wt 11 5
Defender. From Apprentice.

1984–85	Rotherham U	1	—
1985–86		—	—

WARD, Mark

Born Prescot 10.10.62.   Ht 5 6   Wt 9 12
Midfield. From Everton Apprentice and
Northwich Vic.

1983–84	Oldham Ath.	42	6
1984–85		42	6
1985–86	West Ham U	42	3

WARD, Paul

Born Sedgefield 15.9.63.   Ht 5 11   Wt 12 5
Defender. From Apprentice.

1981–82	Chelsea	—	—
1982–83	Middlesbrough	15	—
1983–84		28	1
1984–85		30	—
1985–86		3	—
1985–86	Darlington	35	2

WARD, Steve

Born Derby 21.7.59.   Ht 6 0   Wt 12 13
Midfield. From Apprentice.

1976–77	Brighton	—	—
1977–78		—	—
1978–79		—	—
1979–80	Northampton T	15	2
1980–81	Halifax T	35	1
1981–82		44	7
1982–83		44	1
1983–84		46	3
1984–85		39	4
1985–86		38	1

All appearances include those as substitute

Season	Club	League Appearances/Goals		Season	Club	League Appearances/Goals

WARD, Warren

Born Plymstock 25.5.62.
Forward. From Guisley.

Season	Club	Apps	Goals
1984–85	York C	4	3
1985–86	Lincoln C	21	8
1985–86	*Exeter C*	14	3

WARK, John

Born Glasgow 4.8.57. Ht 5 10½ Wt 11 12
Midfield. From Apprentice.
Scotland Under-21, 29 full caps.

Season	Club	Apps	Goals
1974–75	Ipswich T	3	—
1975–76		3	—
1976–77		33	10
1977–78		18	5
1978–79		42	6
1979–80		41	12
1980–81		40	18
1981–82		42	18
1982–83		42	20
1983–84		32	5
1983–84	Liverpool	9	2
1984–85		40	18
1985–86		9	3

WASSELL, Kim

Born Wolverhampton 9.6.57. Ht 5 8
Wt 11 8
Forward. From West Bromwich Apprentice.

Season	Club	Apps	Goals
1977–78	Northampton T	7	—
1978–79		13	—
1979–80	Aldershot	—	—
From Local			
1983–84	Hull C	1	—
1984–85	Swansea C	2	—
1985–86	Wolverhampton W	2	—

WATKISS, Stuart

Born Wolverhampton 8.5.66. Ht 5 11
Wt 12 0
Defender. From Apprentice.

Season	Club	Apps	Goals
1983–84	Wolverhampton W	2	—
From Local			
1985–86	Crewe Alex	3	—

WATSON, Alex

Born Liverpool 5.4.68. Ht 5 11½ Wt 11 9
Defender. From Apprentice. England
Youth.

Season	Club	Apps	Goals
1984–85	Liverpool	—	—
1985–86		—	—

WATSON, Andy

Born Huddersfield 3.4.67. Ht 5 11 Wt 11 4
Defender. From Apprentice.

Season	Club	Apps	Goals
1984–85	Huddersfield T	—	—
1985–86		—	—

WATSON, Andy

Born Aberdeen 3.9.59. Ht 5 10 Wt 11 10
Midfield. From Sunnyside.
Scotland Youth, Under-21.

Season	Club	Apps	Goals
1976–77	Aberdeen	—	—
1977–78		1	—
1978–79		2	—
1979–80		17	5
1980–81		29	—
1981–82		30	5
1982–83		18	1
1983–84	Leeds U	31	7
1984–85		7	—
1984–85	Hearts	16	3
1985–86		12	—

WATSON, Dave

Born Liverpool 20.11.61. Ht 5 11½
Wt 11 12
Defender. From Amateur. England
Under-21, 6 full caps.

Season	Club	League Appearances/Goals		Season	Club	League Appearances/Goals	
1979–80	Liverpool	—	—				
1980–81		—	—				
1980–81	Norwich C	18	3				
1981–82		38	3				
1982–83		35	1				
1983–84		40	1				
1984–85		39	—				
1985–86		42	2				

WEATHERLY, Mark

Born Ramsgate 18.1.58.   Ht 6 0   Wt 12 0
Defender. From Apprentice.

Season	Club	App	Goals
1974–75	Gillingham	5	1
1975–76		18	5
1976–77		17	2
1977–78		24	2
1978–79		46	2
1979–80		45	1
1980–81		43	1
1981–82		33	1
1982–83		43	10
1983–84		32	9
1984–85		35	2
1985–86		38	7

WATSON, George

Born Stirling 16.9.68.
Midfield. From Apprentice.

1985–86	Ipswich T	—	—

WATSON, Willie

Born Glasgow 23.1.67.   Ht 5 9   Wt 11 0
Defender. From Clyde Juniors.

1984–85	Chelsea	—	—
1985–86		—	—

WEBB, Alan

Born Wellington 1.1.63.   Ht 5 10   Wt 12 0
Defender. From Apprentice.

1979–80	WBA	—	—
1980–81		—	—
1981–82		6	—
1982–83		13	—
1983–84		5	—
1983–84	*Lincoln C*	11	—
1984–85	Port Vale	46	—
1985–86		39	1

WAUGH, Keith

Born Sunderland 27.10.56.   Ht 5 11
Wt 12 2
Goalkeeper. From Apprentice.

1974–75	Sunderland	—	—
1975–76		—	—
1976–77	Peterborough U	32	—
1977–78		26	—
1978–79		46	—
1979–80		46	—
1980–81		45	—
1981–82	Sheffield U	45	—
1982–83		28	—
1983–84		16	—
1984–85		10	—
1984–85	*Bristol C*	3	—
1984–85	*Cambridge U*	4	—
1985–86	Bristol C	44	—

WEBB, Neil

Born Reading 30.7.63.   Ht 5 11   Wt 11 7
Midfield. From Apprentice. England Youth,
Under-21.

1979–80	Reading	5	—
1980–81		27	7
1981–82		40	15
1982–83	Portsmouth	42	8
1983–84		40	10
1984–85		41	16
1985–86	Nottingham F	38	14

Season	Club	League Appearances/Goals	Season	Club	League Appearances/Goals

WEBB, Paul

Born Wolverhampton 30.11.67.
Midfield. From Bilston.

| 1985–86 | Shrewsbury T | — — |

WEBBER, Andy

Born Port Talbot 15.3.63.
Forward.

| 1984–85 | Swansea C | 1 — |
| 1985–86 | Exeter C | 1 — |

WEBBER, Trevor

Born Hennock 5.9.68.
Midfield.

| 1985–86 | Torquay U | 5 — |

WEBSTER, Ian

Born Norton 30.12.65.   Ht 6 1   Wt 10 11
Defender. From Leeds Schoolboy.

1982–83	Scunthorpe U	1 —
1983–84		9 —
1984–85		3 —
1985–86		5 —

WEBSTER, Simon

Born Earl Shilton 20.1.64.   Ht 6 0   Wt 11 7
Defender. From Apprentice.

1981–82	Tottenham H	— —
1982–83		2 —
1983–84		1 —
1983–84	*Exeter C*	26 —
1984–85	Tottenham H	— —
1984–85	*Norwich C*	— —
1984–85	Huddersfield T	16 1
1985–86		41 2

WEETMAN, Darran

Born Oswestry 7.6.68.
Midfield.

| 1985–86 | Wrexham | 1 — |

WEIR, Jim

Born Lesmahagow 24.12.57.   Ht 5 7   Wt 11 7
Midfield. From KSV Hessen

| 1985–86 | Motherwell | 3 — |

WEIR, Michael

Born Edinburgh 16.1.66.   Ht 5 4   Wt 9 2
Midfield. From Portobello Thistle.

1982–83	Hibernian	— —
1983–84		— —
1984–85		12 —
1985–86		7 —

WEIR, Peter

Born Johnstone 18.1.58.   Ht 6 0   Wt 11 9
Forward. From Neilston Juniors. Scotland 6
full caps.

1978–79	St Mirren	6 —
1979–80		26 2
1980–81		28 2
1981–82	Aberdeen	25 2
1982–83		31 6
1983–84		27 5
1984–85		16 3
1985–86		22 5

WELLS, Ian

Born Wolverhampton 27.10.64.   Ht 6 0
Wt 13 0
Forward. From Harrisons.

| 1985–86 | Hereford U | 35 9 |

Season	Club	League Appearances/Goals		Season	Club	League Appearances/Goals	

WELLS, Peter

Born Nottingham 13.8.56.   Ht 6 1   Wt 13 0
Goalkeeper. From Apprentice.

1974–75	Nottingham F	—	—
1975–76		23	—
1976–77		4	—
1976–77	Southampton	24	—
1977–78		30	—
1978–79		19	—
1979–80		25	—
1980–81		30	—
1981–82		10	—
1982–83		3	—
1982–83	*Millwall*	18	—
1983–84	Millwall	15	—
1984–85		—	—
1985–86	Orient	45	—

WELSH, Andy

Born Fleetwood 20.11.62.   Ht 5 5   Wt 8 10
Forward. From Apprentice.

1979–80	Blackpool	—	—
1980–81		1	—
1981–82		—	—
From Local			
1984–85	Bury	—	—
1985–86		1	—

WELSH, Paul

Born Liverpool 10.5.66.   Ht 6 2   Wt 12 4
Defender. From Formby. England Schools.

| 1984–85 | Preston NE | 3 | — |
| 1985–86 | | 17 | 1 |

WEST, Colin

Born Middlesbrough 19.9.67.   Ht 5 7½
Wt 11 0
Forward. From Apprentice.

| 1985–86 | Chelsea | — | — |

WEST, Colin

Born Wallsend 13.11.62.   Ht 6 2   Wt 13 13
Forward. From Apprentice.

1980–81	Sunderland	—	—
1981–82		18	6
1982–83		23	3
1983–84		38	9
1984–85		23	3
1984–85	Watford	12	7
1985–86		33	13

WEST, David

Born Leicester 16.11.64.   Ht 5 10   Wt 11 0
Forward. From Dorchester T.

1982–83	Liverpool	—	—
1983–84		—	—
1984–85		—	—
1985–86	Bristol C	—	—
1985–86	Torquay U	21	2

WEST, Gary

Born Scunthorpe 25.8.64.   Ht 6 2   Wt 12 7
Defender. From Apprentice.
England Youth.

1982–83	Sheffield U	26	1
1983–84		24	—
1984–85		25	—
1985–86	Lincoln C	38	2

WESTLEY, Graham

Born London 4.3.68.   Ht 5 9   Wt 10 11
Forward. From QPR Apprentice. England
Youth.

| 1985–86 | Gillingham | 1 | — |

Season	Club	League Appearances/Goals	Season	Club	League Appearances/Goals

WESTLEY, Shane

Born Canterbury 16.6.65. Ht 6 2 Wt 12 10
Defender. From Apprentice.

Season	Club	App	Goals
1983–84	Charlton Ath	8	—
1984–85		—	—
1984–85	Southend U	12	—
1985–86		36	5

WESTWOOD, Gary

Born Barrow 3.4.63. Ht 6 0 Wt 13 12
Goalkeeper. From Apprentice.

Season	Club	App	Goals
1980–81	Ipswich T	—	—
1981–82		—	—
1981–82	*Charlton Ath*	—	—
1982–83	Ipswich T	—	—
1982–83	*Crystal Palace*	—	—
1983–84	Ipswich T	—	—
1983–84	Reading	5	—
1983–84	*Peterborough U*	—	—
1984–85	Reading	43	—
1985–86		46	—

WHARTON, Ken

Born Newcastle 28.11.60. Ht 5 8 Wt 8 10
Midfield. From Grainger Park BC.

Season	Club	App	Goals
1978–79	Newcastle U	2	—
1979–80		1	—
1980–81		36	—
1981–82		33	5
1982–83		41	5
1983–84		41	4
1984–85		35	6
1985–86		15	2

WHATMORE, Neil

Born Ellesmere 17.5.55. Ht 5 9½ Wt 11 8
Forward. From Apprentice.

Season	Club	App	Goals
1972–73	Bolton W	2	2
1973–74		34	9

Season	Club	App	Goals
1974–75		17	3
1975–76		35	11
1976–77		41	25
1977–78		42	19
1978–79		29	3
1979–80		41	16
1980–81		36	14
1981–82	Birmingham C	24	6
1982–83		2	—
1982–83	*Oxford U*	7	5
1982–83	*Bolton W*	10	3
1982–83	Oxford U	16	7
1983–84		13	3
1983–84	*Bolton W*	7	2
1984–85	Burnley	8	1
1984–85	Mansfield T	26	7
1985–86		31	9

WHEELER, Paul

Born Caerphilly 3.1.65. Ht 5 7½ Wt 9 4
Midfield. From Apprentice.

Season	Club	App	Goals
1982–83	Bristol R	—	—
1983–84		—	—
From Aberaman			
1985–86	Cardiff C	21	2

WHEELDON, Tom

Born Whiston 28.12.57. Ht 5 7 Wt 11 0
Forward.

Season	Club	App	Goals
1976–77	Everton	—	—
1977–78		—	—
From Runcorn			
1981–82	Torquay U	8	—
From Falmouth			
1985–86	Torquay U	8	—

WHELAN, Ronnie

Born Dublin 25.9.61. Ht 5 9 Wt 10 13
Midfield. From Home Farm.
Eire Under-21, 16 full caps.

Season	Club	League Appearances/Goals		Season	Club	League Appearances/Goals	

Season	Club	Appearances	Goals
1979–80	Liverpool	—	—
1980–81		1	1
1981–82		32	10
1982–83		28	2
1983–84		23	4
1984–85		37	7
1985–86		39	10

WHITE, Dale

Born Sunderland 17.3.68.   Ht 5 10   Wt 11 4
Forward. From Apprentice. England
Schools.

Season	Club	Appearances	Goals
1985–86	Sunderland	4	—

WHITE, David

Born Manchester 30.10.67.
Midfield.

Season	Club	Appearances	Goals
1985–86	Manchester C	—	—

WHITE, Dean

Born Hastings 4.12.58.   Ht 5 10   Wt 12 11
Forward. From Chelsea Apprentice.

Season	Club	Appearances	Goals
1978–79	Gillingham	27	3
1979–80		9	3
1980–81		34	5
1981–82		32	12
1982–83		14	3
1982–83	Millwall	14	4
1983–84		27	—
1984–85	Gillingham	—	—
1985–86		—	—

WHITE, Devon

Born Nottingham 2.3.64.   Ht 6 3   Wt 14 2
Forward. From Notts Co Amateur, Radford
Olympic and Arnold T.

Season	Club	Appearances	Goals
1984–85	Lincoln C	7	1
1985–86		22	3

WHITE, Mark

Born Sheffield 26.10.58.   Ht 5 10   Wt 11 12
Defender. From Sheffield W Apprentice.

Season	Club	Appearances	Goals
1976–77	Reading	—	—
1977–78		25	—
1978–79		46	—
1979–80		45	—
1980–81		3	—
1981–82		9	—
1982–83		29	1
1983–84		39	2
1984–85		39	4
1985–86		25	3

WHITE, Steve

Born Chipping Sodbury 2.1.59.   Ht 5 10½
Wt 11 4
Forward. From Mangotsfield U.

Season	Club	Appearances	Goals
1977–78	Bristol R	8	4
1978–79		27	10
1979–80		15	6
1979–80	Luton T	9	—
1980–81		21	7
1981–82		42	18
1982–83	Charlton Ath	29	12
1982–83	*Lincoln C*	3	—
1982–83	*Luton T*	4	—
1983–84	Bristol R	43	9
1984–85		18	3
1985–86		40	12

WHITE, Tony

Born Clacton 3.11.66.   Ht 5 11   Wt 11 3
Defender.

Season	Club	Appearances	Goals
1984–85	Bournemouth	—	—
1985–86		1	—

WHITE, Winston

Born Leicester 26.10.58.   Ht 5 10½
Wt 10 12
Midfield. From Apprentice.

All appearances include those as substitute

Season	Club	League Appearances/Goals		Season	Club	League Appearances/Goals
1976–77	Leicester C	4	—	1982–83		36 1
1977–78		6	1	1983–84		34 1
1978–79		2	—	1984–85		32 —
1978–79	Hereford U	15	3	1985–86		24 —
1979–80		34	2	1985–86	*Wolverhampton W*	2 —
1980–81		43	5			
1981–82		46	8			
1982–83		37	3			
1983–84	Chesterfield	1	—			
1983–84	Port Vale	1	—			
1983–84	Stockport Co	4	—			
1983–84	Bury	29	1			
1984–85		46	4			
1985–86		43	5			

WHITEHEAD, Alan

Born Bury 20.11.56.   Ht 6 3   Wt 12 0
Defender. Local.

Season	Club	League Appearances/Goals	
1977–78	Bury	6	1
1978–79		24	3
1979–80		32	3
1980–81		37	6
1981–82	Brentford	43	3
1982–83		41	1
1983–84		18	—
1983–84	Scunthorpe U	15	—
1984–85		45	4
1985–86		41	3

WHITEHEAD, Clive

Born Birmingham 24.11.55.   Ht 5 10½
Wt 11 5
Forward. From Northfield J.

Season	Club	League Appearances/Goals	
1973–74	Bristol C	12	2
1974–75		14	4
1975–76		22	4
1976–77		41	—
1977–78		33	2
1978–79		30	2
1979–80		40	—
1980–81		31	—
1981–82		6	—
1981–82	WBA	8	1

WHITEHURST, Billy

Born Thurnscoe 10.6.59.   Ht 6 1½   Wt 13 13
Forward. From Mexborough.

Season	Club	League Appearances/Goals	
1980–81	Hull C	26	1
1981–82		36	6
1982–83		36	3
1983–84		37	10
1984–85		40	20
1985–86		18	7
1985–86	Newcastle U	20	7

WHITESIDE, Norman

Born Belfast 7.5.65.   Ht 6 0   Wt 12 8
Forward. From Apprentice.
Northern Ireland, 26 full caps.

Season	Club	League Appearances/Goals	
1981–82	Manchester U	2	1
1982–83		39	8
1983–84		37	10
1984–85		27	9
1985–86		37	4

WHITLOCK, Mark

Born Portsmouth 14.3.61.   Ht 5 11½
Wt 12 2
Defender. From Apprentice.

Season	Club	League Appearances/Goals	
1978–79	Southampton	—	—
1979–80		—	—
1980–81		—	—
1981–82	*Grimsby T*	9	1
1982–83	*Grimsby T*	8	—
1982–83	*Aldershot*	14	—
1983–84	Southampton	16	—
1984–85		22	—
1985–86		14	—

Season	Club	League Appearances/Goals	Season	Club	League Appearances/Goals

WHITTAKER, Brian

Born Glasgow 23.9.56. Ht 6 0 Wt 11 9
Defender. From Sighthill Amateurs.

1974–75	Partick T	1	—
1975–76		1	—
1976–77		36	1
1977–78		35	—
1978–79		36	—
1979–80		35	1
1980–81		34	1
1981–82		28	—
1982–83		35	1
1983–84	Celtic	10	2
1984–85	Hearts	28	1
1985–86		25	

WHITTON, Steve

Born East Ham 4.12.60. Ht 6 0 Wt 12 7
Midfield. From Apprentice.

1978–79	Coventry C	—	—
1979–80		7	—
1980–81		1	—
1981–82		28	9
1982–83		38	12
1983–84	West Ham U	22	5
1984–85		17	1
1985–86		—	—
1985–86	*Birmingham C*	8	3

WHYMARK, Trevor

Born Burston 4.5.50. Ht 5 11 Wt 11 2
Forward. From Diss T.
England Under-23, 1 full cap.

1969–70	Ipswich T	8	1
1970–71		10	1
1971–72		13	3
1972–73		41	11
1973–74		39	11
1974–75		40	10
1975–76		40	13
1976–77		36	14
1977–78		20	9
1978–79		13	1

From Vancouver W/*Sparta Rotterdam*

1979–80	*Derby Co*	2	—
1980–81	Grimsby T	21	3
1981–82		33	11
1982–83		28	1
1983–84		11	1
1983–84	Southend U	19	3
1984–85		19	2
1985–86	Peterborough U	3	—
1985–86	Colchester U	2	—

WHYTE, Chris

Born London 2.9.61. Ht 6 1 Wt 11 10.
Defender. From Amateur.
England Under-21.

1979–80	Arsenal	—	—
1980–81		—	—
1981–82		32	2
1982–83		36	3
1983–84		15	2
1984–85		—	—
1984–85	*Crystal Palace*	13	—
1985–86	Arsenal	7	1

WHYTE, Derek

Born Glasgow 31.8.68. Ht 5 11 Wt 11 5
Defender. From Celtic B.C. Scotland
Schools, Youth.

1985–86	Celtic	11	—

WICKS, Steve

Born Reading 3.10.56. Ht 6 2 Wt 13 2
Defender. From Apprentice.
England Youth, Under-21.

1974–75	Chelsea	1	—
1975–76		19	—
1976–77		34	4
1977–78		41	—
1978–79		23	1
1978–79	Derby Co	19	—
1979–80		5	—
1979–80	QPR	35	—
1980–81		38	—
1981–82	Crystal Palace	14	1

Season	Club	League Appearances/Goals	Season	Club	League Appearances/Goals

Season	Club	Appearances	Goals
1981–82	QRP	9	—
1982–83		14	1
1983–84		31	2
1984–85		33	2
1985–86		29	1

WIGLEY, Steve

Born Ashton 15.10.61.   Ht 5 9   Wt 10 5
Forward. From Curzon Ashton.

Season	Club	Appearances	Goals
1980–81	Nottingham F	—	—
1981–82		—	—
1982–83		4	—
1983–84		35	1
1984–85		35	1
1985–86		8	—
1985–86	Sheffield U	10	1

WIGNALL, Steve

Born Liverpool 17.9.54.   Ht 5 11   Wt 11 11
Defender. From Liverpool Amateur.

Season	Club	Appearances	Goals
1971–72	Doncaster R	—	—
1972–73		23	—
1973–74		38	—
1974–75		35	1
1975–76		23	—
1976–77		11	—
1976–77	*Nottingham F*	—	—
1977–78	Doncaster R	—	—
1977–78	Colchester U	34	2
1978–79		42	4
1979–80		40	3
1980–81		42	1
1981–82		43	—
1982–83		44	4
1983–84		36	8
1984–85	Brentford	36	—
1985–86		28	2

WILDER, Chris

Born Wortley 23.9.67.
Defender. From Apprentice.

Season	Club	Appearances	Goals
1985–86	Southampton	—	—

WILE, John

Born Sherburn 9.3.47.   Ht 60   Wt 120
Defender. From Durham C.

Season	Club	Appearances	Goals
1966–67	Sunderland	—	—
1967–68	Peterborough U	5	—
1968–69		46	1
1969–70		46	4
1970–71		21	2
1970–71	WBA	21	2
1971–72		42	3
1972–73		40	1
1973–74		42	3
1974–75		38	1
1975–76		37	2
1976–77		42	4
1977–78		39	4
1978–79		42	2
1979–80		42	1
1980–81		42	1
1981–82		42	—
1982–83		31	—
1983–84	Peterborough U	32	2
1984–85		41	1
1985–86		14	—

WILKES, Steve

Born Preston 30.6.67.   Ht 5 5   Wt 10 0
Forward. From Apprentice.

Season	Club	Appearances	Goals
1985–86	Wigan Ath	—	—

WILKINS, Ray

Born Hillingdon 14.9.56.   Ht 5 8   Wt 11 2
Midfield. From Apprentice. England Under-
21, Under-23, 80 full caps, Football League.

Season	Club	Appearances	Goals
1973–74	Chelsea	6	—
1974–75		21	2
1975–76		42	11
1976–77		42	7
1977–78		33	7
1978–79		35	3

All appearances include those as substitute

Season	Club	League Appearances/Goals		Season	Club	League Appearances/Goals	
1979–80	Manchester U	37	2	1981–82	Rochdale	6	—
1980–81		13	—	1982–83		37	—
1981–82		42	1	1983–84		27	2
1982–83		26	1	1984–85		25	—
1983–84		42	3	1985–86	Stockport Co	22	—
1984–85	AC Milan	28	—				
1985–86		29	2				

WILKINSON, Paul

Born Louth 30.10.64.   Ht 5 11½
Wt 11 0
Forward. From Apprentice. England
Under-21.

1982–83	Grimsby T	4	1
1983–84		37	12
1984–85		30	14
1984–85	Everton	5	2
1985–86		4	1

WILLIAMS, Alex

Born Manchester 13.11.61.   Ht 6 2
Wt 12 12
Goalkeeper. From Apprentice.
England Youth.

1979–80	Manchester C	—	—
1980–81		2	—
1981–82		3	—
1982–83		17	—
1983–84		42	—
1984–85		42	—
1985–86		8	—

WILLIAMS, Andy

Born Birmingham 29.7.62.
Midfield. From Dudley and Solihull B.

1985–86	Coventry C	8	—

WILLIAMS, Bill

Born Rochdale 7.10.60.   Ht 6 1   Wt 12 11
Defender. Local.

WILLIAMS, Brett

Born Dudley 19.3.68.   Ht 5 10   Wt 11 11
Defender. From Apprentice.

1985–86	Nottingham F	11	—

WILLIAMS, Brian

Born Salford 5.11.55.   Ht 5 9   Wt 12 1
Defender. From Apprentice.

1971–72	Bury	1	—
1972–73		10	1
1973–74		35	9
1974–75		35	1
1975–76		46	5
1976–77		32	3
1977–78	QPR	19	—
1978–79	Swindon T	25	2
1979–80		43	3
1980–81		31	3
1981–82	Bristol R	37	4
1982–83		43	2
1983–84		46	10
1984–85		46	4
1985–86	Bristol C	36	1

WILLIAMS, David

Born Cardiff 11.3.55.   Ht 5 10   Wt 11 8
Midfield. From Clifton Ath.
Wales Under-23, 4 full caps.

1975–76	Bristol R	41	2
1976–77		39	10
1977–78		33	8
1978–79		42	10
1979–80		40	4
1980–81		25	3

Season	Club	League Appearances/Goals		Season	Club	League Appearances/Goals	

1981–82	....	46	11
1982–83	....	25	9
1983–84	....	24	3
1984–85	....	37	6
1985–86	Norwich C...................	39	8

WILLIAMS, Derick

Born Sunderland 5.10.65.   Ht 5 11
Wt 11 10
Goalkeeper. England Schools, Youth.

1983–84	Watford	—	—
1984–85	....	—	—
1985–86	Reading	—	—

WILLIAMS, Gary

Born Wolverhampton 17.6.60.   Ht 5 9
Wt 10 10
Defender. From Apprentice.

1978–79	Aston Villa..................	23	—
1979–80	....	2	—
1979–80	*Walsall*	9	—
1980–81	Aston Villa..................	22	—
1981–82	....	28	—
1982–83	....	36	—
1983–84	....	40	—
1984–85	....	38	—
1985–86	....	25	—

WILLIAMS, Gary

Born Bristol 8.6.63.   Ht 5 8
Wt 10 11
Defender. From Apprentice.

1980–81	Bristol C.....................	1	—
1981–82	....	33	1
1982–83	....	36	—
1983–84	....	30	—
1984–85	Portsmouth	—	—
1984–85	Swansea C...................	6	—
1984–85	Bristol R.....................	—	—
1985–86	Oldham Ath	9	1

WILLIAMS, Gary

Born Nantwich 14.5.59.   Ht 5 9½   Wt 12 0
Defender. From Amateur.

1976–77	Tranmere R.................	1	—
From Djurgaarden			
1980–81	Blackpool	31	2
1981–82	Swindon T...................	38	3
1982–83	....	—	—
1982–83	Tranmere R.................	13	—
1983–84	....	37	3
1984–85	....	32	6
1985–86	....	25	4

WILLIAMS, Geraint

Born Treorchy 5.1.62.   Ht 5 7   Wt 10 6
Midfield. From Apprentice. Wales Youth.

1979–80	Bristol R.....................	—	—
1980–81	....	28	1
1981–82	....	16	—
1982–83	....	35	3
1983–84	....	34	4
1984–85	....	28	—
1984–85	Derby Co.....................	12	—
1985–86	....	40	4

WILLIAMS, Jeremy

Born Didcot 24.3.60.   Ht 5 11   Wt 11 10
Defender. From Apprentice.

1976–77	Reading	5	—
1977–78	....	13	2
1978–79	....	1	—
1979–80	....	15	2
1980–81	....	27	3
1981–82	....	45	—
1982–83	....	41	2
1983–84	....	38	—
1984–85	....	38	1
1985–86	....	31	4

Season	Club	League Appearances/Goals	Season	Club	League Appearances/Goals

WILLIAMS, John

Born Liverpool 3.10.60. Ht 6 2 Wt 14 4
Defender. From Amateur.

Season	Club	App	Goals
1978–79	Tranmere R	1	—
1979–80		3	—
1980–81		27	2
1981–82		44	6
1982–83		35	—
1983–84		20	1
1984–85		43	4
1985–86	Port Vale	36	3

WILLIAMS, Keith

Born Burtwood 12.4.57. Ht 5 9 Wt 11 10
Defender. From Apprentice.

Season	Club	App	Goals
1974–75	Aston Villa	—	—
1975–76		—	—
1976–77		—	—
1976–77	Northampton T	17	1
1977–78		28	1
1978–79		44	2
1979–80		3	—
1980–81		39	2
1981–82	Bournemouth	37	1
1982–83		18	—
1983–84		26	—
1984–85		6	—
1985–86		9	—

WILLIAMS, Mike

Born Mancot 6.2.65. Ht 5 10 Wt 10 12
Midfield. From Apprentice. Wales Youth.

Season	Club	App	Goals
1981–82	Chester	2	—
1982–83		12	2
1983–84		20	2
1984–85	Wrexham	27	—
1985–86		27	—

WILLIAMS, Neil

Born Waltham Abbey 23.10.64. Ht 5 11
Wt 11 4
Midfield. From Apprentice.

Season	Club	App	Goals
1982–83	Watford	—	—
1983–84		—	—
1984–85	Hull	17	3
1985–86		19	3

WILLIAMS, Oshor

Born Stockton 21.4.58. Ht 5 9½ Wt 11 7
Midfield. From Middlesbrough Apprentice.

Season	Club	App	Goals
1976–77	Manchester U	—	—
From Gateshead			
1977–78	Southampton	—	—
1978–79		5	—
1978–79	*Exeter C*	3	—
1979–80	Southampton	1	—
1979–80	Stockport Co	28	1
1980–81		36	6
1981–82		45	9
1982–83		34	2
1983–84		37	6
1984–85		13	2
1984–85	Port Vale	17	3
1985–86		32	3

WILLIAMS, Paul

Born Newton Abbot 20.2.65. Ht 6 0
Wt 11 12¼
Forward. From Ottery St. Mary.

Season	Club	App	Goals
1982–83	Bristol C	11	1
1983–84		8	—
1984–85	Bury	—	—
1985–86	Exeter C	2	—

WILLIAMS, Phil

Born Swansea 24.11.66. Ht 5 10 Wt 10 12
Midfield. From Apprentice.

Season	Club	App	Goals
1983–84	Swansea C	1	—
1984–85		11	—
1985–86		12	3

Season	Club	League Appearances/Goals		Season	Club	League Appearances/Goals	

WILLIAMS, Steve

Born London 12.7.58.   Ht 5 11   Wt 10 11
Midfield. From Apprentice.
England Under-21, 'B', 6 full caps.

Season	Club	App	Goals
1974–75	Southampton	—	—
1975–76		1	—
1976–77		33	—
1977–78		39	5
1978–79		39	—
1979–80		32	2
1980–81		33	4
1981–82		21	—
1982–83		39	3
1983–84		27	3
1984–85		14	1
1984–85	Arsenal	15	1
1985–86		17	—

WILLIAMS, Terry

Born Stoke 23.10.66.   Ht 5 7   Wt 11 0
Defender. From Apprentice.

Season	Club	App	Goals
1984–85	Stoke C	2	—
1985–86		6	—

WILLIAMS, Tommy

Born West Lothian 18.12.57.   Ht 5 10½
Wt 10 12
Defender. From Apprentice.

Season	Club	App	Goals
1976–77	Leicester C	—	—
1977–78		32	3
1978–79		35	2
1979–80		40	1
1980–81		42	4
1981–82		31	—
1982–83		4	—
1983–84		22	—
1984–85		27	—
1985–86		8	—

WILLIAMS, Wayne

Born Delford 17.11.63.   Ht 5 10   Wt 10 10
Defender. From Apprentice.

Season	Club	App	Goals
1981–82	Shrewsbury T	—	—
1982–83		42	4
1983–84		40	—
1984–85		28	—
1985–86		30	1

WILLIAMSON, Bobby

Born Glasgow 13.8.61.   Ht 5 10   Wt 11 0
Forward. From Auchengill B.C.

Season	Club	App	Goals
1980–81	Clydebank	2	—
1981–82		12	1
1982–83		39	23
1983–84		17	4
1983–84	Rangers	17	6
1984–85		1	—
1985–86		23	6

WILLIAMSON, Charlie

Born Sheffield 16.3.62.   Ht 5 10   Wt 11 3
Defender. From Apprentice.

Season	Club	App	Goals
1979–80	Sheffield W	3	—
1980–81		8	—
1981–82		32	1
1982–83		9	—
1983–84		10	—
1983–84	*Lincoln C*	5	—
1984–85	Sheffield W	—	—
1984–85	*Southend U*	10	—
1985–86	Chesterfield	27	1

WILMOT, Rhys

Born Newport 21.2.62.   Ht 6 1   Wt 12 0
Goalkeeper. From Apprentice.
Wales Under-21.

Season	Club	App	Goals
1979–80	Arsenal	—	—
1980–81		—	—
1981–82		—	—
1982–83		—	—
1982–83	*Hereford U*	9	—

Season	Club	League Appearances/Goals		Season	Club	League Appearances/Goals	
1983–84	Arsenal	—	—				
1984–85	*Orient*	46	—				
1985–86	Arsenal	2	—				

WILSON, Kevin

Born Banbury 18.4.61. Ht 5 7 Wt 10 10
Forward. From Banbury U.

WILSON, Clive

Born Manchester 13.11.61. Ht 5 7 Wt 9 10
Forward. Local.

Season	Club	App	Goals
1979–80	Manchester C	—	—
1980–81		—	—
1981–82		4	—
1982–83		—	—
1982–83	*Chester*	21	2
1983–84	Manchester C	11	—
1984–85		27	4
1985–86		25	5

Season	Club	App	Goals
1979–80	Derby Co	4	—
1980–81		27	7
1981–82		24	9
1982–83		22	4
1983–84		32	2
1984–85		13	8
1984–85	Ipswich T	17	7
1985–86		39	7

WILSON, Paul

Born Bradford 2.8.68.
Defender. From YTS.

Season	Club	App	Goals
1985–86	Huddersfield T	7	—

WILSON, Danny

Born Wigan 1.1.60. Ht 5 7 Wt 10 3
Midfield. From Wigan Ath.

Season	Club	App	Goals
1977–78	Bury	12	1
1978–79		46	7
1979–80		32	—
1980–81	Chesterfield	33	3
1981–82		43	3
1982–83		24	7
1982–83	Nottingham F	10	1
1983–84	*Scunthorpe U*	6	3
1983–84	Brighton	26	10
1984–85		38	5
1985–86		33	11

WILSON, Phil

Born Hemsworth 16.10.60. Ht 5 6 Wt 11 3
Midfield. From Apprentice.

Season	Club	App	Goals
1978–79	Bolton W	—	—
1979–80		17	1
1980–81		22	3
1981–82	Huddersfield T	34	2
1982–83		45	6
1983–84		41	3
1984–85		40	3
1985–86		35	1

WILSON, Ian

Born Aberdeen 27.3.58. Ht 5 7½ Wt 10 10
Midfield. From Elgin C.

Season	Club	App	Goals
1978–79	Leicester C	—	—
1979–80		24	2
1980–81		40	1
1981–82		35	—
1982–83		36	8
1983–84		41	—
1984–85		39	1
1985–86		25	2

WILSON, Robert

Born Kensington 5.6.61. Ht 5 10 Wt 11 11
Midfield. From Apprentice.

Season	Club	App	Goals
1979–80	Fulham	2	—
1980–81		35	4
1981–82		43	5
1982–83		40	11
1983–84		16	3
1984–85		39	11
1985–86	Millwall	28	12

Season	Club	League Appearances/Goals	Season	Club	League Appearances/Goals

WILSON, Tommy

Born Paisley 2.8.61. Ht 5 8 Wt 9 7
Defender. From school. Scotland Under-21.

1979–80	Queen's Park	1	—
1980–81		1	—
1981–82		30	—
1982–83	St Mirren	36	—
1983–84		1	—
1984–85		35	—
1985–86		27	—

WIMBLETON, Paul

Born Havant 13.11.64. Ht 5 8 Wt 10 6
Midfield. From Apprentice.
England Schools.

1981–82	Portsmouth	8	—
1982–83		—	—
1983–84		2	—
1984–85		—	—
1985–86		—	—

WINDRIDGE, Dave

Born Atherstone 7.12.61. Ht 5 9 Wt 11 0
Forward. From Amateur.

1978–79	Sheffield U	—	—
1979–80		—	—
1979–80	Chesterfield	—	—
1980–81		2	—
1981–82		34	6
1982–83		42	8
1983–84	Blackpool	34	6
1984–85		39	8
1985–86		16	3

WINNIE, David

Born Glasgow 26.10.66. Ht 5 11 Wt 10 7
Defender. 'S' Form. Scotland Schools,
Youth.

1983–84	St Mirren	8	—
1984–85		30	3
1985–86		20	1

WINSTANLEY, Mark

Born St. Helens 22.1.68.
Defender. From YTS.

| 1984–85 | Bolton W | — | — |
| 1985–86 | | 3 | — |

WINTER, Julian

Born Huddersfield 6.9.65. Ht 6 0 Wt 11 2
Midfield. Local.

1983–84	Huddersfield T	—	—
1984–85		16	2
1985–86		4	—

WINTERBURN, Nigel

Born Nuneaton 11.12.63. Ht 5 10 Wt 10 7
Defender. Local. England Under-21.

1981–82	Birmingham C	—	—
1982–83		—	—
1983–84	Oxford U	—	—
1983–84	Wimbledon	43	1
1984–85		41	4
1985–86		39	1

WISE, Dennis

Born Kensington 15.12.66. Ht 5 6 Wt 9 5
Forward. From Southampton Apprentice.

| 1984–85 | Wimbledon | 1 | — |
| 1985–86 | | 4 | — |

WISHART, Fraser

Born Johnstone 1.3.65. Ht 5 8 Wt 10 0
Defender. From Pollok.

1983–84	Motherwell	6	—
1984–85		—	—
1985–86		26	—

All appearances include those as substitute

Season	Club	League Appearances/Goals	Season	Club	League Appearances/Goals

WITHE, Chris

Born Liverpool 25.9.62.   Ht 5 10   Wt 11 3
Defender. From Apprentice.

Season	Club	App	Goals
1980–81	Newcastle U	2	—
1981–82		—	—
1982–83		—	—
1983–84	Bradford C	45	1
1984–85		45	—
1985–86		33	—

WITHE, Peter

Born Liverpool 30.8.51.   Ht 6 1   Wt 12 0
Forward. From Skelmersdale.
England, 11 full caps.

Season	Club	App	Goals
1970–71	Southport	2	—
1971–72		1	—
1971–72	Barrow	1	—
From Port Elizabeth C and			
Arcadia Shepherds			
1973–74	Wolverhampton W	3	1
1974–75		14	2
From Portland T			
1975–76	Birmingham C	32	9
1976–77		3	—
1976–77	Nottingham F	34	16
1977–78		40	12
1978–79		1	—
1978–79	Newcastle U	39	14
1979–80		37	11
1980–81	Aston Villa	36	20
1981–82		35	10
1982–83		35	16
1983–84		36	16
1984–85		40	12
1985–86	Sheffield U	30	11

WITHEY, Graham

Born Bristol 11.6.60.   Ht 6 0   Wt 11 12
Forward. From Bath C.

Season	Club	App	Goals
1982–83	Bristol R	22	10
1983–84	Coventry C	20	4
1984–85		2	—
1984–85	Cardiff C	22	6
1985–86		5	1

WOLLEN, Andy

Born Swindon 14.11.66.   Ht 5 11   Wt 11 3
Defender. From Apprentice.

Season	Club	App	Goals
1984–85	Swindon T	—	—
1985–86		—	—

WOOD, Darren

Born Scarborough 9.6.64.   Ht 5 10   Wt 11 8
Defender. From Apprentice.
England Schools.

Season	Club	App	Goals
1981–82	Middlesbrough	11	1
1982–83		42	3
1983–84		42	2
1984–85		6	—
1984–85	Chelsea	19	1
1985–86		28	—

WOOD, George

Born Douglas 26.9.52.   Ht 6 3   Wt 14 0
Goalkeeper. From East Stirling.
Scotland, 4 full caps.

Season	Club	App	Goals
1970–71	East Stirling	23	1
1971–72		21	—
1971–72	Blackpool	4	—
1972–73		20	—
1973–74		12	—
1974–75		4	—
1975–76		35	—
1976–77		42	—
1977–78	Everton	42	—
1978–79		42	—
1979–80		19	—
1980–81	Arsenal	11	—
1981–82		26	—
1982–83		23	—
1983–84	Crystal Palace	42	—
1984–85		42	—
1985–86		39	—

Season	Club	League Appearances/Goals		Season	Club	League Appearances/Goals	

WOOD, Nicky

Born Oldham 11.1.66.   Ht 5 11½   Wt 11 1
Forward. From school. England Youth.

Season	Club	App	Goals
1983–84	Manchester U	—	—
1984–85		—	—
1985–86		1	—

WOOD, Paul

Born Middlesbrough 1.11.64.   Ht 5 9
Wt 10 1
Forward. From Apprentice

Season	Club	App	Goals
1982–83	Portsmouth	—	—
1983–84		8	1
1984–85		6	1
1985–86		25	4

WOOD, Steve

Born Bracknell 2.2.63.   Ht 6 0   Wt 11 9
Defender. From Apprentice.

Season	Club	App	Goals
1979–80	Reading	2	—
1980–81		6	—
1981–82		32	—
1982–83		18	—
1983–84		37	3
1984–85		46	1
1985–86		46	4

WOODCOCK, David

Born Darlington 13.10.66.   Ht 5 11   Wt 12 0
Midfield. From Apprentice.

Season	Club	App	Goals
1984–85	Sunderland	—	—
1985–86	Darlington	23	2

WOODCOCK, Tony

Born Nottingham 6.12.55.   Ht 5 10
Wt 11 0
Forward. From Apprentice.
England Under-21, 'B', 42 full caps.

Season	Club	App	Goals
1973–74	Nottingham F	2	—
1974–75		9	—
1975–76		—	—
1975–76	*Lincoln C*	4	1
1976–77	Nottingham F	30	11
1976–77	*Doncaster R*	6	2
1977–78	Nottingham F	36	11
1978–79		36	10
1979–80		16	4
From FC Cologne		81	28
1982–83	Arsenal	34	14
1983–84		37	21
1984–85		27	10
1985–86		33	11

WOODHEAD, Simon

Born Wakefield 26.12.62.   Ht 5 9   Wt 10 6
Forward. From Amateur.

Season	Club	App	Goals
1980–81	Mansfield T	1	—
1981–82		12	—
1982–83		42	3
1983–84		43	1
1984–85		24	2
1985–86	Crewe Alex	—	—

WOODS, Chris

Born Boston 14.11.59.   Ht 6 2   Wt 12 8
Goalkeeper. From Apprentice.
England Under-21, 4 full caps.

Season	Club	App	Goals
1976–77	Nottingham F	—	—
1977–78		—	—
1978–79		—	—
1979–80	QPR	41	—
1980–81		22	—
1980–81	*Norwich C*	10	—
1981–82	Norwich C	42	—
1982–83		42	—
1983–84		42	—
1984–85		38	—
1985–86		42	—

Season	Club	League Appearances/Goals	Season	Club	League Appearances/Goals

WOODS, Neil

Born York 30.7.66.   Ht 5 11   Wt 11 11
Defender. From Apprentice.

Season	Club	App	Goals
1982–83	Doncaster R	4	—
1983–84		7	1
1984–85		6	2
1985–86		30	7

WOODWORTH, Tony

Born Burnley.   Ht 5 10½   Wt 11 6
Goalkeeper. From Apprentice.

Season	Club	App	Goals
1985–86	Burnley	—	—

WORRALL, Gary

Born Salford 4.11.61.   Ht 5 9   Wt 11 8
Forward. From Apprentice.

Season	Club	App	Goals
1978–79	Manchester U	—	—
1979–80		—	—
1980–81		—	—
1981–82		—	—
1982–83		—	—
1983–84		—	—
1983–84	Peterborough U	19	2
1984–85		46	9
1985–86		30	5

WORTHINGTON, Frank

Born Halifax 23.11.48.   Ht 5 11   Wt 11 9
Forward. From Apprentice. England Under-
23, 8 full caps, Football League.

Season	Club	App	Goals
1966–67	Huddersfield T	3	—
1967–68		29	5
1968–69		16	4
1969–70		42	19
1970–71		42	9
1971–72		39	5
1972–73	Leicester C	39	10
1973–74		42	20
1974–75		42	18
1975–76		39	9
1976–77		41	14

Season	Club	App	Goals
1977–78		7	1
1977–78	Bolton W	35	11
1978–79		42	24
1979–80		7	—
1979–80	Birmingham C	19	5
1980–81		36	16
1981–82		20	9
1981–82	Leeds U	17	9
1982–83		15	5
1982–83	Sunderland	19	2
1983–84	Southampton	34	4
1984–85	Brighton	31	7
1985–86	Tranmere R	42	18

WORTHINGTON, Gary

Born Cleethorpes 10.11.66.   Ht 5 10
Wt 10 5
Forward. From Apprentice. England Youth.

Season	Club	App	Goals
1984–85	Manchester U	—	—
1985–86		—	—

WORTHINGTON, Nigel

Born Ballymena 4.11.61.   Ht 5 10   Wt 12 0
Defender. From Ballymena U.
Northern Ireland Youth, 8 full caps.

Season	Club	App	Goals
1981–82	Notts Co	2	—
1982–83		41	3
1983–84		24	1
1983–84	Sheffield W.	14	1
1984–85		38	1
1985–86		15	—

WRIGHT, Billy

Born Liverpool 28.4.58.   Ht 5 11   Wt 11 0
Defender. From Amateur.
England Under-21, 'B'.

Season	Club	App	Goals
1974–75	Everton	—	—
1975–76		—	—
1976–77		—	—
1977–78		4	1
1978–79		39	2
1979–80		41	—

Season	Club	League Appearances/Goals		Season	Club	League Appearances/Goals	
1980–81	....	41	2	1980–81	Oxford U	—	—
1981–82	....	24	2	1981–82	....	10	—
1982–83	....	17	3	1981–82	Southampton	3	—
1983–84	Birmingham C............	40	5	1982–83	....	39	2
1984–85	....	42	2	1983–84	....	29	1
1985–86	....	29	2	1984–85	....	36	—
1985–86	*Chester C*	6	1	1985–86	....	33	3

WRIGHT, Brian

Born Glasgow 5.10.58.   Ht 5 11   Wt 11 3
Midfield. From Phoenix B.C.

1975–76	Hamilton A	—	—
1976–77	....	11	—
1977–78	....	27	1
1978–79	....	20	3
1979–80	....	36	3
1980–81	....	35	6
1981–82	....	37	5
1982–83	....	36	6
1983–84	....	37	—
1984–85	....	35	3
1985–86	....	3	1
1985–86	Motherwell	28	6

WRIGHT, Darren

Born West Bromwich 14.3.68.   Ht 5 10
Wt 11 4
Defender. From Apprentice.

1984–85	Wolverhampton W........	—	—
1985–86	....	1	—

WRIGHT, Ian

Born Woolwich 3.11.63.
Forward. From Greenwich Bor.

1985–86	Crystal Palace	32	9

WRIGHT, Mark

Born Dorchester 1.8.63.   Ht 6 3   Wt 12 1
Defender. From Amateur.
England Under-21, 13 full caps.

WRIGHT, Paul

Born East Kilbride 17.8.67.   Ht 5 8   Wt 10 8
Forward. 'S' Form. Scotland Youth.

1983–84	Aberdeen	1	—
1984–85	....	—	—
1985–86	....	10	2

WRIGHT, Steve

Born Clacton 16.6.59.   Ht 6 0   Wt 11 0
Defender. From Local.

1977–78	Colchester U	1	—
1978–79	....	35	1
1979–80	....	26	1
1980–81	....	17	—
1981–82	....	38	—
From HJK Helsinki			
1983–84	Wrexham....................	37	—
1984–85	....	39	—
1985–86	Torquay U	33	—

WRIGHT, Tommy

Born Dunfermline 10.1.66.   Ht 5 9   Wt 11 0
Forward. From Apprentice.

1982–83	Leeds U......................	4	1
1983–84	....	25	8
1984–85	....	42	14
1985–86	....	10	1

WROE, Mark

Born Manchester 1.6.66.
Midfield.

1984–85	Stockport Co	3	—
1985–86	....	26	4

Season	Club	League Appearances/Goals	Season	Club	League Appearances/Goals

WYLDE, Rodger

Born Sheffield 8.3.54.   Ht 6 1½   Wt 12 0
Forward. From Apprentice.

Season	Club	App	Goals
1971–72	Sheffield W	—	—
1972–73		3	1
1973–74		—	—
1974–75		12	—
1975–76		21	1
1975–76	*Burnley*	—	—
1976–77	Sheffield W	44	21
1977–78		36	9
1978–79		38	14
1979–80		15	8
1979–80	Oldham Ath	10	4
1980–81		29	12
1981–82		35	16
1982–83		39	19
1983–84	Sporting Lisbon	2	1
1984–85	Sunderland	11	3
1984–85	Barnsley	17	4
1985–86		—	—

YALLOP, Frank

Born Watford 4.4.64.   Ht 5 10½   Wt 11 3
Defender. From Apprentice.

Season	Club	App	Goals
1981–82	Ipswich T	—	—
1982–83		—	—
1983–84		6	—
1984–85		10	—
1985–86		34	—

YATES, Dean

Born Leicester 26.10.67.   Ht 6 0   Wt 10 4
Defender. From Apprentice.

Season	Club	App	Goals
1984–85	Notts Co	8	—
1985–86		44	4

YATES, Martin

Born Rawmarsh 19.9.67.
Defender.

Season	Club	App	Goals
1985–86	Barnsley	—	—

YATES, Steve

Born Burton 8.12.53.   Ht 6 0   Wt 13 3
Defender. From Apprentice.

Season	Club	App	Goals
1971–72	Leicester C	—	—
1972–73		—	—
1973–74		2	—
1974–75		13	—
1975–76		—	—
1976–77		4	—
1977–78		—	—
1977–78	Southend U	27	1
1978–79		42	1
1979–80		31	—
1980–81		42	—
1981–82		38	3
1982–83		33	3
1983–84		11	—
1983–84	Doncaster R	27	1
1984–85		17	—
1984–85	*Darlington*	4	—
1984–85	*Chesterfield*	1	—
1985–86	Stockport Co	2	—
1985–86	Burnley	—	—